PRAISE FOR THIS BC

MW01043041

This is an excellent and accessible resource for both students and practitioners of program evaluation. The chapter on 'Using Mixed Methods in Evaluation' alone is worth the investment in this book.

—Debra Bartelli, *University of Memphis*

This text fills a much needed gap by providing an accessible resource for students taking program evaluation for the first time.

—Shane R. Brady, *University of Oklahoma*

The comprehensiveness of the text is its greatest strength. It hits all the right keys. It has an easy readability and an excellent mix of text, graphics, teaching tools.

—Nancy G. Calleja, *University of Detroit Mercy*

With a focus on the practical aspects of evaluation, this textbook also integrates very relevant, and frequently overlooked, theoretical and conceptual frameworks that are extremely valuable for evaluators.

—Sebastian Galindo, *University of Florida*

This book provides students with real-life relatable examples of program evaluation. It's an interesting read, and a must-use in the classroom!

—Heather Lenz, *Case Western Reserve University*

A very interesting and practical introduction to program evaluation. The authors have provided sound arguments for conducting evaluations and a strong introduction to essential considerations in carrying through evaluations for the betterment of the agency, stakeholders, and society as a whole.

—Ted L. Miller, *University of Tennessee at Chattanooga*

This is a thorough guide to conducting evaluation that addresses both concepts and practice. It provides a comprehensive view of all that evaluation entails and delivers that content in a way that is very consumable to readers... well worth keeping beyond the class.

—Richard S. Mohn, *University of Southern Mississippi*

This is an excellent guide for anyone interested in conducting or learning about program evaluation. It looks at evaluation through new lens, recognizing the importance of diversity, the connection of local issues with global issues, and presents the material in a clear, easy-to-follow, and digestible manner.

—Sandra Schrouder, *Barry University, Miami, FL*

Gail Vallance Barrington and Beverly Triana-Tremain have written the quintessential book on evaluation for students new to the science and those who need an updating.

—Randy Schultz, *California State University, Bakersfield*

This text offers a comprehensive yet practical introduction to program evaluation. The authors integrate new approaches, classic frameworks, and practical tools that students can use to design evaluation studies.

—Denna Wheeler, *Oklahoma State University*

Evaluation Time
A Practical Guide for Evaluation

Gail Vallance Barrington

Barrington Research Group, Inc.

Beverly Triana-Tremain

Los Angeles | London | New Delhi
Singapore | Washington DC | Melbourne

FOR INFORMATION:

SAGE Publications, Inc.

2455 Teller Road

Thousand Oaks, California 91320

E-mail: order@sagepub.com

SAGE Publications Ltd.

1 Oliver's Yard

55 City Road

London, EC1Y 1SP

United Kingdom

SAGE Publications India Pvt. Ltd.

B 1/I 1 Mohan Cooperative Industrial Area

Mathura Road, New Delhi 110 044

India

SAGE Publications Asia-Pacific Pte. Ltd.

18 Cross Street #10-10/11/12

China Square Central

Singapore 048423

Printed in the United States of America

Library of Congress Cataloging-in-Publication Data

Names: Barrington, Gail Vallance, 1945- author. | Triana-Tremain, Beverly, author.

Title: Evaluation time : a practical guide for evaluation / Gail Vallance Barrington, Beverly Triana-Tremain.

Identifiers: LCCN 2022013364 | ISBN 9781544339504 (paperback) | ISBN 9781544339511 (adobe pdf) | ISBN 9781544339481 (epub) | ISBN 9781544339498 (epub)

Subjects: LCSH: Evaluation.

Classification: LCC H62 .B339 2022 | DDC 001.4/2–dc23/eng/20220528

LC record available at https://lccn.loc.gov/2022013364

This book is printed on acid-free paper.

Acquisitions Editor: Helen Salmon

Product Associate: Audra Bacon

Production Editor: Vijayakumar

Copy Editor: Christobel Colleen Hopman

Typesetter: TNQ Technologies

Proofreader: Benny Willy Stephen

Indexer: TNQ Technologies

Cover Designer: Gail Buschman

Marketing Manager: Victoria Velasquez

22 23 24 25 26 10 9 8 7 6 5 4 3 2 1

Thank you, Bruce and Wil, for your boundless love, humor, and support. Thanks also to my many students across the years for teaching me how to teach. ~ Gail

I dedicate this book to my four boys! Jack, my husband, and my three sons, Hunter, Hayden, and Holden. How lucky I am to take my life's journey with you. To my mother, I appreciate your steadfast support and your "dig in there and do it" attitude since the beginning. ~ Bev

BRIEF CONTENTS

DETAILED CONTENTS

PREFACE

PURPOSE

Welcome to your new book! We wrote *Evaluation Time: A Practical Guide for Program Evaluation* to give you a deep and intriguing look into evaluation in health, education, and the social sciences. Our approach will help you understand how evaluators measure whether the planned and implemented interventions or services are achieving their goals and objectives. There are several things that are important and special about our book. No matter the stage of program development, we describe the evaluation theories, methods, and tools that are required. Our focus is always on answering the research and evaluation questions most important to the community and organizations in which the evaluation takes place. We also stress the importance of critical and evaluative thinking and self-reflection. We see the importance of context and equity in today's turbulent environment and offer a new stance for evaluators to support global as well as local issues.

AUDIENCE

This book is intended as an introductory program evaluation text for:

- Students who are taking their first course in program evaluation.

- Instructors who are looking for a book that is rigorous and approachable.

- Practicing evaluators and consultants who want to gain more understanding of the theoretical and practical foundations of evaluation.

- Program staff who are responsible for writing evaluation proposals.

- Clients and other funders who want to understand how evaluation can provide evidence to support their decision-making.

- Community stakeholders who want to increase their knowledge and skills about evaluation.

BOOK STRUCTURE

The book is divided into four parts. Each one has three chapters that explore the dimensions of evaluation.

Part I, The Fundamentals of Evaluation, sets the scene by exploring what evaluation is and how evaluators think.

> **Chapter 1, The Scope of Evaluation**, includes an introduction to basic concepts, reasons for doing an evaluation, and differences between research and evaluation. We also discuss the three pillars of evaluation, namely principles, standards, and competencies, and briefly describe evaluation education, training, and professionalization opportunities.

> **Chapter 2, How Evaluators Think**, looks at scaffolds for evaluators' thought using the ladder of evaluation theory as a metaphor. We explore ontology, various paradigms and frameworks, relevant natural and social science theory, and evaluation theory. We end with your program evaluation project and your own epistemology and critical thought.

> **Chapter 3, Program Logic**, examines the golden thread or logic that guides the entire evaluation enterprise and the three key tools, theory of change, program theory, and the logic model, all used to structure evaluation studies.

Part II, Evaluation and the Program Life Cycle, uses the metaphor of a 12-hour clock to describe specific types of evaluation frequently employed at each stage of program development, including the program phase and level of program maturity, along with methods, measures, and key questions for each.

> **Chapter 4, Pre- and Early Program Evaluation**, describes preliminary evaluation processes, including the literature review, stakeholder analysis, needs assessment, program design, and evaluability assessment.

> **Chapter 5, Mid-Cycle Program Evaluation**, presents evaluation activities typically applied during program implementation, including formative, process, and descriptive evaluation, and performance management.

> **Chapter 6, End-of-Cycle Program Evaluation**, examines evaluation activities that occur at the end of a program cycle when decision makers determine if the program should be continued, modified, or closed. Typically, outcome, impact, and summative evaluations are used.

Part III, Evaluation Methods, focuses on the research methods used by evaluators to answer the questions that will help decision makers get the evidence they need.

> **Chapter 7, Using Quantitative Methods in Evaluation**, explores quantitative activities and encompasses credible evidence, types of data, terminology, quantitative designs, strengths and weaknesses, quality issues, and methods of analysis. The chapter ends with an overview of the most common quantitative tool, the survey.

Chapter 8, Using Qualitative Methods in Evaluation, explores qualitative approaches, designs, characteristics, strengths and weaknesses, and ways to ensure quality. The chapter aligns the qualitative process with Bloom's Taxonomy as a way to clarify the type of thought processes required at each level of analysis. The chapter closes with a discussion of the interview to illustrate how qualitative data are collected.

Chapter 9, Using Mixed Methods in Evaluation, describes an approach that is gaining acceptance as a distinct research strategy. When one type of data is not sufficient to gain a holistic understanding of the program under review, a mixed methods design can be used to better understand complex issues. It involves the planned integration of both quantitative and qualitative to draw conclusions about the research question focus groups are often used as a companion tool in mixed methods and so it is described at the end of the chapter as a useful method.

Part IV, Communicating about Evaluation, looks at critical ways that evaluators communicate about their work.

Chapter 10, The Evaluation Plan, examines the two phases of the planning process, the pre-planning process and the preparation of the evaluation plan. Examples are provided for each component.

Chapter 11, Communication, Reporting, and Use, provides ways to communicate throughout the evaluation process. This includes communicating during the evaluation, reporting findings at the end of the evaluation, and supporting use once the evaluation is completed.

Chapter 12, Evaluation Context and the Evaluator's New Stance, explores the importance of the evaluation context, its dimensions, and the role of the evaluator within them. Context is critical to our work because it affects the systems in which our programs are embedded. The chapter discusses current issues and suggests ways that evaluators can tackle the wicked problems that face our world. By linking local problems with global trends, evaluators can use their rare skill set and unique position to bridge the gap between program participants and decision makers. A sense of purpose, balance, and connectedness will let us attain our goal of social betterment and can lead to transformative change.

BOOK FEATURES

In each chapter of the book, you will find special features, such as:

Mind Maps. These guides to thinking orient you to the concepts in the book.

Learning Objectives. Couple these with the Main Ideas at the end of each chapter for an enhanced learning experience.

Lead Stories. These sometimes humorous, sad, or legendary stories relate to some aspect of the chapter topic and are intended to pique your interest about the chapter ahead.

Examples. Many examples of evaluation studies are provided throughout the book that embody the concepts presented.

Metaphors. We use simple metaphors from everyday life to help you visualize the concepts under discussion

Figures, Tables, and Boxes. We understand that as readers you have different learning styles and ways of processing information, so we often present both technical and visual summaries to gain and retain information.

Spotlight on Equity. Each chapter presents a story from the field that highlights real evaluators and their solutions to the equity challenges.

Expert Corner. In every discipline, there are the leaders who set the tone for its practice. Each chapter introduces an evaluation expert who is a deep thinker and has had an impact on the field.

Key Terms/Glossary. Key Terms specific to the evaluation field are bolded the first time they appear in the book. Their definition is provided in the Glossary.

The Main Ideas. The Main Ideas list 10 statements related to important chapter content.

Critical Thinking Questions. Our Critical Thinking Questions push you to think harder and deeper about what you have just read.

Student Challenges. Our Student Challenges encourage you to investigate specific aspects of the evaluation field and apply the concepts in practical ways.

Additional Readings and Resources. This curated list of readings and resources includes related journal articles that illuminate concepts presented in the chapter, tools to use in an evaluation, evaluation examples, books for further reading, and guidance documents on evaluation best practices.

INSTRUCTOR RESOURCES

Resources to accompany this book are available at: https://edge.sagepub.com/barrington-evaluation1e

ACKNOWLEDGMENTS

We wish to thank the many clients we have worked with, the program participants who have shared their lives with us, our students who have challenged us to think harder and deeper about evaluation concepts, and our colleagues who have been so generous with their time and interest. This book would not have happened if it were not for SAGE Publications and their wonderful team. Specifically, thanks to Helen Salmon, Chelsea Neve, and Ivey Mellem for working so closely with us, providing unparalleled encouragement, support, and guidance. Thanks also to team members Audra Bacon, Christobel Colleen Hopman. Benny Willy Stephen, Gail Buschman, and Victoria Velasquez for making our vision a reality. A special shout out to Vijayakumar and TNQ Technologies for their excellent publishing services. We also want to thank our reviewers:

Debra Bartelli, *University of Memphis*

Kasey H. Boyd-Swan, *Kent State University*

Shane R. Brady, *University of Oklahoma*

Nancy G. Calleja, *University of Detroit Mercy*

Kimberly S. Cook, *Texas Christian University*

Sebastian Galindo, *University of Florida*

Amy D. Habeger, *Delaware State University*

Pamela D. Hall, *Barry University*

Daniel Hawes, *Kent State University*

Heather Lenz, *Case Western Reserve University*

Ted Miller, *University of Tennessee at Chattanooga*

Richard S. Mohn, *University of Southern Missouri*

Julie Schroeder, *Jackson State University*

Sandra Schrouder, *Barry University*

Randy Shultz, *California State University Bakersfield*

Denna Wheeler, *Oklahoma State University*

We took your comments seriously and want to thank you for your wise counsel which helped us to broaden our perspective to be more responsive to our reader's needs.

Thanks also to the experts in our Expert Corners who have been so generous with their time and wisdom about theory and practice. Thanks to our contributors who shared their experiences in the Spotlight on Equity and provided examples of ways to make evaluation more equitable. We thank Dr. David Fetterman for introducing us to each other in the first place, without him this book would never have been written.

ABOUT THE AUTHORS

Bev sent an email to Gail asking if she was interested in writing a book about evaluation and that is where this journey began. On July 23, 2018, Gail and Bev met for the first time to discuss what this partnership would look like. We have been delighted to take this journey together and have learned, laughed, solved problems, and gained a new respect for evaluation.

During our four-year writing journey, we had countless conversations about how to engage with you, our reader. Imagine as you read through the chapters that we are walking beside you as we move toward a heightened sense of what evaluation is, what it can do, and how evaluators can strive to make our world a better place.

Gail Vallance Barrington is a Credentialed Evaluator (CE) and a certified teacher. During her 35 years as owner and manager of an independent consulting company, she completed over 130 evaluation studies, mainly in education, health, and research. She has authored articles, book chapters, and the popular book, *Consulting Start-up and Management: A Guide for Evaluators and Applied Researchers* (SAGE, 2012). She has served on the boards of both the American Evaluation Association (AEA) and the Canadian Evaluation Society (CES). Awards include the CES Contribution to Evaluation in Canada Award (2008) and the AEA Alva and Gunnar Myrdal Award for Evaluation Practice (2016). She is a Fellow of the Canadian Evaluation Society (2018) and the Certified Management Consultants of Canada (2014). She holds degrees from McGill University (BA), Carleton University (MA), and the University of Alberta (PhD in Educational Administration). She teaches research and evaluation skills online for Michigan State University.

For more information, see www.barringtonresearchgrp.com.

Beverly Triana-Tremain has at least 35 years of public health teaching and consulting experience. Her areas of expertise are public health, evaluation, and quality improvement. Currently, she serves as Epidemiologist with the University of Oklahoma. As part of the Substance Abuse and Mental Health Administration (SAMHSA) Prevention Technology Transfer Center (PTTC), she supports the preventionist workforce in changing community risk factors for substance misuse and mental health disorders. She received her Bachelor of Science at Texas A & M University—Commerce, and a Master of Science at Texas Woman's University in Exercise Science with an emphasis in Exercise Physiology. She also received her Doctorate of Philosophy in Community Health Studies at Texas Woman's University. She holds a certification in Lean Six Sigma as a Green Belt and is a fellow in the National Public Health Leadership Institute. In 2006, she established Public Health Consulting, LLC, to assist agencies in improving the public health system

For more information, see www.publichealthconsulting.net.

FUNDAMENTALS OF EVALUATION

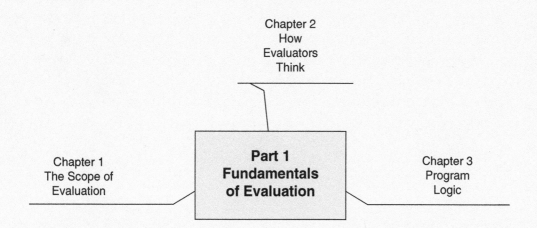

Chapter 2
How
Evaluators
Think

Chapter 1
The Scope of
Evaluation

**Part 1
Fundamentals
of Evaluation**

Chapter 3
Program
Logic

THE SCOPE OF EVALUATION

1. Define program evaluation.
2. List three basic evaluation questions.
3. Identify four main reasons for doing the evaluation.
4. Distinguish between research and evaluation.
5. Recognize the breadth of the evaluation discipline today.
6. Explain how an evaluator can use the three pillars of evaluation.

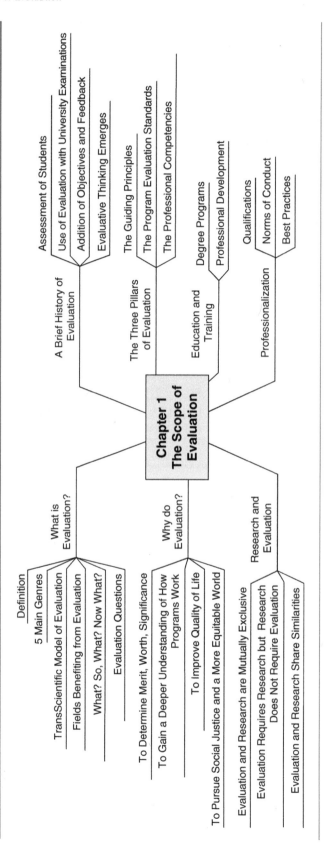

INTRODUCTION

Programs and policies are designed to make positive changes in the world. They affect the lives of people as well as the physical and social environments in which they live. By extension, the evaluations of these programs and policies have intrinsic power, because they serve as a bridge between the organizations that sponsor them and the individuals most affected by the programs and policies in place (McBride et al., 2020). Further, evaluators have extrinsic influence because decision makers and leaders may make significant changes based on the evaluation findings, for example, to expand, revise, replicate, reduce, or terminate the program or policy. It's a big responsibility, and it is one that evaluators willingly accept every day. This chapter will provide you with an overview of evaluation, what it is, and why it is important. The rest of the book will help you learn how to do it.

You may be surprised to learn that you are already an evaluator! You evaluate what car to buy, what school to send your kid to, what to have for dinner. You certainly evaluated which program to enroll in to meet your current educational goals. As a result, because you make decisions every day, you may think that evaluation as a formal decision-making process is unnecessary. It turns out that the personal methods you use to make your decisions are very similar to the ones that organizations use, ranging from thoughtful, evidence-based decision-making processes to the old dartboard approach. Which makes you feel more confident? Which is more likely to produce an effective outcome?

Program evaluation offers a toolbox full of tried-and-true methods and strategies to help programs make better decisions and determine where they need to make improvements. We use the term "program evaluation" throughout the book as an umbrella term, but the processes we describe are just as useful to evaluate projects, services, activities, policies, interventions, and products. Evaluation goes beyond improving how things are done to determining if the program's objectives have been achieved. It can also look at longer-term outcomes to determine impact.

Examples of typical social interventions an evaluator might encounter include an employee mentoring program, a medication compliance intervention, a wellness program for employees, a counseling program for new parents, a no-smoking ordinance, a microloans agency in a developing country, a new graduate program in environmental science, a housing program for homeless youth, or an intervention to reduce falls in the elderly. Other types of evaluations focus on program monitoring, fidelity to an established program model, the potential for scaling an innovation, tracking research dissemination and outcomes, and exploring lessons learned. Finally, evaluation can look at the findings of other evaluations to determine overall quality and best practice.

We need to know that the program has solved a **problem**. Funders want to know if their money has been well spent by supporting this initiative, agencies want to know if they should continue to pursue their current direction or change course, staffers want to know if their work has helped program participants make improvements in their lives.

This chapter provides an overview of program evaluation, what it is and why it is important. It also looks at the similarities and differences between research and evaluation. A brief history of evaluation is provided, looking across its development over the last

70 years to become what is now a worldwide discipline. Because evaluation is grounded in the unpredictable context of people, events, and politics, challenges and ethical dilemmas are commonplace and so the chapter reviews the three pillars of ethical conduct that support evaluators in their work. Last of all, an overview is provided of some of the professional education and training opportunities available to evaluators and those interested in pursuing an evaluation career.

You will also enjoy the resources in this chapter including the Spotlight on Equity, which presents the Graduate Education Diversity (GEDI) Program, our expert Dr. Jean King, Key Terms, Main Ideas, Critical Thinking Questions, Student Challenges, and Additional Readings and Resources.

WHAT IS EVALUATION?

Evaluation is an applied inquiry process used to collect and synthesize information that can then be used to draw conclusions about the situation, significance, or quality of a program or other entity under review. Unlike other types of research, evaluation conclusions encompass not only the evidence obtained but also assign a value or judgment to those findings (Fournier, 2005). It combines (Donaldson & Christie, 2006):

> *systematic inquiry and analysis techniques with an eye toward answering important and fundamental questions about programs, policies, and interventions such as: does it work, why does it work, for whom does it work best, and how do we make it work better?* (p. 249)

Many definitions of **program evaluation** exist, but the one we use most often is by Rossi et al. (2004). It states:

> *Program evaluation is the use of social research methods to systematically investigate the effectiveness of social intervention programs in ways that are adapted to their political and organizational environments and are designed to inform social action to improve social conditions.* (p. 16)

This definition addresses how evaluation borrows methods from social science research to conduct studies. It describes evaluation as systematic, meaning that it is not just an informal activity and that there are theories, frameworks, methods, and processes which have been explored and improved by many evaluators over time. The definition mentions the setting of the program and, as we will see, context is critical to any evaluation. Finally, it provides is a call to action as evaluators seek to find ways to foster social justice in our communities and around the world.

However, not all evaluations focus on social justice. Greene sorted evaluation approaches into five main genres, based on the interests they serve, the values they advance, and the needs of the client (Tarsilla, 2010, p. 211):

1. The efficiency interests of policymakers

2. The accountability and ameliorative interests of on-site program managers

3. Learning, understanding and use

4. Understanding and development interests of direct service staff and affiliates

5. Democratic and social change interests of program beneficiaries and their allies.

In 1991, Scriven described evaluation as a transdiscipline (1991a). He suggests this because it is both extraordinarily multidisciplinary and multirole, as the evaluator typically performs tasks often found in other professions. These include research, instruction, therapy, public relations, administration, entrepreneurship, management, as well as the roles of "arbitrator, scapegoat, trouble-shooter, inventor, conscience, jury, judge, or attorney" (pp. 363–364). In addition, the service role is critical because evaluators have clients, not just readers. He concludes, "evaluation has a nature, a flavor, a gestalt of its own. It is idiosyncratic and complex to the extent that it requires a special kind of paradigm." At an expert lecture at the American Evaluation Conference in 2021, he presented a paper calling for the **TransScientific Model of Evaluation** (Scriven, 2021), where he concluded that "Evaluation is the driving logic of science and of the disciplines outside science (e.g., law, drama, medical practice, journalism, education)."

Source: Chris Lysy/FreshSpectrum.com

Many fields benefit from having evaluation as a professional competency, even if it is not their main focus. Examples of fields benefitting from evaluation are listed in Table 1.1.

TABLE 1.1 ● EXAMPLES OF FIELDS BENEFITING FROM EVALUATION	
• Child and Family Studies	• Human Resource Management
• Counseling	• Human Services
• Community Development	• Nonprofit Organizations
• Criminal Justice	• Policy Analysis
• Education	• Psychology
• Emergency Management	• Public Administration
• Foundations	• Public Health
• Government	• Social Work
• Health Sciences	

Michael Patton (2008, p. 5) points out that in the simplest terms, evaluations answer three basic questions (Figure 1.1, p. 8): What? So what? Now what?

This list of questions provides a way to understand problems and discover new solutions. "What?" asks for the story of the program so that it can be understood, and any issues and problems identified. "So what?" tries to make sense of the facts, examines assumptions

FIGURE 1.1 ⬡ WHAT? SO, WHAT? NOW WHAT?

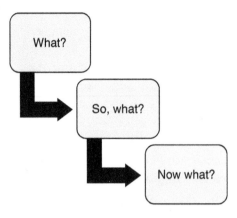

Source: Patton, M. Q. (2008). *Utilization-focused evaluation. SAGE* Publications.

made, looks at who is affected, and explores implications. "Now what?" identifies a course of action and identifies what is needed to make informed decisions (McDowell, 2017; Razzetti, 2019; Tenney & Pew, 2006).

Let's test these basic questions using data literacy as an example.

What?

Data literacy is "understanding what data mean, including how to read charts appropriately, draw correct conclusions from data and recognize when data are being used in misleading or inappropriate ways" (Carlson et al., 2011, p. 5). When someone is data literate, they are confident about their use of data and apply their skills. They need to know where to retrieve data, assess its quality, and interpret it to illuminate the problem they are studying.

So what?

If someone is not data literate, we can assume that they do not know what data to use. They may lack computer skills, or an awareness of what information is available, or be unable to interpret its meaning, or they may experience a fear of numbers in general. If computer literacy is determined to be a barrier, what can be done?

Now what?

A solution could focus first on reducing the amount of anxiety experienced by the individual. Then their computer skills could be assessed and upgraded if needed. They could access online training or work with a trainer or mentor to learn how to use tools and interpret data. Then they could learn how to apply their new skills using mini-cases or scenarios.

Typical evaluation questions might look like those listed in Box 1.1 (Rossi et al., 2004, p. 3):

BOX 1.1 ● TYPICAL EVALUATION QUESTIONS

1. What is the nature and scope of the problem? Where is it located, whom does it affect, how many are affected, and how does it affect them?

2. What is it about the problem or its effects that justifies new, expanded, or modified social programs?

3. What feasible interventions are likely to significantly ameliorate the problem?

4. What are the appropriate intended populations for interventions?

5. Is an intervention reaching its intended population?

6. Is the intervention being implemented well? Are the intended services being provided?

7. Is the intervention effective in attaining the desired goals or benefits?

8. Is the program cost reasonable in relation to its effectiveness and benefits

Source: Rossi, P., Lipsey, M., & Freeman, H. (2004). *Evaluation: A systematic approach.* SAGE Publications.

These critical questions, coupled with the extensive challenges of doing good research in real-world settings, make program evaluation one of the most fascinating fields in social science research. If you like people, love research, are comfortable with constant change, and always need a challenge, then this career is for you.

WHY DO EVALUATION?

Interventions and their subsequent evaluations have the potential to improve lives by telling us what works, what doesn't, and what to do next. For example, a social service agency, government department, school district, public health unit, nonprofit organization, foundation, or other group may need to establish the status of a program to make decisions about its future. They may want to know more about what problems affect their community so that a new intervention can be developed, or more about how a program is working now and how it can be improved, or what difference a current program has made in the community and whether it should be continued. Usually, organizations also want to know what to do next, so most evaluations include recommendations, based on the evidence obtained and feedback provided by stakeholders.

When talking about evaluation, the term **evaluand** is frequently used. It is a term coined by Michael Scriven (2003) to apply to the object of any evaluation or "whatever is being evaluated" (p. 139). For example, a program, service, policy, or product could be an evaluand.

There are four main reasons to conduct an evaluation: to determine merit, worth, and significance; to gain an understanding of how programs work and the difference they can make to stakeholders; to improve quality of life; and to pursue social justice and a more equitable world.

To Determine Merit, Worth, and Significance

The terms merit, worth, and significance are used to attach value to something. According to Greene (1997), evaluators' work, including their findings, is heavily influenced by values, both their client's and their own. Evaluators need to understand what is meant by "good quality."

Merit relates to the intrinsic, context-free attributes and properties of an evaluand. If you are buying an apple, you might prefer one that is sweet, fresh, and symmetrical. Those are intrinsic characteristics of a particular apple. However, if you are planning to make a pie, you may want apples that are tart, not sweet. Or if you are making applesauce, you may not care if the apple is nicely formed. What we value as desirable attributes, therefore, influences the merit of the apple you seek (Lam, 2013).

Worth has extrinsic meaning and so it relates to the value attached to an evaluand in a specific context. Worth requires a thorough understanding of that specific situation. A good apple might be worth $2.00 but one with a large bruise on it might only be worth $0.50. Worth usually has a value attached to it that is equivalent to something else (in this case, money). Thus, it is generally possible to measure worth, whereas merit is more difficult to pin down because it is intrinsic.

Significance depends on the values and meanings ascribed to an evaluand by specific individuals and may have great symbolic value. If the apple comes from a tree that you grew from seed, it has great significance for you and will be treasured and admired. However, the neighbor next door may consider an apple from your tree garbage if it drops onto their carefully manicured lawn.

While the concepts merit, worth, and significance are critical values in evaluation, they are seldom measured directly. Harkreader and Henry (2000) studied a performance measurement system to assess the merit and worth of school reforms made by educational leaders. They found it to be a painstaking endeavor, working their way back and forth "between developing expectations based on the reform, to checking those expectations with data, then unpacking our assumptions and going back to data again" (p. 167). While it was important to investigate plausible, rival explanations before making judgments about merit and worth, in the end, they found it was impossible to link performance measures directly to them as there were too many intervening, unmeasured variables.

Martens (2018) also explored the concepts of merit, worth, and significance in the use of rubrics in evaluation studies, finding that only 20 articles out of 239 mentioned these terms. The authors of these articles "described criteria of *merit* (quality) as opposed to worth (e.g., cost-effectiveness or some sort of value for the money) or significance (importance)" (p. 34) but only about half of them used the terms to reach evaluative conclusions (p. 40). To Martens, it appears that making decisions about merit, worth, or significance is not a simple process. Sirontnik and Oakes (1990) do not view evaluation as simply a way to implement research methods. They depict evaluation "as an ongoing, collaborative, value-driven project of organizational change and improvement" (p. 54).

Scriven (1994) believes that the results are the most frequently desired outcome of an evaluation; however, the findings are the catapult to determine the merit, worth, and significance of the program.

To Gain an Understanding of How Programs Work and the Difference They Can Make to Stakeholders

Evaluations can focus on the activities and events that occur as a program is being delivered (Mathison, 2005, p. 327). They can determine what results are being produced by the operations and if the resources provided to implement the program support the functions the program performs. Evaluation methods dig deeper into how the intervention works and why it works.

Program **stakeholders** are people who have a vested interest in the evaluand and so also in its evaluation (Greene, 2006, p. 397). Typically, they are clustered into four groups:

1. People with decision making authority over the program, such as funders and board members

2. People with direct responsibility for running the program, such as planners, administrators, and staff

3. People who are the intended beneficiaries of the program, as well as their families and communities

4. People disadvantaged by the program, such as those who did not obtain funding for their program because this one was funded instead, or those who could not attend for some reason, or were not selected.

For example, youth from kindergarten through Grade 12 across the United States often participate in out-of-school time (OST) programs, both after school and during the summer months (McCombs et al., 2017). OST programs can offer a variety of options (e.g., after-school clubs, YMCA, Boys & Girls Club), can be academically oriented (e.g., homework support), or can relate to special interests (e.g., sports clubs, theater programs). These large-scale programs are typically funded through a variety of mechanisms, including both public support such as federal, state, and local grants, and private support from tuition and donations. Many stakeholders are involved from policymakers to parents.

When McCombs et al. (2017) conducted a meta-analysis of the many large-scale, rigorous, experimental and quasi-experimental evaluations that had studied these programs, they found that programs were often grouped together without regard for differences among program goals, activities, or the quality of the content provided. They were often judged by a common metric such as achievement test scores. Connecting with stakeholders can help evaluators understand how programs work so they can design effective studies and interpret study results appropriately. These authors recommend that researchers should measure outcomes that align with specific program content and should also explore other factors deemed important to youth development so that policymakers can consider a broader range of outcomes.

To Improve Quality of Life

Quality of life or QOL is a multifaceted concept that is used in many fields that look at outcomes. Wenger et al. (1984) define QOL as "an individual's perceptions of his or her functioning and well-being in different domains of life" (p. 908). It has been adopted by clinicians, researchers, economists, and managers (Carr et al., 1996) as well as by evaluators. It was coined in the United States in the post-war period to describe the effect of material affluence (such as cars, houses, and consumer goods) but has been broadened to also encompass education, physical and mental health, the environment, recreation and leisure time, social belonging, religious beliefs, safety, security, and freedom.

QOL can be thought of as the sum of a range of objectively measured life conditions which can be determined numerically and then compared to a larger population, or as a subjective reaction to life conditions (life satisfaction), measuring the significance an individual places on each domain or subscale (Celestine, 2021).

Many instruments have been designed to measure QOL, for example population surveys and screening tools. Evaluators need to be aware of its limitations, and select a scale suited to the goal of the research rather than choosing one that is popular in the literature. Its use as a generic measure, however, does eliminate more useful information about the actual experiences of the individual. There is good information available on how to select an appropriate QOL questionnaire. For a comprehensive guide on selecting the best QOL questionnaire for your needs, check the Additional Readings and Resources Section for Hyland's (2003) *Brief Guide.*

Purcell et al. (2021) examined the impact of a pilot Whole Health Coaching program for the Veterans Health Administration to determine how the program helped veterans improve their health and quality of life. The program engaged veterans across multiple dimensions of wellbeing and provided coaching to help them develop and implement personal health plans. Using a mixed methods approach, they combined pre-and post-coaching surveys with follow-up qualitative interviews and found that, "although self-reported health goals varied widely, veterans were largely satisfied with their progress toward their goals, often describing that progress as incremental and ongoing after coaching" (p. 9).

To Pursue Social Justice and a More Equitable World

The idea of social justice is underpinned by two concepts: equality and equity. Equality means that all people are entitled to the same rights, freedoms, and opportunities to make the most of their lives and talents. It means that everyone has the same amount of benefit regardless of their existing needs or assets. Equity is the fair treatment of every individual, with access to opportunity, networks, resources, and supports so that they get what they need to survive and thrive. Braverman et al. (2011) define equity in relation to health in the following quotation, but it is just as applicable to any human service:

...is the value underlying a commitment to reduce and ultimately eliminate health disparities. Health equity means social justice with respect to health and reflects the ethical and human rights concerns.... Health equity means striving to equalize opportunities to be healthy. In accord with the other ethical principles of beneficence (doing good) and non malfeasance (doing no harm), equity requires concerted effort to achieve more rapid improvements among those who were worse off to start, within an overall strategy to improve everyone's health. Closing health gaps by worsening advantaged groups' health is not a way to achieve equity. Reductions in health disparities (by improving the health of the socially disadvantaged) are the metric by which progress toward health equity is measured. (p. S151)

An infographic from the Robert Wood Johnson Foundation (2017) provides a visual comparison of equality and equity in a health context (Figure 1.2).

FIGURE 1.2 ⬡ VISUALIZING HEALTH EQUITY: ONE SIZE DOES NOT FIT ALL

Source: Copyright 2017. Robert Wood Johnson Foundation. Used with permission from the Robert Wood Johnson Foundation.

The infographic depicts equality by providing all the cyclists with bikes of the same size; however, for a variety of reasons related to their personal situations, they may not be able to use their bike effectively. In the second image, equity is depicted as each person accessing and using the specific type of bike which best meets their needs.

This then brings us to the idea of fairness in a social context. Social justice refers to the just distribution of wealth, opportunity, and privilege in society. In evaluation terms, it means assessing "whether the distribution of benefits and burdens among members (or groups) of a society are appropriate, fair, and moral" (House, 2005, p. 393). Social justice is directly linked to evaluation because programs and policies directly affect the distribution of benefits and burdens. Despite this conceptual link, House maintains that social justice concerns are often omitted from evaluation discussions, either because evaluators are not well enough versed in the concepts or because adherence can be politically risky.

The dominance of values-free social research in the twentieth century meant that a utilitarian frame prevailed and that overall benefits should be increased as much as possible so that everyone could have more, but how those benefits were distributed was not a major issue (House, 2005, p. 394). However, views on the concept have shifted over time. Eventually, the way that social benefits were distributed became important for evaluators and led to the inclusion of multiple methods and multiple stakeholders in evaluation studies. Even more recently, diverse identities have begun to be considered, giving all stakeholders an effective voice in defining their own needs and negotiating their own benefits (House, p. 395). Several evaluation approaches now give stakeholders roles to play in the evaluation itself, which is a more democratic and participatory approach, but evaluators still differ on what level of involvement is necessary. Social justice continues to be a controversial topic in evaluation although there is growing attention being paid to breaking barriers, creating safety nets, and ensuring economic justice.

In the evaluation of a university-sponsored parent education program (Cooper & Christie, 2005), rather than designing an approach that would be useful to all identified stakeholder groups, the authors shifted their focus to the least powerful stakeholder group, namely the low-income Hispanic parent participants (p. 2249) to emphasize the gap between parents' and educators' notions of empowerment. They cited the admonishment by House (1991) that, "evaluation be socially just as well as true, that it attend to the interests of everyone in society and not solely the privileged" (p. 244). Using a qualitative case study approach, they determined that parents' views were being unwittingly or inappropriately overlooked. They found that educators and administrators needed to share power, validate parents' perspectives, and show sensitivity to culturally relevant values that influenced parents' educational priorities.

RESEARCH AND EVALUATION

How is evaluation different from **research**? This perennial question generates a lot of debate about the differences and similarities of these terms. Research is referred to as the "systematic investigation, including research development, testing, and evaluation, designed to develop or contribute to generalizable knowledge" (Steneck, 2007, p. 39).

There are three ways to view this issue.

Evaluation and Research Are Mutually Exclusive

The first perspective is that research produces generalizable knowledge, is more theoretical, and is more firmly controlled by the researchers; evaluation produces specific, applied knowledge, and is more controlled by those funding or commissioning the evaluation (Rogers, 2014c). The distinction is described by Patton (2017) in Table 1.2, p. 15.

TABLE 1.2 ⬡ DIFFERENCES BETWEEN RESEARCH AND EVALUATION	
Research	**Evaluation**
• Purpose is testing theory and producing generalizable findings.	• Purpose is to determine the effectiveness of a specific program or model.
• Questions originate with scholars in a discipline.	• Questions originate with stakeholders and primary intended users of evaluation findings.
• Quality and importance judged by peer review in a discipline.	• Quality and importance judged by those who will use the findings to take action and make decisions.
• Ultimate test of value is contribution to knowledge.	• Ultimate test of value is usefulness to improve effectiveness.

Source: Patton, M. Q. (2017). Evaluation flash cards: Embedding evaluative thinking in organizational culture. *Otto Bremer Foundation.* ottobremer.org

Evaluation Requires Research but Research Does Not Require Evaluation

The second stance suggests that research is empirical, involves factual description, and generally does not include a judgment about quality. Evaluation is also empirical, but its purpose is to determine the merit, worth, or significance of something—essentially to make a value judgment (Wanzer, 2019). However, evaluation is about more than just conducting the research, its purpose includes learning and capacity building, informing decision making, and improving programming.

Wanzer studied how evaluators and researchers defined program evaluation and differentiated evaluation from research. "Evaluators were more likely to think research and evaluation intersect whereas researchers were more likely to think evaluation is a sub-component of research." According to Wanzer (2020), evaluators saw more differences than researchers in how a study was initiated (purpose, questions, audience) and how it ended (rendering value judgments, disseminating results).

Evaluators rely on good research every time they conduct a literature review so they can base their evaluation design on a foundation of well-supported evidence. When the knowledge is not there, evaluation becomes more developmental and exploratory because the research foundation is weak (Patton, 2017, p. 7). Bloom (2010) states that "evaluation, in contrast to research, is very much influenced by its participants, which includes on-the-dime changes of direction when local evidence supports such change" (p. 2).

Chapel (2012) humorously illustrates how evaluation and research are different:

> *Researchers must stand back and wait for the experiment to play out. To use the analogy of cultivating tomato plants, researchers ask, "How many tomatoes did we grow?" Evaluation, on the other hand, is a process unfolding in real time. In addition to determining numbers of tomatoes, evaluators also inquire about related areas like,*

"how much watering and weeding is taking place?" "Are there nematodes on the plants?" If evaluators realize that activities are insufficient, staff are free to adjust accordingly. (p. 1)

In Figure 1.3, we see that research contributes to a knowledge base and evaluation contributes to program improvement. The dotted line returning from Program to Evaluation suggests that evidence of best practice needs to inform the field.

FIGURE 1.3 ⬢   THE DIFFERENCES BETWEEN RESEARCH AND EVALUATION

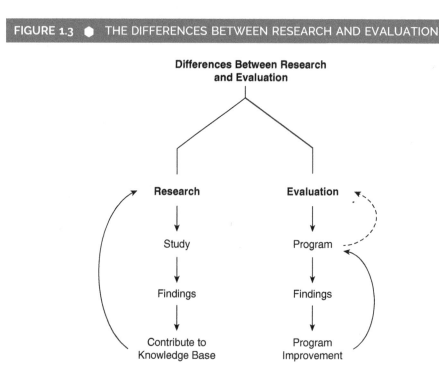

Evaluation and Research Share Similarities

A third view is that the disciplines of research and evaluation share the same overall goal of making life better for people and use many of the same tools, strategies, and methods. Both are based on answering a question, but the evaluation tends to focus on the intervention, processes, impacts, and outcomes. Both start with a design and plan (a research plan or an evaluation plan), both work with data (e.g., qualitative, quantitative, or a combination of the two), both employ approved analysis techniques (e.g., statistics, content analysis), and the results of both types of studies can be submitted for publication in academic journals.

Which perspective resonates with you?

Next we introduce you to our Spotlight on Equity, a feature in every chapter. This first Spotlight is about the Graduate Education Diversity (GEDI) Program, a program of the American Evaluation Association.

SPOTLIGHT ON EQUITY

The Graduate Education Diversity (GEDI) Program: A Pipeline of Emerging Evaluators of Color and Those Underrepresented and Underserved in the Field of Evaluation

AMERICAN
EVALUATION
ASSOCIATION

Source: American Evaluation Association/eval.org

The Graduate Education Diversity (GEDI) Program grew out of the recommendations of the American Evaluation Association (AEA) Building Diversity Initiative (BDI) (1999–2001). The initiative brought together the vision of several diverse groups of evaluators and reflected the views of those AEA members who were becoming aware of the importance of culturally responsive evaluation (CRE) and the need to address diversity issues. The mission was clear: "to develop a cadre of evaluators that were responsive to the needs of underrepresented and underserved groups of color in the United States" (Symonette et al., 2014, p. 12). While first conceived as a fellowship, after discussions with the AEA Board, the concept was expanded to become an internship program that recruited students of color.

Sponsored by the AEA and the W. K. Kellogg Foundation, the first GEDI cohort was welcomed at Duquesne University in 2004. The program's current host site is Community Science.

Program goals include (https://www.eval.org/gedi) the following:

a. Recruit graduate students of color from diverse fields to extend their research capacities in evaluation.

b. Stimulate evaluation thinking concerning diverse communities and persons of color.

c. Deepen the evaluation profession's capacity to work in racially, ethnically, and culturally diverse settings.

Program participants are graduate students of color whose academic focus was not evaluation but who could see a career fit with the internship goals. They are mainly comprised of African American, Hispanic, Native American, and Asian American predoctoral students (Collins et al., 2014, p. 31) and come from a variety of disciplines including public health, education, political science, anthropology, psychology, sociology, social work, and the natural sciences. They share a strong background in research skills, an interest in extending their skills in the field of evaluation, and a commitment to thinking deeply about culturally responsive evaluation practice (https://www.eval.org/Education-Programs/Graduate-Education-Diversity-Internship/Application).

The interns work approximately two days per week at an internship site for a ten-month period from September to June, gaining real-world experience to build their skills and confidence. The GEDI program also provides them with additional support through four multiday intensive trainings, monthly webinars, paid attendance at the AEA Annual Conference and the AEA Summer Evaluation Institute, mentoring, and many networking opportunities. Interns receive a stipend, and their travel expenses are reimbursed. GEDI curriculum and pedagogy is informed by a multidimensional theoretical framework across individual, organizational, community, and professional outcomes (Collins et al., 2014). Each intensive multiday training is associated with specific overarching themes, learning topics, associated readings, and reflective writing assignments. Topics are identified through a needs assessment conducted at the start of the program. Pedagogical practices include one-on-one coaching on culturally responsive and equitable evaluation theory and practice across academic institutions and internship sites. The program prioritizes equity and social justice and emphasizes peer relations and the construction of a familial environment.

At the 10-year mark, Stafford Hood reflected on the development of the program (Hood, 2014, p. 118). He saw the need to increase the number of culturally responsive evaluators worldwide to improve the lot of those who are traditionally disenfranchised. In his view, the GEDI Program has the potential to serve as a model for other programs that wish to target diversity and culturally responsive evaluation.

Now, in its eighteenth year (2021–2022), the program boasts over 130 alumni of the program. Most of them work in major philanthropic, governmental, educational, and nonprofit organizations in the United States. Their hope is to inspire and catalyze a deeper and fuller understanding of the intersection of culture with equity and justice.

The program has empowered students to become adaptive leaders. A case study on leadership, conducted by the sixth cohort, captured the perspectives of 32 former participants as well as from seven members of their own cohort (Aponte-Soto et al., 2013, p. 40). Technical evaluation training was central to their learning, but leadership skills were also prominent. Due to their interactions with influential evaluation mentors and thought leaders in CRE, they have gained the confidence they need to support vulnerable populations. As one GEDI graduate commented (Aponte-Soto et al., 2014):

After participating in GEDI, I have been sought after as an evaluator by organizations in need of evaluation at universities and foundations. In sum, not only do I feel more credible as an evaluator after GEDI, but others also recognize this increased credibility and potential to be a leader in evaluation. (p. 41)

This Spotlight on Equity is based on the contributions of Dr. Sául Isaac Maldonado, Anisha Lewis, Dr. Rodney Hopson, Zachary Grays, and Dr. Brandi Gilbert.

A BRIEF HISTORY OF EVALUATION

To get a sense of the field of evaluation, it is useful to look at how the profession started, how it has continued to grow, and the forces that have influenced it. Understanding changing politics and values over time can provide a useful backdrop for shifts in evaluative thinking and studying the past can provide inspiration and direction for the future and the work that remains. Figure 1.4, p. 19 provides a timeline for the development of the evaluation profession from 1792 to the beginning of the twenty-first century based on the work by several theorists (American Evaluation Association, 2018b; Hogan, 2007; Hoskins, 1968; Mathison, 2005; Reiser, 2001; Stufflebeam et al., 2000; Worthen et al., 1997).

The early roots of evaluation in the United States began in the eighteenth century in 1792, when William Farish invented the first written university examination, using quantitative grades to rank students on their grasp of the practical applications of chemistry (Hoskins, 1968). Horace Mann, the father of modern education, systemized early colonial education by requiring printed tests to determine student achievement. In 1845, under his leadership, the Massachusetts Board of Education employed a comprehensive assessment of student achievement to assess a large school system (Stufflebeam et al., 2000).

In the first half of the twentieth century, Kurt Lewin, a pioneer in action research, contributed to our understanding of how to solve real-world problems with research. Famous for force field analysis, he believed that behavior is a function of the person and their environment.

During the Great Depression in the 1930s, social programs expanded. Unemployment was high and impoverished families struggled. President Franklin D. Roosevelt's New Deal came to their aid through public works projects intended to offer employment assistance (Berkin, 2011) and eventually social programs would become a mainstay in the

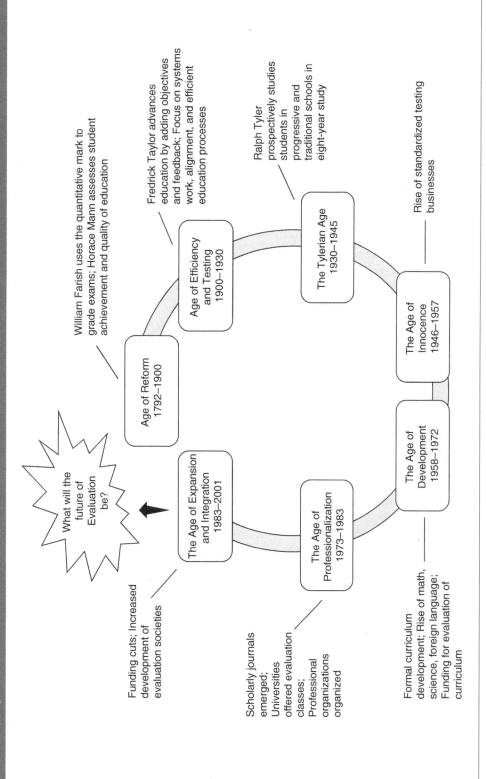

FIGURE 1.4 ● EVALUATION PROFESSION TIMELINE

Source: Adapted from Stufflebeam, D. L., Madaus, C. F., & Kellaghan, T. (2000). *Evaluation models.* Kluwer Academic.

evaluation field. At the time, however, the main developments in evaluation went hand in hand with changes in education.

Fredrick W. Taylor advanced scientific thinking by focusing on observation, measurement, analysis, and efficiency. Educators added objectives to testing to determine the quality of instruction and the effectiveness of school districts. The goal was to add student grades to provide feedback to the student (Worthen et al., 1997).

Ralph Tyler, in the eight-year study, assessed the outcomes of programs in 15 progressive high schools and 15 traditional high schools. He revised educational objectives to include behaviors. After World War II, student evaluation became more sophisticated, with broadening objectives to include the types of learning teachers expected (Reiser, 2001).

When the Russians launched Sputnik, the first Earth satellite, in 1957, a national discussion of preparedness for war began and questions were asked about whether education was adequately preparing American youth (National Aeronautics and Space Administration, 2018). With national defense and security as the top priority, Congress focused on how students were performing in mathematics, science, and foreign languages. Funding focused on educational outcomes. Low-income children became a focal point, and the expectation was that curriculum evaluation would show what worked and how educational outcomes were improved, especially for low-income children (Weiss, 1972).

In the 1960s, after the assassination of President John F. Kenney, President Lyndon Johnson continued the war on poverty, introducing the age of the Great Society. As a result, the government "began to take on more responsibility for the general welfare of its citizens…" (Mathison, 2008, p. 184). Not surprisingly, with the investment, concern grew about program outcomes and their return on investment. Program evaluation as a profession grew out of this need. Evaluators soon found work in contract research firms, universities, and public sector offices (Mathison, 2008). In addition, universities began to train students interested in social serving professions.

In the 1970s and 1980s, evaluators began to be professionalized. Examples of early peer-reviewed evaluation journals include Educational Evaluation and Policy Analysis, Studies in Educational Evaluation, CEDR Quarterly, Evaluation Review, New Directions for Program Evaluation, Evaluation and Program Planning, and Evaluation News (Stufflebeam et al., 2000).

Two American professional evaluation societies were founded in the 1970s: the Evaluation Research Society (ERS) and the Evaluation Network (ENet). They aimed to foster evaluation as both a profession and a science. In 1986, they merged to form the American Evaluation Association (AEA). Meanwhile, responding to similar societal and governmental pressures, the Canadian Evaluation Society (CES) incorporated in May 1981 (Canadian Evaluation Society, 2018). In 1986, the new AEA held its first evaluation conference in Kansas City, Missouri (American Evaluation Association, 2018b).

Evaluation has grown exponentially as the need for evaluative thinking and accountability has become mainstream around the world. The International Organization for

Cooperation in Evaluation (IOCE), founded in 2001, includes many groups involved in advancing evaluation as a profession. It represents international, national, sub-national, and regional Voluntary Organizations for Professional Evaluation or VOPEs ("vo-pee's"). Its goal is to strengthen international evaluation by exchanging evaluation methods and promoting good governance while recognizing the value of evaluation in people's lives. There are currently over 170 VOPEs, large and small, across the globe that are recognized by the IOCE, ranging from the Afghan Evaluation Society (AfES) to the Zimbabwe Evaluation Society (ZES). In total, they represent a membership of almost 52,000 evaluators (International Organization for Cooperation in Evaluation, 2018). As of 2018, the American Evaluation Association (AEA) had approximately 7,300 members representing all 50 states and more than 80 other countries (American Evaluation Association, 2018b).

As Shadish and Luellen commented, social and political climates have influenced evaluation. Funding and types of questions evaluators ask often change with the political tides. However, as they say, "…the need for evaluation seems to be here to stay, as citizens and their representatives prioritize programs and the social problems addressed, as existing programs continue to be scrutinized, and as new and modified programs are proposed" (Mathison, 2005).

Since 2001, there have been several developments in the field of evaluation. Cultural humility, identity and the subjective paradigm, data visualization, and the international growth of evaluation are topics that have blossomed and will continue to influence the work of evaluators.

THE THREE PILLARS OF EVALUATION

Considering the real-world context in which evaluation occurs, where politics, social need, and financial obligation intersect, the evaluator must resolve challenges, conflicts, and dilemmas. To find guidance for completing our work in the best way possible, evaluators rely on the **three evaluation pillars** (Canadian Evaluation Society, 2010) that support reasoned and ethical conduct:

1. The Guiding Principles (the evaluator's conduct)

2. The Program Evaluation Standards (the evaluation work)

3. The Professional Competencies (the evaluator's capacity to do the work)

We will look at each of these important topics.

The Guiding Principles

An essential component for evaluators is to have a clear ethical stance. **Ethics** is defined as norms for conduct, distinguishing between acceptable and unacceptable behavior (Resnik, 2020). Most people learn ethical norms at home, school, religious institution, or other social setting and ideas about right and wrong are so ubiquitous, one might think they are simply commonsense. However, while people may recognize common norms, how they interpret, apply and balance them varies widely. Many disciplines and professions have standards for behavior that suit their particular aims and goals. Researchers in general is guided by ethical norms because of the need to promote knowledge and truth, to minimize error and misrepresentation, to instill values of collaboration and trust among co-workers, to be held accountable to the public, to build public trust in findings, and to promote important social and moral values such as social responsibility, human rights, public health, and safety (Resnik, 2020).

Because evaluation takes place in a political and organizational context, general research norms are expanded to include a focus on stakeholders and decision makers, as well as study participants, and to acknowledge the power, values and norms that underlie their relationships during the evaluation process (Barnett & Camfield, 2016). Morris (2008) states that ethical conflict can arise at any point in an evaluation, from project entry, design, data collection, data analysis, interpretation, and communication of findings, to the ultimate use of the evaluation. However, he continues that a significant minority of evaluators claim to have never encountered an ethical conflict. While this is surprising, perhaps it has to do with the lens through which they view their work. Some may interpret an issue as an ethical challenge, and others may consider it a political, philosophical, or methodological dispute.

As evaluators, we view our work through multiple ethical lenses (Barrington, 2012c):

Values Lens

We form the values lens early. Our culture, race, religion, beliefs, values, and morals shape our worldview and govern our day-to-day behavior. The evaluator's values at the beginning of a project must be acknowledged. At times these may conflict with the values of the program.

Methods Lens

The methods lens results from our research and evaluation training and guides our work processes throughout the life cycle of the evaluation project. Supported by institutional review boards or IRBs, well-designed research protects our human subjects. Three overarching principles include respect for persons, concern for welfare, and justice (Canadian Institutes of Health Research, 2014; U.S. Department of Health and Human Services, 2018).

Conduct Lens

The conduct lens relates to how we do our work and involves the interpersonal realm. All our activities must lead to fostering social equity, communicating effectively, and respecting differences. How we behave is how our clients will remember us.

Business Lens

The business lens is essential in any evaluation project. Whether a formal contract exists or not, the evaluator expects compensation for their work. Regardless of if they are a contractor or an employee, each evaluator must manage the evaluation project, reach a mutual understanding about the scope of work, avoid conflict of interest, respect proprietary and confidential information, and be accountable for project requirements.

The American Evaluation Association (AEA) adopted a set of **Guiding Principles for Evaluators** in 1994. These have been reviewed and updated several times, with member consultation, as part of an evolving process of self-examination by the profession, incorporating member feedback (through surveys and town hall meetings), stories evaluators tell about ethical challenges, and changing societal perspectives. For example, topics related to cultural competence were added in 2004. It is the policy of AEA to review the Principles at least every five years, engaging members in the process (American Evaluation Association, 2018a).

As was stated by AEA in 2004:

> *The principles are intended to guide the professional practice of evaluators, and to inform evaluation clients and the general public about the principles they can expect to be upheld by professional evaluators. Of course, no statement of principles can anticipate all situations that arise in the practice of evaluation. However, principles are not just guidelines for reaction when something goes wrong or when a dilemma is found. Rather, principles should proactively guide the behaviors of professionals in everyday practice.* (p. 3)

Five interconnected principles, as are shown in Box 1.2 should govern the behavior of an evaluator at all stages of the evaluation (American Evaluation Association, 2018a).

BOX 1.2 ● AMERICAN EVALUATION ASSOCIATION

Evaluators' Ethical Guiding Principles

A: **Systematic Inquiry:** Evaluators conduct data-based inquiries that are thorough, methodical, and contextually relevant.

B: **Competence:** Evaluators provide skilled professional services to stakeholders.

C: **Integrity:** Evaluators behave with honesty and transparency to ensure the integrity of the evaluation.

D: **Respect for People:** Evaluators honor the dignity, well-being, and self-worth of individuals and acknowledge the influence of culture within and across groups.

E: **Common Good and Equity:** Evaluators strive to contribute to the common good and advancement of an equitable and just society.

Source: American Evaluation Association. (2018a). *Guiding principles for evaluators and code of ethics.* https://www.eval.org/p/cm/ld/fid=51

Each principle is accompanied by several sub-statements to amplify the meaning of the overarching principle and to provide guidance for its application. The Canadian Evaluation Society also has an Ethics Statement which was first published in 1995. It has three statements about competence, integrity, and accountability, each with a subset of statements about acceptable conduct.

The Program Evaluation Standards

While the Guiding Principles relate to *evaluator conduct*, the Program Evaluation Standards are about the *evaluation work* itself and the key attributes that support its quality. In 1975, a broad-based coalition of professional organizations in the United States and Canada created the Joint Committee on Standards for Educational Evaluation (JCSEE), an incorporated public charity (Joint Committee on Standards for Educational Evaluation, 2011). Each of the 15-member groups sent a representative to the Committee to discuss, interpret and determine evaluation standards resulting in The Program Evaluation Standards: A Guide for Evaluators and Evaluation Users (1981, 1994, 2011). Like the Guiding Principles, the number of editions speaks to evaluators' dedication to and need for these practical guidelines. In addition, scholars and practitioners have scrutinized the standards and input solicited and obtained from national and international reviews, field trials, and national hearings (Yarbrough et al., 2011). Today, the Joint Committee is supported by 17 sponsoring organizations and is a member of the American National Standards Institute. During its 35-year history, its mission has been "to develop and implement inclusive processes producing widely used evaluation standards that serve educational and social improvement" (Yarbrough et al., 2011, p. xviii).

There are five categories of standards and each is accompanied by statements that deal with critical practice issues (see Table 1.3).

TABLE 1.3 ● JOINT COMMITTEE ON STANDARDS FOR EDUCATIONAL EVALUATION		
Standards	**Type**	
Utility Ensure that an evaluation will serve the information needs of intended users.	**U1** Evaluator Credibility **U2** Attention to Stakeholders **U3** Negotiated Purposes **U4** Explicit Values **U5** Relevant Information	**U6** Meaningful Processes and Products **U7** Timely and Appropriate Communicating and Reporting **U8** Concern for Consequences and Influence
Feasibility Ensure that an evaluation will be realistic, prudent, diplomatic, and frugal.	**F1** Project Management **F2** Practical Procedures	**F3** Contextual Viability **F4** Resource Use
Propriety Ensure that an evaluation will be conducted legally, ethically,	**P1** Responsive and Inclusive Orientation **P2** Formal Agreements	**P4** Clarity and Fairness **P5** Transparency and Disclosure

Table 1.3 *(Continued)*

Standards	Type	
and with due regard for the welfare of those involved in the evaluation as well as those affected by its results.	**P3** Human Rights and Respect	**P6** Conflicts of Interests **P7** Fiscal Responsibility
Accuracy Ensure that an evaluation will reveal and convey technically adequate information about the features that determine the worth or merit of the program being evaluated.	**A1** Justified Conclusions and Decisions **A2** Valid Information **A3** Reliable Information **A4** Explicit Program and Context Descriptions	**A5** Information Management **A6** Sound Designs and Analyses **A7** Explicit Evaluation Reasoning **A8** Communication and Reporting
Evaluation Accountability Ensure the responsible use of resources to produce value by documenting and improving evaluation accountability through internal and external metaevaluation and reflection.	**E1** Evaluation Documentation **E2** Internal Metaevaluation	**E3** External Metaevaluation

Source: Yarbrough, D. B., Shula, L. M., Hopson, R. K., & Caruthers, F. A. (2010). *The program evaluation standards: A guide for evaluators and evaluation users* (3rd ed.). Corwin Press.

Table 1.4 outlines the application of the standards and questions to judge the evaluator's work.

TABLE 1.4 ● APPLYING THE PROGRAM EVALUATION STANDARDS		
Standard	**Key Phrase**	**Questions**
Utility	Evaluation has value for stakeholders	• Are those evaluated included in the decision making and design of the evaluation? • Is there a good fit between the evaluators and the needs of the evaluation? • Is the interpretation of findings appropriate? • Does the evaluator prepare clear and useful documents? • Are findings disseminated to a broader audience? • Do stakeholders use the evaluation to make decisions related to whether the program should continue? • Is the evaluation transformative for the organization?
Feasibility	Evaluation is innovative	• Does the evaluation not interfere with the usual routine? • Is the evaluator considering the different lenses through which all those concerned may be viewing the issue? • Does evaluation use resources wisely?

Table 1.4 *(Continued)*

Standard	Key Phrase	Questions
Propriety	Evaluation sets high standards	• Is there a formal agreement of methodology and operations? • Are human subjects treated ethically? • Do the evaluator and stakeholder interact throughout the evaluation? • Is the evaluation complete and fair? • Are results revealed? • Are conflicts of interest shared? • Is evaluation conducted with fiscal care?
Accuracy	Evaluation is right on target	• Is the evaluation explained with the context in mind? • Does the evaluation serve its purpose? • Are procedures used reliable? • Is evaluation described well? • Does the evaluator employ the use of information management to run the evaluation? • Is evaluation reasoning used? • Does the evaluator protect against misconceptions, biases, distortions, and errors in the documentation?
Accountability	Evaluation is defendable	• Do the evaluators document their work? • Do evaluators consult other sources to support their work?

Source: Adapted from Yarbrough, D. B., Shula, L. M., Hopson, R. K., & Caruthers, F. A. (2010). *The program evaluation standards: A guide for evaluators and evaluation users* (3rd ed.). Corwin Press.

Evaluators often work alone or in small groups and can find themselves on an uneven playing field where the client often wields access, resources, and power. On the other hand, evaluation users or clients often have multiple responsibilities and demands placed on them by their organization and can feel torn serving various interests. As a result, both parties can experience role confusion, bias, and poor communication. The Program Evaluation Standards provide meaningful discussion on each topic, offer recommendations for implementation, identify possible hazards, and present a relevant scenario for discussion. When project difficulties arise, this critical book is a great resource.

Many other organizations and government departments have developed norms of evaluation practice. Examples include the United Nations (2019) Development Program Evaluation Policy and the United Kingdom's Magenta Book (HM Treasury, 2020). Ethical protocols and frameworks have also been developed for planning and evaluating in specific contexts, such as in public health in the United States (Kass, 2001). Others address specific populations such as indigenous peoples, for example, the Aotearoa New Zealand Evaluation Standards (Aotearoa New Zealand Evaluation Association, 2015) that reflect New Zealand's bicultural context, and in Canada, the Tri-Council statement for conducting research involving the First Nations, Inuit, and Métis peoples (2018).

The Professional Competencies

With all the focus on ethics and standards, it is not surprising that evaluators turned toward the defining the characteristics of a good evaluator. In 2001, Jean King, Laurie Stevahn, and their colleagues began to explore the possibility of a taxonomy of essential evaluator **professional competencies** (King et al., 2001), and by 2005 they had a validated list of competencies. They define competencies as "the background, knowledge, skills, and dispositions program evaluators need to achieve standards that constitute sound evaluations" (Stevahn et al., 2005).

The American Evaluation Association struck a task force between 2015 and 2018 and engaged AEA members in discussing what makes evaluators distinct as practicing professionals. They developed a list of proposed domains and discussed the pros and cons of evaluator competencies, gathering feedback through a survey, World Café-style listening posts, presentations at conferences, focus groups, and requests for feedback on the AEA website. In 2018, the AEA Board adopted the final list of AEA Evaluator Competencies. Box 1.3 outlines the five domains and the competencies for each (American Evaluation Association, 2018c).

BOX 1.3 ● THE 2018 AEA PROFESSIONAL COMPETENCIES

1.0 **Professional Practice** focuses on what makes evaluators distinct as practicing professionals. Professional practice is grounded in AEA's foundational documents, including the Program Evaluation Standards, the AEA Guiding Principles, and the AEA Statement on Cultural Competence.

2.0 **Methodology** focuses on technical aspects of evidence-based, systematic inquiry for valued purposes. Methodology includes quantitative, qualitative, and mixed designs for learning, understanding, decision making, and judging.

3.0 **Context** focuses on understanding the unique circumstances, multiple perspectives, and changing settings of evaluations and their users/stakeholders. Context involves site/location/environment, participants/stakeholders, organization/structure, culture/diversity, history/traditions, values/beliefs, politics/economics, power/privilege, and other characteristics.

4.0 **Planning and Management** focuses on determining and monitoring work plans, timelines, resources, and other components needed to complete and deliver an evaluation study. Planning and management include networking, developing proposals, contracting, determining work assignments, monitoring progress, and fostering use.

5.0 **Interpersonal** focuses on human relations and social interactions that ground evaluator effectiveness for professional practice throughout the evaluation. Interpersonal skills include cultural competence, communication, facilitation, and conflict resolution.

Source: American Evaluation Association. (2018c). *The 2018 AEA evaluator competencies.*

Evaluator competencies provide a common language and set of criteria to clarify what it means to be an evaluator. The competencies will (American Evaluation Association, 2018c):

- Serve as a roadmap for guiding evaluator education and training

- Encourage members to engage in critical self-reflection about strengths and limitations and find appropriate ways to expand and improve their practice

- Identify ways to improve practice in the field

- Reflect the services evaluators are called upon to perform in multiple contexts

- Recognize the interdependence and overlap of the domains.

They will play a role in moving the field of evaluation toward increased professionalization and improved practice (King, 2020, pp. 7–8). An issue of *New Directions in Evaluation* has documented their development process, but as its editor, Jean King, remarks, "the real work of using the competencies has only just begun" (p. 10).

The Canadian Evaluation Society also began a process to tailor evaluator competencies to the Canadian experience, and through research, member consultation, and expert validation, prepared The Canadian Evaluation Society Competencies for Canadian Evaluation Practice in 2010. Acknowledging that the skills and knowledge for any discipline or profession grows and evolves, influenced by new research and changing environmental circumstances, the CES updated the Competencies in 2018 (Canadian Evaluation Society, 2018). They form the basis of the Credentialed Evaluator (CE) designation.

EDUCATION AND TRAINING

Part of what makes evaluation such an interesting profession is that practitioners come from a wide range of fields and work in an expanding set of contexts such as education, health care, public health, government, policy, development, social services, environment, foundations, and both for-profit and not-for profit organizations.

Stufflebeam (2001) and other writers have suggested that the reputation, impact, and longevity of evaluation as a profession is dependent on evaluation practitioners participating in and applying the lessons learned from high-quality educational experiences (LaVelle, 2018, p. xiv). A recent directory of evaluator education programs in the United States revealed that there are 71 master's and doctoral programs currently operating in the U.S. along with 42 certificate programs (LaVelle, 2018, p. xvi). An inventory conducted in Canada found programs with an emphasis in evaluation are offered by 54 departments in 27 universities across eight Canadian provinces (Hunter & McDavid, 2019, p. 213). American programs are largely offered by university departments of education, educational psychology, and psychology—79.5% of programs were located in these three disciplines (LaVelle, 2014). By contrast, only 21% of evaluation programs were housed in similar departments in Canada; many others were offered in medicine, health, public policy/

administration, management, and social work (Hunter & McDavid, 2019, p. 215). In addition, many disciplines in both countries offer a single course in program evaluation.

Evaluators draw heavily from research methods and could not practice their craft without this methodological expertise (LaVelle & Donaldson, 2015, p. 41) yet despite much being written about the value of qualitative and mixed methods, most programs focus largely on measurement, assessment, and statistics. While methodological and technical expertise are important, evaluators need additional skills in organizational theory and behavior because they spend so much time working in an organizational context. They also need to learn about situational analysis, relationship building, communication, capacity building, negotiation and conflict management, visual data presentation, project and contract management, and reflexivity. Few if any institutions offer courses that focus directly on culturally responsive evaluation (LaVelle, 2018) and other ways of knowing such as Indigenous knowledge, the Black experience, and gendered perspectives.

Many evaluation professionals receive professional development through short courses and workshops offered by professional organizations such as AEA and CES. The Claremont Evaluation Center and The Evaluators' Institute offer short courses and certificate programs. One other popular professional development opportunity, organized by AEA, is held in Atlanta each year and is designed for evaluators, applied researchers, grant makers, foundation program officers, nonprofit administrators, and others, especially in public health.

PROFESSIONALIZATION

Emerging from the discussion on evaluator competencies is the recent global trend toward the professionalization of evaluation. What are acceptable qualifications, group norms of conduct, best practices, and how do we differentiate between the qualified and the unqualified?

While professionalization has long been a topic of discussion among evaluators, Canada was the first to solidify the process. The CES Credentialed Evaluator (CE) designation was initiated in 2010 and there are now over 500 CEs. The holder of the CE designation must provide convincing evidence of requisite skills, knowledge, and practical experience in five competency areas. Applicants must have a graduate degree or equivalent, two years (or equivalent) of evaluation experience, references, and a portfolio which they complete online that describes their use of the competencies. Their submission is reviewed by members of the CES Credentialing Board, comprised of senior evaluation professionals with at least 25 years of evaluation experience. Once the CE is granted, the evaluator must accumulate and report at least 40 hours of continuing education every three years to maintain the designation. A public registry lists the CEs (Canadian Evaluation Society, 2018).

Other VOPEs have begun to formalize the status of evaluators, including Japan, South Africa, and the United Kingdom, while the European Evaluation Society is promoting a

Voluntary Peer Review process. The IOCE is beginning to provide its members with tools for building professionalization.

As Tucker and King (2020) remind us, focusing on short-term, disconnected approaches to professional development does not leverage the collaborative potential available to evaluators working together across organizational barriers and geographic boundaries. "While university evaluator education programs typically focus on motivated, early career evaluators, VOPEs need to articulate and leverage evidence-based career-long training to support members in continuously developing competency skill sets" (p. 161). We need to build multiple pathways to competency development together.

Next, we introduce you to our Expert Corner in which we interview a distinguished evaluator or theorist. Our first expert is Dr. Jean King.

EXPERT CORNER

Dr. Jean King

Dr. King is Distinguished Teaching Professor Emerita in the Department of Organizational Leadership, Policy, and Development at the University of Minnesota where she served as Director of the Minnesota Evaluation Studies Institute for over 20 years. From 2015 to 2018 she chaired the Task Force that developed AEAs Program Evaluator Competencies.

1. *What attracted you to the topic of evaluator competencies and when did you begin your research on this topic?*
   In the late 1990s, I was teaching a doctoral seminar that reviewed the literature on evaluator competencies. We discussed the difficulties of creating a single set for the field. One evening after class, three students approached me, asking why it was so difficult to develop them since their own complex fields (early childhood education, special education, and teacher education) all had long-standing and well-accepted competencies. They wondered what the challenges were in program evaluation. Building on existing lists of competencies and using the latest editions of the Program Evaluation Standards, AEAs Guiding Principles, and the Canadian Evaluation Society's Essential Skills Series as references, our group began a two-year unfunded effort to create and initially validate a set of evaluator competencies. These were ultimately published in 2001 in an article entitled "Toward a Taxonomy of Essential Evaluator Competencies" (King et al., 2001). After that, I was hooked on competencies.

2. *Since that time, of the five competency domains, namely (1) professional practice, (2) methodology, (3) context, (4) planning & management, and (5) interpersonal, which one has evolved the most? How has it changed and why?*
   The competencies needed for effective practice change constantly; they evolve because the contexts in which we work change. Professional practice evolves as theorists develop new approaches, professional associations revise foundational documents, and the role of evaluation in social justice becomes increasingly visible. Methodology changes as both quantitative and qualitative researchers add new techniques and expand existing methods repertoires. Planning and management skills develop as strategic planners and project managers shape their craft in innovative ways, and the need to interact successfully with a growing number of cultures requires enhanced interpersonal competence. To my mind, a better question is which domain has *not* changed as much as the others. I believe that context has remained the most consistent over time, probably because it relates to "understanding the unique circumstances, multiple perspectives, and changing settings of evaluations and their users/stakeholders" (American Evaluation Association, 2018c). The need for this understanding has not changed.

3. *The topic of evaluator competencies has grown worldwide. What has surprised you the most?*
   I am most surprised by the fact that the competencies movement (and professionalization of our field more generally) has only lately taken off globally. Almost 20 years ago, the research on our initial set of competencies showed that participants agreed on 78% of the proposed competencies, with almost unanimous support for "ethical conduct" and "framing evaluation questions." With such a high level of agreement suggesting that it really was possible to come to consensus on a general set of competencies, I wonder why it has taken nearly two decades for this topic to take hold in a practical way. It is true that several VOPEs (including the Canadian Evaluation Society and the European Evaluation Society) have built voluntary credentialing or review processes that use a set of competencies, but the viable possibility of common competencies for all program evaluators—adapted, of course, to specific settings–remains in the process of becoming.

4. *Finally, do you have any words of wisdom for our readers who are just beginning to explore the field of evaluation?*
   As an evaluator I have found it helpful to keep in mind what I call my four rules of life: (1) never panic; (2) work to solve the problem; (3) always keep the big picture in mind; and (4) as my mother taught me—be nice.

Key Terms

Evaluand 9

Equality 12

Equity 12

Ethics 21

Guiding principles for evaluators 23

Merit 10

Problem 5

Professional competencies 27

Program evaluation 6

Program evaluation standards 24

Quality of life 12

Research 14

Significance 10

Social justice 12

Stakeholders 11

Three evaluation pillars 21

TransScientific model of evaluation 7

Worth 10

The Main Ideas

1. In the TransScientific Model of Evaluation, Scriven posits that evaluation is the driving logic for disciplines outside science, such as law, medical practice, journalism.

2. Patton suggests that evaluations answer three questions: What? So what? Now what?

3. Evaluation is an inquiry into a program to answer questions about its merit, worth, significance.

4. Evaluation has three main purposes: (1) to gain an understanding of how program work and the difference they can make to stakeholders, (2) to improve quality of life, (3) to pursue social justice and a more equitable world.

5. Typically, research is used to contribute to a knowledge base; evaluation is used to improve a program.

6. The Guiding Principles cover the evaluator's conduct during their work.

7. The Evaluation Standards set the criteria for the quality of the work.

8. The Professional Competencies lay the groundwork for the evaluator's capacity to do the work.

Critical Thinking Questions

1. Think of a program you know well (e.g., at your child's school, at work) and look at the questions that evaluation should answer. Which of these questions is the most critical one right now? Why do you feel this way? How can an evaluation help to improve the situation for both individuals and the community?

2. What is the role of a person's environment in health equity?

3. In what type of program evaluation dilemma would you seek out the Guiding Principles? When might you need the Program Evaluation Standards for support?

4. Think of a time in your life where you evaluated a problem. What was the topic or issue? How did you know you needed to make a change? What questions did you ask? Who was involved? What did you do to intervene? What were the results of your change? How do you know your life improved?

5. When is the last time you encountered a situation where you questioned someone else's ethics or your own? What was the setting? Why did you have a concern? Was it an apparent ethical concern, or was there a fine line between right and wrong? How did you settle the issue? Do you have a frame or series of questions by which you judge situations for possible ethical problems?

Student Challenges

1. **Livability**. Go to the American Association of Retired Person's (AARP) Livability Index website (https://livabilityindex.aarp.org/). Enter the zip code of your hometown and see the score. What are the strengths and weaknesses that make up your score? What policies in your hometown are based on evidence-based evaluations? Are your findings surprising or what you expected?

2. **Find an Evaluator**. Go to www.linkedin.com and search for "evaluators" or "evaluation." Review your results. How many did you find? What credentials do they have? Where in the world do they practice? In which sectors do they work (e.g., epidemiology, education, business, foundations)? Do their backgrounds interest you?

3. **Evaluation Journals**. The next time you need to do a literature review or write a paper for any class, search for articles within journals dedicated to evaluation. Journals include *African Evaluation Journal*, *Journal of MultiDisciplinary Evaluation*, *Canadian Journal of Program Evaluation*, *Evaluation Journal of Australasia*, *American Journal of Evaluation*, *Evaluation: The International Journal of Theory, Practice and Policy*.

4. **Poverty Clock.** Go to the world poverty clock (https:// worlddata.io/portfolio/world-poverty-clock). This tool provides real-time data on how many residents escape poverty or fall into it in a given time period. Review the heat maps by country. Filter by geography, gender, and age.

Additional Readings and Resources

1. Bechar, S., & Mero-Jaffe, I. (2013). Who is afraid of evaluation? Ethics in evaluation research to cope with excessive evaluation anxiety: Insights from a case study. *American Journal of Evaluation, 35*(3), 364–376. Read about a case study where the client did not want the evaluator to write an evaluation report.

2. Donaldson, S., Gooler, L., & Scriven. (2002). Strategies for managing evaluation anxiety: Toward a psychology of program evaluation. *American Journal of Evaluation, 23*(3), 261–273.
   The authors focus on the concept of anxiety induced by being part of an evaluation. First, the authors define the concept and discuss the fear of a negative evaluation and give some common signs and consequences of excessive evaluation anxiety. Finally, the authors pose strategies for managing evaluation anxiety.

3. LaVelle, J. M. (2018). *2018 directory of evaluator education programs in the United States.* University of Minnesota Libraries Publishing. https://conservancy.umn.edu/bitstream/handle/11299/200790/Directory_full.pdf?sequence=5&isAllowed=y
   This directory provides all the academic evaluation programs in the United States. Included are certificate, masters, and doctoral-level education programs with an evaluation emphasis. Provides required credits, required course with "Evaluation" in the title, required entry courses, and other requirements.

4. Mason, S., & Hunt, A. (2018). So what do you do? Exploring evaluator descriptions of their work. *American Journal of Evaluation, 40*(3), 395–413. This article shares the way evaluators tell others what they do. Describes the reactions by others when evaluators share their work.

5. Pattyn, V. (2014). Why organizations (do not) evaluate? Explaining evaluation activity through the lens of configurational comparative methods. *Evaluation, 20*(3), 348–367.
   The author focuses on the reasons why some organizations evaluate policy, and some do not.

6. Wanzer, D. L. (2021). What is evaluation? Perspectives of how evaluation differs (or not) from research. *American Journal of Evaluation, 42*(1), 28–46. doi:10.1177/1098214020920710

7. Patel, M. (2013). African evaluation guidelines. *African Evaluation Journal*, 1(1), 1–5. https://aejonline.org/index.php/aej/rt/printerFriendly/51/67
   Fourteen African evaluation associations met to discuss the standards by which they would conduct evaluation. Review their standards. Although they used the American Evaluation Association Programme Evaluation Standards, they worked to "develop a checklist for quality evaluation that as suited to African conditions and culture.

HOW EVALUATORS THINK

LEARNING OBJECTIVES

1. Distinguish between concrete and abstract ideas.

2. Explain the difference between the two worldviews that can be held by evaluators.

3. Describe four paradigms prevalent in evaluation along with the perspective on meaning, preferred methods, and critical thinking processes employed in each.

4. Describe some ways that the Socio-Ecological Model is useful in an evaluation context.

5. Identify four possible branches on the Evaluation Theory Tree and give an example of a theorist on each branch.

6. Explain why the assumptions and methodological decisions in any evaluation need to have coherence.

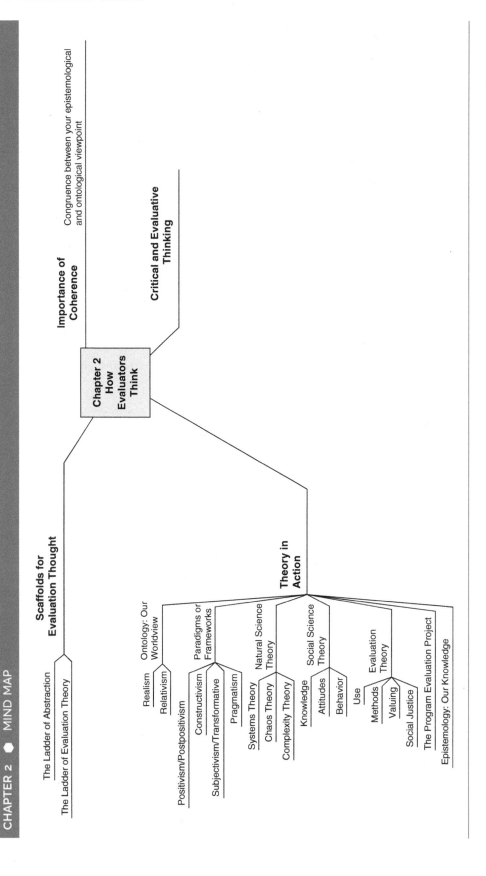

BEV'S PHILOSOPHY OF MORNINGS

I am not a morning person. Ask me to stay up late and accomplish something and I am your person. A few years ago, I came across a book called *Miracle Morning* (Elrod, 2017). The philosophy of this book is simple: the first 10% of your day can dictate and influence how the rest of your day goes. I wanted to try this partly because I have never looked at mornings favorably. Once the sun went down, I came alive. I needed to change my philosophy. The book hypothesized that if you make a set list of activities in the morning, every morning, the quality of your day will be improved. For six minutes (1 minute each), you have Silence, Affirmations, Visualization, Exercise, Reading, and Scribing. I tried this and noticed the benefits the first day.

Source: iStock.com/bruev

It is not only important to have a morning plan but also to have a philosophy about the activities planned. I changed the way I looked at my mornings, took a different approach and it worked. As a result, I was more focused and more energetic. By the end of the week, I was looking forward to my morning!

INTRODUCTION

Bev's morning story gives us a simple example of why having a philosophy is important as a guide to life. This chapter explores how evaluators view the world, how they gain knowledge, and what they do with that knowledge when planning an evaluation project. Evaluators use many terms, sometimes interchangeably, to describe their field. This can be muddy and confusing and often leaves us asking more questions that we had when we started. For this reason, we have gone back to first principles and asked one question, "How do evaluators think?" The answers may be surprising. The work of evaluators is embedded in a long history of scientific thought. How they see the world affects the work they produce.

The chapter is filled with metaphors, from ladders and amoebas to trees and puzzle pieces, all simple devices to illustrate the different ways in which evaluators think about evaluation, social science, and the nature of society. We will distinguish between concrete and abstract thinking, will look at four **paradigms** that underpin different approaches to evaluation, and will review how differing assumptions and frames of reference influence how evaluation theorists think. Whatever their perspective, how they view the world influences how they design, collect, and interpret data. As we often cite evaluation theorists in our work, it is important to understand their philosophical stance to see if it fits with our own. Being able to interpret the through-line of evaluation thought in both your work and that of others will make you an agile and critical thinker.

You will enjoy the resources in this chapter including the Spotlight on Equity, which presents systems thinking in rural medical care, our expert Dr. Donna Mertens, Key Terms, Main Ideas, Critical Thinking Questions, Student Challenges, and Additional Readings and Resources.

SCAFFOLDS FOR EVALUATION THOUGHT

The Ladder of Abstraction

Let's start with a simple and fun metaphor created by S. I. Hayakawa (1939) who wrote a book called *Language in Thought and Action*. It has been used widely to distinguish between very concrete things at the bottom of the ladder, like your favorite Netflix movie, and some very abstract ideas at the top, like the entertainment industry. For our purposes, we use an adaptation of Hayakawa's Ladder (Figure 2.1) to describe Bessie the Cow (Freishtat & Leipzig, 2019).

FIGURE 2.1 ● THE LADDER OF ABSTRACTION

We could visualize it like this, moving from the highest level of abstraction (wealth) down to the smallest level of detail (Bessie):

WEALTH (highest level of abstraction)

ASSETS/ LIVESTOCK

THE HERD

BESSIE THE COW (lowest level of abstraction)

Source: Freishtat, R., & Leipzig, A. (2019). Information acrobat: Climbing the ladder of abstraction.

To climb the Ladder of Abstraction, we start on the ground beside the physical cow. We know she is made up of atoms and molecules. We can actually touch her and give her a pat. As we start to climb the Ladder of Abstraction, we discover that her name is Bessie, a word that stands for her and is a kind of short-cut that incorporates all her particular characteristics. As we climb a little further, we find out that she is part of the "Herd" and shares similar features with the other herd members. Higher up, we learn that she is part of "Livestock" because she shares certain traits with pigs, chickens, goats, and other domestic animals. She represents an asset for the farmer, meaning that she is salable, like all the other assets on the farm. Finally, at the top of the ladder, we see that she represents the concept of wealth. Her monetary value is the only thing that remains at this high altitude. It is a pretty cold and abstract place up there, and we cannot tell that you are referring to Bessie at all when you say the word "wealth."

As we start to climb the ladder, note that we know many details and facts about Bessie. The higher we climb, the fewer details we can carry. Similarly, the more abstract our thinking, the fewer details we can provide. What level should we choose? Of course, the answer is, "it depends." If we want to talk about theory, we will probably find ourselves quite high up the ladder. If we want to talk about a specific evaluation project, we may find yourself quite close to Bessie.

What is the point of this simple metaphor? Evaluators need to be agile thinkers, able to climb up or down the Ladder, depending on the type of information we need. Do we need something that is more abstract? Climb up. If we need something more specific, climb down. People often talk past each other because they are operating on different levels of abstraction. When we ask questions, we need to aim them at the right level so that we get the information we need. Communicating well requires that we understand the level of abstraction that others are using and make sure that these abstractions are derived from the same specific information (Leviton, 2015, p. 241). If we ask a question that is either too general or too specific, we may get the wrong answer. We could end up looking like this unfortunate creature (Figure 2.2, p. 40).

The Ladder of Evaluation Theory

The great evaluation thinker, Michael Scriven, noted that "evaluation is a very young discipline—although it is a very old practice" (Scriven, 1996, p. 395). There has been much discussion about its theoretical and philosophical foundations. In their enthusiasm for the topic, however, evaluation theorists and writers have interpreted and reinterpreted their assumptions and language to explain their worldview until the field of evaluation has been littered with conflicting terminology. Such terms as paradigms, concepts, theories, frameworks, approaches, types, methods, and models are often used interchangeably. One evaluator's theory is another's framework and a third's model. It can be difficult to parse out actual meaning.

FIGURE 2.2   ●   THE COW AND THE LADDER

Source: Scottish Society for the Prevention of Cruelty to Animals, Scottish SPCA.

Why should we worry about philosophy? The answer is simple. If you do not understand the principles and assumptions embedded in your work, your entire evaluation study can be compromised. Muddy thinking leads to unclear study findings that are weak or indefensible. Our goal as evaluators is to affect positive social change and so we want to have the most impact we can. To do this, we need to be clear about our own worldview and know exactly why we choose the methods we do.

The literature on the philosophy of science is confusing, inconsistent, and sometimes, as Crotty (1998) suggests, even impenetrable. For this reason, we have taken a simplified approach, borrowing Hayakawa's metaphor to create our own Ladder—a serviceable and utilitarian tool to use as a scaffold. See the Ladder of Evaluation Theory (Figure 2.3, p. 41).

This visual shows how various theories are used in program evaluation and how they relate to each other. You could start anywhere on the ladder and climb up or down, but for simplicity's sake, we will start at the top which represents your worldview. Ontology, or your view of reality, is the most abstract level. We will climb down slowly, exploring and clarifying each idea until at last, we reach ground level, where any specific program evaluation study is located. Finally, we will step back to admire the overall epistemology or philosophical scaffold we have assembled, made up of the ideas or concepts we have selected that fit best together and provide the strongest foundation for our study.

FIGURE 2.3 ⬢   LADDER OF EVALUATION THEORY

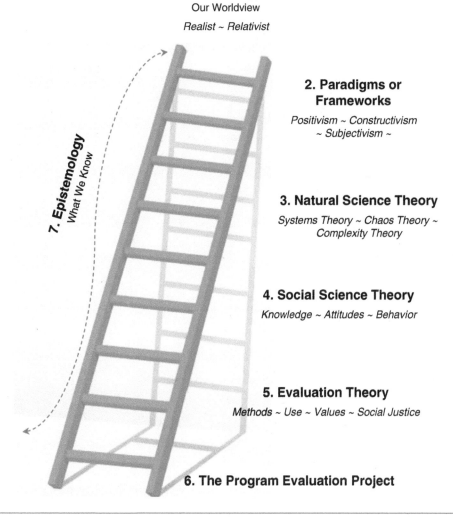

1. Ontology
Our Worldview
Realist ~ Relativist

2. Paradigms or Frameworks
Positivism ~ Constructivism ~ Subjectivism ~

3. Natural Science Theory
Systems Theory ~ Chaos Theory ~ Complexity Theory

4. Social Science Theory
Knowledge ~ Attitudes ~ Behavior

5. Evaluation Theory
Methods ~ Use ~ Values ~ Social Justice

6. The Program Evaluation Project

7. Epistemology
What We Know

Source: istockphoto.com/frans_kuz

THEORY IN ACTION

Ontology: Our Worldview

What we know about the world is our **ontology**. Since Parmenides, who developed this term, philosophers have worried about this fundamental question, "What is reality?" How confident can an evaluator be about the phenomenon we are studying? Who decides what is real? What do we do with conflicting ideas of reality? Our most basic assumptions are of an ontological nature because we must decide if the reality we are investigating is external to the individual (i.e., real substances of the natural universe such as particles, atoms, and genes) or if it is a product of their consciousness (i.e., a subjective or experiential interpretation of reality).

Realism

Realism holds that one reality exists, and humans experience it as "the truth" independent of who is viewing it (Moon & Blackman, 2014). Beliefs about reality include:

- There is only one truth

- Truth does not change

- Observation and measurement discover truth

- Truth can be generalized to other situations.

Relativism

Relativism means that reality exists in the mind of the individual and that each of us creates our own version of reality (Moon & Blackman, 2014). Beliefs about reality include:

- There are multiple versions of reality

- Context shapes reality

- Truth does not exist independent of meaning

- Truth evolves and changes based on experience

- Truth cannot be generalized.

Thus, ontology ranges from realism, where only one reality exists, to relativism, where multiple versions of reality exist side by side.

Let's look at an example. When you see a red traffic light, your instinct is probably to stop your car. We know this is true based on our own experience; however, it may not always be the case. In Italy, for example, a place sometimes known for its cheery dysfunction, Severgnini (2006) explains:

> When many Italians see a stoplight, their brain perceives not prohibition (Red! Stop! Do not pass!). Instead, they see a stimulus. OK, then. What kind of red is it? A pedestrian red? But it's seven in the morning. There are no pedestrians about this early. That means it's a negotiable red; it's a "not-quite-red." So we can go. Or is it a red at an intersection? What kind of an intersection? You can see what's coming here, and the road is clear. So, it's not a red, it's an "almost red," a "relative red…." And what if it's a red at a dangerous intersection with traffic you can't see arriving at high speed? What kind of question is that? We stop, of course, and wait for the green light. (pp. 9–10)

Severgnini suggests that Italians may see a red light as negotiable. Americans do not.

The National Community Anti-Drug Coalition Institute (2009) uses a phrase to help communities understand themselves: "But why, but why here" (p. 22)? These questions focus on why problems, such as teen drinking, occur in their community. The question pushes to understand what it is about the local area that contributes to a high incidence. For example, in one community, alcohol vendors may take a casual approach to checking identification. In another, adults may buy alcohol for youth or condone drinking behaviors (e.g., parents hosting teen drinking parties). In a third community, parents may work actively to support a "dry grad," an all-night party which follows the formal convocation, banquet, and dance where no alcohol or drugs are allowed. Each community has its own unique reality, and it is likely that each approach will produce different outcomes.

Paradigms or Frameworks

We categorize our knowledge in a paradigm or framework to help us interpret the world. Thomas Kuhn (1962), an influential twentieth century science historian, described a paradigm as a coherent tradition of scientific research (p. 11). It attracts a community of practitioners toward shared rules and standards for scientific practice, drawing them away from other schools of thought. Their views reinforce each other's views, and their shared preconceptions and assumptions shape the research approach that they endorse, such as (Kuhn, 1996):

- What to observe
- What questions to ask
- How to structure these questions
- How to conduct an experiment
- What outcomes to expect
- How to interpret the results.

Over time, however, a paradigm's discrepancies and anomalies begin to accumulate. Eventually, a thought revolution occurs, and a new theory emerges that appears to be more relevant than the old one. Kuhn described this as a **paradigm shift** or scientific revolution (Kuhn, 1962, p. 90). An example of a contemporary paradigm shift in medicine is the transition from clinical judgment to evidence-based medicine (Eddy, 1990).

Four paradigms are prevalent in evaluation literature: positivism, constructivism, subjectivism, and pragmatism (Crotty, 1998; Moon & Blackman, 2014). Refer to Table 2.1 on page 44. Each paradigm represents a different set of assumptions about the nature of reality, and each has preferred evaluation methods and ways of thinking critically. Evaluators generally feel more comfortable in one specific paradigm and tend to design their work from that perspective. Over time, however, and depending on the nature of their work, evaluators can move from one perspective to another.

TABLE 2.1 ● FOUR PARADIGMS FOR EVALUATORS

Positivism/Postpositivism	Constructivism	Subjectivism/Transformative	Pragmatism
Only one reality.	Multiple realities.	Meaning exists within the individuals studied.	It depends.
The evaluator discovers reality through observation and experimentation.	The evaluator solves problems through interaction with participants.	The evaluator uses the participants' perspective to interpret reality.	The evaluator focuses on the outcomes and consequences of a specific problem.
Methods: Quantitative.	**Methods**: Qualitative	**Methods**: Mixed	**Methods**: All methods appropriate to the situation
Critical thinking: Deductive	**Critical thinking**: Inductive	**Critical thinking**: Reflective	**Critical thinking**: Abductive

Source: Crotty, M. (1998). *The foundations of social research: Meaning and perspectives in the research process.* SAGE Publications; Moon, K., & Blackman, D. (2014). A guide to understanding social science research for natural scientists. *Conservation Biology, 28,* 1167–1177.

In Figure 2.4, p. 45 we present our model, Miranda, who demonstrates how an individual perceives reality:

- If she is a positivist or postpositivist, she relies on observation and reason to arrive at a singular truth. She tends to use quantitative methods.

- If she is a constructivist, she relies on discussion and interaction with stakeholders and participants to jointly construct a shared version of reality. She tends to use qualitative methods.

- If she is a subjectivist and uses the transformational paradigm, she focuses on feelings, perceptions, and values, usually of marginalized groups. She relies on understanding multiple versions of reality simultaneously. She tends to use mixed methods.

- If she is a pragmatist, she is open to any of these paradigms, depending on the circumstances, and is likely to use at least two in combination.

Let us explore the four paradigms.

Positivism/Postpositivism

Positivism, or more recently postpositivism, is close cousins with realism, logical positivism, objectivism, and empiricism. Positivists see meaning as existing within an object, independent of whoever is observing it. For them, reality exists outside of the individual mind. As Trochim (2006) explains, "the goal of knowledge is simply to describe the phenomena that we experience. The purpose of science is simply to stick to what we can observe and measure. Knowledge of anything beyond that, a positivist would hold, is impossible" (para. 4). Thus, knowledge comes from experimentation. The universe is deterministic and operates by laws of cause and effect. We postulate theories and test

FIGURE 2.4 ● REALITY, MEANING, TRUTH CLAIMS, AND KNOWLEDGE ACCORDING TO VARIOUS EPISTEMOLOGIES

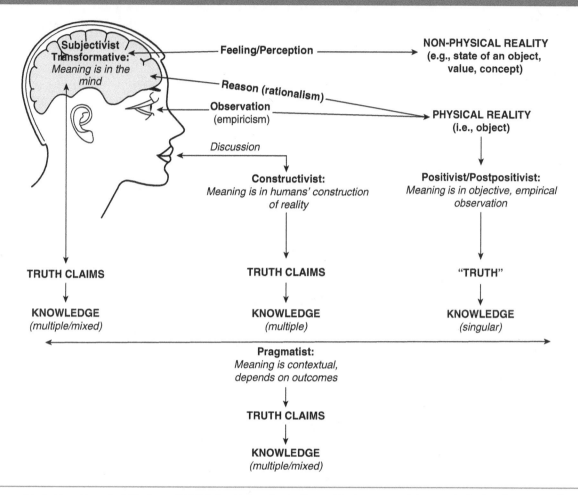

Source: Adapted from Moon, K., & Blackman, D. (2014). A guide to understanding social science research for natural scientists. *Conservation Biology, 28,* 1167–1177. istockphoto.com/juliawhite

them. If we find that our theory does not fit the facts we uncover, we can revise our theory to predict reality better next time.

Since the mid-twentieth century, there has been a shift toward a broader interpretation of positivism. **Postpositivism** uses multiple methods because any one method is prone to error. While the positivist believed the goal of science was to uncover the truth, the postpositivist believes that "the goal of science is to hold steadfastly to the goal of getting it right about reality, even though we can never achieve that goal!" (Trochim, 2006, para. 6). While positivists rely on quantitative methods (e.g., surveys, biometrics), postpositivists can use both quantitative and qualitative methods (e.g., interviews, focus groups, case studies) as valid approaches. Both the positivist and postpositivist believe in empiricism—observation and measurement are the core of the scientific endeavor. This is embodied most closely in the scientific method.

The Scientific Method. Grounded in observation, experimentation, and replication, the **Scientific Method** is based on studying cause–effect relationships in the natural world. To understand the human condition, scientific thought moved away from philosophy and mysticism toward observation and nature. A Muslim scholar, Ibn al-Haytham (c. 965 to c. 1040), wrote the *Book of Optics* in which he described a scientific process grounded in observation, experimentation, and replication. Later, his writings were translated into Latin and influenced European Renaissance thinkers like Galileo (1564–1642), Descartes (1596–1650), and Newton (1642–1726) (United Nations Educational, Scientific and Cultural Organization, 2015). The process became known as the scientific method. It has been the gold standard for studying cause–effect relationships in the natural world ever since and continues to permeate scientific thought today.

Although procedures can vary from one field to another, in general, the steps are shown in Figure 2.5, p. 47.

The value of objectivist research is its focus on validity (applicability of the research in other contexts) and reliability (consistency of results obtained) (Moon & Blackman, 2014).

Foundational ideas in the positivist/postpositivist paradigm include (Patton, 2002, 2015):

- A real, observable, predictable world exists; researchers seek correspondence with it.

- Where scientific credibility is paramount, it is the dominant perspective of policymakers and commissioners of evaluation.

- Its focus is on validity, reliability, and objectivity.

Positivists ask such questions as (Patton, 2015):

- What is going on in the real world?

- What can we establish with some degree of certainty?

- What are plausible explanations for verifiable patterns?

- What is the truth insofar as we can get at it?

- How can we study a phenomenon so that our findings correspond to the real world as much as possible?

Plan-Do-Study-Act (PDSA) Cycle. Often used as an improvement strategy in organizations, the PDSA Cycle is an outgrowth of the scientific method. Moen and Norman (2009) tracked the evolution of scientific thought from the work of Galileo (1564–1642) to the modern day and related it to the work of statistician and management consultant, Edward Deming in the 1950s. Deming created it when he worked with Japanese auto industry leaders, and many credit his ideas about processes as one of the drivers for the Japanese postwar economic miracle

FIGURE 2.5 ● THE SCIENTIFIC METHOD WHEEL

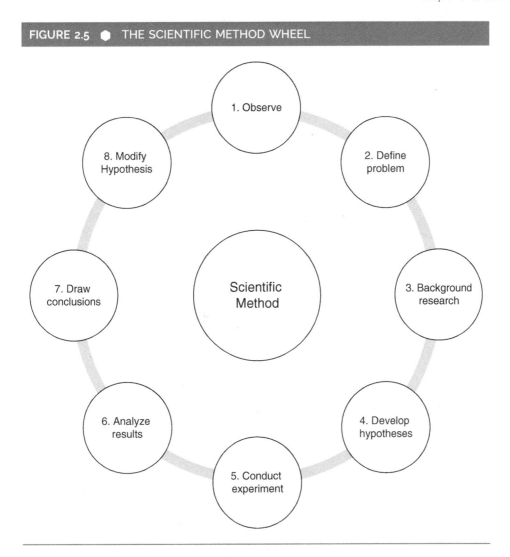

(The W. Edwards Deming Institute, 2019). He taught that using appropriate management principles could increase quality and decrease costs by reducing waste, rework, and staff attrition, and by increasing customer loyalty (Halwes, 1998). Originally known as the Deming Wheel, the PDSA Cycle is still common today, particularly in healthcare (Taylor et al., 2014). See Figure 2.6, p. 48 it offers "a continuous and ongoing effort to achieve measurable improvements in the efficiency, effectiveness, performance, accountability, outcomes, and other indicators of quality in services or processes…" (Riley et al., 2010, p. 5). Data are collected throughout the cycle to determine if a new intervention is more effective than previous practice and conclusions are used by management to inform changes in policy and behavior. We provide more details about the PDSA Cycle in Chapter 5 as a midcycle program evaluation method.

FIGURE 2.6 ● THE PLAN-DO-STUDY-ACT CYCLE

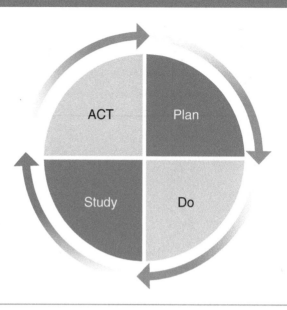

Source: PDSA Model courtesy of The W. Edwards Deming Institute®.

Deductive Thinking. Positivists tend to use deduction as their preferred method of critical thought. The researcher examines the known facts and, like puzzle pieces, tries to fit them into a preexisting framework such as a hypothesis or a conceptual framework. Quantitative inquiry employs deduction (see Figure 2.7).

FIGURE 2.7 ● DEDUCTIVE THINKING

Source: thenounproject.com/Wes Breazell

In this graphic, you can see that something is missing, likely the answer to the research question or hypothesis posed. The data that the researcher collects either prove or disprove (i.e., it fits or it doesn't fit) the research hypothesis. Note how the research is not really interested in the surrounding puzzle pieces but has a clear focus on finding the missing piece.

Milkie and Warner (2011) used deductive reasoning to study the mental health of first graders ($N = 10,700$) who had different classroom environments. The authors based their hypothesis on earlier research and a theoretical understanding of these issues. The authors believed that negative classroom or system characteristics contributed to children's emotional and behavioral issues. These characteristics include lack of basic school supplies, heating, interprofessional relationships of the teachers in the school, excessive paperwork demands on administrators, perceived low-academic standards, and negative behavioral situations of student's peers. The mental health outcomes studied included, for example, attention span, ability to persist at a task, argument frequency, fights, impulsivity, ability to form friendships, display of sensitivity toward others, anxiety, and low self-esteem. In this example, the authors posed a general idea (social science theory) of the way the world works based on their own ideas. Reading the literature, they designed a study to examine the hypotheses, and supported or rejected them based on the analysis of their findings.

The scientific method continues to dominate the fundamental and natural sciences. We rely on scientists to produce findings that are the result of objective, standardized, and replicated experimentation. Historically, evaluation was also dominated by the scientific paradigm; however, sometimes this resulted in evaluations that did not address the issue in question (Mertens, 1999, p. 4). As life is both complex and messy, so programs that attempt to address these tough issues can lead evaluators to avoid or ignore what is deemed to be unmeasurable. In cases like these, other paradigms may be more appropriate.

Constructivism

Constructivism is a paradigm that rejects the idea of objective truth. It is closely linked to constructionism and social constructionism. Meaning is found in the interaction between the subject and the object. Humans construct knowledge as they engage with and interpret the world, so different individuals can construct different meanings about the same object.

For example, Kant challenged the empiricists' claim that research must include measurement (Mertens & Wilson, 2019). The positivist view acknowledges an independent reality and a single universal truth, but social scientists, in trying to understand social phenomena, often work with individuals who hold different, and sometimes conflicting, views of the truth. Rawls (1971) suggested that nobody has privileged access to the truth; all have equal standing, which brings us to the idea of lived experience. A constructivist tries to understand meaning from the perspective of the people who have had the experience (Schwandt, 2000). The value of constructivist research is in generating a contextual understanding of a defined problem, beneficial to stakeholders who need to design contextually relevant responses to social problems.

The key ideas in the constructivist paradigm include (Lincoln & Guba, 1980; Patton, 1990):

- Human perception is a constructed version of reality shaped by culture and language; therefore, we study multiple realities differently.

- Truth is a matter of consensus, and phenomena are only understood within a particular context.

- Stakeholders have different program experiences; one perspective is not more valuable than another despite power differentials.

- Scientists are bound by socially constructed and consensually validated knowledge but can still function in a positivist paradigm.

Constructivists ask questions like these (Patton, 2015):

- How have the people in this setting constructed reality?

- What are their reported perceptions, "truths," explanations, beliefs, and worldviews?

- What are the consequences of this construction for their behaviors and for those with whom they interact?

Inductive Thinking. The type of critical thinking most often used by constructivists is induction. The researcher starts with a puzzle piece or a relevant response to a broad research question. Then they look for other puzzle pieces, or responses, until they find one or more pieces that fit the first one (see Figure 2.8).

FIGURE 2.8 ● INDUCTIVE THINKING

Source: thenounproject.com/Marcio Duarte

By searching and comparing, the researcher slowly starts to develop some other pattern, and slowly, piece by piece, they build connections that develop the story, theory, or description. Induction is frequently used in qualitative inquiry (Mayan, 2009).

Allen, Kaestle, and Goldberg (2010) investigated the process of how young men know and understand menstruation. Evaluators conducted focus groups with 23 young men and then generated a theory based on the qualitative data (i.e., written text of the focus group discussions). Based on this inductive approach of collecting, comparing, and finding connections, the authors developed a theory that young men receive information about menstruation from their sisters.

Subjectivism

Sometimes called the transformative paradigm (Mertens, 2020; Mertens & Wilson, 2019), those who practice **subjectivism** find meaning within the individuals being studied and then interpret the phenomenon using the participants' perspective. As Mertens and Wilson (2019) explain, the transformative paradigm holds

> *the belief that the lives and experiences of diverse groups of people are of central importance in the evaluation to address issues of power and justice. [It] focuses primarily on eliciting and understanding viewpoints of marginalized groups and interrogating systemic power structures through mixed methods to further social justice and human rights.* (p. 548)

Unlike positivism, which looks for a single truth and tries to avoid external influences, and constructivism, which focuses on multiple perspectives and lived experience, subjectivism actively incorporates values, culture, power dynamics, and social justice into its design. As a result, it is an appropriate paradigm for evaluators who are working with marginalized groups so that they can listen to the voices of the oppressed and also address larger systemic issues.

There are many approaches to subjectivism. Main branches include (Magana, n.d.):

- Critical theory—focuses on how injustice and subjugation shape people's understanding and experience of the world

- Queer theory—focuses on sexual orientation

- Indigenous and postcolonial perspectives—focus on challenging existing colonial attitudes, institutions, and practices and understanding problems in their sociocultural context

- Feminist inquiry—focuses on the importance of gender in human relationships and social processes.

The evaluator attempts to understand individuals' knowledge, interests, purposes, and values (Schwandt, 2000). The focus of the inquiry is often on power inequities, the impact of privilege, and how the consequences of these affect social justice. It places central importance on the experiences of marginalized groups (Mertens, 1999):

> *such as women, ethnic/racial minorities, people with disabilities, and those who are poor. The evaluator who works within this paradigm consciously analyzes*

> *asymmetric power relationships, seeks ways to link the results of social inquiry to action, and links the results of the inquiry to wider questions of social inequity and social justice.* (p. 4)

With its ideological lens, subjectivism avoids claiming open-mindedness in favor of the emergent theory. Thus, it is at the opposite end of the research spectrum from positivism. The value of subjectivism or a transformative view is that it reveals how an individual's experience shapes their perception of the world (Moon & Blackman, 2014) and provides essential insight into their behavior.

Reflective Thinking. Critical thinking for the transformative evaluator involves self-reflection and dialogue (see Figure 2.9).

FIGURE 2.9   ●   REFLECTIVE THINKING

Source: thenounproject.com/bmijnlieff

The researcher assesses personal assumptions and positions of privilege, becomes critically aware of how he/she perceives, understands, and feels about the world, and reformulates those assumptions to permit a more inclusive, discriminating, permeable, and integrative perspective (Mezirow, 1990). Reflection leads to dialogue, respect, and collaboration. The transformative evaluator believes that reality exists in the groups' voices.

To ground the research, transformative evaluations use both qualitative and quantitative data collection methods in what is known as a mixed methods approach. The evaluation goes through several cycles of data collection, generally organized in a sequential fashion so that data obtained in the first cycle are used to inform the questions of the next cycle. Sometimes, however, two data collection initiatives are launched simultaneously. (See Chapter 9 for more information on mixed methods.)

Silka (2009) studied Laotians who lived in Massachusetts and became ill after fishing in a contaminated lake. The researchers trained the Laotians to become part of the research team. They conducted blood tests and collected interview data. Their findings were presented at fishing festivals to the Laotian community, providing education on the effects of contaminated fish on their health. Together, they were then able to devise new fishing methods. By using a transformative approach, the team was able to develop relationships with the Laotians, so that their reality could be incorporated into both study outcomes and solutions.

Pragmatism

Pragmatism aligns closely with much of evaluators' work because of its focus on the practical application of ideas and problem-solving in the real world. However, rather than focusing on truth and reality, pragmatism is grounded in consequences and results. Thus, evaluators can use a variety of appropriate methods without being committed to any specific philosophical position.

Pragmatism originated in the United States in the late nineteenth century. It was founded by psychologist William James, philosopher Charles S. Pierce, educator John Dewey, and sociologist George Herbert Mead, all members of the Chicago school of thought. They proposed that consequences determine the meaning of actions and beliefs. Morgan (2014, pp. 26–27) explained three other essential elements of pragmatism:

1. In judging actions, we consider the situations and contexts in which they occur.

2. Actions link to consequences in ways that are open to change.

3. Actions depend on worldviews that are socially shared sets of beliefs.

Rather than emphasizing the nature of reality, pragmatists focus on the outcomes of action. Thus, pragmatism becomes a helpful paradigm for evaluators who work mainly in the realm of program results.

A question for pragmatists is:

• What difference would it make to act one way rather than another?

Decision making becomes a critical link between belief and action (Morgan, 2014, p. 28) and so for evaluators, a pragmatic approach:

accepts that quantitative, qualitative, and mixed research are all superior under different circumstances *[original italics] and it is the researcher's task to examine the specific contingencies and make the decision about which research approach, or which combination of approaches, should be used in a specific study.* (Johnson & Onwuegbuzie, 2004, pp. 22–23)

Rather than using the scientific method, Morgan (2014, pp. 29–30) suggests Dewey's five-step problem-solving framework to reflect on a problem and arrive at an appropriate action. For example, if an evaluator is trying to decide what methods to use in a specific program evaluation, their thinking process might look like.

Step 1 Recognize the problem.

Step 2 Based on existing beliefs, search for a possible solution.

Step 3 Speculate about and suggest a solution or set of actions (a leap of faith).

Step 4 Assess the tentative solution, reflect on its potential effectiveness.

Step 5 Take action.

Looking at Dewey's Steps 3 and 4, for example, you can consider possible explanations, best guesses, speculations, conjectures, and hypotheses; then review, reframe, and revisit until you eventually arrive at the most plausible interpretation (Mayan, 2009; Patton, 2015).

Abductive Thinking. The critical thinking that pragmatists tend to use is known as abduction. It is a kind of in-between type of thinking, not entirely deductive, not fully inductive, but a combination of the two. In a mystery novel by Siger (2010), a police chief inspector used what he called "knitting" to go back and forth between what he knew and the gaps he needed to fill (Figure 2.10). He knit back and forth through his ideas until he could create meaning out of the facts. This knitting back and forth is an excellent way to think about abduction, going from induction to deduction, from framework to data, and back again.

FIGURE 2.10 ● ABDUCTIVE THINKING

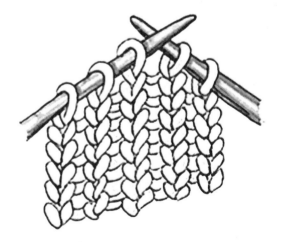

Source: istockphoto.com/Katsiaryna Pleshakova

When we use abduction, we usually have incomplete information, and we search for the likeliest explanation. For example, the thought process that your doctor uses to generate a medical diagnosis is a result of abductive reasoning. Two systems of thinking are at play at each stage of clinical reasoning: "intuitive, fast, and almost unconscious thinking,… and slower, analytical, effortful thinking" (Canadian Medical Protective Association, 2021, para. 2; Croskerry, 2018). This dichotomy of thinking methods is similar to that explained by Kahneman (2011), in which System 1 thinking is fast, intuitive, emotional, and easier, and System 2 thinking is slower, more deliberative, more logical, and more difficult. Abductive thinking incorporates both.

Silver Blaze is a famous story involving the great detective, Sherlock Holmes (Doyle, 1894). It tells about the curious incident of the dog in the nighttime and provides an example of abduction. Holmes solved the mystery by observing what did **not** happen. The fact that the dog did not bark when you would expect it to led Holmes to conclude that the evildoer was not a stranger but rather was someone the dog recognized. That is why the dog did not bark. Holmes drew his conclusions from a fact that did not occur, or a negative fact. The dog did not bark in the night (the result) and moving backward from there, he asked, "Why?" He was able to conclude that the dog knew the intruder (the cause).

Natural Science Theory

Evaluators are eclectic by nature and have often found useful parallels to their work in the physical and biological sciences. Here are three examples of how the natural sciences have influenced evaluation thought: systems theory, complexity theory, and related to the complexity theory, chaos theory.

Systems Theory

An interdisciplinary study of natural systems is attributed to the work of biologist von Bertalanffy (1968). His General Systems Theory looks at the interrelated, interdependent parts of either a natural or artificial entity. A system has boundaries that distinguish it from its environment, and it adapts as needed to protect itself and preserve its purpose. A change to one part of the system affects other parts as well.

Many fields have adopted **systems theory**, including biology, ecology, organizational theory, management, and program evaluation. While in the past, science tried to explain phenomena by reducing them to independent units, von Bertalanffy noted that the interaction between a phenomenon's parts is dynamic, as is the relationship between the phenomenon itself and its environment, all moving parts, all dynamic, all changing.

Think, for example, of a one-celled freshwater amoeba (Figure 2.11, p. 56) swimming in a soupy pond. To survive, it feeds on algae and bacteria and eliminates waste, thus creating

FIGURE 2.11 ● SYSTEMS THEORY AND THE AMOEBA

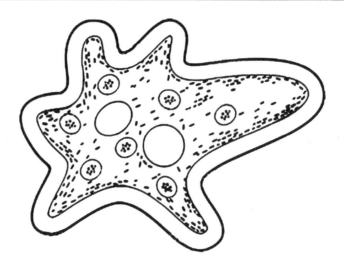

Source: istockphoto.com/mariaflaya

its perfect internal system. By eating the algae, the level of algae on the pond's surface allows water plants to survive through photosynthesis (Berry, 2016). As the plants oxygenate the water, other species have the oxygen they need to survive as well.

Von Bertalanffy described systems as being either closed or open (Frye & Hemmer, 2012). A closed system is one where nothing either enters or leaves the system. We find it very hard to think of any system today that does not interact with its environment. Gail was reminded of this when she visited the Eastern Orthodox monasteries in Meteora, Greece, perched high on remote rocky precipices. They were originally founded by monks who chose a solitary life for contemplation and prayer. However, they found that their survival depended on a rope and pulley system to haul up food and building supplies, as well as new members to their order. The late Fred Boissonnas, a famous Italian photographer, recorded his experience accessing this failed attempt at a closed system (see Figure 2.12, p. 57).

It was not possible to live in a completely closed system and today, we find beautiful monasteries on those rocky outcrops, built piece by piece by the monks and their successors. Thousands of tourists visit them every year, thus contributing to the larger system, the Greek economy. For breathtaking images, see Taylor (2018). It seems, then, that all systems are open to some extent.

An example of a large open system is the public health system (Figure 2.13, p. 58) comprised of "public, private, and voluntary entities that contribute to the delivery of essential public health services within a jurisdiction" (Centers for Disease Control and Prevention, 2020, para. 1).

FIGURE 2.12 ⬡ PROOF OF THE FAILURE OF A CLOSED SYSTEM

Source: thesprotia-news.blogspot.com/Meteora, ascent of Fred Boissonnas with basket

Each part of a system interacts internally with the others, but also interacts with the external environment, made up of clients, funders, stakeholders, the government, and the public. A change in any one of those internal or external components will result in a change in the others.

In early January 2020, the World Health Organization (WHO) announced a mysterious coronavirus-related pneumonia. On January 21, 2020, CDC confirms the first United States coronavirus case. By January 31, 2020, the WHO issues a global health emergency, and it became a public health emergency (American Journal of Managed Care Staff, 2021). In hindsight, there was not one aspect of the global system that has not been impacted: schools, hospitals, grocery stores, business, airlines, churches, the economy, and more. Systems operate best when the individual players in the system are familiar with other parts of the system before a problem occurs, when the system's true function is tested. In chaotic or emergent situations, the players know each other, have created agreements, and understand the functions and roles each other plays, so that in a near seamless manner they can work together to ensure the public's health.

FIGURE 2.13 ● THE PUBLIC HEALTH SYSTEM NETWORK

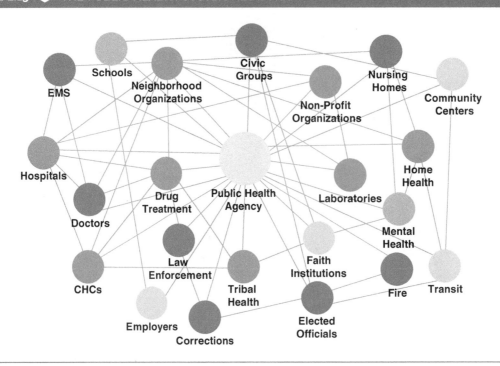

Source: Centers for Disease Control and Prevention. (2020). Original essential public health services framework: The public health system.

The Socio-Ecological Model (SEM). One way to view the interactions between people and their environments has been captured by the Socio-Ecological Model (SEM). Bronfenbrenner (1977) first introduced the model in the late 1970s to understand human development, especially to see how children were influenced by the interactions and relationships of an expanding set of systems. McLeroy et al. (1988), in their seminal article, described a layered framework which "serves to direct attention to both behavior and its individual and environmental determinants" (p. 354). Figure 2.14, p. 59 illustrates their model with the intrapersonal (individual), interpersonal, institutional factors, community factors, and public policy elements. Table 2.2, p. 59 provides examples of each level of the SEM.

Many in the social sciences have adapted the SEM to illustrate various social issues, such as the CDC which has adapted the framework for various health promotion activities (e.g., violence prevention, healthy college campuses, geriatric preventive health, and colorectal cancer prevention) (Kilanowski, 2017). The model can reflect the multiple factors that influence the health system, enabling an examination of the barriers and facilitators at each level.

FIGURE 2.14 ● THE SOCIO-ECOLOGICAL MODEL

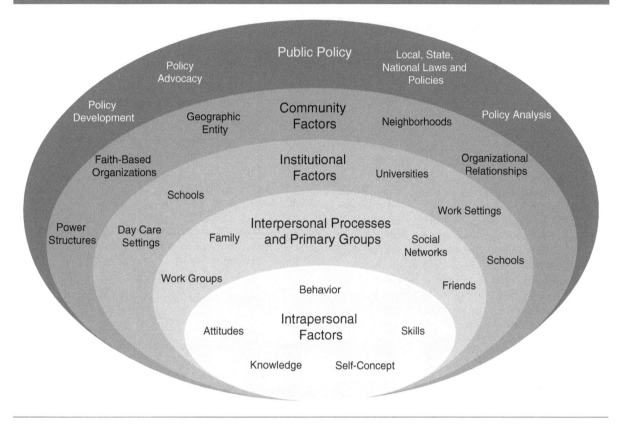

Source: Adapted from McLeroy, K. R., Bibeau, D., Steckler, A., & Glanz, K. (1988). An ecological perspective on health promotion programs. *Health Education Quarterly, 15*(4), 351–377.

TABLE 2.2 ● EXAMPLES OF THE SOCIO-ECOLOGICAL MODEL FOR ENVIRONMENTAL SUSTAINABILITY

Level	Example
Intrapersonal Factors	• Teach children the everyday items that are recyclable.
Interpersonal Processes and Primary Groups	• Post a toolkit to teach families in the community how to reduce, reuse, and refuse in their home.
Institutional Factors	• Create a company-wide environmental plan to reduce waste in purchases.
Community Factors	• Provide recycling centers in neighborhoods or special bins at houses.
Public Policy	• Tax incentives for donating clothing, making energy improvements to homes, buying electric vehicles, using mass transit, bicycling to work • Eliminating or reducing the use of single-use products.

Next, you will read about systems evaluation in rural and remote areas.

SPOTLIGHT ON EQUITY

Systems Evaluation in Rural and Remote Areas

The health outcomes of people living in rural and remote areas are poorer relative to those of people living in urban areas. One major contributor is the lack of proximity to healthcare facilities. For people living in rural states like Wyoming and Montana and provinces like Saskatchewan and the Yukon, it is not uncommon for the nearest healthcare facility to be over an hour away. Early intervention is vital to good outcomes for a heart attack or stroke. Without immediate intervention, such as CPR, brain damage begins to occur in 3 minutes and after 10 minutes most patients will not survive. In a rural emergency response situation, the situation is exacerbated by transport times as the distance to the nearest hospital with lifesaving expertise and equipment can be significant.

Dr. Ralph Renger and his evaluation team addressed these issues in their evaluation of a rural healthcare response system by using systems thinking to enhance their evaluation. It was a particularly informative approach because the ability to get a patient as quickly as possible to a definitive care center (or heart hospital with qualified staff and equipment) depended on the coordination of many moving parts (Renger et al., 2020). People, equipment, agencies, and technology all had to be coordinated for patients experiencing an emergent heart condition to survive. Finding efficiencies in the system could save minutes that could make the difference between life and death. The team chose system evaluation theory (SET) to guide their analysis. SET consists of three guiding principles derived from both system theory and evaluation theories about use, value, and methods (Renger, 2015, p. 17). SET processes reflect these principles and have three main steps: define the system, evaluate system efficiency, and evaluate system effectiveness.

Step 1. Define the system. Before evaluating the system, it must be defined. This involves determining system boundaries, subsystems, processes, relationships, feedback mechanisms, attributes, inputs, and goals. Like building a jigsaw puzzle, the evaluators began by defining the boundary for the study, then filling in the pieces, and then determining how the pieces interacted. They talked with state leaders to identify a goal for the cardiac system. "Getting the patient to definitive care in the shortest time possible" became their shared goal. Then they asked the leaders to identify system elements, and five subsystems were confirmed:

- **Dispatch**: managed by law enforcement.

- **Volunteer Emergency Medical Services**: the first responders to the scene with the local knowledge needed to locate the rural caller and administer CPR.

- **EMS Service with paramedics**: able to administer CPR and lifesaving heart medication.

- **Critical access hospital**: the closest rural hospital, unlikely to have the expertise and equipment needed.

- **Definitive care facility**: with cardiac expertise and equipment, located in an urban center.

The evaluators then worked with representatives of each subsystem to map their standard operating procedures (SOPs).

Step 2. Evaluate system efficiency. To evaluate system efficiency, the evaluators needed to assess the feedback mechanisms and the extent of goal alignment among the subsystems. They conducted a sudden cardiac arrest (SCA) simulation, mimicking an actual event in which people and resources were deployed. The simulation revealed that SOPs were not executed with fidelity. To understand the discrepancies, they applied systems thinking, exploring system wastes, reflex arcs, feedback loops, and cascading failures to identify corrective actions to improve efficiency.

- They found that system waste occurred when the EMTs and the hospital staff both called the same volunteer list to find available drivers. Using a table-top exercise of an evolving cardiac scenario, they identified the overlap and were able to modify procedures.

- Looking at the reflex arc, they identified areas and organization levels used to address issues were higher than necessary. For example, they found that urgent communication was delayed because two different dispatching agencies patched together the responding, volunteer-driven ambulance, and the intercepting ambulance that would take the patient on to the urban hospital. The solution was to ensure that ambulance drivers could communicate with each other directly through a dedicated statewide emergency network.

- They reviewed feedback loops and found that dispatchers, who were law enforcement trained, provided inadequate details about a patient's condition. These individuals now receive training on how to triage the call so that more meaningful information can be passed on to the rest of the system.

- Finally, cascading failures were examined for their impact on the larger system. The simulation had revealed that the heart hospital did not prepare for the patient until they received an EKG. However, the EMS could not send the EKG because there were often connectivity gaps on the road. This resulted in a time delay cascading through the system. The response was to map areas of connectivity on the route so that EMS personnel could proceed there to transmit the vital patient data (Figure 2.15).

Step 3. Evaluate system effectiveness. Having looked at all these elements working together at different levels, the evaluators could now consider the overall emergent system's effectiveness. They were able to synthesize the results of subsystem interactions and interdependencies to determine the emergent system property of lives saved. By streamlining response coordination, over 250 additional lives were saved in a three-year period. As Renger commented, "When the evaluation approach fits the problem and the context, then evaluation results are more meaningful and will have more utility."

FIGURE 2.15 ● KEY SUBSYSTEMS

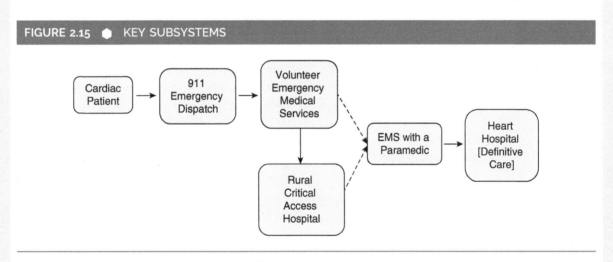

This Spotlight on Equity is based on the contribution of Dr. Ralph Renger.

Chaos Theory

Chaos Theory is a branch of mathematics that looks at dynamical systems highly sensitive to initial conditions. Edward Lorenz was a meteorologist who researched weather and climate predictability. One day when he was running some numbers in a program simulating weather patterns, he discovered that by rounding off one variable of the 12 he was using in his model (e.g., temperature, wind speed) from 0.506127 to 0.506, this tiny alteration drastically transformed the whole pattern of the prediction (Dizikes, 2011).

This property has been captured in mathematics to denote a sensitive dependence on initial conditions, where small differences in the initial conditions of a chaotic system are persistently magnified because of the dynamics of the system (Lauterborn, 2003). This esoteric mathematical finding eventually resulted in the idea of chaos theory which has changed our classical understanding of nature. Unpredictability and nonlinearity have replaced long-standing ideas of determinism and certainty. Lorenz rather imaginatively suggested that even the flap of a butterfly's wing might cause a tornado, and this idea became known as the Butterfly Effect (Chodos & Ouellette, 2003).

As you will probably continue to check the weather forecast every morning, it is heartening to know that Lorenz's work has led to forecasting improvements (Dizikes, 2011):

> wider data collection, better modeling, and "the recognition of chaos" in the weather, leading to what's called ensemble forecasting. In this technique, forecasters recognize that measurements are imperfect and thus run many simulations starting from slightly different conditions; the features these scenarios share form the basis of a more reliable "consensus" forecast. (para. 26)

Chaotic behavior exists in natural systems like weather and climate but can occur spontaneously, as in road traffic or mob behavior (Safonov et al., 2002). A faucet that drips with an irregular pattern could be called chaotic because the predictability of the next drop is difficult to determine (Shaw, 1984). We recognize chaotic behavior in such different areas as irregular heartbeats, epilepsy disorders, riverbed erosion, career uncertainty, and leadership (Burns, 2002; Dizikes, 2011; Iasemidis & Sackellares, 1996; Kumar & Hegde, 2012; Law et al., 2014). Nevertheless, it is still possible to study chaos. There are underlying patterns, constant feedback loops, repetition, and self-organization within this apparent randomness.

A small defiance on the part of Rosa Parks in Montgomery, Alabama, has often been cited as an example of chaos theory in action (Rettie, 2016). She refused to give up her bus seat to a white man and her subsequent arrest launched a bus boycott involving thousands. Her action became a catalyst that fueled the civil rights movement, led to the desegregation of buses, and raised international awareness about racism in the United States (Čirjak, 2020). She is considered the mother of the civil rights movement. Small changes can indeed have large consequences.

Complexity Theory

An offshoot of chaos theory is **Complexity Theory** which examines unpredictable and nonlinear situations in the fields of management, organizational studies, economics, and evaluation. To maintain a balance between flexibility and stability, organizations, communities, and groups respond to turbulence and uncertainty by becoming Complex Adaptive Systems where individuals' actions may not be totally predictable yet to make things more complex, their actions are also interconnected with those of others in the organization (Henry, 2014, para. 3). Examples of complexity theory include how bees swarm and how the stock market operates. Concepts like nonlinearity, emergence, dynamic interaction, adaptation, interdependency, and coevolution have developed to understand what is perceived to be unpredictable. Complexity theory explains why plans, aims, and strategies may not work (Henry, 2014; para. 6) and has changed the way we look at organizational behavior, relationships, and interactions. Henry (2014) provides a useful diagram that compares certainty and agreement (Figure 2.16).

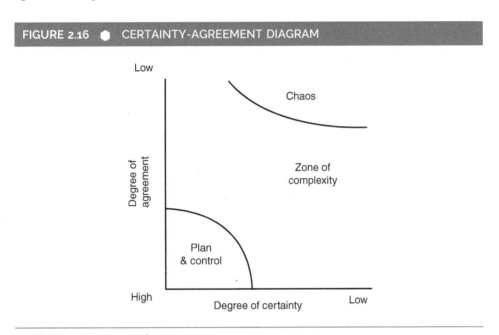

FIGURE 2.16 ● CERTAINTY-AGREEMENT DIAGRAM

Source: Henry, H. (2014, November 3). Complexity theory in nursing. *Independent Nurse.*

Henry describes what happened when a dilapidated community health clinic in Greater Manchester was closed by the Primary Care Trust (PCT) (a branch of the British National Health Service). Health services were moved two miles away and as a result, many residents were unable to access it due to health and transportation issues. Although several alternatives were explored, they failed. The old clinic fell into disrepair, becoming an eyesore and a risk to youth who played on the roof. The residents decided to do something about it themselves. They formed a partnership with service providers, conducted a needs assessment, and held a public meeting. For the first time, residents were able to voice their distress and feelings of being ignored. When the PCT decided to sell the building, the residents approached the community pharmacist who then approached a physician he knew who wanted to open a teaching practice and was looking for a good location.

Together they purchased the clinic site and redeveloped it into a new health center. As Henry comments, "communities on the edge of chaos are fertile ground for complexity theory to work."

Complexity concepts apply to the social change encountered by evaluators. Patton's (2011) **developmental evaluation** approach allows the evaluator to use systems thinking to conduct evaluation under conditions of complexity. The evaluator can track emergent and changing realities, illuminate varying perspectives, and feed back meaningful findings in real time to support the dynamics of innovation (p. 7).

Social Science Theory

As well as natural science theories such as these, social sciences, such as anthropology, sociology, psychology, and public health, have developed theories that often influence evaluators' work. To understand the principles that shape social behavior, evaluators often turn to generalizable and verifiable knowledge found in the social sciences. Donaldson and Lipsey (2006) encourage evaluators to use social science research and empirically based theory to:

- Support initial needs assessment and program design

- Assess the likelihood that a program will accomplish specific objectives

- Guide measurement and design decisions.

For example, deterrence theory, social learning theory, attachment theory, cognitive dissonance theory, social capital theory, public choice theory, and transaction costs theory have all provided explanatory power to evaluation studies. These theories address phenomena related to social programs and the social conditions they intend to improve. They are also helpful in an evaluation context because they can describe practical strategies for program implementation, provide benchmarks for success, offer suggestions about evaluation approaches that others have used, and inform evaluation measurement and design. As Donaldson and Lipsey point out, they can reveal lessons learned about what works or does not work. Evaluators use these theories to measure changes in such areas as knowledge and learning, attitudes and beliefs, and behavior change as well as to understand culture.

Knowledge

One of the earliest approaches (1959) used in evaluation was Kirkpatrick's Four Levels of Learning Evaluation Model. The four levels of training evaluation are Reaction, Learning, Behavior, and Results (Mind Tools Content Team, n.d.). The theory has been used by human resource professionals and evaluators for many years to determine the effectiveness of training programs.

Let us say a health researcher wanted to learn more about Geographical Information Systems (GIS) to create maps out of data. This researcher enrolled in a GIS course and afterward did the following:

- Reported that the training was engaging, informative, and the instructor was easy to follow and helpful (Reaction)

- Was tested on her knowledge of GIS terms and concepts and received a grade of a 90%. She then demonstrated her GIS mapping skills in a project at work (Learning)

- Held a mini-training program for her colleagues and taught them GIS techniques (Behavior)

- Wrote several grant applications for funding new programs and received all three grants because of her ability to do GIS analysis (Results).

A simple analysis indicated that the Return on Investment for the GIS course was high because the cost of the GIS course was a fraction of what she received in funding (Cost-effectiveness).

Attitude

Everett Rogers popularized the Diffusion of Innovation theory in 1962, and it has been frequently used in evaluation. Innovation characteristics, communication channels, time, and social systems all affect the uptake of the innovation (Rogers, 2003). Adopters fall into several categories, depending on the likelihood of their adopting an innovation. They include innovators (i.e., those most likely to adopt the innovation), early adopters, early majority, late majority, and laggards (i.e., those who never will or not likely to adopt the innovation). See Figure 2.17, p. 66 for an illustration of the categories of individuals and the pace at which they adopt interventions.

Valenti and Rogers (1995) studied rural farming practices from the 1920s to the 1940s using the Diffusion of Innovation theory. They found that while hybrid corn was more profitable for the farmer, only a few planted it in the 1920s (i.e., Innovators and Early Adopters). It was not until 1941 that the new strain was adopted by almost the entire community (i.e., Late Majority, Laggards). Through personal interviews with the farmers, they found that there was "considerable farmer reluctance to adopt this highly profitable innovation, a resistance that was very gradually overcome as a farmer talked with his neighbors who already were satisfied adopters" (Valenti & Rogers, 1995, p. 249).

Behavior

A social science theory that is quoted extensively in the behavior change literature is the Transtheoretical Model (Prochaska & Velicer, 1997) (see Table 2.3, p. 66).

FIGURE 2.17   ●   DIFFUSION OF INNOVATION THEORY

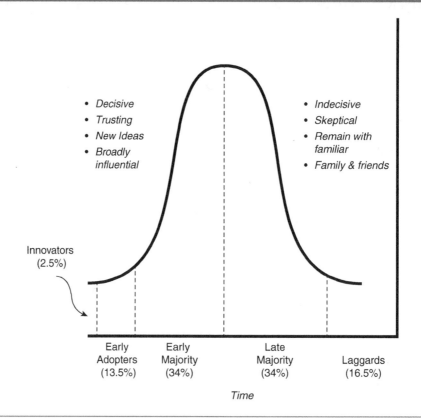

- *Decisive*
- *Trusting*
- *New Ideas*
- *Broadly influential*

- *Indecisive*
- *Skeptical*
- *Remain with familiar*
- *Family & friends*

Innovators
(2.5%)

Early
Adopters
(13.5%)

Early
Majority
(34%)

Late
Majority
(34%)

Laggards
(16.5%)

Time

Source: Based on Rogers, E. (2003). *Diffusion of innovations* (5th ed.). Simon and Schuster.

TABLE 2.3   ●   STAGES OF THE TRANSTHEORETICAL MODEL OF BEHAVIOR CHANGE

Stage	Definition
1. Precontemplation	Not intending to take action.
2. Contemplation	Intend to take action in the next 6 months. See pros, but focus on cons too and this could cause indecisiveness. Can remain in this phase.
3. Preparation	Intend to take action soon (next month). Have a plan of action.
4. Action	Specific behaviors have occurred in the last 6 months.
5. Maintenance	Trying not to go back to old behaviors. Risk for relapse. Increased confidence.
6. Termination	Zero temptation and 100% self-efficacy.

Source: Prochaska, J., & Velicer, W. (1997). The transtheoretical model of health behavior change. *American Journal of Health Promotion, 12*(1), 38–48.

An excellent example of behavior change relates to the risk of falling in older people. Zimmerman et al. (2000) designed a fact sheet for physicians, using the Transtheoretical Model (i.e., Stages of Change). Regarding behavior change, the authors state:

> *Behavior change is seen as a dynamic process involving both cognition and behavior that moves a patient from being uninterested, unaware, or unwilling to make a change (precontemplation); to considering a change (contemplation); to deciding and preparing to make a change (preparation); to changing behavior in the short term (action); and to continuing the new behavior for at least 6 months (maintenance).* (para. 1)

Physicians using the model could measure patients' stage (e.g., precontemplation, contemplation) at the beginning and end of the intervention. Patients' medications could be reviewed to determine if a change was needed. They could do prescribed exercises, change areas in their home that were conducive to falls, and attend a fall prevention program. The physicians were provided a list of conversation topics to use with patients that matched their stage of change. For example, a patient in the precontemplation stage might believe that falling is just part of getting old. The physician could respond with a statement about falling being common but that it can be prevented by simple changes in attitudes and behavior. Another patient, who might be in the preparation stage, might be ready to move to action about preventing falls. The physician could make a referral to a specialist who assists with balance, eye exams, and proper footwear.

Evaluation Theory

Evaluators have developed many valuable ways to tackle evaluation problems. However, we have a secret to share. There is no "real" evaluation theory! Donaldson and Lipsey (2006) reveal "a confusing mix of concepts related to evaluators' notions about how evaluation should be practiced, explanatory frameworks for social phenomena drawn from social science, and assumptions about how programs function or are supposed to function" (p. 57). Evaluation theories are approaches, models, or exemplars, that describe what a good evaluation entails from the perspective of the specific theorist. These are not empirical theories (Alkin, 2004, p. 5). They do not predict an outcome (i.e., involve a hypothesis). Indeed, for positivists, they do not meet the precepts of the scientific method. Newcomers to evaluation find the multiplicity of terms littering the evaluation landscape daunting and confusing.

Nevertheless, prominent evaluation writers and thinkers are currently referred to as *theorists* and so we will simply go with common practice.

Shadish (1998) called evaluation theory "central to our professional identity...and perhaps most important, it is what makes us different from other professions" (p. 1). Alkin and Christie created a metaphor to classify these evaluation thinkers and their ideas (Alkin, 2012; Alkin & Christie, 2004). Known as the Evaluation Theory Tree, it has offered students a much-needed way out of the muddle (Figure 2.18, p. 68).

FIGURE 2.18 ⬡ THE EVALUATION THEORY TREE: USE, METHODS, AND VALUING

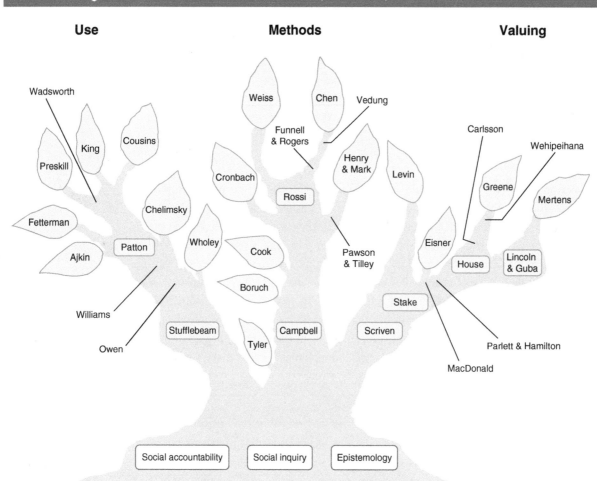

Source: Alkin, M. C. (2012). *Evaluation roots: A wider perspective of theorists' views and influences* (2nd ed.). SAGE Publications.

In the metaphor, the tree trunk represents the foundation of the evaluation understanding established between an evaluator and a client. The tree's three roots provide the foundation for evaluation work. Social accountability is an important motivator for evaluation, systemic social inquiry reflects the need for sound research methods, and epistemology describes the nature of the knowledge on which the evaluation is based (Alkin, p. 11). The tree has three branches, used to organize the different types of evaluation and the theorists who promote them.

- Use theorists focus on how stakeholders go through decision making and how they are going to use the information. They focus on any appropriate method helpful to stakeholders.

- Methods theorists look at obtaining generalizability and constructing knowledge. They focus on quantitative methods and measurement.

- Values theorists stress the importance of placing value on the data we collect. They use multiple perspectives and focus on qualitative or mixed methods.

One criticism is that this tree primarily reflects the work of White Western evaluation theorists and is not inclusive of "evaluation theorists who are feminists, people of color, persons with disabilities, members of the lesbian/gay/bisexual/transgender/queer or questions (LGBTQ) community, communities in economically poor countries, or members of Indigenous groups" (Mertens & Wilson, 2019, p. 40).

However, the tree metaphor has become a powerful tool for students and practitioners alike and scholars continue to add to its value. For example, Carden and Alkin (2012) modified it to include methods from low- and middle-income countries, including indigenous ones. Recently, Mertens and Wilson (2019) added a critical fourth branch on Social Justice as issues of race, identity, diversity, and marginalization continue to gain prominence. Social Justice theorists have an inclusive perspective that focuses specifically on human rights and the viewpoints of marginalized groups. Typically, they use mixed methods (see Figure 2.19).

FIGURE 2.19 ⬢ EVALUATION THEORY TREE: METHODS, USE, VALUES, AND SOCIAL JUSTICE

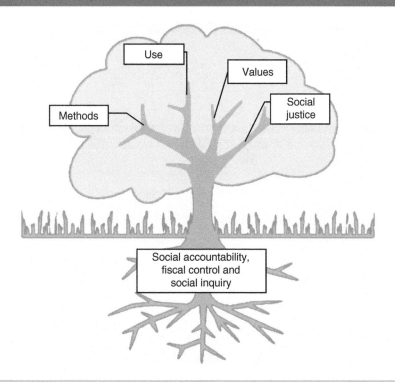

Source: Mertens, D., & Wilson, A. (2019). *Program evaluation theory and practice: A comprehensive guide.* New York, NY: Guilford Press.

Some of the many theorists suggested for the Social Justice branch include those listed in Table 2.4. As awareness grows, the evaluation literature is becoming much more inclusive.

TABLE 2.4 ⬡ SOCIAL JUSTICE BRANCH THEORISTS				
Deliberative Democratic Evaluation	**Feminist**	**LatCrit**	**Indigenous** *African*	**African American/ CRT**
Barry MacDonald	Kathryn Sielbeck-Bowen	Dolores Delgado Bernal	Bagele Chilisa	Stafford Hood
Saville Kushner	Sharon Brisolera	Lilia Fernandez	John Bewaji	Rodney Hopson
Ernest House	Cynthia Dillard	Tara Yosso		Asa Hilliard
Kenneth Howe	Denise Seigart	Daniel Solórzano		Aaron Brown
Jennifer Greene	Bessa Whitmore	**Disability/Deaf Rights**	***Native American***	Leander Boykin
Katherine Ryan	Saumitra SenGupta	Donna Mertens	Marie Battiste	Reid E. Jackson
Human Rights	Sharlene Hesse-Biber	Martin Sullivan	Cheryl Crazy Bull	James Scheurich
Thomas Schwandt	**LGBTQ**	Carol Gill	Joan LaFrance	Gloria Ladson-Billings
Donna Mertens	Jeffrey Todahl	Raychelle Harris	***Maori***	
Marco Segone	Sarah Dodd	Heidi Holmes	Fiona Cram	Henry Frierson
Karen Kirkhart			Linda T. Smith	Veronica Thomas

Source: Mertens, D., & Wilson, A. (2019). *Program evaluation theory and practice: A comprehensive guide* (2nd ed.). Guilford Press.

Interestingly, the four branches align with the four paradigms (Mertens & Wilson, 2019) (see Table 2.5).

TABLE 2.5 ⬤ PARADIGMS AND THE EVALUATION THEORY TREES	
Paradigm	**Branch of Evaluation Theory Tree**
Positivism	Methods
Constructivism	Values
Subjectivism/Transformative	Social Justice
Pragmatism	Use

Many influential evaluation theorists located on these branches are discussed in this book but there are many more, and like real trees, the branches continue to grow and have off-shoots. New theorists emerge all the time.

The Program Evaluation Project

You can see how hundreds of years of philosophy and scientific thought can influence an evaluation project. How we view the world and interpret reality significantly impacts the way we design, collect, and interpret our data. Knowing this background will make you an agile thinker, help you assess your own and other's evaluation thought, and guide you to a strong design for your next evaluation project.

The rest of this book focuses on evaluation projects and how evaluators structure their work. Part 2 examines how evaluators structure their work. It explores how different program phases can be associated with different types of evaluation. In Part 3, we look into what evaluators actually do in their evaluation projects, the types of questions, tools, data collection strategies, data analysis techniques, and reporting and communication processes. Finally, in Part 4, we look at evaluation use in the real world and take on some of the global issues we must incorporate in our work.

Epistemology: Our Knowledge

At last! We have reached the bottom of the Ladder of Evaluation Theory but wait—just a bit more exercise. Climb back up to the top of the ladder, keeping your program evaluation project in mind, and double-check the consistency of your philosophical stance. As with Bessie the Cow, we now see how our project relates to the broader and more abstract philosophical context of evaluation. By understanding our **epistemology**, we can select with confidence the type of evaluation that is needed, including the best design, the most important data to collect, how to analyze it, and how to report it effectively.

Importance of Coherence

Coherence occurs when the parts of something fit together in a "natural or reasonable way" (Cambridge Dictionary Online, n.d. b, para. 2). Mayan (2009) states "Methodological coherence will ensure congruence between your epistemological and ontological viewpoint, your theoretical position/perspective, the method you choose, your research question, and so on" (p. 13).

Evaluation coherence means that the assumptions and choices the evaluator makes regarding purpose, design, methodology, analysis, and interpretation are aligned. Sabarre (2018) argues that:

> *Many practitioners design evaluations around methodology. However, I argue a more holistic approach starts with theory before methodology. Evaluators should first consider the purpose of the evaluation to determine its theoretical foundation, and then develop evaluation questions to inform methodology.* (para. 2)

Evaluators can work from different paradigms, depending on the study, but most tend to be pragmatists, working with the end in mind (i.e., the client's information needs). However, we must avoid the trap of becoming magpies. Although handsome birds, they are known for stealing things, especially shiny objects. As Patton (2002) suggests, we can pick and choose methods "without giving a thought to their philosophical traditions."

Source: iStock.com/bestdesigns

Morse (1999) recommends ensuring methodological coherence by doing an armchair walk-through. The evaluator sits quietly, thinking through the methodological trajectory of their study, and reviews their ontology, paradigm, and theory. In other words, they climb down the Ladder within the context of their specific evaluation study and make sure that their epistemological approach fits together.

So, for example, you cannot take a realist perspective, work within the objectivist paradigm, and do intensive interviews with five participants. How could you draw conclusions and arrive at a single "truth"? Each of the five would have their own worldview. You cannot consider yourself a constructivist and then use a prepost standardized survey with a large population as your only research method. Using a rigorous quantitative design, how can you capture the varying lived experiences of this large group? If you are a pragmatist, you may want to use mixed methods, with both quantitative and qualitative components. You will need to follow approved methodological approaches for each component and then follow the mixed methods guidelines for sequencing and data integration. In each paradigm, you need to stay true to the methodological requirements.

The evaluator must confirm the relevance and fit of the choices made. As Sabarre (2018) concludes: "Focusing on theory at the onset of a project ensures the process (i.e., stakeholder involvement, methodology, data collection, analysis, reporting) is intentional, purposeful, and more useful for the client" (para. 2). If you are faithful to the paradigm you have selected, the quality of your work will shine through.

Source: Chris Lysy/FreshSpectrum.com

Critical Thinking and Evaluative Thinking

In this chapter, we introduced the many layers of evaluation thought, theory in action, and the importance of coherence. Evaluators must engage in **critical thinking**. Paul and Elder (2008) state that "a well cultivated critical thinker: raises vital questions and problems, formulating them clearly and precisely; gathers and assesses relevant information, using abstract ideas to interpret it effectively and comes to well-reasoned conclusions and solutions…" (p. 4). Critical thinking helps us appraise complex problems in society, study data, and arrive at workable conclusions.

More specifically, evaluators use evaluative thinking which aligns with critical thinking. Buckley et al. (2015) suggest, "**Evaluative thinking** is critical thinking applied in the context of evaluation, motivated by an attitude of inquisitiveness and a belief in the value of evidence, that involves identifying assumptions, posing thoughtful questions, pursuing deeper understanding through reflection and perspective taking, and informing decisions in preparation for action" (p. 378). Preskill and Boyle (2008) explain that it is "about getting people in organizations to look at themselves more critically through disciplined processes of systematic inquiry … about helping people ask these questions and then go out and seek answers" (p. 148). Evaluative thinking allows us to continue our inquiry, questioning our assumptions about causes and effects, considering potential solutions, and judging the pathways to change.

Now we move on to look at evaluation in action, starting with program logic. First, though, let's take a moment to meet Dr. Donna Mertens, the evaluation theorist and researcher who added the social justice branch to the Evaluation Theory Tree.

Dr. Donna Mertens

Donna Mertens, Professor Emeritus, Gallaudet University, specializes in research and evaluation methodologies designed to support social, economic, and environmental transformation. Her most recent books include *Mixed Methods Design in Evaluation*, *Program Evaluation Theory and Practice*, and *Research and Evaluation in Education and Psychology*. She is a past President of AEA and a founding Board member of the International Organization for Cooperation in Evaluation (IOCE).

1. *What caused you to update the Evaluation Theory Tree with a new branch on social justice? To what extent has it been accepted so far?*

I have worked with members of many marginalized communities, e.g., deaf people, Indigenous communities, underrepresented racial/ethnic groups, and women. The consistent message they shared was that they were either not being represented in evaluation studies, or they were inaccurately represented. Given the dire consequences of inequities in society, such as lack of access to health care, education, and meaningful employment, I think evaluators have a moral responsibility to design their work so that it consciously addresses issues of human rights and social justice. The Evaluation Theory tree included the branch of values; however, there was nothing explicit about the value of social justice. My hypothesis is that if we explicitly position ourselves as supporting the furtherance of social justice, then we are more likely to see our results used for that purpose. Thus, I added that branch and it has been accepted by many evaluators who share this value.

2. *Transformative evaluation is a term that is becoming widely used in the context of working with marginalized people, particularly in the international development community. How applicable is it in North America?*

The international community is abuzz with the word "transformation," especially as it applies to the achievement of the UN's SDGs or Sustainable Development Goals (United Nations Development Goals, n.d.). I have recommended the application of a transformative lens to evaluations that are used to address the societal transformations needed to achieve the SDGs. North America is not immune to the presence of injustices. We need only to look at headlines in the newspapers to see the incidences of violence against immigrant groups, shooting of unarmed Black men, inequities in resources in many communities of color, lack of access for people who have a disability or are deaf, or the disappearance of Indigenous peoples to convince us that we live in an unequal world. I have worked with communities in 85 countries; I can assure you that the transformative lens for evaluation has applicability in all countries, including North America.

3. *What evaluation strategies would you recommend that are inclusive and supportive of all voices in an evaluation context?*

I recommend a multistage mixed methods design that is informed by the assumptions of the transformative paradigm if we are to legitimately include and support all voices in evaluation studies. This begins with the identification of relevant stakeholders in the particular context. Evaluators should start with such questions as: Who is included? Who is excluded? What needs to be done to respectfully include all stakeholders? What are the cultural issues of relevance in this context? How can we build relationships with the full range of stakeholders that are culturally respectful? These should be followed by a contextual analysis to identify the cultural, historical, and political factors that are relevant. Based on this analysis, interventions and evaluation strategies that are culturally responsive can be developed and tested. Evaluators should examine the effectiveness of programs, as well as the quality of relationships as that will determine the sustainability of an intervention.

4. *Finally, do you have any words of wisdom for those of our readers who are just beginning to explore the field of evaluation?*

Ask yourself this question: "When I leave this world, will I look back on my contributions and say I have contributed to making a more just world?" While communication with our wider community is essential to grow our understanding of how to conduct better evaluation, the inclusion of a transformative lens has the potential to increase all our efforts to create a more just world.

Key Terms

Chaos theory 61
Coherence 71
Complexity theory 62
Constructivism 49
Critical thinking 73
Developmental evaluation 64
Epistemology 71

Evaluative thinking 73
Ontology 41
Paradigm shift 43
Paradigms 37
Positivism 44
Postpositivism 45
Pragmatism 53

Realism 42
Relativism 42
Scientific method 46
Subjectivism 51
Systems theory 55

The Main Ideas

1. Using the Ladder of Abstraction, we begin with ideas at the lowest level of abstraction (concrete) and move upward to ideas that are increasingly abstract.

2. An evaluator must understand the theoretical principles that underpin their study, or their work may be compromised.

3. What we know about the world is our ontology. Are you a realist or a relativist?

4. Paradigms set the foundation for different approaches to evaluation. They help evaluators understand their perspective on reality: positivism/postpositivism (one reality); constructivism (multiple realities); subjectivism/the transformative paradigm (meaning lies within the individual); and pragmatism (it depends).

5. The socio-ecological model provides a framework to study the different layers of influence on a program, including the individual, interpersonal groups, institutions, community, and public policy. Evaluators work across these levels to identify barriers and facilitators and to determine outcomes.

6. The Evaluation Theory Tree separates evaluation theorists into various categories depending on their perspective. The branches include use, methods, valuing, and social justice.

7. Evaluation aims for philosophical coherence. Our perspective reveals the assumptions and the choices we make regarding purpose, design, methodology, analysis, and interpretation.

8. Evaluators should think critically, continually ask questions of hard problems, and seek solutions that are not readily apparent. Critical thinking in an evaluative context is known as evaluative thinking.

Critical Thinking Questions

1. Which of the paradigms most closely aligns with your beliefs? For example, are you a positivist objectivist, constructivist, subjectivist, or pragmatist? Do you find yourself in between two of the paradigms or solidly within one of them?

2. Think about the field in which you hope to practice one day. What paradigm is prevalent in this field? Do you agree or disagree with this focus? How does this paradigm impact the types of evaluations conducted in your field? To what extent do they have a positive impact?

3. Can you remember a time in your life when things did not go as planned and became, instead, chaotic, and unpredictable? What was your response? What would you do differently next time?

Student Challenges

1. **Critically Thinking about your Life**. A well-rounded evaluator thinks critically about their life. You would raise questions about challenges you have, gather information to support a needed change, and arrive at a conclusion about the needed direction that is warranted. If you could change one thing about your life that would exponentially improve your life, what would that be? Identify the one thing you want to change and write a paragraph providing details. When does it happen? Why does it occur? Who is involved? Where does it occur? What precipitates it? What happens after it? What small intervention or strategy, if done, might change the outcome? Try a strategy. Reflect on your selection and write one sentence each day to explain your thinking for 30 days. What outcomes have you seen?

2. **Views of Theorists**. Select one of the theorists mentioned in this chapter. Find their three most recent articles and read them. Identify their important ideas. Do your views align with theirs? Why or why not?

3. **Realist and Relativist Approaches**. Find two articles describing program evaluations in a program area you know well, one using a realist perspective and quantitative methods and the other using a relativist perspective and qualitative or mixed methods.

Your Tasks:

a. Describe the methods used in each article.

b. Observe any differences about the types of conclusions drawn in each one.

c. Decide if a qualitative approach would have yielded different conclusions in the realist article and, similarly, if a quantitative approach for the relativist topic would have elicited different conclusions as well.

d. Determine if you can draw any conclusions from this comparison.

Evaluation Journal Examples:
- *The Canadian Journal of Program Evaluation (free access to all their issues)*
- *New Directions in Evaluation*
- *The American Journal of Evaluation*
- *Evaluation and Program Planning*
- *Evaluation & the Health Professions*
- *Assessment & Evaluation in Higher Education*

Additional Readings and Resources

1. Buescher, T. (1984). Thinking through the evaluation process: An interview with Dr. Joseph Renzulli. *Journal for the Education of the Gifted, 7*(1), 3–11. Several terms from Chapter 2 are used by this author, including pragmatist, evaluation plan, reductionist, evaluation questions.

2. Connor, T. (2018, October 10). *Deductive, inductive, and abductive reasoning.* https://medium.com/10x-curiosity/deductive-inductive-and-abductive-reasoning-c508e6b43097
    Connor has a well-written blog post on deductive, inductive, and abductive reasoning. He posits that to influence others, you need to design your arguments to make a more straightforward case for your position.

3. Dlugan, A. (September 15, 2013). *The ladder of abstraction and the public speaker.* http://sixminutes.dlugan.com/ladder-abstraction/
    This website guides you to becoming an effective speaker and using the ladder of abstraction to frame your presentation delivery.

4. Jones, M., Verity, F., Warin, M., Ratcliffe, J., Cobiac, L., Swinburn, B., & Cargo, M. (2016). OPALesence: Epistemological pluralism in the evaluation of a systems-wide childhood obesity prevention program. *Evaluation, 22*(1), 29–48.
    The authors explain how they apply epistemology to the evaluation research of an obesity prevention program. They look at the intervention at the individual, family, community, and policy levels.

5. McLeroy, K., Bibeau, D., Steckler, A., & Glanz, K. (1988). An ecological perspective on health promotion programs. *Health Education Quarterly, 15*(4), 351–377.
    The authors underscore the importance of visualizing interventions and changes within society through an ecological lens. The article outlines methods for focusing on intrapersonal factors, interpersonal processes, institutional factors, community factors, and public policy.

    Not all programs should be based on how individuals can change but on the best intervention strategies shown through evidence to cause change.

6. Moon, K., & Blackman, D. (2014). A guide to understanding social science research for natural scientists. *Conservation Biology, 28*, 1167–1177. The authors provide a link from the natural scientists to the research world indicating that conservation problems are commonly social problem (p. 1). They discuss the ontological and epistemological positions of the natural scientist and the way these positions can influence how they set up their designs, methodology, interpretation, and conclusions.

7. Mowles, C. (2014). Complex, but not quite complex enough: The turn to the complexity sciences in evaluation scholarship. *Evaluation, 20*(2), 160–175. The author reviews simple, complicated, and complex problems and addresses when best to choose complexity in a program evaluation.

8. Esbensen, F., & Matsuda N. (n.d.). *Changing course: Preventing gang membership* (T. Simon, N. Ritter, R. Mahendra, eds.). Office of Justice Programs and Centers for Disease Control and Prevention. https://www.ojp.gov/pdffiles1/nij/239234.pdf
    This book was a joint venture by the Department of Justice and the Centers for Disease Control and Prevention. It details why gang membership is important to prevent and the attraction for youth to gangs, aligns the attraction to gangs and the prevention of them to the socio-ecological model, and provides a wealth of information as to how individual, relationships, community, and societal factors either promote or discourage joining gangs. The authors give information about what interventions should be employed and how the identification process of gang membership works.

3

PROGRAM LOGIC

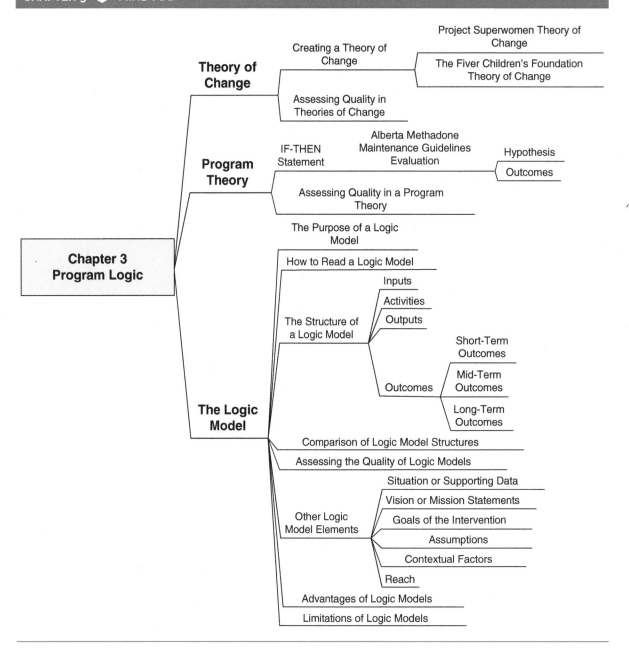

THE GOLDEN THREAD

The great Greek hero, Theseus, had to save the city of Athens from the wicked oppressor, King Minos of Crete. Every nine years, the king demanded a tribute of seven youths and seven maidens to sacrifice to the Minotaur, a terrifying monster with the body of a man and the head of a bull. It lived at the center of the Labyrinth, a complex maze from which no one ever returned. Minos imprisoned his enemies there and they were promptly devoured by the creature. Theseus sailed to Crete, and as he walked along the beach, leading the young Athenians to their doom, he met Ariadne, the beautiful daughter of King Minos. She instantly fell in love with him and opposing her father, decided to help Theseus. She gave him a ball of golden

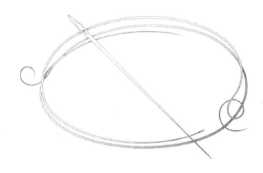

Source: iStockphoto.com/John1179

thread, which he slowly unraveled as he penetrated deeper and deeper into the confusing maze of corridors inside the Labyrinth. He found the Minotaur at the center and killed it with the enchanted sword of Aegeus. He retraced his steps, thanks to the golden thread which he wound back into a ball as he went. He and the rescued Athenians found the young princess waiting impatiently outside the Labyrinth. When they sailed back to Athens, Theseus took her with him (Christou & Papastamatis, 2008; Mark, 2011).

INTRODUCTION

Chapter 3 is about the **golden thread** or program logic that guides the entire program enterprise (Social Ventures Australia, 2012). The evaluator is always on a journey, searching for links between cause and effect, evidence that proves or disproves the relationship between program activities and outcomes. We want to know what happened. Did the program have an impact on human behavior? Was the intervention effective? Program funders, managers, staff, and stakeholders all want to know if their investment and efforts have had an impact on a social issue or problem.

The golden thread reflects the research question posed at the beginning of an evaluation study. It represents the logic that links program purpose to strategy, planning, implementation, and evaluation. It is important to work through this process with stakeholders and together follow the golden thread of logic that runs between the reasons for implementing the program and the outcomes it is expected to achieve. These pathways are not always clear, once the assumptions, beliefs, goals, preconditions, resources, players, and activities are added to the mix. Despite the lack of clarity and overlap of terms that often appear in the evaluation literature, we hope to provide a clear distinction among three important tools used to understand program logic, or the golden thread. They are the Theory of Change, Program Theory or the IF…THEN statement, and the classic Logic Model.

You will enjoy the resources in this chapter including the Spotlight on Equity, which presents the Grand Rapids African American Health Institute (GRAAHI) and their use of logic models, our expert Dr. Stewart I. Donaldson, Key Terms, Main Ideas, Critical Thinking Questions, Student Challenges, and Additional Readings and Resources.

THEORY OF CHANGE

In Chapter 2, we discussed natural science, behavioral science, and social theories. In this chapter, we look inside the program to understand the assumptions and expectations for its success. **Theory of Change (ToC)** is an "organization's story of how and why the world will be different because of what it does" (Taplin & Rasic, 2012, p. 1). It describes change processes by outlining the causal linkages in an initiative (Leeuw & Donaldson, 2015), focusing directly on how change will occur. Developing a ToC occurs early in the program development process when expected outcomes are being identified and prioritized.

Leading evaluation theorist Carol Weiss commented that we can base programs on an implicit or explicit belief about how and why the program will work (Weiss, 1972). In 1995, she proposed that an evaluation

> *…should surface those theories and lay them out in as fine detail as possible, identifying all the assumptions and sub-assumptions built into the program. The evaluators then construct methods for data collection and analysis to track the unfolding of the assumptions. The aim is to examine the extent to which program theories hold. The evaluation should show which of the assumptions underlying the program break down, where they break down, and which of the several theories underlying the program are best supported by the evidence.* (p. 67)

Weiss described a job-training program for disadvantaged youth. The program included job-readiness skills such as dressing appropriately, arriving on the job promptly, and getting along with supervisors and co-workers, as well as basic job skills. She wondered what the underlying assumptions about the program were. Looking at the program design, she posited that program developers thought the youth did not get jobs because they lacked the job skills required and the proper attitudes and habits for work. Program designers had rejected, either implicitly or explicitly, other plausible assumptions about why the youth might be unemployed, such as high unemployment rates, scarcity of entry-level jobs, lack of motivation, family failure to inculcate work values, health problems, transportation issues, lack of childcare—the list of possibilities seemed endless. None of these were powerful enough to overthrow their theory about how to address the issue. Following their logic, she found that many of the program linkages based on these assumptions were problematic. For example, they assumed, *when young people hear of the program's availability, they will sign up for it and will attend regularly.*

Weiss commented that most job-training programs were looking at best case results of a 5–10% increase in employment rates when comparing participants to nonparticipants.

Thus, she made a case for theory-based evaluation (Weiss, 1995, pp. 69–72) because:

1. It focuses on critical aspects of the program

2. It generates knowledge about crucial theories of change

3. It asks program practitioners to make their assumptions explicit and reach a consensus with their colleagues about what they are trying to do and why

4. It influences policy and popular opinion.

Later, Anderson (2004) commented that Weiss "popularized the term Theory of Change as a way to describe the set of assumptions that explain both the mini steps that lead to the long-term goal of interest and the connections between program activities and outcomes that occur at each step of the way" (p. 2).

Bickman (1987) characterized the ToC as "the construction of a plausible and sensible model of how a program is supposed to work" (p. 5). Thus, the ToC provides a deeper inspection of a program to understand outcomes and understand the underlying mechanisms of why it works and for whom and, additionally, what environmental influence could have impacted the results. Vogel (2012) shares the following strategy:

> We use the analogy of Google Maps – this is the territory, this is how we see our bit of the territory, and this is the route that we think is best to take through it (though, like Google Maps, we recognise there may be a couple of different routes across the territory, but we have explicitly chosen one). Based on our understanding of how the territory along the route works, this is how we shall approach the journey, and these are some of the landmarks we expect to see on the way. (p. 5)

In this analogy, travelers could take various routes to their destination. However, they typically choose the one route that is the most direct. Likewise, in evaluation, we are tasked with determining program outcomes from among the many possibilities that exist, searching for that golden thread of program logic that will improve evaluation designs and enhance program success.

Because the ToC relies on a means–ends relationship, Rossi et al. (2004, p. 184) explained that it is essential to define program boundaries, ensuring that all-important activities, events, and resources link to one or more of the outcomes that are central to the program endeavor. A helpful approach is to start with the program benefits and work backward to identify all the activities and resources presumed to contribute to attaining program objectives.

The benefits of using a ToC approach include a clear and testable hypothesis about how the change will occur, a visual representation of how that change will come about, a blueprint for evaluation with measurable **indicators of success**, a consensus among stakeholders about what defines success, and a communication tool.

Creating a Theory of Change

As the Center for Theory of Change explains on their website, "Theory of Change is essentially a comprehensive description and illustration of how and why a desired change is expected to happen in a particular context" (2019a, para. 1). You are filling in the "missing middle" between what a program does and how these activities lead to desired outcomes.

Creating a ToC is a participatory process in which program decision makers and stakeholders identify the conditions they believe must occur to meet their long-term goals. They articulate assumptions about the causal connections between outcomes and interventions, identify indicators for success, and formulate actions necessary to achieve their goals (Center for Theory of Change, 2019a). When developing a ToC, the focus is on the chain of preconditions, not on activities or interventions. The causal links are mapped backward from ends to means and the causal pathways are specified. During the discussions around this mapping process, hidden assumptions surface.

To create a ToC, the Center recommends the following five steps (Center for Theory of Change, 2019b):

1. Identify goals and assumptions

2. Map backward and connect outcomes

3. Develop indicators

4. Identify interventions

5. Write a narrative to explain the logic of the initiative.

Project Superwomen Theory of Change

ActKnowledge and the Aspen Institute Roundtable on Community Change provide an example of a ToC for Project Superwomen, a job preparation program for women who had been victims of domestic violence. Project Superwomen is a coalition of stakeholders including a social service provider, a nonprofit employment training center, and a nonprofit shelter provider for female domestic violence victims. The goal is to help women obtain employment that keeps them out of poverty, off public assistance, and provides provide stability and upward mobility.

Based on a belief that women can learn nontraditional skills and find employers that will hire them, the project's goal is to provide both the training and support needed by this population to enter and remain in the workforce. The assumptions they make about the project are: (1) there are jobs available in nontraditional skills for women and (2) jobs in nontraditional areas such as electrical, plumbing, carpentry, and building management are more likely to pay livable wages, be unionized, and provide job security.

The coalition believed that most of these women would be single mothers coming from abusive situations and would need psycho-emotional counseling, especially low self-esteem, and impaired coping skills. Even those with stable lives might face crises from time to time, thus requiring practical help or psychological support. Based on their resources, the group decided that they could support some types of crises, such as housing evictions or court appearances, but could not be responsible for ultimately stabilizing the lives of their clients. This decision influenced their screening process, ensuring that women entering the program had already settled significant issues, such as substance abuse or foster care.

Here are the steps they used to create a ToC for this program.

1. **Identify outcomes and assumptions**. The long-term outcome for the program was long-term employment at a livable wage for domestic violence survivors. To achieve that goal, the program designers identified three preconditions: (1) survivors attain coping skills, (2) survivors have marketable skills in nontraditional jobs, and (3) survivors know and have appropriate workplace behavior.

2. **Map backward and connect outcomes**. Program designers explored the levels of change that would be necessary to reach these longer-term outcomes. Next, they asked themselves how the project's participants would achieve the three identified preconditions. At each step, the golden thread of program logic was debated and teased out until designers could agree on the best way forward. Finally, they continued to map their ToC framework back to the initial condition, namely the coalition itself.

3. **Develop indicators**. Once they had developed the framework, they measured the implementation and effectiveness of the initiative. Each **indicator** had four parts, outlined here along with a specific answer related to this program:

   • Who is changing? (Women enrolled in the program)

   • How many do we expect will succeed? (Perhaps 90% of the enrolled women)

   • How much is good enough? (A $12 per-hour job for at least 6 months)

   • By when does this outcome need to happen? (within 2 months of graduation)

4. **Identify interventions**. Next, the designers identified the interventions, or activities, that the program needed to offer to bring about the desired outcomes. By doing this, they realized that before women could enroll in the program, they needed childcare. They also had to be ready to commit and attend the program. For all this to happen, they first had to hear about the program. At each step, spot checking occurred to ensure that the program logic was plausible and that the interventions were feasible, given resources available.

5. **Write a narrative**. After completing all the connections in the framework, the team wrote a two-page program description translating their initiative into everyday language.

We provide the final ToC framework for Project Superwomen (Figure 3.1, p. 87).

The Fiver Children's Foundation Theory of Change

The Fiver Children's Foundation is a youth development organization in New York City that takes its name from the book *Watership Down* (Adams, 1975; Fiver Children's Foundation, n.d.a). The novel focuses on the survival, leadership, and courage of a group of rabbits, led by the visionary rabbit, Fiver, who set out to find a better way of life. The foundation benefits children from disadvantaged circumstances. Fiver created a ToC that illustrates the pathways on which foundation activities are based (Figure 3.2, p. 88):

• Education and careers pathway

• Civic-mindedness pathway

• Health and ethics pathway.

The following statement encapsulates their vision: "Ultimately, we want for the Fiver kids what all parents want for their children, for them to grow up to be happy, fulfilled adults who achieve their full potential in life. We want them to have the courage to strive for their dreams, and if they come up short, the resilience to try again. Then, we want them to take what they have learned at Fiver and share it with the world" (Fiver Children's Foundation, n.d.b, para. 1). Within this change model, the mechanisms the Foundation believes will bring about that vision include Fivers demonstrating tolerance and empathy; modeling leadership and advocacy skills; and becoming engaged citizens.

Assessing Quality in Theories of Change

Theories of change are now widely used in evaluation (Mayne, 2017, p. 155). Specific examples can vary greatly and there is limited agreement about what comprises a ToC. Mayne (2017) has provided a set of criteria for assessing the robustness of a ToC, to ensure that it is well articulated, credible, plausible, and logical (p. 158). These criteria can be used as guidelines to assess the strength of a ToC and the intervention it represents (see Table 3.1, p. 89).

FIGURE 3.1 ● PROJECT SUPERWOMEN: A THEORY OF CHANGE

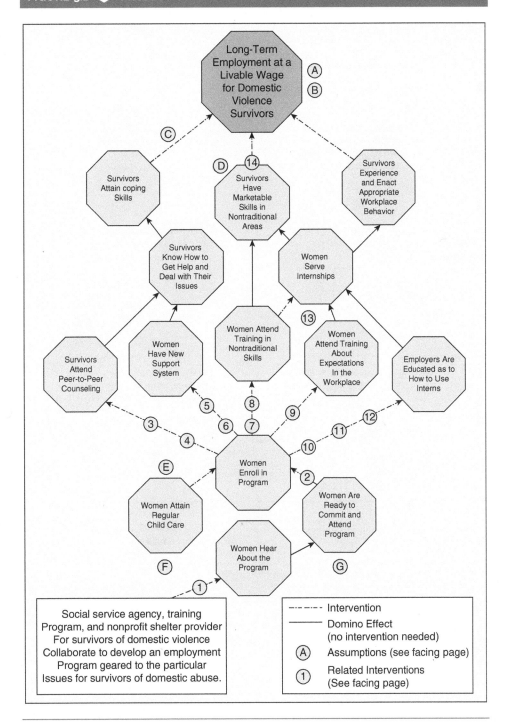

Source: Anderson, A. (n.d.). *The community builder's approach to theory of change: A practical guide to theory development.* The Aspen Institute Roundtable on Community Change.

FIGURE 3.2   ●   THE FIVER CHILDREN'S FOUNDATION THEORY OF CHANGE

FIVER CHILDREN'S FOUNDATION THEORY OF CHANGE

Fivers share what they have Learned with the world

ULTIMATE OUTCOME

Fivers are happy and fulfilled in work, family and life and make positive contributions to society.

Fivers have relevant, market-driven, 21st century skills to succeed in school and careers.

Fivers are engaged citizens.

Fivers make ethical and healthy life choices.

SUMMER INTERNSHIPS

INTENSIVE COLLEGE WORKSHOPS & VISITS

ADVENTURE CHALLENGE TRIPS

ETHICAL DECISION-MAKING & DEBATE CURRICULUM

Fivers understand the connection between education and future success.

Fivers demonstrate leadership and advocacy skills.

Fivers understand the influences that impact decision-making.

ONE-ON-ONE ADVISING ON EDUCATIONAL OPTIONS

ROLE MODELS FROM DIVERSE BACKGROUNDS

Fivers demonstrate curiosity and stay engaged in school.

Fivers demonstrate tolerance and empathy.

Fivers have mentoring relationships with caring adults.

TWO WEEKS AT OUR AWARD-WINNING RESIDENTIAL SUMMER LEARNING PROGRAM, CAMP FIVER

Fivers understand their unique strengths, build social capital, Set basic goals and begin a 10-year character-building journey

TEN YEAR COMMITMENT

EDUCATION & CAREERS PATHWAY

CIVIC MINDEDNESS PATHWAY

HEALTH & ETHICS PATHWAY

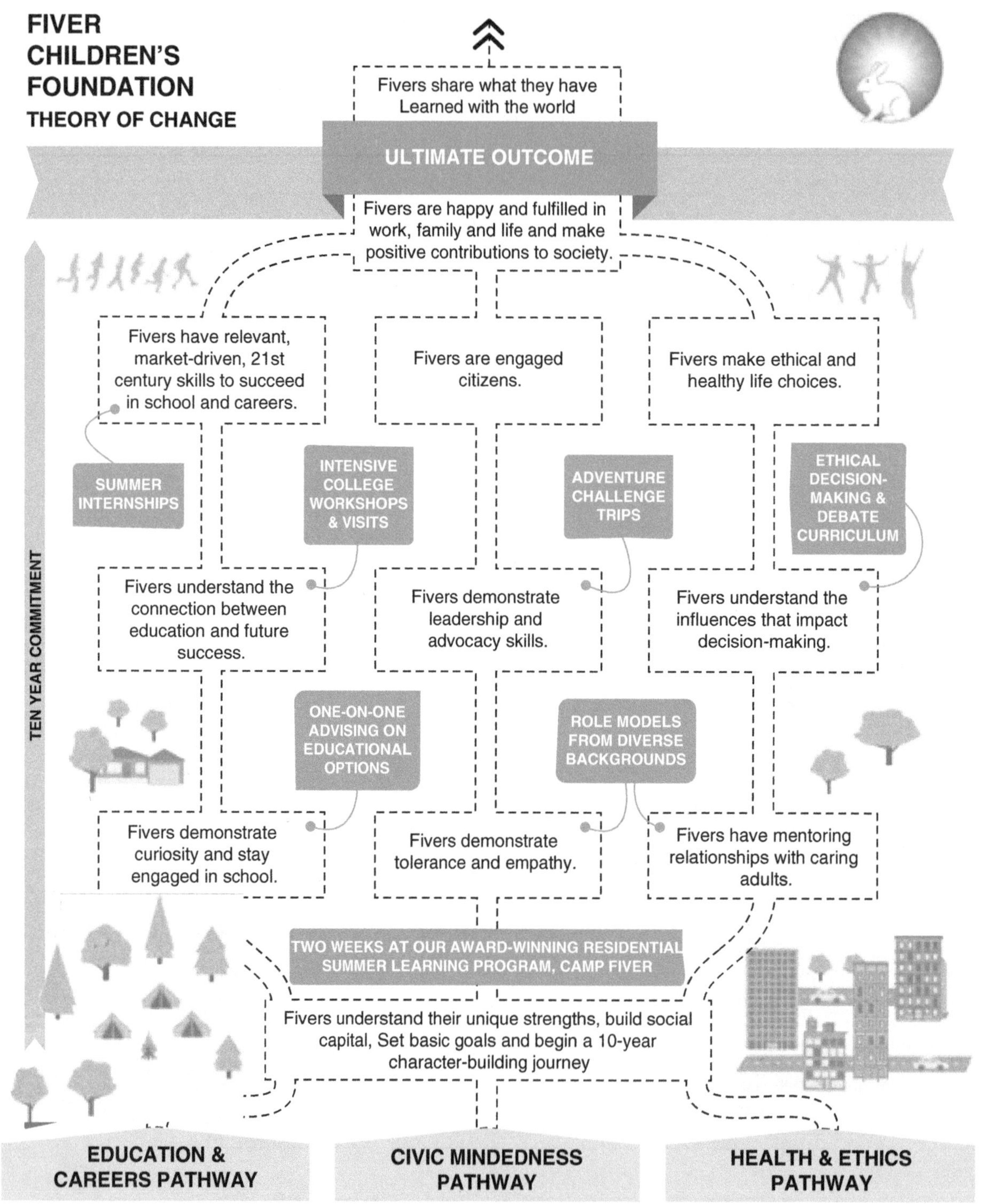

In addition to coming from economically disadvantaged circumstances, Fivers face other daunting and complex challenges of poverty. More than half being raised by single parents and many have had to learn English as second language and acclimate to a new culture. Most of our kids come from groups under-represented in higher education and professional careers, have few examples of academic persistence and are hoping to be the first in their family to attend collage.

Source: Fiver Children's Foundation. (n.d.b). Fiver children's foundation theory of change.

TABLE 3.1 ● CRITERIA FOR THEORY OF CHANGE ANALYSIS

Criteria	Key Questions
Overall Criteria	
Understandable	• Is the logic and structure of the ToC clear?
Agreed	• To what extent is the ToC agreed or contestable?
Level of effort	• Are the activities and outputs of the intervention commensurate with the expected results?
Criteria for Each Result	
Well-defined	• Is the results statement unambiguous?
Plausible timing	• Is the time frame for the result reasonable?
Logical coherence	• Does the result follow logically from the previous result? Is the sequence plausible or at least possible?
Measurable	• Is there a need to measure the result? How can the results be measured? What is the likely strength or status of evidence for the result being realized?
Criteria for Each Assumption	
Well-defined	• Is the assumption unambiguous?
Logical coherence	• Is the assumption a precondition or event for the effect sought?
Justified	• What is the justification for the assumption as being necessary or likely necessary?
Realized	• Is it plausible that the assumption will be realized? Are there at-risk assumptions that should be addressed?
Sustainable	• Is the assumption sustainable?
Measurable	• Is there a need to measure the assumption? How can the assumption be measured? What is the likely strength or status of evidence for the assumption being realized?
Criteria for Each Causal Link	
Independence	• Are the assumptions for the link independent from each other?
A sufficient set	• Are the set of causal link assumptions along with the prior causal factor sufficient to bring about the effect? Is the link plausible?
Strength/Status of evidence	• What is the strength or current status of evidence for the causal link being realized?

Source: Adapted from Mayne, J. (2017). Theory of change analysis: Building robust theories of change. *Canadian Journal of Program Evaluation/LaRevue canadienne d'évaluation de programme, 32*(2), 155–173.

These criteria are best used in a participatory manner involving program designers and implementers as well as the evaluator. The discussion may illuminate (Mayne, 2017):

issues that were not, but need to be, included in the ToC, identify issues about the intervention design that need addressing, and/or identify data that need to be monitored or that need to be addressed in a planned evaluation. (p. 167)

PROGRAM THEORY

Having worked with decision makers and stakeholders to clarify program assumptions, expectations, plans, and preconditions, it is time to focus on the evaluation itself, rather than on the program. The first step is to develop a **program theory**. As Donaldson and Lipsey (2006) explain,

> *At the most practical level, a well-developed and fully articulated program theory can be very useful for framing key evaluation questions and designing sensitive and responsive evaluations…. [It] helps the evaluator and program stakeholders identify the performance dimensions most critical to the program's success and, hence, those that may be the most important to assess.*

A program theory is not one of those grand theories discussed in Chapter 2; instead, it is a very humble and specific statement that explains how a program is supposed to work (Bickman, 1987). Thus, no two program theories are alike; they are all dependent on the components of the individual program.

With a program theory in hand, the evaluator is free to concentrate on appropriate evaluation questions. This focus on questions restrains the evaluator and stakeholders from jumping too quickly to methods and indicators. The methods selected will be "dependent on discussions with relevant stakeholders about what would constitute credible evidence in this context, and what is feasible given the practical and financial constraints" (Donaldson, 2005).

The IF-THEN Statement

The **IF-THEN Statement** represents a program theory and is sometimes described as a conditional sentence. It is the simplest way to describe the golden thread of the program's logic. It encapsulates the research question and the proposed cause and effect logic at play in a program design. The IF statement is a type of hypothesis and is followed by a THEN statement or outcome. The statements represent a thumbnail of your understanding of the logic that links your program components and your program's intended short, intermediate, and long-term outcomes. In the case of evaluation, the IF-THEN statement represents the program designers' core beliefs about how program outcomes will be produced. It follows this pattern:

> *IF we provide the appropriate resources and conduct the planned activities,*
>
> *THEN the identified short-term, intermediate-term, and long-term outcomes will occur.*

Creating a Program Theory: Alberta Methadone Maintenance Guidelines Evaluation

Gail developed a program theory when conducting an evaluation for the College of Physicians and Surgeons of Alberta, the Canadian province where she lives. The project reviewed the development and implementation of Methadone Maintenance Guidelines for physicians. At that time, approximately 10,000 people in Alberta were identified as potential beneficiaries of methadone treatment, yet services were very limited (College of Physicians and Surgeons of Alberta, 2006). There were few clinics, few trained physicians available to provide treatment, and no comprehensive clinical standards or guidelines on the subject. As methadone is a controlled substance in Canada, a physician must obtain a special license to administer it, thus exempting them from criminal charges. The College was involved in issuing these licenses and physicians had to demonstrate that they had sufficient, relevant education, and the experience needed to receive one.

Government funding was received for an 18-month project entitled, *The Development and Endorsement of Alberta-based Methadone Maintenance Guidelines Project*. The project had three goals:

1. Encourage more physicians to obtain methadone licenses for opioid dependency in order to increase access to opioid dependency treatment

2. Contribute to the reduction of illicit drug use, improve the health status of opioid-dependent individuals as a result of access to treatment, decrease transmission of Human Immunodeficiency Virus (HIV), Hepatitis C Virus (HCV), and Hepatitis B Virus (HBV), decrease illegal activity, increase employment, decrease social costs, and decreasing mortality

3. Ensure patient safety in the provision of opioid dependency treatment.

One of the first tasks that Gail undertook was to develop an IF-THEN statement for this evaluation. See Box 3.1.

BOX 3.1 ● HYPOTHESIS AND OUTCOMES FOR IF-THEN STATEMENTS

Hypothesis

- IF the project receives administration and resources, establishes a Guidelines Development Committee, and develops communications, stakeholder consultation, and project evaluation plans—and

- IF the Standards and Guidelines for methadone maintenance treatment (MMT) are developed, approved, and endorsed, used to develop standards for a practice audit process, and launched with appropriate communication, orientation, training, and support—and

- IF training and support are provided, physicians access the Guidelines, a clear role for clinics and community practitioners for MMT is provided, and evaluation occurs....

Outcomes

- THEN trained physicians will find the Guidelines credible and acceptable; understand the disease of addiction; meet registration standards and receive a methadone license; and

- THEN opioid-dependent individuals will experience increased access to treatment, improved health status, and reduced risk of contracting HIV, HCV, and HBV; and

(Continued)

(Continued)

- THEN opioid-dependent individuals will reduce illicit drug use and related illegal activity, and experience improved quality of life and decreased mortality; and

- THEN Albertans will experience improved safety related to methadone treatment, decreased transmission of HIV, HCV, and HBV, decreased social costs, and improved health care.

Assessing Quality in a Program Theory

At the most practical level, a well-developed and fully articulated program theory can be very useful to frame important evaluation questions (Donaldson & Lipsey, 2006, pp. 64–65.) A clear program theory supports the development of a responsive evaluation design. Rather than producing a black-box evaluation which is not transparent and does not respond to change, a program theory-driven evaluation does the following:

- Contributes to an evolving understanding of the program

- Helps formulate relevant evaluation questions

- Produces an evaluation that determines if the program brought about the changes envisioned in that program theory.

THE LOGIC MODEL

While a program's ToC lays out the pathways and preconditions required to achieve specific program outcomes, and while the program theory turns these pathways into a simple hypothesis or golden thread that leads to the desired change, the **logic model** is the tool the evaluator uses to guide the implementation of the evaluation process. It provides a visual map that links the program's inputs, activities, short-term, mid-term, and long-term outcomes.

The logic model provides "a systematic and visual way to present and share your understanding of the relationships among the resources you have to operate your program, the activities you plan, the changes or results you hope to achieve" (W. K. Kellogg Foundation, 2004, p. 1). It is a popular way to illustrate a program, or aspects of a program, and aids in program planning, implementation, and evaluation (MacDonald, 2018).

There are many names for the logic model in the literature and can create confusion (Hurworth, 2008). Other names are blueprint, roadmap, causal chain, or conceptual map (Silverman et al., n.d., p. 9). However, while terms may vary, we have chosen to stay with the term "logic model" because it predominates in the evaluation field today.

Logic models were not mainstream until in the late 1990s when the United Way of America introduced them to measure program outcomes. Then, in 2001, the W. K. Kellogg Foundation furthered the use of logic models with their influential Logic Model Development Guide. Since that time, logic models have become ubiquitous.

The logic model is a one-page visual representation that takes many hours to create. Those who truly understand their program can communicate the elements of it on one page, succinctly enough so that a stranger can understand the program. As the French philosopher and mathematician Blaise Pascal (2012) famously wrote in 1656, "The present letter is a very long one, simply because I had no leisure to make it shorter" (para. 27). It takes time to create a one-page document that resonates with stakeholders.

The Purpose of a Logic Model

Woodward (2010, p. 2) states that "A logic model spells out how the program works. It describes the activities that are a part of the program and the changes you expect if these activities are carried out as planned. It sets out the answer to the basic question: How does change occur in this program"? Table 3.2 delineates the purposes of a logic model.

TABLE 3.2 ● PURPOSES OF A LOGIC MODEL	
Program Planning and Review	• Assesses need for program • Clarifies program goals and assumptions • Determines activities needed to carry out program and achieve its goals • Shows the links between activities, outcomes, and impacts • Helps staff understand their roles and responsibilities • Identifies gaps in programming • Identifies staff and resource needs • Explores likely outcomes and impacts of the program
Program Integrity	• Connects program to overall organization's mission, vision, and overall goals • Monitors program performance • Frames the tools needed to describe the program clearly
Communication	• Portrays program theory graphically • Acts as a tool to help stakeholders understand the purpose of the program • Provides a summary of the program plan • Ensures a common understanding of program among staff, stakeholders, and funders
Evaluation	• Helps evaluators develop evaluation questions and metrics • Focuses on areas where success will be measured • Provides a starting point for quality improvement projects • Improves program accountability • Ensures a focus on outcomes and impacts

How to Read a Logic Model

The W. K. Kellogg Foundation (2004, p. 3) has illustrated how to read a logic model by following the IF-THEN statements from planning through to results (see Figure 3.3, p. 94).

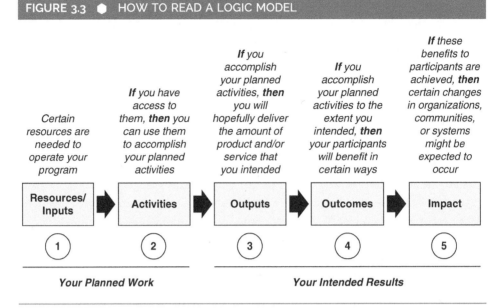

FIGURE 3.3 ● HOW TO READ A LOGIC MODEL

Source: Used with permission from W. K. Kellogg Foundation. (2004). *Using logic models to bring together planning, evaluation, and action: Logic model development guide.*

The Structure of a Logic Model

While the terminology about logic models might vary, the intent is the same: a declaration of planned activities and what you hope to achieve as a result. A complete logic model distills program theory to represent underlying relationships between and among components (MacDonald, 2018). It builds on the program theory or IF-THEN statement and is informed by the causal mechanisms that stakeholders have identified when delineating the ToC. Similar to a flowchart, the logic model is generally a linear arrangement of circles, boxes, and arrows on a one-page document.

Although evaluators design logic models in a variety of ways, the universal elements are **Inputs, Activities, Outputs, Short-Term Outcomes, Mid-Term Outcomes, and Long-Term Outcomes or Impact**.

Each component or bucket is explored in the following sections. Definitions, examples, and sample logic models are provided. Optional elements sometimes found in logic models are also briefly discussed.

Inputs

The first main section of the logic model, Inputs, has to do with program management. What are the human, financial, physical, and philosophical resources needed for the program to take place? Other essential preconditions and supports may include fund-raising, personnel management, facilities acquisition and management, and political liaisons (Rossi et al., 2004, p. 143). Table 3.3, p. 95 provides some examples of Inputs.

In the VERB™ campaign for increased youth physical activity (Huhman et al., 2004), the goal is a media campaign. The logic model describes Inputs, as shown in

TABLE 3.3 ●	EXAMPLES OF INPUTS
Funding	• Money, grants, contracts, loans, in-kind contributions, donations
People	• Staff, volunteers, governing board, partners, money, collaborative agreements
Resources	• Physical infrastructure, technology, equipment, time, policy, laws, or ordinance
Knowledge	• Content expertise, literature review, training, research
Existing Documents	• Materials, philosophical statements, vision for the organization, strategic plan, communication plan, program history, program files and databases

Figure 3.4, p. 96. Inputs for this program are contractors, community infrastructure, partnerships, consultants, staff, and research and evaluation efforts. Long-term outcomes here are the reduction of risky behaviors and ultimately the reduction in chronic diseases.

Activities

The second component of the logic model is devoted to **Activities**. What does the program do? How do participants become engaged with the program? What are the processes, actions, and events needed to implement the program (Kekahio et al., 2014)? How do participants cycle through the services offered that we hypothesized would bring about the desired outcomes? The activities are described in the IF part of the IF-THEN statement. They are the pathways to change depicted in the ToC. Examples of activities are campaigns, programs, coaching, site visits, products, physical structures, media coverage, policies, technology, curriculum, counseling, and networking.

Figure 3.5, p. 97 presents a logic model for the BUZZING program. It hypothesizes that IF students participate in the intervention, THEN they will achieve "empowerment, self-satisfaction, increased motivation, and work ethic, improved health and wellbeing, positive attitude toward employment, and improved employability" (Beaton, 2016, p. 25). BUZZING activities consist of teaching young people to have supportive relationships, positive work experiences, good employment skills, and support for their barriers to employment. Program personnel provide students a mobile application where they journal their activities during the intervention. They also benefit from belonging to a Facebook community and receive training in the hospitality industry. In this logic model, the authors also elaborate on the causes or conditions of the problem and the consequences of unemployment in youth as well as individual and societal ramifications of youth unemployment.

Outputs

The **Outputs** of a logic model directly link from the activities and, when collected and measured, indicate the success of implementation. Outputs are a direct result of the

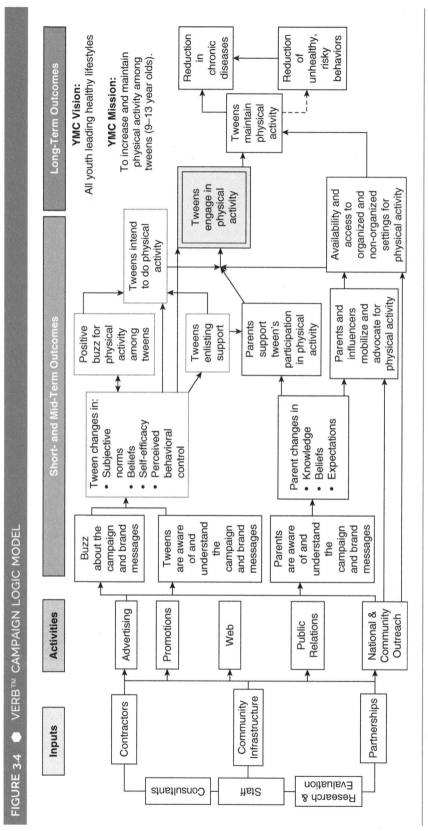

FIGURE 3.4 ⬡ VERB™ CAMPAIGN LOGIC MODEL

Source: Huhman, M., Heitzler, C., & Wong, F. (2004). The VERB™ campaign logic model: A tool for planning and evaluation. *Prevention in Chronic Disease*, 1(3), 1–6. http://www.cdc.gov/pcd/issues/2004/jul/04_0033.htm

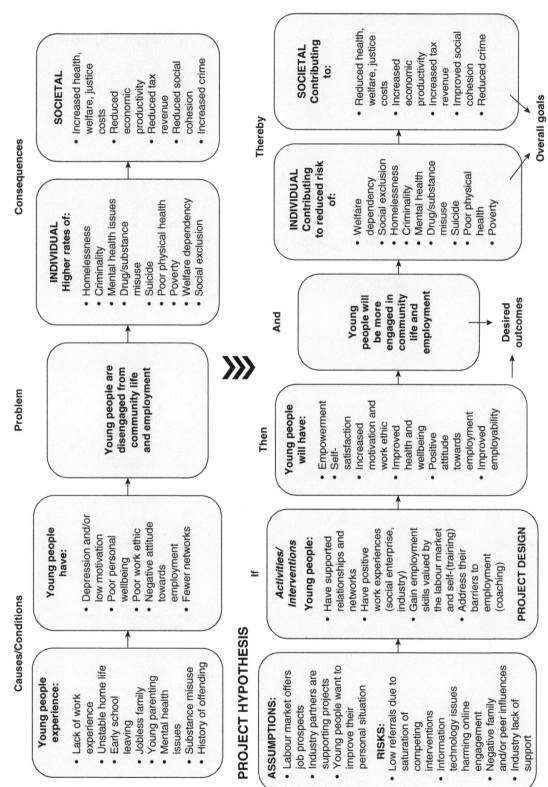

FIGURE 3.5 ● LOGIC MODEL FOR BUZZING PROGRAM

DEFINING THE PROBLEM

PROJECT HYPOTHESIS

Source: Beaton, S. (2016). BUZZING—a theory-based impact evaluation design. *Evaluation Journal of Australasia, 16(4)*, 21–29.

activities and demonstrate that they occurred and are tangible, concrete, and measurable forms of evidence. However, MacDonald (2018) warns us that it is best to avoid representing outputs as specific data points, indicators, or metrics (e.g., number of participants). She comments:

> *this practice can impede discussion of how outputs relate to other components and hinder full examination of options for program evaluation. For example, it is problematic to present outputs as evaluation indicators or metrics when stakeholders have not yet defined overarching evaluation questions or other pieces of an evaluation.* (pp. 2–3)

The logic model in Figure 3.6 illustrates the outputs for a teacher training program on alternative reading strategies (Kekahio et al., 2014, p. 3). Notice that the outputs indicate that the evidence will include the number of resources provided or people served but do not provide the metrics at this stage of the evaluation.

FIGURE 3.6 ● SAMPLE LOGIC MODEL FOR ALTERNATIVE READING STRATEGIES

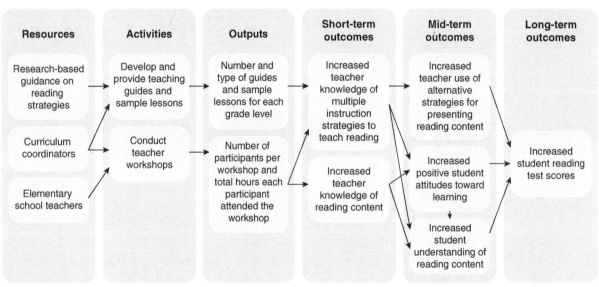

Source: Kekahio, W., Cicchinelli, L., Lawton, B., & Brandon, P. R. (2014). *Logic models: A tool for effective program planning, collaboration, and monitoring (REL 2014–025).* Washington, DC: US Department of Education, Institute of Education Sciences, National Center for Education Evaluation and Regional Assistance, Regional Educational Laboratory Pacific.

Examples of outputs are participation, satisfaction, training developed, website developed, agreements signed, lessons completed, materials distributed, staff trained, and activities implemented.

Outcomes

The **Outcomes** in a logic model are what everyone has been waiting for. What are the expected benefits, changes, or results of the program (MacDonald, 2018)? Typically, evaluators divide outcomes into **short-term outcomes, mid-term outcomes,** and

long-term outcomes, based on a temporal progression from outcomes closest in time to activity experiences to those that occur the longest afterwards that are feasible to measure. This distinction can be described as from proximal to distal. Some logic models also specify impacts as the most long-term aim or desired change (Macdonald, 2018, p. 3). It must be noted, though, that some changes take very little time to occur, but others can take years. It is useful to make a note on the logic model of when the anticipated outcomes are likely to occur. Logic models only include intended outcomes, but the narrative explanation that usually accompanies them can also describe potential unintended outcomes, whether positive or negative. Table 3.4 provides examples of short-term outcomes, while Table 3.5, p. 100 provides examples for mid- and long-term outcomes.

TABLE 3.4 ⬡ EXAMPLES OF SHORT-TERM OUTCOMES	
Type of Outcome	**Example**
	SHORT-TERM OUTCOMES
Awareness	Parents are offered a workshop on STEM (science, technology, engineering, and math) careers for their high school students. The purpose of the workshop is to increase their awareness about the group of disciplines that can serve as a career option for their students. Evaluators will find out to what extent students' awareness has changed.
Perceptions	A corporation has received several complaints regarding workplace sexual harassment. As a result, leadership implements a new training program designed to change perceptions about behavior that employees may not understand is inappropriate. Evaluators will measure the extent to which perceptions have changed.
Beliefs	Programmers provide parents an online intervention designed to talk to their children about racism and prejudice as well as about certain beliefs parents may have about others who are different than they are. The purpose of the training is to educate parents about their ability to influence their child's beliefs about other racial and ethnic groups. Evaluators will measure changes in both parents' and children's beliefs.
Attitude	A local health department has decided to adopt national public health workforce competencies and standards and integrate them into the work plans of all employees. The health department is concerned about certain attitudes of long-time employees. The administrators believe that some employees may feel nervous or defensive. Evaluators will find out the extent to which employees' attitudes change after the standards are implemented compared to their attitudes beforehand.
Knowledge	A financial literacy program designed to teach college students about their money aims to improve their knowledge of debt and the circumstances of using credit cards. The instruction focuses on increasing knowledge related to the actual costs of using credit cards by calculating, for example, the amount the student will pay on a $100 purchase at an 18% interest rate for two years. Evaluators will test students' knowledge about debt and credit cards.

TABLE 3.5   ●   EXAMPLES OF MID- AND LONG-TERM OUTCOMES

Type of Outcome	Example
MID-TERM OUTCOMES	
Decision making	Educators develop an intervention intended to reduce drunk driving by teens. While the standard intervention uses fear-based messages and activities (e.g., video with a mock car accident caused by alcohol, visiting the morgue), this intervention focuses on educating the students about brain science and teenagers and their decision-making ability. Strategies are provided that help students understand how they make decisions about drinking, for example, at a party. Several months after the program, evaluators will ask students to describe any changes to their decision-making skills related to alcohol use.
Skill/Behavior	A company wants to improve the retention rate of its workforce. They start a mentoring program that will provide the new employee several benefits in the new year, including training on project management skills and productivity, and development of an online department dashboard that illustrates the company's status of meeting goals and objectives by department. Evaluators will try to determine which skills are adopted by new employees. Then, later, as a long-term outcome, they will measure retention rates and compare them to rates prior to the program.
LONG-TERM OUTCOMES	
Organizational Behavior	A nonprofit organization wants to increase funding within two years. They brainstorm reasons why their grant writing is not successful. They focus on three strategies to improve their skills: (a) develop logic models for all services in the organization, (b) include more state and local data in proposals, (c) identify staff's particular writing strengths and assign them those parts of the proposals, (d) develop a database of funding priorities with need, funder, focus areas, and application requirements, and (e) develop shared folders that will hold documents frequently requested in proposals and applications (e.g., mission statement, needs assessments, organization strengths, geographic area). Evaluators will establish a tracking system and monitor success rates.
Community Indicators	Program planners in a chronic disease division at the state health department want to understand the benefit of their quit smoking helpline for state residents. They decide to monitor the state's smoking rate by reviewing how many cigarettes are sold by county across the state. Evaluators will track the number of cigarettes sold by county over a three-year period.
Disease Status	A group of psychologists want to study the effect of classical music, rock and roll, and jazz on the number of depressive episodes of those diagnosed with a mental health disorder. The groups of patients are randomly divided to receive one of the music types. Evaluators will compare the number of depressive episodes by subgroup over time.
Death Rates	The purpose of a Prescription Drug Monitoring Program (PDMP) is to improve physicians' opioid prescription practices and prevent patients from using multiple doctors (i.e., doctor shopping) as a way of accessing drugs. The evaluator for a national funded study is interested in tracking the program's effect on the overdose death rate in high-risk counties.

Next, let's find out how the Grand Rapids African American Health Institute (GRAAHI) uses their logic models to develop data profiles.

SPOTLIGHT ON EQUITY

Grand Rapids African American Health Institute (GRAAHI) Using Logic Models to Develop Data Profiles

GRAAHI is a Michigan-based organization designed to increase awareness about the health inequities of African Americans through community service, advocacy, research, and education (CARE). GRAAHI defines health equity as "the practice of providing everyone, especially those with the fewest resources and greatest health disparities, such as Blacks, with enough opportunities, resources, and support to achieve optimum levels of health." As health literacy is an important goal, GRAAHI seeks to educate its stakeholders and website users on the meaning of key health indicators and to provide current information about them.

Andrae Ivy, GRAAHI's Director of Research, developed a pair of logic models including a circular model and a flow chart (both are presented in Chapter 8). Their purpose is to highlight the importance and interconnectedness of health outcomes, health behaviors, and social determinants of health (SDoH). He then used the logic model indicators as a framework for a Health Equity Index (Index) which is available online (https://hei.graahi.org/). It includes:

1. **Health outcomes**—chronic illnesses or conditions that usually require medical attention or treatment (e.g., asthma, high cholesterol)

2. **Health behaviors**—health actions or practices (e.g., binge drinking, tobacco use)

3. **Social determinants of health**—conditions or circumstances that influence people's health in indirect ways (e.g., no high school diploma, home ownership)

GRAAHI's user-friendly, interactive Index models current health statistics by race and ethnicity. It provides Kent County data, disparities, and recommendations;

interactive data maps for Grand Rapids; and, based on findings, recommendations to address health equity issues. The indicators are color coded to show the comparative health status: (1) a green check mark if findings for Kent County or Grand Rapids are better than both the Michigan and the US rates; (2) a yellow exclamation mark if findings for Kent County or Grand Rapids are better than one or the other comparator; or (3) a red "x" if findings for Kent County or Grand Rapids are worse than the two comparators. The information is readily available to public health professionals, students, policymakers, and community members. One stakeholder in the community said, "This site gives additional tools for grassroots organizations that want to engage in this work and move into action and next steps." Index data are updated annually or whenever data become available.

For example, in Figure 3.7, p. 102 we show air pollution at the local, state, and national levels. Note the averages for each and how much higher the local value is than the state and national levels.

Another Index feature compares indicators for subpopulations. Stark disparities are shown in Figure 3.8, p. 102 for prostate cancer deaths and Figure 3.9, p. 102 for infant mortality. Black men experience higher rates of prostate cancer deaths (44.4 per 100,000) compared to White men (16.5 per 100,000) in Kent County, Michigan. Black infants die at a higher rate (16.6 per 1,000) compared to White (3.7 per 1,000) or Hispanic (4.9 per 1,000) infants in Kent County, Michigan.

GRAAHI frequently refers to its logic models to stress the interconnectedness of the indicators. Index findings have been shared at local and national presentations and health seminars and used in reports. For example, GRAAHI led a health literacy campaign in Grand Rapids and presented this information to different organizations around the city. To date, Index usage among community members or average citizens has not occurred as frequently as hoped. However, promotional efforts such as media campaigns are planned to increase Index use.

FIGURE 3.7 ⬢ KENT COUNTY, MICHIGAN, AND NATIONAL AIR POLLUTION DISPARITY

X **Air Pollution**

The average daily measure of fine particulate matter in micrograms per cubic meter (PM2.5) in a county.

Kent County or Grand Rapids-Wyoming Area Rate	Michigan Rate	United States Rate
11.5	8.4	8.6

FIGURE 3.8 ⬢ KENT COUNTY, MICHIGAN PROSTATE CANCER DEATH DISPARITY FOR AFRICAN AMERICAN MEN COMPARED TO WHITE MEN

Prostate Cancer Deaths ⓘ

Rate of men per 100,000 who died of prostate cancer.

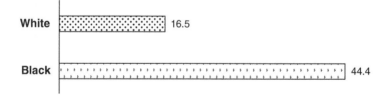

FIGURE 3.9 ⬢ KENT COUNTY, MICHIGAN MORALITY DISPARITY FOR AFRICAN AMERICAN INFANTS COMPARED TO WHITE AND HISPANIC INFANTS

Infant Mortality ⓘ

Rate of live births per 1,000 who died before they turned one year old.

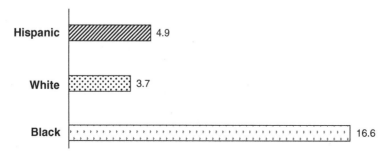

This Spotlight on Equity is based on the contributions of Andrae Ivey and Mikisha Plesco.

Figure 3.10, p. 104 provides a real-world example of a logic model from a trauma-informed initiative in Ohio (Ingoldsby et al., 2020). The program initiates recovery for those victimized by crime and assists in linking prevention and intervention services to children and families experiencing traumatic events. The program initiatives also build the communities' capacity to help young people exposed to violence. Note the short, intermediate, and long-term outcomes for these children and their families. They correspond to a timeline. Among the short-term outcomes are the implementation of a screening tool, resource directory, and a strategic plan, along with increased awareness and networking. While these can be achieved in six months to a year, mid-term outcomes such as victim identification and improved linkages between families and resources will take much longer. The long-term outcome of a well-served system is aspirational and could take decades to come to fruition.

Comparison of Logic Model Structures

One interesting logic model is Bennett's Hierarchy, a more tailored version of the Kellogg model (discussed above). Dr. Claude Bennett with Dr. Kay Rockwell tested the hierarchy for several decades in education and extension programs (Rockwell et al., 2012). It directly addresses educational outcomes including knowledge, attitudes, skills, aspirations, and practice change.

Onkka (2018) compares Kellogg's Model with Bennett's Hierarchy in Figure 3.11.

FIGURE 3.11 ● COMPARISON OF KELLOGG'S MODEL WITH BENNETT'S HIERARCHY

Kellogg Logic Model	Inputs	Activities	Outputs	Short-term Outcomes		Med-term Outcomes	Long-term Outcomes
Bennett's Hierarchy Logic Model	Inputs	Activities	Participation	Reactions	Knowledge Attitude Skills Aspirations	Practice Change	Impact

Source: Onkka, A. (2018, March 13). *What is Bennett's Hierarchy logic model?* Aurora Consulting. Used with permission.

This model helps to tease apart the thorny issues of knowledge acquisition and where best to place them in a logic model. While inputs and activities are the same in both logic models, the outputs in Bennett's Hierarchy focus on aspects of participation, such as audience and scope, frequency, duration, and intensity. Short-term outcomes are split into reactions, often measured by a "happy sheet" at the end of a workshop, and the critical precursors to practice change, namely knowledge acquisition, attitude change, skill application, and aspirations for future use. Mid-term outcomes focus on practice change, on the actual application of learning, and on what participants now do differently because of the training. Long-term outcomes are similar to the Kellogg model, namely impact on a larger scale, such as community- or nation-wide positive changes.

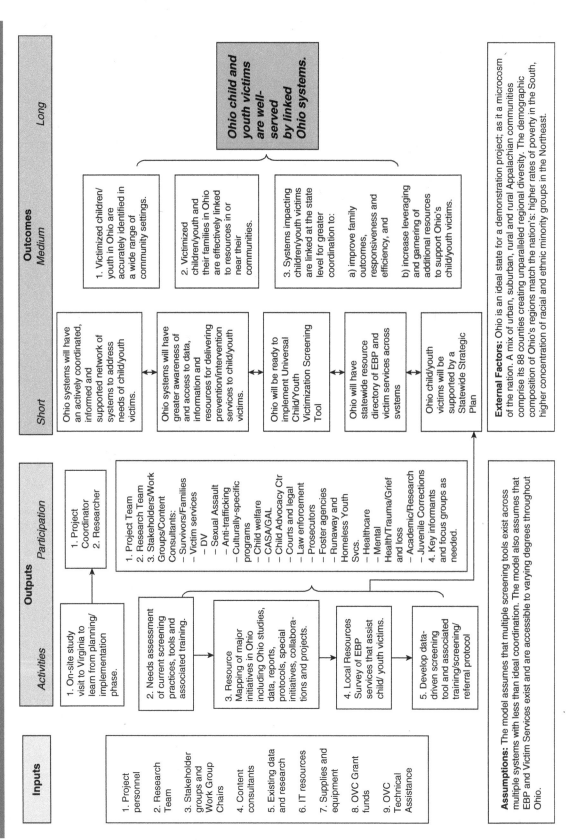

FIGURE 3.10 ● LOGIC MODEL FOR OHIO VISION 21S LINKING SYSTEMS OF CARE FOR CHILDREN AND YOUTH

Inputs

1. Project personnel
2. Research Team
3. Stakeholder groups and Work Group Chairs
4. Content consultants
5. Existing data and research
6. IT resources
7. Supplies and equipment
8. OVC Grant funds
9. OVC Technical Assistance

Outputs

Activities

1. On-site study visit to Virginia to learn from planning/ implementation phase.
2. Needs assessment of current screening practices, tools and associated training.
3. Resource Mapping of major initiatives in Ohio including Ohio studies, data, reports, protocols, special initiatives, collaborations and projects.
4. Local Resources Survey of EBP services that assist child/ youth victims.
5. Develop data-driven screening tool and associated training/screening/ referral protocol

Participation

1. Project Coordinator
2. Researcher

1. Project Team
2. Research Team
3. Stakeholders/Work Groups/Content Consultants:
 – Survivors/Families
 – Victim services
 – DV
 – Sexual Assault
 – Anti-trafficking
 – Culturally-specific programs
 – Child welfare
 – CASA/GAL
 – Child Advocacy Ctr
 – Courts and legal
 – Law enforcement
 – Prosecutors
 – Foster agencies
 – Runaway and Homeless Youth Svcs.
 – Healthcare
 – Mental Health/Trauma/Grief and loss
 – Academic/Research
 – Juvenile Corrections
4. Key informants and focus groups as needed.

Outcomes

Short

Ohio systems will have an actively coordinated, informed and supported network of systems to address needs of child/youth victims.

Ohio systems will have greater awareness of and access to data, information and resources for delivering prevention/intervention services to child/youth victims.

Ohio will be ready to implement Universal Child/Youth Victimization Screening Tool

Ohio will have statewide resource directory of EBP and victim services across systems

Ohio child/youth victims will be supported by a Statewide Strategic Plan

Medium

1. Victimized children/ youth in Ohio are accurately identified in a wide range of community settings.

2. Victimized children/youth and their families in Ohio are effectively linked to resources in or near their communities.

3. Systems impacting children/youth victims are linked at the state level for greater coordination to:

a) improve family outcomes, responsiveness and efficiency, and

b) increase leveraging and garnering of additional resources to support Ohio's child/youth victims.

Long

Ohio child and youth victims are well-served by linked Ohio systems.

Assumptions: The model assumes that multiple screening tools exist across multiple systems with less than ideal coordination. The model also assumes that EBP and Victim Services exist and are accessible to varying degrees throughout Ohio.

External Factors: Ohio is an ideal state for a demonstration project; as it a microcosm of the nation. A mix of urban, suburban, rural and rural Appalachian communities comprise its 88 counties creating unparalleled regional diversity. The demographic composition of Ohio's regions match the nation's: higher rates of poverty in the South, higher concentration of racial and ethnic minority groups in the Northeast.

Source: Ingoldsby, E., Morrison, C., Ruben, J., Melz, H., & Cairone, K. (2020). Using logic models grounded in ToC to support trauma-informed initiatives. Trauma-informed approaches: Connecting research, policy, and practice to build resilience in children and families (ASPE Issue Brief). Office of the Assistant Secretary for Planning and Evaluation (ASPE), US Department of Health and Human Services (HHS).

Onkka states:

> As with any logic model, when you move forward from input (the beginning) to impact (the end), the evidence for your program's value is strengthened. If all you can share in your evaluation is your inputs, activities, and participation, you haven't shown any change in your participants. You've only shown the potential for change and your evidence is supportive but weak. The further along you get, the more evidence you have that your program is achieving its goals. If you can show KASA outcomes, you have stronger evidence for practice change and impact. The further up you go, the better your evidence. (para. 6)

Assessing the Quality of Logic Models

Logic models are ubiquitous these days but they certainly vary in terms of their quality. Community Solutions (2010) developed a rubric to assess logic model quality. It provides useful criteria to describe logic models as either exemplary, satisfactory, or needing improvement. Review Table 3.6, p. 106.

Source: Chris Lysy/FreshSpectrum.com

Other Logic Model Elements

Evaluators are very creative individuals. Each takes a slightly different perspective on what should be included in a logic model, and each produces their own version; however, the basic elements are generally the same. Some of the additional elements that can be found in logic

TABLE 3.6 ● LOGIC MODEL ASSESSMENT RUBRIC

Criteria	Exemplary	Satisfactory	Needs Improvement
a. Comprehensiveness	• more than three items listed for each component • presents a highly comprehensive picture of the program's impacts	• a minimum of three items are listed for each component • presents a relatively comprehensive picture of the program's impacts	• less than three items listed for each component • does not present a comprehensive picture of the program's impacts
b. Correct Placement of Components	• all components are placed in correct columns • client satisfaction listed as an *Output* and not *Outcome* • all *Outcomes* listed demonstrate a horizontal chronological flow from *Short-term* to *Long-term* • all *Outcomes* listed demonstrate a vertical chronological flow within each column	• all components are placed in correct columns • *Outcomes* listed demonstrate a horizontal chronological flow within each column	• components not placed in correct columns • *Outcomes* listed do not have a horizontal chronological flow
c. Correct Presentation of Components	• each *Activity* statement is described using an action-verb • majority of *Outputs* are numerically based, few "deliverables" listed • every *Outcome* listed includes a direction of change	• majority of *Activity* statements are described using an action-verb • majority of *Outputs* are numerically based, few "deliverables" listed • majority of *Outcomes* listed include a direction of change	• *Activities* not described with action-verbs • *Outputs* listed contain many "deliverables" • majority of *Outcomes* do not include a direction of change
d. Underlying Logic	• *Outputs*, and *Outcomes* are linked logically to *Activities*	• *Outputs* and *Outcomes* are linked logically to *Activities*	• no logical linkage between *Activities*, *Outputs*, and *Outcomes* identified
e. Plausible Connections	• connections are highly plausible, i.e., the *Outcomes* listed could realistically arise from the *Inputs* and *Activities* identified • all *Intermediate Outcomes* listed demonstrate a realistic link to the *Long-term Outcomes* identified	• connections are relatively plausible, i.e,. the *Outcomes* listed could realistically arise from the *Inputs* and *Activities* identified • most *Intermediate Outcomes* listed demonstrate a realistic link to the *Long-term Outcomes* identified	• *Long-term Outcomes* could not plausibly arise from the *Short-* and *Intermediate-term Outcomes* identified
f. Readability	• understandable to the lay reader, no jargon included	• understandable to the lay reader, minimal jargon included	• many instances of jargon used, not readily understood by a lay reader
g. Brevity	• fits to one page	• fits to one page	• extends to two or more pages

Source: Community Solutions. (2010). *Logic model assessment rubric.* https://communitysolutions.ca/web/wp-content/uploads/2013/07/Logic-Model-Rubric.pdf. Used with permission.

models include the **situation** or problem statement, data supporting the problem, vision or mission statements, goals of the intervention, assumptions, contextual factors, and reach.

Supporting Data Statement

Usually placed at the top of the logic model, a brief statement uses supporting data to show the need for an intervention. If your logic model is focused on an intervention designed to promote alternatives to opioid use, you could provide a short statement, such as: There was an over 44% decline in opioid prescriptions between 2011 and 2020 (American Medical Association, 2021), however, opioids still take the lives of 136 Americans every day (National Center for Drug Abuse Statistics, 2022). The evaluator can use needs assessment data at the world, national, state, county, or census-tract level to illustrate the need for the program being evaluated. Higher level data are necessary to understand the global and national context, but local data are also effective to gain stakeholder support and funding.

Vision or Mission Statements

Many logic models include an overarching vision or mission statement. For example, at the University of Vermont (2021) the Department of Computer Science (CS) developed a Vision and Mission statement as follows:

> *CS Vision: To be among the nation's premier small research and teaching Computer Science departments* (para. 1)

> *CS Mission: To create, share, and apply knowledge in Computer Science, including in interdisciplinary areas that extend the scope of Computer Science and benefit humanity; to educate students to be successful, ethical, and effective problem-solvers and life-long learners who will contribute positively to the economic well-being of our region and nation and who are prepared to tackle complex 21st Century challenges facing the world* (para. 2)

Goals of the Intervention

Some organizations include their program goals stated broadly. For example, the U.S. Interagency Council on Homelessness (2018) states that:

> *We must design community response that prevent homelessness whenever possible. When we aren't able to prevent it, we must make sure it's a rare, brief, and one-time experience.* (para. 1)

Assumptions

Assumptions, beliefs, and suppositions are tricky. Implicitly or explicitly, they are present in every logic model, linking a cause (intervention) to an effect (outcome). They may or may not be valid. For example, Powell and Black (2003) consider typical assumptions about youth violence prevention programs and then counter them as follows:

- **Social phenomena, such as violence, can be addressed through individual solutions.** The assumption that violence can be solved at the individual level negates the importance of the influence of socioeconomic environments. For example, young people living in poverty must make decisions based on their moment-by-moment needs. As Powell and Black contest, "While there may indeed be wisdom in learning to skillfully avoid potentially violence situations, treating this issue superficially minimizes the real psychological and social consequences that result from these decisions" (p. 51).

- **Interventions should begin as early as possible.** The assumption that the earlier the intervention occurs, the more effective it is likely to be, may be unfounded as younger children may not be ready to receive this type of information. They may not have developed the cognitive and social skills needed to digest the strategies and put them into practice (pp. 49–55).

Thus it is important to really dig into the assumptions that underpin program logic. This example clearly shows the importance of discussing assumptions early in the program design process.

Contextual Factors

Context "is the set of circumstances or unique factors that surround a particular implementation effort" (Damschroder et al., 2009, p. 3). **Contextual factors** relate to the physical, social, and organizational, cultural environment in which the intervention and participants are situated. Cullen et al. (2016) expresses these factors as "external to and operate outside of a programme's control but may influence the implementation of the programme" (p. 9). These factors influence the intervention and, simultaneously, the intervention influences the context in which it is situated (Pfadenhauer et al., 2016, pp. 18–19). In Chapter 12, we discuss the evaluation context in some detail. Every evaluation is influenced by the context in which it is situated.

In 1900, the Michelin Group (n.d.) published the first Michelin Guide. This guide informs travelers where to go to get essentials, such as auto repair and good food. It has become the evaluation tool of chefs around the world; the number of stars assigned to a restaurant is the most highly sought accolade in the industry. "Restaurants may receive zero to 3 stars for the quality of their food based on five criteria: quality of the ingredients used, mastery of flavor and cooking techniques, the personality of the chef in his cuisine, value for money and consistency between visits" (para. 2).

Ottenbacher and Harrington (2008) wanted to identify the contextual factors associated with how chefs innovate their cuisine. The sample consisted of Spanish, German, and American chefs. The researchers conducted interviews to identify factors influencing their culinary innovations. When they probed for context, they found that American chefs cook significantly more meals per day than their colleagues. The volume of customers influenced their innovation practices because they needed to find ways to produce more meals quickly, not because they want to be more creative.

Reach

Reach is the uptake of a program by its intended audience (Belza et al., 2013). Montague (1998) notes that a critical limitation of logic models is "their tendency to focus predominantly on causal chains without reference to who and where the action was taking place" (p. 1). Without reach, Montague continues, evaluators have "the potential to confuse outputs and outcomes…we have often found confusion in terms of what people mean by 'improved access' (e.g., do we mean available? Or do we mean usage by target groups?)" (p. 1).

There are multiple levels of reach, including people, organizations, and communities (Centers for Disease Control and Prevention, 2011b). Reach can be calculated by dividing the number of people actually served by the initial number estimated to receive service. For example, if your program serves 5,000 students in a school system with 15,000 students, your reach would be 5,000/15,000 or 33%.

Advantages of Logic Models

Creating a logic model with a client can be priceless in terms of capacity building and gaining clarity about a program. Logic models lay the groundwork for a strategic plan, act as a valuable training tool for new employees, are a teaching tool for mentors and mentees, and provide a way to retain institutional memory. By working on a logic model together with an evaluator, staff develop a common understanding of program goals and what is needed to achieve success. Staff and stakeholders also experience what Patton (2012, p. 143) calls **process use**. They learn about evaluation from being involved in the evaluation itself. They learn to think evaluatively and begin to understand future interactions with the evaluator about tool development, data collection, and data interpretation. A logic model can also be an educational tool at the board of director's level, expanding members' interest in how their programs actually work. Lastly, logic models can also provide a valuable resource when staff members are writing funding proposals. These discussions can stimulate thinking about needed metrics. While the logic model itself does not usually include indicators, as shown in Figure 3.12, evaluation questions and indicators (data to be collected) flow out of the inputs, activities, outputs, and outcomes. Thus, they become an integral part of the evaluation plan.

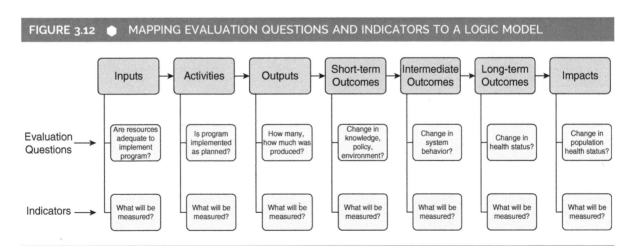

FIGURE 3.12 ● MAPPING EVALUATION QUESTIONS AND INDICATORS TO A LOGIC MODEL

Source: Centers for Disease Control and Prevention. (n.d.). *Evaluation guide: Developing and using a logic model.* Department of Health and Human Services.

Limitations of Logic Models

The first limitation of a logic model is the amount of time it takes to develop one. It can be intimidating to sit down with a group of stakeholders and reach consensus about program intentions. Further, the logic model represents only one reality, and that is a linear one. Programs are not linear; they are organic, expansive, reactive, and unpredictable. Further, the sequence in which activities are depicted may not be sequential. They could be simultaneous, recursive, or lagging. A quick look at any logic model shows that the focus is on outcomes (three boxes for outcomes, only one for program activities). Any number of changes could occur as the program develops. Logic models are rarely updated once the program gets under way. There is an assumption of causal connection. It is impossible to determine at this early stage if the program causes the outcomes, and even once the evaluator is able to trace a history of implementation, causality remains problematic. Finally, logic models do not address values questions such as, "Are we doing the right thing?" and "Should we do this program?"

Despite these shortcomings, the logic model is still useful for the evaluator, administration, staff, and program stakeholders. It provides a common documented understanding of program aspirations and creates a foundation for the development of both the program and its evaluation by defining the elements of success.

EXPERT CORNER

Dr. Stewart I. Donaldson

Stewart I. Donaldson, PhD, is Distinguished University Professor, Executive Director of the Claremont Evaluation Center, and Director of The Evaluators' Institute at Claremont Graduate University. He has taught numerous residential and online courses and published widely on the topics of evaluation theory and practice and on the science of positive psychology.

1. *Why do you think that evaluation discourse has focused so much on theory in the past few years?*

The practice of evaluation continues to grow at a rapid pace all around the world. Some estimates suggest there are now more than 200 evaluation professional societies with more than 55,000 members worldwide. One view of evaluation is that it is a transdiscipline with a core knowledge base that should guide the practice of professional evaluators. The core knowledge base of the transdiscipline is largely made up of evaluation theory and research on evaluation to test evaluation theories. A grand vision moving forward is that sound evaluation theory supported by empirical research is what will guide and improve evaluation practice in the future.

2. *In this chapter, we have tried to clarify the terms program theory, theory of change, and logic model. Do you have any words of wisdom for us?*

Developing program theories, theories of change, or logic models, especially in collaboration with stakeholders, can be a great way to understand the evaluand you are being asked to evaluate. In my experience, most stakeholders really appreciate having a clear conceptual framework that they can use to understand their program or intervention and to use when communicating about or describing it to others. These frameworks can also be very helpful when you are formulating and deciding which evaluation questions to focus on and for providing a context for interpreting evaluation findings. As long as your clients agree, developing a program theory, theory or change, or logic model is a good use of their time and resources. I would encourage you to use one or more of these analytic tools. If they don't see their value, move on and select other tools that better meet your client's needs and/or wants.

3. *We know that you have worked tirelessly with evaluation students throughout your career. What advice can you offer those of our readers who are just beginning to explore the field of evaluation?*

We often joke that a career in evaluation is a great fit for those with a low boredom threshold. That is, it offers so much variety and challenge on a regular basis. Most professional evaluators find themselves working on diverse teams addressing issues that cross multiple fields such as community and global health, psychology and social services, international development, education, public policy, organization and community development among many others. It can also be a very engaging and meaningful career when you align your evaluation projects with your strengths and passions.

Key Terms

Activities 95
Assumptions 107
Contextual factors 108
Golden thread 81
IF-THEN statement 90
Indicators of success 84
Inputs 94

Interventions 86
Logic model 92
Long-term outcomes 99
Mid-term outcomes 98
Outcomes 98
Outputs 95
Process use 109

Program theory 90
Reach 108
Short-term outcomes 98
Situation 107
Theory of change (ToC) 82

The Main Ideas

1. A ToC identifies the change you would expect to see after a program is implemented. The ToC suggests causal linkages between the intervention and the short-, mid-, and long-term outcomes.

2. Indicators of success are data collected by the evaluator that provide a measure of success for the intervention.

3. An IF-THEN statement is the program theory. The evaluator posits that if an intervention occurs then outcomes will result.

4. Logic models identify your inputs, activities, outputs, short-, mid-, and long-term outcomes.

5. There are many purposes of a logic model. They can connect the program to the overall mission of the organization; ensure a common understanding of the program among staff, funders, and stakeholders; and improve program accountability.

6. Inputs can be identified as funding, people, resources, knowledge, and existing documents.

7. The activities in a logic model are the intervention, program, or set of services.

8. The outputs of a logic model directly link from the activities and, when collected and measured, indicate the success of implementation. Outputs are a direct result of the activities and demonstrate that they occurred and are tangible, concrete, and measurable forms of evidence.

9. Evaluators divide outcomes into short-term outcomes, mid-term outcomes, and long-term outcomes, based on a temporal progression from those closest to program activities in time to those the longest afterwards that can feasibly be measured.

10. The quality of logic models can be assessed through their comprehensiveness, correct placement of components, correct presentation of components, underlying logic, plausible connections, readability, and brevity.

11. Other elements in a logic model can include supporting evidence for the program's need, vision or mission statements, goals of the intervention, assumptions, contextual factors, and reach.

Critical Thinking Questions

1. Provide at least one difference between a ToC and a logic model.

2. Differentiate the left half and the right half of the logic model. How are they different? How are they similar?

3. Describe the difference between activities and outputs in the logic model?

4. Why would some suggest starting with outcomes in your logic model and working backward?

5. How would you relate individual health improvement and population health improvement to short- and long-term outcomes?

6. What is one behavior change you have made in the past? What were the steps to making that change? What was your theory of change, from wanting to change to adopt the new behavior?

Student Challenge

A Case Study: K9s for Camo Program. There is an organization in southwest Missouri that aims to provide service dogs to veterans in need at no cost. The program is called K9s for Camo. The program's stakeholders include experienced trainers, veterans, prisoners, a correctional center, shelter dogs, and veterinarians (Lopez, 2021). The relationship between a veteran and a service dog has shown to have positive benefits for the service dog and the veteran. Veterans have improved mental, social, and physiological benefits (American Veterinary Medical Association, 2018). The dogs have improved bonding with the veteran, more physical activity, and preventive care (Barker & Wolen, 2008). K9s for Camo provides a framework that pairs dogs and veterans that are trained to work together as a team. This system has standards and evaluations for each step of their process. The training includes canine behavioral training methodology. The training includes evaluation for temperament, obedience, and task training. The dogs work to earn their American Kennel Club certifications and train to meet the K9s for Camo standards for task performance. The veterans also have access to any guidance or training they may need through the service of the K9s for Camo service dog. The veterans and their dog are encouraged to actively engage in the K9s for Camo community by attending classes for reinforcement. The entire process includes nine steps.

Step 1: Rescue. A shelter dog is identified as potentially having the temperament, or as the founder, John Lopez, calls it, "energy," to become an effective service dog. This is perhaps the most critical step to maximize the rescue's likelihood of long-term success as a service dog. Inappropriate temperament and lack of aptitude can sometimes be masked by training, but usually only partially or temporarily.

Step 2: Evaluation. Candidate dogs are transported to K9s for Camo's home base, where experienced trainers further evaluate the K9s temperament and identify aptitudes for specific service tasks.

Step 3: Fit for Service. In addition to assessing the K9s temperament and aptitudes, we have veterinarians give K9s for Camo recruits a thorough medical exam to confirm they are healthy, physically able to perform his/her tour of duty, and are fit for service.

Step 4: Basic Training. K9s for Camo trainers continue temperament and aptitude assessment of K9 recruits as they begin obedience and home manners training, both at the facility and in trainers' homes.

Step 5: Boot Camp. Offenders at the Ozark Correctional Center, trained members of the K9s for Camo team, provide intensive training for the K9s. They focus on task training and advanced obedience training as the K9s progress to AKC Canine Good Citizens certification.

Step 6: Advanced Certification. K9s return to home base, where trainers hone home manners and task skills, and complete training for AKC Community Canine and AKC Urban Canine certification, as well as K9s for Camo's Public Access evaluation. The K9s stay in trainers' homes and visit restaurants, stores, churches, medical facilities, offices, and schools as they learn to respond appropriately to different stimuli and behave appropriately in diverse environments while performing the supportive tasks for their veteran.

Step 7: Report for Duty. K9s and their veterans are introduced and sent home with instructions for bonding and ongoing training and are provided logs to track their home training regimen as they ready for advanced training.

Step 8: Advanced Training. K9s and their veterans attend weekly training sessions, building their bond by working through the AKC certification process; this time as a team.

Step 9: Service. Once the veteran and K9 team complete advanced training, the former shelter dog is now proudly serving one who serviced us.

Your Task

Based on this case study:

a. State the golden thread for this project.

b. Identify contextual factors of importance for this evaluation project.

c. Identify the program theory (IF-THEN statement)

d. Develop a clear logic model (Inputs, Activities, Outputs, Short-term Outcomes, Mid-term Outcomes, Long-term Outcomes/Impacts).

e. Use your imagination to fill in any gaps in the information provided.

Additional Readings and Resources

1. Leeuw, F. L., & Donaldson, S. I. (2015). Theory in evaluation, reducing confusion and encouraging debate. *Evaluation, 21*(4), 467–480.
The authors present two typologies: Theories of "policy makers, stakeholders, and evaluators underlying their professional work in making policies and doing evaluations" (p. 465) and theories of "scientific theories capable of contextualizing and explaining the consequences of policies, programs and evaluators' actions" (p. 470).

2. Online Logic Model Builders. These are online tools to build your theories of change and logic models.

   a. TOCO (Theory of Change Online). This tool is a web-based online software to design your own theory of change. It provides a graphic ToC and is subscription based. Website shows video on how TOCO works. https://www.actknowledge.org/toco-software/

   b. Dylomo. A free, web-based tool that is interactive with attractive visuals. https://www.dylomo.com/

3. Stevens, J. E. (2013, June 23). A theory of change from Harvard's Center on the Developing Child. *ACES too high.* https://acestoohigh.com/2013/06/03/a-theory-of-change-from-harvards-center-on-the-developing-child/
This 5-minute video illustrates a ToC and the importance of building a foundation for growing children.

4. University of Wisconsin-Madison. (n.d.). *Logic models.* https://fyi.extension.wisc.edu/programdevelopment/logic-models/
The University of Wisconsin-Madison, Program Development and Evaluation, Division of Extension is a site for all things logic models. It contains example, templates, and popular resources on logic models.

5. W. K. Kellogg Foundation. (2004). *Using logic models to bring together planning, evaluation, and action: Logic model development guide.* https://www.wkkf.org/resource-directory/resources/2004/01/logic-model-development-guide.
The W. K. Kellogg Foundation Guide lays the groundwork for developing a logic model as an integral part of a nonprofit mission.

EVALUATION AND THE PROGRAM LIFE CYCLE

Chapter 5
Mid-Cycle Program
Evaluation

Chapter 4
Pre- and Early Program
Evaluation

**Part 2 Evaluation
and the Program
Life Cycle**

Chapter 6
End-of-Cycle Program
Evaluation

PRE- AND EARLY PROGRAM EVALUATION

CHAPTER 4 ● MIND MAP

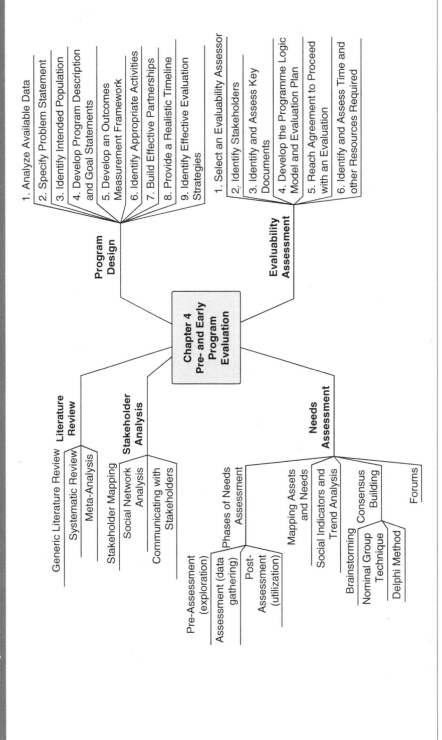

GRIZZLY BEARS AND POLICY CHANGE

On a night in August, more than 50 years ago, two 19-year-old women were killed in separate incidents in Glacier National Park. They were horribly mauled by two different bears in two different areas of the park, at Granite Park Chalet and at Trout Lake. To this day, this haunting coincidence has never been fully explained. What is known is that bears are lured by the garbage left in high-use areas (Dettmer, 2017). Management tended to be lax because there had never been a serious bear–human interaction since the park had been founded in 1910. Garbage

Source: Courtesy of Sequoia and Kings Canyon National Parks

frequently littered campsites and was even used sometimes to lure bears into areas where they could entertain visitors. It was later determined by a forensic expert that at least one of the bears had glass embedded in its teeth and was very emaciated. Excruciating pain as well as hunger had likely enraged the bears and changed their behavior. The women's deaths were the result (Desch, 2007; Olsen, 1996).

Once it was recognized that garbage controlled the bears, bear management began to change. A pack-in and pack-out policy was established. Backcountry campgrounds were established with areas for campfires sepa rate from areas where people pitched their tents. Wire cables were hung between trees for people to hang their food. Education programs were launched about how to stay safe in bear country. Permits were required to limit and track the number of people in the backcountry (Dettmer, 2017). Changes in trash disposal and management, litter prevention, better wildlife management, and increased awareness about preserving the environment have resulted from this tragedy. At all stages, from program design, through implementation, to outcomes and dissemination, program evaluation can measure the success of initiatives like these.

The grim example of these unnecessary deaths (both human and animal) highlights the need for solutions to common problems. Organizations are often confronted with high-stakes issues and are expected to develop systems, processes, or mechanisms to solve them, then implement those solutions, and ultimately determine how well they worked. The life cycle perspective presented in the following three chapters gives the new evaluator a way to wade through the plethora of choices to select the best evaluation for the context, client needs, and available budget.

INTRODUCTION

When well-known evaluator Mary Ann Scheirer was planning some workshops for the U.S. Agency for International Development (USAID) in South Africa, an administrator asked her, "When should we evaluate our programs?" She replied, "All the time! Evaluation methods are useful during every stage of program development, implementation and delivery" (Scheirer, 2012, p. 265). To prove her point, she developed an Evaluation Life Cycle Framework, saying no one type of evaluation alone could do the job. Part 2 of this book uses the life cycle concept to link different types of evaluation to different stages of program maturity. A chronological model is often used to describe the **program life cycle**. It matches evaluation methods to each stage of program development (Love, 2004, p. 67). Figure 4.1 provides a 12-hour clock which represents the three different phases in a program's life cycle (early, mid-, and late).

FIGURE 4.1 ● PROGRAM LIFE CYCLE CLOCK

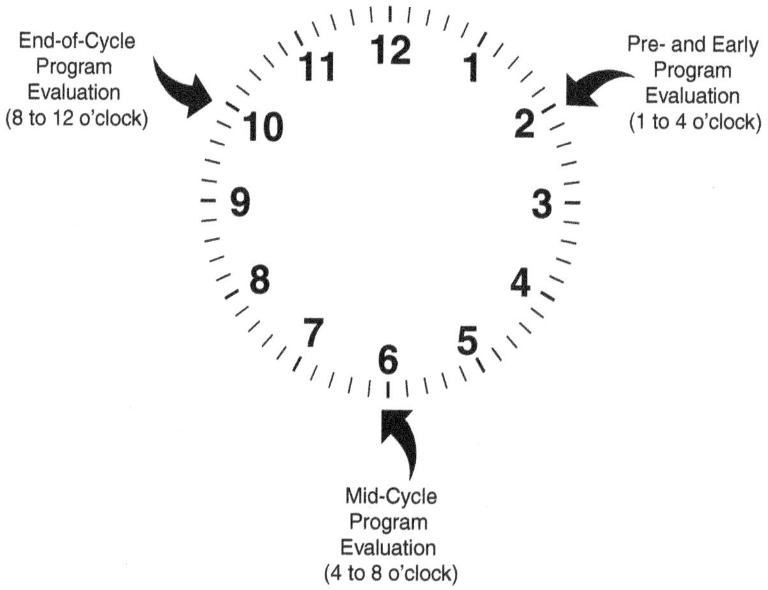

End-of-Cycle Program Evaluation (8 to 12 o'clock)

Pre- and Early Program Evaluation (1 to 4 o'clock)

Mid-Cycle Program Evaluation (4 to 8 o'clock)

Source: istockphoto.com/Tuncaycetin

Table 4.1, p. 121 outlines the organization of the following three chapters which follow this chronology.

Start-up program activities and related evaluations occur early in this imagined 12-hour day; implementation activities occur during the middle of the day; completion, termination, or renewal happens near the end of the day. This 12-hour clock sets the stage for the specific types of evaluation methods frequently employed at each stage. Each chapter in this section is devoted to a component of the program's life cycle: Chapter 4—Pre- and Early Program Evaluation, Chapter 5—Mid-Cycle Program Evaluation, and Chapter 6—End-of-Cycle Program Evaluation. In these chapters, we explore some of the many fascinating ways that an evaluation can be designed.

TABLE 4.1 ● PART 2 CHAPTER ORGANIZATION BY PROGRAM PHASE			
Chronology	**Program Phase**	**Level of Program Maturity**	**Related Chapter**
1:00–4:00 o'clock	Pre- and early program development	Program is envisioned, created, and begins	Chapter 4 Pre- and Early Program Evaluation
4:00–8:00 o'clock	Program implementation under way	Program is in progress	Chapter 5 Mid-Cycle Program Evaluation
8:00–12:00 o'clock	End-of-cycle/review	Program finishes a cycle, starts a new cycle, or is closed	Chapter 6 End-of-Cycle Program Evaluation

Not every program needs every type of evaluation and the evaluator's choice will be dictated by client objectives and resource availability. However, the most effective evaluation matches program maturity and yields the most useful information about program success. We look at the key questions that evaluators ask in each phase of program development and explore some of the evaluation methods used to produce answers.

Chapter 4 addresses the first phase of the program life cycle, **Pre- and Early Program Evaluation**, a critical phase that lays the foundation for successful program implementation. Using our chronological model, pre- and early program evaluation activities would occur between about one o'clock and four o'clock in the program's lifecycle. See Figure 4.2, Pre- and Early Program Evaluation.

FIGURE 4.2 ● PRE- AND EARLY PROGRAM EVALUATION

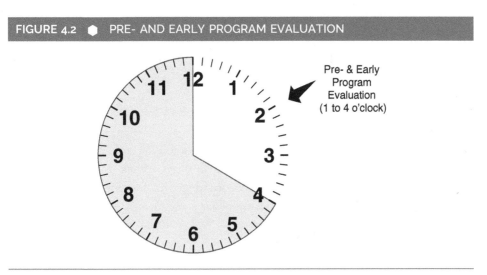

Source: istockphoto.com/Tuncaycetin

Table 4.2, p. 122 expands on our pre- and early program evaluation metaphor by outlining the evaluation types, evaluation methods and measures, and key questions most often used at this point in a program's development. Each of these topics is explored in this chapter.

TABLE 4.2 ● PRE- AND EARLY PROGRAM EVALUATION TYPES

Evaluation Types	Evaluation Methods and Measures	Key Questions
1. Literature Review	• Generic Literature Review • Systematic Review • Meta-analysis	• What have other evaluators and researchers already discovered about this topic? • How did they study it? • What can we learn from the literature to guide our study?
2. Stakeholder Analysis	• Stakeholder Mapping • Social Network Analysis • Communicating with Stakeholders	• Who is concerned about this topic? • How interested will they be in this evaluation?
3. Needs Assessment	• Phases of Needs Assessment • Mapping Assets and Needs • Social Indicators and Trend Analysis • Consensus Building • Forums	• What issue needs to be addressed? • Who is the intended audience? • What kind of service is needed?
4. Program Design	• Nine Steps to Program Design	• What is the purpose of the program? • How will the program be implemented? • How can the evaluator develop an evaluation that supports good program outcomes?
5. Evaluability Assessment	• Six-Step Evaluability Assessment Model	• Is the program ready to evaluate?

You will enjoy the resources in this chapter including the Spotlight on Equity, which presents the Ruth Ellis Center in Detroit, Michigan, our expert Dr. Jim Altschuld, Key Terms, Main Ideas, Critical Thinking Questions, Student Challenges, and Additional Readings and Resources.

THE LITERATURE REVIEW

What made Benjamin Franklin so famous was his love of reading and learning. As a young boy, he loved books and read for an hour a day, five days a week (Simmons & Chew, 2016). Best (n.d.) said, "it's easy to confuse working with learning.... The five-hour [reading] rule is about deliberate learning, not about going to work every day and hoping you might learn something" (para. 8).

Evaluators also love to read, and a **literature review** is foundational to every evaluation project. A literature review is a review of existing studies in the scholarly literature. To get a sense of the field of their present study, evaluators compare and contrast information presented by other researchers about studies that are similar in some way to their proposed project on topics such as data collection methods, findings, and issues. They then synthesize this information into some type of narrative (Collin College, n.d.) which can be as short as a few paragraphs or as comprehensive as a separate report, depending on study requirements and client information needs. Once this important task is completed, evaluators can confidently design a study, building on the lessons learned by others.

Key questions include:

- What have other researchers already discovered about this topic?

- How did they study it?

- What can we learn from the literature to guide our study?

Box 4.1 summarizes elements that influence the extent and nature of the literature review.

BOX 4.1   ELEMENTS THAT INFLUENCE THE LITERATURE REVIEW

- *Time.* Often, evaluations have limited time available, and clients may be pressing for results. This may limit the evaluator's ability to discover significant findings or to interpret the implications of what they do uncover in terms of their own context.

- *Resources.* Depending on the study, support staff such as research assistants may be required to conduct the search which can be extensive and costly. It takes a focused effort to search for the information needed to build on previous work, avoid duplication, omissions, and gaps, and interpret the findings.

- *The research questions.* It is essential to refine the research question carefully so that relevant studies are identified, and time is not wasted reviewing material with little application.

- *Search terms.* The search is facilitated by the careful selection of key words, terms, and phrases that express the concepts under review. Sometimes creating a mind map can help to clarify choices among the many options available.

- *Inclusion/exclusion criteria.* Before launching into the review, it is important to define the parameters of the articles, such as type of publication (e.g., published literature, gray literature or unpublished documents/published in a nonscholarly format, Internet sources, other materials); publication dates (e.g., within the last 10 years); and country of publication (e.g., Unites States only, United States/Europe only, or anywhere).

- *Search sites.* The sources available for the search are important sites, such as Medline, PubMed, ERIC, Sociological Abstracts, CINAHL, PsycINFO, and Cochrane. Scopus and Web of Science are examples of citation indexes. A range of sources is generally preferred to minimize bias and provide a breadth of ideas, interventions, or significant statistical levels (Drucker et al., 2016).

- *Search template.* A literature review template is a helpful tool that outlines essential search elements. The evaluator could create an Excel® or other database spreadsheet for easier entry and analysis of data. This summarizes the research topic, methods used to collect data, study findings, and issues encountered. If several researchers are working on the same search, it also helps to standardize the format of the information obtained.

The literature review is almost universal as a research activity. Not surprisingly, there are many ways to conduct the search. Grant and Booth (2009) created a typology of 14 different types of literature reviews. Here are three of the most common: the Generic Literature Review, the Systematic Review, and Meta-Analysis.

Generic Literature Review

The generic literature review examines published materials from recent or current literature on a range of subjects related to the research question. It can reflect varying degrees of comprehensiveness. The search may involve reviewing several publication databases on the topic, but it does not have to be exhaustive. The evaluator then summarizes the themes in a meaningful fashion, such as using a chronological, conceptual, or thematic structure (Grant & Booth, 2009) and then creating a narrative about the findings. This approach is the most common type of literature review used in evaluations, but the information obtained can be misleading or even biased if the full scope of the issue is not covered or if the quality of the research itself is not reviewed. Because the literature review provides the foundation of the evaluation, it is helpful to explain the process of the search, the studies reviewed, and the rigor of the research process used. That way, the reader can have more confidence in the conclusions drawn by the evaluator and hence on the premise of the evaluation currently under development.

For example, Mallen et al. (2005) conducted a literature review to gather information about best practices for online counseling using email, chat, and videoconferencing. They reviewed telephone counseling, searched for gaps in the literature, and looked for opportunities for new research. The research team used PsycINFO, a peer-reviewed digital database for the behavioral and social sciences. The parameters of their search included all journal articles or chapters up to December 2004. They used the following search terms: *online, Internet, computer-mediated communication, counseling, treatment,* and *therapy.* The search produced 27 relevant studies. They were able to summarize several useful findings and identified some of the benefits and drawbacks of the approaches used by other researchers. Their search raised some critical questions:

- How do in-person counseling and online counseling coexist and interact?

- Does online counseling have the same effectiveness as in-person counseling?

- Do therapists and patients react the same way to each method?

- Which populations are best suited to each method?

Their review provided the basis for their own study and allowed them to design it in a way that incorporated what others had already learned. It also positioned their study to add to the body of knowledge on the topic.

Systematic Review

Another common type of literature review is a Systematic Review. It is narrow in scope and has a specific research question as its focus. It seeks to systematically search for, appraise, and synthesize research evidence and uses most of the elements described above. Information collected in the template includes (Elvik, 2005, p. 230):

- Author information

- Publication year

- Publication type

- Country of publication

- Study design

- Study context

- Estimates of effect

- Standard error of each estimate of effect identified in the search.

The systematic review aims to be as exhaustive as possible, so a wide net is cast. Studies are only included if they have met rigorous inclusion/exclusion criteria. The product is typically a narrative accompanied by a series of tables. The results focus on both what is known and what gaps exist in current knowledge about the topic. Recommendations for practice or future research may also be included.

For example, when seeking more understanding about the influence of gender on personal caregivers, Lindqvist et al. (2004) described using MEDLINE and CINAHL for their search. MEDLINE contains journal citations and abstracts for biomedical literature from around the world. CINAHL is a research tool for nursing and allied health professionals. The authors described their study as follows:

> [Our] review was confined to papers written from 1982–2003. The selected language was English. The search strategies used the search terms home, caregivers, and informal, gender, social support, quality of life, burden, stress, abuse and neglect, multiple diseases. The main focus was on the role of gender on caregivers. The exclusion criteria were the person who received the informal help, newborn babies, children and youth's, literature reviews, editorials, and letters. The initial literature search resulted in 217 articles, of which 65 met the inclusion criteria with reference to gender. (p. 26)

Meta-Analysis

A **meta-analysis** is used to conduct a comprehensive search. It is much more exacting than a systematic review because the results of all the quantitative studies selected will be combined statistically (Grant & Booth, 2009). To combine data from different studies in a valid way, there needs to be similarities across such characteristics as the population, the intervention, and the research question. One approach uses the PICOS framework to search for similar articles. It allows the researcher to categorize by Participants, Interventions, Comparisons, Outcomes, and Study (PICOS). Evaluators may also use inclusion/exclusion criteria or sensitivity analyses. Because this method is strict in its selection criteria, the data sets are generally small.

For example, an early meta-analysis by Pearson (1904) examined the effectiveness of the typhoid vaccine. He reviewed five studies that fit the criteria and used effect size, which indicates how strong the independent variable (vaccine) affected the outcome (typhoid status). He found that, collectively, the results indicated that the vaccine was not effective enough for population use back.

STAKEHOLDER ANALYSIS

The term **stakeholder** originated in management consulting, where it was coined in 1963 at the Stanford Research Institute to describe people who were not stockholders in a company but without whom the firm would not exist (Mendelow, 1987). Patton (2008) has written extensively about the importance of evaluation use. He asks, "Why go to the trouble of conducting an evaluation study if no one uses the results?" He defines evaluation stakeholders as those individuals, groups, or organizations with a vested interest in the evaluation. "They can affect or are affected by an evaluation process and/or its findings" (p. 63).

Key questions about stakeholders include:

- Who is concerned about this topic?

- How interested will they be in this evaluation?

Greene (2006) suggests that there are two primary reasons why stakeholders should be involved in the evaluation: to enhance the evaluation results' usefulness, or to advance values related to equity, empowerment, and social change within the evaluation context. As she contends, stakeholders will likely cause problems if their values are not considered from the beginning of the evaluation process.

Because the world is so interconnected today, a close analysis of stakeholders is more important than ever. As Patton (2008) comments:

in this shared-power world, no one is fully in charge; no organization "contains" the problem. Instead many individuals, groups, and organizations are involved or affected or have some partial responsibility to act…and taking stakeholders into account is a crucial aspect of problem-solving. (p. 63)

To identify stakeholders, ask the following questions as shown in Figure 4.3.

FIGURE 4.3 ● QUESTIONS FOR IDENTIFYING STAKEHOLDERS

Who does the program need to "touch" to be successful?

- Identify these individuals or groups.
- Describe their role.
- Determine their relationship with the program.

Who "touches" the program?

- Determine who is in the program's sphere of control.
- Identify others that the program may influence, either directly or indirectly.
- Determine their relationship with the program.

Box 4.2 identifies potential influential stakeholders who can be an asset to the program.

BOX 4.2   POTENTIAL INFLUENTIAL STAKEHOLDERS

- **Decision makers**. Persons responsible for deciding program initiation, continuation, discontinuation, expansion, modification, or restructuring.

- **Program Sponsors**. Individuals with positions of responsibility in public agencies or private organizations that initiate and fund the program; Sponsors may overlap with decision makers.

- **Evaluation Sponsors**. Individuals in public agencies or private organizations who initiate and fund the evaluation (the evaluation sponsors and program sponsors may be the same).

- **Intended Participants**. Persons, households, or other units intended to receive the evaluated intervention or services.

- **Program Managers**. Personnel responsible for overseeing and administering the intervention program.

- **Program Staff**. Personnel responsible for delivering the program services or functioning in supporting roles.

- **Program Competitors**. Organizations or groups that compete with the program. For instance, a private organization receiving public funds to operate charter schools will compete with public schools also supported by public funds.

- **Stakeholders in the Broader Context**. Organizations, groups, and individuals in the environment of a program with interests in what the program is doing or what happens to it (e.g., other agencies or programs, journalists, public officials, advocacy organizations, and citizens' groups in the jurisdiction in which the program operates).

- **Evaluation and Research Community**. Evaluation professionals who read evaluations and review their technical quality and credibility along with researchers who work in areas related to that type of program.

Source: Rossi, P., Lipsey, M., & Henry, G. (2019). *Evaluation: A systematic approach*. SAGE Publications.

Stakeholder Mapping

Because of the increasingly connected nature of the world, **stakeholder mapping** is essential in any evaluation. As Bryson et al. (2011, p. 2) comment:

> *Choose any public problem—economic development, economic collapse, poor educational performance, environmental resource management, crime, AIDS, natural disasters, global warming, terrorism—and it is clear that "the problem" encompasses or affects numerous people, groups, organizations, and sectors.*

Evaluators overwhelmingly value stakeholder interests, views, influences, involvement, needs, and roles (Alkin, 2004) because significant opportunities may be lost when "the perspectives of stakeholders, cultural sensitivities, and political vulnerabilities are overlooked" (Bryson et al., 2011, p. 3). A number of useful stakeholder identification and analysis techniques can be used throughout the evaluation process. In particular, when planning an evaluation, the evaluator can (Bryson et al., 2011; Subramanian, 2009):

- List evaluation stakeholders

- Identify their interests in the program

- Determine whether they are affected directly or indirectly affected by it

- Using a systems approach with the program at the center of the diagram, map stakeholders as primary or secondary

- Consider how stakeholders interact and influence each other

- Consider stakeholders' degree of power over the outcomes of both the program and the evaluation.

Stakeholder analysis can help to determine how much of a stake, or interest, they have in the evaluation and how much power or influence they bring to bear on the evaluation which can either help or hinder the successful completion of the evaluation (Bryson et al., 2011, p. 5). Eden and Ackerman (1998) created a grid to identify the dimensions of stakeholder power and interest, ranging from low to high on each dimension. Potential actions that an evaluator could take to foster engagement have been added (see Figure 4.4).

FIGURE 4.4 ● THE INTEREST AND POWER OF STAKEHOLDERS

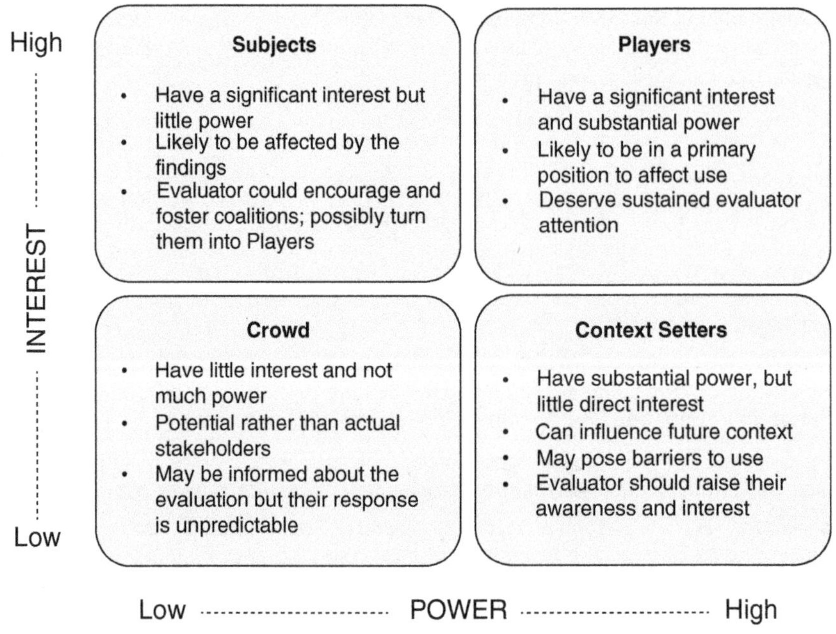

Source: Adapted from Eden, C., & Ackerman, F. (1998). Making strategy. SAGE Publications; Bryson, J. M., Patton, M. Q., & Bowman, R. A. (2011). Working with evaluation stakeholders: A rationale, step-wise approach and toolkit. *Evaluation and Program Planning, 34,* 1–12.

The power versus interest grid helps determine which interests and power bases must be taken into account in order to produce a credible evaluation. As Bryson et al. suggest, the dimensions help to highlight

> *coalitions to be encouraged or discouraged, what behavior should be fostered, and show "buy in" should be sought or who should be co-opted, in part by revealing which stakeholders have the most to gain (or lose) and those who have the most (or least) control over the direction of the evaluation. This information provides a helpful basis for assessing the political, technical, practical, and other risks as the evaluation goes forward. Finally, they may provide some information on how to convince stakeholders to change their views.* (p. 5)

Stakeholders can be organizations as well as individuals. Janssens and Seynaeve (2000) studied a school in Flanders that was considered to be a low-power stakeholder in the school network. It was described as a "Black" school because students' families came from Southern Europe, Turkey, Morocco, former African Belgian colonies, and Central and Eastern Europe. Staff wished to better serve their students by changing the curriculum, attracting a broader mix of students, and gaining power in the school network. Teachers visited other schools in other areas that had succeeded in offering intercultural education and were attracting a mix of children. They brought these ideas back to their own team and, combined with their own skills and competencies, developed a new curriculum of self-experiential learning, project work, creativity, personal responsibility, and multicultural education. The school also established a network of relations with nonschool groups such as Flemish and migrant parents, the local neighborhood, and local shop owners. Shifting their attention away from trying to influence the more powerful groups in the education system, they were able to move outside of their traditional network to rethink their ways of work, collaborating with other groups interested in desegregation. Their new goal of offering high-quality education helped them reframe the nature of success and failure.

Social Network Analysis

One tool that is useful in identifying and understanding stakeholder behavior is Social Network Analysis (SNA). SNA examines social structures by identifying *nodes* representing individual actors, groups of people, organizations, or other things in a network and linking them by ties representing their relationships or interactions. Networks compare to sociograms in which the nodes are points in a graph and the ties are the connecting lines.

In recent years, evaluators have begun to incorporate SNA as a helpful tool because they recognize that "social relationships and networks play a pivotal role in a program or initiative's development, implementation, impact and sustainability" (Fredricks & Carman, 2013, p. 5). According to Fredericks and Durland (2005), SNA can help evaluators understand the overall network embedded in a program or initiative, in terms of its density, connectedness, balance, or centralization; identify subsets within the network, such as cliques and important nodes; identify critical characteristics of the individuals or actors in the network, such as gatekeepers and isolates; and measure the degrees of centrality and similarity for individuals or actors within the network.

Dr. Danielle Varda built a team interested in SNA and created the Center on Network Science. The team built and scaled an organizational network analysis survey tool called PARTNER (Program to Analyze, Record, and Track Networks to Enhance Relationships). The PARTNER tool shows the groups of organizations (networks) and their strength and direction of relationship, characteristics, attributes, and trust. The analysis of data accomplishes four distinct actions:

1. Measures network density, degrees of centralization, and trust

2. Includes individual network scores such as centrality/connectivity/redundancy

3. Values power/influence, level of involvement, and resource contribution

4. Develops individual trust in terms of reliability, support of mission, and openness to discussion.

The organization that uses PARTNER enters their partner's names and contact information into the platform. Then, they develop a survey to collect data in order to understand more about how these organizations interact (e.g., attendance at meetings, common funding stream, and formal and informal interactions). The survey is completed by all partners in their network (e.g., those organizations in a geographic area who work with the same target group). Based on the answers to these survey questions, the PARTNER tool creates a social network map to illustrate the placement of organizations in relation to their peers. By using the tool, users are able to demonstrate to stakeholders, partners, evaluators, and funders how their collaborative activity has changed over time and what progress has been made. Figure 4.5, p. 131 shows how organizations are connected with each other, the importance of their relationship (circle size), and suggested ways to examine these relationships.

Communicating with Stakeholders

Once it is clear which stakeholders will be involved in the evaluation, evaluators can plan a communication strategy to reach stakeholder groups effectively. The degree of their engagement can range across the communication spectrum from informing to consulting, involving, collaborating, and finally, to empowering (Bryson, 2004).

In an evaluation project, it is crucial to know as soon as possible which stakeholders will support the project and which ones will try to block it (i.e., have an emotional reaction). As Rossi et al. (2004) warn, because of the variety of stakeholders involved, someone is likely to be unhappy with the results and so:

> ...it is highly advisable for the evaluator to give early attention to identifying stakeholders, devising strategies for minimizing discord due to their different perspectives, and conditioning their expectations about the evaluation results. (p. 43)

FIGURE 4.5 ● PARTNER TOOL SOCIAL NETWORK MAP

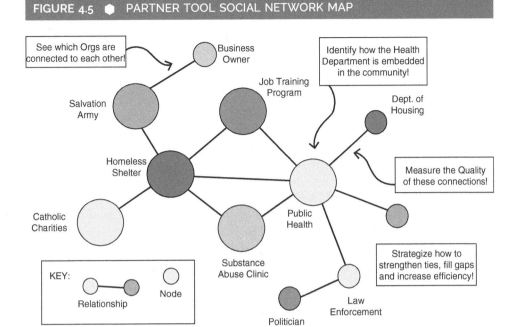

Source: Visible Network Labs. PARTNER Tool. https://visiblenetworklabs.com/partner-platform/

Understanding stakeholders' emotional connection to the project and evaluation can help the evaluator determine an appropriate communication strategy. Clarifying questions can include (Neal, n.d.):

- Do the stakeholders have a positive or negative interest in the outcome of the evaluation? Politically? Financially? Emotionally?

- What motivates them?

- What information do they require from the evaluator?

- What do they currently think about evaluation in general? On what are these opinions based? What do they think about this project?

- Who influences their opinions about evaluation? Whom do they influence with their opinions? Should any of these influencers also be stakeholders?

- How can the evaluator win their support?

- How can the evaluator manage their opposition to the project?

Evaluators frequently work with their clients to establish a steering committee or advisory group composed of representatives from stakeholders. The group can work closely with the evaluator, providing feedback and making collaborative decisions about the study's focus, design, methods, data interpretation, and proposed recommendations.

Balancing the differing perspectives of all these groups takes considerable skill on the part of the evaluator. As Mohan and Sullivan (2006) suggest, the evaluator should be both independent and responsive simultaneously. As they explain, "we lose credibility if we are not independent, and we conduct evaluations that are not useful if we are not responsive" (p. 11). To meet this challenge, we need to manage the project's scope, timing constraints, methods, and legal requirements regarding access to data. Then we should take time to clarify stakeholders' differing concerns, assumptions, and perspectives. These negotiations can result in a "shared construction of the value and social significance of the program" while still respecting "the various ideologies and concerns of different stakeholders" (Rossi et al., 2004, p. 43).

Communicating with the varying levels of stakeholders is important regardless of the type of project and evaluation. Rajkumar (2010) framed the communication activity around the 5Ws (Why, What, When, Where, and Who) and 1H (How). For our purposes, we will focus on the Who, What, and How elements, that is, "Who needs to know What and How do we get the information to them?" The "who" is the person receiving the message. The "what" is the content of the message. The "how" is the medium by which the message gets transmitted to the person or people. See Table 4.3 for examples of the who, what, and how.

TABLE 4.3 ● THE WHO, WHAT, AND HOW FRAMEWORK OF COMMUNICATING WITH STAKEHOLDERS

Who	What	How
• Oppositional audiences	• Crime	• In-person meeting
• Neighborhood associations	• Arrests	• News conference
• Special interest/activists groups	• Police effectiveness	• Email
• Marginalized communities	• Public image and perceptions of the police	• Newsletter
• Victims of crime (family, friends)	• Policing approach	• Nightly news
• Offenders	• Death of an officer	• Radio
• Youth	• Use of force	• Print media
• Parents	• Police misconduct	• Neighborhood meeting
• Business community	• Budget-staffing	• Town hall
• Faith community	• Terrorism	• Community presentations, speeches, meetings
• Nonprofit community	• Immigration	• Reports
• Education leaders	• Influencing behavior	• Brochures
• Elected officials	• Transparency	• Department website
• City/county leadership	• Policy	• Blogging
• Staff in other city/county departments		• Social media
• Surrounding jurisdictions		• Wikipedia
• Civic and social organizations		• Community notification programs
• Law enforcement agencies		
• Courts		
• Attorneys		
• Employees		
• Unions		
• Media		

Source: Stephens, D. W., Hill, J., & Greenberg, S. (2011). *Strategic communication practices: A toolkit for police executives.* Community Oriented Policing Services U.S. Department of Justice. https://cops.usdoj.gov/RIC/Publications/cops-p222-pub.pdf

Police departments, for example, have an ongoing need to communicate to their constituents. They have many different entities needing information quickly or continuously over a period of time. The type of information is not just focused on crime data, but on related issues. How police communicate the information has changed in the last decade and involves more use of technology and smaller pieces of information. For any given public safety threat, there could be an exponential number of element combinations. For example, a higher than usual number of crimes involving youth might involve a police spokesperson using social media and the nightly news to engage parents and the community. That same spokesperson may also engage with education leaders through an in-person meeting about youth and crime.

NEEDS ASSESSMENT

When the evaluator has conducted the literature search and the critical needs of stakeholders, it is time to turn to the social problem. Rossi et al. (2004) define **needs assessment** as to "whether there is a need for a program, and if so, what program services are most appropriate" to meet that need. They add that needs assessment is fundamental "because a program cannot be effective at ameliorating a social problem if there is no problem, to begin with or if the program services do not actually relate to the problem" (p. 102).

In the Pre- and Early Program Phase, key questions include:

- What issue needs to be addressed?
- Who is the intended audience?
- What kind of service is needed?

McDavid et al. (2013) comment that needs assessments are becoming more prevalent due to resource constraints. They have become part of the strategic planning and resource allocation process because:

> health care, education, training, housing, justice, social services, and community infrastructure needs are all contributors to the current interest in needs assessment, with a view to finding the most relevant and effective fit between needs and the design and delivery of programs. (p. 228)

In these circumstances, it is important to objectively conduct needs assessments while acknowledging the context of the program. As Altschuld and Kumar (2010) suggest, "by attending to politics throughout the process, the likelihood of success will increase" (p. 20).

Altschuld and Witkin (2000) developed a useful three-phase model for needs assessment (Altschuld, 2012; Altschuld & Kumar, 2010). Each stage culminates in a decision point. The needs assessment can now be concluded or can continue into the next phase.

Phases of a Needs Assessment

Phase 1. Pre-Assessment (exploration)

In this phase, evaluators set up the management plan for the needs assessment, clarify the general purpose, define areas of need or issues, identify and access available information, scope information sources and data collection methods, and form a needs assessment committee (NAC) to identify concerns and current service gaps. Altschuld strongly supports the creation of the NAC for two reasons: (1) to work collaboratively with the evaluator to obtain organizational commitment; and (2) to galvanize the implementation of recommended changes (McDavid et al., 2013). The committee should be manageable but can include organizational leaders, experts, knowledgeable community members, and those with first-hand experience of the issue. At the end of the phase, evaluators and others decide to collect more data or conclude the needs assessment.

Phase 2. Assessment (data gathering)

This phase may require a significant investment in time, personnel, and resources to collect data. The NAC determines what additional data will be collected and which data collection methods to use. Once gathered, the data are analyzed to understand better the size, cause, and priority of the identified needs. Those involved identify and discuss the gaps between "what is" and "what should be." At this time, high-priority needs and possible solutions begin to emerge along with strategies for implementation. A decision is made at the end of this phase to conclude the assessment process or continue to the action plan.

Phase 3. Post-Assessment (utilization)

Evaluators consider alternative solutions during the final phase, human and material resources and costs are determined, and the optimum solutions for action planning are determined. During this phase, communication strategies and needed bases of support are considered and staff are consulted. Evaluators review the needs assessment results and lessons learned, and the whole process is documented in written reports and oral briefings. It is vital to provide policymakers and program managers with as much convincing evidence as possible if action is to result.

To present a compelling case for the development of any program, transparent, unbiased, and comprehensive information must be collected. Data collection methods commonly used for needs assessments include the survey (Chapter 7), the interview (Chapter 8), and the focus group (Chapter 9). However, a number of other, often inexpensive, data collection options, are also worth considering:

- Mapping Assets and Needs

- Social Indicators and Trend Analysis

- Consensus building

- Forums.

While these methods are useful tools for needs assessments, they may also be appropriate when considering program improvement or determining impact.

Mapping Assets and Needs

When conducting a needs assessment, Altschuld et al. (2014) warn us that too much emphasis on discrepancies or deficits can blind us the importance of also assessing positive assets and strengths. He comments, "when communities note their strengths and what they bring to the table, they can be enabled to move forward in many situations." Thus, he recommends blending assets and needs without favoring either one.

For example, Palihapitiya (2019) worked with "at-risk" youth in Boston to build conflict resolution skills. Using participatory photography to map community assets and needs, the youth gained a voice to narrate their experiences. The findings reached a wide stakeholder group, including policymakers, sponsors, funders, and local communities (Figure 4.6).

FIGURE 4.6 ● ASSETS AND NEEDS MAPPING

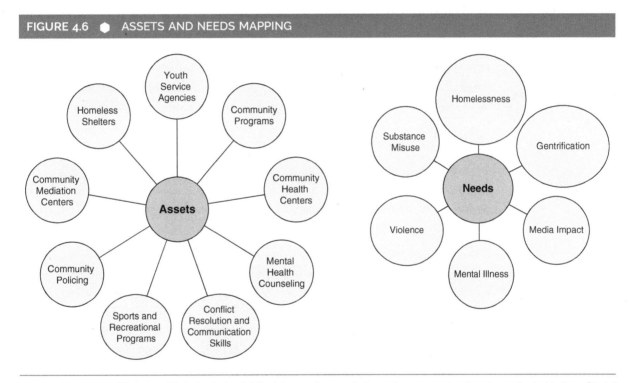

Source: Palihapitiya, M. (2019, June 21). Saying it visually! Participatory photography for needs assessment and asset mapping by Madhawa "Mads" Palihapitiya. Courtesy of Madhawa Palihapitiya and Kristal Corona.

The CDC's Healthy Communities Program (Centers for Disease Control and Prevention, 2021) designed the CHANGE tool for communities interested in creating social and built environments that support healthy living. The purpose of the tool is to gather and organize data on community assets and potential areas for improvement in a community action plan (p. 1). It uses a stakeholder-driven process and creates a foundation for further evaluation activities as change strategies are undertaken. It provides a community snapshot of the policy, systems, and environmental change strategies currently in place using the Socio-Ecological Model (see Chapter 2) to show the multiple influences on community health and barriers to improvement (p. 2). The CHANGE Action Guide outlines the steps needed to develop a community action plan for improving policies, systems, and the environment to support healthy lifestyles and assists with prioritizing community needs and allocating available resources.

Social Indicators and Trend Analysis

The social context of the problem under review must be understood broadly before moving to the individual level. Thus, the evaluator should cast a wide net to estimate the size and characteristics of the desired population. An excellent place to start is with existing data sources. For example, the Current Population Survey of the Bureau of the Census collects annual data on the U.S. population. Available indicators include the composition of households, income, age, gender, and race. The Survey of Income and Program Participation also provides data on unemployment benefits, food stamps, and job training programs (Rossi et al., 2004, p. 110).

Social indicators estimate the size and distribution of the current need. By following indicator trends over time, we can identify changes to conditions. A rough estimate of national program coverage can assess job training, for example. However, these indicators focus mainly on poverty and employment but for many issues, no social indicators exist. In other cases, the national dataset does not provide enough data at the specific state or city level, or may not break down needed target group characteristics.

The search for data may lead to other sources to explain the scope of the problem. For example, information can sometimes be accessed in organizations' records if they provide services to the population in question. In addition, government agencies and large service organizations may keep excellent records, so it is worth checking to see what data are available.

It may be necessary to undertake original research to determine the extent of the issue, but it is an expensive option. A more straightforward approach is to add questions to an omnibus survey. Polling organizations or marketing firms conduct these regularly-scheduled public surveys. There is usually a fee for each question added to the survey. It is a quick way to get a small amount of current data, but timing is critical. For example, the date of the survey administration may not coincide with your data needs.

Once the evaluator has enough data to paint a backdrop for the proposed program, including demographic, geographic, or other contextual information, it is time to address the individual human needs and to understand what is on the minds of community members, local organizations, and individuals (Altschuld, 2014).

Consensus Building

There are numerous group polling methods available. These allow the evaluator to access the thoughts, experiences, and opinions of both groups and individuals. The result is often a consensus or broad agreement about an issue, but if a disagreement occurs, both sides of the argument can be fleshed out. Three consensus-building methods that may be appropriate in an evaluation context include Brainstorming, the Nominal Group Technique (NGT), and the Delphi Method.

Brainstorming

In brainstorming, a group of individuals discuss a topic and generate a list of items to describe that topic. The group can then use this list and prioritize the items. In 1953, Alex Osborn (1953) wrote a book called *Applied Imagination* about a technique to convene a group of people and allow their imaginations to fly untethered. A facilitator sets a topic or issue and the participants were encouraged to brainstorm as many words or phrases. Essentially, the group used their brains to storm a problem (Trott et al., 2016).

Brainstorming is informal and unstructured in style, and participants follow four rules:

1. Generate as many ideas as possible

2. Prioritize unusual or original ideas

3. Combine and refine the ideas generated

4. Abstain from criticism during the exercise.

In this method, facilitators record every idea. First, facilitators tally the frequency of ideas. Then the group identifies the prevailing themes.

While brainstorming unleashes creativity, improves critical thinking, and fosters problem-solving skills, there are contrary opinions about this method. Chamorro-Premuzic (2015) states that "a meta-analytic review of over 800 teams indicated that individuals are more likely to generate a higher number of original ideas when they don't interact with others" (para. 4). Mullen et al. (1991) found that brainstorming results were less effective than had been previously thought. Those participants who are more vocal tend to dominate the discussion and group think eventually starts to limit the generation of new ideas. He found that participants produced more and better ideas when thinking separately, as in the NGT.

Nominal Group Technique (NGT)

The NGT is a straightforward and valuable group process for problem-solving and is particularly useful for needs assessment activities. Andre Delbecq and Andrew H. Van de Ven (1971) developed the technique to generate ideas. The overall group can be quite large but is subdivided into groups of 8–10 people, each with a facilitator/recorder and a flip chart, whiteboard, or wall to which sticky notes can be attached.

The process values all group members equally, avoids group power imbalances, and protects those who hesitate to speak out. First, the facilitator poses the question, and then, participants generate ideas independently, writing each idea on a separate sticky note. Then, using a round-robin process, the ideas are presented one at a time to the group by each individual who explains their intended meaning and attaches their sticky note to the board. At this early stage, brainstorming rules apply, and so all ideas are accepted without analysis or judgment, ideas can piggyback onto other ideas, and the group can generate new ideas. The reporting process continues until all ideas are posted.

Then ideas are clustered, named, and rank-ordered (e.g., top five ideas) by silent voting using sticky dots (five dots for the most important, four for the next, and so on). A discussion may ensue at this point regarding overall meaning and potential next steps. If more than one group is involved, the groups reconvene and share their top ideas. Again, facilitators compile ideas and further ranking occurs if needed. Gail has used this approach many times in her practice and finds that group satisfaction is high because everyone participates equally. In addition, many new ideas and perspectives usually emerge (Moore, 1987).

Delphi Method

The Delphi Method is a forecasting tool named after the Oracle of Delphi and was first used in the Cold War in 1944 by General Henry H. Arnold. It was further developed by Olaf Helmer and Norman C. Dalkey at the RAND Corporation and was generally applied to technological forecasting during the 1960s, particularly in the aerospace and electronics industries. Business forecasters and policymakers began to use it as well.

Based on the assumption that many heads are better than one, it refines and systematically organizes group judgments on complex subjects. Those invited to the group must have the background and expertise needed to judge the worthiness of the ideas. Because data are collected anonymously, the process minimizes the dynamics of group interaction. It is iterative in nature, as several rounds of survey-based data collection occur, each based on the synthesized findings from the previous round. The process culminates in producing a possible scenario, solution, or idea. The Delphi has significantly benefited from web-based versions that compile data in real time.

Mesydel is an online tool for conducting a Delphi and uses collective intelligence to encourage panel conversations about a complex problem. The process involves the selection of a stakeholder panel. Then, in the first round of questions, each person gives their opinion anonymously. Rounds of questions continue until there is a desired level of consensus. See Additional Readings and Resources for more information.

Forums

A forum is a scheduled event where people get together to discuss a subject. They tend to be invitational but can vary widely in size. An example of a large forum is Open Space Technology, where participants drive the agenda in a physically open space such as a warehouse or open-air field. A "marketplace wall" is used to collect all thoughts. World Café is another type of forum where a large group of people meet around a central theme. Leaders pose questions, and after a limited amount of time, groups move to another table for more discussion. Participants create a mind map for all to see as they document their thoughts and ideas. This process is often called "harvesting" or graphical recording.

Mid-sized methods include, for example, Community Conversations and Town Hall Meetings. As described by The Center for Michigan, community conversations with representative groups focus on topics chosen by citizens, such as, for example, student success. Quantitative data are collected using clickers and note takers document qualitative data. Public policy research firms then analyze the data, and a Citizen Agenda report is prepared, paired with the results of separate telephone polling of citizens in an attempt to be as demographically representative as possible.

Examples of small forum methods include the Focus Group (see Chapter 7) and the Deliberative Dialogue. As described by the Canadian Council for International Co-operation (CCIC) (2001), the deliberative dialogue is a way to find common ground for organizational action. "It offers a way to talk about important issues and to wrestle with the hard choices and trade-offs that encompass every issue" (Buchanan & O'Neill, 2001, p. 1). It is reflective, exploratory, and open, and managed by a well-prepared moderator. People with widely differing views can be brought to work together if areas of agreement and difference are clearly defined and common ground identified. Participants must listen to each other to understand their interests and values in order to determine what is best for all concerned. The method is more directed than a discussion but less confrontational than a debate and works well with topics related to diversity and discrimination.

Example of a Needs Assessment

A widely used example of a needs assessment in the United States is the **Community Health Needs Assessment (CHNA)**, which identifies critical health needs and issues through systematic, comprehensive data collection and analysis (Centers for Disease Control and Prevention, 2019). State, tribal, local, or territorial agencies can conduct CHNA to determine the proper allocation of resources. In 2011, the Internal Revenue Service (IRS) added a new requirement for charitable 501(c)(3) hospitals, indicating that an entity must "conduct a CHNA and adopt an implementation strategy at least once every three years" (Internal Revenue Service, 2018).

These changes produce lengthy documents that provide an overall direction for many organizations in a county. To save time, resources, and stakeholders who must work on several initiatives in the same geographic area, agencies such as local health departments and hospitals often join forces to conduct the CHNA collaboratively. Other organizations such as smaller not-for-profits, schools, and businesses can use the results for their strategic planning.

The CHNA can be framed around various categories of indicators or measurable characteristics that describe the health of a population, including life expectancy, mortality, disease incidence or prevalence, or other health states; determinants of health like health behaviors, health risk factors, physical environments, and socioeconomic environments; and healthcare access, cost, quality, and use.

Next, our Spotlight on Equity focuses on meaningful stakeholder engagement in a supportive housing initiative for LGBTQ+ youth in Detroit.

SPOTLIGHT ON EQUITY

Meaningful Stakeholder Engagement: Designing the Evaluation of a Permanent Supportive Housing Initiative for LGBTQ+ Youth in Detroit

Ruth Ellis Center (www.ruthelliscenter.org) pictured in Figure 4.7 is a nonprofit organization that provides trauma-informed services for lesbian, gay, bi-attractional, transgender, and questioning youth and young adults. Services are tailored to Black and brown young people experiencing homelessness, who are involved in the child welfare system or who experience barriers to health and wellbeing. The Center was established in 1999 and is located in metropolitan Detroit. Services include a drop-in center, primary healthcare clinic, counseling, and a number of training programs to increase awareness about youth with diverse sexual orientation, gender identity, and expression (SOGIE).

Homelessness is a common experience among LGBTQ+ youth in Detroit and is particularly acute for trans women of color. For the past few years, Ruth Ellis Center has been planning a permanent supportive housing apartment complex for youth residents and their chosen families. The initiative is known as the Ruth Ellis on Clairmount Center.

Many stakeholders are involved in this project. Systems-level stakeholders include the city government, a nonprofit development company, an architectural firm, the state housing development authority, subject experts, and a network of agencies serving people who are homeless. Onsite service providers include healthcare workers, therapists, behavioral health staff, case managers, other supportive services, and youth peer leaders. A property manager who ensures compliance with federal licensing standards and works to keep residents safe is also involved. Finally, careful attention is being paid to youth voices to ensure that the unique needs of LGBTQ+ youth are central in the structure, processes, and rules within the complex.

The Ruth Ellis Center's Institute secured the services of evaluators Dr. Melanie Hwalek and Victoria Straub from SPEC Associates to design a comprehensive evaluation plan along with the Institute's data manager. Together, the evaluation team documented the evaluation design process and produced a meaningful evaluation plan. Using a stakeholder engagement

FIGURE 4.7   ◆   RENDERING OF REC CENTER

model called Evaluation*Live!*, the evaluators identified key stakeholders who embrace learning, can drive the questions that need to be addressed, and can champion the evaluation within their own organizations. The relationship between the evaluator and stakeholders must be based on trust, equality, and shared responsibility for the evaluation's success. The model typically requires the use of an evaluation advisory group (Roholt & Baizerman, 2012) but this was a somewhat daunting challenge. With so many different players, how could the team engage them in a meaningful way? Their solution was to orchestrate four types of meetings:

1. **Initial meetings** with youth advisors focused on understanding the situation of housing instability among LGBTQ+ youth in metropolitan Detroit so that a "rich picture" of the experience of housing instability could guide the evaluation process.

2. **Large group meetings** with representatives from all the agencies involved in the Clairmount Center development to create a common understanding of big picture issues such as the situation of LGBTQ+ youth facing housing instability and the theory of change. They also provided feedback on the draft evaluation plan.

3. **Subgroup meetings** that focused on the four major components of the theory of change, namely, housing stability, individual goal achievement, engagement with the community, and systems change. They discussed indicators and provided feedback.

4. **Individual interviews** held virtually with advisory group members who had expertise on specific topics such as the housing eligibility screening tool, how to evaluate space from an architectural perspective, tools used to assure compliance of federally supported housing regulations, and types of reports available through the Homeless Management Information System.

Throughout this evaluation planning process, centering, supporting, and meaningfully responding to youth advisors—while avoiding tokenization—was a key consideration. Early on the process, one of the three paid youth advisors asserted, "I want to be a part of this[evaluation process], I really do. However, I do not want to be deemed a poster child for the Ruth Ellis Center. I want whatever feedback I'm giving back, I would like to see it at least be heard, because I don't want to feel like my participation in this is pointless."

The evaluation team spent several weeks preparing for the initial advisory group meeting so that youth advisors would lead the "rich picture" exercise, making their own perspectives on and experiences of LGBTQ+ youth housing instability the central focus of the exercise. Reflecting afterward on that exercise and the messy, highly involved "rich picture" it produced, one youth advisor remarked, "I feel like us as an LGBTQ community, all of these different things, everything that you're illustrating on this paper and how chaotic it is? This is everything that's going through the mind of somebody that's like fifteen, fourteen all of this... just to survive.... This is the reality of it." Another agreed, saying the messy, almost illegible sketch could be a helpful tool, "so we can kind of illustrate," [pointing to the paper] "this is what goes on in our heads when we try to find housing."

The evaluation team worked to keep youth voice, experience, and perspective at the center of the project, involving youth advisors in every stage in the process to inform the development of every document, tool, and plan the evaluation advisory group developed. The entire process involved more than 60 meetings. The indicators and measures that were created made sense to both project stakeholders and field experts, and a comprehensive evaluation framework was produced. This long-term, participatory evaluation planning process has ensured that the data generated from the evaluation will be useful across stakeholder groups. In addition, the process itself offers lessons to those wishing to plan an evaluation of permanent supportive housing and to those designing evaluations of complex initiatives in their own locations.

This Spotlight on Equity is based on the contributions of Dr. Melanie Hwalek and Jessie Fullenkamp.

PROGRAM DESIGN

There is a place for the evaluator at the program design table, especially if they have a systems perspective and can see the interrelatedness of the program, organization, and environment (see Chapter 2). At this critical point, collaborative work between the evaluator and the program design team is the best possible way to design a program. The team provides their knowledge about program participants and their experience working with other similar populations. They also have expertise in program structures and activities that work in similar contexts, and, of course, they know the agency. On the other hand, evaluators offer complementary skills in performance measurement and evaluation. As a result, they can help the designers position the program for successful feedback and evaluation, thus supporting ongoing program improvement.

In the pre- and early program evaluation phase, key questions include:

- What is the purpose of the program?

- How will the program be implemented?

- How can the evaluator develop an evaluation that supports good program outcomes?

Nine Steps to Program Design

The support role played by an evaluator can ensure that the program is positioned from the outset for success. Study the diagram in Figure 4.8 for the nine important steps to program design and then read about each step.

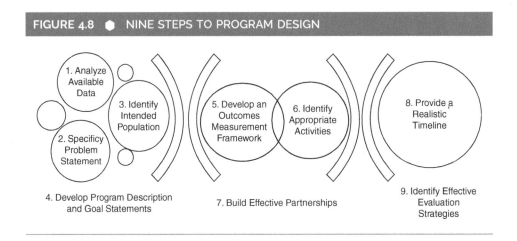

FIGURE 4.8 ● NINE STEPS TO PROGRAM DESIGN

1. Analyze Available Data
2. Specificy Problem Statement
3. Identify Intended Population
4. Develop Program Description and Goal Statements
5. Develop an Outcomes Measurement Framework
6. Identify Appropriate Activities
7. Build Effective Partnerships
8. Provide a Realistic Timeline
9. Identify Effective Evaluation Strategies

Step 1. Analyze Available Data

Transitioning from the needs assessment activities outlined above, if a close analysis of the collected data was not possible at that time, perhaps due to limited resources, now issues can be identified and prioritized. Information should include quantitative data such as trend and population statistics (as available) and qualitative data such as stakeholder views.

Step 2. Specify Problem Statement

Evaluators should clearly express the problem statement to define the issues, put them into perspective, and explain the need or problem in focus (Centers for Disease Control and Prevention, 2013a). Here, data support the problem statement and help justify the program. The evaluator can work closely with the program team to interpret the relevant data. Information in the problem statement should include:

- Severity or extent of the problem
- Affected population(s)
- Associated risk factors and conditions
- Current and/or previously tried solutions
- Context (social, environmental, political, and economic conditions).

Step 3. Identify an Intended Population

Although there may be several possible intended groups, the specific population of interest should be identified (e.g., high-risk pregnant or breastfeeding women with an income of less than $1,300 per month living in metropolitan New York). The evaluator can help to refine the focus, always keeping in mind how program outcomes for the population will be measured. Typical questions include (Association of Family Health Teams of Ontario, 2016):

- Who will benefit from the program?
- Whom are you hoping the program will change?
- How many participants should receive service?
- What are the program's admission criteria?
- How will participants be recruited to the program?
- How will they be retained?

Step 4. Develop Program Description and Goal Statements

Preliminary information may have been developed in the needs assessment but now, it is time to prepare a detailed program description to identify what the program will achieve and what its impact will be. This statement must be clear and specific for use in program marketing materials and funding proposals. In addition, the evaluator can work alongside the program team to craft the program's goals, ensuring that they align with the organization's overall mission, policies, and strategic plan (Association of Family Health Teams of Ontario, 2016). Program planning teams often create SMART goals with five evaluation criteria (Figure 4.9, p. 144).

FIGURE 4.9 ● THE SMART GOAL				
Specific	**Measurable**	**Achievable**	**Relevant**	**Timebound**
Do you provide details about the outcome you are wanting to achieve?	Is there a tool to measure the outcome?	Is the outcome achievable given resources and capacity?	Is the outcome relevant to your organization's strategic plan?	Is the outcome achievable in the time given?

Each goal must have specific details about what is going to change, identification of a tool to measure and collect data, an outcome that is possible, realistic given resources, and the time when the outcome will occur stated.

The evaluator can assist with generating SMART goals to ensure that they are realistic and feasible. Commitment by leadership to their attainment is also essential (Patton, 2012, p. 204).

However, as goals can be exaggerated vision statements crafted to secure funding, it is helpful to ask clarifying questions to make sure that they are grounded in reality (Patton, 2012):

- What are you trying to achieve with program participants?
- If you are successful, how will those who complete the program be different after the program than they were before?
- What kinds of changes do you want to see in program participants as a result of participation?
- When your program works as you want it to, how do those who complete the program *behave* differently? (p. 205)

Sometimes there is confusion between conceptualizing goals and determining how to measure them. By focusing on outcomes and results first, it then becomes easier to focus on how to measure them.

Step 5. Develop an Outcomes Measurement Framework

Once program goals are clear, the changes expected in the participant population resulting from the program are enumerated. Patton (2012, pp. 208, 215) offers a framework that has six separate elements to be specified in order to measure outcomes. In Table 4.4, p. 145, for example, an outcomes framework for a teen parenting program is provided.

Element	Example
TABLE 4.4 ● EXAMPLE OF A FULLY SPECIFIED UTILIZATION-FOCUSED OUTCOMES FRAMEWORK	
Intended subgroup	• Teenage mothers at Central High School
Desired Outcome	• Appropriate parenting knowledge and practices
Outcome Indicator	• Score on Parent Practice Inventory (knowledge and behavior measures)
Data Collection	• Pre- and posttest, beginning and end of the program, 6-month follow-up; district evaluation office will administer and analyze the results
Performance Target	• 75% of entering participants will complete the program and attain a passing score on both the knowledge and behavior scales
Use	• The advisory task force will review the results. The advisory task force consists of the Principal, two teachers, two participating students, one agency representative, one community representative, an associate superintendent, one school board member, and the district evaluator; the task force will decide if the program should be continued at Central High School and expanded to other district high schools • A recommendation will be forwarded to the superintendent and school board

Source: Patton, M. Q. (2012). *Essentials of Utilization-Focused Evaluation.* SAGE Publications.

Step 6. Identify Appropriate Activities

Activities for each objective should be listed, indicating how they will achieve the desired program outcomes (Centers for Disease Control and Prevention, 2013a). The activities should fit closely with the roles, responsibilities, and commitment of staff and the financial and material resources and time available to complete them. Often a series of meetings with the organization's administrators must work through structural and feasibility issues. As the evaluator is not acting as a content expert, they may not be closely involved in these discussions but may obtain information after strategy development. When planning activities, the team should:

- Emphasize organizational priorities
- Promote positive change in the identified issues or risk factors
- Specify the needs of the population yet to receive the program
- Consider the culture of the participants to be served.

Step 7. Build Effective Partnerships

Program partners are often needed to promote program goals. They should represent a broad spectrum of community stakeholders. However, successful coalitions and partnerships do not happen automatically. According to Butterfoss and Francisco (2004), to be effective, a program-community partnership needs a shared mission, meaningful goals, a clear strategic plan, strong leadership, paid support staff, a clear communications and feedback system, an identified line of accountability, and measurable impacts.

When working with partners, the evaluator's role is advisory, but depending on the context, an evaluation of the partnership may be necessary. For example, in her role as an Epidemiologist for the Prevention Technology Transfer Centers (PTTC) of the Substance Abuse and Mental Health Administration (SAMHSA), Bev works with epidemiology workgroups across several states. These are analysts dedicated to using data to make decisions to prevent substance misuse and mental health disorders. She frequently suggests that they evaluate the partnership to determine the experiences and outcomes of the workgroup members.

Granner and Sharpe (2004) studied measurement tools for coalition or partnership characteristics and functioning and found a broad array that lacked conceptual consensus. They recommend that the evaluator identify an overarching theory or framework such as Butterfoss and Kegler's Community Coalition Action Theory (2002); identify specific evaluation objectives based on program needs; and identify measurement tools with adequate validity and reliability.

Step 8. Provide a Realistic Timeline

An evaluation takes time and must consider the complexity of the organization, the activities planned, and requirements of the funders. Evaluation scheduling must be arranged so that organizational deadlines can be met. Sometimes, decisions are made 6–9 months before the implementation of a recommendation may occur, as in a policy change affecting school functioning. A brilliant evaluation report delivered after the decision has been made is of little use, so the evaluator needs to understand the organization's decision making cycle in order to integrate with critical decision points.

Step 9. Identify Effective Evaluation Strategies

Because the evaluator has worked collaboratively with the program team, evaluation strategies should flow smoothly from these program design steps. Program goals and objectives should be measured regularly, allowing progress to be charted and fed back to staff to make adjustments as needed. Williams (2019), who has applied systems concepts to evaluation thinking for many years, suggests that the evaluator needs to ask the following six evaluation questions continuously:

1. What is the intervention's purpose?

2. What is the scope and focus of the intervention and evaluation?

3. What ought to be the consequences of the evaluation and what evaluation purposes promote those consequences?

4. What are the criteria (or values) that should underpin the judgment of merit, worth, and significance?

5. What questions inform the data collection that leads to the judgment of criteria?

6. How can the feasibility of the evaluation be ensured?

In Bev's work with a teen pregnancy prevention program, she used the socio-ecological model to illustrate the effect teen pregnancy had on the student, parents, school system, and community. An intervention for parents as well as the students was desired, so Bev became involved in this process to ensure that the program could be evaluated. She reviewed the literature for parenting concepts related to communicating with teens, and using a mind mapping tool, worked with the program team to define the purpose and components of the intervention and to craft the evaluation questions. For example, "Was the teacher highly skilled at teaching parent's communication concepts with their teens?" was a process-oriented question for the parents. One outcome evaluation question was: "To what extent are the parents more confident talking to their child after the classes than before?" Outcome results indicated that 85% of the parents were ready to talk to their child about sexual health and knowledge, teen pregnancy, and prevention topics.

EVALUABILITY ASSESSMENT

A client asked Gail to evaluate a job skills training program at a local community college. The staff assured her that the data needed for the evaluation were readily available. It was all "in the database." So she dug a bit further and found out that there were actually three databases, one for the college registrar, one for the program, and one for the government funder. The databases all used different platforms, and students had been assigned different ID numbers in each one.

Further, support was lacking. The individual who had set up the registrar's database was no longer available, the government database was now under construction, and staff had not updated the program's database for two years due to resource issues. It turns out that this is a pretty typical scenario in complex organizations. Systems are often dysfunctional, out of date, or inaccessible, despite the faith that staff have in them. Gail had to start over and determined that an evaluability assessment (EA) was in order.

Evaluability assessment (EA) is defined as follows:

> *An evaluability assessment examines the extent to which a project or program can be evaluated in a reliable and credible fashion. It calls for the early review of a proposed project or program in order to ascertain whether its objectives are adequately defined and its results verifiable.* (United Nations Office on Drugs and Crime, 2019)

An EA is a quick and relatively inexpensive method to determine the actual status of a program and its readiness for a full evaluation. It is often needed because, sadly, as Wholey (2004) commented, an evaluation will probably not result in improved program performance if the following circumstances exist:

- The evaluator and intended users of the evaluation disagree on the goals and measurement criteria intended to be used to evaluate the program.

- The program goals are unrealistic given the program design, resources available, and activities underway.

- The cost of the data collection is unreasonable.

- Policymakers and managers are unable or unwilling to change the program based on evaluation information (pp. 33–34).

It is better to identify these issues before launching into an expensive and time-consuming evaluation process. An EA asks the following key question: *Is the program ready to evaluate?*

EA has had a checkered history. Wholey and his colleagues initially developed it in 1979 in response to the many extensive survey evaluations prevalent at the time, many using sophisticated quasi-experimental designs. Unfortunately, evaluators often discovered little or program impact (Trevisan & Walser, 2015). In addition, the expense of running these no-effect studies was hard to justify, and both government funders and evaluators were getting frustrated. Finally, Wholey (1979) wished to prepare programs for the outcome evaluations that would happen later.

While Wholey's approach focused mainly on assisting program managers, evaluators also began to involve stakeholders (Trevisan & Walser, 2015). In the 1980s, however, the use of EAs declined, partly because although programs were often not ready for an evaluation, the political pressure for outcomes was intense. Also, funding for EAs competed with that for regular outcome evaluations. As a result, they fell out of favor. By the mid-1990s, a shift in opinion occurred. EAs came back into vogue because evaluation readiness had become accepted as an essential component of the program's life cycle. The enactment of the U.S. Government Performance and Results Act (GPRA) in 1993 meant that all federal agencies were accountable for program results and so all types of evaluation gained in perceived value. In addition, EAs have been adopted in international development evaluation, expanding the boundaries of conventional EA use to include portfolios of programs (rather than single programs), policy areas, and strategic plans (Davies, 2013).

Thurston and Potvin (2003, p. 457) supported a participatory approach to EA in the health professions, as a helpful method to manage resource allocation in any social change program. EA results in better articulated programs and ongoing learning. It can also be a guide to the development of future evaluation activities (p. 466). Their six-step EA model includes:

1. Select an evaluability assessor.

2. Identify stakeholders.

3. Identify and assess important documents.

4. Develop the program logic model and evaluation plan.

5. Reach agreement to proceed with an evaluation.

6. Identify and assess time and other resources required.

According to Trevisan and Walser (2015), EA is a valuable precursor to various evaluation approaches, both qualitative and quantitative. It determines:

- If the program theory aligns with the program as implemented in the field

- The likelihood that the program will yield positive results as currently implemented

- The feasibility of, and best approaches for, further evaluation activities. (p. 14)

Evaluability Assessment Example: Engaging Stakeholders to Improve Data Collection in Evaluability Assessments

The U.S. CDCs' Division for Heart Disease and Stroke Prevention worked with evaluators to conduct an EA of the Community Health Team Model in St. Johnsbury, Vermont. Joanna Elmi contributed this case study (Trevisan & Walser, 2015). In the model, teams of community health workers (CHWs) working in hypertension control linked clients to economic, social, behavioral health, and other community supports in the community. Their goal was to reduce the economic and social issues that effectively posed barriers for clients to manage their health issues.

When interviewing the CHWs and other team personnel, the evaluators found that the client data currently being collected included:

- Number of clients served

- Incoming and outgoing referrals

- Planned action items.

The EA findings suggested that evaluators needed more detailed information about each client encounter, including additional demographic data, the purpose for a visit, and life satisfaction and well-being measures. As Elmi commented, "this would allow the program to track actual services delivered, monitor changes in clients' needs, and measure the impact of CHW services on clients' life conditions" (Trevisan & Walser, 2015, p. 56).

The team was so receptive to this suggestion that they developed a standard intake and follow-up form. It became one of the special data sources for the evaluation that was later conducted and helped assess the impact of the team's model on participants' quality of life. Later, the evaluators provided technical assistance to refine the form further and created an electronic version compatible with electronic hospital records.

The evaluators observed that because team members had created the intake form collaboratively, they had ownership of the tool, resulting in its universal uptake. The EA also documented the program's readiness for a thorough evaluation by documenting intended outcomes. This process strengthened the team's understanding of their own goals and built their capacity for the upcoming program evaluation.

Next, in our Expert Corner, we present needs assessment expert, Dr. Jim Altschuld.

Dr. Jim Altschuld

Jim Altschuld, Professor Emeritus at Ohio State University OSU, is a charter member of the American Evaluation Association and a member of one of its predecessor organizations starting in 1979. At OSU he taught program evaluation, needs assessment (NA), and basic methodology and conducted evaluations and research studies (mostly on NA). He has written eight books, edited numerous NDE and other journal issues, and published many articles. It has been his honor to have received local, state, and national (AEA) awards for his work which continues to the present.

1. *You have been called the patron saint of needs assessments (NA), although you deny it (Altschuld, 2015). Still, you have spent a good deal of your career promoting needs assessments. Do you see an increase in its use over that last ten years? If so, to what do you attribute that change?*

Recent books and articles (research, applied) about NA are available. There is a small, vibrant, 30-year plus Topical Interest Group (TIG) on NA at AEA (the only national group on the topic) with some but not many new members over time. Some TIG sponsored presentations have been well attended, and others have had limited participation. There is NA training at AEA's annual meeting, the Evaluators' Institute, and other venues. NA concepts are embedded in university evaluation courses and in texts like this one and others. These are positive indicators attesting to continuing vitality and the integration of NA into evaluation practice, and the latter was not always the case.

Above is good news for NA but underlying the text authors' questions are the ideas of increase and change and in that light, I must be more moot/tempered. As of 2014, there was not a stand-alone NA course in evaluation-specific curricula worldwide! The only national NA group is stable, and doing well but it is in more in a holding pattern than one of growth. Substantive articles about implemented assessments and improving methodology are not plentiful in the literature. Thus, a more thoughtful reply to the inquiries would be to see what the future might bring—will the glass be even less full, remain sort of half-empty/full, or much fuller?

2. *You have stressed the importance of balancing assets with deficits when looking at program needs. Do you have some suggestions about the best way to do that?*

A well-done assessment will determine the highest priority needs out of many, what their nature is, and what might be causing them, etc. Beyond that, action plans to resolve needs must be developed and part of this activity will require identifying assets and resources currently available (or those that might become available). To obtain such information, it is best to have a working NAC consisting of a variety of agency and stakeholder individuals who are knowledgeable about communities—groups within them, service providers, how to locate existing sources of data, how to access organizations, and so forth.

Use that group to find assets/resources. Have them interview key informants who tap into the heartbeat of a community (realtors, police and fire personnel who are liaisons with the population, local reporters, clergy and church groups, civic associations, businesses in specific locations, municipal planners, managers of transportation systems) and ask them who or what should be sought out to resolve the need. Compile what is found and see where it coalesces and what emerges from it. Also, briefly skim the literature for studies of assets/resources similar to yours as well as instruments and techniques (e.g., surveys, questionnaires, PhotoVoice, crowdsourcing, others) that could be used/adapted for the specific circumstance.

3. *What advice can you offer to those of our readers who are just beginning to explore the field of evaluation?*
Carefully think about your purposes for looking into the field (to do evaluations, to become an evaluation researcher, to learn about evaluation as it fits into a management role, and so on) and after that find a practicing evaluator to gain another perspective. In addition, it might be beneficial to contact AEA for ways and sources to further your exploration.

Key Terms

Community health needs
    assessment (CHNA) 139
Evaluability assessment 147
Generic literature review 124
Literature review 122

Meta-analysis 125
Needs assessment 133
Pre- and early program evaluation
    121
Program life cycle 120

Social network analysis 129
Stakeholder 126
Stakeholder mapping 127
Systematic review 124

The Main Ideas

1. The program life cycle starts at the established need for the program and continues through to the determination of its future service.

2. Pre- and early program evaluation is an important phase that consists of literature reviews, stakeholder analysis, needs assessments, program design, and evaluability assessment.

3. Evaluators should dedicate a deliberate amount of time reading the literature and understanding the theories, programs, methods, and approaches used in evaluation.

4. Literature reviews help the evaluator understand what has been discovered about a topic, how it was studied, and guide the purpose and activities of the evaluation study.

5. Stakeholders could be described as having low- or high-interest and power in terms of the program under study.

6. Stakeholder communication can consist of who you are going to tell, what you are going to tell

them, and how you are going to tell them the important information.

7. Needs assessments consist of an exploration phase, data gathering activities, and utilization of the data collected or located to justify an intervention or service.

8. During data gathering activities of a needs assessment, the evaluator and stakeholders can understand the evaluand better through a study of social indicators and trend analysis, consensus building, and forums.

9. Evaluators can play an integral part of the program design process, setting the program up for a well-designed evaluation study.

10. An evaluability assessment can help prepare the program for a future evaluation. Not every program is ready for an evaluation; some have under-developed goals, missing documents, or poorly defined variables and instruments to measure them.

Critical Thinking Questions

1. Think of a policy change that needs to occur at your school, in your community, or in an organization you know. What is the topic related to this policy change? Why is there a needed change? What are the challenges with changing this policy or creating a new policy? Why would encouraging behavior change around this topic not be appropriate?

2. Explain why we used a clock metaphor for the program phases. How does that help you understand how time relates to the program and its maturity level?

3. Conduct a mini literature review. Select a topic you are interested in and use a search engine (e.g., EBSCO Host, and Google Scholar) to yield articles. How many articles did you find? What journals published articles on this topic? What were the features of the articles?

Student Challenges

1. **Life as an Intervention**. Think of your life and how you live it as an intervention. Using a mind mapping tool, such as Mindomo, MindMup, Lucidchart, Coggle, Creately, Scapple, Canva, Mindmeister, or Padlet, create a mind map of all the stakeholders connected to you.

2. **Stakeholder Involvement**. Think about a program you are familiar with that you might evaluate someday. If you cannot think of one, use the program in which you are currently enrolled. Using sticky notes to organize your material, do the following:

   a. List the stakeholders that could be involved and organize them into a stakeholder map.

   b. Organize the stakeholders into primary (directly affected by the program) and secondary (indirectly affected).

   c. Use Eden and Ackerman's 1998 Power versus Interest grid to map stakeholders according to their power and interest. Which stakeholders might be more engaged users of a future evaluation of this program and why?

   d. Patton suggests (2012, p. 136) that if an evaluator does not identify key stakeholders and users prior to launching into the evaluation, there could be problems and misunderstandings along the way. What types of problems might occur in your scenario?

3. **Evaluation Across the Globe**. Visit the International Organization for Cooperation in Evaluation (IOCE) website and see the national evaluation organizations in the IOCE database (https://ioce.net/interactive-map). Get involved! Select several of interest on the interactive map, such as the South African Monitoring and Evaluation Association, Australasian Evaluation Society, Swedish Evaluation Society, or United Kingdom Evaluation Society. Note their resources, activities, conferences, membership, journals published, and other information.

Additional Readings and Resources

1. Bebow, J., & Pratt, P. (2013). The public's agenda for public education. *The Center for Michigan*. https://centerformich.files.wordpress.com/2019/08/publics-agenda-for-public-ed.pdf
   This report on public deliberation highlighted how engaged Michigan residents decided what type of changes and innovation they would like to see in their children's public education. The shared ground vision was for more arduous teacher training and greater education accountability. The legislature responded by expanding the preschool availability and creating more difficult teacher certification tests.

2. Bryson, J. M., Patton, M. Q., & Bowman, R. A. (2011). Working with evaluation stakeholders: A rationale, step-wise approach and toolkit. *Evaluation and Program Planning, 34*(1): 1–12.
   This useful article stresses stakeholder analysis, essential to the design of a credible evaluation. It presents a range of relevant techniques to inform the development and implementation of an evaluation design.

3. Centers for Disease Control and Prevention. (2010). *Community Health Assessment and Group Evaluation (CHANGE) Action Guide: Building a Foundation of Knowledge to Prioritize Community Needs*. U.S. Department of Health and Human Services. https://www.cdc.gov/nccdphp/dnpao/state-local-programs/change-tool/about.html
   The CHANGE tool provides a structure for community coalitions to develop their own community action plan. CHANGE is a data collection process that defines areas for improvement in a community. These areas could be increased physical activity, improved nutrition, reduced tobacco use and exposure, and chronic disease management. A community team plans and implements the CHANGE model. It includes Excel® spreadsheets for data collection with schools, hospitals, worksites, and community organizations.

4. Oster, A., Wejnert, C., Mena, L., Elmore, K., Fisher, H., & Heffelfinger, J. (2013). Network analysis among HIV-infected young black men who have sex with men demonstrates high connectedness around few venues. *Sexually Transmitted Diseases, 40*(3), 206–212.
   The authors use network analysis to gather graphical information about the incidence of HIV and other sexually transmitted infections. Researchers recruited Black men who have sex with men (MSM) and are HIV positive and interviewed them. The focus of the interview questions was the year prior to the HIV diagnosis. Network maps are visually displayed, showing main and casual partnerships, HIV status, and gender of the partner.

5. Pennel, C., McLeroy, K., Burdine, J., & Matarrita-Cascante, D. (2015). Nonprofit hospitals' approach to community health needs assessment. *American Journal of Public Health, 105*(3), e103–e113.
   According to the 2010 Patient Protection and Affordable Care Act, nonprofit hospitals create a CHNA with implementation strategies. This article describes the methods and strategies used to complete this mandate. In addition, the authors provide criteria that describe the quality characteristics.

6. Xiao, Y., & Watson, M. (2019). Guidance on conducting a systematic literature review. *Journal of Planning Education and Research, 39*(1), 93–112.
   This article focuses on creating a structure or typology of literature reviews. The authors also outline a literature review process, from formulating the research problem to reporting the findings.

MID-CYCLE PROGRAM EVALUATION

1. Distinguish between formative and summative evaluation.

2. Describe four types of formative evaluation.

3. Summarize four reasons for using a process evaluation.

4. Distinguish between a literature review and a document review.

5. Explain why the case study is the most frequently used method for implementation evaluation.

6. Differentiate between performance indicators, performance standards, and performance measurement.

7. Suggest reasons why evaluators frequently use monitoring and evaluation in international contexts.

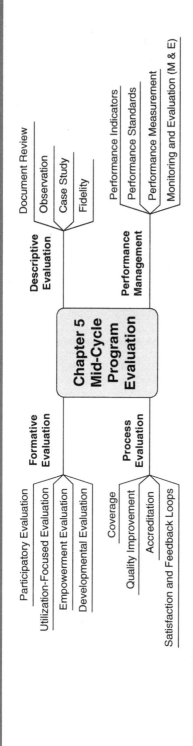

Chapter 5 Mid-Cycle Program Evaluation

Formative Evaluation
- Participatory Evaluation
- Utilization-Focused Evaluation
- Empowerment Evaluation
- Developmental Evaluation

Process Evaluation
- Coverage
- Quality Improvement
- Accreditation
- Satisfaction and Feedback Loops

Descriptive Evaluation
- Document Review
- Observation
- Case Study
- Fidelity

Performance Management
- Performance Indicators
- Performance Standards
- Performance Measurement
- Monitoring and Evaluation (M & E)

A KILLER ASTEROID IS HEADED OUR WAY

On March 26, 2019, space officials discovered an asteroid at a magnitude of 21.1, and it was determined to be potentially hazardous. Based on its size, speed, and distance from the earth (0.05 astronomical units), astronomers predict it will reach earth on April 20, 2027. So, in 2027, an asteroid that was now about 35 million miles away had a 1% chance of hitting the United States. This space object could wipe out any town. How could our planet defend itself? How would populations evacuate and where would they go?

Source: **istockphoto.com/adventtr**

Space explorers created this hypothetical scenario so that scientists worldwide could figure out how to deflect such an albeit remote possibility. The Center for Near-Earth Object (NEO) Studies at the National Aeronautics and Space Administration (NASA) considers alternate approaches to responding to such a disaster. Although there is no identified threat, NASA "estimates there are over 300,000 objects larger than 40 meters that could pose an impact hazard and would be very challenging to detect more than a few days in advance" (National Science and Technology Council, 2018, p. 3). The U.S. government released an action plan identifying goals over the next 10 years to prepare for this "low-probability, high-consequence threat" (Greenfieldboyce, 2019, para. 17).

Exercises that test readiness processes were central to activities at the 2019 Planetary Defense Conference. The conference's purpose was to place the aeronautical community in situations where they had to make decisions quickly and develop recommendations about how to increase readiness for such a disaster. Organizers arranged tabletop exercises with oral presentations about the evolving threat. A leadership group was selected, and in an open letter, over 100 planetary scientists, physicists, and engineers supported the development of a kinetic impactor to deflect the orbit of such an asteroid.

An evaluation of this simulation activity would need tools and strategies to understand its effectiveness. Evaluation questions might include:

- To what extent did the participants who attended the conference represent certain stakeholder groups?

- How did the tabletop activity foster discussion among participants?

- What ideas about disaster readiness were generated?

- Was a consensus achieved? Why or why not?

- What recommendations emerged from the conference?

- Which recommendations warranted further exploration?

- What lessons did participants learn from this exercise?

- What are the next steps?

INTRODUCTION

In Chapter 4, we looked at Pre- and Early-Program Evaluation processes. Now, we progress to Mid-Cycle Program Evaluation, which is midday on the clock, typically between four o'clock and eight o'clock in the program's lifecycle. See Figure 5.1, Mid-Cycle Program Evaluation.

FIGURE 5.1 ◆   MID-CYCLE PROGRAM EVALUATION

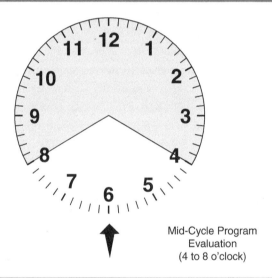

Mid-Cycle Program
Evaluation
(4 to 8 o'clock)

Source: istockphoto.com/Tuncaycetin

During this phase, the program is in progress and service delivery is underway. These implementation activities are of great interest to program managers, sponsors, and funders. The evaluation types associated with this program timeframe provide timely feedback that is critical to program improvement.

Mid-Cycle Program Evaluation or implementation evaluation, as it is often called, is a family of approaches, concepts, and methods that focus on the actual operation of a program "once it moves from the drawing board and into action" (Love, 2004, p. 64).

It has garnered greater attention in recent years as organizations become more attentive to achieving measurable results. As Love suggests, we focus on:

identifying and meeting the needs of the customer or citizen, delivering high-quality programs, continuously improving business and service delivery processes, applying evidence-based practices, demonstrating accountability for achieving outcomes, and using performance measures to bridge the gap between strategic planning and program implementation. (p. 64)

Each of these activities relies heavily on data. Evaluators can help organizations strengthen programs, achieve results, and build a performance-oriented culture. Several groups are interested in knowing about processes, "a prerequisite for explaining or hypothesizing why a program did or did not work as expected" (Rossi et al., 2019, p. 101). Program managers want to know the extent of implementation, what issues have emerged, how they can take corrective action, and how organizational development and learning can be supported. Sponsors and funders have an oversight role and are concerned about fiscal responsibility. Evaluators need to understand causation so they can examine the program theory or what a program "should" be doing to determine what constitutes adequate performance.

Table 5.1, p. 160 expands on our mid-cycle clock by outlining the evaluation types, evaluation methods and measures, and key questions most often used during the implementation process. Each of these topics is explored in this chapter.

You will enjoy the resources in this chapter including the Spotlight on Equity, which presents the Youth GO Program, our expert Dr. Michael Quinn Patton, Key Terms, Main Ideas, Critical Thinking Questions, Student Challenges, and Additional Readings and Resources.

The following sections explore four types of implementation evaluation: formative evaluation, process evaluation, descriptive evaluation, and performance management.

FORMATIVE EVALUATION

The most well-known types of evaluation are **formative evaluation** and **summative evaluation**, introduced by evaluation guru Michael Scriven in 1967 (Shadish et al., 1991). These terms have become lodged in the evaluation literature and in the vocabulary of both evaluators and clients. Scriven (1991b) described them as follows:

Formative evaluation is evaluation designed, done, and intended to support the process of improvement, and normally commissioned or done by, and delivered to someone who can make improvements.

Summative evaluation is the rest of evaluation: in terms of intentions, it is evaluation done for, or by, any observers or decisions makers (by contrast with developers) who need valuative conclusions for any reasons besides development. (p. 20)

Scriven went on to clarify the distinction between them by famously quoting the analogy provided by Stake: "When the cook tastes the soup, that's formative evaluation; when

TABLE 5.1 ● MID-CYCLE PROGRAM EVALUATION TYPES		
Evaluation Types	Evaluation Methods and Measures	Key Questions
1. Formative Evaluation	• Participatory Evaluation • Utilization-Focused Evaluation • Empowerment Evaluation • Developmental Evaluation	• Is the program being delivered as intended? • What is helping or hindering program development? • How are stakeholders engaged in the program from conception throughout ending? • Are short-term outcomes promising? • What areas need improvement?
2. Process Evaluation	• Coverage • Quality Improvement • Accreditation • Satisfaction and Feedback Loops	• Is the program reaching the intended participants? • How well are program activities being implemented? • Does the program comply with expectations and applicable standards? • Are participants satisfied with the services they received?
3. Descriptive Evaluation	• Document Review • Observation • Case Studies • Fidelity	• Is the program being implemented according to plan? • What differences are observed across sites?
4. Performance Management	• Performance Indicators • Performance Standards • Performance Measurement • Monitoring and Evaluation (M & E)	• Is the program meeting its goals and objectives?

the guest tastes it, that's summative evaluation" (Scriven, 1991b, p. 19). Many evaluators have come to believe, as Patton (1996) comments, "that the world of evaluation has grown larger than the boundaries of formative and summative evaluation, though this classic distinction remains important and useful" (p. 131) and it does provide us with a needed entry point to our discussion of both mid-cycle/implementation evaluation (Chapter 5) and end-of-cycle/outcome evaluation (Chapter 6).

Key mid-cycle questions include:

- Is the program reaching the intended participants?

- Is the program being delivered as intended?

- What is helping or hindering program development?

- Are short-term outcomes promising?

- What areas need improvement?

Several variations of formative evaluation have emerged that keep program improvement and organizational learning in the foreground: participatory evaluation, utilization-focused evaluation, empowerment evaluation, and developmental evaluation.

Participatory Evaluation

Experienced community builders know that involving stakeholders in the evaluation process is the best way to meet community needs. The goal of **participatory evaluation** is to improve program performance by empowering stakeholders and participants so that they can control and own evaluation decisions at all stages of the evaluation process, from design to data collection to reporting (Fetterman et al., 1995; Kranias, 2017). Over the last 20 years, participatory evaluation has become a touchstone for collaborative, community-based evaluation approaches.

Cousins and Leithwood (1986, p. 360) reviewed 65 evaluation studies and found that evaluation use was strongly evident when "users were involved in the evaluation process and had a prior commitment to the benefits of evaluation." In participatory evaluation, practitioners bring their deep understanding of program context and content to the table. The evaluator brings their technical skills, such as study design, statistical analysis, and technical reporting, and then trains staff in the evaluation process, but they share project control with practitioners. In this way, evaluations can be responsive to local needs but remain rigorous enough to satisfy most critics.

Some of the advantages of the participatory approach are included in Figure 5.2 (Cousins & Earl, 1995; Eberhardt et al., 2004; Estrella & Gaventa, 1998; USAID, 2011).

FIGURE 5.2 ● ADVANTAGES OF THE PARTICIPATORY APPROACH

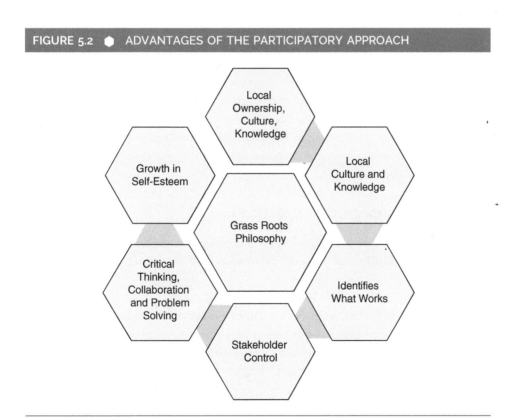

Participatory evaluation also has some disadvantages (Cousins & Earl, 1995; Eberhardt et al., 2004; USAID, 1996; Zukoski & Luluquisen, 2002):

- Demands significant time, resources, and a commitment to the process

- Evaluators need strong facilitation skills

- Participants need to represent all key stakeholders

- Building a climate of trust can be challenging

- May be viewed as less objective due to stakeholder involvement

- Takes participating staff away from regular duties

- May be dominated or misused by some stakeholders to further their own interests

- May not be appropriate for the more technical aspects of evaluation

- Cultural knowledge and understanding may be lacking. and will need to be supported. (Fawcett et al., 2003; Rabinowitz,n.d.; Sette, n.d.)

An example of a participatory evaluation involved a school health promotion project called *Mi Escuelita or My Little School* (Eberhardt et al., 2004) and involved a number of village schools in the Alitplano region of Bolivia. The primary goal was to provide alternative education through hygiene, health, and nutrition training. Selected communities received greenhouses, latrines, water pumps, trees and seeds, kitchen tools, and a nutrition curriculum. Some project sites progressed more successfully than others and so a participatory evaluation was undertaken to identify the factors that predicted project success. The evaluators facilitated and documented the evaluation process, staff collected and compiled the data, and villagers offered feedback, providing insight into the variables that affected program success and contributing to the action plan. Findings indicated that the most important success indicator was the increased desire of villagers to have these innovations in their own homes.

Utilization-Focused Evaluation (U-FE)

Based on the belief that evaluations should be judged by their utility and actual use, Patton developed **Utilization-Focused Evaluation (U-FE)** in 2002. As he said (Patton, 2013):

> *Evaluators should facilitate the evaluation process and design any evaluation with careful consideration of how everything that is done, from beginning to end, will affect use. Use concerns how real people in the real world apply evaluation findings and experience and learn from the evaluation process.* (p. 1)

Like participatory evaluation, U-FE gives a central role to stakeholders and espouses a problem-solving approach that calls for creative adaptation in response to changing conditions (Christie, 2003, p. 21). The actual evaluation process increases participants' "sense of control, deliberation, and reflection about their own lives and situations" (Patton, 2008, p. 173).

U-FE is a highly personal and situational approach to evaluation and has substantial implications for the use of a program's evaluations (Patton, 2004, p. 282). Use depends on the presence of an identifiable individual or group who personally care enough about the evaluation and its findings to see that it gets used. However, a U-FE evaluator should also place more importance on those people who are not inclined to use the evaluation—who are intimidated by it, indifferent toward it, or generally hostile to the concept of evaluation (p. 383).

Patton (2008, pp. 37–38) states that U-FE can include any evaluative purpose (formative, summative, developmental), any kind of data (quantitative, qualitative, mixed), any kind of design (such as naturalistic or experimental), and any kind of focus (processes, outcomes, impacts, cost-benefit). In our experience, however, U-FE tends to be used in a formative context where program improvement is the objective. Its overwhelming success as an evaluation approach has heightened awareness about the importance of users and use and no evaluator today would forget to pay attention to these concepts, regardless of the type of evaluation they are conducting. Box 5.1 outlines the steps involved in U-FE.

BOX 5.1 ● STEPS TO UTILIZATION-FOCUSED EVALUATION

1. Assess program/organizational readiness for evaluation.

2. Ensure evaluator has the facilitation skills required to lead U-FE change.

3. Identify, organize, and assess primary intended users.

4. Identify, assess, understand, and act on situational factors that may affect use.

5. Assist users in identifying and agreeing on the major focus for the evaluation priority uses for findings.

6. Design evaluation to lead to useful findings.

7. Explore potential use of findings by using simulated findings as a learning experience for users prior to collecting data.

8. Keep users informed and involved through all stages of data collection.

9. Facilitate data analysis and interpretation among users to increase their understanding, ownership, and commitment to use.

(Continued)

(Continued)

10. Work with users to use the findings and learnings from the evaluation process in intended ways.

11. After the evaluation, follow up to determine the extent to which intended use was achieved.

Source: Adapted from Patton, M. Q. (2008). *Utilization-focused evaluation* (p. 35–38). SAGE Publications; Patton, M. Q. (2012). *Essentials of utilization-focused evaluation.* SAGE Publications.

An example of a U-FE is described by Zamberg et al. (2020). The global pandemic of 2019 caused concern all over the world. This team of healthcare professionals and medical students needed a strong communication effort to relay valid health information about COVID-19 to other health professionals thereby reducing misinformation and allowing the needed measures and medical treatment to be implemented. To do this, the team developed a mobile platform called "Head to Toe." The platform provides an "institutional knowledge dissemination solution and consists of iOS and Android mobile apps where medical students and health professionals can access medical content organized by medical specialties, such as local and international guidance, clinical skills videos, and administrative material. Yahoo Flurry provided the data for user activity and what content was viewed (i.e., patterns and trends). The research and evaluation team used the platform during the pandemic to communicate with personnel in the Children's Hospital. The result was that doctors received up-to-date information about the virus. A U-FE method was employed, and a demonstration of use was given to the leadership of the hospital. Data collected included average and total number of users and sessions per day, average usage time per user per day, and total and specific number of content views per day.

Users were also asked to complete an open-ended survey to report the effect the platform had on the physician's daily practice, effectiveness, and the ability of the platform to reassure the physicians of the appropriate treatment for challenging COVID-19 patients. One of the main goals of this study was to limit the amount of random information physicians were exposed to about COVID-19 and focus their attention on sources of valid information. Results of the study revealed that the relay of information from local, national, and international authorities pertaining to new COVID-19 information was more successful on this platform. The swift provision of the information helped doctors create response plans and protocols during the outbreaks and reassured them about quality clinical decision making. The authors also highlighted the needs assessment benefit from the platform. Doctors were able to provide insight and data into what was lacking on the platform and what was needed to perform their duties. The doctors on this platform were operating in a "real-time" environment simply because the communication quality "would be harder to achieve with classic methods as emails, which may be hard to sort and find, or with printed material, especially when frequent content updating is necessary" (p. 6).

Empowerment Evaluation

While the goal of participatory evaluation and utilization-focused evaluation is increased use of evaluation findings due to participation in the evaluation process, **Empowerment Evaluation (EE)** has the goal of emancipation or empowerment for those that have been oppressed (Alkin and Christie, 2004, p. 56). Based in community psychology, the approach uses evaluation concepts and techniques to foster self-determination by helping communities monitor and evaluate their own performance (Fetterman, 1994, p. 1). Introduced by David Fetterman in 1993, EE aims to (Fetterman & Wandersman, 2005):

> *increase the probability of achieving program success by (1) providing program stakeholders with the tools for assessing the planning, implementation, and self-evaluation of their program, and (2) mainstreaming evaluation as part of the planning and management of the program/organization.* (p. 28)

The emphasis of EE is on fostering self-determination and sustainability through program development, improvement, and lifelong learning. It is particularly suited to the evaluation of comprehensive community-based initiatives or place-based initiatives. It offers a role to stakeholders in all aspects of the evaluation, essentially empowering program staff and clients to conduct their own evaluations. Stakeholder involvement is mandatory in almost all aspects of the process (Christie, 2003, p. 29). Community stakeholders are best situated to understand the problems they are experiencing and by being deeply engaged in the evaluation process, they are more likely to believe in the results. The evaluator's role becomes one of collaborator and facilitator rather than expert and counselor (Zimmerman, 2000). The evaluator helps program staff members and participants determine the types of evidence required to document and monitor progress to their goals in a credible way. Capacity building occurs in EE as communities learn to collect their data, develop strategies, and monitor their work as they implement the evaluation (Fetterman et al., 2015).

There are three steps in the EE process (Fetterman, 2001, p. 23):

1. Determine a mission, vision, or unifying purpose

2. Take stock or determine where the program stands, including strengths and weaknesses

3. Plan for the future by establishing goals and helping participants determine their strategies to accomplish program goals and objectives.

EE is guided by 10 specific principles. See Box 5.2, p. 166.

BOX 5.2 ● EMPOWERMENT EVALUATION PRINCIPLES

1. **Improvement**—helps people improve program performance; it is designed to help people build on their successes andreevaluate areas meriting attention

2. **Community ownership**—values and facilitates community control; use and sustainability are dependent on a sense of ownership

3. **Inclusion**—invites involvement, participation, and diversity; contributions come from all levels and walks of life

4. **Democratic participation**—participation and decision making should be open and fair

5. **Social justice**—used to address social inequities in society

6. **Community knowledge**—respects and values community knowledge

7. **Evidence-based strategies**—respects and uses the knowledge base of scholars in conjunction with community knowledge

8. **Capacity building**—enhances stakeholders' ability to conduct an evaluation and to improve program planning and implementation

9. **Organizational learning**—evaluation data are used to help organizations learn from their experience, building on successes, learning from mistakes, and making mid-course corrections

10. **Accountability**—focused on outcomes and accountability; functions within the context of existing policies, standards, and measures of accountability asks, "Did the program accomplish its objectives?"

Source: Fetterman, D. M., & Wandersman, A. (2005). *Empowerment evaluation principles in practice.* Guilford Publications.

The extensive involvement of program participants in the actual program evaluation process has often raised questions about rigor, objectivity, bias, and privilege. Fetterman's (2001, pp. 102–106) arguments are countered in Figure 5.3, p. 167.

EE continues to flourish in projects from Silicon Valley to the remote areas of Amazonia. Nevertheless, concerns about the centrality of stakeholders remain. As Stufflebeam (1994, p. 323) suggests, fostering self-determination has not been the guiding purpose of evaluation in the past, which is to determine the merit, worth, or value of a program. Yet, since it was introduced, the subjectivist or transformative paradigm (see Chapter 2) has gained ground in evaluators' work with marginalized groups. How does the evaluator adequately represent the interests of all stakeholders? How much of an advocate should the evaluator be? Issues such as these continue to generate important discussions in the modern conception of our practice.

Bev worked with Fetterman on a tobacco prevention initiative in Arkansas for the CDCs Minority Initiative Sub-Recipient Grant Office (MISRGO). Coalitions participated in regular evaluation training and used EE for their evaluation activities (Fetterman et al.,

FIGURE 5.3 ● COUNTER ARGUMENTS TO QUESTIONS OF EMPOWERMENT RIGOR

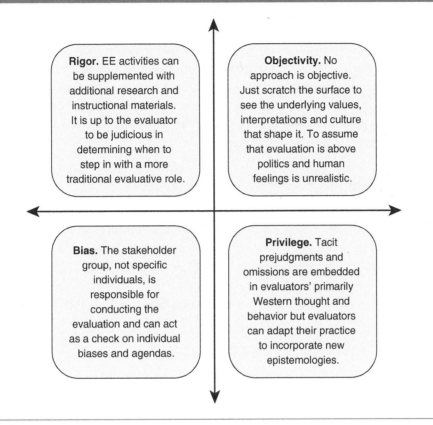

Rigor. EE activities can be supplemented with additional research and instructional materials. It is up to the evaluator to be judicious in determining when to step in with a more traditional evaluative role.

Objectivity. No approach is objective. Just scratch the surface to see the underlying values, interpretations and culture that shape it. To assume that evaluation is above politics and human feelings is unrealistic.

Bias. The stakeholder group, not specific individuals, is responsible for conducting the evaluation and can act as a check on individual biases and agendas.

Privilege. Tacit prejudgments and omissions are embedded in evaluators' primarily Western thought and behavior but evaluators can adapt their practice to incorporate new epistemologies.

Source: Fetterman, D. M. (2001). *Foundations of empowerment evaluation.* SAGE Publications.

2015). Coalitions in Arkansas worked on tobacco prevention priority activities, such as the following:

- Encourage voluntary smoke-free perimeter policies

- Educate parents and law enforcement officers about the benefits of smoke-free environments in cars (Act 811)

- Gather petition signatures for smoke-free environments

- Establish smoke-free parks.

A novel feature was the presence of a "critical friend" or coach to help guide and assist stakeholders during program planning, implementation, and evaluation. Together they developed a dashboard to monitor their progress. For example, the dashboard had the following metrics:

1. Baseline (the number of people using tobacco in their community)

2. Goals (the number of people they expected would stop using tobacco by the end of the year)

3. Benchmarks (the number of people who stopped using tobacco each quarter)

4. Actual Performance (the number of people who stopped using tobacco compared to goals and benchmarks to determine progress).

Grantees used these metrics to monitor program implementation and to make mid-course corrections, substituting ineffective strategies with potentially more effective ones. The dashboard enabled legislators, sponsors, grant coordinators, and evaluators to see if progress was being made across grantees. Bev remembers that one of the most unique aspects of this grant was showing policymakers the power of collective action, instead of individual action, on the part of the grantees.

Developmental Evaluation

Many organizations, including philanthropic foundations, have only a general notion of their goals. They want to respond to changing conditions quickly and so need real-time data for decision making. In response, Patton pioneered **Developmental Evaluation (DE)**, a type of formative evaluation well suited to social innovation in uncertain, dynamic, and complex environments where outcomes are unclear or where continuous progress, ongoing adaptation, and rapid responsiveness are needed (1996, p. 135).

For example, Tim Broadhead, President and CEO of the J. W. McConnell Family Foundation, described their needs as follows (Dozois et al., 2010):

> As this Foundation shifted its funding to complex, long-term initiatives that are not so much pre-planned as emergent, the inadequacy of the usual evaluation methods became evident. We needed a compass, not a roadmap. We needed to know we were on the right track, not that we had arrived at a pre-determined spot, on budget, and at the specified time. (p. 7)

DE could answer questions like the following (Parkhurst et al., 2016, para. 3):

- What is emerging as the innovation takes shape?
- What do initial results reveal about expected progress?
- What variations in effects are we seeing?
- How have different values, perspectives, and relationships influenced the innovation and its outcomes?
- How is the larger system or environment responding to the innovation?

DE "focuses on understanding an innovation in context and explores how both the innovation and its context evolve and interact over time. Its real-time feedback allows for quick course corrections, critical to success in conditions of complexity" (Parkhurst et al., 2016, para. 8). It can be an important strategic learning tool for funders and practitioners as they facilitate systems change and can be useful in contexts such as the following (Patton, 2011, pp. 334–335):

- New, innovative programs where outcomes are uncertain

- Ongoing programs that need to respond to changing conditions

- Multi-agency evaluations with complicated interactions, unclear outcomes, and unexpected events and crises

- Humanitarian crises where relief agencies and emergency teams need coordination and assistance

- Major system changes initiatives where a new direction is required.

The evaluator's function is to infuse development teams with an evaluative perspective and to support real-time learning, decision making, and development by using the interventions shown in Figure 5.4 (Dozois et al., 2010).

FIGURE 5.4 ● DEVELOPMENTAL EVALUATION (DE) INTERVENTIONS

Type of Developmental Evaluation (DE) Intervention	Definition and Examples
Asking Questions	Good questions create openings, expose assumptions or misapprehensions, push thinking, surface values, highlight common ground, and reveal differences that, if not dealt with, could impede development (or, if looked at appreciatively, could become a strength). Ideally, they result in the release of new or tied-up assets in a system (e.g., the capacity to capitalize on a relationship, use a hidden skill, draw on in-kind resources, or set an idea in motion).
Facilitating	All of the practices associated with quality facilitation can be used to good effect with developmental evaluation, including active listening, surfacing assumptions, clarifying, synthesizing, ensuring a diversity of voices are heard, and ensuring that the conditions in the room support learning.
Sourcing or Providing Information	Bringing information into the system is another key form of intervention. This can take many forms. For example, it might involve surfacing tensions and concerns by conducting stakeholder interviews and sharing the themes that emerged with the group. Or it might involve doing some research around promising practices, alerting the group to a complementary initiative, identifying a helpful resource, or conducting an environmental scan.
Mapping and Modeling	Helping the group to articulate, extend, clarify, and correct their mental models is critical to adaptive development. DEs play a significant role in helping to surface assumptions and visually map out the political, economic, social, and cultural forces, interconnections, barriers, and leverage points relevant to the initiative.
Pausing	There are times when a pause in the action would be very helpful. For example, when ideas are being generated and dismissed before there's really time to give them some thought, or when someone is heading down a conceptual path that no one else is following. A DE can ask the group to pause and then support whatever action is most needed (e.g., clarification, synthesis, thoughtful consideration, group discussion, celebration).
Reminding	In the chaos of complexity, it's very easy to lose touch with the core intent of the initiative or forget agreed-upon principles. Groups can become focused on chasing the next best thing and lose track of higher level purposes. Effective DEs help stakeholders to align their thinking and conduct with their vision and values by reminding them of the agreements they've made about their principles and priorities. Another aspect of "reminding" is to serve as lore keeper—someone who keeps track of past failures and successes so that the group can build on the learning that has gone on before. Bringing the history of an initiative forward is also part of this; understanding how and why decisions were made helps to orient new members as well as informs others who are doing similar kinds of work.
Matchmaking	Matchmaking can involve connecting the group with people, organizations, resources, or ideas. Any DE can play this role, but the connections will likely be more meaningful if you have some experience and expertise with the system you are trying to influence. It can also help the group to consider social resources available to them (e.g., existing connections, potential champions or door-openers) that they are not yet leveraging.

Source: Adapted from Dozois, E., Langlois, M., & Blanchet-Cohen, N. (2010). *DE 201: A practitioner's guide to developmental evaluation.* The J.W. McConnell Family Foundation and the International Institute for Child Rights and Development.

While evaluating a childcare worker licensing and curriculum renewal initiative, Gail discovered that a traditional approach to evaluation was not appropriate (Barrington, 2010). Initially, she had designed a formative evaluation with a logic model and a survey for each of the project's four strategies, but there was an urgent demand for workers to renew their licenses. After meeting the dynamic and irrepressible project team, it was clear there would be no stopping them and it was also clear that their strategies would be in a continuous state of development throughout the project. Luckily, she was familiar with DE, so she began to respond to the project on the go, running alongside the development team. She asked evaluative questions, applied evaluative logic, created evaluation tools, collected real-time data, and fostered reflection to support ongoing decision making. For example, she:

- Designed surveys for use the following week

- Developed measurement tools for an expert review panel meeting to be held within a few days

- Developed a curriculum template and compared traditional and modularized curricula for 60 courses that were in development until the end of the project

- Reviewed multiple-choice test item development and validated the results as they were being developed

- Interviewed rural childcare workers and their instructors about their experiences with remote supervision

- Conducted a deliberative dialogue about report recommendations with a group of fractious college administrators who seldom agreed on anything.

Never had her work been so interesting, so intense, or so time-consuming, and never had her evaluative skills grown so rapidly; in fact, she took the lessons learned from this project into her practice and still uses them today.

PROCESS EVALUATION

Process Evaluation focuses on service delivery. It examines what a program is, what activities are implemented, who receives services, and whether it is operated as intended or according to some standard (Rossi et al., 2019, p. 92).

Key questions include:

- Is the program reaching the intended participants?

- How well are program activities being implemented?

- Does the program comply with expectations and applicable standards?

- Are participants satisfied with the services they received?

The CDC (2008, p. 8) identifies the four primary purposes of process evaluation (see Table 5.2, p. 171).

TABLE 5.2 ● FOUR PRIMARY PURPOSES OF PROCESS EVALUATION		
Purpose	**Evaluation Activities**	**Sample Questions**
1. Program monitoring	Track, document, and summarize the inputs, activities, and outputs of a program. Describe other relevant characteristics of the program and its context.	• How much money do we spend on this program? • What activities are taking place? • Who is conducting the activities? • How many people do we reach? • What types of people do we reach? • How much effort (e.g., meetings, media volume) did we put into a program or specific intervention that we completed?
2. Program improvement	Compare the inputs, activities, and outputs of your program to standards or criteria, your expectations/plans, or recommended practice (fidelity). Relate information on program inputs, activities, and outputs to information on program outcomes.	• Do we have the right mix of activities? • Are we reaching the intended audience? • Are the right people involved as partners, participants, and providers? • Do the staff/volunteers have the necessary skills?
3. Building effective program models	Assess how the process is linked to outcomes to identify the most effective program models and components.	• What are the strengths and weaknesses within discrete components of a multilevel program? • What is the optimal path for achieving a specific result (e.g., getting smoke-free regulations passed)?
4. Program accountability	Demonstrate to funders and other decision makers that you are making the best possible use of program resources.	• Have the program inputs or resources been allocated or mobilized efficiently?

Source: Centers for Disease Control and Prevention, Office on Smoking and Health. (2008). Introduction to process evaluation in tobacco use prevention and control. https://www.cdc.gov/tobacco/stateandcommunity/tobacco_control_programs/surveillance_evaluation/process_evaluation/pdfs/tobaccousemanual_updated04182008.pdf

An excellent place to start a process evaluation is with the program theory (see Chapter 3). The first three segments of the logic model, namely Inputs, Activities, and Outputs, provide the evaluator with more detail about what a program includes, its function over time, and how it links to outcomes. Alkin and Vo (2018, p. 171) comment that this information allows the evaluator to form conclusions about program implementation, strengths and weaknesses, and improvements needed. In the following section, we examine four important aspects of process evaluation: coverage, quality improvement, accreditation, and feedback.

Coverage

Coverage refers to the extent to which our desired population accepts the program and participates to the levels specified in the program design (Love, 2004, p. 82; Rossi et al., 2019, p. 104). In other words, to what extent did the program reach the intended audience? Coverage is one of the fundamental measures of program implementation and helps to ensure program accountability.

An analysis of coverage can reveal that participation in the program by different subgroups may be affected by bias, or the extent to which some subgroups participate more than others (Rossi et al., 2019, p. 104). Bias can arise from self-selection, intentional "creaming" of easier-to-serve clients, lack of awareness or timely program feedback, or service restrictions. Typically, programs can only afford to serve a fraction of potential clients, so it is important during program planning to define group characteristics clearly so that the program can reach them.

Program staff need to be concerned about both the over-coverage of some subgroups and the under-coverage of others. To measure the extent of this problem, we need to identify the important characteristics of the intended population, typically age, gender, ethnicity, race, socioeconomic status, geographic location, and other eligibility criteria identified by the program design. In addition, as Love suggests (2004, p. 83), we should identify issues associated with potential participation, such as transportation, childcare, language translation services, literacy supports, program location, and hours of operation. Finally, we should be open to unanticipated barriers that may emerge through discussion with actual and potential program participants.

For example, in a prenatal nutrition program for high-risk women that Gail evaluated, attendance was very low in one community, even though the program was offered at the health unit located on the First Nations' reserve where the women lived. When she interviewed women about other health issues, she asked them why they did not participate in this program. They explained that because the community was so small, everyone knew who was going to the health unit, and they were not necessarily ready to share their pregnancy with the world. However, when programmers moved the offering to the local school and changed the time to coincide with that of a pottery class, attendance increased significantly. No one could tell which program the women were attending.

Quality Improvement

In Chapter 2, we mentioned Quality Improvement (QI) and one of the most widely used QI tools, the four-step Plan-Do-Study-Act (PDSA) cycle. This quality is supported by the ISO, the International Organizational for Standardization. They have over 165 country members from Afghanistan to Zimbabwe. These standards are internationally recognized as "the best way of doing something" (International Organizational for Standardization, n.d., para. 1). Examples of what they set standards for are products, environmental impacts, reduction of waste, accidents in the workplace, energy management to cut consumption, and food safety.

QI requires a systems perspective and the use of criteria-based metrics in methodical and routine ways. Attention to variation is critical because the more variation you have, from day to day and from task to task, the less that quality can be assured. Evaluation helps to identify those processes in need of improvement. Essential to these changes is the readiness of individuals within the organization to accept change and modify their behavior.

The PDSA Cycle, depicted by Massoud et al. (2001) in Figure 5.5, p. 173, can uncover where variation occurs in a process. The first step is to identify a problem in the organization through a brainstorming exercise, for example. The second step is to collect and analyze data about that problem to determine how it affects the quality of the service. Step 3 is an early supposition about what changes need to occur to improve quality. What intervention, if implemented, will change the data from baseline to the subsequent measurement? Step 4 is

FIGURE 5.5 ⬠ THE PLAN, DO, STUDY, ACT CYCLE

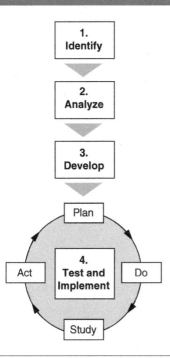

Source: Massoud, R., Askov, K., Reinke, J., Franco, L., Borstein, T., Knebel, E., & MacAulay, C. (2001). *A modern paradigm for improving healthcare quality.* Developed by the USAID-Funded Quality Assurance Project.

the iterative cycle that includes: P-plan for change, D-do the intervention and collect data, S-study the data to determine the extent of change that has occurred, and A-act or implement the intervention. If quality is not yet sufficiently improved, the cycle is repeated.

The hallmark of a PDSA Cycle is its reliance on the use of QI tools throughout each of the steps. These tools allow teams to drill deeper into a problem and uncover possible solutions. Typically, small groups of individuals engage in a PDSA exercise.

Table 5.3, p. 174 provides an example of how a local high school could resolve a trash problem at their football stadium.

Bev often teaches QI and reinforces using QI tools for data collection and analysis. Figure 5.6, p. 175 provides examples of some of the tools she uses.

Accreditation

While certification and credentialing focus on an individual's competencies, **accreditation** assesses the level of quality of an organization against a set of standards established by an impartial and independent accrediting body. For example, there are accrediting bodies for hospitals and other healthcare organizations, state and local health departments, schools, universities and colleges, police, fire, construction, and laboratories.

The accrediting body creates standards that detail what an institution must do to attain a certain level of quality. The accreditation process typically has several phases, including a self-assessment, an application process, a site visit, scoring, feedback, and the final accreditation decision.

TABLE 5.3 ● USING PDSA TO RESOLVE A TRASH PROBLEM AT A LOCAL HIGH SCHOOL

Element of PDSA	Activity	Example
1. Identify	Identify a problem you want to solve.	• Too much trash in the stadium after the games. • Janitorial staff spend too much time picking it up.
2. Analyze	Collect data to better understand the problem.	• Students take pictures of the trash. • They counted 300 pieces of trash on average at the end of a game. • The school receives three complaint calls per week from neighbors about trash flowing into their yards.
3. Develop	Develop the characteristics of an intervention to reduce the effects of the problem.	• The community needs to be involved. • Students need to be involved. • Trashcans are needed at more locations. • Reminder announcements need to be made more frequently. • A reminder email/text will be sent to students and parents to keep the stadium clean.
4. Test and Implement	(a) Plan to make the change and document who is responsible for it.	• 10 student volunteers will stand at identified positions at either end of bleacher rows. • They will distribute trash bags at one end and collect them on the other end. • Attendees will place the trash in the bags and pass them on. • At least 10 trash cans will be placed strategically throughout the facility and checked every hour for capacity. Aim 1: At our next home game, the amount of trash beneath the bleachers by the end of the game will decrease by about 75% (baseline was 300) as measured by the janitorial staff. Aim 2: By the end of the season, there will be no calls made to the school by neighbors complaining about the trash as reported by the front office.
	(b) Do: Conduct the study.	• Conduct the intervention and collect data.
	(c) Study: Review data to determine if the intervention caused a change in the problem.	• Students report that trash has decreased by 90%. • Complaint calls from neighbors have ceased.
	(d) Act: If successful, institutionalize the results across the organization. If not successful, revise and repeat the process.	• The trash management process becomes routine practice. • Staff and students plan to use these QI strategies in other areas of the school.

FIGURE 5.6 ● EXAMPLES OF QUALITY IMPROVEMENT TOOLS

Brainstorming. The team is asked, "Why do new mothers not keep their WIC appointments?" The team lists answers in a random fashion and then drills deeper into the problem to uncover a solution.

Affinity Diagrams. The team is asked, "Why do staff not want to participate in QI Cycles?" The generated items are organized into subgroups or themes. Then they are organized into broad categories such as: *Knowledge, Skill, and Does not Understand Connection to Work.*

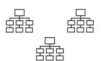

Fishbone or Root Cause Analysis. The team is asked, "Why do parents not stay up to date with immunizations?" They brainstorm reasons and then group the common themes into causal relationships on the fishbone branches. This diagram then shows the specific causes of an event. (Ishikawa, 1968).

Flowchart. The team is asked, "What steps are necessary to complete a specific product or service?" They may be confused about the order of the necessary steps. A flowchart of important tasks demonstrates their expected sequence and is beneficial for staff training.

Source: Istockphoto.com/kemalbas, RaulAlmu, Boris25, pseudodaemon

In 1988, public health leaders identified a need to strengthen work processes because the public health system was "in disarray" (Walker, 1989). In 1994, a framework for essential public health services was developed to carry out the mission of public health and was updated in 2020. Leaders identified three core functions for state, county, and tribal public health systems: assessment, policy development, and assurance. A framework was developed to promote the health of people in all communities and to remove systemic and structural barriers that have resulted in health inequities such as, "poverty, racism, gender discrimination, ableism, and other forms of oppression" (Centers for Disease Control and Prevention, 2020).

Surrounded by three core functions of assurance, assessment, and policy development, the 10 Essential Public Health Services include:

1. Assess and monitor population health status, factors that influence health, and community needs and assets

2. Investigate, diagnose, and address health problems and hazards affecting the population

3. Communicate effectively to inform and educate people about health, factors that influence their health, and how to improve it

4. Strengthen, support, and mobilize communities and partnerships to improve health

5. Create, champion, and implement policies, plans, and laws that impact health

6. Utilize legal and regulatory actions designed to improve and protect the public's health

7. Assure equitable access to individual services and the care needed to be healthy

8. Build and support a diverse and skilled public health workforce

9. Improve and innovate public health functions through ongoing evaluation, research, and continuous quality improvement

10. Build and maintain a strong organizational infrastructure for public health.

Figure 5.7 depicts these core functions and services (Centers for Disease Control and Prevention, 2021).

FIGURE 5.7 ◆ THE 10 ESSENTIAL SERVICES OF THE PUBLIC HEALTH SYSTEM

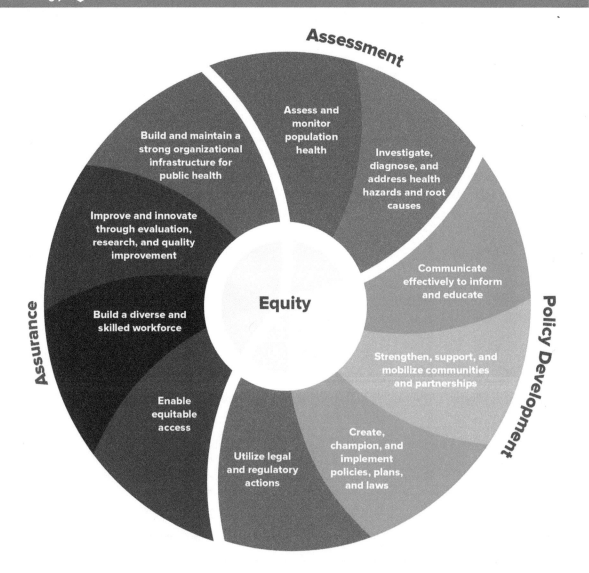

Source: Centers for Disease Control and Prevention. (2021, March 18). *The public health system and the 10 essential public health services.*

The framework provides the basis for The National Public Health Performance Standards (NPHPS). When seeking accreditation by the Public Health Accreditation Board (PHAB), public health departments must go through a lengthy review process. There are hundreds of statements (measures) for which they must provide the evidence that they are meeting the required standard. For example, typical documents include a strategic plan, community health assessment, quality improvement plan, meeting agendas, minutes, written processes manual, data collection instruments, policies and procedures, emergency management plans, and outbreak investigations. Reviewers examine these documents to judge them against the established criteria for each essential service.

It can take months and sometimes years to prepare for accreditation, but the benefits are substantial. Health departments report (NORC, 2016) that accreditation helps them, for example, better identify their strengths and weaknesses, promote transparency, and be more competitive in funding opportunities.

Satisfaction and Feedback Loops

Clients' feedback about their program experience seems to be such obvious evaluation data that it does not need discussion. As we know, just about every commercial service offered today comes with a tag-along customer satisfaction survey, most of them online. Typical discussions about the limitations of client feedback revolve around bias – participants may not recognize or acknowledge program benefits, they may not want to appear critical and so may overrate the program, or their dissatisfaction may make it less likely that they return the feedback questionnaire at all.

Regardless of their flaws, as Rossi et al. (2019, p. 134) comment, "direct ratings by recipients of the benefits they believe the program provided them, or not, are useful feedback for a program." Perhaps, as Guijt (2014) claims, feedback loops are a better approach. Rather than being a "one-off" evaluation moment, routine, continual monitoring of program implementation provides regular insights into progress toward program goals and can also alert staff about emerging issues. The concept of a "loop" means a two-way flow of information, which makes good sense from a participatory evaluation perspective.

In peacebuilding evaluation, feedback mechanisms allow groups or individuals affected by agency programs to influence the design, management, and evaluation. Information can flow from clients to those who are implementing, assessing, or funding, but it can also flow back again from the program to clients in a genuine loop which involves "the collection, acknowledgment, analysis, and response to the feedback received" (Bonino et al., 2014). Figure 5.8, p. 178 provides an example of a fully functioning feedback mechanism and an incomplete feedback loop.

Effective feedback mechanisms support "the collection, acknowledgment, analysis, and response to the feedback received, thus forming a closed feedback loop" (p. 4). Listening to participants should be a standard practice, but methods for implementing dynamic

FIGURE 5.8 ● CLOSED AND OPEN FEEDBACK LOOP

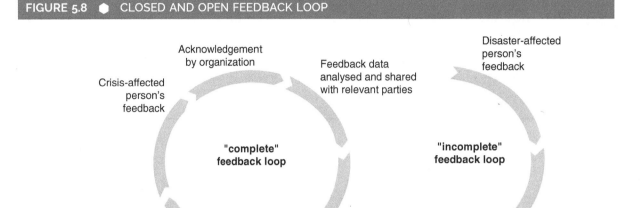

Source: DME for Peace. (2014, December 3). *Using feedback effectively in peacebuilding contexts.* DME for Peace.

feedback loops are still developmental in terms of vocabulary, principles, accepted best practices, and reliable measurements (Davenport, 2013). A critical element of these feedback mechanisms is that both participants and staff must see value in the process. Participants need to know leaders will respect their opinions, and staff must value the feedback as an additional source of information worth collecting.

Further, organizations must be honest with themselves and program participants about their ability to make any desired changes. As DME for Peace (2014) comments, "To install a feedback mechanism without any real ability to make changes undermines the purpose of an effective feed-back loop" (para. 15). The challenge for evaluators and managers is to build trust to demonstrate that feedback can directly impact decision making and service delivery (Davenport, 2013).

Next, let's read about the Youth GO Method, a participatory focus group method used with systematically marginalized youth.

SPOTLIGHT ON EQUITY

The Youth GO Method:

Conducting Effective Participatory Focus Group Research with

Systematically Marginalized Young People

Drs. Sara T. Stacy and Danielle Chiaramonte have developed, utilized, and refined the Youth Generate and Organize (Youth GO) focus group process. It is a participatory approach involving young people in research and evaluation (Stacy et al., 2018, 2020). Youth GO aligns with the existing resources and capacities already present within community-based settings and uses developmentally appropriate techniques to elevate youth voices by engaging young people in collecting, analyzing, and interpreting data.

When conducting projects that impact the lives of youth, evaluators can–and should–consider using tools to meaningfully engage young people in evaluation as they have unique knowledge, expertise, and insights. This is particularly important for projects impacting young people who are traditionally and systemically marginalized as their voices are often strategically left out from these systems.

Dr. Stacy has used it in her work with school and afterschool settings, including projects that explored the educational and programming needs and assets of students living in low-income housing (Stacy et al., 2018) and the experiences of Black and brown students within Community Schools (Stacy et al., 2020). Dr. Chiaramonte has used Youth GO to understand power and oppression in healthcare access among transgender and gender diverse (TGD) youth and young adults.

Youth GO can be delivered in-person or virtually, using a combination of video conferencing (e.g., Zoom) and Jam board (via Google). The process includes five steps in which youth generate data, learn qualitative analysis techniques, code and categorize the data, and discuss the findings (Figure 5.9).

- **Pre-Focus group: Goal setting and design**. Before beginning, the team determines goals, develops the protocol, trains facilitators, and pilot tests sessions.

- **Stage 1: Climate setting**. Sessions begin with introductions, an overview of goals, and co-creation of rules to guide discussion and manage group dynamics. Facilitators present an icebreaker to build rapport and trust among participants (e.g., *"What is something you love or something about yourself that you wish people asked you about more?"*)

- **Stage 2: Generating**. Prompts are revealed on a flip chart and read aloud. Participants are encouraged to individually reflect, write down responses on sticky notes, and place them onto the flip chart. Facilitators clarify and probe responses. This process is repeated for all prompts.

- **Stage 3: Organizing.** Participants learn how to code and theme data with a sorting game where they create categories, organize, and re-organize items based on different instructions. After, facilitators support youth in the process of collaboratively organizing and interpreting the data from Stage 2. They place organized responses onto different colored papers and create a label to signify a theme.

- **Stage 4: Selecting.** Participants work to identity central categories for the themes that emerged in the previous stage. Participants and facilitators discuss and define meaningful categories for each theme. These definitions are recorded, refined, and agreed upon.

- **(optional) Stage: Theoretical exploration.** Participants engage in a deeper discussion of the generated themes considering similarities

---

FIGURE 5.9 ● YOUTH GO STEPS

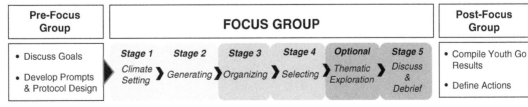

and differences on flipcharts. This process is akin to analytic memoing (Saldaña, 2016) and works well with older participants.

- **Stage 5: Debrief and discussion**. Finally, youth participants are encouraged to reflect on the Youth GO process through a group discussion guided by the facilitators.

- **Post-Focus group: Compile results and define actions.** Facilitators take detailed notes to clarify discussions, listen to recordings, add contextual detail, and note personal reflections.

In applying this approach across multiple settings and with multiple populations, the researchers have found Youth GO to be adaptive, flexible, and feasible to implement. It is particularly useful for rapid evaluation as it can be implemented cheaply and quickly. Finally, participants and facilitators of Youth GO have overwhelmingly reported enjoying the process. They report feeling valued and respected because they are able to share their stories, analyze the data as a group, meet other local youth, and learn new skills.

As one youth facilitator said: *"I've never done anything with college. I haven't even gotten my GED yet...I didn't expect to like it as much as I did...I learned research skills, focus group skills, other stuff that I don't have the words for, but I know how to do. It's been a really nice experience.*

A participant commented: *The team did a great job validating and really seeing each and every individual that was in my focus group. We did not feel like research subjects. This experience was great!*

This Spotlight on Equity is based on the contributions of Drs. Sara Stacy and Danielle Chiaramonte.

DESCRIPTIVE EVALUATION

Descriptive evaluation is a type of implementation evaluation that provides detailed information about what happens in the program and how it operates (Patton, 2008, p. 301). In this section, we explore four data collection methods that are commonly used in descriptive evaluations:

- Document Review

- Observation

- Fidelity

- Case Studies.

Key questions include:

- Is the program being implemented according to plan?

- What differences are observed across sites?

Document Review

The first stop for an evaluator who wants to learn more about a program is a review of program documents and records. This behind-the-scenes look at program processes helps the evaluator to understand how the program began and how it changed over time. The types of data routinely collected are apparent (Patton, 2015, p. 377).

It is important to distinguish between a document review and a literature review (see Chapter 4). A literature review analyzes and discusses published articles and reports on a topic to prepare for the development of a new evaluation or research project. A document review requires similar analysis techniques but focuses on a wide variety of unpublished documents and records that tend to be internal to an organization. Its main purpose is as a preamble to study design, as discovered records could act as a baseline for later comparison with data collected in the evaluation.

The reasons to conduct a document review include (Centers for Disease Control and Prevention, 2018):

1. To gather background on program history, philosophy, and operations

2. To determine if implementation reflects program plans

3. To gather information needed to develop other data collection tools

4. To answer *what* and *how many* types of evaluation questions.

Much useful information already exists in an organization and if the evaluator can unlock this history, all other evaluative activities will be better informed. Mogalakwe (2006, p. 221) suggests that the use of documentary sources can be just as good as, and sometimes more cost effective than, using surveys, in-depth interviews, or participant observation.

Nearly all programs keep records, and they can often reveal information about service delivery. Whether hard copy or electronic, they can be a good source of data about client characteristics, participation rates, types and intensity of services offered, and information about outputs and early outcomes, all valid for monitoring service delivery.

As Love comments (2004):

When combined in an implementation evaluation, these data can demonstrate whether the program delivery was faithful to the program plan, implementation differences by program site or client characteristics, and the relationship between implementation and outcomes. (p. 82)

Advantages of the document review as a data collection method include (Bretschneider et al., 2016; Centers for Disease Control and Prevention, 2018):

- Relatively inexpensive

- Provides a good source of background information

- Provides a global perspective

- Is unobtrusive and can be conducted without participant consent

- Can be easily tabulated

- Provides a behind-the-scenes look at the program that may not be directly observable

- May identify issues not evident by other means

- Can assist in the development of data collection tools.

Disadvantages include:

- Desired information may not be available

- Information can be misinterpreted as the reviewer may not have all the relevant background and context

- Information may be inapplicable, disorganized, inaccurate, incomplete, out of date, or difficult to understand

- There may be potential bias as not all documents may have survived

- It can be time-consuming to collect and review.

Programs differ widely in the quality and extensiveness of their file-keeping and data entry capabilities, storage, and maintenance. Agency resources and staffing are a significant consideration, but good administrative processes are also needed to set up and maintain record-keeping systems. As Rossi et al. (2019, p. 107) point out, all records systems are subject to some degree of error. They can be incomplete or contain incorrect or outdated information. They can also become inaccessible when placed in long-term data storage. Therefore, if the evaluator needs to review program records for an implementation evaluation, it is usually prudent to first examine the records for accuracy before deciding to use them as a data source (Rossi et al., 2019, p. 107).

Program records can be extensive and are a rich resource that is available to the evaluator who is willing to do a little digging. Examples include strategic plans, websites, brochures, client handouts, staffing lists, agendas, minutes, organization charts, policy manuals, and quarterly and annual reports (Alkin and Vo, 2018, p. 72; Love, 2004, p. 87; Patton, 2015, pp. 276–278).

Often, other data collection methods are needed to supplement the information in available documents. For example, when critically reviewing the elements of the evaluation design in 12 large federal evaluations, Howell and Yemane (2006) compared each program's documentation with its evaluation report. Their intent was to determine the range of questions the evaluations addressed, the appropriateness of the evaluation designs for answering the evaluation questions, whether the evaluation designs were followed closely, and whether results from the evaluations were disseminated to improve the programs or similar programs or to learn from evaluation methods.

The documents reviewed include the following (p. 122):

- Enabling legislation for the program and, if applicable, the evaluation

- Program statement of work

- Program grantee application

- Evaluation statement of work

- Program logic model

- Design report and/or evaluation work plan

- Survey instruments

- Office of management and budget clearance package

- Interim and final evaluation reports

- Other dissemination products (e.g., conference presentations, reports, and/or articles).

They found that most evaluations did not provide clear information about the study design. As a result, it was often necessary to review multiple documents and to conduct follow-up interviews to identify the components of each design.

Better information can be obtained when a document review template is developed. This tool can establish a common set of guidelines, ensuring accuracy, clarity, completeness, and consistency across reviewers. While each template will vary to fit the information needs of a particular evaluation, generally, it should contain the rationale and purpose of the evaluation; information about the actual review process, such as document reference, date reviewed, and reviewer; and information related to the evaluation questions. Of course, no document will provide information on every question but by listing them all in the template, relevant information will not be missed.

Observation

Evaluators often classify, count, rate, or describe various objects, conditions, or behaviors (Alkin, 2018, p. 131; Cohn et al., 2004, p. 211). Observation allows us to move from "work as imagined" (i.e., what should happen, what we think happens or what we are told happens) to "work as done" (what really happens) (Catchpole et al., 2016, p. 1). Many fields have incorporated observation into implementation evaluation including teaching, healthcare, art, sports, construction, mental health, libraries, and public works, to name a few. An accurate, systematic technique is required to assess conditions consistently. The evaluator becomes a human instrument, using eyes, ears, and other senses as evaluative tools. Training is essential so that observations are comparable across observers.

When evaluators use rating scales, a detailed description of the meaning of each point on the scale should be provided. In some cases, photographs or diagrams can serve as benchmarks (e.g., to assess alternate street cleaning programs). The prompts allow raters to assign precise grades to the conditions they see. Accuracy and consistency among raters and across time are vital. As Greiner (2004, p. 212) suggests, trained observers can provide accurate and reliable quantitative measures when properly used. The quantified data that are produced through observation assist in measuring implementation processes especially when collected over time.

Other, more naturalistic approaches to observation are also valid and produce qualitative data. Alkin (2018, p. 131) describes observation as "careful watching" that can continue over time until patterns or trends emerge. The role of the evaluator can vary from being an external observer not involved in the program activities under scrutiny to a participant-observer with direct involvement in the action, trying to balance participation with simultaneous attempts to observe and take notes.

> *The role that evaluators play has implications for the detail of notes they might take, for their understanding of the context, their impartiality (or bias), or their better understanding of the implications of actions or events.* (Alkin, 2018, p. 131)

Protocols, or the rules for recording information, can vary from structured tools, like a checklist, to unstructured notes, like a blank page. Evaluators use observation checklists when documenting a prescribed activity or behavior. Depending on the design, a checklist leaves little room for note-taking and elaboration but does allow for the efficient capture of data in the field (Alkin, 2018, p. 132).

For example, if we want to observe a new teacher in the classroom, we might develop a checklist like the one provided in Table 5.4. A mentor teacher can complete the observation and provide a check mark for the number of times they observe certain behaviors in the new teacher. After the observation, the mentor can identify areas for improvement and discuss them with the new teacher, elaborating on their actions from memory.

TABLE 5.4 ● NEW TEACHER OBSERVATION CHECKLIST

Model New Teacher Behavior	Check if Demonstrated
a. Addresses students by name	☐
b. Looks students in the eye	☐
c. Moves around the room	☐
d. Dresses professionally	☐
e. Pauses 10 seconds after asking the question	☐
f. Commands knowledge of the content	☐
g. Creates fluid transitions between topics	☐
h. Holds a good pace	☐
i. Allows students to practice content	☐
j. Uses stories and humor to relay content	☐
k. Handles interruptions quickly	☐

Using a blank notebook to take observational notes, what Alkin calls a "write-like-mad" approach, the volume of detail may be significant. However, mobility is limited as the evaluator is pinned in the corner writing feverishly. A more subtle method is to jot down important words or sketch images that can be transposed into more complete notes later. This technique provides more flexibility, but the evaluator's memory may be flawed. Preparing companion commentaries or memos to support the observational notes can bolster the quality of the observational data produced. A quick voice memo on the evaluator's mobile phone can capture some of the less measurable aspects of an observation and can be transcribed later for inclusion in study data.

Observational data are an incredibly rich source of information. They capture contextual details and participant perspectives unavailable to the evaluator using any other method. To limit bias and systemic error, the evaluator should be clear on the role observation will play in data collection, provide observer training if more than one evaluator is involved, pilot test the tool in a comparable setting, and maintain quality control by reviewing data at the end of each observation session.

Case Studies

According to Love (2004, p. 88), the case study is the most frequently used method for implementation evaluation. It tells stories. It allows you to integrate qualitative, quantitative, or mixed methods data from various sources to paint an in-depth picture and understand the complexities of a particular project, program, organization, or individual's situation within a real-life context.

Robert K. Yin (1989, p. 14) explains that the need for case studies arises out of a desire to understand a complex social phenomenon. The evaluator can retain the holistic and meaningful characteristics of events, activities, and interventions, especially when their boundaries are unclear. The case study can answer important *how* and *why* questions. It is the next best thing to "being there."

There are at least four uses for case studies (Yin, 1989, p. 25):

- To explain the causal links in an intervention that are too complex for more structured research designs

- To describe the real-life context in which an intervention occurs

- To illustrate or describe in a journalistic way the intervention itself

- To explore those situations where the intervention has no clear, single set of outcomes.

Despite its descriptive mode and story-like packaging, a case study is an empirical form of inquiry that uses multiple sources of evidence organized into an evaluation framework to answer a set of evaluation questions regarding one or more units of analysis. Findings are not generalizable from a realist's perspective (see Chapter 2), but any relativist will recognize the case study's ability to value context and present multiple versions of reality.

Although some researchers criticize case studies for lack of rigor, Lincoln and Guba's (1985) qualitative or relativist criteria still apply today. Mayan aligns them with typical realist criteria (2009, p. 102) in Table 5.5.

TABLE 5.5 ⬣ ELEMENTS OF CASE STUDY RIGOR COMPARED TO REALIST RIGOR		
Case Studies Element of Rigor	Replaces	Definition
Credibility	Criterion of Internal Validity	Assesses whether the findings make sense and represent the phenomenon accurately. It is enhanced by member checks, such as having the draft case study report reviewed by key informants, prolonged engagement, repeated visits, and cross-checks of different data sets to ensure consistent findings.
Transferability	External Validity	Assesses the applicability of the findings to other settings. Primary themes, supported by detailed description, will resonate with readers and increase their understanding of a phenomenon while keeping variability in mind.
Dependability	Reliability	Provides the evaluator with the opportunity to review decisions regarding the evaluation using an audit trail or chain of evidence.
Confirmability	Objectivity	Ensures that findings are logical throughout data collection and analysis; uses abductive thinking to scrutinize the data and entertains all possible explanations, confirming or disconfirming alternative interpretations until the most plausible explanation is reached.

Source: Mayan, M. J. (2009). *Essentials of qualitative inquiry.* Left Coast Press.

While conducting case study research looks like fun, and that all you need to do is "tell it like it is," nothing could be further from the truth because:

> *the demands of a case study on a person's intellect, ego, and emotions are far greater than those of any other research strategy. This is because the data collection procedures are* not *routinized.* (Yin, 1989, p. 62)

To manage the continual interplay between theoretical issues and the data being collected, the evaluator must be well-trained, able to take advantage of unexpected opportunities, and experienced enough to thwart potentially biased procedures. In addition, the extensive data cross-checking and triangulation required means that the evaluator must have excellent analytical skills. Finally, the case study must be so well written that it reads like a story, albeit with extensive evidence to back it up. All this and the project must be within time and budget constraints too.

Despite these challenges, descriptive case studies can make complex projects accessible and interesting for a nonscientific audience. The scope of the case study format is flexible and wide ranging, from short descriptions of individual project sites to multilevel explorations of strategy implementation.

The World Bank conducts many case studies in a development context (Morra & Friedlander, 1999). For example, the Operations Evaluation Department (OED) reviewed World Bank support for small- and medium-sized industries in Sri Lanka to determine the impact of the Bank's funding strategy. Multiple data sources were used, including project data, economic data, a survey of more than 300 firms in Sri Lanka (half as beneficiaries of the program, the other half as a control group), and structured interviews with participating financial institutions. The central finding was that Bank support was an essential aspect of Sri Lanka's development strategy. Bank loans had a desirable effect on income distribution and industrial development and played a role in developing a more diversified private-sector economy, contributing to a more effective financial infrastructure, and generating jobs, particularly for lower-skilled workers.

Fidelity

When reviewing a program, you can say, "It worked!" but unless you can describe and assess the details of the program's operations, you will not be able to answer the question, "What worked?" (King et al., 1987, p. 9). Not knowing about implementation limits the usefulness of findings and contributes to confusion about why programs succeed or fail. Fidelity assessment is one way to determine the "extent to which the program was implemented consistently with underlying theory, design, and philosophy" (Saunders, 2016).

As Chen (1990, p. 198) has stated, without documentation and/or measurement of a program's adherence to an intended model, there is no way to determine why the program failed. Figure 5.10 depicts two reasons for program failure.

FIGURE 5.10 ● REASONS FOR PROGRAM FAILURE

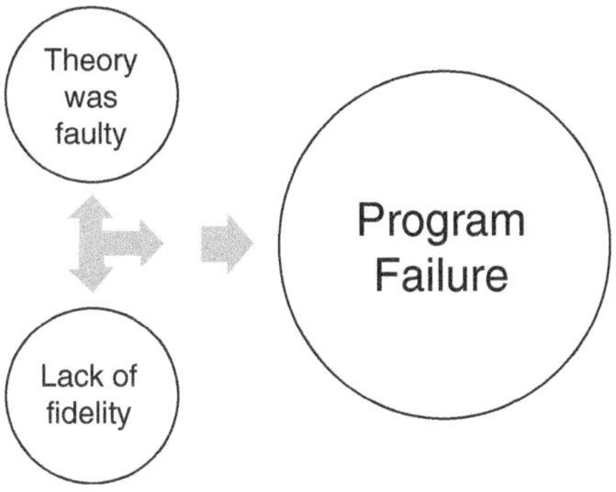

Source: Adapted from Chen, H. (1990). *Theory-driven evaluations*. SAGE Publications.

Key questions for fidelity are:

1. How unique is the program to others having the same outputs, outcomes, and impacts?

2. How do participants react to the program?

3. How well do the programmers implement the program?

4. How does delivery of the program align with the written description of the program?

5. What is the uptake of the program by participants?

Mowbray et al. (2003, p. 316) explain that administrators want to know how adequately a program model has been implemented. Fidelity measures the degree to which the program is offered with the same components, intensity, and duration as those specified by the program designer (Kubiak et al., 2019). Evaluators want to know that the implementation was plausible enough to produce the identified program effects to track the causal links between activities and outcomes. Finally, as in mental health, for example, practitioners want to know if the treatment delivered adhered to the recommended protocol.

Evaluators can establish fidelity criteria by drawing critical components from a specific program model that has proven to be effective, by gathering expert opinions, or by conducting qualitative research through site visits and interviews. They can then develop and test a rating scale. Experts can then use the scale to measure fidelity by reviewing documentation and records, conducting site observations or interviews, or watching videotapes of interventions. Program staff and participants can also provide ratings by completing surveys or interviews (Mowbray et al., 2003, pp. 323, 327–328).

Choices need to be made about whether to use easily accessible, observable, and measurable indicators which may skirt vital issues, or more subtle and harder-to-access indicators that may better reflect adaptation in a dynamic environment. When faced with this tension, Patton (2008, p. 318) asks users to evaluate which approach is more appropriate: adaptation to local conditions or adherence to an implementation blueprint.

Kubiak et al. (2019) evaluated a law enforcement training program that provided police officers with techniques that were developmentally appropriate for youth with mental health issues. The evaluators examined program implementation in two counties using training observations, officer interviews, and pretests and posttests. They found that there was positive change in both the officers' knowledge and attitudes about these youth, and in their reported behaviors toward them. The implementation evaluation was able to highlight the feasibility, fidelity, and acceptability of the program.

PERFORMANCE MANAGEMENT

Performance Management is the umbrella term that describes a systematic process to measure, monitor, and report on an organization's progress toward strategic and program goals. Performance Management "is the practice of actively using performance data to improve the public's health through the strategic use of performance standards and measures, progress reports, and ongoing QI" (National Association of County and City Health Officials, 2018, p. 4). Performance management systems produce measurable improvements in the quality of services and benchmark outputs and outcomes. Evaluators can support organizations by helping them define necessary elements in the performance measurement process.

The key question is as follows:

- Is the program meeting its goals and objectives?

Other more specific management questions might include:

1. How do we know what is working?

2. Is staff working according to agreed-upon standards?

3. What incentives will employees respond to?

4. What gaps are there in performance and what will reduce them?

Because government and nonprofit organizations operate in the glare of public scrutiny in both the traditional media and social media, they continually face demands for accountability and transparency. Since the early 1990s, performance management has been adopted by business leaders worldwide as the solution to this need (McDavid et al., 2013, p. 5; Wholey & Newcomer, 1997, p. 92).

Central agencies in the United States, including the U.S. Federal Office of Management and Budget (OMB) and the General Accounting Office (GAO), use performance management extensively. The GAO performs a range of oversight activities, "a vast majority of which are conducted in response to congressional mandates or requests" (Government Accountability Office, 2018). In 2018, the GAO received requests from 90% of the standing committees of Congress and 43% of their sub-committees.

In Canada, a 2016 Policy on Results requires all federal departments and agencies to provide a five-year rolling departmental evaluation plan and report their results to the Treasury Board Secretariat (TBS) (Government of Canada, 2016).

Healthcare leaders use performance management extensively, typically moving their organizations through an annual iterative management cycle. It provides them with the information needed to achieve the desired results. The cycle includes defining indicators and standards, collecting data, reporting, and improving quality based on results. The Public Health Performance Management System (Figure 5.11, p. 190) integrates these core performance management practices in the following framework (Public Health Foundation, n.d.):

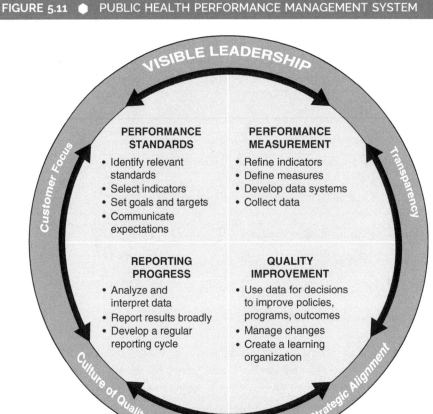

FIGURE 5.11 ● PUBLIC HEALTH PERFORMANCE MANAGEMENT SYSTEM

Source: Public Health Foundation. (n.d.). About the performance management system framework. http://www.phf.org/focusareas/performancemanagement/toolkit/Pages/PM_Toolkit_About_the_Performance_Management_Framework.aspx

The terminology associated with performance management systems can be unclear and so we clarify here three basic components: performance indicators, performance standards, and performance measurement.

Performance Indicators

Performance indicators or key performance indicators (KPIs) are the critical markers used to gauge progress toward intended goals. Their selection is an essential evaluation activity because they focus attention on what matters the most in judging program improvement. Governments and politicians set goals and report on progress in the interest of public accountability. That means that the performance indicators need to be credible, relevant, valid, transparent, and meaningful (Patton, 2008, p. 258).

Choosing what to measure involves identifying several broad dimensions of important performance and then sub-dividing them into the specific indicators that capture essential characteristics of that dimension. While there is a wealth of possible choices, an implementation evaluation cannot explore every avenue. Therefore, the actual indicators selected must be only those considered essential to decision making. The Washington State Department of Health (2009) developed a health indicators workbook that illustrated their indicators. They defined public health indicators as a "snapshot of population health status and health determinants and public health system performance" (Slide 2). Indicators are important because local or state health departments can use them to compare themselves to other geographic areas and can compare themselves to their own performance over time (i.e., trend analysis). Washington State identified 32 indicators grouped into five categories. Examples include childhood unintentional injury hospitalization, first trimester prenatal care, and teen smoking. The data yielded from these observations allow the evaluator to demonstrate outcomes from program interventions in those areas and provide an indication of wise use of investment dollars.

Performance Standards

When judging the importance of evaluation findings, critical questions for any evaluator are: "Compared to what? What were we expecting? What is good enough?" For example, an evaluator might encounter a question like this: Did the program serve at least 80% of the individuals meeting the criteria? From where does the 80% come? Is it a more appropriate aim than 70% or 90%? What is the rationale for its selection?

Many programs have established professional standards, particularly in health and medicine, where leaders explicitly state practice guidelines and managed care standards. However, we often find evaluation criteria in the program goals and objectives or the requirements of funders and sponsors. Sometimes these statements lack specificity (e.g., empower women to take control of their lives), and evaluators and stakeholders must translate them into acceptable, observable, and concrete performance standards (Rossi et al., 2019, p. 15).

One way to think about performance measures is to understand the four dimensions: effect, effort, quantity, and quality. These are elements that can be used in how you write measures. Take the 2 × 2 (quadrant) in Figure 5.12, p. 192. The four quadrants derive from the intersections of quantity and quality with effort and effect (Clear Impact, n.d.). What is clear in the table is the distinction between what the program team did (effort) and what outcomes occurred (effect). Additionally, another distinction is the number of deliverables (quantity) and how well the team delivered those outcomes (quality).

Rossi et al. (2019) suggest that staff can find performance benchmarks in professional standards, expert opinion, or the needs or wants of the selected community. Staff must have thoughtful conversations to determine satisfactory performance levels, such as expected numbers, percentages, rates, or ratios.

FIGURE 5.12 ● QUADRANT TABLE OF PERFORMANCE MEASURES BY EFFECT, EFFORT, QUANTITY, AND QUALITY

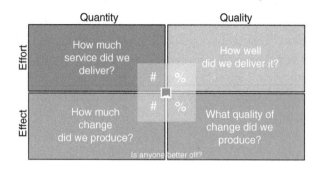

Source: Clear Impact. (2016). Example performance measures you can use for your program or service: Designing effective performance measures. *Clear Impact.* https://clearimpact.com/results-based-accountability/example-performance-measures-can-use-program-service/# www.clearimpact.com. Used with permission.

Performance Measurement

Performance measurement is the actual process of measuring performance using the agreed-upon indicators and standards as part of the performance management system to produce information about the performance story. Organizations use many approaches to performance measurement, such as the balanced scorecard and the KPI. The balanced scorecard was created in 1987 by Art Schneiderman and was updated a few years later by Kaplan and Norton. It consists of both financial and nonfinancial measures, hence the term "balanced." The typical scorecard is a four-cell matrix of the dimensions to be measured, including financial measures, customer measures, internal business processes, and learning and growth (Kaplan & Norton, 1996). Each dimension is described in terms of objectives, measures, targets, and initiatives. See Figure 5.13, p. 193 and the description of the four dimensions that follows.

- Financial measures reflect corporations' vital concern with their budget and bottom line.

- Customer measures highlight an organization's need to understand its customers, the reasons for their loyalty, and which products and services align best with their needs and values.

- Internal business processes relate to the organization's purpose, mission, and services provided and focus on efficiency and customer satisfaction.

- Learning and growth is a dimension that measures both employee and leadership capacity to improve and inspire others. A culture of personal and professional improvement is desired.

Scorecards are about transformation and change in the organization, not just about checking off tasks completed. Therefore, it is essential for staff to understand the causal

FIGURE 5.13 ⬡ A BALANCED SCORECARD

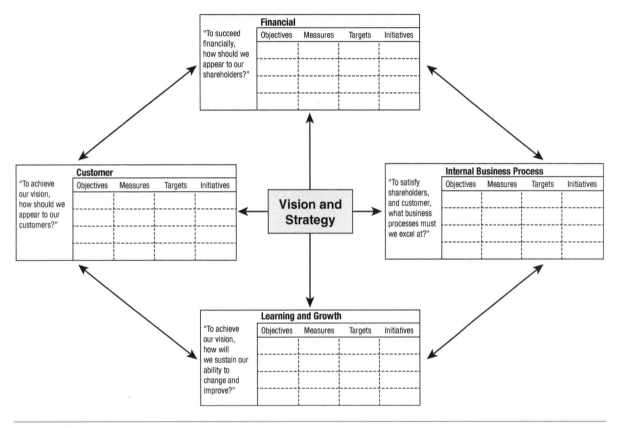

Translating Vision and Strategy: Four Perspectives

Source: Kaplan, R. S., & Norton, D. P. (2007, September–October). Using the balanced scorecard as a strategic management system. *Harvard Business Review, 74*(1), 75–85.

links between their strategies and expected outcomes, similar to creating a program theory (see Chapter 3).

As Arthur Omolo, Chief Financial Officer of the Kenya Red Cross, commented, "The balanced scorecard has changed the conversation on strategy and increased the focus on consistent monitoring of the strategy…. [It] guides our day to day decisions and activities" (p. 1). See additional resources and readings for an interesting case study about the Kenya Red Cross Society and how they developed a balanced scorecard for strategic planning and management.

Monitoring and Evaluation (M & E)

Curry (2018) believes that **Monitoring and Evaluation** (M & E) "represent two elements of the enterprise of assessing the merit or worth of an organization or program, encompassing assessment of both performance and impact for a broad range of different audiences and purposes" (p. 147). The World Bank (2007) defines monitoring as a continuing function that aims primarily to provide…an ongoing intervention with early indications of progress, or lack thereof, in the achievement of results (p. 1).

It defines evaluation as, "the systematic and objective assessment of an on-going or completed project, program, or policy, and its design, implementation and results." Perhaps the best way to compare and contrast M & E is to present a case study. The Highlife Project (Office on Drugs and Crime, 2006, pp. 8–9) was designed to engage young people in projects and activities primarily for substance misuse prevention. In this example, monitoring activities occurred as follows:

- A team meeting after each class to discuss what was successful and how they needed to adapt

- Designating one team member to observe the classes and report back what they witnessed

- Completing a short form after each class to describe how many children were involved in the activities, what activities were held, and documenting any unplanned events that occurred

- Holding monthly team meetings with a discussion of the implementation. Managers reviewed these "minutes."

In contrast, evaluation activities occurred in the following ways:

- Administering a questionnaire to the youth that explores their satisfaction with the activities, any improvements that could be made in the classes, and issues related to drugs

- Interviewing the towns people to determine what effect the classes had on the community

- Holding a leader and staff meeting at the end of each activity period and comparing what happened with their goals and objectives.

Monitoring is often referred to as process evaluation because its nature is to collect data during the implementation of the program. Evaluation in an M & E context is sometimes referred to as impact evaluation because its nature is to understand what results occurred because of the program (Frankel & Gage, 2016).

Supplies distributed, the quality of a service, how well the service reached the intended audience, and a gain in knowledge or attitude are all examples of how we could monitor. Monitoring each of these examples would require us to tally the number completed. Evaluation is concerned about whether the participants were impacted by the program on some indicator, such as pregnancy, disease, death, reduce substance misuse. Participants are measured before the program begins and measured at the end and statistical results indicate if there was a change in the indicator measure.

Patton (2008) states that "the phrase M & E makes the marriage of monitoring and evaluation explicit" (p. 129). A good analogy, in Figure 5.14, would be a trip you are going to take in your car. Monitoring would include all those activities needed as the trip begins and gets under way (e.g., fill up with gas, pack needed items, take the most efficient route). Evaluation, in an M & E context, refers to the outcomes you achieved as part of that trip (e.g., arrival at final destination).

FIGURE 5.14 ● AN ANALOGY FOR M & E

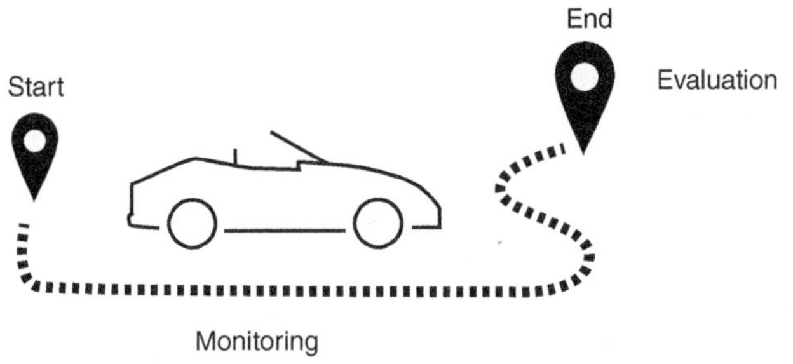

Monitoring data collection methods might include field monitoring, social audits, grievance and complaints reviews, financial reviews, and case studies. Typical monitoring questions might include:

- Did all the children receive 80% of the lessons?

- What level of quality did the participants receive the intervention?

- Did the parents return the informed consent for participation in the intervention?

- What is the attrition rate of participants enrolled in the study?

- What is the time to completion for delivery of the immunizations?

- What reactions do stakeholders have to the intervention delivery and early findings?

- Were the training materials received and read by all the participants?

- How were funds used compared to the intended budget allocations?

Evaluation studies would use comparison/control groups, large sample sizes, and a mixture of quantitative and qualitative methods. Types of evaluation work would include infrastructure studies using economists and engineers to assess the effectiveness and economic impact of infrastructure developed or thematic evaluations on specific issues of interest such as gender, micro-finance, and corruption. Typical evaluations questions would be much more extensive in scope. For example, questions would focus on such impacts as:

- Have our programs reduced poverty? Have they reached the poor?

- Are projects cost effective compared to other mechanisms?

- Do they promote improvement in local governance?

- Has transparency, participation, and inclusion increased, especially of women and vulnerable groups?

- Do they improve social relations and cohesion?

- Do they reduce incidents of conflict?

At the Girls not Brides Campaign, their immediate goal is to end child marriage. Child marriage is defined as "any formal marriage or informal union where one or both parties are under 18 years of age" (Girls not Brides, 2017, p. 5). The Campaign considers three questions important to any M & E project:

1. What do I want to measure?

2. How will I measure it?

3. How will I communicate my findings and to whom?

Here are a few indicators used by the Girls not Brides Campaign (p. 57). Can you identify the element in the indicator that makes it a monitoring or an evaluation indicator? Answers are at the end of the chapter.

1. Girls have an increased knowledge about the negative effects of child marriage and knowledge and skills to claim their sexual and reproductive health and rights (SRHR).

2. Number of teachers and health workers completing child marriage and SRHR teacher training.

3. A reduction in 20% in the occurrence of child marriage in the project area by the end of the project period.

4. Number of by-laws prohibiting child marriage developed in the project area by the end of the project period.

5. Number of girls delaying marriage until after the age of 18 in the project area by end of the project period.

Stakeholders and context are an important part of M & E success. Singh (2012) describes typical M & E projects for community-driven development (CDD) programs supported by the World Bank. Characteristics include a turnover of resources and decision making power to the poor communities. They receive funds, decide on their use, plan and execute the chosen local projects, and monitor services that result. The objective is to improve "not just incomes but also people's empowerment, the lack of which is a form of poverty as well" (World Bank, 2009). M & E serves both the information needs of managers, who need ongoing information about program delivery, and the needs of external stakeholders, particularly donors and funding agencies, whose interest in the accountability of resource use is vital.

However, as evaluation thinker Burt Perrin (2002) warns us, closed-ended accountability evaluations can be misleading if they focus only on predetermined results without providing explanatory information about the changing program context, environment, and activities. We discuss context and its importance in Chapter 12. Programs should adopt a learning approach and be accountable for demonstrating outcomes. In this way, staff can reflect on findings and then make changes to help programs meet their needs and improve social, economic, and environmental conditions.

Now it's time to present our expert, well-known theorist Dr. Michael Quinn Patton.

Dr. Michael Quinn Patton

Michael Quinn Patton, PhD, is an independent consultant, past president of the American Evaluation Association (AEA), and former faculty member at the University of Minnesota. He is a well-known author, trainer, and workshop presenter and has worked with organizations and programs throughout the world. Among his books are *Utilization-Focused Evaluation* (fourth edition), *Qualitative Research and Evaluation Methods* (fourth edition), *Developmental Evaluation*, and *Principles-Focused Evaluation*. Notable awards include the Alva and Gunnar Myrdal Evaluation Practice Award and the Paul F. Lazarsfeld Evaluation Theory Award, both from AEA.

1. *Developmental Evaluation (DE) has become very popular in recent years. It seems to have expanded beyond your initial concept of using it for social innovation – or has it? Do you think evaluators and program managers see themselves as social innovators? What are your thoughts on the prevalence of DE today?*

Developmental Evaluation has developed to include ongoing adaptation, which is an incremental form of innovation but still innovation. It is also being applied to systems transformation on a global scale. What has emerged most unexpectedly is principles-focused DE. Evaluators and program managers who see themselves as principles-driven (rather than procedures-based) embrace ongoing development and adaptation and understand these processes as innovative in contrast to maintaining the status quo or fidelity implementation (ensuring that prescriptive practices are followed exactly).

I think DE's prevalence flows from the realization that evaluation takes place in complex dynamic systems and an evaluation approach based on complexity theory, which DE is, was welcomed for alignment and appropriateness. I also hear from DEers that it's more fun, creative, engaging, and useful than traditional fixed-design approaches.

2. *Throughout your career, you have continually explored and developed new ways of thinking about evaluation, and we have all benefited from your journey. Any tips about what might be next on your agenda?*

My new book is *Blue Marble Evaluation* (Patton, 2020). *Blue Marble* refers to the iconic image of the Earth from space without borders or boundaries, a whole Earth perspective. We humans are using our planet's resources, and polluting and warming it, in ways that are unsustainable. Many people, organizations, and networks are working to ensure the future is more sustainable and equitable. Blue Marble evaluators enter the fray by helping design such efforts, provide ongoing feedback for adaptation and enhanced impact, and examine the long-term effectiveness of such interventions and initiatives. Incorporating the Blue Marble perspective means looking beyond nation-state boundaries and across sector and issue silos to connect the global and local, connect the human and ecological, and connect evaluative thinking and methods with those trying to bring about global systems transformation.

Evaluation as a transdisciplinary, global profession has much to offer in navigating the risks and opportunities that arise as global change initiatives and interventions are designed and undertaken to ensure a more sustainable and equitable future. It is essential for planners, implementers, and evaluators at the beginning of their work together to routinely analyze the sustainability and equity issues presented by the formulation of the intervention and the implications for evaluation. Blue Marble evaluation premises and principles provide a framework for that initial review, ongoing development and adaptation, and long-term evaluation of systems transformation contributions and impacts.

3. *What advice can you offer those of our readers who are just beginning to explore the field of evaluation?*

Evaluation offers a way to contribute to a better world, as Blue Marble Evaluation makes clear. You don't have to hide or abandon your values and passions to be an evaluator. Instead, you acknowledge and channel your values and passions through rigorous evaluative thinking and engagement.

Key Terms

Accreditation 173

Coverage 171

Descriptive evaluation 180

Performance Management 188

Developmental evaluation (DE) 168

Empowerment evaluation (EE) 165

Formative evaluation 159

Mid-cycle program evaluation 158

Monitoring and evaluation 193

Participatory evaluation 161

Performance measurement 192

Process evaluation 170

Summative evaluation 159

Utilization-focused evaluation (U-FE) 162

The Main Ideas

1. Four types of implementation evaluation are formative, process, descriptive, and performance management.

2. Formative Evaluation types are Participatory Evaluation, Utilization-Focused Evaluation, Empowerment Evaluation, and Developmental Evaluation.

3. Participatory Evaluation includes the goal to involve stakeholders as much as possible encouraging them to make decisions about evaluation design through to communicating with stakeholders about what happened.

4. Utilization-Focused Evaluation involves stakeholder's input about program improvement and focuses on the user, whereas Empowerment Evaluation involves stakeholders developing the evaluation process.

5. When the goal is social innovation, Developmental Evaluation helps with real-time learning and working with complexity.

6. Process Evaluation types are coverage, quality improvement, accreditation, and satisfaction.

7. Coverage is whether the program reaches the population intended. Quality Improvement (QI) studies help organizations determine where they can improve as a system through better organization of their processes, work habits, and structures. Accreditation validates the meeting of organizational or national standards and the use of satisfaction and feedback loops seeks to improve the two-way communication channels between the community and the evaluator.

8. Descriptive Evaluation types, such as document review, observation, case study, and fidelity, provide details about program function and operation. The evaluator can conduct a document review to understand a program better, observe a program being implemented, write a case study to reflect what is occurring during program implementation, and conduct fidelity measurements to determine if the program is actually being implemented as intended.

9. Performance Management is a global term to include performance indicators, performance standards, performance measurement, and monitoring and evaluation. The key questions for performance management focus on the program meeting its goals and objectives.

Critical Thinking Questions

1. Using concepts you learned about the logic model in Chapter 3, in what part of the logic model is implementation evaluation located? Why?

2. How do quality improvement tools create data by which you can then solve problems? How are they useful in uncovering issues about a problem? Give an example.

3. Describe why Patton developed the Utilization-Focused Evaluation Framework. How is it beneficial for those who remain with the program just evaluated?

4. What is one similarity and one difference between Participatory Evaluation and Developmental Evaluation?

5. What are at least five transformations that people in the community may have if they participate in an Empowerment Evaluation?

Student Challenges

1. **PDSA Cycle for your Life**. Identify a challenge in your life. Review the Quality Improvement section. Evaluation Method. Work through the PDSA Cycle with this problem. What is something new that you realized about this problem?

2. **Your Life in a Fishbone**. American Society for Quality. (2021). *Learn about quality: Quality topics A to Z.* https://asq.org/quality-resources/ learn-about-quality. Explore the range of terms related to quality improvement in a variety of fields. For a Fishbone template in Excel, click on "Fishbone (Ishikawa) diagram template." Use the Girls not Brides Report provided in Additional Readings and Resources and make a fishbone diagram of the influential factors that lead girls and boys to marry early.

Additional Readings and Resources

1. Girls not Brides. (2017). *Design for success! A guide to developing end child marriage projects and how to fundraise for them*. The Global Partnership to End Child Marriage. https://www.girlsnotbrides.org/documents/850/Girls-Not-Brides-Design-for-Success-Toolkit_Final-ENG-high-res.pdf

   This toolkit identifies the steps to planning and executing an M & E effort. The content is based on the goal of reducing child brides around the world. Content includes project design and fundraising.

2. Omolo, A. (2010). *Our experience with the balanced scorecard strategy development process*. Kenya Red Cross.

   An interesting case study by the Kenya Red Cross Society describes how they developed a balanced scorecard for strategic planning and management. Omolo describes the case at www.balancedscorecard.org/Portals/0/PDF/KenyaRedCrossBSC.pdf; and presents the scorecard at: www.balancedscorecard.org/Portals/0/PDF/KenyaRed%20CrossScorecard Poster.pdf

3. Patton, M. Q. (2012, May 4). Planning and evaluating for social change: An evening at SFU with Michael Quinn Patton, Part One [Video]. YouTube. https://www.youtube.com/watch?v=b7n64JEjUUk

   Internationally known Dr. Michael Quinn Patton discusses social change and innovation in a lecture in Canada.

4. Patton, M. Q. (2013). *Utilization-focused evaluation (U-FE) checklist*. Western Michigan University. https://wmich.edu/sites/default/files/attachments/u350/2014/UFE_checklist_2013.pdf

   This resource is a checklist that identifies the 17 steps for U-FE. The premise of U-FE is that stakeholders should utilize evaluations.

5. Public Health Accreditation Board. https://phaboard.org/

   To see standards and measures based on the 10 essential services, click on "Accreditation Process" and "Standards and Measures for Initial Accreditation." The over 250 page document outlines all the specific standards and measures local county health departments must comply with to receive accreditation.

6. Todd, A. W., Newton, J. S., Horner, R. H. Algozzine, K., & Aligozzine, B. (2014). *TIPS II training manual: TIPS fidelity checklist*. https://www.pbis.org/resource/tips-fidelity-checklist
   The TIPS-FC (Team Initiated Problem Solving Fidelity Checklist) allows an evaluator to monitor the progress of the TIPS intervention so that the foundations of the intervention are met. The fidelity checklist has the item to be scored, data sources, scoring criterion, and checklist for marking completion of item.

Answers

1. Monitoring
2. Monitoring
3. Evaluation
4. Monitoring
5. Evaluation

END-OF-CYCLE PROGRAM EVALUATION

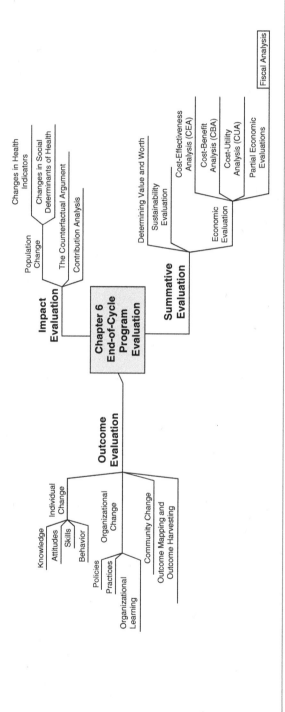

TRAFFIC JAM AT 29,000 FEET

Nepal is known as home to Mt. Everest, the most prominent mountain on Earth's surface. In 1953, Sir Edmund Hillary was the first to scale the 29,000-foot peak. Climbers still view Mt. Everest as the ultimate challenge. Every year, about 380 permits are issued. It costs at least $45,000 for the permits, fees, and a Sherpa guide. Until recently, there were no eligibility or fitness requirements.

Source: istockphoto.com/DanielPrudek

Due to the popularity of the climb, waiting in line has become the new norm as climbers and their support teams mount and descend. It is a race against the clock, and at the Death Zone, above 26,000 feet, the real challenge begins. At this altitude, the human body slowly starts to die. Lack of oxygen, fatigue, and risk of falling can make a climber sluggish and disoriented. If another climber falls ill or is in distress, people just pass them and continue because stopping to help could cause their own deaths. Some have suggested that officials should establish "climbing ethics."

More than 300 people have perished on this climb and over 200 bodies remain on the mountain. As Ithal (2019) explains:

> If someone dies on Everest, it's almost impossible to retrieve their body, especially in the Death Zone. Due to unbearable weather conditions, severe lack of oxygen, pressure on dead weight, and the fact that many bodies on Mount Everest are completely frozen onto the mountain face, most corpses are left exactly as they fall. Attempts are sometimes made to retrieve the body of a loved one, but those expeditions can cost upward of $25,000 and are extremely dangerous for the retrieval team. Overall, standard protocol is to simply let these figures, frozen in the final moments of death, become a permanent addition to the rocky terrain. For the past two decades, climbers have used the body of "Green Boots" [because he died wearing green boots] to gauge how far they had left to go on their own race to the summit. (para. 4)

The increased traffic and deaths have resulted in recent changes to the Nepal Department of Tourism's Mountaineering Expedition Regulation. They include:

- Climbers must have summited a 7,000-meter peak before attempting Everest.

- No one can climb solo.

- No climber over the age of 75 will be accepted.

- No individual who is blind or is a double amputee will be accepted.

New regulations hopefully will mitigate these unfortunate outcomes by reducing injury and death on the mountain. Therefore, it will be very important to evaluate the policy and rule changes and track the outcomes on Mt. Everest.

INTRODUCTION

In Chapters 4 and 5, we discussed Pre- and Early and Mid-Cycle Program Evaluation. In Chapter 6, we complete our program chronology by looking at the end of the program cycle when decision makers determine if the program should continue, be modified, or close. Types of evaluations that are prevalent during this phase are outcome, impact, and summative evaluations. For example, outcome evaluation aims to understand the individual and organizational changes that occur. Impact evaluation looks at population changes, and the extent to which the program has contributed to the changes that occurred. The outcomes harvesting method is also reviewed. Summative evaluation draws conclusions about whether the program should continue to provide services, modify them, or close. It also looks at sustainability and economic considerations.

In this chapter, we complete our chronological trip through the program life cycle. We focus on how evaluators and their clients determine if the program should be continued or modified. It is at this point that a program's effectiveness is determined. Ways to measure change become a central concern and many important decisions rest on the evaluation findings. Using our chronological model, End-of-Cycle activities would occur between about eight o'clock and midnight. See Figure 6.1.

FIGURE 6.1 ◆ END-OF-CYCLE PROGRAM EVALUATION CLOCK

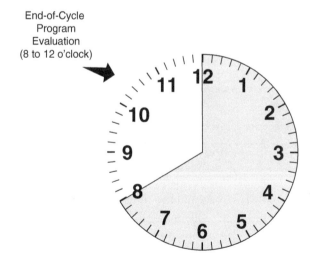

End-of-Cycle
Program
Evaluation
(8 to 12 o'clock)

Source: istockphoto.com/Tuncaycetin

Related evaluation topics, key questions, evaluation types, and evaluation measures are outlined in Table 6.1, p. 207. These topics are explored in this chapter. While the terms often overlap, we have selected three broad types of evaluation to discuss: outcome evaluation, impact evaluation, and summative evaluation.

TABLE 6.1 ● END-OF-CYCLE PROGRAM EVALUATION: EVALUATION TYPES, EVALUATION METHODS AND MEASURES, AND KEY QUESTIONS

Evaluation Types	Evaluation Methods and Measures	Key Question
1. Outcome Evaluation	Individual Change: Changes in knowledge, attitudes, skills, and behavior	To what extent have the participants changed their knowledge, attitudes, skills, and/or behavior as a result of the program?
	Organizational Change: Changes in policies, practices, and organizational learning	How has the organization changed as a result of the program?
	Community Change: Changes in employment rates, poverty reduction, etc.	How has the community changed as a result of the program?
	Outcome Mapping and Outcome Harvesting	What changes have occurred in the behavior, relationships, activities, or actions of the people, groups, and organizations with whom a program works directly?
2. Impact Evaluation	Population Change: Changes in Health Indicators Changes in Social Determinants of Health	Did the program bring about the intended changes in the intended population?
	The Counterfactual Argument	What would have happened if the program had not been offered at all?
	Contribution Analysis	To what extent did the intervention contribute to outcomes?
5. Summative Evaluation	Determining Value and Worth	Should the program be continued, changed, or terminated?
	Sustainability Evaluation	How can the evaluator help the program to continue to provide services and benefits over time?
	Economic Evaluation	Was the intervention worth the cost?

You will enjoy the resources in this chapter including the Spotlight on Equity, which presents the Power Up! Program, our expert Dr. John Mayne (1943–2020), Key Terms, Main Ideas, Critical Thinking Questions, Student Challenges, and Additional Readings and Resources.

OUTCOME EVALUATION

Rossi et al. (2019) define an outcome as the state of the intended population or social condition that the program is expected to change (p. 320). Unlike outputs, which relate directly to program services received, **outcome evaluation** examines actual accomplishments, like changes experienced by service recipients. While programs often claim impressive outcomes, we must also ask: Did the changes result from the program itself or from some other external influence? How confident can we be that the program contributed to the outcomes we see? Let's look at program outcomes, or changes wrought by the program, at the individual, organization, and community levels.

Individual Change

Knowledge, Attitudes, Skills, and Behavior are a cluster of outcomes often measured in the evaluation of educational and other social programs because of their focus on learning and performance.

The key evaluation question is:

> *Did the participants change their knowledge, attitudes, skills, or behavior due to the program?*

See Figure 6.2 for definitions of these terms.

FIGURE 6.2   ◆   KNOWLEDGE, ATTITUDES, BEHAVIOR, AND SKILLS

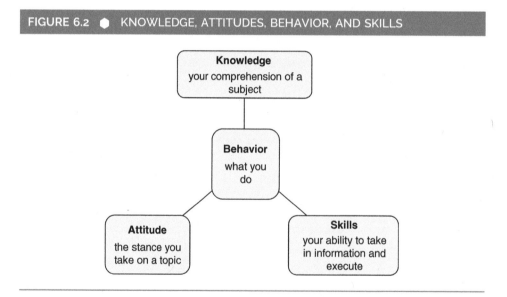

Evaluators must write a clear statement of the targeted change, whether in circumstances, status, level of functioning, behavior, attitude, knowledge, or skills. This detail helps guide the evaluation of outcomes. Patton (2008, pp. 244–245) provides some practical examples of outcomes in Table 6.2, p. 209.

Selecting the best measures for assessing outcomes is critical to the quality of the evaluation. However, most important program outcomes tend to be multidimensional and reflect complexity in both the program's context and participants' behaviors.

TABLE 6.2 ● EXAMPLES OF PROGRAM PARTICIPANT OUTCOMES

Type of Change	Illustration
Change in circumstances	Children safely reunited with their families of origin from foster care
Change in status	Unemployed to employed
Change in behavior	Truants will regularly attend school
Change in functioning	Increased self-care Getting to work on time
Change in attitude	Greater self-respect
Change in knowledge	Understand the needs and capabilities of children at different ages
Change in skills	Increased reading level Able to parent appropriately
Maintenance	Continue to live safely at home (e.g., the elderly)
Prevention	Teenagers will not use drugs

Source: Patton, M. Q. (2008). *Utilization-focused evaluation*. SAGE Publications.

For example, the Supporting Healthy Marriage Project, funded by the U.S. Department of Health and Human Services and Administration for Children and Families (Lundquist et al., 2014) examined individual outcomes. In 2001, the project began to help couples planning marriage to use resources that improved their attitudes, knowledge, and skills about parenting and marriage (U.S. Department of Health and Human Services, 2014a). The evaluation sought to discover such program outcomes as:

- Marital stability and relationship quality
- Attitudes and expectations regarding the marriage
- Parenting attitudes and behaviors
- Adult and child well-being
- Child development (e.g., cognitive, social, emotional, health)
- Economic outcomes for families.

Note in the list the complex, intended behavior change in relationships between the parents and the children, the parents' attitudes toward the role of parenting, the wellness of the parents and child, and finally, changes in managing finances and financial status. There are many factors that influence parenting behaviors, child reactions, and financial status.

Rossi et al. (2019, p. 124) suggest the evaluator think comprehensively about outcomes. Consultation with stakeholders can ensure the evaluation continues to reflect their initial hopes and desires for the program. Revisiting the program theory and logic model is warranted because the environment could have changed and there may be unanticipated outcomes that arise as well. It is quite likely that no one single outcome will reflect the fundamental changes to overall program results.

Diversifying measurement activities also ensures a broader and less biased representation of program effects and makes for a more robust evaluation study. Rossi et al. (2019) suggest selecting from "observations, records, responses to interviews and questionnaires, standardized tests, physical measurement, and the like."

While standardized tools may sometimes be appropriate, the evaluator often finds that no preexisting questionnaire covers the required topics. In addition, there is usually limited time available for the evaluator to develop the measures, so frequently, the decision is to use informal measures. Issues of reliability, validity, and sensitivity may result. To counteract possible threats to rigor, the evaluator often uses multiple strategies. For example, they may use mixed methods involving both quantitative and qualitative tools (see Chapter 9), comparing results across data types (called triangulation), and, further, consult with stakeholders to verify results, an essential strategy for most evaluation studies.

Organizational Change

When working with organizations, the evaluator often needs to capture changes in organizational policies and practices as well as in organizational learning to understand organizational growth.

The key evaluation question is:

How did the organization change as a result of the program?

However, outcomes can be wide-reaching. If discussions about outcomes are very narrow (e.g., related only to funding issues), all the collateral, supportive, and linking work that may have occurred can be missed (Mensing, 2017). In an environment where resources tend to be shrinking anyway, this omission of essential outcomes can have a significant impact on future decisions. Organizations should look across all aspects of operations.

Some examples of organizational outcomes and their definitions are listed in Table 6.3.

TABLE 6.3 ◆ EXAMPLES OF ORGANIZATIONAL OUTCOMES	
Term	**Definition**
1. Service outcomes	• Provide evidence about the interactions of clients and services within the parameters of funding or reimbursement requirements.
2. Staff-client relationships	• Produce positive changes in clients and affected by job performance, staff training, support, selection, and turnover.
3. Organizational learning outcomes	• Create and transfer knowledge gained from experience over time.

Table 6.3 *(Continued)*

Term	Definition
4. Social capital outcomes	• Build reciprocity and trustworthiness based on connections among individuals, small groups, and networks.
5. Organizational climate outcomes	• Focus on work groups, departments, and the overall organizational level that can often predict productivity and profitability (West & Luybovnikova, 2015).
6. Organizational leadership outcomes	• Explore the networks of power, authority, and politics (Hardy, 2015).
7. Inter-organizational outcomes	• Enhance relationships, interdependencies, and collaboration through mutual learning, innovation, enhanced reputation, and cost savings (Ebers, 2015).

Undoubtedly the veterans in the United States have earned and deserve the best healthcare available. They fight for the cherished rights of "Life, Liberty, and the Pursuit of Happiness." In 2021, there are about 19 million U.S. veterans (Schaeffer, 2021). Out of 10 government agencies, the Veterans Affairs (VA) was perceived favorably by 65% of the public, whereas the U.S. Postal Service received a 91% favorable rating (Pew Research Center, 2021). In 2015, the VA launched a massive transformation to "enhance the entire veterans' experience with the agency" (Miller, 2015, para. 9). The transformation centers on 12 Breakthrough Priorities. The stimulus to gain ground on these priorities is veteran trust. Less than 50% of veterans said they trust the VA, as reported by the U.S. Department of Veterans Affairs (2016a). The VA set trust targets of 70% and then 90% as part of this transformational effort (Blackburn et al., 2021). Note that of their Breakthrough Priorities, the first eight priorities outlined below focus on Veterans and the last four focus on internal work processes (U.S. Veterans Administration, 2016b, p. 5).

1. Improve the Veteran Experience
2. Increase Access to Healthcare
3. Improve Community Care
4. Deliver a Unified Veteran Experience
5. Modernize Contact Centers
6. Improve the Compensation and Pension Examination
7. Develop a Simplified Appeals Process
8. Improve the Employee Experience
9. Staff Critical Positions
10. Transform the Office of Information and Technology

11. Transform the Supply Chain

12. Continue to Reduce Veteran Homelessness.

The above list is "what" the VA wanted to change. The following provides examples of "how" they have worked and continue to work to make organizational changes and achieve greater efficiency and effectiveness. They also stated that "we design and evaluate all of our plans and programs through the eyes of the Veterans they're meant to serve. It's the Veteran-centric approach" (U.S. Department of Veterans Affairs, 2016, p. 14).

- Eliminate need for a physical signature. Enrollment for VA services can occur by phone or online.

- Use SAIL (Strategic Analysis for Improvement and Learning), an internal measures tool, that measures patient satisfaction, length of stay, coordination of care, safety, mortality, and 26 quality and efficiency measures. SAIL allows the VA to identify system weaknesses on a quarterly basis and to launch a plan to improve quality.

- Design mobile apps as a self-management tool to aid families in times of emotional distress. There are PTSD Coach, CBT-I Coach for insomnia and Mindfulness Coach for meditation practice, Moving Forward for problem-solving skills.

- Designed the Veteran Journey Map that illustrates distinct stages of the Veterans life. This map is aligned with the products of the VA so they can provide timely support along the way.

Community Change

Philanthropic organizations and government agencies would like to know the impact that their grants have on people's lives in impoverished communities in areas such as housing, employment, and health.

The key evaluation question is:

To what extent has the community changed as a result of the program?

Frequently, agencies work together on community change projects. Collaboration is a prerequisite to partnership sustainability. Hogue (1993) distinguished five levels of community linkage, including networking, cooperation or alliance, coordination or partnership, coalition, and collaboration. Frey et al. (2006) commented that assessing collaboration is often difficult because there are few valid and reliable instruments to measure change in the level and pattern of collaboration. They used Hogue's indicators when evaluating a Midwest school district's implementation of a Safe Schools, Healthy Students initiative. The grantor believed that program sustainability once funding ceased was a necessary ingredient of a successful collaboration, and so the evaluators designed a Levels of Collaboration survey to measure the depth of involvement of the agencies (see Table 6.4). In this example, ABC Hospital has measured their linkage with other partners in the community (e.g., coalitions, churches). Networking is the most basic form of linkage between partners and is not collaborative. Collaboration, which is more sophisticated and higher on the scale, indicates partners belong to one system and consult each other often in their work (e.g., the collaboration between the hospital and the health department).

TABLE 6.4 ● LEVELS OF COLLABORATION SCALE

Partner Name: ABC Hospital	Partners				
	Community Coalitions	Churches	Local Public Health Department	Law Enforcement	School District
1. **Networking** • Aware of organization • Loosely defined roles • Little communication • All decisions are made independently		✔			
2. **Cooperation** • Provide information to each other • Somewhat defined roles • Formal communication • All decisions are made independently	✔				✔
3. **Coordination** • Share information and resources • Defined roles • Frequent communication • Some shared decision making					
4. **Coalition** • Share ideas • Share resources • Frequent and prioritized communication • All members have a vote in decision making				✔	
5. **Collaboration** • Members belong to one system • Frequent communication is characterized by mutual trust • Consensus is reached on all decisions			✔		

Source: Adapted from Frey, B. B., Lohmeier, J. H., Lee, S. W., & Tollefson, N. (2006). Measuring collaboration among grant partners. *American Journal of Evaluation, 27*(3), 383–392.

Data from their survey were then plotted on a map to depict visually the complex collaborative relationships. Areas of high and low collaboration then became apparent, as did areas of disagreement. Their partners, including respondents, district administrators, teachers, principals, and grant partners found the visual representation valuable and persuasive.

Many agencies and foundations are beginning to sit down together to develop measurement strategies. For example, organizations dealing with poverty reduction have made some headway. For nearly 20 years, the Tamarack Institute has worked with a number of funders and partners on Vibrant Communities Canada. This initiative supports cities and local leaders in order to develop and implement large-scale change to end poverty using collaborative strategies to engage citizens and institutions.

Working with the Ontario Trillium Foundation, the Tamarack Institute set out to develop community change indicators. Looking at ten different approaches to measuring the change in community poverty levels, they found most common indicators of change in poverty included (Weave et al., 2010, p. 9):

- Income and poverty rate
- Ability to gain employment
- Access affordable housing
- Access to quality education
- Access to affordable childcare.

Now in its third phase, the network includes over 47 communities across Canada and has successfully fostered local collaborations through bringing businesses, community organizations, and government together to create local jobs, deliver innovative social programs, and craft housing and transportation policies that promote inclusion for vulnerable residents (J.W. McConnell Foundation, 2020).

The network has also expanded into the United States. The United Way of Central Iowa is a member of the Vibrant Communities Cities Reducing Poverty network and, since 2015, 36,000 central Iowans have become financially self-sufficient (Lynch et al., 2020). As a recent Tamarack post reported,

> *This is incredibly significant to the community, as it marks the first time in recent memory that Central Iowa has seen a reduction in poverty. The good news reflects well on the hard work of United Way of Central Iowa and their partners, the value of a Collective Impact approach to poverty reduction, and the importance of a robust measurement strategy.* (Vibrant Communities Canada, 2018, para. 1)

Thus, it appears that measuring community change is possible when funders, thinkers, and grassroots organizations come together with a shared vision to develop outcome measures.

Outcome Mapping and Outcome Harvesting

Organizations often struggle to measure and demonstrate lasting change because "longer-term outcomes often occur a long way downstream from program implementation and may not take the form anticipated" (Earl et al., 2001, p. viii). The complexity of the international development process makes it very difficult to assess outcomes and impacts quickly and so some evaluators look instead at outcomes in terms of behavior change. The focus is on contribution to outcomes while recognizing the importance of impact as the ultimate goal toward which programs work (p. 1).

The key question is:

> *What changes are expected to occur, or have occurred, in the behavior, relationships, activities, or actions of the people, groups, and organizations with whom a program works directly?*

Outcome mapping is a prospective activity and is conducted at the planning stage of a program. "Rather than attempting a "rolling-up" of evaluation information from a number of disparate activities, outcome mapping provides a method for a program to set overall intentions and strategies, monitor its contributions to outcomes, and target priority areas for detailed evaluation studies" (Earl et al., 2001, p. 5). It offers a continuous system for thinking holistically and strategically about intended results. Figure 6.3 provides a model of the three stages of outcome mapping.

FIGURE 6.3 ● THE STAGES OF OUTCOME MAPPING

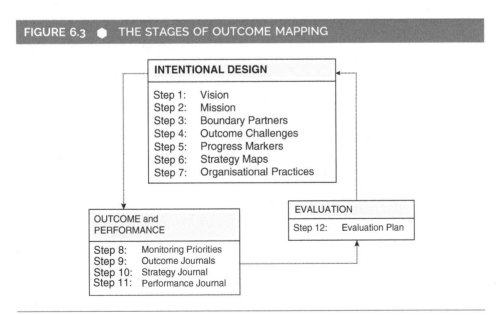

Source: Earl, S., Carden, F., & Smutylo, T. (2001). *Outcome mapping: Building learning and reflection into development programs.* International Development Research Center. https://www.idrc.ca/en/book/outcome-mapping-building-learning-and-reflection-development-programs

Outcome harvesting, on the other hand, is retrospective. It "does not measure progress towards predetermined objectives or outcomes, but rather, collects or "harvests" evidence of what has changed and, then, working backwards, determines whether and how an intervention contributed to these changes" (Wilson-Grau, 2015, para. 1; Wilson-Grau et al., n.d.).

This method is particularly useful in complex situations where cause and effect are not yet fully understood and stakeholders want to know about effectiveness. Outcome harvesting is used for end and midterm evaluations as well as monitoring. One component of outcome harvesting mentioned in Chapter 4 is document review. Existing project documents can help the evaluator identify changes and what aspects of the intervention may have contributed to them. Another essential piece is engaging directly with informants to review the outcomes which have been identified in order to verify them, complete with missing information and add any additional outcomes. Figure 6.4 outlines the six steps in outcome harvesting.

FIGURE 6.4 ● STEPS IN OUTCOME HARVESTING

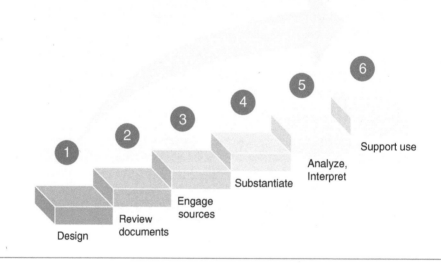

Source: Adapted from Wilson-Grau, R. (2015). Outcome harvesting. BetterEvaluation. https://www.betterevaluation.org/en/plan/approach/outcome_harvesting##OH_what_is_OutcomeHarvesting.

IMPACT EVALUATION

Impact evaluation addresses the following critical question:

Did the program bring about the intended changes in the intended population?

This may be the most valuable type of evaluation in the eyes of stakeholders, funders, decision makers, and policymakers.

The focus of an **impact evaluation** is the cause-effect relationship. Thus, rather than asking a simple question like, "Did A cause B?" evaluators find themselves in much more contingent territory, asking, "To what extent did A contribute to B's outcomes?" knowing what we do about context and personal agency and other still-to-be-determined factors.

For example, in a job training program designed to reduce unemployment, if the program is effective, the likelihood of participants obtaining jobs is increased. However, even in a very successful program, it is not likely that every participant will get a job (Rossi et al., 2019, p. 142). As a result, evaluators often look at the average effect across all participants.

Many other factors that have nothing to do with the actual training program can come into play, such as economic conditions and job availability, prior skills, experience, and personal constraints (e.g., childcare and transportation). However, maybe some participants would have found a job, even without the program.

Another worry is, "How much of the program did they access? Every class or just a few?" This leads us to the dose-response question. Typically, one would expect that attending more classes would lead to a greater likelihood of getting a job, but that may not be true. To push the issue even further, "Which classes were the ones that may have made the difference?"

Maybe, some sub-groups were more successful than others. If we can find out who prospered and who did not, we can glean some beneficial information for program designers. Also, if programmers offer the service at several sites, we need to explore fidelity and variation in program implementation. Finally, we need to see any side effects resulting from participation in the program. That is, "What else happened?" Table 6.5 provides a list of the common questions addressed in impact evaluation.

TABLE 6.5 ● COMMON QUESTIONS ADDRESSED IN IMPACT EVALUATION BY EVALUATION OBJECTIVE

Impact Evaluation Objectives	Questions to be Answered
Average impact	• What is the average difference in the desired outcomes that is attributable to the influence of the program?
Subpopulation average impacts	• What is the average program impact on relevant outcomes for different important subpopulations?
Dosage effects	• Are some program services or higher quality services associated with better outcomes?
Fidelity of implementation	• How closely does program implementation match the program plan for the intended implementation? • How much does the fidelity of program implementation vary across time, sites, or individuals? • Is greater fidelity of implementation associated with more significant program effects?

Source: Rossi, P., Lipsey, M., & Henry, G. (2019). *Evaluation: A systematic approach.* SAGE Publications.

It is easy to see how a simple question can quickly become more complex. As Davidson (2000) suggests, the wise evaluator will determine early in the evaluation what evidence is required to infer causality and then design the evaluation to get that information. However, she warns us to always bear in mind the dangers of preconditioning ourselves to look only for what we expect to find.

Population Change

Program impact can be difficult to measure but one area that has been particularly successful is in population health. On a broad scale, evaluation can measure health change. In 1947, the World Health Organization moved away from a bio-medical model that focused exclusively on biological factors and excluded psychological, social, and environmental factors to a more holistic definition of health as "a state of complete physical, mental, and social well-being and not merely the absence of disease or infirmity" (World Health Organization, 2006, p. 1).

Measuring health variables can occur at the individual level, as, for example, when you have your blood pressure measured, or at the population level, when researchers assess aggregate measures such as rates, averages, and medians. Health indicators and the social determinants of health are explored in the following sections.

Changes in Health Indicators

Health indicators describe specific populations' healthcare needs, measure risk levels, and forecast disease outbreaks. In addition, they can help to explain why some individuals are healthy and others are not. Identifying and monitoring health indicators can improve decision making at the system level and so can be helpful in evaluations to show the results of health interventions thus informing health policies, programs, and services.

In 1979, the U.S. Surgeon General, Julius Richmond, published a report entitled, "Healthy People: The Surgeon General's Report on Health Promotion and Disease Prevention." It focused on reducing preventable death and injury and included national health promotion and disease prevention goals for a 10-year period. These goals continue to be updated each decade. By identifying reliable indicators and developing consistent ways to measure them, the field of epidemiology has taken a significant step forward. In addition, the data make it possible to communicate with both medical professionals and the public about the current state of the nation's health. It is also possible to disaggregate data to the state and local levels to identify areas needing targeted efforts for improvement.

In the Healthy People 2020 (U.S. Department of Health and Human Services, 2014b) report, which includes science-based 10-year national objectives for improving the health of all Americans, there are more than 1,200 objectives, 26 leading health indicators (LHIs), and 12 key topics. A progress report in March 2014, stated that 14 of the 26 indicators (53.9%) had either shown improvement (38.5%) or met (15.4%) their target. From looking at the graph in Figure 6.5, p. 219, for example, you can see how useful this information can be for policymakers, decision makers, and program managers. Officials noted fewer adults smoked, fewer children were exposed to second-hand smoke, more adults met physical activity targets, and fewer adolescents used alcohol or illicit drugs.

From broad statements such as these, it is possible to drill down to specific indicators and targets. For example, one objective was to reduce the suicide rate in all populations per 100,000. From the chart in Figure 6.6, p. 219, you can see the suicide rate since

FIGURE 6.5 ◆ STATUS OF THE 26 HP2020 LEADING HEALTH INDICATORS MARCH 2014

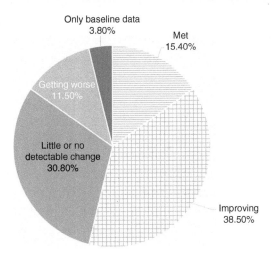

Source: U.S. Department of Health and Human Services. (2014). *Healthy people 2020: Leading health indicators progress update.* Office of Disease Prevention and Health Promotion. https://www.healthypeople.gov/2020/leading-health-indicators/Healthy-People-2020-Leading-Health-Indicators%3A-Progress-Update

FIGURE 6.6 ◆ SUICIDE RATE TREND LINE WITH TARGET BY 2020

Suicide (age adjusted, per 100,000 population)
By Sex

2020 Baseline (year): 11.3 (2007)   --- 2020 Target: 10.2   **Desired Direction:** ↓ Decrease desired

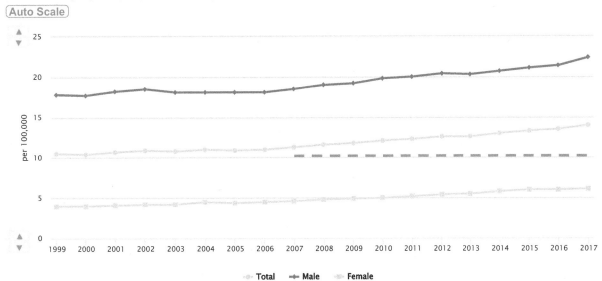

Source: Centers for Disease Control and Prevention. (2021). *Suicide (age adjusted, per 100,000) by total.* National Center for Health Statistics and U.S. Census Bureau, National Vital Statistics System-Mortality. https://www.healthypeople.gov/2020/data/Chart/4804?category=2&by=Sex&fips=-1

1999–2017 is more for males than females in any year. The objective is to reduce the overall suicide rate per 100,000 to 10.2 in 2020 (dashed line). It was 10.5 per 100,000 in 1999 and continued an upward trend to 14 per 100,000 (dotted line) in 2017. The Healthy People 2020 website also provides interventions for each of these objectives and targets. For depression, evaluated interventions, such as music therapy, screening in children ages 11 years and younger, and interventions for primary prevention of suicide in college settings are provided with the data.

Changes in Social Determinants of Health

Reaching beyond the traditional boundaries of healthcare and public health are broader factors that influence people's health. For example, the health outcomes for those who have low income and also live in impoverished regions tend to be more negative than those who are well-off and live in affluent areas. The complex interacting forces that cause these disparities are known as the Social Determinants of Health (SDH or SDOH). Together they influence the health of populations and include the factors shown in Figure 6.7.

FIGURE 6.7 ● SOCIAL DETERMINANTS OF HEALTH

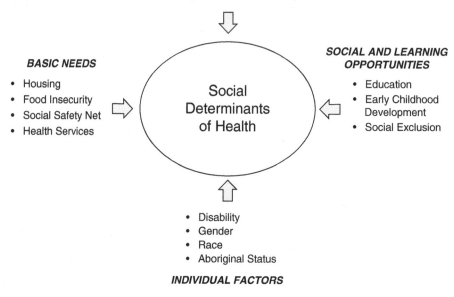

Source: Adapted from Mikkonen, J., & Raphael, D. (2010). *Social determinants of health: The Canadian facts.* York University School of Health Policy and Management.

As the Kaufman Family Foundation illustrates (Figure 6.8), these factors can be grouped into different domains.

FIGURE 6.8 ● W. K. KAUFMAN'S SOCIAL DETERMINANTS OF HEALTH

Social Determinants of Health

Economic Stability	Neighborhood and Physical Environment	Education	Food	Community and Social Context	Healthcare System
Employment	Housing	Literacy	Hunger	Social integration	Health coverage
Income	Transportation	Language	Access to healthy options	Support systems	Provider availability
Expenses	Safety	Early childhood education		Community engagement	Provider linguistic and cultural competency
Debt	Parks	Vocational training		Discrimination	
Medical bills	Playgrounds	Higher education		Stress	Quality of care
Support	Walkability				
	Zip code / geography				

Health Outcomes
Mortality, Morbidity, Life Expectancy, Healthcare Expenditures, Health Status, Functional Limitations

Source: Artiga, S., & Hinton, E. (2018, May 10). *Beyond health care: The role of social determinants in promoting health and health equity.* KFF. https://www.kff.org/racial-equity-and-health-policy/issue-brief/beyond-health-care-the-role-of-social-determinants-in-promoting-health-and-health-equity/

Addressing the social determinants of health not only reduces long-standing disparities in health and healthcare but in addition, relate to social, economic, and environmental conditions. For example, the County Health Rankings is based on a community health model that emphasized the many factors that influence how long and how well we live. The rankings use more than 30 measures to help communities understand how healthy their residents are. Figure 6.9, p. 222 presents this model which can be explored interactively online (University of Wisconsin Population Health Institute, 2022).

Using the social determinants, state Medicaid agencies and select providers are exploring ways to collect and use patient information to better direct population-level strategies. National organizations are also beginning to standardize data collection and measurement protocols using these SDOH indicators.

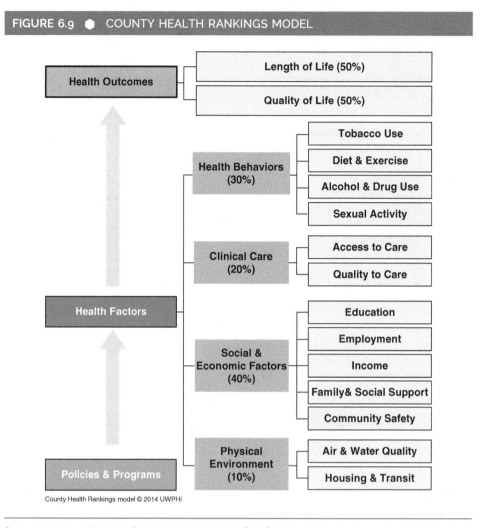

FIGURE 6.9 ● COUNTY HEALTH RANKINGS MODEL

County Health Rankings model © 2014 UWPHI

Source: University of Wisconsin Population Health Institute. (2021). *County health rankings model.* https://www.coun-tyhealthrankings.org/explore-health-rankings/measures-data-sources/county-health-rankings-model

Disaster mitigation is an area that has adopted some of these indicators, operational-izing them in the Social Vulnerability Index (SVI) developed by the Agency for Toxic Substances and Disease Registry of the Centers for Disease Control and Pre-vention. Social vulnerability is the "potential negative effects on communities caused by external stresses on human health. Such stresses include natural or human-caused disasters, or disease outbreaks. Reducing social vulnerability can decrease both human suffering and economic loss" (Agency for Toxic Substances and Disease Registry, 2015, para. 1).

People experiencing a disaster may not respond to it in the same way. Some are more prepared and have more resources than others. The Index uses 15 U.S. census variables to help community leaders identify geographic areas warranting extra attention in disaster preparation or recovery (Figure 6.10, p. 223).

| FIGURE 6.10 ● OVERALL VULNERABILITY SCORE AND DISASTER |

Overall Vulnerability	Socioeconomic Status	Below Poverty
		Unemployed
		Income
		No High School Diploma
	Household Composition & Disability	Aged 65 or Older
		Aged 17 or Younger
		Older than Age 5 with a Disability
		Single-Parent Households
	Minority Status & Language	Minority
		Speak English "Less than Well"
	Housing & Transportation	Multi-Unit Structures
		Mobile Homes
		Crowding
		No Vehicle
		Group Quarters

Source: Agency for Toxic Substances and Disease Registry. (2015). *CDC/ATSDR Social vulnerability index.* Centers for Disease Control and Prevention. https://www.atsdr.cdc.gov/placeandhealth/svi/index.html

Government policies have a direct impact on the social determinants of health through regulatory legislation and funding decisions. For example (Canadian Public Health Association, n.d., para. 3)

> *implementing employment laws that provide employment security, benefits during and if these jobs end, deciding whether to fund early child development programs or supports to seniors, foster care programs, or continuing education can have very different health impacts upon different segments of the population.*

Informed decision makers can strengthen these factors, promote health, and reduce health inequalities, and evaluators can generate some of the evidence needed to turn policy into action. Many resources exist for assessing and measuring the Social Determinants of Health. While the precise causal pathways between social factors and health are not fully understood (Bonnefoy et al., 2007, p. 11), there is enough evidence to act while we continue to explore these complex interrelationships.

The Counterfactual Argument

Here is another impact question to consider:

> *What would have happened if the program had not been offered at all?*

While this question might be seen as rhetorical at best, researchers often explore the counterfactual scenario as a means of testing the impact of the program under review.

Unlike the laboratory situation where a control group does not receive the intervention, "the challenge of evaluation is that the work is performed in the rough-and-tumble world of everyday life" (Rossi et al., 2019, p. 147).

Using the less stringent real-world control group, while not a perfect solution, may be a helpful way to explore the counterfactual. By looking at the outcomes for individuals who did not participate in the program and yet are like the program group in other ways, it is possible to make some comparisons with those who did participate. What makes the research difficult is that nonparticipants' outcomes are frequently missing, and it is difficult to predict what "might" have happened.

A number of statistical procedures have been developed to address this problem such as matched comparisons, propensity scores, and regression analysis. The most well-known approach is the randomized control trial in which one group of randomly selected participants does not receive the intervention and then their outcomes are compared with those who did (see Chapter 7). More qualitative options include asking informants or experts to predict what would happen in the absence of the intervention or by using baseline information as an estimate of the "before" program scenario. For a detailed tip sheet on linking interventions to outcomes and impacts see BetterEvaluation (2013) in the Additional Readings and Resources.

Another place to look for nonparticipants is the program's wait list; but even there, selection bias could affect who took the program or did not for such reasons as self-selection (i.e., personal motivation to be on the wait list) or staff selection (i.e., creaming the best off the wait list). Whatever approach is finally selected by the evaluator, it is important to ask the question, "Are the participants better off than they would have been if they had not participated in the program?"

Contribution Analysis

Experimental or quasi-experimental designs may be neither practical nor feasible in an evaluation. Hence, another way to look at these tricky cause and effect questions is Contribution Analysis (CA), a theory-based approach for evaluating programs in complex and dynamic settings. It helps to reduce uncertainty about program achievement when traditional experimental designs are not appropriate (Biggs et al., 2014). The method enables the evaluator to look at supportive conditions and alternate explanations that may affect program achievement. As its initiator, Mayne (2008) states:

> The essential value of contribution analysis is that it offers an approach designed to reduce uncertainty about the contribution the intervention is making to the observed results through an increased understanding of why the observed results have occurred (or not!) and the roles played by the intervention and other internal and external factors.

When the program has an articulated theory of change (ToC), CA can provide the evidence needed to draw some plausible conclusions about the program's contribution to outcomes. So, the key evaluation question becomes:

To what extent did the intervention contribute to outcomes?

Mayne (2008) outlines six steps to use when conducting a CA which help to build what he calls "the contribution story." It consists of:

...a well-articulated presentation of the context of the program and its general aims, along with the strategies it is using to achieve those ends; presenting a plausible program theory leading to the overall aims (the logic of the program has not been disproven; there is little or no contradictory evidence and the underlying assumptions appear to remain valid). (p. 22)

Biggs et al. (2014) used CA to judge the contribution of a nutrition program in primary schools in Australia. The program encouraged increased fruit, vegetable, and water consumption among primary school children. Programmers delivered Crunch&Sip® to 14 different health services in over 2,000 schools. While several randomized control trials had confirmed the efficacy of fruit and vegetable programs in schools and demonstrated an overall increase in fruit consumption, the studies were costly. In addition, they did not necessarily explain why the program worked or what assumptions and underlying mechanisms influenced program outcomes.

Box 6.1 sets out the interpretation of Mayne's six steps based on the experience of these authors.

BOX 6.1 ● PRACTICAL PRINCIPLES OF APPLYING MAYNE'S SIX STEPS TO CONTRIBUTION ANALYSIS

Step 1: Set out the cause-effect issue to be addressed

- Acknowledge that program improvement is an iterative process.
- Have a reasonable understanding of the current situation and whether the program is being implemented according to plan.
- Understand program strengths, limitations, and threats before agreeing upon cause-effect questions.

Step 2: Develop the postulated theory of change and risks to it, including alternative explanations

- Have realistic expectations about how a program can contribute toward set targets.
- Create a logic model (or results chain) depicting sequential actions from input to results and measured.

(Continued)

(Continued)

- Have a good understanding of social and economic issues which may affect program outcomes.

- Consider the links between each activity. It is important to understand "how" activities are progressed through the postulated logic model.

Step 3: Gather existing evidence on the theory of change

- This step can be run simultaneously with Step 2.

- Identify all relevant stakeholders directly involved in program implementation and stakeholders who may influence outcomes.

- Gather the evidence available and assess the quality of the evidence.

- Start identifying gaps in the evidence.

Step 4: Assemble and assess the contribution story and the challenges to it

- Start shaping the contribution story.

- Assess the strengths and weaknesses of the intervening steps in the program logic, accounting for other influencing factors not previously identified.

Step 5: Seek out additional evidence

- Use secondary evidence to confirm or refute expert knowledge or judgments.

Step 6: Revise and strengthen the contribution story

- It is a continuous process (Mayne, 2012).

- Reassess program strengths and weaknesses through continuous improvement processes.

- Revisit Step 4 (Mayne, 2012).

Source: Biggs, J., Farrell, L., Lawrence, G., & Johnson, J. (2014). A practical example of contribution analysis to a public health intervention. *Evaluation, 20*(2), 214–229.

While children enjoyed the program and asked for it, the CA allowed the evaluators to verify that some of the assumptions underpinning the program logic were flawed, including:

- Health services actively promoted the program

- Schools received support in adopting the program

- Teachers' capacity increased to understand nutritional requirements

- The program was user-friendly and quickly adopted

- Schools were willing to adopt the program

- Programmers embedded curriculum components in school activities

- Fruit and vegetables were available.

By articulating this list of assumptions, programmers realized the flaws in their ToC. For example, teachers found the delivery process onerous and confusing, the activities were just another set of demands placed on schools by external agencies, not all students had access to fruit and vegetables to bring from home, teacher training was recommended but not necessarily implemented, and parent support was mixed.

The CA also helped them look for alternative explanations for outcomes and found that several factors (e.g., parent's diet) influenced children's consumption of fruit and vegetables. In addition, external factors such as friends and media also affected their consumption. Finally, a separate nutrition and physical activity program implemented in some schools had provided teachers with relevant training, which probably increased their knowledge and motivation, while teachers at other schools did not share this benefit.

The theory-based review enabled by CA allowed the evaluators to move beyond questions of efficacy to identify triggers to success and enabled designers and practitioners to sharpen the planning and infrastructure of the program.

Next, we invite you to read about outcome harvesting and building power for women and girls in our Spotlight on Equity.

SPOTLIGHT ON EQUITY

Outcome Harvesting and Building Power for Women and Girls

Comic Relief, a major charity based in the United Kingdom, has the vision of a just world, free from poverty. Through its Power Up! initiative, it supports a diverse cohort of grantees in the United Kingdom, sub-Saharan Africa, and south Asia. The goal is to build power for women and girls on issues of paramount importance to them. The initiative reaches such groups as Indigenous women, feminist groups, LBTQI and women's movements, refugees, sex workers, women in prison, home-based workers, elected women representatives and girls at school with safety and equity issues. During its first year, independent learning coordinator Dr. Barbara Klugman facilitated grantees in creating peer learning groups on movement-building, feminist leadership, research and advocacy on gender-based violence, and monitoring and evaluation. Comic Relief asked her "to explore 'if and how this work is leading to women and girls involved having more power within their contexts,' defining power as agency to 'define, decide, do'" (Klugman, 2021, p. 3).

To answer Comic Relief's question, Klugman reviewed the October 2020 annual reports from 17 grantees, along with those of six additional grantees' partners. Using the Outcome Harvesting method, she identified the grantees' outcomes and contributions, and then interpreted their significance in relation to the evaluation question. Then she asked each organization to review her findings and to provide more specific information where clarification was needed.

Through her analysis, she compiled 242 outcomes and 184 contributions (some of these were overlapping in influence). She then categorized them by social actor, type of outcome, and type of strategy. In addition, she developed a power framework (see Figure 6.11, p. 229). She used this to interpret the type of power grantees used that had contributed to each outcome demonstrated, thus articulating the significance of the outcomes in relation to Comic Relief's question.

The power framework moves from individual power, where individuals break through the barriers of social, cultural, or economic disempowerment to take action, to the power of organizations and movements gained through growing their numbers and linkages to others, to the influence of their voices on public and political discourse or narratives, to their influence on those with "power over," that is decision makers at different levels

of society (Klugman, 2021, p. 7). There is a nonlinear interplay across and between public perspectives, narratives, and norms on one hand, and political change on the other—whether at the community, institutional, or societal level. Four broad types of power were evident in the outcomes (percentages and number of instances provided):

- **Power within/internal agency—27% (65)**

  Grantees gave examples of "power within" as women described their increased sense of confidence, dignity, and self-esteem, influenced by the efforts of grant-funded activities. In her analysis, Klugman only included outcomes where the women took action based on their increased agency. For example, during one country's first COVID-19 lockdown, an organization of precarious women workers established self-protection groups and equipped the women with self-defense skills, plus the vests and boots needed for this training. It also provided knowledge on how to create safe spaces as well as how to combat violence against women. Thirty women in different locations joined these groups.

- **Power of organizations and movements—30% (73)**

  Social movements are a way to mobilize power by people who are structurally disempowered, who do not own the means of production or sit in the political hierarchies, or who are subjected to discrimination or stigma. By organizing together, they build institutional capacity to act collectively. For example, one grantee reported the creation of the Feminist Festival with participation of over 315 activists including women, transgender, and gender nonconforming human rights defenders from 31 countries. An early outcome was that 38 Women Human Rights Defenders participated in an advisory group prior to the festival.

- **Narrative power—25% (60)**

  Grantees and their partners used their movement power to influence narratives by decision makers or carried by the media. For example, one grantee undertook continuous training and engagement with traditional and local or villages leaders. They then played a key role in educating their communities against gender-based violence.

- **Influence on institutional power—18% (44)**

Institutional power was defined as when decision makers actually shifted institutional policy or practice influenced directly or indirectly by grantees or their partners. For example, a grantee sent out a COVID-19 women's survey to collect the opinions and experiences of women during lockdown and to gain a picture of the disproportionate effects of the pandemic on women. Their report recommendations have been used by public health commissioners to shape services and, where required, to be more responsive to gender needs.

In terms of future impact, Klugman found that her request for clarification regarding groups' reports, and a consultation workshop on the draft findings, helped them reflect on what they had chosen to report. They expressed great interest in taking time to engage together about the power categories, noting potential overlaps, and differing perspectives on framing. She welcomes the possibility of reviewing and rethinking the framework together. Eighteen out of the 19 organizations expressed interest in learning more about how to do this kind of outcomes and power analysis and 16 indicated that they thought an adapted version of the framework would be useful for their own organization's approach to learning. Power Up! will likely repeat the outcome harvesting and power analysis process in the third year of the program when more outcomes have had time to emerge (Figure 6.11).

FIGURE 6.11 ● TYPES OF POWER SHIFTED BY POWER UP! GRANTEES

Power Within		Movement Power				Narrative Power	Institutional Power	
Individual internal authority or agency that prompts action	Individual actions that generate collective power	Organizational	Bonding	Bridging	Linking	Influencing discourse of the media, community and political leaders	Influencing politicians, government officials, traditional leaders to take actions in support of our issue	Influencing service providers

Source: Klugman, B. (2021). *How has work funded by Comic Relief's power up program contributed to shifts in women and girls' power?* Barbara Klugman Concepts.

This Spotlight on Equity is based on the contribution of Dr. Barbara Klugman.

SUMMATIVE EVALUATION

You are tired of grocery shopping and cooking! You search online for a meal service and find one that fits your needs. You sign up for a membership and stay with this service for six months. In the end, you need to decide whether you should continue this service and if it meets your needs. You ask:

1. Did I receive the number of meals I purchased per week?

2. Did I save on my grocery bill each month?

3. Is my family healthier as they eat better, more nutritious foods?

4. Do I want to continue this service?

5. Is this service worth it?

You will recognize these questions from our previous discussion of evaluation types. The first question looks at outputs (i.e., number of meals received). The second question examines short-term outcomes (i.e., effect on the monthly family budget). The third question reviews impacts (i.e., family health status). The last question is the focus of this section and is a summative evaluation question.

Determining Value and Worth

Scriven (1991a) defines **Summative Evaluation** as being:

> …*conducted* after *completion of the program (for ongoing programs, that means after stabilization) and* for *the benefit of some* external *audience or decision-maker (for example, funding agency, oversight office, historian, or possible future users), though it may be* done *by either internal or external evaluators or a mixture. The decisions it services are most often decisions between these options: export (generalize), increase site support, continue site support, continue with conditions (probationary status), continue with modifications, and discontinue.* (p. 340)

He says that summative evaluations are much more likely to involve external evaluators for reasons of credibility than formative evaluation. In addition, when evaluators conduct a summative evaluation, the aim is to report *on* the program, not *to* it.

Thus, the key question for a summative evaluation is:

> *Should the program be continued, changed, or terminated?*

Taxpayer's money frequently supports human service programs, so we assume that these programs will benefit society. Funders expect program managers to use resources effectively and efficiently (Rossi et al., 2019, p. 11). It renders a judgment about the program's overall performance, generally for decision makers who have a responsibility for program oversight. A summative evaluation tends to have high stakes because, as Wholey (1996) suggests, it is used for accountability, policy and budget decision making, and for legislative action. As a result, the evaluation information produced must be of enough credibility to warrant these actions.

Typically, the evaluator functions relatively independently and although they may access stakeholders for input, they do not participate in decisions about the evaluation itself. Communications about evaluation findings are formal, relying mainly on a written final report. At this point, further communication between the evaluator and the program becomes very limited or ceases altogether. It may be for this reason that evaluators do not report most summative evaluations in the literature. Instead, they remain closely held by the organizations that commission them. Interestingly, a number of summative evaluations conducted for the Government of Canada are now available on the web, likely due to the expanded evaluation policy and the desire for transparency espoused by that government.

For example, the Canada School of Public Service (CSPS) underwent a three-year initiative to examine its learning program for government employees in order to put a more accessible, relevant, and responsive learning platform in place (Government of Canada, 2018a). The program's delivery and management, programming, business model, and support strategies were all reviewed, first with a formative evaluation in 2016 to provide a mid-term assessment, and then a summative evaluation, once the initiative was completed to examine intermediate- and long-term outcomes. Among the key evaluation questions were the following:

1. Should the school's statutory mandate and revenue and spending authorities be adjusted to reflect its new mandate and business model?

2. Was the amount reallocated to the school aligned with the ongoing expenditures required to deliver the new business model?

3. Are the school's revenue and spending authorities appropriate?

4. Is there an increase in learner satisfaction?

5. Is the school's curriculum relevant to public servants and the Government of Canada?

6. Has a standard core curriculum been established?

7. Can the school provide evidence of the outcomes of training it delivers?

8. Is there an increase in the level of knowledge acquired by learners and are they applying what they learn on the job?

Data collection for the CSPS summative evaluation included five sources of evidence (Figure 6.12, p. 232). The evaluators synthesized the data using evidence matrices and prepared a technical report for each line of evidence. Next, the evaluators took the findings from these separate evidence sources and triangulated them to maximize the reliability and credibility of the findings. Finally, evaluators linked the findings and conclusions to a series of recommendations. School officials reviewed the recommendations to ensure they were realistic and implementable.

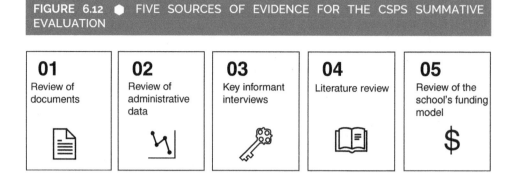

FIGURE 6.12 ● FIVE SOURCES OF EVIDENCE FOR THE CSPS SUMMATIVE EVALUATION

Source: Government of Canada. (2018). CSPS strategic directions initiative integrated summative evaluation. *Canadian School of Public Service.* https://www.csps-efpc.gc.ca/About_Us/currentreport/sdi-ise/index-eng.aspx

Sustainability Evaluation

Schroeter (2010) defines **sustainability evaluation** as:

> *the determination of the merit, worth, and significance of efforts to continue a given evaluand (i.e., evaluation object) beyond the removal of initial program resources: What is the level of sustainability of your evaluand? How well is the evaluand sustained? Should it be sustained?* (p. iii)

Hutchinson (2010) reviewed program sustainability assessment tools in the literature and found four recurring definitions of program sustainability:

- Termination of major or seed funding

- The continuation of program delivery through a network of agencies, regardless of original program participation (i.e., spinning off)

- The extent to which pilot programs or new practices become "taken up" and embedded as core programs or practices within an institution or host agency (i.e., institutionalization)

- The maintenance of program benefits in a community occurs over the long term by developing increased community capacity.

There are many reasons to help programs sustain themselves, but perhaps the greatest one is to help them continue to exist and serve their missions (Scheirer & Dearing, 2011). Thus, the key question for sustainability evaluation is:

- How can the evaluator help the program continue to provide services and benefits over time?

Calhoun (2012) and her team developed a model of eight domains (Figure 6.13) that influence a program's sustainability over time.

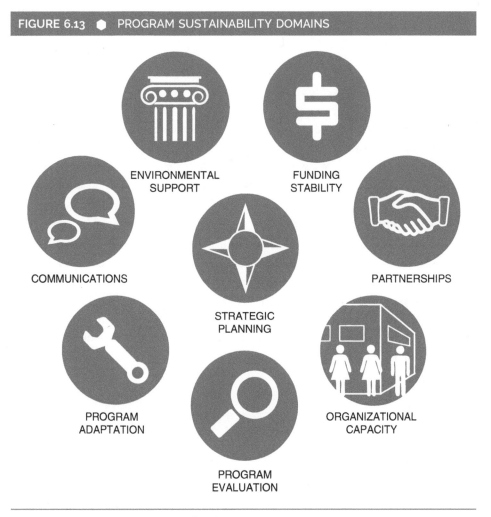

FIGURE 6.13 ◉ PROGRAM SUSTAINABILITY DOMAINS

ENVIRONMENTAL SUPPORT

FUNDING STABILITY

COMMUNICATIONS

STRATEGIC PLANNING

PARTNERSHIPS

PROGRAM ADAPTATION

PROGRAM EVALUATION

ORGANIZATIONAL CAPACITY

Source: **Washington University in St. Louis. (2021).** *Program sustainability tool.* Center for Public Health Systems Science – Brown School. https://www.sustaintool.org/

The authors developed a tool with a series of questions to obtain information about each of these domains. Based on this assessment, the evaluator can identify a program's areas of sustainability, strength, and challenge to inform sustainability planning.

Economic Evaluation

When the dust settles at the end of an evaluation, there may still be a few questions in decision makers' minds. "What did the program cost?" "Was it worth the effort?" Additionally, you may ask, "Compared to what?"

Economic Evaluation may have the answers we need if we are willing to look for them. First, it has to do with the inputs and outputs related to program activities or the costs and consequences, as some prefer to call them. Second, it has to do with choices, and because resources are scarce (namely people, time, facilities, equipment, and knowledge), a decision made among different possible uses of those resources becomes a rich source of information. With those two characteristics in mind, a definition emerges. Drummond et al. (1987) define economic evaluation as "the comparative analysis of alternative courses of action in terms of both their costs and consequences" (p. 8).

The key question is:

Was the intervention worth the cost?

Several types of economic evaluation may help determine alternative courses of action in terms of program costs and consequences, even if the alternative is doing nothing by not offering the program at all. We will briefly explore four types: Cost-effectiveness Analysis, Cost-Benefit Analysis, Cost-Utility Analysis, and Partial Economic Evaluations.

Cost-Effectiveness Analysis (CEA)

Cost-Effectiveness Analysis (CEA) allows both the costs and effects of alternative programs with similar goals to be analyzed even when the outcomes are not monetary, and programmers cannot easily convert them into dollars. For example, the U.S. Department of Veterans Affairs (2021) uses the QALY or Quality-Adjusted Life Year. This QALY is an outcome measure that takes into consideration the quantity and quality of the life. Researchers try to determine the ability of an intervention that is being evaluated to produce a high QALY rating (Box 6.2).

BOX 6.2 ● COST-EFFECTIVENESS ANALYSIS OF TWO QUIT SMOKING PROGRAMS

This CEA examines and compares the effectiveness of two different programs where the objective is for clients to quit smoking long term (i.e., more than a year). You do not know the monetary value of preventing a heart attack (impact), but you can estimate how much is saved by quitting smoking (outcome). Here are some steps to follow in conducting the CEA.

1. **Write S.M.A.R.T. Objectives.** (See Chapter 4.) In the evaluation plan, write all S.M.A.R.T. program objectives (e.g., "By December 31, 2019, there will be a 10 % reduction in smoking among those participating in the Heart Health Program as measured by baseline and posttest surveys." Do not include ultimate objectives in this analysis (e.g., "reduce cardiovascular disease by enhancing fitness").

2. **Calculate Total Program Costs.** Record the total costs to implement the program (e.g., staff, training, curriculum, transportation, and babysitting costs for clients, space, materials, phone, and postage).

3. **Define Program Outcomes.** Include risks incurred by the participants (e.g., risk of admission/readmission to hospital). Include costs for immediate savings for clients, such as money saved by not purchasing cigarettes. Subtract these savings from program costs.

(Continued)

(Continued)

4. **Conduct a sensitivity analysis.** Since the results of cost-effectiveness analysis are highly dependent on the assumptions used to estimate both the cost and the outcomes, it is essential to examine the effects of variable factors on the analysis.

5. **Calculate CEA.** In Table 6.6, examine the different programs and calculations of a CEA.

Program A costs $10,000. Program A can treat 100 clients, so that is $100 per client for treatment ($10,000 ÷ 100 clients = $100 per client). There is a long-term quit rate recorded for Program A at 25%. Your program, regardless of how many people quit, still costs you $10,000. Only 25 clients quit (100 × 25% = 25 clients). To calculate the CEA, take $10,000 ÷ 25 = $400 for Program A.

TABLE 6.6 ● EXAMPLE CALCULATION OF CEA					
	Cost (Investment)	Number of Clients	Cost per Client	Quit Rate (%)	Cost Per Client Who Quits
Program A	$10,000	100	$100	25	$400
Program B	$20,000	100	$200	60	$333

Program B can also treat 100 clients but costs $200 per client for treatment ($20,000 ÷ 100 = $200 per client). Program B has a much higher long-term quit rate at 60%. Program B still costs $20,000 to implement. With 60 clients quitting long term, this equates to 60 people (100 × 60% = 60 clients). To calculate the CEA, take $20,000 ÷ 60 = $333 for Program B.

Comparing these two programs, Program B costs more to implement, but it is more effective with a higher quit rate and lower cost per client who quits than Program A. Therefore, Program B is more effective.

Source: Barry, P., & DeFriese, G. (1990). Cost-benefit and cost-effectiveness analysis for health promotion programs. *American Journal of Health Promotion, 4*(6), 448–451.

Cost-Benefit Analysis (CBA)

Cost-Benefit Analysis is probably the most well-known type of economic evaluation. CBA determines whether a program is "worth it" (Barry & De Friese, 1990), but it is challenging to do this analysis well. It compares only the costs and benefits of one service or program that can be expressed in a ratio of dollar costs to dollar benefits and thus represents the net benefit (or loss) of one program and then compares it with another (Drummond et al., 1987). When the costs and benefits are easily quantifiable in monetary terms, it is useful to measure program payoff. However, it can be challenging (though not impossible) to translate effects such as disability days avoided, life-years gained, medical complications avoided into monetary terms (Box 6.3, p. 236).

BOX 6.3 ● COST-BENEFIT ANALYSIS OF TWO PROGRAMS

This CBA, for example, hypothetically distinguishes two separate programs, one that is operated by an external consulting wellness team (Program A) and the other is operated by staff within the organization (Program B). The company has 10,000 employees. The external program (Program A) costs $2 million and the benefits are predicted to be worth $10 million. Conversely, the internal program (Program B) costs only $1.5 million and its expected benefits will be $6.5 million. Which one is a better choice? The answer is in the benefit to cost ratio yielded.

Steps to Calculate CBA

1. Determine the costs of the program.

2. Determine the benefits of the program.

3. Divided the costs by the benefits.

4. Compare the ratio of the two programs.

Sample Calculation of CBA

Program A		Program B	
Benefit/Cost Ratio = $\frac{\$10,000,000}{2,000,000}$ = 5 to 1		Benefit/Cost Ratio = $\frac{\$6,500,000}{1,500,000}$ = 4.3 to 1	

Our CBA reviews that the external program (Program A) yields a more significant (higher at 5 to 1) benefit to cost ratio, that is, for every $1 spent on programming, the yield is $5 in benefits. For Program B, the ratio is less (4.3 to 1), meaning that for every $1 spent, the yield is $4.30 in benefits. In this scenario, Program A, the externally operated wellness program for the employees in the corporate organization, would be a better choice.

Source: Barry, P., & DeFriese, G. (1990). Cost-benefit and cost-effectiveness analysis for health promotion programs. *American Journal of Health Promotion, 4*(6), 458–451.

Cost-Utility Analysis (CUA)

Cost-Utility Analysis looks at evaluating alternatives according to a comparison of their costs and the estimated utility or value of their outcomes (Levin, 1983, pp. 116–128). It allows a broader range of qualitative and quantitative data to inform the decision, but the effectiveness assessments may be subjective and prevent replicability unlike the more stringent CEA and CBA (Box 6.4, p. 237).

Partial Economic Evaluations

There are many reasons why an evaluator may not easily measure a program's economic outcomes. First, the program may still be in operation. Second, multiple systems may be involved in program implementation, such as in community initiatives, making it challenging to tease out relevant data. Third, program length may be so long that a complete analysis is unrealistic. However, decision makers may want to know, "Is our program on course?" To

BOX 6.4 ● COST-UTILITY ANALYSIS OF TWO SCHOOL PROGRAMS

In a hypothetical example of a CUA, Levin (1983) describes the process used by educational administrators to choose between two instructional strategies. They cannot afford a formal evaluation. They are looking at two outcomes, reading and mathematics, in each program, rather than a single criterion. Somehow, they need to make an overall evaluation that combines them both. Using CUA they can use available data to make probability statements on achieving particular results and can use a common utility scale. They can draw on all kinds of data, such as the nature of the curriculum, teacher strengths, or results from other school districts which have used the same strategies to help them make their decision.

- First, they use the information available to ascertain the probability of achieving specific educational outcomes (i.e., an increase in test scores of a grade-level equivalent) in each of the instructional programs.

- Here, they use their judgment to determine that the probability of raising average student mathematics and reading performance is .5 for Instructional Strategy A.

- In contrast, the assessment of Strategy B is that there is a lower level of probability (.3) of increasing math scores by a grade-level equivalent but a much higher probability of raising reading scores a similar amount (.8).

- Then they rate the utility of each educational outcome in terms of the value or desirability they place on these outcomes, using a 0–10-point cardinal, or equidistant, scale.

- Then, they use similar calculations to those used for CEA and CBA and divide the costs by the expected utility. This produces a cost-utility ratio for each alternative. Their calculations are provided in Table 6.7.

TABLE 6.7 ● LEVIN'S HYPOTHETICAL ILLUSTRATION OF COST-UTILITY ANALYSIS

	Instructional Strategy A	Instructional Strategy B
Probability of raising math performance by grade-level equivalent	.5	.3
Probability of raising reading performance by grade-level equivalent	.5	.8
Utility of raising math performance by grade-level equivalent	6	6
Utility of raising reading performance by grade-level equivalent	9	9
Expected utility	[(.5) (6)] + [(.5) (9)] = 7.5	[(.3) (6)] + [(.8) (9)] = 9
Cost	$375	$400
Cost-utility ratio	$50	$44

Based on this calculation, it appears that the cost of $50 per point of utility for Strategy A compared to $44 for Strategy B suggests that decision makers should choose Strategy B.

Source: Levin, H. M. (1983). Cost effectiveness: A primer. New Perspectives in Evaluation. SAGE Publications.

respond to this demand, creative evaluators develop ways to answer at least part of this question, but as their work often feeds into larger-scale evaluations, it is seldom reported.

We provide an example of a partial economic evaluations: a fiscal analysis of program expenditures across community partners.

Fiscal Analysis. Brechter et al. (2005) conducted a fiscal analysis of federal, state, and local public dollars spent on children at two points in time as part of the Urban Health Initiative, an evaluation funded by the Robert Wood Johnson Foundation. The initiative sought to improve health and safety outcomes for children and youth in five cities. Features include collaboration among local voluntary, private-sector, and public-sector leaders, data-driven planning practices, and financial assistance to one lead agency to support partners' activities. The evaluators looked for data regarding the total amount spent on children's services, the amount spent per child, and the amount spent on different types of services. They did not explore effectiveness as their findings would feed into a large-scale evaluation in 10 years. Instead, they analyzed public expenditures on children in each of the initiative's cities in three-year intervals to measure the change in the scale of public expenditures and their allocation between remediation and prevention.

They looked at audited financial data, unpublished data on expenditures, and estimates based on numbers and percentages of clients under age 18 where programmers pooled money for the total population. In addition, they reviewed the ToC, conducted site visits, and interviewed key informants. They were then able to identify per-child and total expenditures for children's services by primary function (e.g., education, housing) and by the city at two points in time, 1997 and 2000. They were able to track changes over time, by city, and by function, and compared results to national benchmarks to determine trends. In this way, the researchers were able to reveal several important insights (Brechter et al., 2005):

- The relative amount of public spending devoted to children's services did not increase.

- By looking at the mix of local, state, and federal funding, they found that in four of the five cities, the state share was more significant than the federal share; and the local government was the smallest source of funds in all but one city.

- Changes in education spending grew more slowly than total education spending across the United States.

- However, the largest share of total initiative spending was devoted to public schools in each city. No other single category came close.

- Distinctions between preventive and corrective services and expenditures were less clear than anticipated.

These interim findings, interpreted in the context of the ToC, provided a benchmark for the more significant long-term evaluation, and allowed data-sharing with individual sites, so they could make mid-course corrections.

Brecher et al. (2005, p. 186) warn us that economic evaluations are difficult and expensive to conduct. In addition, evaluators need a deep understanding of public budgets and accounting practices and may not have developed these skills in what is often considered a social science career. Rather than seeing this as a hurdle, Brecher et al. (2005) recommend that evaluators select a team of researchers to work together, including someone with economic training. Each team member can offer their strengths and contribute to a deeper understanding of program effects.

Next, we report our interview with Dr. John Mayne, who developed and explored the concept of contribution analysis, among many other accomplishments.

EXPERT CORNER

Dr. John Mayne 1943–2020

Dr. John Mayne was an independent advisor on public sector performance, with a focus on international development evaluation and results-based management. Previously, he was with the Office of the Auditor General of Canada and the Treasury Board Secretariat. In 1989 and in 1995, he was awarded the Canadian Evaluation Society Award for Contribution to Evaluation in Canada. Toward the end of his life, his interests were on approaches in complex settings for strengthening impact evaluation and building useful theories of change. We were fortunate to interview him prior to his death.

1. *You have brought the concept of contribution analysis to the forefront in evaluation thought. What initiated your interest in this topic?*

At the time, I was focused more on monitoring than evaluation and wondered what one could say about causality using only monitoring-type data. It seemed to me that there must be many situations where evaluation data, much less data from experimental designs was available, and yet one would like to be able to conclude something about causal issues with respect to an intervention. This led me to think about forms of theories of change that modeled how interventions worked to bring about change, and how they could be the basis for making causal claims. Somewhat later, when working more on evaluation, I became aware of parallel thinking in evaluation on using theories of change for exploring causality issues. With the advent of more complex interventions becoming the norm and experimental designs less practical, forms of contribution analysis became seen as a way of exploring causality in such settings.

2. *Recently, your work has explored Theories of Change in complex settings. Why do you think this topic is gaining momentum today? What types of organizations are finding the approach useful?*

Today, many, if not most, interventions being looked at are taking place in complex settings and may themselves be complex, with many actors involved, numerous intervention components, and different locations and levels of government. In such settings, a ToC—a model of how the intervention works—is needed to understand if and how the intervention is making a contribution. A well-developed ToC can play several roles, helping to (1) develop understanding and agreement about an intervention, (2) design an effective intervention, (3) manage an intervention, (4) develop a framework for evaluation and monitoring, and (5) unpack the complexity involved. An increased focus on ToCs follows. I would argue that any organization that wants to understand and learn about its interventions would find ToCs useful.

3. *What advice can you offer those of our readers who are just beginning to explore the field of evaluation?*

Explore! Evaluation opens the possibility for you to get involved with and explore just about every field of social science, as well endless intellectual and practical challenges. And of course, the opportunity is there to make a difference.

Key Terms

Contribution analysis (CA) 224
Cost-benefit analysis 235
Cost-effectiveness analysis 234

Economic evaluation 233
Outcome evaluation 207
Outcome harvesting 215

Outcome mapping 215
Summative evaluation 230
Sustainability evaluation 232

The Main Ideas

1. Three types of End-of-Cycle program evaluation are outcome evaluation, impact evaluation, and summative evaluation.

2. Outcome evaluation refers to changes within the individual, organization, and community.

3. Individual changes refer to knowledge, attitudes, skills and behavior, whereas organizational change considers adoption of new practices or policies, or group learning. Community change indicates movement in larger social issues, such as poverty or unemployment.

4. An impact evaluation determines if the program has made the intended changes on the intended population.

5. Population level changes are on a global scale and usually require large scale interventions that reach many people and can take years to witness.

6. In a Counterfactual Argument, evaluators try to understand what would have happened if the program had not occurred.

7. In a Contribution Analysis, the evaluator seeks information about the linkage between the intervention and the noted outcomes, but also other potential causes surrounding the program that could have contributed to the outcomes instead.

8. Summative Evaluation involves asking whether the program should be continued or not (determining worth and value).

9. Programs that achieve sustainability cease need for external funding, continue to operate, become institutionalized, and increase the community's capacity.

10. Economic evaluations focus on the inputs and outputs of a program and seek to determine if the program was worth the cost.

Critical Thinking Questions

1. Countries provide data on a national, state, regional, and local level. Justify the reason for needing each of these levels independently and how each contributes separately to the whole picture of health?

2. Review the online Sustainability Tool created by the Center for Public Health Systems Science in the

Additional Readings and Resources section. Gain an understanding of each element of sustainability in this tool. For each of the eight dimensions in the model, identify why and how sustainability would be challenging for an organization. Give one specific example for each dimension.

Student Challenges

1. **Evaluation Types**. Which of the evaluation types, methods, and approaches in this chapter most resonated with you? Go to a search engine and find an article in an evaluation journal about your area of study or interest. Read the article and determine if it matches any of the evaluation types we have presented in the last three chapters. What did you learn? Were there common concepts presented? How did reading the article enhance your learning?

2. **Collaboration Levels**. Identify an organization, list the many partners it works with, suggest areas where collaboration is likely to be very high or very low and explain why.

3. **Economic Evaluation**. A hospital wants to know if it implements a new pharmacy bar coding system if the benefits would outweigh the costs spent on the new intervention compared to their existing method. They know the cost of the adverse drug events (ADE) to be $2 billion per year nationally and at individual hospitals it is about $2,200 per ADE and $4,685 per preventable ADE. The new bar coding system will cost $2.24 million. The net benefits were reported to be $3.49 over five years. The evaluators would compare this new bar coding system to their current protocol. What type of economic evaluation would be most suitable for this scenario (Maviglia et al., 2007)?

Additional Readings and Resources

1. BetterEvaluation. (2013, May). *Understand causes of outcomes and impacts.* https://www.betterevaluation.org/sites/default/files/Understand%20Causes%20-%20Compact.pdf
   This tip sheet provides strategies for better understanding how you can relate interventions to outcomes and impacts. Suggestions are given for supporting causal attribution, comparing results ot the counterfactual, and investigating possible alternative explanations.

2. Center for Public Health Systems Science. (2021). *Program sustainability tool.* Washington University in St. Louis. https://www.sustaintool.org/
   This online tool allows the user to provide responses to statements to determine a sustainability score on environmental support, funding stability, partnerships, organizational capacity, program evaluation, program adaptation, communications, and strategic planning.

3. Hillemeier, M., Lynch, J., Harper, S., & Casper, M. (2004). *Data set directory of social determinants of health at the local level.* U.S. Department of Health and Human Services, Centers for Disease Control and Prevention. https://www.cdc.gov/dhdsp/docs/data_set_directory.pdf
   This publication outlines the social determinants of health, such as economy, employment, education, political, environmental, housing, medical, governmental, public health, psychosocial, behavioral, and transport. In addition, the tool provides examples of data sets for each dimension, such as the Census Bureau, National Center for Education Statistics, School Health Policies and Programs Study, Environmental Protection Agency.

4. Schroeter, D. (2010). *Sustainability evaluation checklist.* https://www.researchgate.net/publication/282862008_Sustainability_Evaluation_Checklist
   This tool provides direction on measuring an organization's sustainability currently and in the future and allow users to understand their capacity and where their strengths and weakness are related to sustainability.

EVALUATION METHODS

Chapter 8
Using Qualitative Methods
in Evaluation

Chapter 7
Using Quantitative Methods
in Evaluation

**Part 3
Evaluation
Methods**

Chapter 9
Using Mixed Methods
in Evaluation

USING QUANTITATIVE METHODS IN EVALUATION

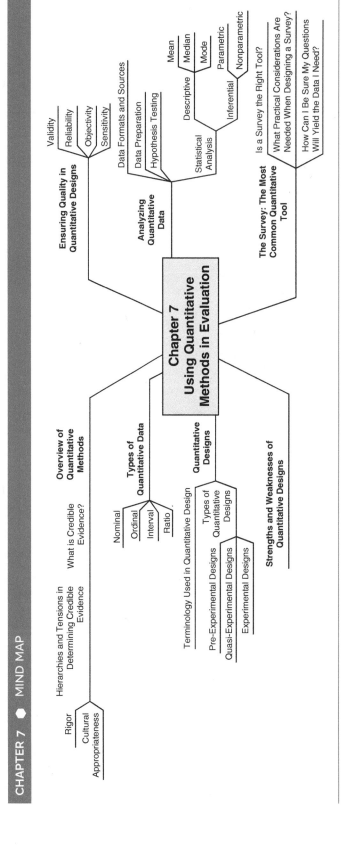

DATA AND THE DISHWASHER

Kaizen in Japanese means change for the better. No word could be more appropriate for this chapter, which is about collecting and analyzing data to make the world a better place. The Gemba Academy provides an excellent demonstration of Kaizen. In a popular YouTube video called Kitchen Kaizen, a little girl unloads the utensil basket in the dishwasher and makes multiple trips back and forth to the cutlery drawer. The narrator times the minutes and distance walked per day, week, and year for her. The narrator represents these values in the Before-Kaizen metrics (see Table 7.1).

The Kaizen Team then brainstorms ways in which they could improve the "system." They develop three options:

- The utensils could be loaded with all the spoons together, knives together, and forks together in the dishwasher basket.

- The little girl could move the silverware tray drawer across from the dishwasher.

- The basket could be taken out of the dishwasher and placed by the drawer, eliminating the trips back and forth.

Source: iStockphoto.com/deepblue4you

The little girl implements these improvement methods and records the After-Kaizen metrics (also in Table 7.1). The recorder documents improvements in time to complete the process (in seconds) and distance walked (in feet and miles over time). These calculations reveal remarkable improvements. In this Kaizen demonstration, we see that change for the better occurs because of data collection, brainstorming, and improvement strategies. Repeated data collection allows us to measure the improvements made.

TABLE 7.1 ⬢ KITCHEN KAIZEN COLLECTION AND ANALYSIS OF DATA			
	Comparison		
	Before Kaizen	After Kaizen	Improvement
Time to complete process (seconds)	1:25	0:38	0:47
Distance walked per day (feet)	60	6	54
Distance walked per week (feet)	420	42	378
Distance walked per year (feet)	21,840	2,184	19,656
Distance walked per year (miles)	4.14	0.41	3.72

Source: Adapted from Gemba Academy, gembaacademy.com

INTRODUCTION

Evaluators love data. Their eyes light up when they see a spreadsheet, a dashboard, or a list of themes, categories, and codes. Working with data puts them right in their comfort zone. In the chapters in this section, we use the term **research methods** to describe quantitative, qualitative, and mixed methods. Evaluators use the same methods as other researchers; they just use them for a different purpose. While other researchers try to advance knowledge generally, evaluators focus on asking the most likely questions to help decision makers get the evidence they need to make good decisions. There is always a link between the questions asked and potential changes to a program, policy, or project.

Source: Chris Lysy/FreshSpectrum.com

There are two main types of data—quantitative or numerical data and qualitative or descriptive (often text-based) data. A third important approach, called mixed methods, finds ways to combine both quantitative and qualitative data in the same study. Because evaluation covers such a broad spectrum of both topics and uses, each of these approaches is appropriate in certain contexts and so we have devoted a chapter to each one. We designed Chapter 7 to help you understand the kinds of quantitative data evaluators use, how they collect them, and how they analyze them. Chapter 8 focuses on qualitative methods, and Chapter 9 on mixed methods.

This chapter outlines the types of methods, data, and analyses used in a quantitative design. In this first section, we clarify the differences between quantitative and qualitative data and consider what constitutes credible evidence. Some of the hierarchies and tensions present in the fields of research and evaluation are described. Then we look at types of quantitative designs, including pre-experimental, quasi-experimental, and experimental, and examples are provided. We review some of the strengths and limitations of these designs, including bias and representativeness, and explore quality in quantitative design. Issues associated with ensuring quality include validity and an examination of internal and external validity and potential threats associated with each, reliability, objectivity, and sensitivity. We explore the analysis of quantitative data and look at the uses of various websites which provide examples of accessible, high-quality data for comparison purposes. Descriptive and inferential statistics are discussed, and examples are provided. We end the chapter with a look at the survey, the most common quantitative tool used in evaluation, and provide some tips to consider when designing one.

You will enjoy the resources in this chapter including the Spotlight on Equity, which presents a report on the grandmother perspective, our expert Dr. Mel Mark, Key Terms, Main Ideas, Critical Thinking Questions, Student Challenges, and Additional Readings and Resources.

OVERVIEW OF QUANTITATIVE METHODS

This section provides a brief overview of quantitative methods. It looks at what constitutes credible evidence, explores the hierarchies and tensions in quantitative methods, and clarifies the four types of quantitative data.

What Is Credible Evidence?

The purpose for conducting an evaluation is to understand people and populations and how a program or intervention can make a difference in a participant's life. To make good evaluative decisions, we need evidence. What is evidence? Who decides what constitutes good evidence? What methods will provide use with the evidence we need?

Evidence-Based Practice (EBP) is based on the belief that our practice should be formulated and driven by scientific evidence. In the 1970s, Archie Cochrane of the Cochrane Collaboration strongly urged that the strategies used in medicine should be assessed to determine their effectiveness. If resources are tight, he posed, then we should use the best available evidence to determine our actions. Cochrane supported the randomized clinical trial (RCT) as the best available quantitative design to determine evidence. Many disciplines have since adopted the evidence-based phrase, such as conservation, dentistry, nursing, philanthropy, policing, education, business, and public health.

Websites are available in a variety of disciplines that provide searchable databases of effective EBP strategies. These include, among others:

- Best Evidence Encyclopedia (BEE) from Johns Hopkins University School of Education's Center for Data-Driven Reform in Education

- What Works Clearinghouse (WWC) for educational programs operated by the National Center for Education Evaluation, and Regional Assistance (NCEE)

- EBPs Resource Center by the Substance Abuse and Mental Health Administration (SAMHSA) dedicated to preventing mental health disorders and substance use disorders.

Hierarchies and Tensions in Determining Credible Evidence

Debates on what constitutes credible evidence have echoed through evaluation communities for many years. Two issues are rigor and cultural appropriateness.

Rigor. Coryn (2007) describes the hierarchies of evidence often used to judge research, mainly in quantitative research, and these often form the basis by which research quality is judged. They usually consist of the criteria of validity, reliability, and objectivity (see below). In terms of clinical interventions, for example, they include from highest to lowest in terms of quality or rigor (pp. 25–26):

1. Systematic reviews and meta-analyses

2. Well-designed randomized controlled trials

3. Well-designed trials without controls (e.g., single-group pre-post, time series, or matched case-controlled studies)

4. Well-designed nonexperimental studies from more than one center

5. Opinion of respected authorities, based on clinical evidence, descriptive studies, or reports of expert committees.

This hierarchy is grounded in the quantitative tradition and is often used as the benchmark for all research. As you can see, all qualitative research is collapsed in the lowest level of the hierarchy under the term "descriptive studies." When one considers the sheer number of excellent qualitative studies that have become part of the research canon, this seems unnecessarily harsh and favors those with a realist perspective.

Perhaps it is not surprising that a major tension emerged in both research and program evaluation about the perceived value of quantitative versus qualitative data. The debate shook the evaluation community for more than 20 years. At times, the language used seemed to equate scientific research with randomized trials, and RCTs were often described as the "gold standard" against which all other research was compared. Qualitative researchers fielded criticism for not meeting these realist criteria.

Scriven (2006) explains that these standards are, at least in part, the result of social scientists trying to replicate the natural sciences and the ideal embodiment of the scientific theory. He commented, "The correct standard, or basis, in science or outside it, for such conclusions is that they can be demonstrated or established beyond a reasonable doubt" (p. 1).

The What Works Clearinghouse, created in 2002, was designed to vet educational research considered scientific enough to inform educational practice (Gersten & Hitchcock, 2009, p. 78). They prioritized proposals that used randomized experiments (Mark, 2009, p. 217). The controversy that ensued, as Mark (2009) explains, was due to different assumptions about what constituted the right research question. Advocates of RCTs and quasi-experimental designs assumed it was valuable to assess the average effectiveness of educational interventions. Critics preferred questions that looked at processes, relationships, and context. Patton (2015) comments that to treat experimental designs as the gold standard was to cut off serious consideration of alternative methods. It channeled millions of research and evaluation dollars to support a specific method rather than looking for the most appropriate way to answer a specific question in a specific context.

Schwandt (2009, p. 201) offers three criteria to assess the quality of evaluation evidence. Figure 7.1, p. 251 illustrates the combination of relevance, credibility, and probability.

Mark (2009, p. 235) concludes that if the key research question relates to the effects or outcomes of an intervention, such as, "Did the new math program lead to improved student performance?", then experimental and quasi-experimental designs would be appropriate to produce credible evidence. If, on the other hand, the research question relates to students' lived experience in the program, or to program context, interactions, and other specifics, then qualitative methods would produce more useful information

FIGURE 7.1 ● CRITERIA FOR QUALITY OF EVALUATION EVIDENCE

Relevance
Does the information bear directly on the hypothesis or claim in question?

Credibility
Can we believe the information?

Probability
How strongly does the information point toward the claim or hypothesis under consideration?

Relevance Credibility Probative Force

Source: Adapted from Schwandt, T. A. (2000). Three epistemological stances for qualitative inquiry: Interpretivism, hermeneutics, and social constructivism. In N. K. Denzin, & Y. S. Lincoln (Eds.), *Handbook of qualitative research* (pp. 189–214). SAGE Publications. Source: Slidemodel.com

(p. 230). In the end, the evaluator must explain the research question and the choice of research methods selected to answer it.

Cultural Appropriateness. Another emerging tension is about the appropriateness of research methods for minority cultural groups. Community fit is often overlooked. Callejas (2021), with the National Latino Behavioral Health Association, defines the concept of community-defined evidence, as a "set of practices that communities have used and determine by community consensus over time, and which may or may not have been measured empirically but have reached a level of acceptance by the community" (p. 1). Another term, practice-based evidence, was defined by the National Indian Child Welfare Association (NICWA) as:

> knowledge derived from systematic observation of community, culturally based practices, and the outcomes they produce. PBE helps stakeholders better understand the effectiveness of a practice in context. Such evidence respects the community's view of a successful outcome and helps identify what should be measured to evaluate a program's effectiveness. (p. 3)

Isaacs et al. (2005) raised concerns related to many mental health research designs for tribal communities:

- Inadequate inclusion of ethnic and cultural groups in study samples
- Lack of analyses on the impact of ethnic, linguistic, or cultural factors
- Limited resources devoted to research on culturally specific practices
- Lack of theory development related to the relationships between culture, mental health disorders, and treatment

- Absence of culturally relevant treatment outcomes

- Limited involvement of ethnically and culturally diverse researchers.

With regard to suicide prevention programs, for example, Sahota and Kastelic (2012), state:

> *The large sample sizes needed for "reasonable effect sizes" or "statistical significance" are not available in many AI/AN [American Indian/Alaskan Native] community suicide prevention programs. Randomized clinical trials may be unappealing to many communities, particularly with an issue as sensitive as suicide prevention, because one group of community members would not be provided the intervention under study.* (p. 107)

One Sky Center (n.d.), a national resource center for health, education, and research in American Indian/Alaska Native communities, examines programs for best practices and determines their value for Indian Country holding consensus meetings to "combine science, practice, and culture-based knowledge" (para. 3).

For example, the Positive Indian Parenting (PIP) program is practice-based evidenced. PIP is an 8–10 week program developed by the National Indian Child Welfare Association (n.d.). The program provides practical- and cultural- based training for American Indian and Alaska Native (AI/AN) parents using the values and attitudes consistent with AI/AN child-rearing in conjunction with modern parenting practices. The use of storytelling, cradleboard, harmony, nature, behavior management, and praise are all strategies in this program. It addresses the "history impact of boarding schools, intergenerational trauma and grief, and forced assimilation of parenting…" (para. 1).

TYPES OF QUANTITATIVE DATA

Four **types of data** are commonly used in evaluation. These are known as the Stevens typology and include Nominal, Ordinal, Interval, and Ratio (Stevens, 1946). To remember these four types, use the acronym NOIR as shown in Figure 7.2, p. 253.

Read the statements below and see if you know the data type. The answers are at the end of the chapter.

1. If an evaluator asks whether a group of individuals in the criminal justice system has reoffended in the last year (i.e., a yes/no question), what type of data are collected?

2. If evaluators ask a group of participants their yearly income in dollars, what type of data are collected?

3. If data collectors ask homeowners taking a class on money management to respond to the statement, "This class helped me manage my money better," and a 5-point scale is provided, from 1 (*not at all*) to 5 (*most definitely*), what type of data are collected?

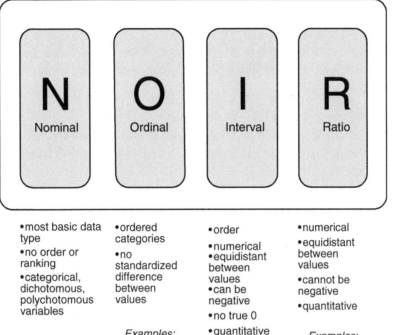

FIGURE 7.2 ● TYPES OF DATA

- most basic data type
- no order or ranking
- categorical, dichotomous, polychotomous variables

Examples:
race, ethnicity, country, gender, intervention group, vaccine status

- ordered categories
- no standardized difference between values

Examples:
Likert Scale, age groups, economic group, pain score, program satisfaction, stage of cancer

- order
- numerical
- equidistant between values
- can be negative
- no true 0
- quantitative

Examples:
temperature, intelligent quotient, time during day, GPA

- numerical
- equidistant between values
- cannot be negative
- quantitative

Examples:
age (years), weight, number of participants, income per month

4. A community foundation oversees a grant to improve students financial literacy knowledge. The students are in elementary, middle school, and high school. What type of data is used to describe the groups of students?

By studying the logic model and working with stakeholders, the evaluator can determine the metrics, indicators, and sources of information needed to measure and ultimately answer the evaluation questions.

QUANTITATIVE DESIGNS

In this section, we review common terms used in quantitative designs and then examine various quantitative designs including pre-experimental, quasi-experimental, and experimental, look at some of the strengths and limitations of them, including bias and representativeness, and explore quality in quantitative design through the topics of validity, reliability, objectivity, and sensitivity.

Terminology Used in Quantitative Design

Before exploring the common quantitative designs used in evaluation, it is helpful to understand some of the terminology.

- **Subjects** (sometimes called treatment groups) are the individuals that are studied in an evaluation. The evaluation measures how they change due to the program.

- **Control group** are study subjects that do not receive the intervention. While they are not involved, they are still measured in the same way as the treatment group to see any differences in their outcomes can be attributed to the program.

- **Comparison group** are study subjects that may receive another type of intervention, usually simultaneously. Their outcomes are compared to those of the treatment group.

- **Randomization** relates to the way the study population is selected. Each individual has an equal chance of being selected or not selected as a subject in either the treatment or the control group. The evaluator must ensure that both groups are similar in ways that are important to the study from the outset.

- A **variable** is a characteristic or attribute of study participants that can be measured or observed and is likely to vary across the group. Examples include gender, age, socioeconomic status, attitudes, or behaviors such as racism, social control, political power, or leadership status. Because variables can change over time, one variable can affect or predict another in a cause–effect way.

- An **independent variable** is a variable that influences the outcomes in a study, for example, the intervention, treatment, or program. It is called independent because it stands alone and cannot be changed by the other variables being studied.

- A **dependent variable** is dependent on other factors and may change as a result of the intervention. Evaluators are interested in studying the causes for this change.

- **Notation** provides a visual way to help the reader understand the procedures of a specific research design. A standard notation system, provided by Campbell and Stanley (1963, p. 6), is still widely used today to describe experimental designs. There are three important players: **X**, **O**, and **R**.

  - **X** is the independent variable and refers to intervention, treatment, or program and may result in a change in the dependent variables being measured. For example, if we use a college stress-reduction class as an example, the independent variable could be the actual class.

- **O** is the observation or measurement of the dependent variables that is recorded on an instrument or measurement tool. It will give you information about the dependent variable. In our example, the observation could be the measurement of blood pressure.

- **R** indicates a random assignment of students. In our example, we could randomly select college students from their freshman year to participate in the class.

Types of Quantitative Designs

Three main quantitative designs are used in evaluations to determine the effect of a program on a group of subjects and to identify such outcomes as knowledge, attitudes, skills, behaviors, and other changes. They include:

1. Pre-experimental designs

2. Quasi-experimental designs

3. Experimental designs.

Pre-Experimental Designs

There are two types of pre-experimental designs, the single case, and the one group, pretest/posttest design. **Pre-experimental designs** have no randomization and there is only one group involved. In addition, they tend to be very convenient and low cost, two reasons why evaluators often use them.

Single Case Study. The single case study's notation, shown below, includes the intervention (X) and observation or measurement using a survey or instrument (O). You cannot claim causality in this design, but you can describe the results. Let us say you design a study about getting a good night's sleep. You go to bed at a recommended time and use an app to monitor your sleep duration. The notation looks as follows:

$$\textbf{X} \quad \textbf{O}$$

One-Group, Pretest–Posttest Design. If you choose the one group, pretest–posttest design, there is an observation before the intervention (e.g., baseline measurement or O_1); then the intervention occurs, and then another observation occurs (i.e., O_2). This approach can help the evaluator determine changes based on the intervention, but there is no control group and no randomization. In our sleep example, you would use the app on the first night but would not change your usual bedtime routine, thus producing a baseline measure (O_1). On the second night, you would avoid using screens at least one hour before bedtime and monitor your sleep with the app (O_2). Then you would compare the two measures of sleep duration (O_1 compared with O_2) to see if there is a difference.

$$\textbf{O}_1 \quad \textbf{X} \quad \textbf{O}_2$$

Quasi-Experimental Designs

Quasi-experimental Designs mean "as if" it were experimental, but it is not. Two quasi-experimental designs are common in evaluation studies, the nonequivalent (pretest/posttest) control group design, and the interrupted time-series design. There is no random assignment to groups in these studies.

Nonequivalent Control Group Design. The nonequivalent (pretest/posttest) control group design has two selected groups without random assignment. Both groups take a pretest and posttest, but only the experimental group receives the treatment or intervention. The evaluator recruits a control group similar to the treatment group regarding sociodemographic status, age, or health status; for example, to limit differences between the two groups.

The notation for this design has two rows. The first row represents the treatment group, which receives X, the intervention, and the second row is for the control group, which, as you can see, neither receives the intervention nor participates in the program.

$$\mathbf{O_1} \quad \mathbf{X} \quad \mathbf{O_2}$$

$$\mathbf{O_1} \qquad \mathbf{O_2}$$

For example, evaluators tested students' attitudes on vaping using a 10-item survey. Students are then provided a 30-minute tutorial about the dangers of vaping and its implications for their health. After the tutorial, the students take the same 10-item survey, and scores are compared. The comparison will reveal if there is a change in their knowledge and attitudes regarding vaping. Next, a control group takes a survey at two points in time but does not receive the tutorial. Finally, analysts compare the scores for the study group and the control group.

Interrupted Time Series. This is a useful design, especially in population health. It is often used, for example, when considering changes to public health legislation. A time series is a series of longitudinal observations "interrupted by an intervention at a known point in time" (Bernal et al., 2017). The design can involve a single group, both before and after a treatment, or include a control group, but neither group is randomly assigned. Instead, evaluators observe both groups over time, but only one receives the intervention.

A large Canadian healthcare employer implemented a disability management policy, which included an emphasis on early contact, supervisor training, and the integration of union representatives in return-to-work (RTW) planning (Mustard et al., 2017). Interviewers met with employers over a six-year period: for three years before policy implementation and for three years once it was in place. Results indicated 624 work disability episodes in the treatment group compared to 8,604 in the comparison group. The RTW policy was also associated with a more significant reduction in disability duration.

The notation for this study might look as follows:

$$O_1 \quad O_2 \quad O_3 \quad X \quad O_4 \quad O_5 \quad O_6$$

Experimental Designs

In **experimental designs**, the evaluator randomly assigns participants to treatment groups. Typical experimental evaluation designs include the posttest-only control group design and the pretest–posttest control group design.

Posttest-Only Control Group Design. Is the simplest experimental design. Evaluators randomly assign participants to treatment or control groups, but only the treatment group receives the intervention or program. Then, they measure both groups with the posttest.

The notation is as follows:

$$R \quad X \quad O$$
$$R \qquad O$$

For example, two groups of veterans with posttraumatic stress are randomly chosen and assigned to the treatment (X) group or to the control group. First, the researchers train the treatment group on how to work with a service dog. Then, they measure blood pressure after the veterans have worked with their service dog for six weeks. Meanwhile, the control group is getting their measurements taken as well (e.g., blood pressure); however, they do not receive experience with a service dog. Then, they compare the data from the intervention group with the data from the control group.

Pretest/Posttest Control Group Design. The pretest/posttest control group design is a classic design. It involves randomly assigning participants to two groups. The researchers administer a pretest and a posttest, but only the treatment group receives the intervention. The notation is as follows:

$$R \quad O_1 \quad X \quad O_2$$
$$R \quad O_1 \qquad O_2$$

If the evaluators had employed a pretest/posttest control group design in the veteran's study above, the study would be the same except that the blood pressure of both groups would be measured both before and after the period in which the study group worked with their service dogs.

Researchers and evaluators often conduct longitudinal studies over a more extended period. Measurement can occur several times before and after the intervention. For example, in the above study, veterans with a similar length of service in the military are randomly assigned to the treatment or control group. Remember, the individual variable is the treatment (i.e., receiving the intervention). In the same study, the treatment again is working with a service dog. Prior to the intervention, researchers measure the veterans in both groups on a series of indicators, or dependent variables, such as blood pressure, heart rate, depression, anxiety, blood sugar, and epileptic seizures in the past month (i.e., dependent variables). These indicators are measured three times over 90 days, or once every 30 days. Then the treatment group receives their assigned dog for six months, but the control group veterans receive no service dog although, they are measured in the same way as the treatment group. Six weeks into the intervention, measurement begins again, and both groups are measured three times, or every 30 days, using the same dependent variables. The results are then compared. This longitudinal design would have the following notation.

$$R \quad O_1 \quad O_2 \quad O_3 \quad X \quad O_4 \quad O_5 \quad O_6$$
$$R \quad O_1 \quad O_2 \quad O_3 \qquad O_4 \quad O_5 \quad O_6$$

STRENGTHS AND LIMITATIONS OF QUANTITATIVE DESIGNS

All designs have their strengths and limitations. Johnson and Onwuegbuzie (2004) provide a list of strengths and limitations for quantitative designs in Table 7.2.

TABLE 7.2 ● STRENGTHS AND LIMITATIONS OF QUANTITATIVE DESIGNS

Strengths

- Quantitative research is useful for studying large numbers of people.
- Provides precise, quantitative, numerical data.
- Data collection is relatively quick (e.g., internet and phone interviews).
- Data analysis is less time-consuming (using statistical software).
- Findings can be generalized when the data are based on random samples of sufficient size.
- The research design can eliminate the confounding influence of many variables.
- The research results are independent of the researcher.
- Those using the findings may favor quantitative designs more than qualitative designs.

Limitations

- The researcher's design may not reflect the community culture.
- Knowledge produced may be too abstract and general for direct application to specific local situations, contexts, and individuals.
- Lack of complete control over the context or setting of the intervention.
- Lack of an interaction between data collector and participant to find out more about the responses.
- Often there are missing data on instruments and surveys.

Source: Adapted from Johnson, R. B., & Onwuegbuzie, A. J. (2004). Mixed methods research: A research paradigm whose time has come. *Educational Researcher, 33*(7), 14–26.

Next, let's read about using the grandmother perspective to report disaggregated data as described by the British Columbia of Office of the Human Rights Commissioner.

SPOTLIGHT ON EQUITY

Disaggregating Data: The Grandmother Perspective

FIGURE 7.3 ⬡ REPORT ON THE GRAND-MOTHER PERSPECTIVE

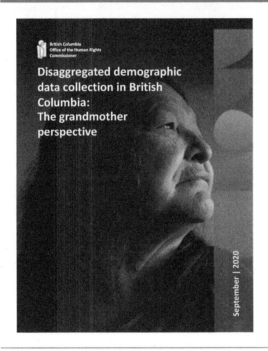

Source: British Columbias Office of the Human Rights Commissioner. (2020, September). *Disaggregated demographic data collection in British Columbia: The grandmother perspective.*

> *First Nations governments are not wanting to operate with the big brother mentality that we've all been groomed into believing in relation to what data does to us—it's more like we want to come from the grandmother perspective. We need to know because we care.* (p. 14)

This comment by Gwen Phillips of the Ktunaxa Nation, a First Nations Data Governance Initiative Champion, was central to the development of a framework for disaggregated data collection in British Columbia (BC), Canada, in 2020 (British Columbia's Office of the Human Rights Commissioner, 2020).

Powerful statements are made possible by disaggregated data. For example:

- Some 56% of Black Canadians report layoffs or reduced working hours during COVID-19 (African-Canadian Civic Engagement Council and Innovative Research Group, 2020).

- Only 25% of Indigenous communities in British Columbia have basic internet access (The Union of B.C. Indian Chiefs, 2020).

- More than 40% of homeless youth are LGBTQ2S+ (True Colors United, 2020).

Disaggregated data provide subcategories of information, for example, by ethnic group, gender, occupation, or educational status. Surveys frequently ask respondents to identify themselves using categories such as these and then anonymized data are used for statistical analysis. Aggregated data group people together, whereas disaggregated data can show the inequity and relationships among categories.

Facing an urgent need for disaggregated data during the COVID-19 pandemic, John Horgan, the BC Premier, invited Kasari Govender, the Human Rights Commissioner, and Michael McEvoy, the Privacy Commissioner, to inform policy development regarding the collection of race-based, Indigenous, and other disaggregated data. The aims of their subsequent research project were: (1) to provide foundational principles for the BC government to use when undertaking disaggregated data collection to address systemic racism and other forms of oppression; (2) targeted recommendations to embed these principles in a legislative framework; and (3) immediate recommendations to move forward on specific data projects (Figure 7.3).

Standard research practice and typical data disaggregation have harmed, and continue to harm, marginalized communities. Risks can include increased stigma and systemic oppression. Big data are commodified and repurposed with insufficient consideration for the negative impacts on human rights, treaties, social cohesion, and democracy. Equity may not be considered when using disaggregated data as a tool; instead, the focus may be on increasing the response rates and quantity of data collected which can lead to further stigma and discrimination. Problems can include undermining community initiatives for external/funder-oriented objectives, triggering trauma in participants, not sharing results with participants, not providing opportunities for communities to respond to study findings, having limited or no relevance for community members, using research as a delaying tactic, and diverting community resources from more appropriate activities.

Oppressed communities have experienced further stigma and marginalization when research has been used as a tool for control and surveillance, For example:

- The Department of Indian and Northern Affairs Canada collected demographic information on Indigenous households to support the establishment and operation of residential schools.

- Japanese British Columbians were documented, tracked, and forcibly relocated to internment camps in the interior of the province during the Second World War (Price, 2020).

- Between 1950 and 1990, the Canadian Government exposed and removed LGBTQ2S+ members in the public service, keeping extensive records on individuals and "suspect" activities (Levy, 2018).

- Toronto's Black Public Health Collective warned that race-based data collection on COVID-19 at times resulted in "greater police presence in 'COVID hotspots' and pathologized Black communities as 'sick,' reinforcing harmful narratives (Black Public Health Collective, 2020).

In undertaking this project, the researchers acknowledged the grief, fear, and anger that marginalized people and communities hold, and that data collection can increase trauma if handled poorly. It was their mission to provide pathways to healing with equity as a continual focus. Dr. Kwame McKenzie, physician and professor in the Department of Psychiatry at the University of Toronto, emphasizes the important difference between tools, process, and purpose. Disaggregated data are merely a tool, and depending on the context and aim, it must be accompanied by a process that supports the purpose of reducing systemic racism and oppression and achieving equity.

Facing a two-month deadline, the Commissioners Office went to the community first. Two community dialogue sessions and multiple one-on-one consultations were held with community and academic leaders from diverse Black, Indigenous and People of Color (BIPOC), LGBTQ2S+ and disability communities. Further one-on-one consultations were held with other experts, local leaders, and government. A literature review and policy analysis were conducted. Grounded in critical race, disability and queer theory, the demographic categories were recognized as social constructions not biological facts.

Report recommendations include: (1) enact the Anti-Discrimination Data Act (ADDA) to legislate the collection, use, and disclosure of demographic data for social change; (2) develop data standards that provide guidelines for data collection; (3) ensure that a framework for these standards includes an equity impact process; (4) ensure that the framework includes the purpose of the project, uses a respectful process, involves the community, and defines the scope and limitations of data collection, use, and disclosure. While the framework is being established, the government should begin immediately to collect disaggregated demographic data in health care, mental health, policing, corrections, poverty reduction, education, gender-based violence, and child and family development. Finally, all data disaggregation processes should embrace the grandmother perspective—to be caring but not controlling.

The Spotlight on Equity is based on a report by the British Columbia Office of the Human Rights Commissioner.

ENSURING QUALITY IN QUANTITATIVE DESIGNS

Four measurement properties can help to ensure the quality of the data to be collected: **validity, reliability, objectivity, and sensitivity.**

Validity

In their classic paper, Campbell and Stanley (1963) distinguished between internal validity and external validity (p. 5). These important terms are discussed below.

Internal Validity

"**Internal validity** is the basic minimum without which any experiment is uninterpretable: Did in fact the experimental treatments make a difference in this specific experimental instance?" (Campbell & Stanley, 1963, p. 5). It refers to the confidence you have that your independent variable caused your dependent variable (Trochim, 2020). To a large extent, internal validity is the ability of your study to avoid confounding or the possibility that there is another independent variable interacted with your results.

Hoyle et al. (2001) state that "internal validity refers to the extent to which the short term and/or long-term outcomes of a program…can truly be attributed to it or if these outcomes could have been caused by something else" (p. 13). If a study shows a high degree of internal validity, we can conclude we have strong evidence of causality. If a study has low internal validity, then we must conclude we have little or no evidence of causality (Michael, n.d.).

One issue relates to the possibility of confounding variables. Skelly et al. (2012) state that "confounding factors may mask an actual association or, more commonly, falsely demonstrate an apparent association between the treatment and outcome when no real association between them exists" (p. 10). Ewert and Sibthorp (2009) explain that "it becomes unclear whether the actual treatment caused the effect, or the presence of the confounding variable influenced the outcome. For the variable to be confounding it must (1) be associated with the independent variable of interest, and (2) be directly associated with the outcome or dependent variable" (p. 377).

Kim and Crutchfield (2004) studied the effect that an aftercare program at Transition House (independent variable) had on homeless women with children. Those who were in recovery were the most vulnerable due to high-risk environments and severe stress. Dependent variables on the Program Outcome Scale, administered three months after discharge, included drug relapse, noncompliance or full compliance with rules/regulations, attendance at regular meetings, and positive behavioral and attitudinal change. The evaluators were careful to consider potential confounding variables in this case. After reviewing the literature, they determined that family and social support received by the women during and after care was a substantial predictor of subsequent recovery. As a result, they revised their question to ask, did the Transition House program cause a change in the women's score or did the receipt of family and social support act as a confounding variable? See Figure 7.4.

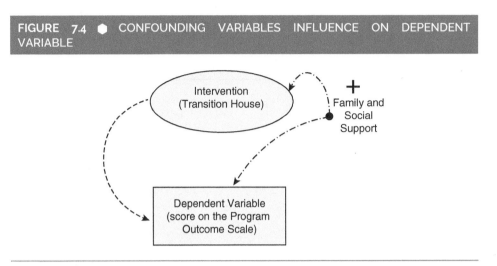

FIGURE 7.4 ● CONFOUNDING VARIABLES INFLUENCE ON DEPENDENT VARIABLE

Source: Adapted from Kim, S., & Crutchfield, C. (2004). An evaluation of substance abuse aftercare program for homeless women with children using confounding variable-control design. *Journal of Drug Education, 34*(3), 213–233.

Careful analysis of potential confounding variables for the population under study is important.

Another example is provided in the following scenario by Puddy and Wilkins (2011):

> *A school-based violence prevention program focuses on educating adolescents about pro-social conflict resolution to decrease violence. The school also makes major changes to the physical structure of the school (i.e., increased lighting and visibility) to decrease incidents of violence. In this case, could reductions in violence-related outcomes be attributed to the pro-social conflict resolution strategy? Could these changes in violence also be attributed to the physical changes made to the school? To address internal validity, the evaluation of the violence prevention program would have to use a research design that enables the researchers/practitioners to determine whether reductions in violence are due to the violence prevention program, physical changes to the school, neither, or both.* (p. 13)

The evaluator must be aware not only of the study variables but of other variables that could be closely associated with the study's original independent variable and which could be exerting a confounding influence on results.

Threats to Internal Validity. One effective way to look for flaws within the study itself is to examine its internal validity. Threats to internal validity can compromise our confidence that a relationship exists between the independent and dependent variables. Creswell and Creswell (2018, pp. 170–171) identify common threats to internal validity and actions evaluators can take to counteract them in Table 7.3, p. 263.

TABLE 7.3 ⬢ THREATS TO INTERNAL VALIDITY	
History	Time passes during a study and participants will experience other events in their life. Groups will need to experience the same events.
Maturation	Participants in a study are naturally aging and developing more knowledge and skills. This influences the results. Selection of participants who will change at the same rate should be considered.
Mortality	Participants in either the treatment or control group can drop out of the program for many reasons. So, changes and outcomes for these missing participants are unknown. The evaluator can select a larger sample to account for dropouts. It may also be possible to compare dropouts' outcomes with those who remain.
Selection bias	Participants in the study may have special characteristics that lead them to perform differently on the outcomes than other participants. The evaluator should use random selection to ensure traits have the potential to be spread among the groups.
Regression to the mean	Recruitment may yield participants with extreme scores, but these can moderate during the program. Typically, scores regress toward the mean over time. The evaluator can select participants without extreme scores at the outset.
Diffusion	Participants in the treatment and control groups communicate with each other during the study. This cross-contamination influences the outcomes in each group. Therefore, the evaluator can keep the groups as separate as possible or select groups unlikely to interact (e.g., different locations).
Testing	Participants become familiar with the measure and remember responses for later testing. The pretest cues subjects about the posttest. The evaluator can have a longer interval between pretest and posttest.
Instrumentation	For some reason, the instrument changes between pretest and posttest and thus compromises comparability. The evaluator can make sure to use the same measure at both times.

Source: Adapted from Creswell, J. W., & Creswell, J. (2018). *Research design: Qualitative, quantitative, and mixed methods approaches.* SAGE Publications.

Ways to enhance internal validity include randomization, use of a control or comparison group, repeated data collection procedures on the same variables over time, and exploring and mitigating in advance confounding variables that could potentially influence outcomes in advance (Puddy & Wilkins, 2011).

External Validity

External validity asks the question of generalizability: "To what populations, settings, treatment variables, and measurement variables can this effect be generalized?" (Campbell & Stanley, 1963, p. 5). External validity refers to the extent to which causal relationships determined by the evaluation results can be generalized to and across individuals, settings, and time (Michael, n.d.).

As evaluators strive to have a more significant societal impact and as systematic reviews of evaluations become more common, external validity becomes of greater interest. As Avellar et al. (2017) comment:

Questions of external validity may be of particular interest to practitioners who often must make decisions on what to offer their clients. Practitioners who believe that the research samples and context are substantially and substantively different than their own may be concerned that the reported effects would not be realized in their situation. (p. 284)

Threats to External Validity. External validity can be compromised if inaccurate generalizations are drawn from the findings of a study. Common threats and possible evaluator actions to counteract them are described by Creswell and Creswell (2018, p. 172) in Table 7.4.

TABLE 7.4 ● THREATS TO EXTERNAL VALIDITY	
Selection and program interaction	If the characteristics of participants selected for the study are very specific, the results cannot be generalized to individuals who do not have those characteristics. The evaluator can measure additional groups with different characteristics.
Setting and program interaction	If the setting where measurement occurred is unique, results cannot be generalized to other settings. The evaluator can conduct additional measurements in new settings to see if the same results occur.
History and program interaction	Because the measurements occur at a specific point in time, the results cannot be generalized to past or future situations. The evaluator can replicate the study later to determine if the same results occur.

Source: Creswell, J. W. (2015). *A concise introduction to mixed methods research.* SAGE Publications.

Avellar et al. (2017) provide a useful list of questions for the evaluator to consider when determining if an intervention might work in a particular context:

- Has the intervention been tested in a similar location in terms of urbanicity, demographics, or policy context?

- Has the intervention been tested in a similar service delivery context?

- Has the intervention been tested on participants similar to my intended population regarding age, gender, socioeconomic status (SES), race and ethnicity, or other characteristics?

Additionally, the authors indicated that for purposes of future comparison, specific characteristics need to be provided in evaluation reports to assess external validity. These include the number of studies, number of settings, description of study site characteristics (e.g., state, city, density, setting), description of study sample characteristics (e.g., age, gender, socioeconomic status, race, or ethnicity), and description of the intervention (e.g., dosage, components, delivery format, staff training, and cost). Finally, they recommend that evaluators develop reporting guidelines for external validity. This would ensure that crucial information is reported across studies and supports the conduct of systematic reviews. This information is then extracted and summarized and supports the design of future studies.

It must be kept in mind, though, that generalization can never be fully justified because it involves extrapolation into an unknown future population not represented by the current study sample (Campbell & Stanley, 1963, p. 17). Assumptions or "best guesses" must be made which should make the evaluator both cautious and diligent in their search for comparability.

Reliability

If someone else repeats the same research with the same population, the same results should be achieved. This is known as Reliability. It also describes the ability of an instrument to yield the same results when used repeatedly. Variation in the results is considered a measurement error. As Rossi et al. explain (2019), a postal scale is reliable to the extent that it reports the same weight for the same type of envelope every time it is measured. However, some types of measures tend to be more reliable than others. For example, measurements of physical characteristics tend to use standard devices (e.g., a scale or ruler) and tend to produce more consistent results than measures of psychological characteristics such as IQ. Standardized tests tend to be more reliable than measures based on recall. In addition, participants' responses to written or oral questions posed by evaluators may be unreliable. As Rossi et al. (2019) caution, "Differences in the testing or measuring situation, observer or interviewer differences in the administration of the measure, and variations in the respondent's recall or engagement in the measurement process will contribute to unreliability" (p. 128). Finally, it is not always safe to assume that a reliable measure in one setting will be reliable in another, especially in a cultural context (see Chapter 12).

There are several common ways to enhance reliability.

Internal Consistency

This type of consistency determines the degree to which a set of related items on an instrument designed to measure the same general topic elicit the same type of answer. For example, to measure customer satisfaction, a call center's survey may include three different questions scattered throughout the list of questions to measure overall satisfaction. Response categories might include Strongly agree/Agree/Neutral/Disagree/Strongly disagree (Statistics How To, 2020a). The questions might be:

1. I was satisfied with my experience.

2. I will probably recommend your company to others.

3. If I write a review online, it would be positive.

If the survey has good internal consistency, respondents will answer the three questions similarly (e.g., agree to all three or strongly disagree to all three). Conversely, if they do not answer these questions in a similar way, it is an indication that the survey is poorly designed and is not reliable.

Test–Retest Reliability. This type of reliability is a process used to measure consistency. An instrument is administered twice to the same people under similar circumstances where the outcome should not change. This measurement can determine if the scale is reasonably stable over time with repeated administrations (Creswell & Creswell, 2018, p. 154). For example, a test can be administered to students on Monday, then administered the following Monday again. The two scores are then correlated (Statistics How To, 2020). A high correlation would indicate good reliability, and a low correlation, poor reliability. While technically a good idea, the outcomes could naturally have changed between the two testing periods. In this example, students could have received feedback on their first version of the test and remembered the corrections, gained knowledge, or remembered the test from the last time. Any of these could bias the results.

Objectivity

Objectivity stems from the realist ontology, namely that truth can be discovered through observation and measurement and exists independently in the external world, regardless of who is measuring the data. As the Stanford Encyclopedia of Philosophy (Reiss & Sprenger, 2020) states, "objectivity is often considered an ideal for scientific inquiry, as a good reason for valuing scientific knowledge, and as the basis of the authority of science in society." Objectivity is intrinsic to the scientific method and expresses the idea that "the claims, methods and results of science are not, or should not be influenced by particular perspectives, value commitments, community bias or personal interests." It stands at the other end of the paradigm continuum from subjectivity (see Chapter 2). Today, many evaluators debate whether objectivity is attainable or desirable, but it remains foundational to science.

Sensitivity

Sensitivity is the extent to which the values on a measure change when there is a change or difference in the thing being measured (Rossi et al., 2019, p. 130). To detect changes in program outcomes, the measures used must be sensitive to change. For example, a physician's scale is set to measure an individual's body weight and is likely to produce a valid and reliable result, whereas a truck scale on an interstate highway is not sensitive to measures under a few hundred pounds. Thus, evaluation tools must be sensitive to the type of change being measured.

There are two main ways that program evaluation measures may be insensitive to changes brought about by the program (Rossi et al., 2019, p. 130):

1. The measure is not targeted to program outcomes. It may include elements that are unrelated to the program under review. For example, a math tutoring program for elementary students focused on fractions and long division. The evaluator chooses the state's required math achievement test as a measure of program outcomes but, the test includes items with a broad range of math problems and thus obscures the students' performance on fractions and long

division. A more sensitive measure would align with the topics covered by the program.

2. The measure only detects individual differences. Diagnostic measures do not capture group changes that may have resulted from the program or intervention. For example, most standardized psychological measures, such as those that measure personality, clinical symptoms, cognitive abilities, are helpful to detect the severity of an individual's problem. However, when the measure is applied before the program to a group of individuals who vary widely on the characteristic of interest, it is likely there will be variations afterward as well ,and the program effect will be lost among the individual differences. Individual differences should not be conflated with group differences. In an impact evaluation, the evaluator should select a measure that is sensitive to differences in the dependent variable across the group.

ANALYZING QUANTITATIVE DATA

Once respondents return the surveys, the challenge of data analysis begins. With quantitative data, this usually involves statistics. "Statistical methods involved in carrying out a study include planning, designing, collecting data, analyzing, drawing meaningful interpretation, and reporting the research findings. The statistical analysis gives meaning to the meaningless numbers, thereby breathing life into a lifeless data" (Zulfiqar & Bhaskar, 2016, p. 662).

It must be remembered that reductionism, an integral part of the scientific method, is the key to the mathematical science of statistics which is used in virtually all scientific fields today to collect, organize, and interpret data and to reduce complex data into simple elements. Statistics allows people to use a limited sample to understand larger populations, look for meaningful trends and changes, and support decision making about issues involving uncertainty.

Data Formats and Sources

Data come in many formats. Sometimes paper surveys are used, and the data must be entered into a spreadsheet or database program before analysts can interpret it. This is an example of primary data, that is, data that are newly generated. This data entry process can take significant staff hours. Sometimes numerical answer sheets are used and need to be scanned, requiring an electronic reader to digitize the information. Or, the participant can enter their data into a laptop or phone. Most surveys now are electronic, and the use of survey software significantly reduces the time required for analysis, although sometimes surveys have open-ended questions that evaluators need to analyze using qualitative coding and theming methods (see Chapter 8).

Other data formats may also be needed which are not compatible with the evaluator's usual analysis tools. Examples include historical data or data from other surveys. There can be significant work involved in interpreting and exporting these unfamiliar data to a generic spreadsheet for further analysis.

Secondary data sources are also available for analysis. They compile previously collected data that are archived for public use. Examples include:

- Census data

- Government websites with data repositories

- Organizational records

- Newspapers

- Social media (Twitter®, Blogs)

- Internet (search trends).

With the onset of big data in the early 2000s (Thompson, n.d.), the term "data mining" has come into use. It involves "sifting through massive datasets to uncover patterns, trends, and other truths about data that aren't initially visible...." (Calvello, 2020). While data mining has been used mainly in business and industry so far, as tools improve, it will allow social scientists to look for patterns, sequences, and meaning in large data sets. This information can support evaluative data and can help inform decision making.

The U.S. Census Bureau provides a treasure trove of data that are collected every 10 years. Evaluators can download data sets defined by geography, people, income, education, employment, housing, health, business and economy, families and living arrangements, and race and ethnicity.

There are so many useful data repositories available. Here are a few:

- **Global Health Observatory** from the World Health Organization provides health data for countries from Afghanistan to Zimbabwe. Indicator examples are dementia policy and legislation, tobacco control, violence prevention, and air pollution.

- **U.S. Bureau of Labor Statistics** provides information on the labor market and characteristics. Variables include inflation and prices, employment, unemployment, productivity, workplace injuries, and pay and benefits.

- **Prison Policy Initiative** focuses on producing information to support justice in states with high incarceration rates. Variables include national data on state prisons, local jails, federal prisons, geographic data, state-level criminal justice data by race/ethnicity, and gender.

- **Canadian Research Data Centre Network (CRDCN)** for micro data from Statistics Canada. The CRDCN is a premier research and training platform for the quantitative social and health sciences in Canada. Variables include crime and justice, energy, education, health care, seniors, and aging.

- **Youth Risk and Behavioral Survey (YRBS)** by the Centers for Disease Control is located on the Youth Online website. Evaluators can analyze national, state, and local Youth Risk Behavior Surveillance System (YRBSS) data from high-school and middle-school surveys conducted during 1991–2019. The focus is health, alcohol/drug misuse, violence, sexual orientation, and many other variables.

As an example, we produced Figure 7.5 with census data on the percentage of Texas' counties living below the poverty line. Then, we converted raw data into quartiles and mapped the quartiles using the free online mapmaker Tableau Public (public.tableau.com). The map has varying shades of gray to indicate whether people in that county on average live above poverty (better) or below poverty (worse). The darker the gray, the higher percentages of people living below poverty; the lighter the gray, the lower the percentages of people living below poverty. This map can illustrate the context in which an evaluation is situated, which is useful for both the evaluator and stakeholders. Note in the

FIGURE 7.5 ● POVERTY IN THE STATE OF TEXAS

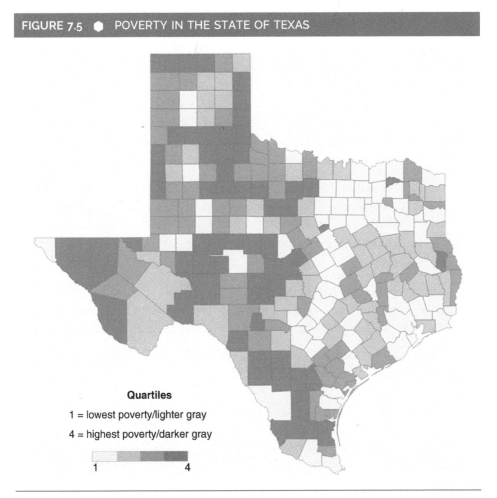

Quartiles

1 = lowest poverty/lighter gray

4 = highest poverty/darker gray

1   4

Source: public.tableau.com/U.S. Census Bureau

map, the clusters of counties in the northeast with low poverty and the clusters of higher poverty in the far west and central Texas. Tableau, the online map making tool used to create this map, can be an excellent tool for evaluators to take a data set (i.e., an Excel file with raw data and variables) and illustrate for stakeholders the various situational variables in which the program is operating.

Data Preparation

"Writing a codebook is an important step in the management of any data analysis project" (Bélisle & Joseph, n.d.). An evaluator should create a codebook before data analysis. This codebook systematically provides a simple and unique label for each survey variable. These labels then help inform statistical processes and ensure that all the evaluators working on a project interpret the data in the same way. Then a template or workbook is set up in Excel® for this study's data set. Next, the data manager enters the variable names at the top of each column. Finally, each respondent is assigned a row for their data.

There are conventions for assigning specific codes, such as for categorical response data (e.g., replacing Yes and No with numbers such as 1 and 2), for dates (e.g., day/month/year), and the responses of other check-box types of data.

Once research team members approve the codes and template, the next step is to clean the data. Data cleaning is essential because "not all data is *good* data" (Pickell, 2019). The evaluator must identify and purge duplicate data, anomalous data, inapplicable data, and any inconsistencies that could skew the analysis to generate inaccurate results. Missing data requires special attention. It is possible to delete those respondents with missing data or replace the missing values with that variable's mean or median value (Tunguz, 2018). There are also other methods and conventions, but they are beyond the scope of this text.

It seems that 60% of data scientists say that they spend most of their time cleaning data, and perhaps not surprisingly, 57% also comment that it is their least enjoyable task in the whole data analysis process (Pickell, 2019). Still, the myriad issues associated with standardizing the data must be resolved during the data preparation process to avoid significant errors later.

When this process is complete, the evaluator has a clean data set in a spreadsheet template. These large spreadsheets then serve as a repository of all the quantitative data collected in the study. Next, the analyst can transfer the Excel® file to a statistical package for analysis.

While evaluators can conduct some simple analyses in Excel®, statistical software is the typical choice of evaluators. A few examples follow:

- SPSS (Statistical Package for the Social Sciences)
- Stata
- SAS/STAT.

Hypothesis Testing

The purpose of using statistical methods is to test a hypothesis (see Chapter 2 on the Scientific Method). A **hypothesis** can be in the form of a null hypothesis or an alternative hypothesis. A null hypothesis is stated in the negative meaning that there is no significant relationship or difference between the variables or groups under study. Of course, the evaluator is hoping that there will be a difference, but this counter-intuitive approach helps to avoid confirmation bias. An alternative hypothesis would be that there is a significant difference between the variables. Evaluators reject or accept null hypotheses statements based on their study findings.

Evaluators, when writing the evaluation plan, will include the analysis planned for their data. They will write their null hypotheses, choose the appropriate tests (discussed later), and the significance level at which they will reject or fail to reject their null hypotheses. This significance level is what we call the p value and can be set at .05 (or 95% confident), .01 (99% confident), or .001 (99.99% confident). These values indicate the likelihood that the significance occurs by chance if the null hypothesis is true. Therefore, if you set your p value before your study at .05, you are willing to accept a 5% error that you have made a mistake by rejecting the null hypothesis. The flip side is that you are 95% confident that you should reject the null hypothesis. An evaluator enters their data for their participants into statistical software (see previous section), and it computes the values for the statistic and provides a p value. The evaluator compared this calculated p value to the set p value before the study (i.e., .01, .05, and .001).

In a study by Fuscaldi et al. (1998), program staff observed teen parents. A treatment group received the program and were compared with a comparison group who received no program. Factors of interest included continuing their education, self-sufficiency, self-esteem, and parenting practices. Researchers then tracked the birth of a subsequent child after the program. The null hypothesis was as follows: "There is no significant difference in the number of children born to the intervention mother's post-program versus the comparison mothers post-program." The authors found that 38% of the comparison mothers gave birth to another child two years after having their first child, whereas only 11% of the program mothers delivered another child. This null hypothesis was rejected because the p value threshold was set at .05, and the resulting p value was less than .05. The conclusion was that there was a significant difference in the number of children born to mothers who took the program compared to those in the comparison group.

Statistical Analysis

In this section, we will introduce **descriptive statistics** and **inferential statistics**. Descriptive statistics describe the study data in terms of their centrality or their reflection of a normal distribution. There are two types of inferential statistics, parametric and nonparametric. Parametric statistics have specific assumptions that the evaluator makes about the data if it is normally distributed. Nonparametric statistics make no assumptions about the data. For an overview of descriptive and inferential (i.e., nonparametric and parametric) tests, see Table 7.5.

TABLE 7.5 ● TYPES OF STATISTICS			
Type	**Description**		**Test**
Descriptive Statistics	Summarize a data set with the mean, median, and mode or their central tendency		• Mean • Median • Mode
Inferential Statistics	**Parametric Statistics**	**Equivalent**	**Nonparametric Statistics**
	Assumes a normal distribution and ratio or interval data		Does not assume a normal distribution and typically uses ordinal or nominal data
	Independent samples *t* Test	→	Mann-Whitney Test
	Dependent Samples *t* Test	→	Wilcoxon Signed-Ranks Test
	One-Way Analysis of Variance (ANOVA)	→	Kruskal-Wallis Test
	Pearson Correlation	→	Spearman Correlation

Descriptive Statistics

Descriptive statistics are "a suite of statistics that summarize the characteristics and distribution of a set of data values. In classical statistics, descriptive statistics of a data series include its 'minimum,' 'maximum,' 'range,' 'percentile,' 'mean,' 'median,' 'mode,' 'mean deviation,' 'standard deviation,' 'variance,' 'skewness,' and 'kurtosis.' Descriptive statistics represent information that can be used as the basis for comparing how data series differ" (Lee, 2020, p. 13). To clarify, see Box 7.1.

BOX 7.1 ● TYPES OF DESCRIPTIVE STATISTICS

5   10   12   15   19   34   82

The **mean** is the sum of all the data points divided by the number of data points. In the list of numbers above, what is the mean? If you guessed 25.28, that is correct (or 177 divided by 7).

The **median** is the middle of a list of sorted numbers in order. So, if you have the exact numbers above, can you identify the median? If you said 15, that is correct. However, if there is an even number of data points, you average those two numbers, giving you the median.

The **mode** is the score (or scores) that is repeated the most often. If all the numbers only occur once, there is no mode.

We call these **measures of central tendency** because they describe the center of the group of data or whether they are normally distributed.

A **normal distribution** is where most of the scores in a data set gather around the mean value. This is also termed a bell-shaped curve (see Figure 7.6).

FIGURE 7.6 ● NORMAL DISTRIBUTION

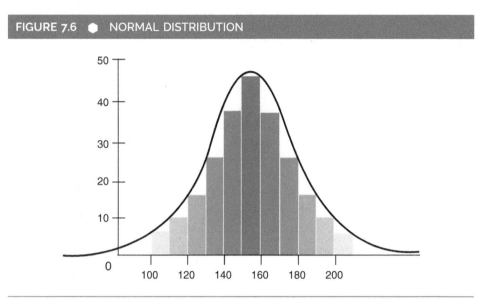

Source: istockphoto.com/lamnee

Inferential Statistics

Inferential statistics, as defined by Chawla and Deorari (2005), "implies using statistical methods for making inferences (generalizations) from the results obtained from the sample to the population from where the sample was selected" (p. 259). Inferential statistics are divided into Parametric and Nonparametric tests.

Parametric and Nonparametric Tests. When we use parametric tests, we make assumptions about our data. For example, we assume that the data are randomly selected from the population of interest and are normally distributed. Parametric tests compare means. Nonparametric tests do not require a normal distribution with the data. Several types of parametric tests are discussed below. We also give the parametric test alternative if assumptions are not met.

The Dependent Sample t Test (or Paired Sample t Test). This test compares two means that are collected from the same sample or group of people. For example, let us say you are evaluating an exercise program that includes a group of smokers. You measure the number of cigarettes they smoke per day before the program and after the program. This comparison is analyzed using the paired *t* test because the same group of individuals is measured before and after the program. Their scores are paired and analyzed to determine a difference. The null hypothesis is as follows: "There is no significant difference in the number of cigarettes smoked daily before and after completing the exercise program." The independent variable is the class; the dependent variable is the number of cigarettes smoked. Using the dependent sample *t*-test formula, the *t* value is calculated with a formula using the means. When they are compared, the results are $t = 12.12$, $p = .03$. The "t" here is an abbreviation for "test". Remember our earlier discussion about the p value. The p simply means the probability of our result being due to chance. Here, we have a $p = .03$. So, there is a 3% chance our differences are due to chance. We reject our null hypothesis because the p value (.03) is less than .05 meaning that your results have reached significance. That is, there is a significant difference between the number of cigarettes smoked before the program versus after the program.

[The nonparametric alternative to a dependent Samples t Test is a Wilcoxon-Rank Sum test. Remember, this means that the test can be used with data that may not have a normal distribution, meaning that they may not cluster around the mean.]

The Two-sample t test compares the means of two independent groups of people from a selected population. For example, let us say that you created a test to measure the differences between two independent groups of students. One group receives a 12-week class on sexual risk avoidance. The other group receives no training. Evaluators administer a pre- and posttest to measure students' knowledge, behavior, and attitudes related to sexual risk avoidance. They run an independent samples t test and the results are expressed as $t = 1.99$, $p = .04$. The p value is less than .05, so we may reject the null hypothesis indicating a significant difference between the test scores for the two groups.

[The nonparametric alternative to a Two-sample t test is a Mann-Whitney U test.]

Analysis of Variance. An ANOVA compares the means of three or more independent groups. Unlike the t test, "it imposes no restriction on the number of means. Instead of asking whether two means differ, we can ask how three, four, five, or [means] differ" (Howell, 1997, p. 299). In a product evaluation, Marras and Kroemer (1980) studied the design of distress signal devices for boaters who find themselves in an emergency. They hypothesized that distress signal devices designed with users in mind (i.e., ergonomically) would perform better for the boater than those that were not. Programmers divided the participants into Group 1 (fully complied with proposed ergonomic recommendations), Group 2 (partially complied with HF/E recommendations), and Group 3 (no compliance with HF/E recommendations). Analysts run six tests to judge the operation of the devices. Analysis indicated that two of the ANOVAs were significant at the .05 level. For example, the amount of time it took to unpackage the distress signal devices and latches of the devices was significant, $F(2,27) = 15.17$, $p < .05$. This result is arrived at by comparing the means of the different groups. Ultimately, the authors concluded, "the better the design complied with Human Factor/Ergonomic recommendations, the more performance time was reduced" (p. 395).

[The nonparametric alternative to an ANOVA is a Kruskal-Wallis Test.]

Pearson Correlation. Known as Pearson's r, the Pearson product-moment correlation coefficient (PPMCC) is a measure of linear correlation between two sets of data. It is the ratio (r) between the covariance of two variables and the product of their standard deviations. It is denoted with an r and is represented between -1 and $+1$ (where 1 represents an unrealistically perfect correlation). This measure indicates the extent to which two numeric variables are associated when plotted on an X–Y axis (i.e., X is the horizontal axis and Y is the vertical axis). The question is, "As one measure increases, does the other one increase or decrease, or is there no relationship?" A positive (+) sign indicates a positive relationship, and a negative (−) sign indicates a negative relationship. At 0 there is no relationship.

Barnes et al. (2018) studied the correlation between personal health history and depression self-care practices. In this study, the author found that several chronic conditions correlated positively with the score on a depression screening ($r = .31, p < .001$). Furthermore, as the number of chronic care conditions increased, so did the score on the depression screening. See Figure 7.7 for sample correlations.

FIGURE 7.7 ● TYPES OF CORRELATIONS

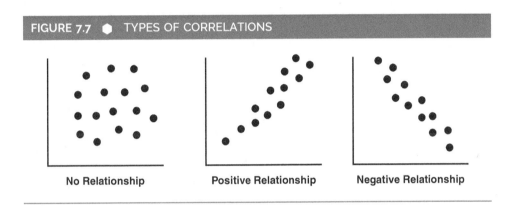

No Relationship   Positive Relationship   Negative Relationship

[The nonparametric alternative to a Pearson Correlation is a Spearman Rho Correlation.]

Understanding the differences between groups of subjects who did or did not receive an intervention is essential to an evaluator's practice. They must be aware of certain errors that could affect study conclusions in a significant way. A Type I error means that the null hypothesis is rejected when in fact it is true. A Type II error means that the null hypothesis is not rejected but it is false.

There are other assumptions and specific details of parametric and nonparametric testing beyond this chapter's scope. If, as an evaluator, you are required to conduct these tests, it is advisable to consult with a professional who has training in this area. Nevertheless, having a basic understanding of statistics is helpful when conversing with a statistician.

Here is an example of an evaluation using quantitative methods.

Example of an Evaluation with a Quantitative Design: Factors Precipitating Suicidality Among Homeless Youth

Homeless youth are at risk for many public health problems. Kidd (2006) studied the factors that precipitated suicidality among homeless youth. The study focused on the indicators that increase their likelihood of suicide. The study group included 208 students who were at least 24 years of age or younger and displaced in the last year. Using a survey, the researchers explored the youth's past experiences, street context, physical health, drug-related factors, self-esteem variables, and suicidality. Measures were scored on an ordinal scale. For example, they measured suicidality using statements from an existing instrument (e.g., I thought about plans to kill myself). These statements used a scale of $1 =$ never to $4 =$ all of the time.

Results indicated that 55% of females and 40% of males reported at least one attempt $(t = 2.07, p < .05)$, which showed significant differences in gender attempts. In addition, the average suicidality attempts when they were at home were significantly higher than attempts on the street $(t = 4.79, p < .001)$. The authors also found that shortly after the youth left home, suicidal attempts reduced significantly.

THE SURVEY: THE MOST COMMON QUANTITATIVE TOOL

Surveys are one of the most popular tools used to collect evaluation information. They are a research method "used for collecting data from a pre-defined group of respondents to gain information and insights on various topics of interest" (Bhat, 2020, para. 1). Surveys allow the evaluator to collect data in a systematic and standardized way, asking the same questions to all respondents. As Taylor-Powell and Hermann (2000) explained, the data collected in a survey can help make inferences about the population of interest. It is useful when, as these authors explain:

> your evaluation questions and information needs are best answered by the people themselves. Often, we want people's own reports of their opinions and behaviors. Often there are things we cannot see directly, such as attitudes and beliefs, Or we may not be able to observe people's actions...so, we have to ask them. (p. 3)

There are many types of surveys, such as questionnaires, quizzes, polls, and standardized instruments. They can be administered in person, on the phone, by mail, by email, or online. If you chose an online format, there are various online survey services available such as Survey Monkey, Survey Gizmo, Qualtrics, Zoomerang, Zoho, and others. However, these services do not ensure the quality of the survey. It is up to the evaluator to ask the right questions in the right way. And, as we mentioned earlier, as evaluators are usually up against tight deadlines and limited budgets, they must be well versed in survey design and survey software use before launching into survey development. The quality of the data collected will only be as good as the survey's design itself.

Surveys can be conducted at one point in time, at repeated intervals, or concurrently at multiple sites or with multiple samples. They can be challenging to design, but once finalized, they are efficient to administer, are relatively low in cost, and can be straightforward to manage. Unfortunately, they have become so common that it takes extra effort on the part of the evaluator to persuade potential respondents to participate.

In the 1970s, Dillman (1978) created the Total Design Method (TDM) to deal with nonresponse issues. He based his ideas on social exchange theory to explain why individuals are motivated to engage in certain behaviors. He proposed designing interesting questions that respondents would see as useful and easy to answer, including clear reasons why answering the survey would be useful to others, personalizing the correspondence, and providing contact information. All of these suggestions are considered essential components of survey design today. When used with mail and telephone surveys, the approach garnered response rates of 60–70% (Dillman, 1978).

He later responded to changing technology, including computerization, the internet, and electronic surveys, by revising his approach and renaming it as the Tailored Design Method (also TDM). His focus shifted from reducing nonresponse rates to dealing with the most common sources of error, i.e., sampling, coverage, measurement, and nonresponse. He continues to update his approach, providing guidance for producing effective survey designs and considering "the predominant rapid-fire asynchronous communication that now dominates societies throughout the world" (Dillman, 2014).

There are many useful texts and courses available on survey design, and it is not our intention here to cover all aspects of question development, sampling, dissemination, analysis, and reporting. Instead, we answer some quick questions on survey design.

Is a Survey the Right Tool?

Like every other data collection method, a valid and meaningful survey design takes time, energy, and resources. The evaluator must determine if a survey is the most appropriate tool to get the information required, if it will have buy-in from respondents, and if the information produced will answer the evaluation questions. Taylor-Powell and Hermann (2000) suggest answering these questions before setting out to design a survey:

1. What are the evaluator's abilities and skills in terms of survey design and management? Are there others who can help?

2. What is the purpose of the evaluation?

3. What questions will the evaluation seek to answer?

4. Who will use the information?

5. How will they use the information?

6. What is the timeline?

7. What resources are available, such as money, time, and people to support survey design, implementation, and analysis?

What Practical Considerations Are Needed When Designing a Survey?

Table 7.6 provides a summary of some practical considerations for survey design.

TABLE 7.6 ● PRACTICAL CONSIDERATIONS FOR SURVEY DESIGN	
Stakeholder involvement	• Stakeholder involvement increases commitment to the evaluation and to the likelihood of evaluation use. • Stakeholders can help to clarify the audience, provide access details, and review draft wording.
Cost of survey implementation	• Costs include staff time, equipment, software, survey dissemination costs, and analysis (if subcontracted). • Use a spreadsheet to outline tasks, dates, persons responsible, resources needed, and costs (Taylor-Powell & Hermann, 2000).
The analysis plan	• Write the analysis plan before administering the survey. Once it has gone out, you cannot change it. • Review issues of reliability, validity, objectivity, and sensitivity to ensure that the quality data needed is obtained. • Determine analysis procedures, how data will be disaggregated for sub-group, and how results will be presented. • Ensure that required expertise and software are available. • Ensure that there is enough time for data entry, coding, analysis, stakeholder consultation, and reporting before the study deadline. • Develop a survey design matrix to cross-reference evaluation objectives with data sources, sampling strategies, data collection methods, analysis plans, and other design features (Newcomer & Triplett, 2004).
Survey drafts	• Write a "compelling introduction" (Newcomer & Triplett, 2004) to capture the participant's interest. • Think carefully about the number and type of questions, scales, sequence of the questions, instructions, layout, and overall look and feel of the tool. • Get feedback from a variety of colleagues and friends. • Prepare to write several drafts.
Pilot testing	• Pilot-test the draft survey to a few respondents who are as similar as possible to the sample. • This is the most valuable step in the whole survey development process; it offers a controlled setting to try out the tool (Taylor-Powell & Hermann, 2000). • Then take any corrective action needed.
Access issues	Response rates can be increased if you are sensitive to access issues: • Are respondents' email addresses, phone numbers (cell or landline), or physical addresses available? Are they transient or homeless? If so, where do they hang out? • Do they have strong literacy skills? What is their reading grade level? • Do they need the information translated into other languages? If so, which ones? • Are they physically able to write a response or should the survey be read to them?
Survey scheduling	• Understand the rhythms of your organization and intended group to plan survey timelines: • Work backward from the point when decisions makers will use the findings. • Consider the intended group's scheduling issues (e.g., exam week, spring break, and arrival of seniors' monthly pension checks). • Major religious holidays and vacation periods are usually poor choices for survey dissemination.

How Can I Be Sure My Questions Will Yield the Data I Need?

Many resources are available on survey construction. Box 7.2 provides a summary of 15 principles of questionnaire construction (Johnson & Christensen, 2020, p. 172).

BOX 7.2 ● PRINCIPLES OF QUESTIONNAIRE CONSTRUCTION

Principle 1. Make sure the questionnaire items match your research objectives.

Principle 2. Understand your research participants.

Principle 3. Use natural and familiar language.

Principle 4. Write items that are clear, precise, and relatively short.

Principle 5. Do not use "leading" or "loaded" questions.

Principle 6. Avoid double-barreled questions.

Principle 7. Avoid double negatives.

Principle 8. Determine whether an open-ended or a closed-ended question is needed.

Principle 9. Use mutually exclusive and exhaustive response categories for closed-ended questions.

Principle 10. Consider the different types of response categories available for closed-ended questionnaire items.

Principle 11. Use multiple items to measure abstract constructs.

Principle 12. Consider using multiple methods when measuring abstract constructs.

Principle 13. Use caution if you reverse the wording in some of the items to prevent response sets in multiitem scales.

Principle 14. Develop a questionnaire that is easy for the participant to use.

Principle 15. Always pilot test your questionnaire.

Source: Johnson, R. B., & Christensen, L. (2020). *Educational research: Quantitative, qualitative, and mixed approaches* (7th ed.). SAGE Publications.

Quantitative data can help evaluators understand the differences between groups of individuals and their differing responses to independent variables such as program implementation. Lipsey and Corday (2000) state that:

> *The strength of experimental methods for outcome evaluation is the scientific credibility with which they answer questions about the effects of intervention on the social conditions they are intended to ameliorate. They answer these questions, however, chiefly in terms of whether there were mean effects on the outcome variables examined and, sometimes, what the magnitudes of those effects were. As valuable and relevant as this information is, it leaves much of the story untold. Knowing what services were delivered and received, what difference that made to the individuals receiving them, whether individuals responded differently, and generally, why certain effects were or were not found is also valuable and*

relevant. These additional concerns cannot be easily addressed by experimental methods within the practical and ethical constraints inherent in social programs. Qualitative methods can tell much of this story and, in that regard, are a worthwhile adjunct to even the most comprehensive and rigorous experimental design. (p. 368)

We will explore qualitative methods next in Chapter 8. First, however, let's meet researcher and theorist, Dr. Mel Mark, in our Expert Corner.

EXPERT CORNER

Dr. Mel Mark

Mel Mark is Professor of Psychology at Penn State College of the Liberal Arts. He has edited a dozen books and is author of more than 130 articles and chapters in books. For much of his career, Dr. Mark has applied his background in social psychology and his interest in research methods to the theory and practice of program evaluation. He has served as President of the American Evaluation Association and as Editor of the *American Journal of Evaluation*. Dr. Mark's awards include the American Evaluation Association's Lazarsfeld Award for Contributions to Evaluation Theory.

1. *To what extent do you think the recent focus on credible and actionable evidence in evaluation has impacted current evaluative thinking?*

That's a good question. I'll focus on the "actionable" part. To some extent, thinking about actionable evidence echoes a point Lee Cronbach and colleagues emphasized 40 years ago. They talked about the importance of "leverage," of attending to where evaluative evidence could make a difference. Imagine you're doing evaluations for a foundation, and one program that it funds is a sacred cow because it was the brainchild of the foundation's founder. An evaluation designed to give a thumbs up or thumbs down judgment about the program may not have any leverage. In contrast, an evaluation looking at better (versus worse) ways of implementing the same program seems far more likely to be acted on. Of course, actionability is partly a function of evidence quality as well as its potential for leverage.

2. *Has the gold-standard debate been resolved? If so, what was the defining argument? If not, what issues are still outstanding?*

It's probably rare to have complete consensus about whether a raging debate has been resolved—and maybe even consensus about what the central issue was. However, I think it's accurate to say there has at least been some movement toward resolution. A broad way of stating the central issue in the debate is that it involved whether the randomized trial is the gold standard for evaluation or not. But that's a silly assertion. Randomized experiments, or RCTs (for randomized controlled trial), are relevant only for a subset of evaluation questions. RCTs may be relevant for a question such as "Did program X lead to improvement on outcome Y?" But they wouldn't be relevant for questions such as "How well was the program implemented" or "To what extent were services delivered to the entire population of eligible clients, and what impediments existed to better coverage?"

A narrower statement of the debate would involve the claim that RCTs are the gold standard for causal inference. But randomized experiments aren't usually a good method for a major class of causal questions, specifically ones that start with an observed phenomenon and look backwards for its cause. An example would be, "What caused the high rate of dropouts in the treatment condition?" There's also the argument that randomized trials aren't needed to assess the effectiveness of all interventions, with examples like the effects of Velcro vests on gunshot fatalities or the effects of parachutes on landings of people who've jumped from an airplane. No RCTs have been done on these topics. So, if RCTs are to be thought of as a gold standard, this only really holds in certain circumstances, such as when we're interested in estimating the effects of a program on an outcome of interest, and the program's effects aren't "ginormous," and there are other factors that affect the scores, like individual differences and maturation and history, that can obscure the treatment's effects. Well, those circumstances are probably common when programs are being evaluated so you can see that even this limited gold standard claim is important but there are several important caveats. Some have to do with generalizability or external validity, others with feasibility and potential ethical issues, others with the larger portfolio of evaluation questions that may be of interest and methods to address them. Etcetera. Does that count as a resolution?

3. What advice can you offer those of our readers who are just beginning to explore *the field of evaluation today?*

After reading this chapter, perhaps they won't be surprised that I suggest they develop a range of methodological and statistical skills. But that's hardly enough. They should also strive for experiences to increase their interpersonal skills, facilitation skills, and judgment in terms of evaluation. They should read a lot, including about what's called evaluation theory. Don't be a one trick pony. Perhaps most importantly, enjoy the ride. Most evaluators make a decent living while doing work aimed at making a positive difference in the world. That's not a bad gig.

Key Terms

Comparison group 254
Control group 254
Dependent variable 254
Descriptive statistics 271
Experimental designs 257
Hypothesis 271
Independent variable 254

Inferential statistics 271
Normal distribution 273
Notation 254
Objectivity 266
Pre-experimental designs 255
Quasi-experimental designs 256
Randomization 254

Reliability 265
Sensitivity 266
Subjects 254
Surveys 276
Types of data 252
Validity 261
Variable 254

The Main Ideas

1. There are tensions in determining credible evidence that includes the rigor and elements of cultural appropriateness.

2. Types of data include nominal, (categories), ordinal (ordered categories), interval (equidistant values with no true 0), and ratio (equidistant values and a true 0).

3. Many terms can help you understand quantitative design.
   - Evaluations often use an intervention group and a comparison or control group to determine the differences of an intervention on a group of participants.
   - The independent variable is the intervention in which the participants participate and is hypothesized to be the cause of change in the dependent variable, the outcomes or impact.
   - Notation is a visual representation of the activities (i.e., intervention, observation, and randomization) that will occur in a study.

4. Pre-Experimental Designs and Quasi-Experimental Designs have no randomization of participants into groups, whereas Experimental Designs provide randomization of participants into an intervention or control/comparison group.

5. There are several strengths and weaknesses to any design. Strengths of quantitative designs are:
   - the use of large numbers of people
   - generalization to a large population can occur if larger samples are used
   - data collection is relatively quick

   - analysis can be time-consuming
   - designs are independent of the researcher

   Limitations of quantitative designs include:
   - do not offer complete control over the context in which the data collection occurs
   - missing data pose a problem during analysis

6. There are four measurements that can raise the level of quality in studies:
   - Validity can be distinguished between internal and external validity. Internal validity is the ability to contribute the outcomes to an intervention. External validity is the ability to generalize the findings to larger populations.
   - Reliability is, for example, the ability of an instrument design (e.g., psychological test) to measure an outcome variable, to produce the same results when used repeatedly without an intervention.
   - Objectivity stems from the idea that truth can be discovered through measurement and is independent of the external world.
   - An instrument that can detect small changes in a population when they have occurred is deemed sensitive.

7. Evaluators develop hypotheses to reflect their supposition about the relationship between variables or differences between the variables before the intervention and after the intervention.

8. Descriptive statistics are typically calculated to provide the mean, mode, and median of a data set and give the central tendency.

9. Parametric statistics assumes a normal distribution and uses ratio or interval data, whereas nonparametric statistics does not assume a normal distribution and uses ordinal or nominal data.

10. There are many considerations when designing and implementing a survey, such as question wording and design, order, timing, feasibility, readability, delivery method, and analysis.

Critical Thinking Questions

1. What would quantitative and qualitative designs look like if you drew a picture to represent them?

2. How would you change one type of data to another type (i.e., NOIR)?

3. Explain why the control group or comparison group do not get the intervention as the treatment group, but they are measured on the same variables?

4. What is the temporal placement of the typical independent variable and dependent variable(s)?

5. How can certain variables confound the results of an evaluation? Why is confounding a concern for the evaluation team?

6. How can notation help the evaluator communicate with stakeholders on the design of the evaluation?

7. The quality of the data collected is only as good as the survey or data collection tool. What are three examples of how the evaluator works to ensure future quality data through development of the survey?

Student Challenges

1. **Study on Post-Effects**. You want to conduct a study on the post-effects of an intervention designed to improve study habits. You are interested in understanding the effect on the overall grade point average. State the null hypothesis for this study. What are the independent and dependent variables?

2. **Study Design**. Design a study using the same null hypothesis as in the last challenge. Again, use concepts from the chapter, including types of data, terminology related to quantitative design (e.g., notation), type of quantitative design, and descriptive and inferential statistics.

3. **Knowing the Terminology**. Read the following article on a communication mobilization and intervention project and answer the questions: Abramsky, T., Devries, K., Kiss, L., Nakuti, J.,

Kyegombe, N., Starmann, E., Cundill, B., Francisco, L., Kaye, D., Musuya, T., Michau, L., & Watts, C. (2014). Findings from the SASA! Study: A cluster randomized controlled trial to assess the impact of a community mobilization intervention to prevent violence against women and reduce HIV risk in Kampala, Uganda. *BMC Medicine, 12*(122), 1–17. https://bmcmedicine.biomedcentral.com/track/pdf/10.1186/s12916-014-0122-5.pdf

a. What is the independent variable?

b. What are the dependent variables?

c. What was the purpose of randomization?

d. Compare the Initial Outcomes and the Impact columns of the SASA! Logic Model. How are they inherently different?

Additional Readings and Resources

1. Dillman, D. A., Smyth, J. D., Christian, L. M. (2014). *Internet, phone, mail and mixed-mode surveys: The tailored design method* (4th ed.). John Wiley.
The new edition of Dillman's classic text has been updated and revised. It covers all aspects of survey research and features expanded coverage of mobile phones, tablets, and the use of do-it-yourself surveys. His unique Tailored Design Method is also thoroughly explained.

2. Jenkins-Guarnieri, M., Horne, M., Wallis, A., Rings, J., & Vaughan, A. (2015). Quantitative evaluation of a first-year seminar program: Relationships to persistence and academic success. *Journal of College Student Retention, 16*(4), 593–606.
This paper on student success focused on high rates of attrition and the concern for college leadership. The authors provided students a first-year seminar program that included content for intellectual, personal, and professional development. The team compared the students receiving the seminar program to those who did not receive it. An important comparison was persistence from the first semester into the second semester.

3. Nurse Killam. (2014, March 14). Nominal, ordinal, interval and ratio: How to remember the differences [Video]. YouTube.
In this short video, learn the difference between types of data.

4. Vogt, W., & Johnson, R. B. (2016). *The SAGE Dictionary of statistics & methodology: A nontechnical guide for the social science* (5th ed.). SAGE Publications.
Vogt and Johnson (2016) provide a clear and concise dictionary of the most useful statistical terms and methodology. Straightforward and easy-to-understand language provides a useful resource for the student or experienced evaluator.

5. Wetherill, M., Williams, M., Taniguchi, T., Salvatore, A., Jacob, T., Cannady, T., Jernigan, V. (2018). A nutrition environment measure to assess tribal convenience stores: The THRIVE study. *Health Promotion Practice, 21*(3), 410–420.
The authors developed an instrument to measure the food quality of convenience stores frequented by American Indians in rural Oklahoma. The article focuses on developing the Nutrition Environment Measures Survey for Tribal Convenience Stores (NEMS-TCS). This instrument assessed four food environment domains: food availability, pricing, quality, and placement.

Answers

1. Nominal
2. Ratio
3. Ordinal
4. Ordinal

USING QUALITATIVE METHODS IN EVALUATION

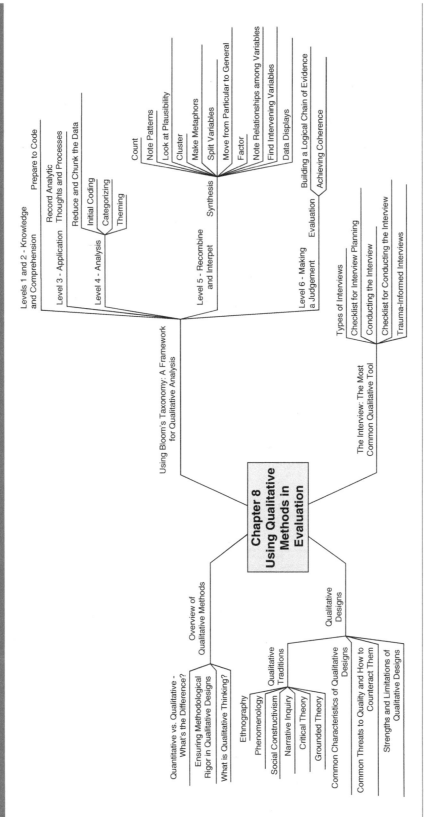

TINY BABIES AND QUALITATIVE RESEARCH

Qualitative expert Maria Mayan (2001, pp. 9–10) tells the following story:

Recently, I was invited to talk about qualitative inquiry to a group of pediatric organ transplant surgeons and specialists. Since the 1960s, astonishing transplant research has been conducted, saving the lives of neonates, infants, and children. In our local hospital we know the number of infants born each year with congenital heart disease and neonatal cardiomyopathy; we know how many infants receive heart transplants each year, we track success rates; and we record infection and rejection rates. But what do all of these numbers mean?

 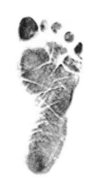

Source: istockphoto.com/ryasick

This reminded Mayan of the quote, "Everything that can be counted does not necessarily count; everything that counts cannot necessarily be counted" (Cameron, 1963, p. 13).

She noted the following questions the professional group had pondered:

- Why do some parents choose not to proceed with a transplant?

- What is a "successful" transplant and according to whom?

- Given the likelihood of growth and developmental delays following transplant, do parents ever regret their decision to proceed?

Many people want to know the stories behind the numbers. Mayan cites Agar and Kozel (1999) who suggest that the best way to do this is to "go out and listen to the people [to] whom the numbers referred, listen to their words and learn from their actions" (p. 1936). They remind us that "each data point is a person with a biography …who can show and tell what it is in their life that the data point reflects" (p. 1936). Qualitative inquiry allows us to walk into the world of stories, reasons, explanations, and human experience. It helps us understand the "why" behind the "what."

INTRODUCTION

In Chapter 8, we discuss a second type of evaluation design, namely qualitative evaluation. This approach allows us to look for meaning in people's lives and the context in which they live that experience. We consider the differences between quantitative and qualitative designs and discuss ways to ensure methodological rigor in qualitative inquiry. Then we look at what having a qualitative orientation means, or how to achieve an understanding of the elusive story behind the numbers. Six social science traditions are described that frequently are found in evaluation studies, and a summary table presents their roots, foundational questions, main ideas, and typical data collection methods. Some common characteristics of all qualitative studies, along with threats to quality, and the strengths and limitations of qualitative designs, are described. Then qualitative analysis is discussed, and, using Bloom's Taxonomy, a framework for data analysis and synthesis is explored. An example of a qualitative evaluation is provided and the chapter closes with an overview of the most common qualitative tool, the interview.

You will enjoy the resources in this chapter including the Spotlight on Equity, which presents the experience of two evaluators in Old Crow, Yukon, our expert Johnny Saldaña, Key Terms, Main Ideas, Critical Thinking Questions, Student Challenges, and Additional Readings and Resources.

OVERVIEW OF QUALITATIVE METHODS

This section provides a brief overview of qualitative methods. It explores the main differences between quantitative and qualitative approaches, looks at what constitutes rigor in qualitative research, and explores qualitative thinking.

Quantitative Versus Qualitative—What's the Difference?

Before reviewing the many aspects of qualitative methods, it is useful to understand the differences between quantitative and qualitative designs. Figure 8.1 provides some of their main differences.

FIGURE 8.1 ● MAIN DIFFERENCES IN QUANTITATIVE AND QUALITATIVE METHODS

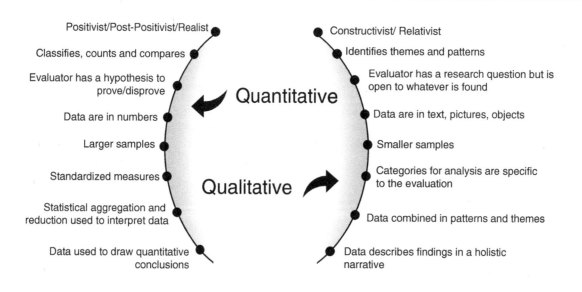

The methods used to collect quantitative and qualitative data both answer a research question but as Maxwell (2013, p. 290) explains, they have different strengths and logic, and as a result, they are often used to address different kinds of questions. For example, quantitative researchers tend to see the world in terms of variables, and they look for statistical relationships among those variables. On the other hand, qualitative researchers explore the processes that connect people, situations, and events.

The **evaluation questions** posed determine what data collection methods are required. That is, depending upon the intention of the evaluation questions, the evaluator will be directed toward a quantitative, qualitative, or mixed-methods design. For example, if an organization hires an evaluator to determine the work climate for employees, how might they approach this? What do they want to know? How can they find the answers to the evaluation questions? Review these potential questions:

1. How supportive is the administration to employees professional and personal life?

2. What are strengths of the organization?

3. What are challenges while working at the organization?

4. How many days of the week do you feel productive at work?

For example, the last question could produce simple quantitative data. The average response might be "three days per week." While useful, the evaluator will not gain a behind-the-scenes understanding about why employees are only productive three days out of five. To determine how the employees define "productive," what situations cause them to be unproductive, what negative influences exist in their environment, or what physical spaces cause them to be unproductive, the evaluator needs to ask some open-ended questions and these will produce qualitative data.

Figure 8.2 provides some sample questions along with the type of data most likely to answer them.

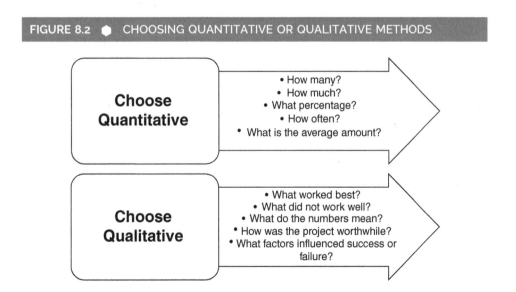

FIGURE 8.2 ● CHOOSING QUANTITATIVE OR QUALITATIVE METHODS

Choose Quantitative
- How many?
- How much?
- What percentage?
- How often?
- What is the average amount?

Choose Qualitative
- What worked best?
- What did not work well?
- What do the numbers mean?
- How was the project worthwhile?
- What factors influenced success or failure?

Source: Olney, C., & Barnes, S. (2013). *Collecting and analyzing evaluation data: Planning and evaluating health information outreach projects.*

Ensuring Methodological Rigor in Qualitative Designs

Miles and Huberman (1984, p. 16) observe that qualitative studies are rich in descriptions of settings, people, events, and processes, but typically say little about how the researcher got the information and almost nothing about how conclusions were produced. As Sal-daña (Miles et al., 2020, p. 4) suggests in his reimagining of their classic text, the trustworthiness of qualitative findings is a significant challenge. Issues include (1) adequacy of sampling; (2) generalizability and transferability of findings; (3) credibility, trustworthiness, and the **quality** of conclusions and recommendations; and (4) utility of findings in the world of policy and action.

One reason for this concern may be that, in the past, qualitative researchers had no established convention or cannon to inform their methodology. For example, Mayan (2009, p. 103) examined the proliferation of potential criteria for judging quality in qualitative research and found 15 different sets of criteria—and that was only between the years of 1981 and 2006.

Guba and Lincoln (1981) proposed the criteria of **trustworthiness, dependability,** and **confirmability** to replace the familiar quantitative terms of validity, reliability, and objectivity and these appear to have stood the test of time. Based on a discussion by Coryn (2007), we provide a side-by-side comparison of these criteria (see Figure 8.3).

FIGURE 8.3 ● COMPARING RIGOR IN QUANTITATIVE AND QUALITATIVE DESIGNS

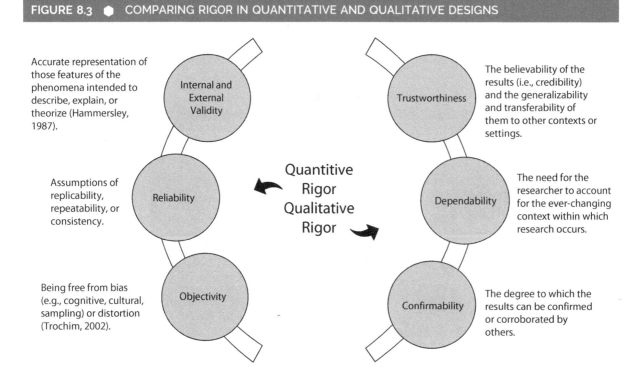

Accurate representation of those features of the phenomena intended to describe, explain, or theorize (Hammersley, 1987).

Internal and External Validity

The believability of the results (i.e., credibility) and the generalizability and transferability of them to other contexts or settings.

Trustworthiness

Assumptions of replicability, repeatability, or consistency.

Reliability

Quantitive Rigor
Qualitative Rigor

Dependability

The need for the researcher to account for the ever-changing context within which research occurs.

Being free from bias (e.g., cognitive, cultural, sampling) or distortion (Trochim, 2002).

Objectivity

Confirmability

The degree to which the results can be confirmed or corroborated by others.

Source: Coryn, C. L. S. (2007). The holy trinity of methodological rigor: A skeptical view. *Journal of MultiDisciplinary Evaluation, 4*(7), 26–31.

These criteria reflect the different paradigms in evaluation theory. The quantitative criteria emerge from an objectivist stance that anticipates a single reality or truth revealed through observation and experimentation. The qualitative criteria suggest a constructivist or subjectivist stance where multiple realities exist in a changing context and where the evaluator and study participants need to interact as they interpret and solve problems.

What Is Qualitative Thinking?

Saldaña (Miles et al., 2020) explains that when we use a qualitative orientation:

> We affirm the existence and importance of the subjective, the phenomenological, and the meaning making at the center of social life. Our goal is to register and transcend these processes by making assertions and building theories to account for a real world that is both bounded and perceptually laden—and to test these assertions and theories in our various disciplines.
>
> Our tests do not use the deductive logic of classical positivism. Rather, our explanations flow from an account of how human actions produced the events we observed. We want to account for events rather than simply document their sequence. We look for an individual or a social process at the core of events that can be captured to provide a causal description of the most likely forces at work. (p. 5)

For Mayan (2009, p. 25), qualitative inquiry allows us to ask a research question and a conversation ensues. Moving away from the post-positivist perspective, the evaluator may choose instead to achieve a broader understanding of a **phenomenon**, the elusive story behind the concrete numbers. We are brought to a fundamental question—what is reality? Is there one singular, verifiable reality, or are there multiple, socially constructed realities? Qualitative researchers assume that there are multiple realities and multiple truths because qualitative research is rooted in a relativist ontology and a constructivist paradigm (see Chapter 2). This means that the results of any qualitative study represent only one possibility of many and are historically, culturally, and socially constructed. In addition, values, ethics, politics, and power are infused in the study.

We also know that the clients who hire evaluators tend to adhere to the dominant scientific perspective of a single, objective, and verifiable reality. Many believe that "The right data are out there if only we can find them" or "The self has no place in the research process."

The strength of qualitative data lies in their focus on "naturally occurring, ordinary events in natural settings" (Miles et al., 2020, pp. 7–8), with the emphasis on lived experience and the meanings people place on the events, processes, and structures of their lives and connecting them with the broader social context. As these authors explain, "We can go far beyond snapshots of 'what?' or 'how many?' to just *how* and *why* things happen as they do—and even *assess causation* as it actually plays out in a particular setting (p. 8)."

The evaluator must advocate for the appropriate use of qualitative and quantitative research—always in service of answering the research question. If an evaluator has not thought through the purpose of the evaluation, the role of the evaluator, the methods selected for data collection, and the approaches used for analysis and synthesis of the data, then their study's rigor and credibility will not stand up to scrutiny. Qualitative research is not achieved just by "doing" a focus group or "running" a series of interviews. We need to think qualitatively.

QUALITATIVE DESIGNS

Qualitative Designs are a more subjective examination of participants' experiences related to the phenomenon under study. We focus on three areas: (1) **qualitative traditions**, (2) common characteristics of qualitative designs, and (3) some of their strengths and limitations.

Qualitative Traditions

To gain a working knowledge of qualitative design, evaluators must understand the social science traditions on which it is based. While there are many possibilities to consider, we have selected six traditions that frequently permeate qualitative evaluation designs. Each is discussed briefly below.

Ethnography

An ethnographic lens can be helpful in an evaluation to describe the cultural reality of a group or community. **Ethnography** is a type of field research useful in process evaluations to understand how complex interventions operate in an environment or context. Morgan-Trimmer and Wood (2016) suggest that it is characterized by long-term participant observation, unstructured interviews, documentary analysis, and the use of an evaluator's field notes, all employed within a holistic and flexible approach to data collection. As Hammersley and Atkinson (1983) explain, "The ethnographic researcher participates, overtly or covertly, in people's daily lives for an extended period of time, watching what happens, listening to what is said, asking questions; in fact collecting whatever data are available to throw light on the issues with which he or she is concerned" (p. 2). Perhaps the most classic ethnographic study is *Street Corner Society,* in which Whyte (1943) provided vivid portraits of city life and recorded the social world of street gangs in Boston's North End.

Phenomenology

Husserl and Heidegger provide the philosophical foundation for Phenomenology. Van Manen (1990) popularized phenomenology to seek a more profound and fuller meaning of the lived experience of study participants. As Stone explains (1975), the evaluator becomes a participant observer, systematically recording his/her reactions and feelings and those of the participants. This intermingling of perspectives creates the evaluation milieu which surrounds the target of the evaluation. After intensive involvement, interaction, and identity with the participants, the evaluator takes "an existentialist's leap from their immersed role to evaluating summatively their reaction to the total behavior of the group in a dispassionate and judicious way" (p. 65).

In an evaluation of a mentorship program for student nurses and midwives in Southeast Scotland, Neades et al. (2017) undertook a small-scale qualitative phenomenological study and used participant questionnaires and focus groups to capture the experience of mentored students, mentors, and service managers. While they found that the approach produced rich and detailed data, the sheer volume of data was unexpected and negatively impacted study timelines and workload responsibilities.

Social Constructivism

Guba and Lincoln, long-time partners and qualitative theorists, wrote extensively about a naturalistic approach to evaluation (1981). They explained that naturalistic inquirers focus on multiple realities, that "like the layers of an onion, nest within or complement one another. Each layer provides a different perspective of reality, and none can be considered more 'true' than any other" (p. 57). Rather than taking a singular, positivist stance, the naturalistic evaluator is open, exploratory, and complex, diverges into multiple truths, and focuses on patterns and differences. Truth results from social interaction and the determination of shared meaning among a group of people. Truth is only understood in the study's specific context. Lincoln continued to work on this constructivist perspective after her partner's death and produced *The Constructivist Credo* (2013), which distills their long conversation on the topic into a set of principles.

A constructivist approach is often found in the evaluation of teaching and learning in online environments because it acknowledges different learning styles and rates of progress. Iofciu et al. (2012) describe the use of a constructivist evaluation of science education. Tools included: (1) self-evaluation for students to judge the quality of their work based on evidence and explicit criteria; (2) peer review of student papers using a peer-review worksheet designed by the instructor; (3) graphic organizers for students to personally track performance; and (4) portfolios of a student's best work to reflect the growth of their learning. The approach allowed students to reflect on their skill acquisition and to obtain feedback from both their peers and the instructor.

Narrative Inquiry

Narrative inquiry treats the story as valid data and involves interpreting it, placing it in context, and comparing it with other stories. Stories capture the individual's experience more intensely than any other format, so it is not surprising that they provide a valid tradition for the evaluator. As the term "story" casts an appealing aura to what might otherwise be a threatening interview situation, sharing stories allows people to relax and have more confidence in the research process. Story as narrative or case study provides an "especially translucent window" into the human experience (Patton, 2015, p. 128). A narrative study is essentially a story about participants' stories (Mayan, 2009, p. 50).

The use of narrative has long been an important part of evaluations (Salm & Stevens, 2016, para. 1) and usually starts with either a group interview, a story circle, or an individual interview. Evaluators can record information in many ways, from standardized questionnaires to open-ended comments. In addition, evaluators can use different analysis methods to interpret the transcribed text by determining codes, themes, anecdotes, and exemplars or identifying the most significant changes.

Participants can also tell stories visually. Photovoice is a data collection method that entrusts cameras to the hands of people so that they can record their own experience, using "the immediacy of the visual image to furnish evidence and to promote an effective, participatory means of sharing expertise and knowledge" (Wang & Burris, 1997). These authors used photovoice to conduct a participatory needs assessment for the Yunnan Women's Reproductive Health and Development Program in two counties in China. Taking photographs allowed rural women to document their experiences with lack of water, transportation, and childcare and enabled them to add their voices to the policymaking process.

Gail has used photovoice with her online evaluation students (Barrington, 2021). Using a smartphone or camera, they took three photos that captured the challenges and benefits of being an online student during a pandemic. Then they discussed them with their peers and reflected on the experience. Themes of loneliness, isolation, impact on family, and reliance on technology emerged, topics that might not have been evident to their instructor otherwise.

Critical Theory

Critical theory comes with a basket of traditions, such as Feminist Inquiry, Queer Theory, Indigenous and Postcolonialism, Critical Race Theory, and others. Their commonality is that they focus on reflective assessment and critique society and culture to address "issues of power inequities, the impact of privilege, and consequences of these for achieving social justice" (Mertens, 2019, p. 159) (see Chapter 2). These traditions are rooted in the philosophies of Kant, Marx, Habermas, Friere, and others who are concerned with race and ethnicity, gender and sexual orientation, class, culture, disability, and political status—any characteristic associated with marginalization and social inequity.

Because evaluation occurs in a social context, it is inherently a political activity. Mertens (2009, p. 48) comments that "discrimination and oppression are pervasive, and that evaluators have a moral responsibility to understand the communities in which they work in order to challenge societal processes that allow the status quo to continue."

Jackson et al. (2018) used a subjectivist or transformative framework for a needs assessment in a Hispanic community in Greenfield, Texas, an area that had the lowest median income, the greatest number of children under 18 living in poverty, and the highest percentage of families on public assistance programs in the city. While other studies had identified gaps in the infrastructure, the existing data were too generalized for decision makers to know how to institute change. A transformative design allowed them to hear the voices of community members. It provided greater insight into the power of community relationships, how a lack of trust constrained them, and why agencies needed to adopt a social justice framework to ensure community change.

Grounded Theory

Grounded theory is a set of qualitative strategies that are systematic, flexible, comparative, and iterative. It relies on the interplay between the researcher and the data and uses an inductive approach. Evaluators collect and analyze qualitative data to construct theories or meaning grounded in the data. As Charmaz (2014, p. 1) explains, it "invokes iterative strategies of going back and forth between data and analysis, uses comparative methods, and keeps you interacting and involved with your data and emerging analysis." The evaluator tries to identify why and how people behave in certain ways by moving from the specific to the general to build an explanatory theory. Many kinds of data can be included, such as the texts from intensive interviews, logs or diaries, public documents, files, databases, participant observation, and case studies. A strength of the method is that it provides clear procedures to analyze data such as coding, diagramming, and memoing, thus adding standardization and rigor to the analysis process.

Initially developed by Glasser and Strauss (1967), Charmaz (2014) expanded it in her excellent resource, *Constructing Grounded Theory*. It is one of the most influential traditions in evaluation today, although evaluators often use it informally and may not acknowledge or even know that it as the source of their methodology. For example, in a health evaluation, Foley and Timonen (2015) used grounded theory to explain how and why people with Amyotrophic Lateral Sclerosis (ALS) interacted with healthcare services. After completing and scrutinizing their interview codes, they found that "the experience of loss permeated all interviews and was *the* central experience for participants and shaped how they engaged with health care services" (p. 1203). Thus, grounded theory proved to be a valuable method to capture variation in participant experience while being rigorous, credible, and "do-able."

Table 8.1, p. 296 provides a summary of these qualitative traditions, their disciplinary roots, foundational questions, key ideas, and typical data collection methods.

TABLE 8.1 ● QUALITATIVE TRADITIONS IN EVALUATION				
Tradition	Roots	Foundational Questions	Key Ideas	Typical Data Collection Methods
1. Ethnography	Anthropology	• What is the culture of this group of people?	• An outsider's perspective • Interpretation from a cultural perspective/cultural competency • Organizational studies • Virtual ethnography	• Participant observation • Intensive fieldwork
2. Phenomenology	Philosophy	• What is the meaning, structure, and essence of the lived experience of this phenomenon for this person or group of people?	• Focus is on retaining the essence of lived experience and making sense of how people experience it • The subjective experience becomes a person's reality and how they interpret the world • An assumption that shared experience can be analyzed and compared	• Participant observation • In-depth interviews • Photovoice • Reflection • World Café
3. Social Constructivism	Sociology	• How have the people in this setting constructed reality? • What are their reported perceptions, "truths," explanations, beliefs, and worldview? • What are the consequences of their construction for their behaviors and for those with whom they interact?	• Multiple realities must be captured because perception is a constructed version of reality • Truth is a matter of consensus; phenomena are only understood within the context • Stakeholders have different program experiences; one perspective is not more valuable than another despite power differentials	• Open-ended interviews • Observation • Critical analysis and deconstruction • Relation between investigator and investigated
4. Narrative Inquiry	Social Sciences Literary Criticism Non-fiction	• How can this narrative or story be interpreted to understand the person and world from which it comes? • How can this narrative be interpreted to understand and illuminate the life and culture that created it?	• Lived experience • People's stories are the data • Tales from the field • The text of stories is central to the interpretation	• Narrative analysis • Life history and biography • Personal stories and autobiography • Historical memoirs • Creative nonfiction • Case studies

Table 8.1 *(Continued)*

Tradition	Roots	Foundational Questions	Key Ideas	Typical Data Collection Methods
5. Critical Theory, Feminist Inquiry, Queer Theory, Indigenous, and Postcolonialism, Critical Race Theory	Sociology Political Philosophy Literary Criticism	• What does a particular subjectivist perspective reveal and inform about how and why the world works as it does?	• Importance of being culturally respectful • Promotion of social justice • Furtherance of human rights • Addressing inequalities • Reciprocity • Community strength and resilience • Role of power, privilege, dominant values and ideology in oppression and subjugation • Results are interpreted through a specific lens such as race, ethnicity, class, gender, sexual orientation and disability • The goal is not only to study but to change society	• Transformative evaluation • Social justice perspective • Participatory, collaborative and empowerment approaches
6. Grounded Theory	Social Science	• What theory emerges from systematic and ongoing comparative analysis and is grounded in fieldwork to explain what is observed?	• Inductive theory building • Testing emergent concepts through fieldwork • Analysis is the interplay between evaluators and the data • Data can be quantitative or qualitative • Provides a set of coding procedures to standardize analysis	• Interviews • Focus groups • Document analysis • Participant observation • Case studies

Sources: Adapted from Patton, M. Q. (2002). *Qualitative research and evaluation methods.* Thousand Oaks: CA: SAGE Publications; Patton, M. Q. (2015). *Qualitative research and evaluation methods.* Thousand Oaks, CA: SAGE Publications; Mayan, M. J. (2009). *Essentials of qualitative inquiry.* New York, NY: Routledge; Mertens, D. (2019). *Research and evaluation in education and psychology.* Thousand Oaks, CA: SAGE Publications.

Common Characteristics of Qualitative Designs

No matter which qualitative method you choose, they all share some essential characteristics (Creswell & Creswell, 2018, pp. 181–182; Patton, 2015, p. 46). We have organized these common characteristics into the topics of participants, design, data collection, and the self.

Participants

Participants' Meaning. The evaluator does not focus on the meaning they bring to the study or what others commonly describe in the literature. Throughout the evaluation, they focus on the meaning held by the participants regarding the problem or issue under study.

Purposeful Sampling. Cases for study (e.g., people, organizations, communities, cultures, events, and critical incidences) are selected because they are "information rich" and illuminative. They offer useful manifestations of the phenomenon of interest; the goal of sampling is insight about the phenomenon, not an empirical generalization from a sample to a population.

Holistic Account. Evaluators report multiple perspectives, identify the many factors involved in the issue under study, determine how they interact, and create a complex picture that approximates real life.

Design

Emergent Design. In the initial design, the evaluator does not prescribe the inquiry too tightly as parts of the research process may shift when they enter the field and begin to collect data. In addition, the inquiry process can be adapted as understanding deepens or situations change. For example, the questions, the forms of data collection, and the study participants and sites can all shift and change based on emergent findings.

Data Collection and Analysis

Multiple Sources of Data. Evaluators do not rely on a single source for their data. For example, they gather information from documents, interviews, correspondence, and observation notes. **Data analysis** cuts across data sources and uses a variety of methods or software to reduce the data to obtain a greater understanding of the participants and/or the problem and the influence of the intervention on the outcomes.

Inductive and Deductive Data Analysis. Evaluators organize the data from the ground up. They work inductively to create categories, themes, and patterns to develop increasingly abstract units of information. Then based on these themes, they work deductively to determine if more evidence is needed.

Natural Setting. Evaluators tend to collect data where participants experience the phenomenon, or program, under study. Real-world situations are studied as they unfold; the evaluator is open to whatever emerges.

The Self

Evaluator as Key Instrument. The evaluator is the research instrument. While they may use a protocol to record the data, they are the mechanism through which the information is gathered and interpreted.

Reflexivity. The evaluator reflects on their role and how their background, culture, and past experiences shape their assumptions and how they interact with the study.

Memo writing provides a means to reflect on how these personal experiences may shape their interpretation.

As Maxwell (2013, p. 87) warns, there is no cookbook approach to qualitative design. In true qualitative fashion, "it depends." One of the critical issues is how the evaluator describes their study. Does their language reflect a structured, objectivist, deductive, and closed-ended perspective or is it unstructured, constructivist, inductive, and open to emergent developments?

"Structured approaches can help to ensure the comparability of data across individuals, times, settings, and other researchers, and are particularly useful in answering questions that deal with *differences* between people or settings" (Maxwell, 2013, p. 88). Less structured approaches focus on the phenomenon under study, trading generalizability and comparability for internal validity and contextual understanding and revealing the processes that lead to specific outcomes.

Evaluators are pragmatists by both nature and design. They conduct their evaluations for decision makers who need the information as soon as possible. These clients have structured timelines, limited budgets, and various constituents or stakeholders who demand answers. Neither the evaluator nor the client has the luxury of exploring a topic of interest for its own sake. A highly inductive, loosely designed study may not be feasible.

How then can an evaluator be a qualitative researcher? The answer lies in the structure of the evaluation. The logic model and evaluation plan are generally quite structured because they may be part of the funding proposal used to support the study or because clients, stakeholders, and steering committees want a clear indication of the evaluator's plans. A highly emergent process is seldom an option. Fortunately, while the evaluation plan can be very detailed in survey design, sampling, and analysis plans, it can be quite flexible in other areas. Within a delineated structure, there is still room for flexibility. It is simply a question of framing the areas "we do not know" within the broader study parameters. For example, evaluators can use focus groups to identify further areas of exploration. A snowball design can turn interviews into a journey of discovery. An evaluability assessment can identify areas where emergence is more likely to be successful than preordained plans.

One evaluation approach that relies on an emergent, qualitative design is Developmental Evaluation (Patton, 2011). This type of formative evaluation is well suited to social innovation, which tends to occur in uncertain, dynamic, and complex environments where the path to success is not clear or where continuous progress, ongoing adaptation, and rapid responsiveness are needed (see Chapter 5).

Common Threats to Quality and How to Counteract Them

There are several common threats to the quality of qualitative designs (Caudle, 2004, pp. 427–428; Mayan, 2009, pp. 92–93), and these are presented in Table 8.2, p. 300.

Threat	Description
TABLE 8.2 ● COMMON THREATS TO QUALITY IN QUALITATIVE DESIGNS	
Inaccurate or incomplete data	Evaluators only tell part of the story; some data are missed or ignored; they overvalue some data; and the evaluator can be rushed or fatigued.
Misinterpretation of the data's meaning	The evaluator's background, training, values, and assumptions may influence their interpretation.
Uneven weighting	The evaluator may tend to overweight facts believed to be accurate and ignore or forget data not consistent with their reasoning; may see confirmatory evidence but not that which contradicts; and may select pithy quotes to make a point that may not be representative of the data.
Failure to document the chain of evidence	The evaluator may only provide cursory information about the evaluation scope, methodology, analytical decisions, and evidence-based conclusions.
Sequential analysis	The evaluator may not analyze the data iteratively by not working abductively across data collection, coding, and analysis; may miss important "gems" that could significantly change the nature of the research.
Use of a predetermined theory or framework	The evaluator may look for confirmation of assumptions held at the initiation of the study.

Source: Caudle, S. L. (2004). *Qualitative data analysis: Handbook of practical program evaluation* (2nd ed.). John Wiley & Sons, Inc; Mayan, M. J. (2009). *Essentials of qualitative inquiry.* Left Coast Press.

Many tools are available to counteract these threats. Popular procedures used throughout the research process include (Mayan, 2009, pp. 108–111; Lub, 2015, pp. 1–8):

During Study Design

- Methodological coherence to ensure congruence between the evaluator's epistemological and ontological viewpoint, theoretical position, research questions, and data collection methods (see Chapter 2)

- Appropriate and adequate sampling that includes participants who can speak to the topic and provide rich data

- Evaluator responsiveness and the ability to be a critical thinker.

During Data Collection

- Prolonged engagement and observation in the field—long enough to adequately represent the subject under investigation

- Audit trails that document the evaluator's processes and choices through audio files, notes, and memos

- Concurrent data collection and analysis so that the design and processes can be refined as needed.

During Data Analysis and Synthesis

- Member checks that involve systematic feedback from stakeholders, key informants, and participants on the effectiveness of data collection processes and the accuracy of the evaluator's interpretation

- Peer debriefing through an external evaluation of the research process by peer reviewers or devil's advocates. Both evaluators and peer reviewers must continually ask:

  - Can the data support the findings?

  - Are the conclusions logical?

  - Can methodological choices be justified?

- Negative case selection or a conscious search for outliers

- Theorizing at both the micro-level (the data) and the macro-level (the literature), "inching forward without making cognitive leaps" (Morse et al., 2002, p. 6).

Goodyear et al. (2014) see quality in qualitative evaluation as grounded in a cyclical and reflective process that is facilitated by the evaluator. There are five distinct elements needed to achieve a high-quality evaluation (p. 251). These include:

1. The evaluator must first bring a clear sense of personal identity and professional role to the process. It is a matter of understanding who you are, what you know, and what you need to learn.

2. The evaluator needs to engage stakeholders and develop trusting relationships from the outset and throughout the evaluation.

3. High-quality evaluation relies on sound methodology, systematically applied, that is explicitly shared with stakeholders.

4. Conducting quality evaluation can only be accomplished by remaining "true" to the data; in other words, hearing participants as they are, now how the evaluator wants them to be.

5. Skillful facilitation of the process by the evaluator results in learning by all involved.

These elements are summarized in the model in Figure 8.4, p. 302.

Strengths and Limitations of Qualitative Designs

Evaluators are human, and, like them, all methods, techniques, and strategies have their strengths and their limitations. Qualitative methods let you travel deeper into the attitudes or ways of thinking behind the numbers (Gaille, 2018). Qualitative research has many strengths but there are some limitations. Review Table 8.3, p. 302 for a summary.

FIGURE 8.4 ● CYCLE OF QUALITY IN QUALITATIVE EVALUATION

Source: Goodyear, L., Jewiss, J., Usinger, J., & Barela, E. (2014). *Qualitative inquiry in evaluation: From theory to practice.* Jossey Bass.

TABLE 8.3 ● STRENGTHS AND LIMITATIONS OF QUALITATIVE METHODS

Strengths of Qualitative Methods	Limitations of Qualitative Methods
• Complex phenomena can be explored. • Focus is on the particular, the personal, and the specific. • Applied in natural settings rather than controlled environments. • Situations are dynamic, emergent, and changing. • The framework and tools can be quickly revised as new information emerges. • Produces rich description and detail which can be more powerful and compelling than quantitative data. • Subtleties are discovered that are often missed by quantitative approaches. • A tentative theory is developed and can be refined based on more information.	• Findings cannot be generalized due to small sample size. • The information produced remains situated in the study context. • Study quality is dependent on the individual skills of the evaluator; and can be influenced by personal biases and idiosyncrasies. • Rigor is more difficult to maintain, assess, and demonstrate. • It takes more time, money, and effort for data collection and analysis than an equivalent quantitative study. • Findings can be more difficult and time-consuming to characterize in a visual way. • Qualitative data may have lower credibility with administrators and commissioners of evaluation.

Source: Johnson, R. B., & Onwuegbuzie, A. J. (2004). Mixed-methods research: A research paradigm whose time has come. *Educational Researcher, 33,* 14–26; (p. 20); Anderson, C. (2010). Presenting and evaluating qualitative research. *American Journal of Pharmaceutical Education, 74*(8), 1–7. https://doi.org/10.5688/aj7408141

Next, in our Spotlight on Equity, you can read about the experiences of two evaluators above the Arctic Circle.

SPOTLIGHT ON EQUITY

Honouring Community Voices:

The Evaluator Experience in Old Crow, Yukon

In 2008, the Yukon Department of Education decided to create a vision for secondary school programming in the Territory's capital city, Whitehorse. Evaluators Linda Lee and Larry Bremner of Proactive Information Services Inc. were asked to identify issues that would impact secondary school programming, program improvement, systemic change, and facility requirements for the new high school then in the planning stage. They share their reflections with us.

Our review was complex and multifaceted. We began by reviewing the literature and then conducted a program inventory, document review, and key informant interviews with department staff. Then we visited schools in Whitehorse, interviewing educators and holding focus groups with students. We surveyed all secondary school students, teachers, and a number of community members; interviewed community stakeholders, and held public consultations. Although we needed to complete this rather daunting task within less than a year, we realized that something important was still missing. Students from the many small Northern communities who came to Whitehorse for their secondary schooling, as well as their families and communities, had not been contacted, yet their input was critical if programming was indeed to change.

Our planned process was to train Indigenous students at Yukon College so they could go into the communities and conduct the interviews. They would know the community context and protocols, and they would also benefit by learning how to conduct interviews themselves.

We met with the Yukon First Nations Education Advisory Committee, made up of representatives and Elders from the 13 Yukon First Nations, and proudly presented our idea. We were met with a long silence. Then they began talking among themselves and finally, an Elder spoke up and suggested that our idea was not a good one. We needed to go to the communities ourselves. We had the power to write the report, so we needed to hear the community voices and the stories firsthand if we were to reflect their realities properly in our report.

We immediately agreed and asked the members of the Advisory Committee to select four diverse communities for us to visit. One of these was Old Crow, a Vuntut Gwitchin community of about 300 people, located within the Arctic Circle on the banks of the Porcupine River in the Northwest area of the Yukon Territory (Figure 8.5, p. 304). It was accessible only by air.

Luckily, we were linked with a community Elder who was able to facilitate our visit to the community. We arrived at the Old Crow airport in June at the time of the summer solstice when there was 24 hours of daylight (Figure 8.6, p. 305). The Elder met us and took us by all-terrain vehicle to the nursing station. We spent our first night there, before moving to the only bed and breakfast in the community.

Over the next three days, the Elder took charge of our tour. He led us to the First Nations office and introduced us to everyone and we had conversations in offices and hallways. He took us on learning walks in the community where we talked with parents and community members. We were invited to a community feast and were introduced. We spoke to many people. We visited the school and listened to the experiences of students and educators. We took a trip down the beautiful Porcupine River with Old Crow secondary students who were home for the summer. We had conversations with them on the river's banks when we stopped for a cookout. We listened to Elders at the abandoned site of Rampart House, an old Hudson's Bay trading post established in 1890 on the Alaskan border (Vuntut Gwitchin First Nation, 2022).

We heard their voices and stories. What came through was the frustration that students experienced when they were streamed into dead-end programs as soon as they arrived in Whitehorse. As one student explained, the school staff said:

You are from Old Crow, so you go into this course.

The result of this quick sorting process was that the students gained only a high school completion certificate instead of a graduation diploma. Parents were not informed of the implications of this decision and remained unaware that their children would not be accepted into postsecondary programs upon completing school.

FIGURE 8.5 ⬡ OLD CROW IN THE YUKON

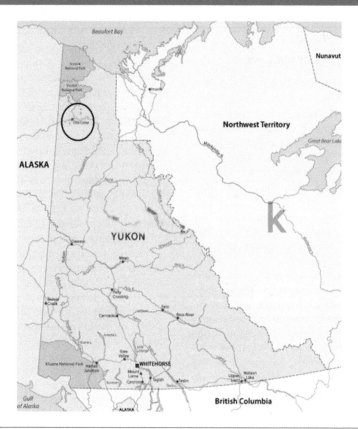

Source: istockphoto.com/Rainer Lesniewski

We heard how difficult it was to leave home and to stay in a residence down the street from the old Whitehorse Residential School. As one Elder told us:

The cover has changed, but the book remains the same.

We heard how overwhelmed they felt in the noise and bustle of a school with more students in it than in their whole community. As one young man told us:

Every day [in Whitehorse] brings a different feeling. When the geese fly over you feel homesick. When the snow comes, when the caribou come, you want to be home.

The parent of a former student voiced her frustration:

I still feel my daughter missed out on so much. It's similar to my own situation growing up in the residential school system. We weren't given a voice back then. And today we still don't have a voice to share our concerns, where people who educate our children will really take the time to listen, where our children can get the best of both worlds—the traditional upbring, culture, language, and traditions and integrate it into the modern school system where they will come out winners....able to hold their own in any situation they are challenged with, instead of walking away and saying 'I quit; it's too hard to deal with.' I speak for people who cannot speak for themselves, and I don't want our children, here in our community, to miss out any more than they have.

As we reflect on our time in Old Crow, we think how privileged we were to be welcomed into the community.

FIGURE 8.6 ◆ AT THE OLD CROW AIRPORT

Source: **Larry K. Bremner and Linda E. Lee.**

The voices we heard were powerful and the stories, often distressing. People in Old Crow told us of the importance of 'being on the land' and, for us, being in Old Crow—on the land and on the water—immersed us in the context and increased our understanding of the stories we heard.

The voices from the community visits strengthened our report and led us to reflect that Yukon, like many jurisdictions across Canada, lives with cultural and racial tensions that often play themselves out in public institutions. Yukon has the advantage of being a "younger" jurisdiction where history may be more easily overcome and Indigenous knowledge and cultures can be treated as significant assets. However, the educational system needed to recognize that the many First Nations families who send their children to secondary school in Whitehorse must deal emotionally with the legacy of residential schools, as well as with systemic barriers. Despite this reality, there was incredible opportunity to move forward in the spirit of equity and inclusion. While not all the recommendations from our report were implemented, educational policy changes did result. One of the recommendations led to a dual credit pilot program at Yukon College for high school students, and the report informed the *Yukon First Nations Joint Education Action Plan 2014–2024 (Yukon First Nations, 2014).*

This Spotlight on Equity is based on the contributions of Larry K. Bremner and Linda E. Lee.

QUALITATIVE ANALYSIS—OVERVIEW

In this section, we look at qualitative data analysis, strategies to deal with some of the associated issues, how to think critically about the data, and the three steps involved in **data reduction**.

First, we need to clarify what data we are talking about. Typically, Qualitative data can consist of "interview transcripts, participant observation field notes, journals, documents, open-ended survey responses, drawings, artifacts, photographs, video, Internet sites, email correspondence, academic and fictional literature, and so on" (Saldaña, 2016, p. 4). In this section, we often use the generic term "document" when any of the above forms of communication might be involved.

Then we need to look more closely at how we analyze data. While inquiry process itself is the source of rich, well-grounded, and often vivid information, it is important to use credible analytic methods to produce reliable findings. In the past, evaluators may have chosen to use "whatever works" to analyze their qualitative data, glossing over their analysis processes. However, as Mayan (2009, p. 85) points out, if we say merely, "The categories emerged from the data," our work will be discredited. This explanation is no longer considered sufficient. "Procedures must be reported that align with accepted qualitative analysis methods which are being documented more and more frequently in the literature" (p. 85).

The classic approach uses a hybrid blend of ethnography and grounded theory (Miles et al., 2020). The evaluator must move:

> *from one inductive inference to another by selectively collecting data, comparing and contrasting this material in the quest for patterns or regularities, seeking out more data to support or qualify these emerging clusters, and then gradually drawing inferences from the links between other new data segments and the cumulative set of conceptions.* (p. 6)

The process is iterative. The evaluator cannot collect all the data first and then hibernate in their office to conduct the analysis. This would be a big mistake because:

> *it rules out the possibility of collecting new data to fill in gaps or to test new hypotheses that emerge during analysis. It discourages the formulation of rival hypotheses that question a fieldworker's routine assumptions. And it makes analysis into a giant, sometimes overwhelming task that frustrates the researcher and reduces the quality of the work produced.* (Miles et al., 2020, p. 62)

The evaluator should structure their qualitative study or the qualitative components of their study (as in a mixed-methods design—see Chapter 9) so that they can conduct at least a portion of the data collection and analysis concurrently. Cycling back and forth between existing data and strategies for future data collection enhances the tools, the processes, and the results. For example, it is possible to conduct a pilot study or a phased approach to data collection to allow for revision and improvement as understanding expands. Early findings can be circulated in interim reports to generate further discussion and interpretation.

Recall the three types of critical thinking described in Chapter 2 (deductive, inductive, and abductive). Neither entirely deductive nor inductive, abduction allows the qualitative evaluator to "knit back and forth" between what is known and what is still unknown. The evaluator begins to work backward, starting with the data to consider possible explanations, best guesses, speculations, conjectures, and hypotheses. Then, by returning to the data, re-framing it, and naming it, at last one arrives at the most plausible interpretation, hypothesis, or theory (Mayan, 2009, p. 87; Patton, 2015, pp. 560–562).

Some of the issues encountered by the evaluator who conducts a qualitative study include:

- Labor intensiveness

- Frequent data overload

- Time demands to process and analyze data

- The adequacy of sampling

- The generalizability and transferability of findings

- The credibility, trustworthiness, and quality of conclusions

- The utility of the findings in a world of policy and action.

On the flip side, we live in the best of all possible worlds today because evaluators have support at their fingertips. Two crucial options can reduce the daunting tasks associated with **data preparation**:

1. The evaluator can transcribe the interview using transcription software that is freely available on the internet. If time is pressing and the budget permits, another option is to contract with an electronic data transcription service. These are generally both speedy and reasonably priced and usually charge by the word.

2. Computer-assisted qualitative data analysis software is available. Once learned, programs such as NVivo, MAXqda, QDA Miner, or ATLAS.ti can lessen the load significantly. Creswell and Creswell (2018) point out that software is a superior choice to laborious hand coding because these programs can store, locate, and use qualitative data efficiently. Although expensive, they offer good tutorials and demonstration files. In addition, some programs have specific low-cost versions available to students.

Another less formal solution for small data sets is to link codes and notes to relevant text with the comments function in Word. The comments are then cut and pasted into Excel® for further analysis. Bazeley's (2013) excellent text, *Qualitative Data Analysis: Practical Strategies* provides screen shots and examples of different software solutions. She explains several pathways to analysis.

While we do not have space here for a more extensive discussion of these data preparation processes, we heartily endorse their use. No software will replace the critical analysis and sheer thinking time required to interpret qualitative data. The analysis will always be time-consuming, but these time savers can shorten the process and decrease the evaluator's stress level.

The challenge that accompanies good qualitative analysis is that it is neither quick nor easy. It requires the evaluator to make sense of large amounts of data. As Patton comments

(2015), "this involves reducing the volume of raw information, sifting the trivial from the significant, identifying significant patterns, and constructing a framework for communicating the essence of what the data reveal" (p. 521).

USING BLOOM'S TAXONOMY—A FRAMEWORK FOR QUALITATIVE ANALYSIS

Bloom's Taxonomy offers an analytic framework that clearly distinguishes between the thought processes required at different levels of analysis. Devised by Bloom (1956) and his colleagues, the Taxonomy classifies learning objectives into three domains: cognitive, affective, and psychomotor. It is an explanation of the cognitive domain that has resonated greatly with educators over the years, and it has utility for evaluators as well. When we collect data and try to figure out what it means, we approach our data as learners. Bloom reminds us that an evaluator's higher-order thinking is preceded by lower-order knowledge. His framework offers a useful checklist to ensure that we use due diligence as we move from concrete to abstract knowledge in the cognitive hierarchy.

In Figure 8.7, we overlay Bloom's taxonomy with the associated steps in the qualitative analysis thought process.

FIGURE 8.7 ⬢ BLOOM'S TAXONOMY AND QUALITATIVE ANALYSIS

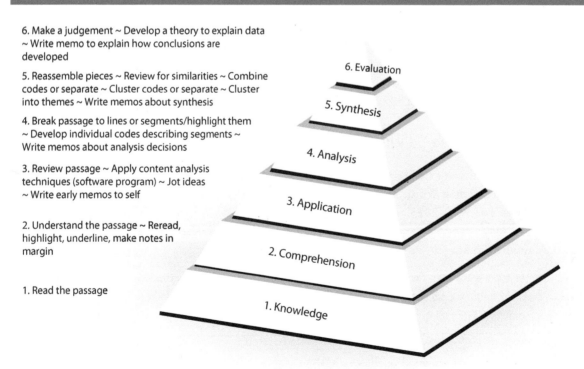

6. Make a judgement ~ Develop a theory to explain data ~ Write memo to explain how conclusions are developed

5. Reassemble pieces ~ Review for similarities ~ Combine codes or separate ~ Cluster codes or separate ~ Cluster into themes ~ Write memos about synthesis

4. Break passage to lines or segments/highlight them ~ Develop individual codes describing segments ~ Write memos about analysis decisions

3. Review passage ~ Apply content analysis techniques (software program) ~ Jot ideas ~ Write early memos to self

2. Understand the passage ~ Reread, highlight, underline, make notes in margin

1. Read the passage

6. Evaluation
5. Synthesis
4. Analysis
3. Application
2. Comprehension
1. Knowledge

Source: Adapted from Bloom, B. S. (1956). *Taxonomy of educational objectives: The classification of educational goals.* David McKay Co. Inc./slidemodel.com

Levels 1–6 are described in the following sections along with the analytical activities required.

Levels 1 and 2—Knowledge and Comprehension

Prepare to Code

We start at the bottom of Bloom's Taxonomy at Knowledge and Comprehension for this early stage of the analysis process. Before beginning to code a document, a critical first step is to explore the data, carefully reading the whole document to remind oneself of the depth and breadth of the content (Bazely, 2013). It builds "a contextualized and holistic understanding of the people, events, and ideas being investigated, and the connections within and between them" (p. 101).

Once the evaluator completes a thorough reading, it is time to start looking for patterns in the data. They then reread the document, this time more slowly and start to become saturated with the information, looking at and thinking about each element, highlighting sections of the text, and making comments in the margins (marginalia) as desired.

Level 3—Application

Record Analytic Thoughts and Processes

As we move up the pyramid, we arrive at the Application stage, where the recording of analytic ideas begins to occur. The highlighted sections and marginalia quickly turn into jottings or ideas, keywords, and questions noted as they arise. This written form of self-reflection starts the analysis process, and the evaluator must record it. Qualitative evaluators customarily write their preliminary thoughts or "musings" to record their thought processes both for themselves and others. It is a habit that continues throughout data collection, analysis, and writing (Bazeley, 2013, p. 103). Rather than being close-ended or jumping to conclusions, this form of writing is like having a discussion with oneself. It enhances the depth of analytic thinking. Recording these analytic thoughts as they arise often provides, as Miles and Huberman (1984) so eloquently describe, "sharp, sunlit moments of clarity or insight—little conceptual epiphanies" (p. 74).

An excellent way to keep track of these jottings is to start a research journal. A journal is more useful than the marginalia because you do not need to return to each original document to find the observations. While personal, these rough notes become a vital source of ideas for later analysis and report writing. Further, as evaluations are often long-term in nature, these immediate notes capture many ephemeral observations that the evaluator may forget over the longer term.

Bazely (2013, pp. 102–103) suggests:

1. Summarize critical points (referenced and dated).

2. Update these notes as new ideas emerge.

3. Write about what you have learned and note the ideas stimulated by the information in the document.

4. Create a diagram that captures processes described or discussed in the document.

While the research journal is often a hand-written notebook, the next step in recording the evaluator's thought processes is the memo. Memos are integrated into the data analysis software and so may be digital. They form the crucial first link in the chain of evidence between preliminary codes and the document's final theory or overall interpretation. They move beyond personal observations or jottings and begin to formalize the analysis process, creating a retrievable record of reflections and thoughts about the data analysis process. A critical question to keep in mind is: "Would another evaluator arrive at the same conclusions?"

Miles et al. provide advice on memo writing (2020, pp. 91–92):

- When an idea strikes, stop what you are doing and write the memo.

- Memo writing begins as soon as researchers generate the first field data and eventually produce the final report. The number of different ideas addressed by memos starts to stabilize or achieve what grounded theorists call "saturation," when about one-half or two-thirds of the data are collected (Miles et al., 2020, p. 91).

- To keep memos sortable, add a descriptive caption. They can be stored and retrieved either physically (e.g., index cards) or electronically. Most qualitative analysis programs offer a memo function.

- Remember that memos are about ideas and the researcher's interpretation process; they are not quotations or examples of the data.

Memo writing continues throughout the rest of the analysis process.

Level 4—Analysis

Reduce and Chunk the Data

Data reduction is the heart of the coding process and reflects the Analysis stage in Bloom's Taxonomy. Saldaña (2016, p. 14) provides a useful model that demonstrates the transition from codes to theory. As the evaluator moves from very small chunks of information on the model's left side to fewer and larger ones on the right side, the concepts become clustered and combined into increasingly large buckets of information. His model is in Figure 8.8, p. 311.

You can see that the data on the left represent the lines of text in the document we would code. We assign labels or codes to chunks of text. Sometimes when we revisit this text, they need to be revised, combined, or split, as shown. Then larger categories are produced that contain similar or clustered codes. Again, some categories may need to be split or combined as needed. The end point of this highly inductive analysis process is to arrive at an overall assertion about meaning. An assertion is a synthesizing statement confirmed by the evidence found in the codes and categories (Bazeley, 2013, p. 192). We refer to this statement as an emergent theory or hypothesis. We must test it further, but it is a first best guess at the overall data.

FIGURE 8.8 ● THE TRANSITION FROM CODES TO THEORY

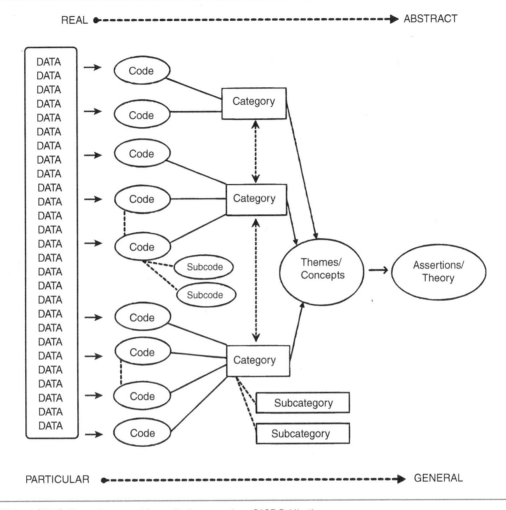

Source: Saldaña, J. (2016). *The coding manual for qualitative researchers*. SAGE Publications.

There are three steps needed to reduce and chunk the data:

1. Initial coding

2. Categorizing

3. Theming.

Initial Coding

Coding is the first step in the data reduction process. A code is the smallest discrete element or chunk of meaning in a document. The chunk does not need to be a sentence because a sentence may include more than one topic, but alternatively, sometimes several sentences relate to a single topic. The data chunk is as big as it needs to be to encapsulate a single idea or topic. A descriptive name or label, usually a single word, is then assigned to it. This label is the code.

There are many ways to code data. While Saldaña (2016) has identified 33 different coding strategies, two types are common in grounded theory approaches:

- Descriptive coding—a word, or short phrase, often a noun, to describe the basic topic of a passage

- Gerund coding—words ending in *-ing*, derived from a verb, connotes action or a sequence of events.

Box 8.1 provides a brief reflective passage on parenting, coded twice, once with descriptive coding, and again with gerund coding.

BOX 8.1 ● USING DESCRIPTIVE AND GERUND CODING[1]

Text	Descriptive Coding
Lately I have been wondering if I expect too much of my son. He gets all mixed up in his homework, is overtired, can't think straight, and spends hours doing one straightforward assignment when he should just be relaxing and enjoying family life like all the other kids in his class: he has misread the instructions and has to do the whole thing again; he has a thousand ideas for a report on gorillas, but can't seem to get it together to write even the opening sentence.	• Parental dilemma • Son overburdened • Son's listlessness • Son's lack of focus • Abundant ideas • Lack of initiative

Text	Gerund Coding
Lately I have been wondering if I expect too much of my son. He gets all mixed up in his homework, is overtired, can't think straight, and spends hours doing one straightforward assignment when he should just be relaxing and enjoying family life like all the other kids in his class: he has misread the instructions and has to do the whole thing again; he has a thousand ideas for a report on gorillas, but can't seem to get it together to write even the opening sentence.	• Questioning expectations for son • Expressing concern for the son's homework issues • Missing family life • Comparing son to his peers • Misinterpreting instructions • Redoing work • Coming up with ideas • Lacking initiative to get started

Source: van Manen, M. (1984). Practicing phenomenological writing: Robbie's mother's experience with parenting. *Phenomenology + pedagogy, 2*(1), 20–21. The University of Alberta. "Robbie's Mother's Experience with Parenting." https://ejournals.library.ualberta.ca/index.php/pandp/article/viewFile/14931/11752. Thanks to Raymond Adda, former student in PSY 884 at Michigan State University, for his assistance with this analysis. February 28, 2019.

[1]Thanks to Raymond Adda, former student in PSY 884 at Michigan State University, for his assistance with this analysis. February 28, 2019.

When you compare these two approaches, you can see that descriptive coding focuses on topics and appears like a shopping list. It seems to limit or bound the meaning. Gerund coding provides a strong sense of action, sequence, and fluidity. It reveals possibilities and encourages the evaluator to see things from the participant's perspective (Charmaz, 2014, p. 121).

Another third common approach to coding, often used by evaluators, is *a priori* coding. Using this method, the evaluator works with a preprepared list of anticipated codes that are based on the evaluation questions, logic model, or data collection framework. This deductive approach focuses the analysis on sought-after concepts. In a rush to meet a client's need for specific information, the evaluator may limit coding to preassigned topics and may skip over other unexpected findings. Grounded theory can enhance findings by revealing unexpected linkages and nuances that sometimes seem bothersome and extraneous. Once the evaluator has searched deductively for important study topics, a second, open-ended review of the data can be revealing. The evaluator can ask, "What else are the data telling me?" We can add new codes as unanticipated findings illuminate the interpretation.

Codes allow data to be retrieved and clustered in preparation for further data reduction. Code generation seems daunting at first, but the topics usually stabilize quite quickly as we reach saturation. Good resources on coding include Bazeley (2013), Charmaz (2014), and Saldana (2016).

Categorizing

Categorizing is the second step in the data reduction process, sometimes referred to as pattern coding, focused coding, or axial coding (Miles et al., 2020, p. 79). Categorizing allows the evaluator to develop meaningful clusters of similar data (Hseih & Shannon, 2005) by recoding groups of similar codes at a slightly more abstract level and attaching a new label. These higher-level categories allow the evaluator to organize, index, and sort topics more quickly. Using a software program, database, or spreadsheet enhances this process.

The evaluator makes constant comparisons among groups of codes to ensure that the topics are similar enough to be grouped. If they do not fit together well, the evaluator can decide to expand the category, split it, transfer codes to different categories, or discard the code as irrelevant (Spiers, 2015). As the process draws the evaluator into a detailed understanding of the document, patterns of meaning emerge, such as causes, explanations, relationships, or concepts (Miles et al., 2020, p. 80). Mayan (2009, p. 95) suggests that to account for the data in a meaningful but manageable way, the researcher should restrict the number of categories to 10–12 categories when analyzing the text of a typical interview, much reduced from the initial expansive set of codes.

Theming

The third step is theming. The researcher creates large buckets of related data that combine the information to tell the story buried in the document. Themes are the few top-level points that capture key findings. Mayan (2009) again provides some guidance:

> *Newcomers often confuse or do not understand the difference between categories and themes. Themes are thoughts or processes that weave throughout and tie the categories together. Theming, then, is the process of determining the thread(s) that integrate and anchor all categories. To form themes, the researcher returns to the "big-picture" level and determines how the categories are related. You will typically have only one to three themes. If you have more, you are likely not abstracting enough.* (p. 97)

The researchers derive the themes from a thoughtful, evidence-based data reduction and reflection process and summarizes each one as a brief phrase.

Level 5—Recombine and Interpret

Synthesis

Once the researcher condenses the data into manageable units, it is time to pull them back together, compiling a new, much briefer, informed whole which sheds light on the original evaluation questions. This recombination occurs at the **synthesis stage** in Bloom's Taxonomy.

This section provides a brief overview of Miles and Huberman's (1984) ten classic strategies to synthesize data as well as an eleventh strategy described in their new text (Miles et al., 2020), namely data displays. These include four different ways to visualize the data, including narrative description, matrices, flowcharts, and graphics.

Count. It may be surprising to find that numbers have a place in qualitative research, but counting is still helpful to look at distribution and proportion. What is no longer acceptable is to base conclusions on frequency counts. Just because 26 participants mentioned one topic and four others said something different, there is no guarantee that the following 30 participants would respond in the same way, or, indeed, if you asked the first 30 the same question a second time, they would respond as they had before. It is a good idea to know when counting is appropriate and when it is not. Three good reasons to resort to numbers include (1) to see meaning quickly in a large batch of data, (2) to verify a hunch or hypothesis, and (3) to keep yourself honest by protecting against bias in the analysis (Miles et al., 2020, p. 279).

Note Patterns. Categories allow the evaluator to pull together much material to explain it in a meaningful and parsimonious way. Seeing patterns is almost intuitive but finding them is useful; the evaluator must avoid expecting a pattern to become the norm and then looking only for it. Instead, the evaluator must remain open to the possibility of disconfirming evidence, and in a sense, play devil's advocate, continuing to ask, "Does this make sense?"

Look at Plausibility. We are all good meaning finders and usually assign some meaning to chaotic or random events, even if it is inaccurate. Things may "feel right," but this initial impression may be false. Plausibility becomes the refuge of those who are too quick to conclude (Miles et al., 2020, p. 275). It acts as a signpost or pointer, drawing attention to a conclusion that looks reasonable. However, the evaluator must ask, "What is it based on?" and then dig deeper to see if there is more support. Lack of plausibility can also be helpful. When something does not make sense, we tend to rule it out, but puzzling findings can be extraordinarily rich, and the evaluator needs to probe them well.

Cluster. We cluster things together to understand a phenomenon better by grouping and then conceptualizing items with similar patterns or characteristics. We use an iterative sorting process, comparing and aggregating as we go. For example, we ask, "What things are like or unlike each other?" We group them accordingly. As the evaluator clusters the data, the concepts get more abstract and further removed from the original item. Like packing a suitcase, we can put many miscellaneous items together, but our job as a coder is to make sure that the items are similar enough in meaning to fit together.

Make Metaphors. A metaphor is a figure of speech that compares two things without expressing the relationship between the two. It is possible to imply meaning. That "unstatedness" stimulates the imagination, and connections are made. It may seem that metaphor has no place in the field of evaluation because of our need to obtain as accurate a representation of reality as possible. Neutral language may not capture the feelings or values that evaluators often need to describe. The metaphor unites reason and imagination and lies halfway between empirical facts and the conceptual significance of those facts (Miles et al., 2020, p. 278). Metaphors are compelling for stakeholders who may not have the technical language so often used in evaluation.

Split Variables. The direction of our analysis and synthesis activities is toward integration and reduction, but sometimes you have to say, "Stop! These things do not really go together. It's not one variable; it's two or three." Sometimes you need to unbundle a variable, which seemed to work well at first but eventually became combined with too many disparate items, which now the evaluator should regroup. The goal is to avoid burying significantly different variables in the same category but at the same time to avoid having too many variables with only a hair's difference between them. "When you divide a variable, it should be in the service of finding coherent, integrated descriptions and explanations" (Miles et al., p. 281).

Move From Particular to General. Moving from particular to general is both a conceptual and theoretical activity. The evaluator shuttles back and forth or up and down the Ladder of Abstraction (see Chapter 2) between first-level data and more general categories. The process evolves through successive iterations, back and forth, up and down, until the category is saturated, and more data do not add new meaning.

Factor. Factoring is a statistical technique used to represent numerous variables by a smaller number of unobserved and usually hypothetical variables. Most of the tactics described here are data reduction and pattern-making exercises. When you derive a pattern or a category, you hypothesize that these disparate facts go together in some way and have *something* in common. That *thing* that they have in common is called a factor. Thus, it is a pattern of a pattern or a category of categories. Ultimately, we must ask if the factor (i.e., uber category) makes a meaningful difference or just a decorative wrapping (Miles et al., 2020, p. 283).

Note Relationships Among Variables. Once we are clear about the variables or themes, our next question is, "What is their relationship to each other?" Using abductive thinking, we work back and forth between variables to determine their relationships. Data displays such as matrices and flowcharts (discussed in the next section) are helpful ways to visualize them.

Find Intervening Variables. Finally, it seems sometimes as if two variables ought to go together, but they only seem to have a tepid or inconclusive relationship. Other times, two variables do go well together, but there seems to be no reason they should. In both cases, it may be that a third hidden variable is confusing the relationship. For example, look at the following formula:

$$A \rightarrow [Q] \rightarrow B$$

You can see in this formula that A and B are disrupted by Q. Ask yourself, "What does Q stand for?" Then, it is time to go back to the data and hunt for Q. Qualitative inquiry goes beyond the linear cause–effect thought process to look at multiple, often interactive influences. For example, if you had asked Bob if the Quit Smoking program caused him to stop smoking, as the evaluators claimed, he might have told you that the reason he quit was that his friend had just died of lung cancer, an intervening variable that had nothing to do with the program. Evaluators need to probe and question to make sure that such hidden variables do not exist.

Data Displays. The volume of data involved in qualitative research is cumbersome, unwieldy, and dense. Even a small study can yield several hundred pages of text and boxes of files. In our highly visual culture, attention spans are short (sometimes as short as a sound bite), and so evaluators must work to capture readers' attention. It is often better to show the results first and then provide more detail for those who want it. Here are four ways to portray synthesized data and capture the reader's attention: (1) narrative description, (2) the matrix, (3) the flowchart, and (4) the creative graphic.

Narrative Description. While not a visual display, written narratives paint a picture in words. Everyone loves a story and there are so many stories to tell in every evaluation study. Often, one carefully selected, eloquent quotation from a program participant can do more to capture a decision maker's attention than any table of statistics. Another type of story is the case study. Clients welcome these because they communicate the sense of what it is like to be there—at a program site, in a practitioner's shoes, responding like the client to a specific phenomenon such as a service, activity, event, or treatment.

For example, Smith et al. (1999) evaluate the benefits of a therapeutic massage program in an acute care setting. They captured the outcomes identified by patients, and analyzed surveys and narrative reports by 70 patients, 14 healthcare providers, and 4 massage therapists. One of their conclusions was: "Pain relief was one of the most frequently mentioned benefits of massage therapy within the hospital setting" (p. 6). But that statement did not have the same impact as this supporting quotation:

I always get headaches and wake up with them in the night, and I didn't get a headache last night and I don't have one now. I haven't had one since the massage. I think the massage therapy is one of the most beneficial treatments that the hospital can offer to patients. It helped me tremendously. (p. 6)

The Matrix. A matrix sometimes called a table or grid, is "essentially the 'intersection' of two lists, set up as rows and columns" (Miles et al., 2020, p. 105). It is an economical way to depict relationships between two or more variables that might not be evident without this side-by-side comparison. It collapses data into an efficient framework and sets the stage for deeper questioning and more detailed analysis.

For example, Patton (2015) described a high school dropout program that focused on reducing absenteeism, skipping classes, and tardiness. An external team of change agents worked with teachers to study the problem. Their observations and interviews uncovered two critical dimensions:

- Teachers' beliefs about what kind of program intervention was effective with dropouts

- Teachers' behaviors toward dropouts on a continuum from taking responsibility to shifting it to others.

The qualitative analyst working with the data had struggled to find patterns that would express the different roles teachers played in the program. But when the two dimensions were crossed in a matrix format, "the whole thing immediately fell into place" (pp. 560–561). Each cell represented a different role for the teacher, and by working back and forth between the matrix and the data, the researcher was then able to generate labels and a full description and analysis of the diverse and conflicting roles teachers played (Patton, 2015, p. 561). Table 8.4 presents the matrix.

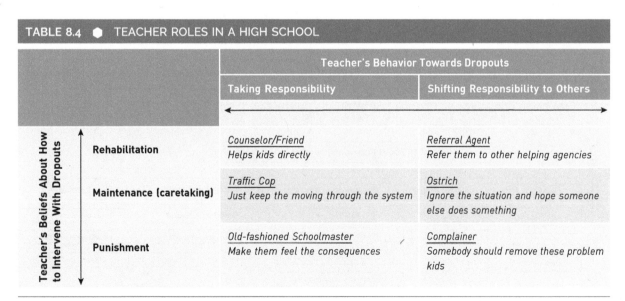

TABLE 8.4 ● TEACHER ROLES IN A HIGH SCHOOL		
	Teacher's Behavior Towards Dropouts	
	Taking Responsibility	**Shifting Responsibility to Others**
Rehabilitation	*Counselor/Friend* *Helps kids directly*	*Referral Agent* *Refer them to other helping agencies*
Maintenance (caretaking)	*Traffic Cop* *Just keep the moving through the system*	*Ostrich* *Ignore the situation and hope someone else does something*
Punishment	*Old-fashioned Schoolmaster* *Make them feel the consequences*	*Complainer* *Somebody should remove these problem kids*

(Row label: **Teacher's Beliefs About How to Intervene With Dropouts**)

Source: Patton, M. Q. (2015). *Qualitative research and evaluation methods.* SAGE Publications.

The Flowchart. Flowcharts are conceptual maps or diagrams representing workflows or processes, sequences of events, and various relationships in complex systems. Topics are presented in boxes or nodes and link the variable connections with lines. A flowchart maps sequences and relationships with more fluidity than a static matrix as multiple connections, and complex relationships can be displayed simultaneously.

The position of the nodes can imply distance from each other, centrality, and number of connections. In addition, evaluators can represent the directionality of relationships with single, bidirectional, or multidirectional arrow heads. Additionally, they can represent the strength of connections with visual elements such as varied line widths and lengths, and different fonts, shading, and colors.

In evaluation, the most ubiquitous flowchart is the logic model, which depicts how planned activities in an intervention will produce the desired results. It can be linear or nonlinear, simple or complex, but generally depicts a hypothesis about cause and effect. For example, the Grand Rapids African American Health Institute's Health Equity Index in Figures 8.9, below, and 8.10, p. 319, demonstrate two different ways to depict the same relationships. Which of these two flowcharts do you think is more accessible to stakeholders?

FIGURE 8.9 ● EXAMPLE OF A FLOWCHART LOGIC MODEL FOR EQUITY

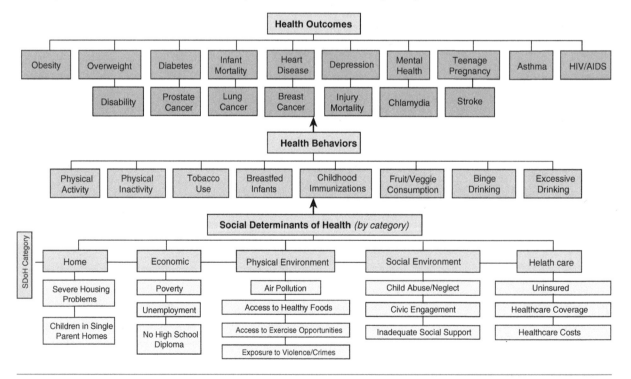

Logic Model (flowchart)for GRAAHI's Health Equity Index

Grand Rapids African American Health Institute (GRAAHI)

Source: Grand Rapids African American Health Institute. (2020). Logic models. Health Equity Index of the Grand Rapids African American Health Institute. https://hei.graahi.org/Logic-Model

FIGURE 8.10 ● EXAMPLE OF A CIRCULAR LOGIC MODEL FOR EQUITY

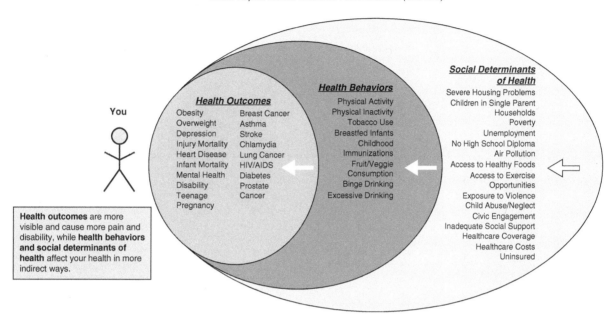

Logic Model (Circular) **for GRAAHI's Health Equity Index**
Grand Rapids African American Health Institute (GRAAHI)

Source: Grand Rapids African American Health Institute. (2020). Logic models. Health Equity Index of the Grand Rapids African American Health Institute. https://hei.graahi.org/Logic-Model

The Creative Graphic. Over the last 10 years, the world of data visualization has blossomed. Graphic representation is an act of creative data reduction and synthesis that, at its best, "evokes from its reader an at-a-glance understanding of the entire study" (Miles et al., 2020, p. 110). Graphics provide a display option that moves beyond the static matrix and the linear flowchart to reimagining findings in action. While not limited to qualitative research, graphics encapsulate the overall meaning and make the findings come alive.

Venn diagrams illustrate relationships as multiple integrated and overlapping circles. Each circle depicts a set of concepts, and their overlap indicates variables held in common. For example, the habits and attitudes needed by a student to be career-ready are depicted in a simple Venn diagram (see Figure 8.11, p. 320).

More complex graphics can illustrate concepts holistically and are limited only by the creativity of the evaluator. Scales et al. (2018) conducted a longitudinal multi-case study to investigate how four novice teachers learned to use their professional judgment in their literacy instruction. This trajectory is illustrated in Figure 8.12, p. 320.

The graphic provides an instant, overall explanation of the learning process experienced by new teachers. "Rather than displaying their results as a linear model across time, the trajectory design illustrates the holistic, interwoven, and spiraled nature of beginning teacher development" (Miles et al., 2020, p. 114).

FIGURE 8.11 ● HABITS AND ATTITUDES FOR THE CAREER READY STUDENT

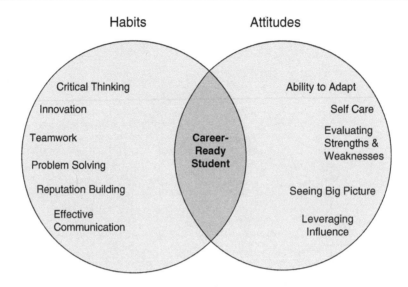

Source: Tim Elmore/Growing Leaders

FIGURE 8.12 ● TRAJECTORY OF LEARNING TO USE PROFESSIONAL JUDGMENT

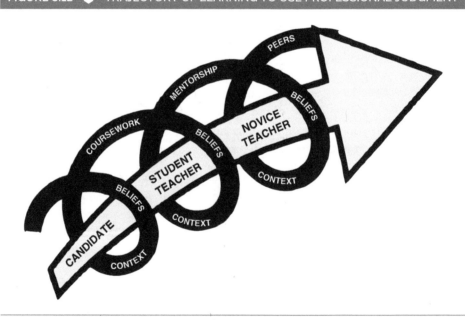

Source: Scales, R. Q., Wolsey, T. D., Lenski, S., Smetana, L. Yoder, K., Dobler, E., Grisham, D. L., & Young, J. R. (2018). Are we preparing or training teachers? Developing professional judgment in and beyond teacher preparation programs. *Journal of Teacher Education, 69*(1), 7–21.

Level 6—Making a Judgment
Evaluation

Making a judgment about the meaning of the data or drawing conclusions about them is the final step in the data interpretation process. It is found at the peak of Bloom's pyramid. Throughout the entire analysis process, this has been our end point, to develop a theory that explains the overall meaning of the data. Two steps are involved in the judgment process: (1) building a logical chain of evidence and (2) achieving coherence (Miles & Huberman, 1984, pp. 227–229).

Building a Logical Chain of Evidence. How do you pull together all the discrete pieces of information into a meaningful whole? It is a gradual construction of the evidential trail, starting with an initial sense of the main factors, then plotting the logical relationships on a tentative mental map, and then testing them against subsequent waves of data collection using constant comparison. You need to find a variety of instances in which informants mention the same topics or themes and identify the same causal links or reasons for the relationship. You compare these findings to see if they agree. Then you eliminate alternate explanations and countervailing evidence and determine if stakeholders can verify the claims. By modifying, refining, testing, and going back and forth with increasing focus, eventually, clarity is achieved. If all these checks and rechecks align and the relationships you are attesting make sense, then the chain is complete from antecedents to outcomes.

Achieving Coherence. In the end, how do you reach the integrated core of meaning? Bazeley (2013, pp. 357–358) has some suggestions:

- Write the basic storyline and answer the question, "What seems to be going on here?" based on what you know from the data.

- Identify or create a central concept or theme that ties it all together. Test its explanatory power by matching all the categories and themes to it.

- Use diagrams to help focus your ideas about relationships between this central concept and the other categories and themes.

- Once the central concept is confirmed, look for all the elements, such as the processes, actions, strategies, and emotions that are embedded within it.

- Retell the story of the data centered around this main concept, arriving at last at some answers to the evaluation questions that led us down this path in the first place.

- Check for gaps and inconsistencies.

- Fill in descriptive details for each element of the story.

- Depict the process by creating a causal model or flowchart.

- Be prepared to defend your conclusions by describing the progressive steps you took through your data analysis and synthesis process (as recorded in your memos).

Now, let us look at an example of a qualitative evaluation.

Example of an Evaluation With a Qualitative Design: The Girls Just Wanna Have Fun Evaluation

The Girls Just Wanna Have Fun program (Bean et al., 2015) was a community-based physical activity and life skills program in eastern Ontario for girls between the ages of 11 and 16 from low-income families. The program had been evaluated at the end of its first year and was now in its second year. It was held in a Boys and Girls Club facility and involved a 75-minute program session once a week during the school year. It was largely based on two models about positive youth development. In the program, the youth chose the physical activities they wanted to engage in and the leaders then selected and integrated appropriate life skills activities.

The purpose of the evaluation was twofold:

- To gain an understanding of ongoing successes and challenges after the second year of program implementation

- To examine how adaptations made because the first year's evaluation had had an impact on the program.

The study involved 13 semistructured interviews with the youth and program leaders. Participants were reminded of their rights to confidentiality and anonymity, parental consent was received for the youth before their involvement, and the leaders provided written consent before their interviews. Study procedures were approved by the Research Ethics Board at the authors' university.

An inductive–deductive thematic analysis was conducted, using a priori coding that built on the findings of the first evaluation and descriptive coding as a second, more flexible exploration of the data. The interview transcripts were read and reread independently by the first two authors. They used NVivo to identify codes, organize the themes, and link supporting quotations. They then met to discuss any discrepancies in their coding and to come to an agreement about the themes. The third author then verified the themes and ensured that the categories were coded accurately and represented the data, and that the selected quotations supported the themes.

The analysis revealed that applying lessons learned from the first evaluation had made a significant difference, specifically, finding better space for the program, improving transportation, and using smaller groups for life skills rather than one large group. In addition, the findings suggested continuing to implement successful strategies from the first year including providing field trips and community involvement, offering leadership roles to the youth, and having positive relationships with the adults in the program. Some ongoing challenges were also identified: competing extracurricular activities for participants limited involvement, the use of electronic devices during program time was a distraction, and the length of program sessions was too short.

The authors concluded that "researchers and practitioners must consistently evaluate physical activity-based programs and use the findings to adapt the program to better meet the changing needs of community-based partners…and youth participants" (p. 39). As a result of these positive evaluation efforts, the Boys and Girls Club integrated the program into their regular programming and sought to offer it at multiple locations.

THE INTERVIEW—THE MOST COMMON QUALITATIVE TOOL

The **interview** is the most frequent qualitative tool used in evaluation studies. As Patton remarks (2015, p. 423) we live in an "interview society." From the latest news reporter to Oprah and Dr. Phil, it seems like anyone can ask anybody about anything. The popularity of the interview may be its undoing because so many interviews are done so badly that the credibility of the method may be undermined. It is difficult for the average person to distinguish between an interview done by a talk show host and an interview done by a serious social scientist. For this reason, then, evaluators need to prepare very carefully and conduct themselves with decorum because when an interview is done well, it "takes us inside another person's life and worldview. The results help us make sense of the diversity of human experience" (Patton, 2015, p. 426).

In this section we look briefly at the types of interviews, provide checklists for planning an interview, and summarize the five steps involved in conducing one. Finally, we introduce trauma-informed interviewing, which may provide some guidance for situations where evaluators interact with participants who have experienced intense physical and psychological stress.

Types of Interviews

Generally, interviews fall into three types: structured, semistructured, and unstructured.

- Structured interviews tend to be used in large studies where the interviewer uses a standardized or closed set of questions, often similar to a questionnaire in form. There may be a preset series of answers to select from, rather than open-ended questions. The interviewer asks the questions in the same order, retaining the same wording from one interview to the next.

- Semistructured interviews combine closed or preestablished questions with broader open-ended ones. The interviewer can leave questions out or change the order as the interview unfolds.

- Unstructured interviews are informal or conversational. The interviewer has a list of topics and can pursue them based on the natural flow of the conversation and can probe and ask follow-up questions as needed. Sometimes the interviewee is involved in determining what the questions will be, particularly in trauma-informed interviewing.

Checklist for Planning the Interview

Before the evaluator shows up at the interview site, a great deal of preparation has occurred. Often a series of interviews will be conducted with program staff or participants and the evaluator may spend a couple of days on site. Because time is short, the process needs to be streamlined. Based on our own field experience, here is a checklist of planning considerations:

- ☐ Link questions to evaluation questions determined when the study is designed.

- ☐ As with surveys, word questions to be clear and likely to elicit the desired information.

- ☐ Select language carefully and be mindful of potential connotations.

- ☐ Fulfill IRB requirements if needed.

- ☐ Make the Consent Form as user-friendly as possible.

- ☐ Respect all research and evaluation ethics.

- ☐ Practice the protocol several times, run a pilot test, and continue to revise until the interview flows smoothly.

- ☐ Organize the complex task of setting up the interviews: (1) Work with supervisors or program staff to gain access permission to the facility and staff; (2) Select interviewees; (3) Invite them to participate; (4) Schedule interviews; (5) Organize logistics such as using a private interview room (away from the work site and prying eyes).

- ☐ Have a fallback plan if some participants do not show up.

- ☐ Check to make sure the tape recorder is in good working order (and remember to turn it on!).

- ☐ Dress appropriately to fit in with the setting.

Checklist for Conducting the Interview

There are five stages for the qualitative interview, is described as a conversational partnership (Mayan, 2009; Rubin & Rubin, 2005):

- ☐ Introduce yourself, set the topic, and put the participant at ease.

- ☐ Ask the easy questions first, show empathy, and demonstrate interest in what the participant has to say.

- ☐ Ask the tough questions or address the more sensitive topics later once rapport has been established.

- ☐ Tone down the emotional level toward the end of the interview, sometimes by a brief return to the less sensitive information obtained in #2 above. Finish on a positive note.

☐   Close the interview with a thank you, provide your contact information, both for the participant to contact you if they have additional thoughts later and to ask permission to follow up with them if you have any questions. Offer feedback about study results, if appropriate, such as a copy of the report or summary.

Trauma-informed Interviews

Often, evaluators find themselves in areas of conflict, whether domestic or international. Particularly in human services and international development, the evaluator may encounter participants who have experienced intense physical and psychological stress. For example, traumatic events might include acute events such as death, accidents, catastrophic illness, war, displacement, or natural disasters; interpersonal trauma, such as rape, intimate partner violence, human trafficking, stalking, or bullying; community violence, military combat, or PTSD; insidious trauma such as racism, sexism, heterosexism, homophobia, ageism, or discrimination based on disability or other characteristics; and historic trauma such as slavery and the oppression of Indigenous peoples.

Recently, specific methods have emerged about how to conduct trauma-informed interviews. For example, see the Substance Abuse and Mental Health Administration (2017), *A Guide to GPRA Data Collection Using Trauma-informed Interviewing Skills*. Jennings (2004) defined a trauma-informed approach as one that "would be experienced by all involved as a profound cultural shift in which consumers and their conditions and behaviors are viewed differently, staff respond differently, and the day-to-day delivery of services is conducted differently" (p. 21).

Retraumatization can occur in a situation or environment that resembles an individual's original trauma either literally or symbolically, which then causes difficult feelings associated with the original issue to arise (Buffalo Center for Social Research, 2015). Participating in the interview or the actual relationship between an interviewer and a participant can initiate unsettled feelings for those with trauma as they must retell their story or simply feel unsafe emotionally.

It is not surprising that the effects of trauma can influence a participant's behavior during an interview. As the Office for Victims of Crime (n.d.) explains, "Memory loss, lack of focus, emotional reactivity, and multiple versions of a story can all be signs of trauma exhibited during interviews. Interviewers should be familiar with the signs of trauma and not assume the victim is evading the truth. For example, lack of linear memory is often a sign of trauma, so it may be helpful during initial interviews to ask, 'What else happened?' instead of 'What happened next'" (para. 5).

The Buffalo Center for Social Research identifies five principles for trauma-informed care that can inform the interview process (Buffalo Center for Social Research, 2015) (see Figure 8.13, p. 326).

Extra time should be allotted for each interview (15–20 minutes are suggested) to allow for any required breaks during the process. Rushing the interview may leave the person feeling unheard, misunderstood, and unsupported. The interviewer also needs additional time

FIGURE 8.13   ●   THE FIVE PRINCIPLES OF TRAUMA-INFORMED CARE

Safety	Choice	Collaboration	Trustworthiness	Empowerment
Definitions				
Ensuring physical and emotional safety	Individual has choice and control	Making decisions with the individual and sharing power	Task clarity, consistency, and Interpersonal Boundaries	Prioritizing empowerment and skill building
Principles in Practice				
Common areas are welcoming and privacy is respected	Individuals are provided a clear and appropriate message about their rights and responsibilities	Individuals are provided a significant role in planning and evaluating services	Respectful and professional boundaries are maintained	Providing an atmosphere that allows individuals to feel validated and affirmed with each and every contact at the agency

Source: Buffalo Center for Social Research. (2015). What is trauma-informed care? Buffalo Center for Social Research.

between interviews to process the experience because secondary traumatization (to themselves) is also a potential risk and so self-care is important. While these principles and guidelines may be essential when interviewing at-risk respondents, in fact, using them in any interview situation can send the message that the interviewer respects and values the interviewee—always an important communication strategy for the evaluator.

Now, let's introduce our expert, Johnny Saldaña, a well-known qualitative research methodologist.

EXPERT CORNER

Johnny Saldaña

Johnny Saldaña is the Professor Emeritus of Theater in the Herberger Institute for Design and the Arts in the School of Music, Dance, and Theater at Arizona State University (ASU) where he taught from 1981 to 2014. He has been involved in the field of theater education as a teacher educator, drama specialist, director, and researcher. His works have been cited in over 15,000 research studies conducted in over 130 countries. Saldaña's research methods in longitudinal inquiry, ethnotheatre, coding, and qualitative data analysis have been applied and cited by researchers internationally in disciplines such as K-12 and higher education, business, the social sciences, technology, government, health care, and medicine.

1. *How has your wide experience in theater affected your approach to qualitative inquiry?*

Theater artists are trained to think conceptually, symbolically, and metaphorically. These design principles transfer into my qualitative data analytic work when I create codes, categories, and themes. My work as an actor, playwright, and director also enables me to "think theatrically" as I observe social life performed in front of me. I have been taught to look deeply into fictional characters' motives, tactics, values, and emotions that drive dramatic action, and these same qualities can be seen in participants as they go about their daily lives. I utilize my creativity whenever possible in social science endeavors and especially in my nonfictional writing. I am a storyteller both on the stage and on the page. I take my students and workshop participants through physical and verbal improvisation exercises to demonstrate how a *research studio* is an innovative space for learning unique insights about the human condition.

2. *What was going through your head when you were revising Miles and Huberman's iconic text on qualitative data analysis?*

I had taken two courses in qualitative data analysis in which Miles and Huberman's (1994) text was required reading, so I was intimately familiar with their methods. Their text, however, was sometimes overwhelming with its meticulous detail and visual magnitude. My goal was to revise their book into the version I wish I would have had as a student. I edited the extraneous passages and some of the more convoluted profiles and developed what I felt was a streamlined and better organized text.

My commission by SAGE Publications was to update Miles and Huberman's work, not to transform it into my own. For the third edition revision in 2014, I stayed relatively faithful to their original vision and methods. But for the fourth edition in 2020, the text evolved so that, in addition to their classic matrix and network displays, graphics were added as a third analytic modality. As I reviewed qualitative research studies in journal article formats, I was impressed with the creative array of graphic designs for displaying analytic findings. Miles and Huberman's book needed to showcase these unique visual methods since "think display" was their classic mantra. I never met Miles and Huberman in person, but I am deeply honored to continue their research legacy for a new generation of qualitative researchers.

3. *What advice can you offer those of our readers who are just beginning to explore the field of qualitative evaluation?*

Approach your evaluation ethnographically. Learn as much as you can about the culture of your field site. Its ethos (values system) will inform you of the participants' ways of working. The question I've asked of others that's yielded the richest information is: "What, to you, is important for me to know?"

Key Terms

Bloom's Taxonomy 308
Confirmability 290
Data analysis 298
Data preparation 307
Data reduction 310
Dependability 290

Ethnography 292
Evaluation questions 289
Grounded theory 295
Interview 323
Phenomenon 291
Qualitative designs 292

Qualitative traditions 292
Quality 290
Synthesis stage 314
Trustworthiness 290

The Main Ideas

1. There are differences in quantitative and qualitative designs.
   - Quantitative designs are based on a positivist/postpositivist/realist mindset, have standardized measures, set hypotheses, and use data to draw quantitative conclusions.
   - Qualitative designs are based on a constructivist/relativist mindset, identify themes and patterns, and findings may be represented in a holistic narrative.

2. In qualitative designs, the evaluator and the study participants interact with one another, help each other, interpret problems and work to solve them. Guba and Lincoln (1981) proposed trustworthiness, dependability, and confirmability as criteria of rigor.

3. Qualitative research has its roots in ethnography, phenomenology, social constructivism, narrative inquiry, critical theory, and grounded theory.

4. A qualitative design could include:
   - Multiple sources
   - Purposive sampling
   - Participants help to interpret the issue
   - Acknowledgement of evaluator as evaluation tool
   - The design can change as findings evolve.

5. Threats to qualitative designs are missing data, misinterpreting the meaning of the data, failure to document the activities of the study and chain of evidence as the study continues, missing important data gems, and seeking data to support pre-existing notions about the issue.

6. Strengths of qualitative methods include:
   - Can study complex phenomena
   - Applicable to natural settings
   - Study design can be changing and dynamic
   - Produces rich data.

   Limitations include:
   - Findings are not generalizable
   - Quality of findings is dependent upon the skills of the evaluator
   - Credibility of findings may not be acceptable with stakeholders.

7. Bloom's Taxonomy offers a framework for the processes involved in qualitative research, including:
   - Knowledge (reading the passage)
   - Comprehension (understanding the passage)
   - Application (reviewing the passage and content analysis)
   - Analysis (coding or breaking the passage into categories and themes)
   - Synthesis (reassembling and finding similarities, combining codes)
   - Evaluation (making a judgment about meaning).

Critical Thinking Questions

1. How do qualitative and quantitative methods answer different evaluation questions?

2. Why is the evaluator described as "the research instrument" in qualitative inquiry?

3. Why are qualitative methods more time-consuming and labor-intensive than quantitative methods?

4. How can Bloom's Taxonomy explain qualitative process?

5. How does the evaluator conduct the three steps to qualitative analysis: (1) coding, (2) categorizing, and (3) theming?

6. Why would an evaluator want to use a visual method to communicate the findings of a qualitative inquiry?

7. If the case study of *Girls just Wanna Have Fun* were a quantitative study, how would the design have been different?

8. When does an evaluator need to consider using a trauma-informed approach when conducting interviews?

Student Challenges

1. **Coding Approaches**. Continuing to explore Robbie's mother's experience with parenting, use this second excerpt to code the passage below using descriptive coding (a word/noun or short phrase that describes the topic in this sentence/partial sentence). Then code the same passage a second time using Gerund Coding (an ing-word/verb to connote action in this sentence/partial sentence). Reflect on the two processes. Comment on which approach you like better and why.

   So yesterday I looked at Robbie's file at school. I felt guilty in a way, resorting to that, especially since those numbers have so little to say about a person. And my love and hopes for him are unconditional of course, don't depend on his achievement or IQ scores. But the numbers weren't supposed to tell me whether Rob is special or not—they were supposed to tell me whether it is alright for me to tease, prod, and cajole him about his homework, and say, "Hey, you lazy schmuck, get some of this work finished in school instead of fooling around," or maybe, "Of course, you can't think straight when you're so tired. You'll have to get home earlier

   and do this homework before supper." (van Manen, 1984, p. 21).

2. **Deeper Exploration of Quantitative Data**. Select an issue you are familiar with for which quantitative data is readily available (e.g., incidence of incarcerated individuals from a particular race or ethnic group or number of children with specific learning disabilities in public schools). In one or two pages or in a class discussion, answer the following questions.

   • What do these numbers tell you about the issue?

   • What do the numbers not tell you about the issue?

   • What is missing?

   • What kind of information do you need to complement your understanding of the issue?

   • Construct a research question that focuses on the stories behind the numbers (Mayan, 2009, p. 21). *Source:* Mayan, M. J. (2009). *Essentials of qualitative inquiry*. Routledge.

Additional Readings and Resources

1. Bazeley, P. (2013). *Qualitative data analysis: Practical strategies*. SAGE Publications.
   A book by Pat Bazeley offers practical strategies throughout the entire qualitative research experience. Topics include designing and managing the analysis through to developing conclusions based on the data collected. Provides the theoretical basis for qualitative data collection and offers many useful screen shots of software programs.

2. Carmichael, T., & Cunningham, N. (2017). Theoretical data collection and data analysis with gerunds in a constructivist grounded theory study. *Electronic Journal on Business Research Methods, 15*, 59–73.
   The authors studied the coaching process using the constructivist grounded theory. They are careful in the selection of the first participant to start the study and discuss the conversion of data coded into gerunds as discussed in this chapter.

3. Charmaz, K. (2014). *Constructing grounded theory*. SAGE Publications.
   This book by Kathy Charmaz is recommended for those wanting to know more about how to conduct grounded theory studies. Topics include gathering rich data and conducting interviews with the grounded theory approach. Chapters also include a focus on coding the interview, memo-writing, and sampling.

4. Dinesen, B., & Andersen, P. (2006). Qualitative evaluation of a diabetes advisory system, DiasNet. *Journal of Telemedicine and Telecare, 12*, 71–74.
   This study evaluates the technological use of a system designed to help those who are diabetic become advocates and learners in their own care. Patients entered data, and then a review by the diabetes team was conducted, thus reducing the number of hyperglycemia and hypoglycemia cases. Qualitative interviews and focus groups were held with patients and healthcare professionals.

9

USING MIXED METHODS IN EVALUATION

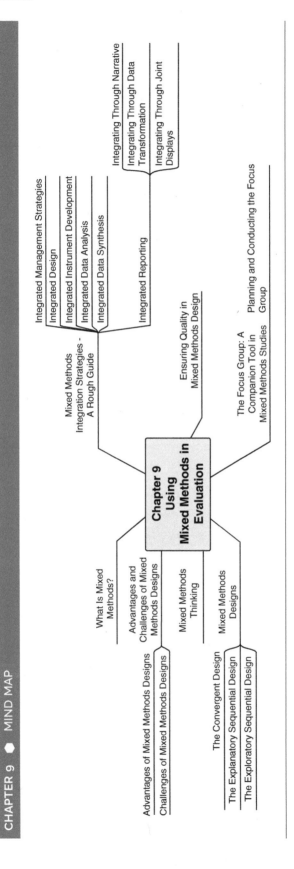

**Chapter 9
Using
Mixed Methods in
Evaluation**

Mixed Methods
Integration Strategies -
A Rough Guide

- Integrated Management Strategies
- Integrated Design
- Integrated Instrument Development
- Integrated Data Analysis
- Integrated Data Synthesis
- Integrated Reporting
  - Integrating Through Narrative
  - Integrating Through Data Transformation
  - Integrating Through Joint Displays

Ensuring Quality in
Mixed Methods Design

The Focus Group: A
Companion Tool in
Mixed Methods Studies

Planning and Conducting the Focus Group

What Is Mixed
Methods?

Advantages and
Challenges of Mixed
Methods Designs

- Advantages of Mixed Methods Designs
- Challenges of Mixed Methods Designs

Mixed Methods
Thinking

Mixed Methods
Designs

- The Convergent Design
- The Explanatory Sequential Design
- The Exploratory Sequential Design

JELL-O® AND MIXED METHODS

As noted mixed methods researcher David Morgan recalls, his first experience combining qualitative and quantitative methods was for his dissertation (Morgan, 2014). He found it to be an exhilarating process but confessed that making sense of it all was another matter. After his defense was over, he asked his committee members what they thought of his efforts. One of his advisors compared it to "…a Jell-O® salad in which a number of things were held together by something that wasn't nearly as interesting as the bits and pieces themselves" (p. 4). Morgan admitted that he felt the same way. He concluded, "Even though both the qualitative 'bits' and the quantitative 'pieces' had much to offer, I

Source: iStockphoto.com/AlasdairJames

hadn't found a successful approach to integrating them" (p. 5). The challenge for him became how to connect both the qualitative and quantitative methods in a research design in a way that purposefully integrated both.

INTRODUCTION

Chapter 9 focuses on mixed methods design, an approach often used in evaluation that has now gained acceptance more broadly as a distinct research strategy. It involves the planned integration of both quantitative and qualitative data to draw conclusions about the research question based on the strengths of both methods. Mixed methods is required when one type of data is not sufficient to gain a holistic understanding of the phenomenon being studied. We present the advantages and challenges of mixed methods designs and explore how mixed methods thinking allows the evaluator to engage with multiple research traditions and different ways of knowing. Dewey's Five-Step Model of Inquiry provides a framework to help us think through the types of research questions that should be addressed in a mixed methods study. Three common mixed methods designs are explained including the convergent, explanatory sequential, and exploratory sequential designs. For each of these designs, a shorthand notation, a diagram, and an example of a program evaluation study using the design are provided. A rough guide of data integration strategies is presented; it is rough because mixed methods requires a hands-on approach that is responsive to changing circumstances and new discoveries along the research journey. Suggestions are provided for integration strategies for design, instrument development, data analysis, data synthesis, and reporting.

You will enjoy the resources in this chapter including the Spotlight on Equity, which presents the evaluation of an alternate lawyer licensing pathway, our expert Dr. Jennifer Greene, Key Terms, Main Ideas, Critical Thinking Questions, Student Challenges, and Additional Readings and Resources.

WHAT IS MIXED METHODS?

As Mertens (2018) points out, evaluators have intuitively used **mixed methods** for many years, "possibly because they sensed that the programs, policies, products, systems, and organizations they were asked to evaluate were complex and that use of a single approach or type of data collection would not capture that complexity" (pp. 6–7). In fact, evaluators are frequently asked to explore "wicked problems" or those for which only an imperfect understanding exists. These complex problems are more likely to be clarified through diverse methods and multiple solutions. Evaluators routinely combine multiple types of data, multiple methods of data collection, and multiple perspectives. They are often asked to make program specific generalizations and causal claims and decision makers seem comfortable accepting evaluations that combine, for example, outcome monitoring with administrative data, surveys with interviews, or program administrators' perspectives with those of program participants.

However, mixed methods as a distinct strategy is relatively recent, dating from the last decades of the twentieth century when it emerged as a defined methodology. Mixed methods is not just about mixing quantitative and qualitative data in the same study; rather, it involves the planned **integration** of data collection, analysis, and synthesis prior to drawing conclusions (Bazeley, 2018, p. 7), and making sure that the data integration plan is clear before conducting the study.

Creswell (2015) defines mixed methods as:

> *An approach to research in the social, behavioral, and health sciences in which the investigator gathers both quantitative (closed-ended) and qualitative (open-ended) data, integrates the two, and then draws interpretations based on the combined strengths of both sets of data to understand research problems.* (p. 2)

In mixed methods, the evaluator collects and analyzes both quantitative and qualitative data in response to a research question or hypothesis, integrates the two forms of data and their results, and organizes the procedures into specific research designs, framing them within theory and philosophy (Creswell & Plano Clark, 2018, p. 5).

Not all situations require mixed methods. As Creswell and Plano Clark (2018) explain, sometimes qualitative research is needed "to explore a problem, honor the voices of participants, map the complexity of the situation, and convey multiple perspectives" (p. 7). Other times, quantitative research is necessary "to understand the relationship among variables or determine if one group performs better on an outcome than another group" (p. 7). The goal always is to match the methods to the research question.

The National Institutes of Health (2018, p. 3) suggests that mixed methods is an approach that:

- Focuses on research questions that call for real-life, contextual understandings, multilevel perspectives, and sociocultural influences

- Uses rigorous quantitative methods that assess the magnitude and frequency of variables and rigorous qualitative methods that explore the meaning and understanding of constructs

- Involves multiple sources and types of data to capture complex phenomena (e.g., geospatial types, in-depth informant interviews, survey questionnaire responses, text messages, and visual content including emoji, photos, video, and other graphics)

- Systematically integrates and triangulates different types of data to maximize the strengths and counterbalance the weaknesses of each data type

- Develops and integrates conceptual and theoretical frameworks into the development of research questions.

Mixed methods seems the most appropriate choice when the research is in support of one of the following purposes (Greene, 2007, pp. 98–104; Greene et al., 1989; Johnson & Onwuegbuzie, 2004, p. 22):

1. **Triangulation**—convergence and corroboration of results from different methods with different strengths and limitations can be used to assess the same phenomenon and thus offsets bias and increases confidence in findings.

2. **Complementarity**—while convergence is not expected, many different choices are offered that can elaborate, enhance, illustrate, and clarify the results of one method with the results from another.

3. **Initiation/Reframing**[1]—the discovery of paradoxes, divergence, and contradictions can lead back to a reassessment of the research question and allow the researcher to pursue the puzzle further.

4. **Development**—the use of findings from one method can help develop or inform a second method, for instrument development or conducting a series of interconnected studies that build on new information as it is obtained.

5. **Expansion**—the scope and range of inquiry can be broadened by using different methods for different study components and allows for the use of creative methods as well as more traditional approaches.

Typically, mixed methods are required where one type of data may be insufficient. Mixed methods are best used when a need arises to (Creswell & Plano Clark, 2018, pp. 8–12):

- Learn what questions need to be asked

- Explain initial results

---

[1]Note: Originally called Initiation by Greene et al. (1989), it seems to us that Reframing is a more descriptive term.

- Obtain more complete and corroborated results

- Enhance understanding of an experimental study

- Describe and compare different data sources for a more holistic understanding

- Connect multiphase or multiproject studies.

Some researchers may be daunted by the idea of combining qualitative and quantitative methods. An early study by Greene et al. (1989) found that 44% of the 57 mixed methods evaluation studies they reviewed conducted analyses that were completely independent of each other. An additional 32% integrated data only at the interpretation stage. Just five studies integrated data and analysis prior to final interpretation and conclusions.

Yet Johnson and Onwuegbuzie (2004, p. 17) suggest that mixed methods research can provide a more workable solution and produce a superior product to a single method approach. Mixed methods resolve many research issues because, as Creswell (2015, p. 15) explains

> ...quantitative research does not adequately investigate personal stories and meanings or deeply probe the perspectives of individuals. Qualitative research does not enable us to generalize from a small group of people to a large population. It does not precisely measure what people in general feel. In short, all research methods have both strengths and weaknesses, and the combination of the strengths of both provides a good rationale for using mixed methods....

Advantages and Challenges of Mixed Methods Designs

When considering a mixed methods design, it may be helpful to review the advantages and challenges of the approach (Creswell & Plano Clark, 2018, pp. 12–17; Johnson & Onwuegbuzie, 2004, p. 21).

Advantages of Mixed Methods Designs

It is important to understand the advantages of this approach because it may be necessary to convince clients and stakeholders of its use if mixed methods is not familiar to them. Mixed methods builds on the advantages of quantitative rigor and qualitative richness and the strengths of one make up for the weaknesses of the other. The evaluator is free to use all the methods possible to address a research problem and is thus less constrained by precedence. Mixed methods research provides more evidence about a research question than either component can alone. It answers broader, more complex questions and offers new insights that go beyond the individual results of the separate components. A mixed methods design can become increasingly strong and more targeted if the first component's findings inform the design of the second component. Jointly, the methods can produce stronger and more complete evidence because of the convergence and corroboration of findings, or if differences are found, the exploration of reasons for divergence.

Challenges of Mixed Methods Designs

On the other hand, there are some notable challenges to consider. As Morgan (2014) comments, a mixed methods design:

> ... often involves more than twice as much work as using a single method, since you must not only use each separate method effectively but also integrate them effectively. Simply having more results or different kinds of results does not inherently improve your work; in addition, you must bring those results together in a way that demonstrates the value of your additional effort. (p. 4)

Given the demand for additional time and resources, feasibility issues must be addressed. Creswell and Plano Clark (2018, p. 15) suggest asking the following questions:

- Is there sufficient time to collect and analyze two different types of data?

- Are there sufficient resources to collect and analyze both qualitative and quantitative data?

- Are the skills and personnel available to complete the study?

The scheduling of data collection and analysis activities can be problematic as they are more interdependent than in traditional approaches. It can be difficult for a single researcher to carry out both components because of the different skill sets required, and if a team is used, leadership and coordination are required. Working within two different paradigms is challenging and requires constant conversation and negotiation. Some individuals (including clients, stakeholders, and team members) may need training on the essential requirements. It may be necessary to conduct working sessions where exemplary mixed methods studies are discussed prior to planning the study at hand.

MIXED METHODS THINKING

Greene (2007), a pioneer in the mixed methods field, focuses on values. For her, **mixed methods thinking** requires a mental model that invites dialogue about multiple ways of seeing and hearing, of making sense of the social world, and of regarding that which is valued. Using mixed methods allows the evaluator to engage with difference in a meaningful way and allows them to support the goal of social justice For Greene, mixed methods thinking requires the evaluator to challenge themselves in several ways.

- To understand the complexity of the social phenomena being studied, the evaluator must engage in multiple and possibly discordant perspectives, bringing the political and value dimensions of the work to the foreground.

- Using a broad mental model, the evaluator invites dialogue and multiple philosophical and theoretical stances, embracing convergence, consonance, and consensus to triangulate findings while, at the same time, valuing divergence, dissonance, and difference.

- Engaging with difference through multiple ways of knowing, the evaluator incorporates diverse traditions, designs, and processes, locates their own values and ideological stance in their work, and sees context as multifaceted, dynamic, and socially constructed.

Therefore, mixed methods thinking requires the evaluator to calmly approach differing stances comfortably and bring them closer for inspection, analysis, and interpretation. They must also learn to triangulate differing views and appreciate them all, while alternating between the different ways of gaining knowledge used to make a judgment about the data used for conclusions. For evaluators, conducting complex mixed methods studies requires metacognition or to routinely "think about your thinking" (Chick, 2013) while integrating ideas from different paradigms. Mertens (2015a, p. 13) stresses how important it is for an evaluator to be aware of the philosophical assumptions that shape their worldview. These include:

- Axiology—the nature of ethics and values

- Ontology—the nature of reality

- Epistemology—the nature of knowledge and the relationship between the evaluator and stakeholders

- Methodology—the nature of systematic inquiry.

In terms of the evaluator's worldview, mixed methods can fit comfortably in one of two paradigms (see Chapter 2). Mertens (2018, p. 21) stresses that the subjectivist, or as she calls it, the transformative paradigm, is a good fit for mixed methods because it supports "the use of culturally responsive strategies that are needed to respectfully engage with a diverse set of stakeholders…who hold varying levels of power within the context, thus increasing the possible use of findings for transformative purposes" (p. 21).

She suggests (2015b, p. 4) that a mixed methods mindset allows the evaluator to ask the complex evaluation questions that are more appropriate for our dynamic and uncertain world. Examples of transformative questions include:

- How can we understand the context and experiences of diverse communities in culturally appropriate ways, especially for those who are displaced or from low-income households?

- How can we capture the complexities inherent in moving forward to a more resilient, healthy path of growth and development?

On the other hand, mixed methods also fits the ontological perspective of pragmatism, where the focus is on the outcomes of a specific question or problem and the methods are selected accordingly. Morgan (2014) takes this middle-of-the-road position somewhere between objectivism and constructivism. For him, complex decisions require the researcher to find points of complementarity between the different types of knowledge produced by quantitative and qualitative methods.

Johnson and Onwuegbuzie (2004, p. 16) comment that pragmatism helps improve communication among researchers from different paradigms and can uncover ways to mix their research fruitfully. They see this middle ground as a workable position, especially for those engaged in long-standing dualistic debates such as postpositivism versus constructivism or quantitative versus qualitative.

For a pragmatist, the environment is not fixed but is in flux and requires adaptive behaviors from evaluators. When you are faced with difficult or complex situations and are unsure how to respond, pragmatism asks the key question, "What difference would it make to act one way rather than another" (Morgan, 2014, p. 28)? To find a solution, you need to think through the likely consequences of different courses of action and select the one most likely to resolve the original uncertainty. The evaluator must decide which approach or combination of approaches is most likely to answer the evaluation questions.

Dewey's Five-Step Model of Inquiry in Figure 9.1, p. 340 provides the evaluator with a way to think about what research questions to ask and which methods will best address these questions (Morgan, 2014).

Morgan (2014, p. 8, pp. 29–31) describes the model as follows:

1. Select the problem or research question, understand that it is beyond your current experience, and be aware that you have no obvious solution for it.

2. Reflect on the nature of the problem using your current philosophical stance.

3. Speculate about possible ways to address the problem, such as a tentative research design; use an "if-then" approach to explore various options (abductive thinking) to determine if planned methods will produce results that address the research question; identify the most promising course of action.

4. Assess the nature of your tentative solution and reflect on potential outcomes, again based on your philosophical stance.

5. Take action. Collect and analyze your data; compare study outcomes with your original goals; reassess and revise your beliefs based on this research experience.

Rather than debating theoretical differences, Johnson and Onwuegbuzie (2004) conclude, "the mixed methods approach provides the best opportunity for answering important, multi-faceted research questions with workable, practical solutions" (p. 15).

FIGURE 9.1 ● DEWEY'S FIVE-STEP MODEL OF INQUIRY

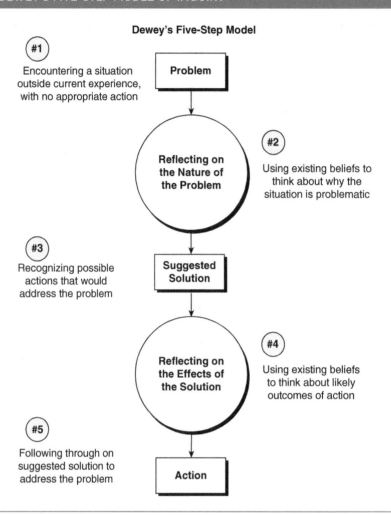

Dewey's Five-Step Model

#1 Encountering a situation outside current experience, with no appropriate action

Problem

#2 Using existing beliefs to think about why the situation is problematic

Reflecting on the Nature of the Problem

#3 Recognizing possible actions that would address the problem

Suggested Solution

#4 Using existing beliefs to think about likely outcomes of action

Reflecting on the Effects of the Solution

#5 Following through on suggested solution to address the problem

Action

Source: Morgan, D. L. (2014). *Integrating qualitative & quantitative methods: A pragmatic approach.* SAGE Publications.

MIXED METHODS DESIGNS

Over the years, scholars have advanced various typologies about how qualitative and quantitative methods should be combined. After much discussion in the literature, there now seems to be some agreement about the most common mixed methods designs. They include (1) **convergent**, (2) **explanatory sequential**, and (3) **exploratory sequential** mixed methods designs (Creswell & Plano Clark, 2018, p. 60). Each of them reflects a different intention on the part of the researcher regarding the purpose they hope to achieve by mixing methods. In this section, each of the core mixed methods designs is described, along with their shorthand **notation**, a diagram, and a study example.

First, however, it is useful to understand the shorthand system used in mixed methods. A series of notations was developed by Morse (1991) to symbolize the different mixed methods designs. They include the use of uppercase and lowercase letters, and symbols such as the plus sign, equals sign, and arrow. The notation helps to explain the relationship between the qualitative and quantitative components of any mixed methods study by highlighting each method's priority and sequence (Johnson & Onwuegbuzie, 2004, p. 20):

- Priority can be given to either the qualitative or quantitative component of a study, or both can have equal status. The dominant component is presented in UPPER CASE letters (emphasized method) and the secondary component in lower case (deemphasized method). If both are equally important, they are both presented in UPPER CASE.

- The sequence in which the components occur is part of the design. They can happen either sequentially and are described with a plus sign (+) or concurrently and described with an equal sign (=). The use of an arrow (→) reflects the decision to analyze and interpret the first component of the study to inform the design of the second component.

The Convergent Design

The notation for a convergent design is:

$$QUAL + QUAN$$

The convergent design is used when both the quantitative and qualitative methods are used to explore the same research question, and the evaluator intends to bring the results together at the end of the study so that they can be compared or combined. This allows a fuller understanding of the problem, validates one set of findings with the other, or determines if participants responded the same way across both methods (Creswell & Plano Clark, 2018, p. 66). Data tend to be collected simultaneously. Parallel construction is essential to enable later data integration but the data from each component are analyzed separately. After the results are merged, the researcher can determine to what extent the quantitative results are confirmed by the qualitative results (or vice versa). However, there is no guarantee that results will converge or that they will provide a stronger and more consolidated conclusion.

A general diagram for the convergent design is presented in Figure 9.2.

FIGURE 9.2 ● THE CONVERGENT DESIGN

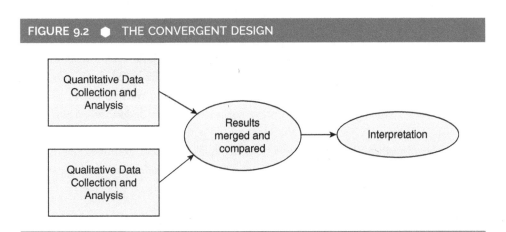

Source: Creswell, J. W., & Plano Clark, V. L. (2018). *Designing and conducting mixed methods research* (3rd ed.). SAGE Publications.

An example of a convergent mixed method design is the study by Classen et al. (2007). It studied older driver safety using a convergent design to integrate the main findings of the Fatality Analysis Rating System (FARS), a national crash data set, with perspectives on safety factors of drivers over the age 65 and other stakeholders. The findings from the two study components were integrated using a socioecological framework. Eleven multicausal factors for safe elderly driving were identified that integrated environmental factors with behavioral and health factors. The researchers then developed a framework for a targeted health promotion plan.

The Explanatory Sequential Design

The notation for an explanatory sequential design is:

$$\text{QUAN} \rightarrow \text{qual}$$

In this explanatory sequential design, the quantitative component has greater emphasis in addressing the study's purpose and the qualitative methods that follow help to explain the quantitative results. The study has two distinct phases but uses the same research question. The quantitative strand can help to focus subsequent qualitative tools or data collection methods; the qualitative strand builds on the results of the first component. It is possible that the emphasis is on the second, qualitative strand which is informed by the prior quantitative data collection; in that case, the notation would be **quan → QUAL**.

A general diagram for the explanatory sequential design is presented in Figure 9.3.

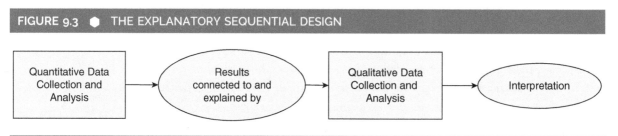

FIGURE 9.3 ● THE EXPLANATORY SEQUENTIAL DESIGN

Source: Creswell, J. W., & Plano Clark, V. L. (2018). *Designing and conducting mixed methods research* (3rd ed.). SAGE Publications.

An example of an explanatory sequential mixed methods study is provided by Banyard and Williams (2007) who examined how women recovered from childhood sexual abuse. The quantitative component involved structured interviews with 80 women at two points in time over seven years; the qualitative piece consisted of open-ended interviews with a subset of 21 survivors. Quantitative findings showed patterns of both stability and change on an index of resilience across multiple domains; qualitative data examined the dynamic quality of recovery over time such as the role of "turning points" across the lifespan. The notation in this case is **QUAN → qual**.

The Exploratory Sequential Design

The notation for an exploratory sequential design is:

$$QUAL \rightarrow quan$$

In an exploratory sequential mixed methods design, the evaluator implements the qualitative methods first to explore a phenomenon and this component has greater emphasis in addressing the study's purpose. The quantitative methods that follow assess the extent to which the initial qualitative findings can be generalized to a larger population. It is also possible to emphasize the second quantitative strand; in that case the notation would be **qual → QUAN**.

As Creswell and Plano Clark (2018) explain, "Building from the exploratory results, the researcher conducts a development phase by designing a quantitative feature based on the qualitative results. This feature may be the generation of new variables, the design of an instrument, the development of activities for an intervention, or a digital product, such as an app or website. Finally, in the third phase the investigator quantitatively tests the new feature…grounded in the initial qualitative perspectives of participants" (p. 67).

A general diagram for the exploratory sequential design is presented in Figure 9.4.

FIGURE 9.4 ● THE EXPLORATORY SEQUENTIAL DESIGN

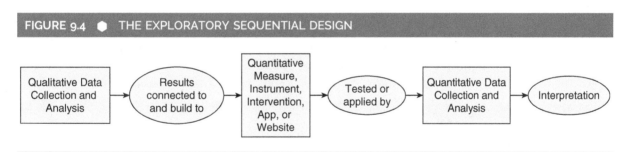

Source: Creswell, J. W., & Plano Clark, V. L. (2018). *Designing and conducting mixed methods research* (3rd ed.). SAGE Publications.

An example of an exploratory sequential mixed methods study is provided by Betancourt et al. (2011). They evaluated a family strengthening intervention to assist families facing mental health problems with HIV-infected children in Rwanda. The first phase included exploratory interviews with children and their caregivers. The thematic analysis that resulted led to a review of the literature to find relevant standardized measures that were then used along with additional new measures in a survey for pre- and posttest assessments in the program. The notation in this case is **qual → QUAN**.

To think through your design decisions, Creswell (2015, pp. 48–49) recommends considering whether you want to merge two databases or connect them. This will lead to either a convergent design (merging the data) or a sequential design (connecting the data). Then other factors can be incorporated, such as a theoretical framework or a particular values lens. The skill sets and philosophical orientations of the researchers must also be considered. Finally, relevant literature should be reviewed to see how different mixed methods designs are used and reported.

The next section outlines some ways to integrate mixed methods throughout the evaluation process.

MIXED METHODS INTEGRATION STRATEGIES—A ROUGH GUIDE

While design typologies and notations are helpful, the critical issues are found within the process of each individual study as the evaluator determines how the different components will interact. Some evaluators may be tempted to conduct a survey and then throw in some focus groups to add "color" to the final report, but this is not a mixed methods study. The design must be intentional from the initial design of the project. Decisions about when and how integration will occur are critical to study success.

However, mixed methods studies are not fixed but continue to evolve throughout their implementation because the real-world environments in which evaluators work are very complex. Change is inevitable. For example, in their mixed methods study of family involvement in school and children's educational development, Weiss et al. (2005) learned:

> …that mixed methods approaches could only be rough guides and that intentional designs might have to give way to real-world problems of data availability and deadlines. Accordingly [they] developed a sense of [their] mixed methods work as a dynamic hands-on process, guided only very generally by mixed methods analytic models. (p. 61)

Like a travel book that suggests adventure and illumination, mixed method designs are rough guides that tend to be modified as conditions change. If the trains are not running or an exciting new museum upends your original agenda, immediate travel plans can change, but you are still on the same trip and you still have the same destination. Similarly, while specific processes in a mixed methods study may be challenged by unexpected events or new discoveries made along the way, the original research purpose and the research questions remain the same although they can be refined as new knowledge is revealed.

From its inception, a mixed methods study should focus on how strategies will be managed so that a "conversation" can be maintained between the quantitative and qualitative components. As Bazeley (2010) explains:

> Integration can be said to occur to the extent that different data elements and various strategies for analysis of those elements are combined throughout a study in such a way as

to become interdependent in reaching a common theoretical or research goal, thereby producing findings that are greater than the sum of the parts. (p. 432)

Tight integration between qualitative and quantitative members of the research team is essential to extract the true value from a mixed methods approach. Several useful integration strategies are summarized here for consideration (Bazeley, 2012, 2018; Burch & Heinrich, 2016; Datta, 2001). It should be noted that these suggestions can be combined as needed to address the evolving evaluation context. The integration strategies are depicted in Figure 9.5.

FIGURE 9.5 ● MIXED METHODS INTEGRATION STRATEGIES

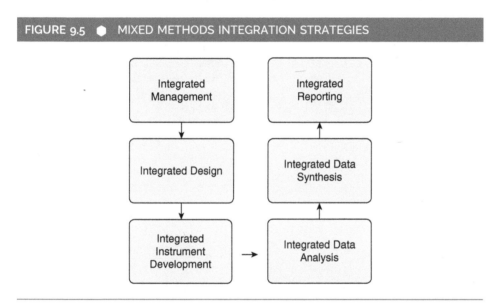

Source: Adapted from Bazeley, P. (2012). Integrative analysis strategies for mixed data sources. *American Behavioral Scientist, 56*(6), 814–828; Burch, P., & Heinrich, C. J. (2016). *Mixed methods for policy research and program evaluation.* SAGE Publications; Datta, L. (2001). Mixed methods evaluation: The wheelbarrow, the mosaic and the double helix. *Evaluation Journal of Australasia, 1*(2), 33–40.

Integrated Management Strategies

Examples of some useful integrative management strategies are summarized in Figure 9.6, p. 346 (Datta, 2001, p. 37; National Institutes of Health, 2018, p. 13). They include teamwork, co-project managers, a common vision, adequate staff and resources, decision-making protocols, data comparability, and conflict resolution.

Integrated Design

An important element in a mixed methods study is when, where, and how the different components will come together. As Bazeley (2018) remarks, "planned strategies for integration need to be considered during the design stage of a study, so that its importance is established early and it remains in focus as an issue" (p. 30). Integration need not happen at only one point of interface but can have multiple intersections. Researchers can

FIGURE 9.6 ⬡ INTEGRATIVE MANAGEMENT STRATEGIES

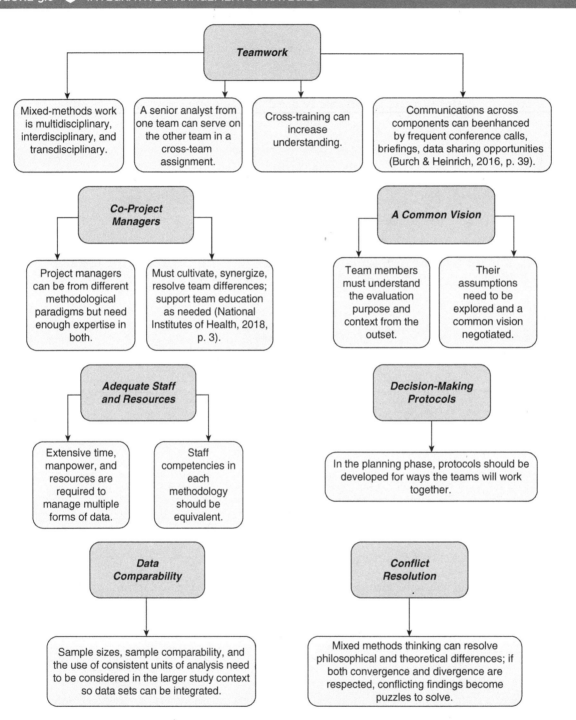

Source: Adapted from Datta, L. (2001). Mixed methods evaluation: The wheelbarrow, the mosaic and the double helix. *Evaluation Journal of Australasia,* *1*(2), 33–40; National Institutes of Health Office of Behavioral and Social Sciences. (2018). *Best practices for mixed methods research in the health sciences* (2nd ed.).

include specific decision points throughout the study to stop and look intentionally for ways that one component can inform another.

Wooley (2009) looked at the lives of young people, aged 18–25 years, in Derby, England, and the variations in their personal agency/sense of control across six socio-structural contexts defined by gender and institutional setting. She wanted to understand the structure–agency interplay as these young adults made transitions to adulthood and to explore the significance of gender and agency in shaping lives. The study was undertaken in two phases. Phase 1 involved an overarching conceptualizing strategy, a survey ($n = 300$), and seven focus groups ($n = 47$ in total). In Phase 2, eight individual interviews were conducted. Wooley's research design is presented in Figure 9.7.

FIGURE 9.7 ● WOOLEY'S MIXED METHODS RESEARCH DESIGN

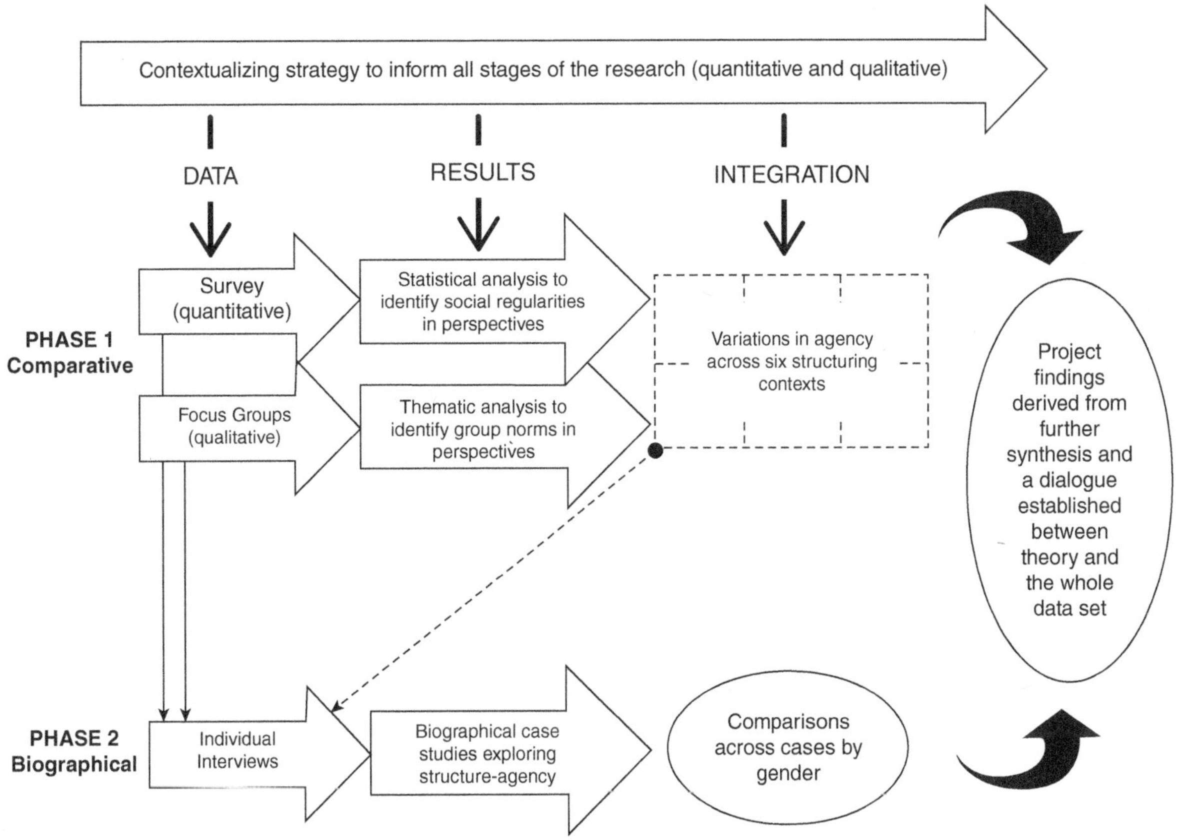

Source: Wooley, C. M. (2009). Meeting the mixed methods challenge of integration in a sociological study of structure and agency. *Journal of Mixed Methods Research, 3*(1), 7–25.

Wooley (2009) concluded that an important consideration for mixed methods researchers is to be explicit about how analyses and findings from complementary data sets will be linked. Wooley explains:

> the analytic framework developed from a flexible, iterative process rather than from the sequence of steps perhaps conveyed earlier. It might appear, for example, that the research questions were the primary drivers propelling the analyses forward, but it was not as clear-cut as this in practice. The research questions became more clearly formulated only once the factors had been identified and the decision to use these to guide further analyses had been taken. The factors fell into neat groups that made sense in relation to existing theoretical literature, and it was on this basis that the four empirical research questions were specified. Thus, in producing integrated analyses and findings there was a dialogue between ideas and evidence throughout. Although the project developed in a flexible, iterative manner, it is nevertheless evident that the features that allowed the integration of data, analyses, and findings in the latter stages were present within the research design from the beginning. (p. 22)

While Woolley based her initial design on the theoretical constructs of agency and structure to make meaning, evaluators often use a logic model or theory of change as their framework because their interests lie in the study's causal linkages. The purpose of many evaluations is to understand how the intervention contributes to specific outcomes and what those outcomes may be.

Burch and Heinrich (2006) suggest that the logic model can clarify:

> … the purpose of an intervention and what is required to effect change, serving as a reference and guide for planning and executing the research activities, and monitoring progress and identifying opportunities for mid-course improvements. Logic model linkages provide a structure to explore program assumptions and can indicate whether qualitative or quantitative methods will produce the most useful results. (pp. 35–36)

Integrated Instrument Development

Mixed methods are often used to develop more responsive tools; so, for example, the first method (whether qualitative or quantitative) informs the design of the second. For example, the design of a quantitative instrument can be based on the findings of documentary analysis, qualitative interviews, or focus groups. Survey data can be used to identify either a sample or an issue to be investigated qualitatively (Bazeley, 2012, p. 819). Questions that surface at site visits can be elaborated and expanded on in surveys; results from surveys and databases can direct observations, interviews, and other subsequent data collection methods (Datta, 2001, p. 37). The interplay of methods is the true strength of a mixed methods design.

Berman (2017) designed an exploratory sequential mixed methods study to understand faculty's data management behaviors and challenges at the University of Vermont (UVM) so that relevant research data services could be developed. The three research questions focused on how faculty manage and share their research data, particularly in the long-term, the challenges or barriers they faced when managing their research data, and the type of institutional data management support they needed. In the first phase of the study, semistructured interviews were held with faculty who had received National Science Foundation (NSF) grants, and their data management plans were also analyzed. This information was coded, and the elicited themes were used to develop a survey which was administered to all UVM faculty and researchers. Berman's research design is provided in Figure 9.8.

FIGURE 9.8 ● EXPLORATORY SEQUENTIAL MIXED METHODS RESEARCH DESIGN

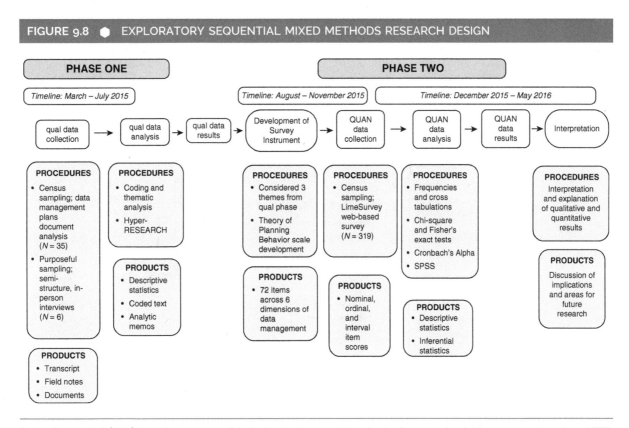

Source: Berman, E. A. (2017). An exploratory sequential mixed methods approach to understanding researchers' data management practices at UVM: Integrated findings to develop research data services. *Journal of eScience Librarianship*, 6(1), e1104. Licensed under CC-BY-SA 4.0

Berman found that the mixed methods design provided a deeper insight into UVM researchers' data management practices and the challenges they faced in the management of digital data than would have been possible with a single research method.

Integrated Data Analysis

Comparative analysis can be conducted when more than one data set is available simultaneously. As Li et al. (2000, p. 120) explain, while the bulk of the work is done with the traditional analysis methods associated with each component of the study (as described in Chapters 7 and 8), "data integration is the process that weaves what has been discovered into a coherent piece." The authors describe two analytic approaches: (1) parallel tracks analysis and (2) cross-over tracks analysis. Figure 9.9, p. 350 depicts these two approaches.

FIGURE 9.9 ◆ PARALLEL AND CROSS-OVER TRACKS ANALYSIS

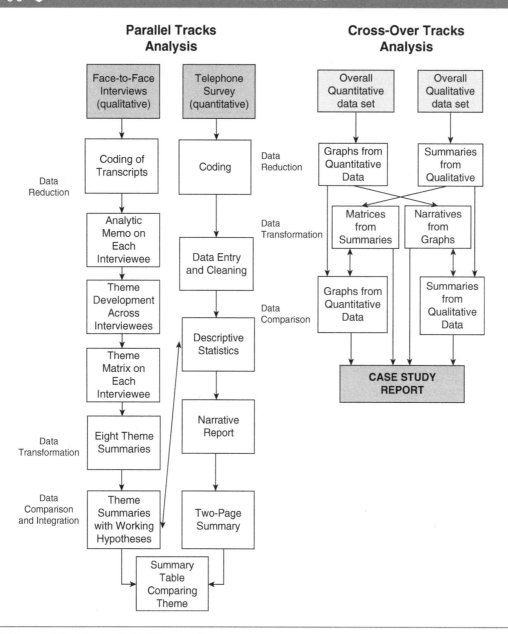

Source: Li, S., Marquart, J. M., & Zercher, C. (2000). Conceptual issues and analytic strategies in mixed-methods studies of preschool inclusion. *Journal of Early Intervention, 23*(2), 116–132.

In the **parallel tracks analysis**, research activities proceeded separately "through the steps of data reduction and transformation until the point of data comparison and integration" (Li et al., 2000, p. 120). They describe the separate analysis of two different studies on families' perspectives on preschool inclusion; one study involved in-person interviews with 112 families; the second study was a telephone survey based on information gleaned from the interviews.

The studies produced summary data by method—eight themes summarized from the interview data and a two-page synopsis of survey data. Data were synthesized by creating a table organized by the eight themes; the survey findings were matched by theme to facilitate comparisons. As they explain:

> *This iterative process of going back and forth between the two data sets enhanced our ability to build upon and expand the understandings we were developing. It allowed us to incorporate both types of data for a more complete understanding of family choices and satisfaction with an inclusive program.* (p. 123)

In the **cross-over tracks analysis**, both qualitative and quantitative data were analyzed concurrently. Li et al. (2000, p. 126) comment, the analysis "moves back and forth continually between both data sets throughout the stages of data transformation, comparison, and integration." Their study involved case studies of 16 programs to determine barriers and facilitators of pre-school inclusion (p. 125). Data were integrated by structuring the case study report according to the main themes that emerged from their analysis (p. 130). The themes were further interpreted by the research team by returning to the data sources to look for more detail, visiting, re-visiting, and discussing the themes as they emerged. The resulting synthesis was then incorporated into a case study report.

The study by Classen et al. (2007) on older driver safety (discussed above) provides a clear diagram of their data analysis plan. It shows that quantitative and qualitative data would be analyzed separately and compared and integrated in the final stage of the study (see Figure 9.10, p. 352).

Integrated Data Synthesis

The analysis of mixed methods data can lead to the production of tables, matrices, diagrams, spreadsheets, case studies, databases, and other creative compilations. The challenge then becomes how best to pull the pieces together. For example, specific research questions can be linked to analyzed data sets and organized into data workbooks or catalogs of information (Barrington, 2014). Data can then be extracted by specific topic into cross-tool data summaries. A clear and consistent numbering system, such as one linked to the original evaluation logic model, can help to organize comparisons.

Triangulation, where convergence is expected, can increase certainty through methods that cancel out each other's limitations (Datta, 2001, p. 39). It can improve the validity of evaluation findings, an important step in "the process of embedding complex empirical data in a more holistic understanding of that specific situation" (Mathison, 2005, p. 423). As Datta suggests (2001, p. 38), triangulation makes sense when two or more data sources considered independent take on the same question and can cancel out biases. When different methods produce similar results, that convergence can increase confidence in study conclusions (Morgan, 2014, p. 69) by eliminating bias and dismissing rival explanations. However, Datta warns that triangulation can also produce inconsistent and

FIGURE 9.10 ● DATA ANALYSIS PLAN FOR OLDER DRIVER SAFETY

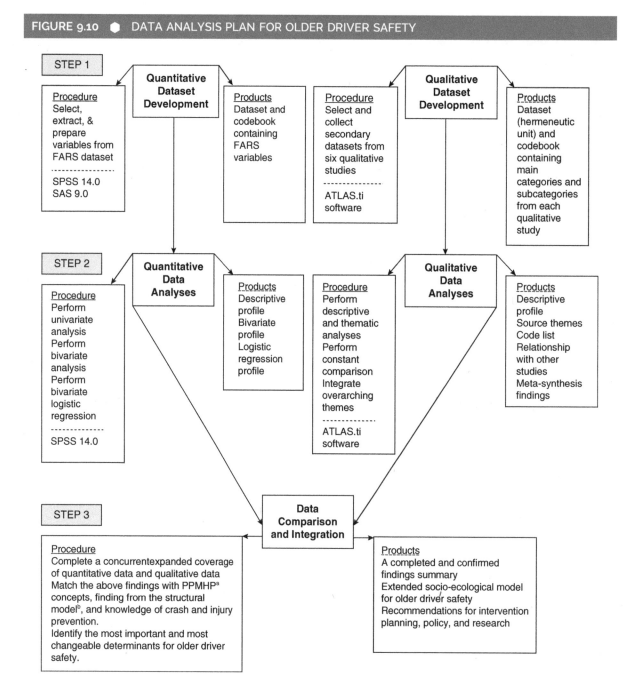

Source: Classen, S., Lopez, D., Winter, S., Awadzi, K. K., Ferree, N., & Garvan, C. W. (2007). Population-based health promotion perspective for older driver safety: Conceptual framework to intervention plan. *Clinical Interventions in Aging, 2*(4), 677–693.

contradictory findings. These can be equally valuable and can be resolved by further analysis of existing data, such as by increasing the granularity of the analysis, or by collecting more data. Datta recommends avoiding premature closure of the analysis. Unexplained findings offer a good opportunity for the evaluation team to draw stakeholders into the discussion to help interpret meaning.

Data triangulation is frequently used in evaluation studies. Ammenwerth et al. (2003) described a case study of the evaluation of a nursing documentation system in four wards in different hospital departments. Standardized questionnaires measured nurses' attitudes before introduction of the new software, three months after its introduction, and again at the nine-month mark. Once the data were analyzed, focus groups were designed and held with both staff and management of each ward. Triangulation of data uncovered both complementary and divergent results. Together they provided a better picture of adoption and attitude change on the four wards and stimulated further discussion.

Data complementarity is a data synthesis technique used when convergence is not necessarily expected. Overlapping but different issues or questions can be explored, and it can provide an enriched understanding of the phenomenon (Li et al., 2000, p. 123). Analysis is often concurrent, as the researchers shuttle back and forth between data sets.

Classen et al. (2007, p. 7) developed a multimethod metamatrix template to compare and integrate significant study findings. They compared and integrated the quantitative data extracted from a national crash data set (the 2003 FARS) using logistic regression with comparable qualitative findings from their systematic review and meta-synthesis of narrative articles that illustrated stakeholder perspectives on safety factors. These findings were further organized by factors in the Precede-Proceed Model of Health Promotion (PPMHP) which provided the theoretical model on which they based their research.

Their template, in Figure 9.11, p. 354 clearly shows how the data would be synthesized, and it is easy to envision how the final report would flow from this careful organization of study data.

Integrated Reporting

There are several approaches to integrating qualitative and quantitative data when reporting study findings. Fetters et al. (2013) identify three approaches: (1) integrating through narrative; (2) integrating through data transformation; and (3) integration through joint displays.

Integrating Through Narrative

The researchers describe the qualitative and quantitative findings in a single report or series of reports (Fetters et al., 2013, p. 2142). The results can be woven together on a theme-by-theme or concept-by-concept basis (such as by research question or logic model topic).

An example of an integrated narrative approach is provided by Meijering and Weitkamp (2016). They explored the everyday mobility practices and wellbeing of older adults in the Netherlands using GPS tracking data, daily travel diary entries, and in-depth interviews. The comparison of GPS and self-reported data identified differences in their storylines.

FIGURE   9.11 ● EXAMPLE OF INTEGRATING QUALITATIVE AND QUANTITATIVE FINDINGS MULTIMETHOD METAMATRIX TEMPLATE

The Precede-Proceed Model of Health Promotion (PPMHP) Domain

Quantitative   **Significant finding from the logistic regression model**

Description and interpretation of the significant finding

	Referent category	Level 1	Level 2
		Significant protective or risk factor	*Significant protective or risk factor*
Qualitative	Description and interpretation of a comparable theme from the meta-synthesis, corresponding to the above mentioned finding from the logistic regression model	Description and interpretation of a comparable theme from the meta-synthesis, corresponding to the above mentioned finding from the logistic regression model	Description and interpretation of a comparable theme from the meta-synthesis, corresponding to the above mentioned finding from the logistic regression model
	Relevant data (quotes) from the stakeholders with citations	*Relevant data (quotes) from the stakeholders with citations*	*Relevant data (quotes) from the stakeholders with citations*
Comparison or Integration	Synopsis and interpretation of the compared data.		
Discussion	Compared or integrated findings discussed in terms of the existing literature, the PPMHP and implications for intervention planning.		

Source: Classen, S., Lopez, D., Winter, S., Awadzi, K. K., Ferree, N., & Garvan, C. W. (2007). Population-based health promotion perspective for older driver safety: Conceptual framework to intervention plan. *Clinical Interventions in Aging, 2*(4), 677–693.

For example, Angela, an 81-year-old widow, who lived in a suburb, walked to the supermarket every day. Sometimes she took a different route, depending on the weather. Her efforts to explain her travels were not sufficiently detailed for the interviewer to be sure of the exact routes she had taken. For example, she said:

> *It's always windy down there, and it's extra fierce....But I can also, then I take the other corner and the street back there...so I take that street over there, and that's not so windy.* (p. 204)

Her travel diary did not explain why the changes were made; however, the GPS data provided precise clarification of her weather-related diversions. At least one trip included a significantly longer route due to the wind. For the researchers, the integration of data from different methods generated a layered understanding of these adults' mobility issues and secured new insights. It allowed them to formulate research questions that could not have been asked previously such as examining the impact of weather conditions on mobility.

Integrating Through Data Transformation

Two forms of data transformation appear in the evaluation literature: quantitizing and qualitizing. One type of data is converted, or transformed, to the other type of data so that it can be combined and analyzed together.

Quantitizing qualitative data "refers to the process of assigning numerical (nominal or ordinal) values to data conceived as not numerical (Sandelowski et al., 2009, pp. 209–210) such as words or visual displays. Converting text into numbers is often done to facilitate pattern recognition or to discern regularities or peculiarities that might not be seen otherwise in the data (p. 210). Numerical data can be produced in support of numerical coding for ranking, sorting, and counting. The approach tries to produce objective, systematic, quantitative, and replicable interpretations of textual data (Krippendorf, 1980, p. 21). The converted data can then be combined with quantitative data for statistical analyses. We must caution that quantitizing qualitative data has tended to fall out of favor in recent qualitative research thought; however, there are situations where it remains a powerful tool.

As Sandelowski et al. remark (2009, p. 219):

> *Numbers have tremendous rhetorical appeal, in part, because of their association with scientific precision and rigor. They substitute the simplification and security of numerical precision for the complication and ambiguity of narrative. The issue is whether numerical precision can satisfactorily grab enough of the complexity of narrative both to understand and communicate it.* (p. 219)

An example of quantitizing qualitative data is provided by Srnka and Koeszegi (2007) who studied the online negotiation behavior of 80 graduate students in business administration at universities in Vienna and Taiwan. Students from the two universities were paired and then responded to a scenario by negotiating topics of price, quality, delivery, and payment. The transcripts of their electronic messages during the negotiation process were unitized, coded, and categorized. Ultimately, they were condensed into nine main categories, each with up to seven subcategories for a total of 40 categories. These were then analyzed using descriptive statistics, exploring for correlation patterns, and testing theory using nonparametric tests. The results suggested that electronic negotiations are "highly content-focused and…require a lot of process coordination, while there is little interpersonal communication when establishing a relationship in e-negotiations" (pp. 49–50). This differed from face-to-face negotiations (as reported in the literature) in which relationship building is much more important. The researchers considered this finding to be an important contribution to theoretical knowledge about negotiations.

Qualitizing quantitative data works in the reverse. Quantitative data are transformed into qualitative data. This happens more often than we realize, such as, in the verbal description of survey scores. If, for example, survey participants indicate their age as in the

50–59 age category, that group might then be described verbally as "middle aged" (Sandelowski, 2000, p. 253). This kind of profiling is often done to describe samples and interpret research results and can enhance pattern matching across data sets (Almutairi et al., 2014).

Qualitizing can add descriptive precision or interpretive richness to quantitative data (Onwuegbuzie & Leech, 2019) to allow the researcher to absorb the context more fully (p. 104) or to make the data more reader-friendly. In a sense, it is backwards engineering that returns scaled items to their original verbal concepts, and there are very few examples in the literature of its use (Nzabonimpa, 2018; Onwegbuzie & Leech, 2019). As Nzabonimpa (2018) comments, "the process amounts to driving back to [the] operationalized and underlying concept that led to numerical responses in the first place" (p. 14).

In his doctoral dissertation, Nzabonimpa (2018) investigated both data conversion processes, he converted narratives into numerical data and numerical data into narratives in mixed methods research while studying students' attitudes toward their choice of subjects taken in school (among other topics). When he looked at complementarity of data across both surveys and interviews, some topics could not be transformed. Tone of voice spoke volumes in the interviews, but the surveys could not pick up the nuances. So, for example, when he asked girls about their choice of school subjects, there were some who wanted to break barriers into the science subjects which were traditionally the stronghold for boys. As he describes:

> *Their burning desire to overcome the gendered stereotypes are only traceable in their tone and sense of revolt against all sorts of socio-cultural stereotypes that have for long undermined their opportunities to excel in science. Except for the narrative content, these language tones and sense of revolt are not easily quantitizable, unless the process is confined to counting participants whose tone and revolt are raised against the patriarchal order.* (p. 12)

Another example of nontransformability was in respondents' use of silence. As he said, "In a self-administered survey questionnaire, silence leaves blank, unanalyzable space, but silences in face-to-face interviews are manifestly meaningful…giving a glimpse into something" (p. 13). He concluded that some types of data cannot easily be rendered into another form or subjected to conversion.

Integrating Through Joint Displays

Joint displays allow the evaluator to integrate the data visually to draw out new insights or generate new inferences. Examples include data in a figure, table, matrix, or graph (Fetters et al., 2013, p. 2142). Mapping key concepts can also be helpful. Guetterman et al. (2015) analyzed 19 mixed methods studies in published health-related literature that provided joint displays. The most prevalent types of displays were statistics-by-themes and side-by-side comparisons although other innovative displays were found such as aligning mixed results to theory or to policy recommendations. They found that joint displays provide a structure to discuss integrated analysis and support the synergy created by this approach.

Bazeley (2018, p. 133) provides many examples of the use of visual artifacts such as videos and photographs in joint displays. These are enabled by the powerful qualitative analysis data software programs available today.

In Berman's (2017) studies of UVM research data management needs, the two strands of data were integrated in a joint display where quotes from the interviews were compared and contrasted to results from the Data Management Practice (DMP) document analysis and the statistical analyses of the survey data. An excerpt is provided below in Table 9.1.

TABLE 9.1 ◆ JOINT DISPLAY COMPARISON

Theme	In-Person Interviews	Data Management Practice (DMP) Document Analysis	Survey
Research Question 1a. Data Management Activities: *Metadata*	"Metadata? I have written some things to help the grad students work with the data more efficiently. Like, 'Here's a standard and here's a good script that checks to make sure that your files are conforming to that standard.' It's not very formalized."	• 25.7% (N = 35) of DMPs mentioned specific metadata standards.	• 28.1% of survey respondents (N = 178) generate metadata standards
Research Question 1b. Data Management Activities: *Data Sharing*	"I like sharing data when it's possible. Sometimes there are Non-Disclosure agreements on these things. It would be nice to make available once we are able to get some papers out, because there is a notion of being scooped.	• 20% (N = 35) of DMPs do not share data because of specific data sharing restrictions. • 94.3% (N = 35) of DMPs share data via publications or presentations.	• 4% of survey respondents (N = 208) "always" or "often" do not share data • 25.6% (N = 199) are "significantly limited" in sharing data because of confidentiality concerns • 23.8% (N = 199) are "significantly limited" in sharing data because of lack of time, personnel, or available infrastructure • 15.6% (N = 199) are "significantly limited" in sharing data because of intellectual property concerns
Research Question 1c. Data Management Activities: *Long-Term Data Preservation*	"We want to keep (the data) around (on external hard drives), but it's not going to updated."	• 48.6% of DMPs (N = 35) deposit data into repositories. • 91.4% of DMPs (N = 35) use hard drives or external media to store data long term.	• 7.7% of survey respondents (N = 208) deposit data into repositories • 64.7% of survey respondents (N = 208) use external hard drives or media to store data long term

Source: Berman, E. A. (2017). An exploratory sequential mixed methods approach to understanding researchers' data management practices at UVM: Integrated findings to develop research data services. *Journal of eScience Librarianship, 6*(1), e1104. Licensed under CC-BY-SA 4.0.

Berman (2017) comments that the integration of the different data strands in the study allowed them both a deeper dive into researcher experiences and an accurate measure of data management activities. As a result, they were able to recommend a robust plan to update their research data services.

In another mixed methods study, Ihrig et al. (2018) focused on the STEM (Science, Technology, Engineering, and Mathematics) opportunities for students in disadvantaged rural settings. The author's study was a concurrent, triangulation mixed methods design. Questions answered through data collection centered around the perceptions, attitudes, and aspirations of the educators and the students. Qualitative data were gathered from teachers and quantitative data from students. For the teachers, data were collected using an open-ended survey and a focus group which gathered their perceptions of the benefits and challenges they had experienced when implementing the STEM program, perceived support from administration for STEM, and how the program had affected their teaching. A close-ended, structured survey was administered to the students at the close of the school year. It contained items that assessed satisfaction with the STEM program, and its effect on their learning, motivation, and ability.

Table 9.2 shows linkages between findings for the teachers and students.

TABLE 9.2 ● PARALLEL FINDINGS FROM THE MIXED METHODS EVALUATION DATA FOR THE STEM PROGRAM	
Teachers	**Students**
• Benefited from creating an academically more challenging STEM program.	• Benefited from participating in the STEM program.
• Wanted to continue their role in the program.	• Wanted to continue their role in the program.
• Critical thinking skills were enhanced in their work.	• Critical thinking skills were enhanced in their work.
• Better understood the individual attention needs of high-performing students.	• Benefited from the individual attention given.

Source: Adapted from Ihrig, L., Lane, E., Mahatmya, D., & Assouline, S. G. (2018). STEM excellence and leadership program: Increasing the level of STEM challenge and engagement for high-achieving students in economically disadvantaged rural Communities. *Journal for the Education of the Gifted, 41*(1), 24–42.

Next, let's read about how the evaluation of an alternative lawyer licensing pathway benefited from using a mixed methods design.

SPOTLIGHT ON EQUITY

Pathways to the Profession Pilot:

Evaluation of An Alternate Lawyer Licensing Pathway Using Mixed Methods

The Law Society of Ontario (LSO), founded in 1797, determined in 2008 that, based on trends in population growth, the demand for Articling positions would continue to outpace supply. Articling is an essential component of the lawyer licensing process and includes a mandatory, transitional, experiential training component, typically in a law firm. By 2011, the rising number of unplaced Articling candidates led to the establishment of an Articling Task Force, which explored, among other things, reasons for the lack of Articling positions.

The Task Force received numerous submissions from equity-seeking groups such as racial minorities, recent immigrants, mature candidates, those from Indigenous populations, and those who identify as LGBTQI+. Nearly all these groups rejected the status quo Articling pathway as it failed to solve the placement shortages that they believed disproportionately affected them. The Task Force recommended developing and piloting an alternative pathway to lawyer licensing, which became known as the Law Practice Program (LPP). It would be delivered by contracted universities with expertise in the development and delivery of professional experiential programs, adult learning, and use of technology in advanced education.

A key goal of the LPP was to increase the access to justice for people from traditionally marginalized communities, often disadvantaged by the race and culture power dynamics of dominant class privilege in Ontario. Due to academic scheduling, the LPP was eight months long, compared to the ten months required in the Articling pathway. It was divided between standardized course work and assessments, and a co-op work placement arranged by the contracted university. The nontraditional LPP was in some ways advantageous to lawyer candidates from marginalized communities because unlike Articling, a work placement did not rely on a candidate's connections, law school affiliation, or appearance. Participation in either pathway was an option to all candidates. Satisfactory completion of either option enabled candidates to challenge the LSO's Bar Exams, and if successful, to practice law in Ontario.

Dr. A. Sidiq Ali, Managing Director of Research & Evaluation Consulting (RaECon), was lead evaluator of the five-year pilot project. The evaluation used a culturally responsive (CRE) lens and paid specific attention to culture and race, and the power differentials between them. Mixed methods suited the CRE approach because it aimed to capture the demographics, data, experiences, and outcomes of these culturally diverse groups within the imbalanced power dynamic the program sought to redress. The evaluation was designed to compare the two options, both annually and over time, using quantitative data such as demographics and standardized assessments, and qualitative data that captured the candidates' experiences and outcomes in each pathway. See Figure 9.12, p. 360 for the mixed methods data collection process.

The program was contentious in the established legal community as it had the potential to alter power dynamics. Members from the larger firms argued that the LPP would provide "second tier" experiential learning, as these larger legal firms believed that only they provided the highest quality training, and many indicated they would not participate in placing candidates from the LPP in their firms. Over the first two years of the pilot, employers failed to participate in adequate numbers in the evaluation focus groups. Ultimately, the data collection strategy was modified to a postprogram survey distributed by new lawyers from each pathway to their current supervisor/employer. This strategy increased employer participation and added important data on the results of competency development in each pathway.

Still, after Year 2, a call came from the established legal community to drop the LLP and it was paused indefinitely. The evaluators shifted their data collection efforts to a new source—the public. The evaluators' Year 2 report (Ali et al., 2016) with preliminary findings was made public by the LSO, posted on their website with an open invitation for commentary on the decision to halt the program. Through this outreach, the public (i.e., the residents of Ontario), those whom the LSO is responsible to protect through its regulatory mandate, and those most likely to benefit from increased access to justice through an additional licensing pathway, were given a voice on the matter. Over 200 written submissions were received. An overwhelming majority of them called for a reinstatement of the LPP and Pilot for Years 3 through 5.

Use of a mixed methods design enabled the identification of emerging trends that indicated the LPP was successful in providing high-quality, experiential legal training. The LSO decided that the evaluators' Year 4

FIGURE 9.12 ●   PLANNED MIXED METHOD DATA COLLECTION AND ANALYSIS FOR THE PATHWAYS TO THE PROFESSION PILOT

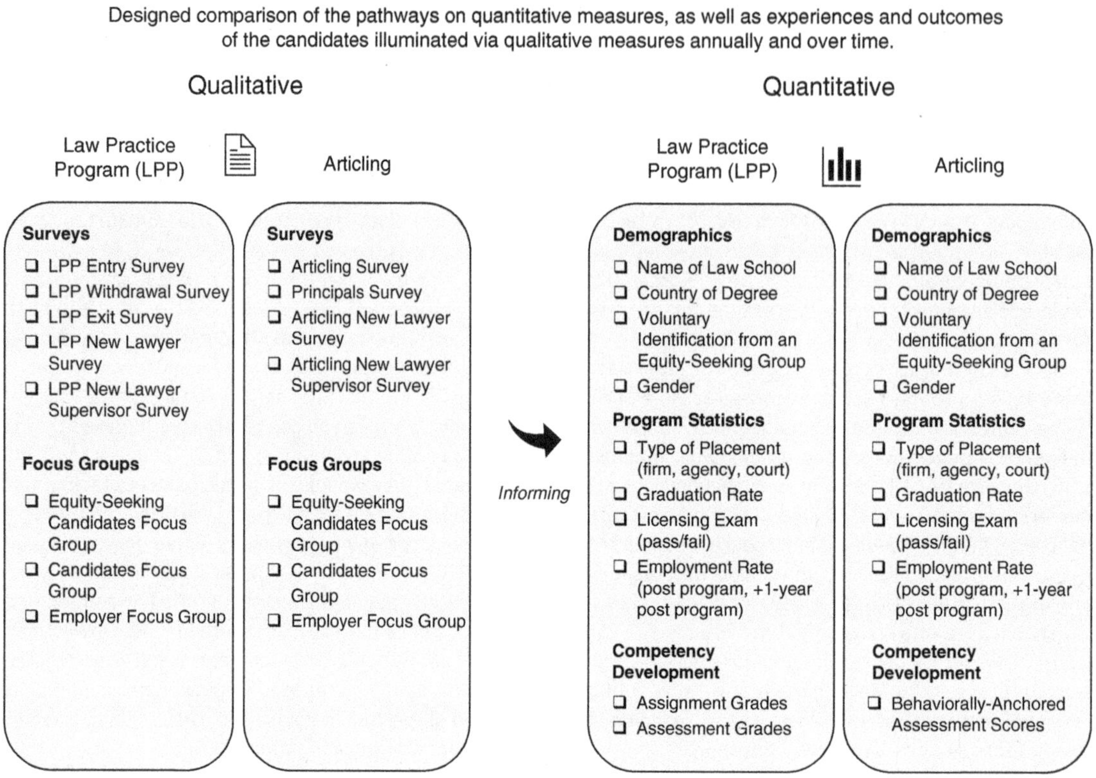

Designed comparison of the pathways on quantitative measures, as well as experiences and outcomes of the candidates illuminated via qualitative measures annually and over time.

Qualitative

Law Practice Program (LPP)

Surveys
- ❑ LPP Entry Survey
- ❑ LPP Withdrawal Survey
- ❑ LPP Exit Survey
- ❑ LPP New Lawyer Survey
- ❑ LPP New Lawyer Supervisor Survey

Focus Groups
- ❑ Equity-Seeking Candidates Focus Group
- ❑ Candidates Focus Group
- ❑ Employer Focus Group

Articling

Surveys
- ❑ Articling Survey
- ❑ Principals Survey
- ❑ Articling New Lawyer Survey
- ❑ Articling New Lawyer Supervisor Survey

Focus Groups
- ❑ Equity-Seeking Candidates Focus Group
- ❑ Candidates Focus Group
- ❑ Employer Focus Group

Informing

Quantitative

Law Practice Program (LPP)

Demographics
- ❑ Name of Law School
- ❑ Country of Degree
- ❑ Voluntary Identification from an Equity-Seeking Group
- ❑ Gender

Program Statistics
- ❑ Type of Placement (firm, agency, court)
- ❑ Graduation Rate
- ❑ Licensing Exam (pass/fail)
- ❑ Employment Rate (post program, +1-year post program)

Competency Development
- ❑ Assignment Grades
- ❑ Assessment Grades

Articling

Demographics
- ❑ Name of Law School
- ❑ Country of Degree
- ❑ Voluntary Identification from an Equity-Seeking Group
- ❑ Gender

Program Statistics
- ❑ Type of Placement (firm, agency, court)
- ❑ Graduation Rate
- ❑ Licensing Exam (pass/fail)
- ❑ Employment Rate (post program, +1-year post program)

Competency Development
- ❑ Behaviorally-Anchored Assessment Scores

Source: A. Sidiq (Sid) Ali

report (Ali & Backlund, 2016) provided enough information about the benefits of the LPP, such as its "broad scope of practice areas" and "innovative approach" to legal training that resonated especially among candidates from marginalized communities, to warrant termination of the pilot. Year 5 of the study was canceled and by vote of the LSO's elected benchers, on December 10, 2018, the LPP joined Articling as a permanent pathway to lawyer licensing in Ontario.

This Spotlight on Equity is based on the contribution of Dr. A. Sidiq (Sid) Ali.

ENSURING QUALITY IN MIXED METHODS DESIGNS

Because paradigms, mental models, and methodological traditions are combined in a mixed methods study, how can quality be judged? Greene (2007, pp. 166–167) suggests that we use traditional criteria to judge the quality of the method used (i.e., quantitative or qualitative) but then take a broader, more integrative stance to judge the quality of the inferences, interpretations, and conclusions made about the data. We need to check for data that support any interpretive statements, multiple and diverse types of data, and researcher awareness of the different methodological traditions involved.

Greene (2007) concedes that mixed methods research provides some knotty problems when interpreting multiple, interactive assumptions and stances or when judging quality. However, these multiple perspectives offer an invitation to "invoke the imagination and creativity as a part of rationality. In these ways they well illustrate a mixed methods way of thinking" (p. 174).

Based on the evolving literature on mixed methods, Creswell and Creswell (2018, p. 214) have developed a checklist of questions for researchers to consider in the design of a mixed methods study (see Figure 9.13).

FIGURE 9.13 ● QUALITY CHECKLIST FOR THE DESIGN OF A MIXED METHODS STUDY

❑ Is a basic definition of mixed methods research provided?

❑ Are the reasons (or justification) given for using both quantitative and qualitative data in your study?

❑ Does the reader have a sense for the potential use of mixed methods research?

❑ Are the criteria identified for choosing a mixed methods design?

❑ Is the mixed methods design identified?

❑ Is a visual model (a diagram) presented that illustrates the research strategy?

❑ Are procedures of data collection and analysis mentioned as they relate to the chosen design?

❑ Are the sampling strategies for both quantitative and qualitative data collection mentioned for the design?

❑ Are the procedures for validation mentioned for the design and for the quantitative and qualitative research?

❑ Is the narrative structure of the final study mentioned and does it relate to the type of mixed-methods design being used?

Source: Creswell, J. W., & Creswell, J. (2018). *Research design: Qualitative, quantitative, and mixed methods approaches.* SAGE Publications.

Finally, let's look at an example of a mixed methods study.

Example of an Evaluation Using an Exploratory Sequential Mixed Methods Design: Telling It All—A Story of Women's Social Capital

Hodgkin (2008) examined gender in relation to the concept of social capital, defined as the norms and networks that enable people to work collectively to address common problems in regional Australia. As a feminist researcher, she located her study within the transformative research paradigm (Mertens, 2015a) which provided a framework to address issues of social justice and to recognize the disenfranchised. In Stage 1, she explored her first research question, "Do men and women have different social capital profiles?" She used a survey previously designed and validated by the South Australian Community Health Research unit in Adelaide to describe, explore, and explain aspects of social, community, and civic participation. Six participation types were measured: social participation (informal, in public spaces, and group activities), civic participation (individual and collective), and community group participation (a mix of social and civic). The survey was mailed to a random sample of 4,000 households and 1,431 (or 35%) were completed and returned.

Data were analyzed using SPSS. Of the respondents, 71.2% were female and 28.8% male, and the data file was divided by gender (the independent variable). A total score was computed for each respondent on the six participation types (dependent variables), and a one-way between-groups multivariate analysis of variance was performed. In addition, multivariate analysis of variance (MANOVA) was also conducted to compare the mean differences between men and women on a combined dependent variable of participation.

Women reported higher levels of individual social participation and activities with a group focus or community group focus particularly activities with children, while in contrast, men reported higher participation in more formal activities such as service clubs, social clubs, sporting clubs, and political parties or trade union groups. Men also reported slightly higher involvement in civic activities.

A second research question was then explored, namely: "Why do women participate more in social and community activities than in civic activities?" When the survey was circulated, an additional form was included that requested expressions of interest to participate in interviews. From the 75 women who responded, 12 were selected for inclusion in the qualitative component. They were interviewed twice, one week apart, and were asked to keep a diary of their activities during the intervening period. In the first interview, they were asked to describe a week in their lives and how they viewed their lives as different from their partner's. The diary provided a focus for the second interview. The data were analyzed using narrative analysis. As Hodgkin explained, her intent was:

>...to analyze the data in successive stages, looking for plot, characters, metaphors, interpretations, and cultural norms; how the stories compared and contrasted; and how the researcher was viewed by the participant. (p. 305)

A careful analysis of the transcripts revealed three motivational themes:

- Wanting to be a "good mother"

- Wanting to avoid social isolation

- Wanting to be a good citizen.

Integration of the quantitative and qualitative findings provided a more powerful story. The quantitative data revealed a different participation pattern among men and women, namely that the predominant pattern for women was informal sociability whereas for men it was associational life. The qualitative data provided Hodgkin with an opportunity to delve into the motivations behind those participation patterns among women. She found that participants' experiences of conflict, exclusion, and guilt influenced their choices. A mixed methods approach allowed her to capture both the statistics and the stories of genderized patterns of participation, a topic which had previously received little attention in the social capital literature.

THE FOCUS GROUP: A COMPANION TOOL IN MIXED METHODS STUDIES

A **focus group** is not simply a group interview. It is a formal discussion of between approximately 6–12 people, selected from a population of interest, and led by a trained facilitator. Its purpose is to collect in-depth information on a specific topic. As Morgan explains, while the focus group is a researcher-constructed data collection tool, it belongs to the group's participants. It is their conversation and interaction that generate the data (Morgan, 2018a). As Patton (2015, p. 475) points out, it is not a decision making or problem-solving tool, and so there is no need to reach a consensus. "The object is to get high-quality data in a social context where people can consider their own views in the context of the views of others."

Focus groups can be used for a variety of purposes (The Health Communication Unit, 2002).

- Exploratory focus groups are used to increase understanding of an issue, to generate hypotheses, to develop concepts, to pilot test the construction of questionnaires, or to help interpret study results.

- Phenomenological focus groups seek to understand the lived experiences and outlook of respondents (such as program participants, consumers, or opinion leaders).

- Clinical focus groups are used to examine unconscious motivation or predispositions, often used to interpret buyer behavior patterns or to gain information about patients' perceptions of their illness or treatment (Tausch & Menold, 2016).

Kreuger and Casey (2009) identify some essential characteristics of a focus group:

1. The focus group must involve people who possess certain characteristics that are related to the study's intended group.

2. The group process must produce qualitative data in relation to the research topic.

3. The data are generated through a focused discussion led by a moderator.

4. Several focus groups should be held so that the same questions can be asked to several groups to identify common themes and trends in the data gathered (Jenkinson et al., 2019).

However, there are few examples in the literature of studies that use the focus group as the sole data collection method. Ecological researchers Nyumba et a. (2018) reviewed focus group discussions that were reported in 170 different articles on the topic of biodiversity and found that the focus group was rarely a stand-alone method. Nearly 85% (144 of the 170 studies) used focus groups in combination with other methods in the same study. Their review highlighted serious gaps in reporting as more than half of the studies ($n = 101$) did not report the sample size or group size ($n = 93$) and over 30% ($n = 54$) did not mention the number of focus group discussion sessions held. Further, the studies rarely provided a rationale for why the focus group method was selected.

It seems that while focus groups are a very common tool, they are not always awarded the same respect or scrutiny as more traditional methods. Worse, focus group data are often used to generate survey questions and are ignored once the statistical data are in or the pithy quotes are identified. No attempt is made to integrate this cache of rich data with survey findings (Bazeley, 2018, p. 13). Without integrating these findings with the results from other methods, questions can be left unanswered, deeper insights unexplored, and there is a greater likelihood that inappropriate conclusions may be drawn.

While mixed methods studies often use focus groups as a companion tool, there is work to be done to harness the qualitative power they harbor. On the positive side, creative combinations of methods, including focus groups, are becoming more prevalent. For example, Guichard et al. (2017) conducted focus groups in conjunction with concept mapping to explore the possible use of a team analysis tool aimed at reducing social inequities in health. They found that the two methods were complementary and provided both concrete and operational ideas, highlighting the issues and challenges associated with putting such a tool into active practice (p. 174).

The traditional single focus group remains the norm, but Nyumba et al. (2018, p. 24) identify a number of other flexible formats, including:

- Two-way focus groups where one group discusses the topic and the other group observes it and then holds their own discussion based on this information

- Dual-moderator focus groups where each moderator performs a different role in the same group

- Dueling-moderator focus groups where the moderators purposefully take opposite sides on an issue or topic

- Respondent-moderator focus group where the researchers recruit a group member to take the temporary role as moderator

- Online focus groups using Zoom, conference calling, chat rooms, or other shared media

- Mini focus group when an adequate pool of participants cannot be obtained; two to five experts are selected

- The one-question focus group when staff schedules are very complex. The focus group is attached to the end of a prescheduled staff meeting and one key question is posed by the researchers (Barrington, 2015).

Planning and Conducting the Focus Group

Operationalizing a focus group is more complicated than it sounds. It takes significant time and human as well as financial resources to organize one. Such tasks as recruiting; confirming participation; securing a space; arranging for honoraria, transportation, parking, and childcare; obtaining refreshments; and organizing transcription services all take more time than anticipated. As a result, it is important to plan carefully.

A great deal of useful information is available on how to prepare for and conduct a focus group (Morgan, 2018; Nyumba et al., 2018; Tausch & Menold, 2016; The Health Communication Unit, 2002). Figure 9.14, p. 366 provides a quick overview of the focus group process.

Some recommendations for best practice in focus groups (Nyumba et al., 2018, p. 29) include:

1. A clear rational for the choice of discussion method, the selection of participants, and the analysis and interpretation methods planned.

2. A facilitator with effective research skills and group management techniques.

3. A report which includes adequate information on the research design, data collection methods, analysis methods, and intended audience.

4. Awareness of, and strategies to counteract, issues of bias, dominance, the halo effect, and groupthink.

5. A clear pathway between focus group data and other results obtained in the study.

Now, it's time to hear from Dr. Jennifer Greene, noted theorist on the topic of mixed methods.

FIGURE 9.14 ⬡ OVERVIEW OF THE FOCUS GROUP PROCESS

①

Select Participants

✓ Topic is of interest to researcher and participants.

✓ Focus groups have high recruitment failure (Morgan, 2018).

✓ Continuously contact potential participants to reinforce importance of study for their intended group.

✓ Over-sample to recruit at least 20% more than needed.

✓ Aim for groups with similar experience, viewpoints, demographics.

✓ Use purposive sampling; segment the target population accordingly.

✓ Number of groups depends upon budget, complexity of topic, emergent themes, saturation of topic.

②

Prepare for Focus Group

✓ Select an attractive venue without distractions.

✓ Provide refreshments.

✓ Gather equipment, consent forms, name tags.

✓ Prepare a well-developed Discussion Guide with right questions, stakeholder input, research questions/purpose, script, discussion questions.

✓ Hire experienced moderator and research assistant for support.

③

Design the Questions

✓ Pose general questions with probes to stimulate discussion.

✓ Approximately 10 questions per 2-hour session.

✓ Questions ordered broad to narrow, easy to difficult.

✓ Provide introduction, purpose, recording plan, consent, confidentiality, facility details, ground rules.

✓ Question segments: 1-2 warm-up; 3-6 key content; 1-2 for wrap up.

✓ Thank you; explain what will happen to results.

④

Moderate the Session

✓ Moderator follows the Discussion Guide but is essentially the research instrument.

✓ Create a nonthreatening, supportive climate, refrain from reaction to participants, limit personally speaking.

✓ Ensure that desired information is collected and follow through on conversational themes.

✓ Record, observe discussion; probe, pause, reflect, facilitate interaction, flow of discussion, and observe non-verbal cues.

✓ Control the opinionated; elicit responses from the reluctant.

✓ Assistant observes non-verbal interactions and group dynamics, takes notes to supplement data; manages equipment and ensure recording works.

Source: Adapted from Morgan (2018), Nyumba et al. (2018), Tausch and Menold (2016), and The Health Communication Unit (2002).

EXPERT CORNER

Dr. Jennifer Greene

Jennifer C. Greene is Professor Emerita of Educational Psychology at the University of Illinois at Urbana-Champaign. Her work has focused on the intersection of social science methodology and social policy, concentrating on advancing qualitative and mixed methods approaches to social inquiry. She aspires to being both methodologically innovative and socially responsible and promotes a value-engaged approach to evaluation. Her publication record includes the coeditorship of the *Sage Handbook of Program Evaluation* and authorship of *Mixed Methods in Social Inquiry*. Greene is a past president of the American Evaluation Association.

1. *As a pioneer of mixed methods in evaluation, your contribution to conceptual frameworks continues to reverberate in the field of evaluation. To date your article with Caracelli and Graham (1989) has received over 7,500 hits. Why do you think that is the case?*

The work presented in this article came from an integrative review of the character of both existing mixed methods theory and recent mixed methods evaluation studies conducted in the 1980s. Specifically, "in this study, a mixed method conceptual framework was developed from the theoretical literature and then refined through an analysis of 57 empirical mixed-method evaluations" (Greene et al., 1989, p. 255). This interplay of conceptual thinking and empirical practice, maintaining respect for both, generated an enriched portrait of mixed methods evaluation in the 1980s, along with a clear agenda for further development of both mixed methods theory and practice.

This review generated a comprehensive set of reasons for mixing methods, vital dimensions of mixed methods design, and direct connections between purposes and design. The review also signaled mixed methods topics that warranted further work, for example, integrated data analysis, thereby offering a research agenda for future mixed methods development.

2. *How relevant is mixed methods thinking in today's unpredictable and complex environment? What new lessons can it offer us?*

It is important to first acknowledge that all social science methodologies are anchored in specific assumptions and values. In postpositivism, social phenomena are assumed to be real, universal, and predictably controllable; and generalizable causal theory is of highest value. In constructivism, social phenomena are assumed to take different forms in different contexts, which are importantly constituted by local norms and cultures; so contextual understanding is of highest value. And critical social scientists focus on revealing societal structures that systematically privilege some people and disempower others.

By definition, a mixed methods approach to social inquiry respectfully engages the assumptions, stances, and values of more than one methodological tradition. Mixed methods studies seek "better understanding" through the thoughtful inclusion of diverse lenses, standpoints, and values about the phenomena being studied. In a study of adolescent gender identity, for example, a theory-based survey can be well complemented by narrative group interviews. This mix can foster meaningful dialogue between broad portraits of adolescent development and local stories of actual youth experience.

So, mixed methods perspectives and values are potentially highly relevant to today's fractured and troubled societies. Mixed methods work supports shared journeys toward knowledge, mutual respect, and an ethic of listening well with both your mind and your heart.

(Continued)

(Continued)

3. *What advice can you offer those of our readers who are just beginning to explore the use of mixed methods in evaluation?*

Read a variety of authors on both the "theory" and the practice of mixing methods in evaluation. Shared ideas abound—especially about key dimensions of mixed methods design. Divergent ideas also abound, notably within conversations about the politics and values that accompany, even energize mixed methods evaluations.

Start small, for example, with a modest mix at the methods level (interview and questionnaire) and then gradually work up to mixes at the level of methodology (case study and survey study) and perhaps reach the level of philosophy (constructivism and postpositivism).

Be thoughtfully creative! The domain of mixed methods remains dynamically unfinished and genuinely welcoming of new perspectives on mixing, along with their adventuresome authors.

Key Terms

The Main Ideas

1. Mixed methods design involves the intentional mixing or integration of quantitative and qualitative data during data collection, analysis, synthesis, and forming conclusions.

2. Mixed methods build on the advantages of quantitative rigor and qualitative richness. The strengths of one make up for the weaknesses of the other and using both can provide more information than using either one alone. The methods can yield stronger findings and more complete evidence because of convergence and corroboration of findings; however, if findings contradict each other, the evaluator and stakeholders can explore and look deeper for reasons.

3. Mixed methods increase the amount of work for the evaluator, thus being a major challenge of the design. Users of mixed methods need to understand their available time, resources and skills for analyzing various types of data.

4. Dewey's Five-Step Model of Inquiry provides a preliminary method for determining appropriate methods for a mixed methods study design.

5. Notation for mixed methods designs involves a shorthand of qual, quant, QUAL and QUANT, and represents both study emphasis and sequence of activities.

6. The convergent design involves two concurrent strands, both qualitative and quantitative. The results integrated at the end of the study to formulate conclusions.

7. In the explanatory sequential design, the quantitative strand occurs first, and the results are further explored through qualitative methods.

8. In the exploratory sequential design, the qualitative strand occurs first, and the analysis of findings informs further quantitative research.

9. Integration of the qualitative and quantitative strands of a study can occur at various points, from management to design, instrument development, data analysis, data synthesis, and reporting.

10. Integrative reporting occurs through narrative, data transformation, and joint displays.

11. Quality is important in mixed methods design. Evaluators should justify why a mixed approach is warranted, identify the specific type of mixed methods design, describe their sampling procedures well for each method, and visually depict the strategies for the design.

12. Focus groups are a popular tool used in mixed methods designs to gain understanding of an issue, generate hypotheses, and pilot test questionnaires. They also deepen the evaluator and community's understanding of participants' lived experience.

Critical Thinking Questions

1. Could mixed methods be described more as an approach to design and sequencing rather than as a methodology? Why or why not?

2. What is the role of integration in mixed methods designs? Provide some examples.

3. Why are the elements of timing and emphasis important when it comes to the design of the mixed methods study? How would timing be illustrated in a notation? How would emphasis be illustrated in a notation?

4. What if someone wanted to conduct a mixed methods study on your life? Identify three quantitative questions they would ask about you in an interview and identify three qualitative questions they would ask. How could the evaluator integrate the separate studies?

5. Why are focus groups often poorly described in the literature? How should the practice be improved?

Student Challenge

1. **The Case of Operation Reach-Out** (Patton, 2015). You have been asked to design a mixed methods evaluation for a comprehensive program known as Operation Reach-Out. It is aimed at high school students who are at high risk educationally. They may have poor grades, poor attendance, or poor attitudes toward school. Their health may be vulnerable due to poor nutrition, a sedentary lifestyle, or high drug use. They also may be candidates for delinquency, feeling alienated from dominant societal values, running with a "bad" crowd, or feeling angry.

The program consists of experiential education internships through which these high-risk students get individual tutoring in basic skills, part-time job placements that permit them to earn income while gaining work exposure, and an opportunity to participate in peer-group discussions aimed at changing health values, establishing a positive peer culture, and increasing social integration.

Your challenge:

1. Create a mixed methods purpose statement for this evaluation.

2. Propose a mixed methods design based on the information in this chapter.

3. Suggest data collection methods.

4. Provide the appropriate notation for your design.

5. Consider potential challenges and limitations that may result from your design.

Additional Readings and Resources

1. Garnet, B. R., Becker, K., Vierling, D., Gleason, C., DiCenzo, D., & Mongeon, L. (2017). A mixed-methods evaluation of the Move it Move it! Before-school incentive-based physical activity program. *Health Education Journal, 76*(1), 89–101.
Garnet et al. (2017) discuss the lack of physical mobility with young people and families. The program quantitatively evaluated the number of miles ran/walked and the ability to perform on mathematics testing. Qualitative structured interviews were conducted with the school personnel. Findings indicated that increased academic performance and behavioral outcomes were correlated with participation in the fitness programs that occurred before and after school.

2. Hong, Q. N., Pluye, P., Fabregues, S., Bartlett, G., Boardman, F., Cargo, M., Dagenais, P., Gagnon, M., Griffiths, F., Nicolau, B., Cathain, A., Rousseau, M., & Vedel, I. (2018). *Mixed methods appraisal tool (MMAT)*. McGill University. http://mixedmethod sappraisaltoolpublic.pbworks.com/w/file/fetch/127916259/MMAT_2018_criteria-manual_2018-08-01_ENG.pdf
This appraisal tool in Part I allows users to score studies on the methodological quality criteria. Categories of study designs include qualitative, quantitative randomized controlled trails, quantitative nonrandomized, quantitative descriptive, and mixed methods. Part II of the tool provides a deeper examination of the study designs by providing a series of questions that allows the user to determine the quality of the design chosen.

3. Ihrig, L., Lane, E., Mahatmya, D., & Assouline, S. (2018). STEM excellence and leadership program: Increasing the level of STEM challenge and engagement for high-achieving students in economically disadvantaged rural communities. *Journal for the Education of the Gifted, 41*(1), 24–42.
This article focuses on the high-achieving student in economically disadvantaged and rural settings who may not have access to STEM participation at the highest levels. The authors used a mixed methods approach to study the experiences of a cohort of students and their teachers who participate in an out of school STEM curriculum.

4. Martí, J. (2015). Measuring in action research: Four ways of integrating quantitative methods in participatory dynamics. *Action Research, 14*(2), 168–183.
This study uses action research to blend quantitative and qualitative methods. They discuss four specific methods for integrating the qualitative and quantitative approaches. They present quantitative evaluation to measure and qualitative research as a method of understanding a population of interest.

5. USAID. (2013). *Technical note: Conducting mixed-method evaluations.* Bureau of Policy, Planning and Learning. https://www.usaid.gov/sites/default/files/documents/1870/Mixed_Methods_Evaluations_Technical_Note.pdf
This 14-page toolkit provides an overview of and rationale for mixed methods designs. Several examples illustrate the use of this design to answer evaluation questions. Parallel, sequential, and multilevel types are discussed. Evaluators are encouraged to use a design matrix, as data collection, analysis, and reporting are thoroughly reviewed.

COMMUNICATING ABOUT EVALUATION

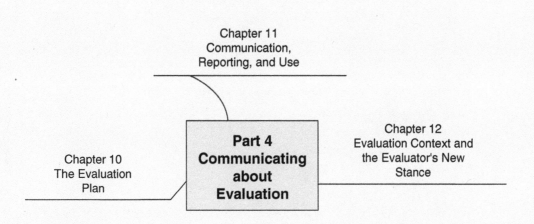

Chapter 11
Communication,
Reporting, and Use

**Part 4
Communicating
about
Evaluation**

Chapter 12
Evaluation Context and
the Evaluator's New
Stance

Chapter 10
The Evaluation
Plan

THE EVALUATION PLAN

LEARNING OBJECTIVES

1. Explain why an evaluation plan is an essential component of an evaluation project.

2. Explain why stakeholder engagement must continue throughout the evaluation process.

3. List the important tasks which must be completed prior to writing the evaluation plan.

4. Describe ways in which the logic model and the evaluation plan are linked.

5. Clarify the reasons why a Data Collection Matrix (DCM) or evaluation framework provides a scaffold for the evaluation study.

6. Explain why a policy of "no surprises" is essential when working with clients and stakeholders.

7. Identify the main topics in the management section of the evaluation plan and explain why they should be elaborated prior to conducting the evaluation.

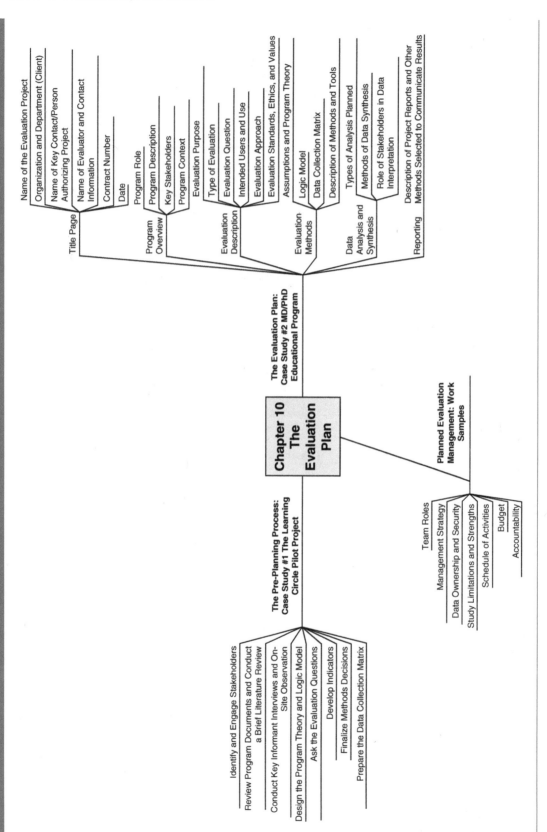

Chapter 10
The Evaluation Plan

The Evaluation Plan: Case Study #2 MD/PhD Educational Program

Title Page
- Name of the Evaluation Project
- Organization and Department (Client)
- Name of Key Contact/Person Authorizing Project
- Name of Evaluator and Contact Information
- Contract Number
- Date

Program Overview
- Program Role
- Program Description
- Key Stakeholders
- Program Context

Evaluation Description
- Evaluation Purpose
- Type of Evaluation
- Evaluation Question
- Intended Users and Use
- Evaluation Approach
- Evaluation Standards, Ethics, and Values
- Assumptions and Program Theory

Evaluation Methods
- Logic Model
- Data Collection Matrix
- Description of Methods and Tools

Data Analysis and Synthesis
- Types of Analysis Planned
- Methods of Data Synthesis
- Role of Stakeholders in Data Interpretation

Reporting
- Description of Project Reports and Other Methods Selected to Communicate Results

The Pre-Planning Process: Case Study #1 The Learning Circle Pilot Project
- Identify and Engage Stakeholders
- Review Program Documents and Conduct a Brief Literature Review
- Conduct Key Informant Interviews and On-Site Observation
- Design the Program Theory and Logic Model
- Ask the Evaluation Questions
- Develop Indicators
- Finalize Methods Decisions
- Prepare the Data Collection Matrix

Planned Evaluation Management: Work Samples
- Team Roles
- Management Strategy
- Data Ownership and Security
- Study Limitations and Strengths
- Schedule of Activities
- Budget
- Accountability

THE FRANKLIN EXPEDITION, A PLANNING DISASTER

On a Monday morning in May 1845, two ships set out from England to chart the northwest passage through the Canadian arctic. For a long time, merchants had wanted a quick way to reach India and China. The ships, known as the *HMS Erebus* and the *HMS Terror*, were especially equipped for Arctic conditions and had reinforced steel bows to cut through the ice. The captain was Sir John Franklin, a 59-year-old explorer who had been on several previous Arctic expeditions. There was a crew of 129 members on board. The ships carried the latest surveying equipment, a cannon weighing 680 pounds, and three years of provisions, including hastily prepared tinned food, over 1,000 pounds of raisins, and 580 gallons of pickles. They also had 1,000 books, an accordion, and a daguerreotype camera (Shapton, 2016).

Source: istockphoto.com/mashuk

However, the expedition met with disaster. Both ships became icebound and were locked in the Arctic waters for more than two years. By April 1848, 24 men had died, including Franklin himself. The remaining crew abandoned the ship and walked across the frozen wasteland and sea ice to reach the mainland. Most of the men died during this march, and the rest died afterward, hundreds of miles from known outposts. Researchers believe that various misfortunes killed them, including starvation, emaciation, severe hypothermia, scurvy, tuberculosis, and possible suicide.

The mystery of the disaster has fascinated people for over 100 years. Search parties began in 1850 and over 90 have followed, including one sent by Lady Franklin herself. Finally, in 2014, a search team led by Parks Canada located the wreck of the *Erebus*, and two years later, the Arctic Research Foundation found the wreck of the *Terror*, mysteriously located over 46 miles away from its companion ship (Davison, 2020).

In the end, it was information gleaned from Inuit oral history that put the puzzle pieces together although these stories had been discounted from the beginning. Researchers continue to unravel the mystery about what happened in this, the worst disaster in the history of British polar exploration.

Appropriate planning is an essential component of any exploratory endeavor, whether it is an expedition into uncharted territory or an upcoming evaluation where, indeed, a lot is unknown. In planning the Franklin Expedition, context and experience should have been considered instead of accepted practice. The seaman could have avoided several challenges. Appropriate clothing and footwear for Arctic temperatures, supplies such as food and medicine for what were already well-documented illnesses, and staff with the appropriate skills in leadership and exploration could have aided survival. In hindsight, it is easy to say, but better planning might have saved lives and spared their families the tragic outcome.

Of course, evaluation is on a much smaller scale, but when an evaluation flounders or fails because of poor planning, there can be many serious consequences. Evaluators and stakeholders may waste resources and money, ruin relationships and goodwill, and cause programs to fail. Most importantly, program participants may lose essential services.

A strong evaluation plan sets the parameters for how the study will proceed, helps to troubleshoot potential issues, and ultimately supports further program development.

INTRODUCTION

The evaluation plan is the focus of Chapter 10. First, we explain why it is considered the essential first step to the entire evaluation project. Then two case studies and other work samples are used as exemplars for the preplanning work and the actual plan itself. Preliminary work includes eight steps: identifying key stakeholders, reviewing program documents, interviewing key informants, designing the program theory and logic model, asking evaluation questions, developing indicators, finalizing methods decisions, and preparing the Data Collection Matrix (DCM). Writing the evaluation plan includes seven elements: the title page, program overview, evaluation description, evaluation methods, data analysis and synthesis, reporting, and evaluation management. We delve further into some of the important project management tasks that benefit from planning. Finally, we close the chapter with a discussion on evaluation plan accountability.

You will enjoy the resources in this chapter including the Spotlight on Equity, which presents an evaluation for community-based climate change adaption, our expert Dr. Katrina Bledsoe, Key Terms, Main Ideas, Critical Thinking Questions, Student Challenges, and Additional Readings and Resources.

Source: Chris Lysy/FreshSpectrum.com

THE PREPLANNING PROCESS: CASE STUDY #1 THE LEARNING CIRCLE PILOT PROJECT

We like to think of the **evaluation plan** as the base camp for an evaluation project. It is the place where you gather your resources, check your equipment, and plan your strategy. Once the plans are in place, it is much easier to begin the evaluation expedition.

As Francisco et al. (2000) explain:

> *There is no better way to get started with an evaluation than to develop an evaluation plan. Good evaluation planning involves identifying who the key audiences for the evaluation findings include, posing relevant and useful evaluation questions, and using evaluation measures and designs that will answer those questions to the satisfaction of key stakeholders.* (p. 126)

Figure 10.1, p. 379 illustrates some of the critical reasons for preparing an evaluation plan.

Case Study #1: The Learning Circle Pilot Project involved the evaluation of a learning circle pilot project at the Bethany Care Society, a long-term care center (2014). The administrators had noticed that traditional educational initiatives did not transfer into

FIGURE 10.1 ● REASONS FOR AN EVALUATION PLAN

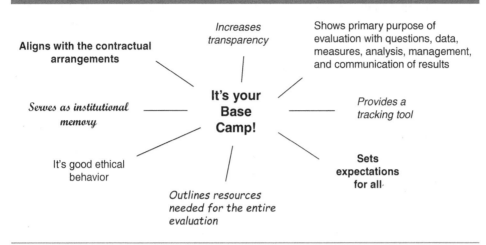

practice change on their long-term care wards, and so this pilot project was initiated to test a collaborative learning model. They hoped it would be a more effective way for health-care workers to transfer best practices to their work. The Learning Circle project was small in scope and included three learning circles, each comprised 6–8 participants and a facilitator. They met once a month for six months. Each circle addressed a different theme and had a different staff mix.

This section describes the pre-planning processes that were used to prepare for the written evaluation plan. Figure 10.2 provides a checklist of the eight preplanning activities that occur prior to preparing the written evaluation plan.

FIGURE 10.2 ● THE EIGHT PRE-PLANNING ACTIVITIES CHECKLIST

❑ Identify and Engage Stakeholders
❑ Review Program Documents and Conduct a Brief Literature Review
❑ Conduct Key Informant Interviews and On-Site Observation
❑ Design the Program Theory and The Logic Model
❑ Ask the Evaluation Questions
❑ Develop Indicators
❑ Finalize Methods Decisions
❑ Prepare the Data Collection Matrix

Each of these eight preplanning activities is described in the following sections. We have anonymized this information for privacy reasons.

Identify and Engage Stakeholders

Stakeholders have a particularly important role in evaluation (see Chapter 4). "Failure to attend to the interests, needs, concerns, powers, priorities, and perspectives of stakeholders represents a serious flaw in thinking or action that too often and too predictably leads to poor performance, outright failure, or even disaster" (Bryson et al., 2011, p. 2). While their involvement is essential throughout the evaluation process, stakeholders' perspectives, cultural sensitivities, and political vulnerabilities are critical especially during the planning stage.

Important **stakeholder identification** activities in the planning phase include: (1) listing the stakeholders, (2) identifying the interests of each (both in the program and in the evaluation), (3) diagramming their interrelationships and influence, and (4) determining the sources of their power. With this information, the evaluator can seek common ground across stakeholder groups, uncover their motivations, and increase the likelihood that their networks will benefit from the evaluation.

Stakeholders can be recruited from the following groups (see Figure 10.3).

FIGURE 10.3 ● SOURCES FOR STAKEHOLDER RECRUITMENT

Once the appropriate stakeholders are identified, the evaluator can establish an **Evaluation Working Group** (EWG). The Centers for Disease Control and Prevention (2011) suggest that stakeholders are much more likely to buy into and support the evaluation if they are involved in the evaluation process from the beginning. Although program leads can invite many potential stakeholders, the CDC recommends selecting those who can directly benefit from the evaluation results. Between eight to ten members is suggested as an appropriate size for the group (p. 11).

Stakeholders can contribute to the following evaluation tasks (p. 7):

- Determine and prioritize key evaluation questions (KEQs)

- Pretest data collection instruments

- Facilitate data collection

- Implement evaluation activities

- Increase the credibility of analysis and interpretation of evaluation information

- Use evaluation results.

As Holden and Zimmerman (2012, p. 10) point out, it is essential to define the stakeholders' roles in the working group and to structure their input. Depending on the size of the evaluation and the political volatility of its environment, it may be important to develop a written description of members' roles and the expectations held for their contribution. For example, in a complex study environment with many interests at play, a stakeholder **Memorandum of Understanding (MOU)** can be prepared to outline the purpose of the working group, the role of individual members, the evaluator's expectations for their involvement, their time commitment, the schedule of meetings, communication strategies, and the decision making process to be used. While not a legal contract, the MOU ensures that each member clearly understands their commitment and how their participation can benefit both the program and their context. The clarification of expectations helps avoid surprises and prepares stakeholders for the review of the final report.

The evaluation plan for the Learning Circle Pilot Project described stakeholder engagement as follows (Box 10.1):

BOX 10.1 ● STAKEHOLDER ENGAGEMENT

Because the learning circle process itself is collaborative, democratic, responsive, and staff are committed to organizational learning, the evaluator will use an Appreciative Inquiry (AI) (Preskill & Catsambas, 2006) approach. The Vice President, staff educators/learning circle facilitators, and the evaluator will comprise the EWG and will meet regularly to discuss study plans and interpret results.

Review Program Documents and Conduct a Brief Literature Review

A **review of program documents** enables the evaluator to gain a deeper understanding of the evaluation questions. It provides insight into the organization and its culture and can provide background on the program's history and current context. The CDC (2018) explains when to use a document review:

- To gather background information

- To determine if implementation reflects program plans

- To inform the development of data collection tools for the evaluation

- To provide basic descriptive information about the program (e.g., number and type of participants, personnel, and costs).

The review is like thumbing your way through the program's filing cabinet to determine what has happened from program initiation to the present. Often a good place to start is with the program's original funding proposal and relevant documents related to its inception. It is possible to understand the program's original goals and objectives, intended target group, and initial implementation strategies. Depending on how long the program has been operating, a lot may have changed over the years.

Documents can include (Centers for Disease Control and Prevention, 2018; Patton, 2015, p. 376):

- Job descriptions of program staff

- Organization charts

- Rules and regulations relevant to the program

- Annual reports

- Financial and budget records

- Staff correspondence

- Meeting minutes

- Program materials

- Program logs (sign-in sheets, etc.)

- Routine client records

- Case management software or other systems used

- Newsletters, artifacts, marketing materials, websites, and social media

- Other official or unofficial documents generated by or for the program.

At this early point in the project, it is not necessary to analyze all these files and records, but it is important to determine which documents are available and which ones are not. Often staff make assurances about the availability of documents and data which may not be accessible. This can be for various reasons such as faulty recollection, removal of records to storage, degradation of digital files, outdated software, or missing gatekeepers.

Once the evaluator understands what information is available, what it looks like, and how and where it is stored, it is much easier to plan the analysis process and the time required for the document review. The document review process is discussed in Chapter 4.

A Document Review Checklist that standardizes the criteria used in the review process is a useful tool (Bretschneider et al., 2016). There are many templates available on the Internet. Table 10.1 provides a simple example.

TABLE 10.1 ● SAMPLE DOCUMENT REVIEW CHECKLIST					
Document Title or Type	Location	Document's Author and Date	Informs Evaluation Question Number	Key Points or Note for Additional Review Later	Reviewer and Date

Sometimes, particularly in the case of new programs, documents may not be available for review. Important concepts may emerge that require a deeper understanding, and a brief literature review may be required (see Box 10.2).

BOX 10.2 ● LITERATURE REVIEW
In this small pilot project, there were no internal documents to review because the learning circles had not been initiated. Instead, the evaluator conducted a brief literature review. Relevant concepts were searched to inform the plan, including adult learning, experiential learning, quality circles, and AI.

Conduct Key Informant Interviews and On-Site Observation

Armed with more information about the program background and context, the evaluator can then conduct a brief set of open-ended interviews with **key informants**. Gaining perspective on stakeholder perceptions before launching into the evaluation can deepen the evaluator's understanding of the types of issues that may surface and can provide information about which data collection methods are likely to be the most effective. The number of stakeholders will vary depending on the size and complexity of the program, but generally, between three to six interviews are sufficient. Candidates include program

initiators, opinion leaders, knowledgeable staff, and representatives of funders and beneficiaries. The evaluator should explain that their input will help to shape the evaluation
design.

Suggested topics include:

- Perceptions of program accomplishments compared to stated goals and intended
  impacts

- Examples of program successes

- Areas that raise a concern or need improvement

- Biggest surprises about the program

- Recommendations of additional data sources

- Most pressing issues.

This high-level view of the program can provide helpful preliminary information. It allows
the evaluator to gauge the organizational culture and the nature of current relationships
within the program. In addition, sometimes, simply meeting with these individuals can be
quite eye-opening, as was the case in the Learning Circle Pilot Project (Box 10.3).

BOX 10.3 ⬡ KEY INFORMANT INTERVIEWS

To clarify the program's intent and refine the evaluation approach, the evaluator conducted
a key informant interview with the Vice President to discuss the reasons for project
initiation and to explore expectations for the pilot.

She also attended a Learning Circle team meeting to conduct a group interview. She
quickly discovered that the project was embedded in a turbulent environment. Staff were
anxious and upset, and their work routines had been disrupted. In addition, several significant events had occurred or were ongoing during the study, which heightened their
sense of unease. These included:

- A current accreditation process was making heavy demands on staff.

- Government funding had just changed, affecting management structures. For example,
  managers who had been responsible for one unit were now managing two.

- Budget cutbacks were leading to job losses, staff relocation, and position changes due
  to seniority.

- A major city flood had affected many staff who had experienced disruption in their
  personal lives.

- Staff turnover was a continuing problem.

These revelations caused the evaluator to choose an AI approach. Staff were relieved that
the evaluation was not yet another negative issue to contend with but was, rather, a
positive force during a difficult period.

Design the Program Theory and Logic Model

The evaluator based the evaluation plan on the logic model. As Braverman and Engle (2009) explain, "The causal links can identify potentially important mediators or intermediate variables necessary to make the desired changes happen" (p. 3). In their extension education context, they described these linkages: "the program creates short-term *knowledge* change, which leads to intermediate-term *behavior* change, which finally leads to long-term *impact* such as improved personal health or economic sustainability" (p. 3).

Discussions about the logic model can be an excellent team-building exercise with the EWG because it is a nonthreatening way to explore program assumptions and expectations. It can also engender good conversation about how evaluation findings will be used. This early meeting can establish positive relationships and build collaborative decision making processes to sustain the project (Box 10.4).

BOX 10.4 ● LOGIC MODEL DEVELOPMENT

Due to the stressful environment and lack of time available to EWG members, the evaluator reviewed the project purpose and evaluation objectives and developed a draft logic model to reflect the program theory and assumptions as she understood them. She then reviewed the draft with the EWG. Members offered feedback and she revised accordingly.

The Learning Circle Pilot Project purpose was:

> *To test the learning circle approach to facilitate knowledge transfer by creating a series of learning circles.*

The evaluation's objectives, as outlined by the Vice President, included:

1. To contribute to the understanding of the Bethany Care Society concerning workplace learning and knowledge translation by evaluating the Learning Circle Pilot Project.

2. To contribute evaluation findings to the future research agenda of the funder.

3. To build evaluation capacity among team members and other staff at Bethany and at partner organizations.

A copy of the revised logic model is presented in Figure 10.4, p. 386 (Bethany Care Society, 2014).

Ask the Evaluation Questions

Rossi et al. (2019) define evaluation questions as those "developed by the evaluator, evaluation sponsor, and/or other stakeholders that define the issues the evaluation will investigate. They should be stated in terms that can be answered using methods available to the evaluator and in a way useful to stakeholders" (p. 318).

Davidson (2009) suggests that evaluation questions should cover the "big picture" issues (pp. 8, 10–11). They must be "actionable," meaning that the answers must be direct,

FIGURE 10.4 ● LEARNING CIRCLES PILOT PROJECT

Process			Outcomes		
1.0 Inputs	**2.0 Activities**	**3.0 Outputs**	**4.0 Immediate Outcomes**	**5.0 Intermediate Outcomes (2013)**	**6.0 Ultimate Outcomes (2014–2015)**
1.1 Funding & research agenda 1.2 Adult learning principles 1.3 Prepared facilitators 1.4 Appropriate topics 1.5 Management & operational support in Bethany & participating organizations 1.6 Evaluation plan using Appreciative Inquiry (AI)	**Learning Circle Process** 2.1 Training in Learning Circle concept 2.2 Selection of background materials 2.3 Participant preparation 2.4 Learning Circle discussions 2.5 Experiential learning 2.6 Reflective observation 2.7 Abstract Conceptualization 2.8 Active experimentation 2.9 Feedback loops 2.10 Staff participate in evaluation	**Participants:** 3.1 Assess their learning outcomes 3.2 Enhance their capacity in target skills & knowledge 3.3 Apply target skills & knowledge in workplace 3.4 Experience enhanced confidence in self-directed learning **Facilitators:** 3.5 Demonstrate enhanced leadership capacity **Evaluation:** 3.6 Is conducted; report is prepared	4.1 Practice is changed in target areas 4.2 Understanding of learning circles for workplace learning & KT is increased 4.3 Evaluation capacity for team & staff is enhanced 4.4 Unanticipated outcomes & side effects are identified 4.5 Additional research topics are identified 4.6 Recommendations are advanced to funder 4.7 Understanding of AI for evaluation is increased	5.1 Care for residents in target areas is improved 5.2 The learning circle approach to workplace learning is expanded at Bethany 5.3 Strategies are developed for learning circles at partner organizations. 5.4 Funder's research agenda is enhanced.	6.1 Workplace learning & KT at Bethany & partner organizations improve practice 6.2 Additional funding for research on innovative learning models is obtained by funder

Source: Bethany Care Society. (2014). *Learning circles pilot project final evaluation report.* Gail V. Barrington.

explicit, and warrant action, such as, for example, continuing to fund the program. She suggests that there should be no more than about seven of these big picture questions, covering most or all of the topics she presents in a "cheat sheet" (Box 10.5) for evaluators. These questions can be tailored to any evaluation.

BOX 10.5 ● DAVIDSON'S TEMPLATE FOR EVALUATION QUESTIONS

- What was the quality of the program's content/design, and how well was it implemented?

- How valuable were the outcomes to participants, to the organization, the community, and the economy?

- What were the barriers and enablers that made the difference between successful and disappointing implementation and outcomes?

(Continued)

(Continued)

- What else was learned (about how or why the effects were caused/prevented, what went right/wrong, lessons for next time)?

- Was the program worth implementing? Did the value of the outcomes outweigh the value of the resources used to obtain them?

- To what extent did the program represent the best possible use of available resources to achieve outcomes of the greatest possible value to participants and the community?

- To what extent is the program or aspects of its content, design, or delivery likely to be valuable in other settings? How exportable is it?

- How strong is the program's sustainability? Can it survive/grow in the future with limited additional resources?

Source: Davidson, E. J. (2009, November 12). *Improving evaluation questions and answers: Getting actionable answers for real-world decision makers* [Presentation]. Context and Evaluation American Evaluation Association Conference, Orlando, FL, United States.

These broad questions can then be "unpacked" into specific, measurable evaluation questions like those found in the **DCM**. They lead directly to indicators that the evaluator will use to craft the data collection tools. For example, in the Learning Circle case study, the EWG focused their interest on specific components of the logic model (2.0 Activities, 3.0 Outputs, and 4.0 Immediate Outcomes). Box 10.6 provides an example of how the evaluator developed questions for topic "2.4 Learning Circle Discussions."

BOX 10.6 ● QUESTION DEVELOPMENT FOR "2.4 LEARNING CIRCLE DISCUSSIONS"

To get a sense of the learning circle discussion process, the evaluator observed a circle meeting at the beginning of the project. Afterward, she discussed her observations with the facilitator and clarified her understanding of the meeting structure, process, and discussion. She gained a mental picture of the types of interactions that would be likely to occur in other learning circle meetings.

Based on this observation, she developed some questions to elicit information about the discussion process. Then she obtained feedback from the facilitators, and the questions were further clarified.

For example, questions related to 2.4 on the logic model, "learning circle discussions," were expanded in the DCM as follows:

2.4.1 How did learning circle discussions proceed?

2.4.2 To what extent did the facilitators use group process skills?

2.4.3 To what extent were the issues discussed relevant to circle members' workplace contexts? To their current learning needs?

2.4.4 What helped or hindered circle members' ability to discuss topics openly?

2.4.5 How did the discussion process vary by circle?

Stufflebeam (1999a, p. 5) reminds us that evaluators must consider trade-offs between comprehensiveness and specificity as evaluators make choices in the final list of evaluation questions. These include choices about the feasibility and the availability of data, the extent of stakeholder collaboration, the burden of data collection on staff, specific characteristics about the program and its target group that can impact data collection, the budget and other resources, scope, scheduling and time allotted for the project, evaluation team member skills and qualifications, and environmental constraints and context (Centers for Disease Control and Prevention, 2011; Saunders et al., 2005).

Develop Indicators

Once evaluators develop the questions, it is time to define the indicators. As Taylor-Powell et al. (1996) explain, "Indicators answer the question, 'How will I know it?' It is the indication or observable evidence of accomplishments, changes made, or progress achieved" (p. 8). Typically, indicators provide evidence about performance or outcomes. Performance indicators often measure program activities and processes against desired target levels. Outcome indicators focus attention on goal achievement. As Patton (2008, p. 257) reminds us, "What gets measured gets done." Indicators must be well-developed and appropriate and are central to the selection of the data collection tools.

Continuing the example of "2.4 Learning Circle Discussions," here is what the evaluator did to define indicators to measure "2.4.2 To what extent did the facilitators use group process skills?" (Box 10.7).

BOX 10.7 ● INDICATOR DEVELOPMENT FOR "2.4.2 TO WHAT EXTENT DID THE FACILITATORS USE GROUP PROCESS SKILLS?"

As learning circles were a new initiative and neither the facilitators nor the evaluator had readily available criteria to measure group process skills, the evaluator reviewed relevant literature to identify appropriate indicators. She developed a list of criteria to judge the effectiveness of the facilitators' group process skills based on the work of Christensen (1983). These included:

- Provide leadership

- Offer communication, clarification and summarization

- Be sensitive to individual and group learning needs

- Promote cohesion

- Promote trust and confidentiality

- Encourage full participation, collaboration, and shared responsibility.

These criteria would become the indicators used to measure the effectiveness of the facilitator's group process skills.

Finalize Methods Decisions

The last two preplanning activities, finalizing methods decisions and preparing the DCM, generally coevolve as ideas coalesce and the pieces start to fall into place. Having moved from evaluation topics to questions to indicators, now it is time to consider the best way to obtain the needed information.

Both divergent and convergent thinking are needed (Cronbach et al., 1980, pp. 227–228). Divergent thinking allows the evaluator to cast a broad net and consider the many possibilities on offer, but convergent thinking is influenced by four factors: (1) uncertainty around program outcomes, (2) how likely the study recommendations will be enacted, (3) the cost of answering the evaluation questions, and (4) how much information the questions will produce. In this back-and-forth decision making process, the evaluator weighs the answers and shifts resources, time, and evaluation activities back and forth until an adequate balance is achieved (Cronbach et al., 1980, p. 261).

The evaluator must also consider the rigor of the evidence, defined by Braverman and Arnold's (2008) as "the strength of the design's underlying logic and the confidence with which conclusions can be drawn" (p. 72). Choices range from high-rigor options to moderate ones. Braverman and Engle (2009) comment that evaluators "have to make smart, thoughtful, and sometimes difficult decisions about methodology, weighing benefits and costs to find the most suitable overall plan" (p. 8).

Sometimes evaluation situations require the highest methodological rigor despite the costs; at other times, a more moderate confidence level may be acceptable if resources are limited. Braverman and Engle (2009) conclude, "A moderately rigorous evaluation can be appropriate if it will answer the primary questions with a level of confidence that is acceptable to the program's stakeholders" (p. 9). Box 10.8 outlines data collection decisions for our example, "2.4 Learning Circle Discussions."

BOX 10.8 ● DATA COLLECTION DECISIONS FOR "2.4 LEARNING CIRCLE DISCUSSIONS"

Moving back and forth between the DCM, study objectives, time allotted, and budget limitations, the evaluator planned to use the following tools to answer the questions identified for "2.4 Learning Circle Discussion."

1. **Learning Circle Tracking Sheet**. A tracking sheet was designed to obtain process information about each learning circle meeting (e.g., date, number of attendees, materials used, concerns, or issues) and facilitator satisfaction with group process skills based on Christensen (1983).

2. **Evaluator Observation**. The evaluator planned to take informal notes during observations at Meeting #3 and Meeting #6.

3. **AI Focus Groups**. Using AI, the evaluator designed participant focus group questions. She planned to conduct a one-question focus group (see Chapter 9) after learning circle meetings #3 and #6.

(Continued)

(Continued)

Focus Group 1 *(after Learning Circle Meeting #3)*

[The question is based on AI concept, "Inquire:" to appreciate the best of "what is."]

Think back on your experience with the learning circle so far and remember when you felt most energized by it. What happened? What contributed to this success?

Focus Group 2 *(after Learning Circle Meeting #6)*

[The question is based on Appreciative Inquiry concept, "Imagine:" to determine what might be, and consider possibilities, creating and validating the vision.]

Imagine this learning circle has continued for another 6 months. What changes have happened in your workplace as a result? Why have these changes happened?

Figure 10.5, p. 391 provides the Tracking Sheet used to measure the learning circle discussion process at each learning circle meeting.

Prepare the Data Collection Matrix

The **Data Collection Matrix** (DCM), or evaluation framework, is the scaffold on which the evaluator builds the evaluation. It links the evaluation questions back to the overarching research questions, the evaluation objectives, and the logic model, and forward to measurement indicators, appropriate data collection tools, and data sources. The DCM is helpful not only during the design stage but throughout the study. Here are some of its uses.

Creates a Shared Understanding of the Project

Stakeholders are consulted about the DCM and confirm its use. Thus, it documents a shared understanding of the evaluation process. As part of the work plan, it can be attached to the evaluation contract as an appendix to provide a detailed outline of planned work. If stakeholders raise questions later about study scope, perhaps suggesting more or different questions, sources, or using different tools, the matrix provides a reminder of the agreed-upon design.

Acts as a Concrete Work Plan

As the evaluation progresses, additional topics (and columns) can be added to the DCM to support work processes. Examples include data sources, schedules, personnel responsible for specific tasks, and due dates.

Maintains Study Focus

The matrix keeps the research focused and manageable, so evaluators use resources wisely to collect the most pertinent information. However, as new study information emerges, such as new intended groups, new sites, or a clearer understanding of specific topics, it can be revised to reflect these new circumstances. As Raimondo and Vaessen (2019) point out, it is not a one-shot deal; instead, it is a living document that evolves in response to a changing context. It helps the evaluator keep the evaluation focused and manageable in the face of the unexpected challenges that occur in real-world evaluation, responding to such questions as "Are we on track? Are we asking the questions we need to ask now? What has changed?"

FIGURE 10.5 ● EXAMPLE OF AN EVALUATION TRACKING SHEET

Learning Circle Evaluation: Tracking Sheet

Circle Operation

Please provide the following information:

Today's Topic:	# Attendees:	Date :
	# Absent:	

Please describe any scheduling concerns related to this meeting:

Please describe any coverage issues related to participants' attendance at this meeting:

What background materials were used today?

Please rate their appropriateness and comment as needed:

Not effective 1	2	3	4	Very effective 5	NA
☐	☐	☐	☐	☐	☐

Use of Your Group Process Skills Today

Select the number that best reflects your satisfaction with your use of group process skills while facilitating this Learning Circle meeting. If you did not use the skills, indicate *Not Applicable (NA)*.

Group Process Skill	Very dissatisfied 1	2	3	4	Very satisfied 5	NA
1. Leadership	☐	☐	☐	☐	☐	☐
2. Communication, clarification & summarization	☐	☐	☐	☐	☐	☐
3. Sensitivity to individual & group learning needs	☐	☐	☐	☐	☐	☐
4. Promoting group cohesion	☐	☐	☐	☐	☐	☐
5. Promoting trust & confidentiality	☐	☐	☐	☐	☐	☐
6. Encouraging full participation, collaboration & shared responsibility	☐	☐	☐	☐	☐	☐

What group process skill worked particularly well for you today? Why was it so successful?

Provides a Coding System for Study Tools

The individual items in each study tool can be coded to the DCM to ensure the evaluator maintains a link to the study design. The codes also support the development of an evidence trail which the analysts can use to retrace the source of specific findings.

Guides Data Analysis

Both qualitative and quantitative data can be organized into workbooks, catalogs of information, or spreadsheets to assist with analysis. Data can be organized in sequence by DCM code number, indicator, and theme. Then cross-tool data summaries can be prepared that triangulate all the information obtained, using the DCM code numbers (Barrington, 2012b).

Provides a Systematic and Recognized Outline for the Final Report

As stakeholders are already familiar with the logic model and DCM structure, a final report that walks through the same topics supports their confidence in the research process. Having the DCM in the evaluation plan helps them visualize how the evaluation will be implemented and which topics the results are likely to address (Lavinghouze & Snyder, 2013). Box 10.9 presents item "2.4 Learning Circle Discussions" as it is fleshed out in the DCM to describe the measurement process.

BOX 10.9 ● DATA COLLECTION MATRIX DEVELOPMENT PROCESS

Example: 2.4 Learning Circle Discussions

"2.4 Learning Circle discussions" has been extracted from the DCM as an example. The full DCM addresses all relevant topics identified in the logic model.

Evaluation Topics	Evaluation Questions	Indicators	Data Collection Tools and Sources
2.4 Learning Circle discussions	2.4.1 How did Learning Circle discussions proceed? 2.4.2 To what extent did the facilitators use group process skills? 2.4.3 To what extent were the issues discussed relevant to Circle members' workplace contexts? To their current learning needs? 2.4.4 What barriers or facilitators influenced Circle members' ability to discuss topics openly? 2.4.5 How did the discussion process vary by Circle?	Group process skills (Christensen, 1983): • Leadership • Communication, clarification, and summarization • Sensitive to individual and group learning needs • Promotes cohesion • Promotes trust and confidentiality • Encourages full participation, collaboration and shared responsibility	Learning Circle Tracking Sheet AI Focus Groups Evaluator Observation

Next, we invite you to read about a strategy in South Africa to guide evaluation planning for community-based climate change adaptation.

SPOTLIGHT ON EQUITY

Evaluation Planning for Community-Based Climate Change Adaptation

In South Africa, climate variability and change are having drastic consequences for low-income and disadvantaged communities dependent on natural resources for their sustenance and livelihood. Resource-poor smallholder farmers needed a decision making process to support district- and local-level climate change adaptation. The Mahlathini Development Foundation (www.mahlathini.org) is a nongovernmental organization that designs and implements innovative projects to promote collaborative, pro-poor agricultural innovation. It works in partnership with local and provincial governments, other nonprofit organizations, and rural communities.

A collaborative knowledge creation and mediation process was conducted in several provinces in the Eastern Cape, Limpopo, and KwaZulu-Natal. Support was provided to smallholder farmers in climate-smart agriculture (CSA) practices and small agribusiness enterprise development to improve sustainable livelihoods, social agency, and productivity. Strategies included agro-ecology, water and soil conversation, conservation agriculture, sustainable food gardening, livestock integration, rangeland management, and water harvesting. The goal was to increase farmer's adaptive capacity so they could manage their agricultural and natural resources better to reduce their vulnerability and risk due to climate change. It was the first program of its kind in South Africa that looked at building smallholder farmer and community resilience from a systems perspective (Patton, 2010).

The Foundation was keen to conduct an evaluation to ensure that the principles, practices, and support underpinning the CSA model worked in different community contexts. The Foundation's M&E team included Internal Evaluator, Samukelisiwe Mkhize, who led the monitoring and evaluation activities for the project and shared this story. The team consisted of seven members. They worked in 19 communities with 500 farmers, using a participatory, developmental evaluation approach. It was vital that local communities participated in evaluation planning, to determine what was to be evaluated, when it was to be evaluated, and what methods and indicators would be used.

The team developed participatory learning processes to ensure the engagement of a wide range of stakeholders with varying interests. They also wanted to ensure that the evaluation assessed the interventions to inform the next phase of farmer-led experimentation of CSA practices. In their view, the farmers' knowledge of their own context would help them respond to climate variability, testing local adaptive strategies and new CSA practices to increase their agricultural coping strategies and to improve their livelihoods. Furthermore, they saw the border between the projects and the evaluation as almost inseparable (Patton, 2010), which supported the use of a developmental approach. They had to accommodate both the high level of complexity and uncertainty of climatic conditions, and the varying nature of participating communities in terms of their geographic, social, and economic systems.

Due to the geographic spread of the program and the variety of interventions involved, a clear communication and knowledge management plan was crucial. Because the team worked closely with program coordinators, farmers, researchers, and stakeholders, they were able to develop real-time feedback and other innovative communication strategies for continuous improvement. Village-level learning groups were coordinated by local facilitators selected by the farmers. The facilitators held weekly dialogues where smallholder farmers, program staff, and the M&E team could discuss the evaluation and mediate and share meaning among themselves.

To gain a contextual understanding of community diversity, the team conducted stakeholder mapping and situational analysis with smallholder farmers, using participatory rural appraisal tools such as rich picture (Figure 10.6, p. 394). Rich pictures are mental and then illustrated models of how a group of stakeholders view a situation or a community and its processes. This method allows peoples to create a sketch of their shared understanding of a complex situation. Other tools the team used included developing timelines and conducting community walkthroughs to understand the impacts of climate change in each community. These activities were facilitated in the community's local language so that historical events and experiences

FIGURE 10.6 ● MODEL OF PROJECT SYSTEMS

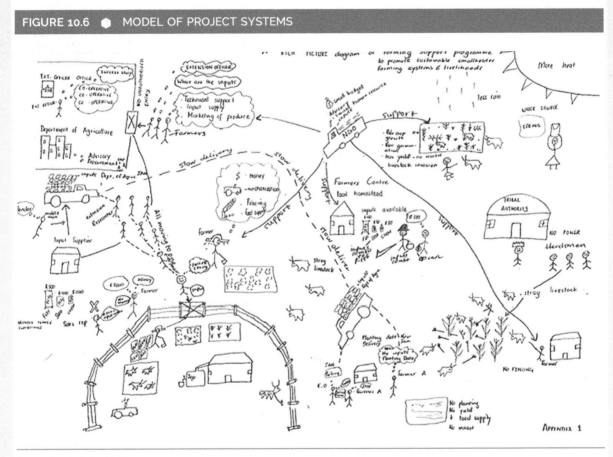

Source: Samukelisiwe Mkhize

related to climate change could be captured and local adaptation measures identified.

Representatives from each community were convened at a participatory planning workshop to determine the priority interventions to be evaluated. It was held in the homestead of one of the participants. At the request of the farmers, several local and provincial government officials, representatives of nonprofit agencies working in the area, and local and traditional authorities were also invited to share meaning and co-create action plans. It was a critical step as these stakeholders would continue to provide essential support to implement findings at a later stage.

At the workshop, the smallholder farmers selected the CSA practices they would adapt locally, using a negotiated decision making process in their small learning groups. With the assistance of the M&E team,

they thought deeply about the indicators, interpreting them according to their own needs, contexts, and priorities (Figure 10.7, p. 395).

Collectively they crafted integrated and systemic outcome and impact indicators, including, for example, new indicators such as *social agency,* instead of more commonly used indicators such as *increase in production* or *income.* As one of the farmers shared:

This workshop has allowed us to think deeper about the indicators. For us as farmers, for example, the cost indicator is not just about savings cost but also the income generation of each practice as this is how we make our decisions locally. Therefore, when we measure each practice and prioritize them, we have to think about all these factors. Are we saving money?

FIGURE 10.7 ● WORKSHOP DECISION MAKING EXAMPLE

PRACTICE	Increase H₂O Availability	Increase H₂O Storage/ Access	Increase Soil Fertility	Cost	Increase Crop Quality	Labour	Time	Total
Jojo Tanks	3	3	1	2	2	1	2	14
Underground Tank	3	3	1	1	3	1	1	13
Tunnel	2	2	3	1	3	1	1	13
Diversion Furrows	3	2	1	2	3	2	2	15
Mulching	2	2	3	3	3	3	3	19 ①
CA/No till	3	2	3	3	3	2	2	18 ②
Furrows and ridges	2	2	2	3	3	2	2	16 ④
Tower Garden	2	3	3	3	3	2	2	18 ②
Keyhole Gardens	2	3	3	3	2	2	2	17 ③

Source: Samukelisiwe Mkhize

Are we able to make more money? How much money are we using? Also, we have to weigh these practices across the set of indicators collectively, if we are making money and saving cost, is it at the expense of high labour? Can this practice be implemented in groups? Does it increase social/ collective agency in the community? When we think of indicators, we need to do this, about our needs as smallholder farmers and community.

These community-derived indicators, along with others identified by the team, formed the integrated indicator framework used to assess CSA practices. The learning groups provided the basis for continued engagement and discussion between stakeholders and farmers. In this way, local planning capacity was built, a very different approach from the traditional method of gathering predefined information to be analyzed outside of the community.

This Spotlight on Equity is based on the contribution by Samukelisiwe (Samke) Mkhize.

THE EVALUATION PLAN: CASE STUDY #2 MD/PHD EDUCATIONAL PROGRAM

Once these pre-planning activities are completed, it is time to craft the written evaluation plan. While there are probably as many styles for an evaluation plan as there are evaluators, the basic elements of the plan are generally the same. Table 10.2 outlines the seven key elements of an evaluation plan.

TABLE 10.2 ● SEVEN KEY ELEMENTS IN THE EVALUATION PLAN	
1. Title Page	• Name of the Evaluation Project • Organization and Department (Client) • Name of Key Contact/Person Authorizing Project • Name of Evaluator and Contact Information • Contract Number (If Appropriate) • Date
2. Program Overview	• Program Role • Program Description • Key Stakeholders • Program Context
3. Evaluation Description	• Evaluation Purpose • Type of Evaluation • Evaluation Questions • Intended Users and Use • Evaluation Approach • Evaluation Standards, Ethics, and Values
4. Evaluation Methods	• Assumptions and Program Theory • Logic Model • Data Collection Matrix (Including Evaluation Questions, Indicators, Methods, Data Sources, and Tools) • Description of Methods and Tools
5. Data Analysis And Synthesis	• Types of Analysis Planned • Methods of Data Synthesis • Role of Stakeholders in Data Interpretation
6. Reporting	• Description of Project Reports and Other Methods Selected to Communicate Results
7. Evaluation Management	• Team Roles • Management Strategy • Data Ownership and Security • Study Limitations and Strengths • Schedule of Activities • Budget

In the following discussion, we move to Case Study #2, the MD/PhD Educational Program. It is an advanced medical education program designed for exceptional students who wish to have both an MD and a PhD so that they can pursue careers as clinical investigators. Excerpts from the evaluation plan are provided. The information is anonymized for privacy reasons.

Remember that each evaluator is different; each evaluation is unique. This evaluation plan represents one of many possible ways of presenting the information and is illustrative, not prescriptive.

Title Page

The first element of the evaluation plan, the title page, is a critical component. As the plan is usually the first report prepared by the evaluator, it sends an important message about the evaluator's professionalism and competence. As a result, it is a good idea to give considerable thought to its layout and design. See Box 10.10 for a sample title page.

BOX 10.10 ● EVALUATION PLAN TITLE PAGE

Organization's Logo

MD/PhD Program
Evaluation Plan

An Examination of the MD/Phd Program's Merit and Significance to Inform Decision Making about Its Future

Prepared for:

Funding Agency
Attention: Project Manger
Address
Phone Numbers
e-mail

Prepared by:

Evaluator
Company Name
Address
Phone Numbers
Email address
Website

Date

The title page should center the evaluation project's name, the organization's name, and the department for which the evaluation is conducted (i.e., the client). Also, the person who authorized the evaluation project and can approve the completed project should be named. The evaluator's name, phone, website, and email should be clearly presented for easy access. Contract information such as a file number should also be displayed if needed. Finally, it is important to include the plan submission date for future reference.

Program Overview

As the program is the focus of the evaluation, the evaluator should present a brief program overview to set the scene for the plan that follows. It includes a thumbnail sketch of the program's role within its organization, a clear description of its objectives and activities, an acknowledgment of essential stakeholders, and an overview of essential contextual factors that may impact the evaluation.

Program Role

The program role should be described so that stakeholders can understand how the program fits with other parts of the organization. See Box 10.11 for an example.

BOX 10.11 ● MD/PhD PROGRAM ROLE

The funder has been supporting medical research for over 20 years. Of its organizational goals, the eighth goal relates most closely to its support of this program:

> To maintain research education and training programs and to encourage exceptional students to pursue research careers.

The objective of the MD/PhD program is:

> To allow exceptional candidates wishing to pursue careers as Clinical Investigators an opportunity to pursue MD and PhD degrees simultaneously.

Program Description

Stakeholders should understand how the program works and what will be evaluated. The description should be brief but clear. Even at this early stage, readers need to be guided toward aspects of the program that the evaluation will scrutinize, thus helping to define the evaluation's boundaries and managing stakeholders' expectations about what the evaluation will and will not produce. Williams and Britt (2014) indicate that setting boundaries is not optional. They continue:

> For projects, critical boundary setting decisions take place during project design and again when designing the project's performance monitoring and evaluation plan. Such decisions include determining the purpose of the intervention, who or what does and does not benefit, what kind of measurement is appropriate to assess whether in real life the intervention is delivering the purpose to the beneficiaries, what resources are allocated and how they are monitored, and finally the basis upon which to judge whether or not the intervention is being supported by stakeholders. Monitoring the implications of those boundary decisions throughout the life of the project is an important means of tracking the project's relationship to the local system in which it is embedded. (p. 7)

The description should use some of the program's terminology to indicate that the evaluation is grounded in the program's documentation. For example, the program's purpose and objectives can be quoted directly from essential documents such as funding proposals, annual reports, brochures, or the program's website. In addition, specific examples of program activities and strategies can be used to help readers visualize how the program operates. It is also important to identify intended outcomes and impacts as this will foreshadow the upcoming logic model. See Box 10.12 for the Program Description.

BOX 10.12 ● MD/PhD PROGRAM DESCRIPTION

The program's objective is *to provide an opportunity for exceptional candidates who wish to pursue careers as clinical investigators to study for the MD and PhD degrees simultaneously.* The relevant university programs will provide highly motivated students with the fundamental knowledge and research experience required to equip them for investigative careers while concurrently providing educational experiences in clinical disciplines. In addition, they will be trained to bring a scientific approach to their clinical experiences and a clinical perspective to their research. The program is small in scope and accepts approximately seven students per year. Since program inception, 31 students have received funding through this program.

Key Stakeholders

Key stakeholders should be acknowledged as early as possible because the evaluator will want to engage them at several critical points in the evaluation process. Identifying them at the beginning of the study helps develop their sense of ownership of the evaluation by suggesting their involvement in decisions about methods, results, and recommendations. This sense of shared purpose starts the capacity-building process and will continue throughout the evaluation (Centers for Disease Control and Prevention, 2011). Once established, the evaluator can list the EWG members in the evaluation plan. Sometimes, their photos and brief bios can be included, linking them more closely to the study process and adding the weight of their endorsement to study credibility. See Box 10.13 for an example of stakeholder identification.

BOX 10.13 ● MD/PhD STAKEHOLDER IDENTIFICATION

Stakeholders include the following:

- Representatives from relevant university faculties
- Funder staff member
- Project manager
- A representative of the program's alumni
- The funder's President and CEO
- Dean of Medicine
- Dean of Health Sciences
- Two members-at-large from the university research community.

Program Context

The evaluator has obtained vital information about the program context through the document review and key informant interviews. At this time, the evaluator should include unique characteristics, conditions, assumptions, and other circumstances of the program environment in the plan. (See Chapter 12 for a more fulsome discussion on context.) This early identification of potential issues keeps everyone apprised of challenges that may affect the evaluator's ability to collect data. Where possible, the plan can identify strategies that can work within or mitigate these constraints, referring to the upcoming section on methodology for details. See Box 10.14 for an example of program context.

BOX 10.14 ● MD/PhD PROGRAM CONTEXT

The MD/PhD Program is arduous, but successful students learn the multitasking and organizational skills necessary for a dual career. Graduates also have the skills to conduct research, publish, and compete for funding simultaneously. The time between graduation and a career as an independent clinician-scientist tends to be shorter for graduates of the program than those who independently pursue the two degrees. Graduates already have a history of research publications and can look forward to commanding higher salaries than researchers with a PhD.

The main program issue is the length of time to complete, which can last upwards of nine years. In addition, there is a personal toll on family life. Costs are significant even when students obtain full funding. Some students complete the program with a heavy debt load. As a result, attrition rates are a potential issue, although they have been relatively low in this program.

The funder has the policy to evaluate all programs every four years, so they commissioned this study. Decision makers wish to determine the advisability of continuing the program and review available data on application pressure, award rate, the performance of successful candidates, and opinions and perspectives of university partners. However, as intermediate- and long-term outcomes will not be available for at least 7–12 years, the evaluation will focus mainly on implementation.

Evaluation Description

The evaluation description is a central element of the evaluation plan. Readers must understand the purpose and scope of the evaluation, the type of evaluation planned, the KEQs, intended users and uses, the evaluation philosophy or approach, and how the evaluation will address evaluation standards, ethics, and values.

Evaluation Purpose

The evaluation purpose is often closely linked to upcoming decisions about the program's future. Other common reasons for conducting an evaluation include informing program improvement, policy decisions, resource allocation, practice guidelines, capacity building, or other specific organizational needs. Above all, the evaluation must answer the critical questions asked by the client. From the outset, then, everyone must be clear about the evaluation purpose. See Box 10.15, p. 401 for an example.

The general intent of the MD/PhD program is to train students to become clinician-scientists so the time between research conducted and application of research findings can be reduced. Professionals generally recognize the importance of the MD/PhD Program; however, student enrollment has been declining. The funder is determined to support this program so that high-quality students can be attracted to enroll. Since the program's inception in 2000, the funder has paid increasing attention to the results of outcome evaluations in other equivalent programs. An EWG was established in 2005 to oversee the program's first evaluation initiative to develop baseline data.

Type of Evaluation

The type of evaluation depends mainly on its position within the life cycle. Refer to our discussion in Chapters 4–6 on the types of evaluation most relevant for different program stages, including needs assessments, evaluability assessments, and evaluations that focus on process, outcomes, effectiveness, or impacts. All decisions about methods will flow from the determination of the evaluation type needed for this study. See Box 10.16 for the type of evaluation recommended in this case.

BOX 10.16 ● MD/PhD—TYPE OF EVALUATION RECOMMENDED

Funder representatives have indicated that they were interested in supporting program development. Accordingly, evaluators plan a **formative evaluation** to help shape program performance by providing helpful feedback to planners, administrators, funders, and partners interested in optimizing program effectiveness.

This plan provides a rigorous evaluation process to respond to the overarching evaluation questions and ensures that the study outcome is of sufficient credibility under scientific standards to provide a confident basis for action and withstand any criticism to discredit it.

Evaluation Questions

KEQs are similar to the research questions in a research study. However, the analysis provides answers to the high-level questions in the evaluation, not specific questions asked in a survey or interview (BetterEvaluation, 2016a). These questions link directly to the evaluation objectives and should be developed by considering "the type of evaluation being done, its intended users, its intended uses (purposes), and the evaluative criteria being used" (BetterEvaluation, 2016). See Box 10.17 for the evaluation questions in our example.

BOX 10.17 ● MD/PhD EVALUATION QUESTIONS

This evaluation will address two overarching evaluation questions:

1. What is the merit and significance of the MD/PhD Program?

2. How can evaluation findings inform the program's future design, delivery, and ongoing evaluation?

Intended Users and Use

By defining the purpose of the evaluation, the **intended users** and planned use of evaluation findings may already be implied because they go together. Patton (2008) has explored this relationship extensively in his utilization-focused evaluation approach, which is "evaluation done for and with specific intended primary users for specific, intended uses" (p. 37). Because these people care about the evaluation and its findings, they can influence evaluation use and impact.

A brief paragraph can adequately explain the intended use of findings; however in most cases, the very real political agenda is hidden from view. Thus, it is up to the evaluator to navigate these tricky waters throughout the evaluation, ensuring that the right users have access to the findings. See Box 10.18 for an example of intended use of findings.

BOX 10.18   ⬡   MD/PhD EVALUATION: INTENDED USE OF FINDINGS

The funder and stakeholders within the MD/PhD program have indicated that program improvements may well result from a review of study findings, thus enhancing the truly formative nature of this evaluation. In addition, the evaluation findings will inform the program's future design and delivery if continued support for the program is warranted and approved by the funder.

Evaluation Approach

There are many approaches to consider when designing an evaluation. Typically, the evaluator combines their own experience and knowledge with the information needs of stakeholders and quickly narrows the field to one or two top choices. In the case of the MD/PhD program evaluation, it was apparent that the evaluation needed to fit within such stakeholder-involved approaches as collaborative, participatory, and empowerment evaluations. Of these, a collaborative approach seemed the most appropriate as stakeholders wanted the evaluator to take charge of the evaluation while engaging them in ongoing consultation and feedback (Fetterman et al., 2017, p. 2). See Box 10.19 for the evaluation approach used in this case.

BOX 10.19   ⬡   MD/PhD EVALUATION: A COLLABORATIVE APPROACH

As evaluators, we believe the evaluation methodology selected should mirror the evaluated program's philosophy. In addition, the partnerships essential to this program suggest that a collaborative evaluation approach is required. Here are some ways we can collaborate:

Collaboration With the Evaluation Working Group (EWG):

At the first EWG meeting at the end of September, we will:

1. Review the draft Logic Model, DCM, Project Plan, and Project Tools

2. Discuss any final suggestions for change

3. Discuss the intended uses of the final evaluation report

(Continued)

(Continued)

4. Develop a list of stakeholders for interviews

5. Discuss focus group logistics

6. Obtain lists of students and supervisors

7. Make revisions as appropriate.

At the second EWG meeting at the end of February, we will:

1. Discuss the draft Evaluation Report

2. Finalize conclusions and recommendations

3. Make revisions as appropriate.

Collaboration With the Program Manager (PM)

We plan to work closely with the PM, including:

- Communications weekly by conference call or e-mail throughout the project period to provide an update on study activities, progress, and emerging issues

- In-person meetings to be scheduled as needed

- A joint review of draft tools and other study documents before submission to the EWG

- Monthly status reports to update study progress, ensure accountability, and provide milestones for billing.

Evaluation Standards, Ethics, and Values

Stakeholders can discern the quality of an evaluation by using a set of program evaluation standards that identifies how a good evaluation should be completed and reflects the shared principles of the evaluation community. As discussed in Chapter 1, before the evaluator finalizes the plan, they need to adopt standards to guide their practice and review them with key stakeholders (Rossi et al., 2019, p. 271). Thus, the evaluation plan offers an excellent opportunity to remind stakeholders that the evaluator is aware of and adheres to these guidelines. It also strengthens an evaluator's position to claim membership in a professional evaluation organization that promotes best practice. We cannot overstate the value of reminding stakeholders of this important link to the broader evaluation community.

See Box 10.20 for a statement on adherence to standards.

BOX 10.20 ● MD/PhD EVALUATION STATEMENT ON ADHERENCE TO STANDARDS

The Program Evaluation Standards (Joint Committee, 2018) identify principles that should be addressed in every evaluation. They include utility, feasibility, propriety, and accuracy. It is not accidental that Utility is addressed first—it is essential that this evaluation will address the information needs of intended users; in particular, that it is "planned, conducted, and reported in ways that encourage follow-through by Stakeholders, so that the likelihood that the evaluation will be used is increased" (Utility Standard U7). We are committed to promoting open-mindedness, compassion, and collaboration in all our evaluation activities.

Evaluation Methods

In the methods section of the evaluation plan, all the evaluator's preplanning work begins to pay off. The thinking and negotiating that have already occurred make it relatively straightforward to document the assumptions and the draft program theory, logic model, and DCM.

After consultation with stakeholders in the organization, the evaluator can provide a detailed description of the plan's proposed evaluation methods and tools. See Box 10.21 for an outline of the data collection methods planned for this case.

BOX 10.21 ● MD/PhD EVALUATION DATA COLLECTION METHODS

The methods proposed for this study are outlined as follows:

Literature Scan
Research and evaluation studies on similar programs will be reviewed. Sources will include online journal databases (PubMed, ERIC, "gray literature"), unpublished reports, and background program documents. A Document/Literature Review Template has been developed to increase standardization and consistency in review. Relevant data will help to inform the development of other evaluation tools.

Key Informant Interviews ($n = 3$)
Key informants from three similar programs will be interviewed and asked to reflect on their program and share lessons learned. A draft list of contacts has been prepared, and it is hoped that at least three of these individuals will be available to participate.

Student Survey With Optional In-Depth Follow-Up ($n = 45$)
An online student survey will be developed for the program's students, including:

- Funded students
- Nonfunded students
- Students who are currently "away" from the program
- Students who have withdrawn or otherwise left the program
- Graduates of the program.

Survey participants will be informed that an optional in-depth telephone interview is available should they desire to provide additional unstructured feedback.

Supervisor Interviews ($n = 18$)
Administrative staff will provide a complete list of supervisors so that the evaluators can draw a random sample. Supervisors of both funded and nonfunded students will be interviewed by telephone. However, an email version of the questions will be provided to those for whom a telephone interview is not convenient.

Stakeholder Interviews ($n = 15$)
Key university stakeholders will be interviewed by telephone, including Program Coordinators, Program Administrators, Program Dean, Dean of Graduate Studies, and Registrar. Staff at the funding agency will also be interviewed, either in-person or by phone, including Grant Director, Grant Administrator, and Vice President, Programs.

Data Analysis and Synthesis

The data analysis section includes a basic description of the various analysis methods planned.

Types of Analysis Planned

As Rossi et al. (2019, p. 282) comment, the data analysis plan will be different for qualitative and quantitative data, and also, as we learned in Chapter 9, if the study is a mixed-methods design, will ensure that mixed methods are analyzed appropriately. It is too late, once the data are collected, to decide what to do with them.

The evaluator must create an open-ended and transparent plan incorporating both the known and the unknown. An excellent way to organize the data analysis plan is by the KEQs. Often the tools are designed to address more than one KEQ and so data will need to be clustered by question. The DCM also provides an organizational structure to manage the more granular data obtained from each survey and interview question. See Box 10.22 for an explanation of the quantitative data analysis plan. A similar level of detail would be used to explain qualitative analysis and data integration strategies.

BOX 10.22 ● MD/PhD EVALUATION: QUANTITATIVE DATA ANALYSIS PLAN

The quantitative data obtained from the student survey will be analyzed using the Statistical Package for the Social Sciences (SPSS). The survey is designed with a number of branching questions that divide respondents into various subgroups such as program year, funding status, and area of specialization.

The data will be entered into a database developed for each survey, and analyses will be conducted in SPSS. If the error rate per variable exceeds 2%, further error checks will be made by running frequencies. If the error rate for any variable exceeds 2%, the variable(s) in question will be inspected in all original surveys for accuracy of data entry. In addition, the minimum and maximum values, means, and standard deviations of each variable will then be inspected for plausibility. When entries outside the possible range are detected, the original survey forms will be consulted, and corrections made. Analysis techniques will involve descriptive and inferential techniques depending on the information will be sought. Following data analysis, the information will be compiled into pie graphs, bar charts, and tables as appropriate to illustrate key findings.

Methods of Data Synthesis

Once analysis is complete, it is time for synthesis—which, if you remember Bloom's Taxonomy, is a higher-order level of thinking (see Chapter 8). The evaluator transfers the data into manageable and accessible formats (see Chapters 7–9 for examples). Next, so patterns may become evident, the evaluator reviews, interprets, and organizes the study findings. The evaluator can then determine if the findings "agree, disagree, reinforce, subvert, explain or contradict" the evaluation questions (Warwick & Clevenger, 2011, p. 1). Finally, by synthesizing the data, the evaluator will determine if there are links between the data and the evaluation questions or if, indeed, no links exist.

Role of Stakeholders in Data Interpretation

An excellent opportunity is provided at this point for stakeholders to gain a clear overview of the complexities involved in data synthesis and interpretation. By sharing a summary of data with them, they can offer their own views on important emergent findings. See Box 10.23 for an example.

BOX 10.23 ● MD/PhD EVALUATION: DATA SUMMARY

A data summary will be prepared, which compiles a synthesis of all data collected across the data collection tools by DCM topic. This important document enables the triangulation of findings. It will improve validity, eliminate bias, and dismiss rival explanations for evaluation conclusions. Key themes will be identified (as well as any important outliers) and will provide a holistic understanding of the program. Summary tables will be prepared, and representative quotes selected for inclusion in the final report. A meeting will be held with stakeholders to review summary tables and to share their thoughts and interpretation of emergent findings.

Reporting

While some evaluators see the final report as the ultimate "product" of the evaluation because it answers the research questions and assists stakeholders in interpreting findings and their implications (Rossi et al., 2019, p. 284), others think that a final report is only "one of many mechanisms for facilitating use" (Patton, 2008, p. 507). The evaluator will need to have a conversation with priority stakeholders to determine their specific reporting needs.

These days, thanks to click technology, people's attention spans are very short. As a result, evaluators need to use their creativity to prepare a brief, visually compelling, and interactive report that captures and holds stakeholders' interest. This takes more time and effort than typical report preparation, so a careful analysis of communication strategies is needed to determine how best to relay the findings. (See Chapter 11 for more information on reporting.) See Box 10.24 for a list of planned reports for this case.

BOX 10.24 ● MD/PhD EVALUATION: REPORTING PLANS

The following reports are planned for this study:

1. Evaluation Work Plan (i.e., this document) includes Logic Model, DCM, Task Schedule, Methodology, and Draft Instruments:

   - Document/Literature Review Template

   - Environmental Scan Interview Protocol

   - Student Telephone Internet Survey

(Continued)

(Continued)

- Supervisor Telephone Interview Protocol

- Key Stakeholder Interview Protocol.

2. Biweekly status reports provide information on current project status and task completion. Emerging issues will be identified.

3. Draft Final Evaluation Report, assessing findings related to the project's key questions will include an introduction and project overview, a description of the program environment, a section on study methodology and limitations, a detailed section on findings with appropriate tables and charts, tentative conclusions and recommendations. A bibliography, and copies of the project instruments will be provided in the Appendix. The Draft Final Evaluation Report will be circulated to the EWG to obtain feedback, and a PowerPoint presentation will be prepared and presented.

4. Final Evaluation Report will incorporate changes provided by the EWG to the extent that the evaluator deems them to be both feasible and appropriate.

5. An Executive Summary will be prepared.

6. A one-page Infographic will be prepared for broader circulation.

PLANNED EVALUATION MANAGEMENT: WORK SAMPLES

The last element in the evaluation plan relates to **evaluation management**. While management issues were discussed briefly in the project proposal, now they must be expanded to describe the upcoming work, based on the more detailed understanding which the evaluator has acquired through this planning process. Now, the evaluator views the study from the perspective of a manager to ensure that implementation follows the plan as intended, or if changes are warranted, that they are reasonable and well documented. We draw here on examples from our evaluation files. The elements of the management plan are outlined in Figure 10.8.

FIGURE 10.8 ● ELEMENTS OF THE MANAGEMENT PLAN

- ❑ Team Roles
- ❑ Management Strategy
- ❑ Data Ownership and Security Plans
- ❑ Study Limitations and Strengths
- ❑ Schedule of Activities
- ❑ Budget
- ❑ Accountability

Team Roles

Evaluation personnel were described in the proposal but in the evaluation plan, roles, responsibilities, and limits to authority are described. Contracting relationships are often quite complex and need to be carefully teased apart so that the evaluator is clear on lines of authority and accountability. Once an organization receives a grant to conduct an evaluation, it is common for the organization to hire an evaluator through a subcontract. These arrangements can lead to complex reporting relationships. Figure 10.9 illustrates the team for one recent evaluation conducted by the authors.

FIGURE 10.9 ● SAMPLE EVALUATION TEAM AND ROLES

Project Officer (Local Foundation/ Funder)

- Sent out a Request for Proposals for an evaluation of this funded project.
- Requires evaluation at end of first year of project.
- Future funding for the project depends upon evaluation findings.

Role on Project
- Selects the winning proposal.
- Manages the contract and provides the funds.
- Chairs the Evaluation Working Group (EWG).
- Communicates with the Grantee.
- Is responsible to Foundation Board for successful project outcomes.

Project Director (Dean at Local Community College/Grantee)

- Wrote winning proposal.
- Manages this project.

Role on Project
- Receives quarterly grant payments.
- Has fiscal responsibility.
- Liaises with/is accountable to Foundation for this project.
- Is responsible to senior College administration for management role.
- Hires Evaluator to conduct this evaluation.
- Hires new Research Assistant to work on this and other evaluation projects.
- Communicates with Evaluator on resource requirements and project status.
- Provides Project Officer monthly progress reports.
- Provides Project Officer with a draft agenda and relevant materials for all EWG meetings.
- Attends EWG meetings.
- Is responsible for all project deliverables.

Research Assistant (Employee at Community College)

- Hired by the Dean to work on this evaluation and other projects as needed.
- Reports to the Project Director.

Role on Project
- Conducts literature search.
- Assists Evaluator in coordinating project tasks.
- Assists Evaluator in communicating with project sites and participants.
- Manages survey.
- Enters data.
- May do some report preparation.
- Other tasks as needed.

Evaluator (Works for Small Consulting Firm)

- Hired by Dean on a sub-contract basis to evaluate this project.
- Reports to the Project Director.

Role on Project
- Designs the evaluation framework and evaluation tools.
- Leads data collection and analysis.
- Meets regularly with Research Assistant and provides coaching as required.
- Prepares project status reports for Project Director.
- Prepares materials for EWG meetings.
- Attends EWG meetings to report on evaluation status.
- Prepares evaluation reports and submits them to the Project Director.

Source: SlideModel.com

Management Strategy

The evaluator oversees the implementation of the evaluation plan and is responsible for problem-solving as issues arise. The best management strategy is communication, communication, and more communication. From the outset of the project, a communication system must be established to track assigned tasks. It should include a schedule of critical dates, milestones or deliverables, and methods of communication (such as in-person or virtual meetings, e-mail correspondence, and written status reports). Strategies to troubleshoot issues should be established at this early point so that protocols are already in place should an issue arise. "It is particularly important to agree on how unforeseen issues that affect the implementation of the evaluation and may jeopardize particular milestones and/or deliverables will be raised, escalated and resolved" (BetterEvaluation, 2016).

By implementing a policy of "no surprises," the evaluator can maintain routine communication with key stakeholders. In our view, a monthly status report is the best client communications tool (Barrington, 2017a). Typically, stakeholders love these brief one-to-two-page reports because they receive a regular update on task completion, unanticipated problems, and other pertinent information. It also allows them to deal with questions about the evaluation that they may receive from their superiors. See Box 10.25 for the description of a status report strategy.

BOX 10.25 ● SAMPLE STATEMENT OF STATUS REPORT STRATEGY

Because we value communication with our clients, we will keep you apprised of our progress with a monthly status report. This will provide you with a regular deliverable and a predictable milestone. In addition, it will include an update on task completion, some brief comments on study progress, the identification of any emerging issues, and other pertinent information.

Data Ownership and Security

As Scassa (2018) comments, "The rapid expansion of the data economy raises serious questions about who owns data and what data ownership entails" (p. 1). Universities have varying policies about data ownership. For example, Harvard University owns all research data for all projects conducted at the University, and principal investigators and all other researchers are stewards and custodians of the data (Harvard University, 2019). On the other hand, The University of British Columbia and the researchers who collect the data have joint ownership (The University of British Columbia, n.d.). However, evaluation data typically belong to the client, commissioner, or funder of the project, and this can cause some confusion, especially if university researchers are involved in the project. Therefore, the evaluator needs to be very clear about their data ownership rights. Generally, permission is required to present study findings at a professional conference or publish an article that incorporates study data or study experiences.

A primary responsibility for the evaluator is to safeguard the data collected. Study data are vulnerable to exposure through hacking, leaking, error, and theft. Czechowski et al. (2019) recommend that evaluators have a **data management plan** that identifies how data will be handled at each stage of the evaluation project, providing information on storing, sharing, and disposing of data. Evaluators should:

1. Determine the extent to which the data reveal participant identity

2. Assess the level of risk associated with a potential breach of confidentiality

3. Decide to what extent data should be secured.

The evaluation plan should explicitly state how the evaluator will handle the data during the study and afterward. Examples of more complex data management templates are available on the internet. Box 10.26 provides a simple data ownership and security plan.

BOX 10.26 ● SAMPLE DATA OWNERSHIP AND SECURITY PLAN

All primary and secondary data collected and obtained in this evaluation study belong to [the client]. Privacy of information is protected as stipulated in the provisions of [relevant legislation]. Strict confidentiality of all data and information acquired in the course of project work will be maintained. Information and data acquired will not be shared by the evaluation team in any form that would allow identification of any one individual. Once the study is completed, electronic materials will be delivered to [the client]. They will be deleted from the evaluators' computers and servers. Printed material will be shredded. Our servers have security measures and firewalls in place, and we will make every effort to keep all evaluation project information confidential. In addition, all evaluation staff sign a confidentiality agreement upon being contracted or hired.

Study Limitations and Strengths

In any study, evaluators can anticipate many barriers, roadblocks, or issues that can impact the smooth functioning of the evaluation. Rather than ignoring them and hoping that they do not materialize, or worse, waiting until the end of the study to identify the limitations now too late to address, wise evaluators list potential limitations or risks that may impact the evaluation. Frequently, they also offer suggestions for how to avoid or mitigate some of these risks. Of course, there will always be issues, and many of them are likely to be unanticipated, but the evaluator can demonstrate foresight by managing as many of them as possible. It is also wise to remind the client of the strengths that the evaluator brings to the project. See Box 10.27, p. 411 for a sample statement of evaluation limitations and strengths.

BOX 10.27 ● SAMPLE STATEMENT OF EVALUATION LIMITATIONS AND STRENGTHS

Evaluation limitations and risks:

- Data collection during a vacation period could impact response rates.

- Program outcomes are likely to be limited as the implementation period has been relatively short.

- There is a lack of baseline data against which to measure change.

- There are limited benchmark data from similar programs.

- Attribution issues may be unclear; for example, participant decisions to withdraw may be personal and not related to funding availability.

- The potential exists for a positive response bias in survey results from funded applicants.

Evaluation strengths:

- Extensive involvement of staff and stakeholders in study design, data access, instrument development, and report preparation helps to ensure appropriateness, relevance, and clarity.

- An innovative evaluation design incorporates the findings from each data collection strategy in the design of subsequent strategies (mixed methods).

- Rapid turnaround of emerging information supports timely decision making.

- Evaluator adherence to the Guiding Principles of the American Evaluation Association enhances ethical practice.

- Accepted and documented research and evaluation methods will be used for all evaluation activities.

Schedule of Activities

Often a **Gantt chart** is used to display proposed study activities. This is a simple chart that includes "proportionate, chronologically scaled timeframes for each evaluation task. The chart provides an overview of the entire evaluation process that illustrates when evaluation activities will begin and how long each will continue" (Taylor-Powell et al., 1996, p. 20). Table 10.3, p. 412 presents a simple schedule for a three-month evaluability assessment in the form of a Gantt chart. Many scheduling programs are available, such as Asana, Smartsheet, Monday, Trello, and Zoho. These allow the evaluation team, multiple stakeholders, and the client to work collaboratively on evaluation schedules and other planning activities.

Budget

As Britt (2020) comments, "Evaluation expenses are highly situational and there are no magic formulas for calculating costs" (para. 1). However, as more detailed information has

TABLE 10.3 ● SAMPLE SCHEDULE OF EVALUATION PROJECT ACTIVITIES THREE-MONTH EVALUABILITY ASSESSMENT PROJECT

Task	January 2020	February 2020	March 2020
Project Management & Status Reports			
Project management and monthly Status Reports *(Ongoing)*			
Coordinate and communicate with Project Manager			
Deliverables: Work Plan (January 31) & Monthly Status Reports (February 29 & March 31)	●	●	●
● **Develop Draft Evaluation Plan:**			
Review background documents			
Meet staff and kick off project			
Revise logic model			
Develop Data Collection Matrix			
Prepare Draft Evaluation Plan			
● **Validate Plan with Stakeholders**			
Meet with Project Manager to plan team meetings/debrief			
Review additional documents			
Meet with committees & teams to obtain feedback, discuss data collection issues and strategies, revise Plan			
Validate the Evaluation Plan with the Evaluation Steering Committee			
Revise Plan as needed			
● **Develop/Select Tools**			
Search for/review proposed tools			
Develop additional tools as needed			
Obtain feedback from Data Analysts			
Complete Evaluability Assessment Report/Evaluation Plan			
Deliverable: Evaluability Assessment Report & Evaluation Plan (March 31, 2020)			●

Legend	● Deliverable

been obtained during the preplanning phase, evaluators can now more accurately apportion the budget than they did when writing the proposal, although the bottom line must remain unchanged. These costs are relatively straightforward to present. Table 10.4 presents a sample budget for personnel costs.

TABLE 10.4 ● SAMPLE BUDGET FOR PROJECT PERSONNEL COSTS

Phases/Tasks	Senior Evaluation Advisor	Evaluation Consultant	Total (Person-days)
Phase I: Planning and Design			
Evaluation logic model, DCM, and detailed planning	6.00	2.50	**8.50**
Phase II: Fieldwork			
Review of program documents and data	0.75	1.25	**2.00**
Student surveys	0.75	4	**4.75**
Planned Interviews	1.5	4.25	**5.75**
Review of relevant literature to inform future strategies	1.0	2.0	**3.00**
Phase III: Reporting			
Analysis, data visualization, reporting, and follow-up	6.75	10.0	**16.75**
Total (Person-days)	**16.75**	**24.00**	**40.75**
Per Diem Rates	XX	XX	
Cost	$—————	$—————	$—————

Source: Frédéric Bertrand

The evaluator can estimate other direct costs. It is important to determine them as accurately as possible. Otherwise, the evaluator may find themselves paying for additional expenses beyond the contracted amount. Depending on the study, direct costs may include, for example:

- Travel, meals, and accommodation
- Local transportation
- Transcription services
- Data entry services
- Translation (if appropriate)
- Administrative costs such as printing courier, and supplies.

Generally, the budget does not include software costs. Clients expect the evaluator to have subscriptions to the appropriate programs. All expenses associated with running an evaluation business (such as rent and insurance) are also excluded. If an evaluator uses their own staff members on a project, the budget can only include their actual days or partial days spent doing project work.

Accountability

As Alkin and Vo (2018, p. 41) explain, organizations commission evaluations in various ways. Evaluations conducted within an organization are called **internal evaluations** and are conducted by staff members who are already directly accountable to the organization being evaluated. There is a useful literature available on the topic of internal evaluation (see Love, 1991). Most evaluations, however, are **external evaluations** conducted by evaluators who are not employees. Organizations like government departments, not-for-profits, foundations, educational and health organizations, and other agencies and groups commonly hire evaluators. Each of these organizations manages its accountability processes and structures slightly differently. Therefore, the external evaluator needs a contract tailored to their specific evaluation project to clarify and formally describe their relationship with the organization.

Rather than assuming that everything will be fine and that a handshake is enough to seal the deal, it is essential that the evaluator clearly understands their agreement. The reality is that once the client has accepted the evaluator's proposal, an implicit contract is in place. Now the evaluator must produce the work at the price and within the time frame proposed. This arrangement tends to be one-sided, and unless the organization states the terms of the agreement in writing, the balance of power remains with the client.

The written contract increases the likelihood of a successful project outcome. There may be many challenges during the evaluation, but nothing provides a more solid foundation for this business arrangement than a written contract. Whether it is a formal document or a simple letter of agreement, there are several compelling reasons for its use (Barrington, 2012, p. 207; Rogers, 2014a). A written contract:

- Clarifies the financial relationship
- Identifies who will perform the work
- Indicates both client and evaluator responsibilities
- Protects against project scope creep
- Provides ways to manage conflict
- Protects against litigation
- Provides a schedule of tasks
- Identifies deliverables
- States total project budget, payment methods, conditions, and timeframes.

Stufflebeam (1999b) provides an exhaustive checklist on evaluation contracts which is worth reviewing. As he says:

> *Advance agreements on these matters can mean the difference between an evaluation's success and failure. Without such agreements the evaluation process is constantly subject to misunderstanding, disputes, efforts to compromise the findings, attack, and/or withdrawal—by the client—of cooperation and funds.* (p. 1)

Rather than being intimidated by a contract, the evaluator should take the time to understand its terms, ask for changes if needed, and sign it before work commences.

Now it is time to introduce an expert who has worked with many different organizations and agencies, Dr. Katrina Bledsoe.

EXPERT CORNER

Dr. Katrina Bledsoe

Katrina L. Bledsoe, PhD is a Senior Evaluation Specialist and Research Scientist with Education Development Center and a Partner with Strategic Learning Partners for Innovation in Washington, DC. She works with philanthropic, community-based organizations, and federal agencies such as the National Science Foundation, on evaluation design, data collection, evaluation partnering, and technical assistance. She is a widely published author and serves as Chair of the American Evaluation Association's Graduate Education Diversity Internship Workgroup.

Source: Education Development Center.
https://www.edc.org/staff/katrina-bledsoe

1. *In your work as an evaluator, professor, mentor, and guide, you have seen many evaluation plans. What is the one key characteristic you expect to see?*

Although there are many key characteristics that need to be considered in an evaluation plan, the main aspect I look for is how the stakeholders and community will be engaged. Without good stakeholder/community engagement and a plan about how you are going to manage that engagement and relationship, even if the rest of the plan reads "perfectly," it's unlikely to go well. Over the years, I have found that a key focus of evaluation is really not the intervention, program, or initiative; it's the people. A good relationship with stakeholders is the key piece to a credible evaluation because an evaluation is actually a joint venture with the stakeholders. Therefore, evaluators need to think about and plan for who will be at the table, the kind of relationship communities want to have, how everyone will communicate, and how the relationship/engagement will be maintained over the long term.

2. *An evaluator designs an evaluation plan to support decision making throughout the evaluation process. Can you describe a situation where the plan did indeed help to guide decision making and another where it did not? What was the difference between these two cases? What were the outcomes?*

One of my best evaluation plans was developed with a foundation. The plan had to be altered several times, but it was considered the guide for theory of change development, working with stakeholders, etc. We regularly revisited the plan at monthly meetings to serve as a grounding factor and to orient us on where to go next. All stakeholders had access to it and could make suggestions. The plan also served as a historical record for the work that had been accomplished.

A time when the evaluation plan did not guide decision making was on a project with the US State Department. The plan was complicated, and we later realized that it was more of a requirement than an actual guide. Further complicating the issue was the presence of multiple stakeholders in multiple countries who did not have access to the plan or the conversation and did not always understand or know the strategies that were used.

The key difference between the two experiences was stakeholder engagement. In one evaluation, all stakeholders were on the same page about the plan and the work. In the other, multiple stakeholders were left out of the conversation and were unaware of what was happening.

3. *What advice can you offer those of our readers who are just beginning to explore the field of evaluation?*

One piece of advice is to realize that evaluation is a creative and innovative venture. You have to be creative and innovative in how you plan, go about the work, and deliver products. Be prepared to pull from a variety of sectors, disciplines, and experiences to do good, credible evaluation.

Key Terms

Data Collection Matrix 390
Data management plan 410
Evaluation management 407
Evaluation plan 378
Evaluation Working Group 381

External evaluations 414
Gantt chart 411
Intended users 402
Internal evaluations 414
Key informants 383

Memorandum of Understanding
(MOU) 381
Review of program documents 382
Stakeholder identification 380

The Main Ideas

1. The evaluation plan is the base camp for evaluators.

2. Before writing the evaluation plan, the evaluator should spend time with eight pre-planning activities:
   a. identify and engaging stakeholders
   b. review documents
   c. conduct key informant interviews and on-site evaluation
   d. design program theory and logic model
   e. ask evaluation questions
   f. develop indicators
   g. finalize methods decisions
   h. prepare the Data Collection Matrix (DCM).

3. The EWG engages stakeholders in an ongoing process to determine evaluation questions, test instruments, facilitate data collection, implement the evaluation, increase credibility of analysis and interpretation, and use the evaluation results.

4. Key informant interviews enable the evaluator to obtain insider information from knowledgeable individuals connected to the program.

5. Evaluators and stakeholders answer questions using the tools and methods determined by the evaluator and the EWG.

6. The DCM, or evaluation framework, provides the evaluation questions, evaluation objectives, indicators, data collection tools, and data sources.

7. The evaluation plan consists of the title page, program overview, evaluation description, evaluation methods, data analysis and synthesis, and reporting.

8. Management of the evaluation includes activities that clarify team roles, strategies for managing the process of the evaluation, data ownership and security issues, study limitations and strengths, schedule of activities, budgeting, and accountability.

9. The evaluator acts as a manager and ensures implementation follows the plan as intended.

10. Planned accountability increases with the development of a written contract between the evaluator and the client.

Critical Thinking Questions

1. Why would the evaluation plan be referred to as the "base camp" of the evaluation project? Give three reasons why this thinking is beneficial for the success of the evaluation project.

2. When you start an evaluation, the organization's logic model may not suit your needs. What do you do? Describe different solutions to this problem.

3. How does the DCM help you answer the evaluation questions?

4. In what ways can an evaluation management plan anticipate potential issues?

5. What risks should a data management plan address? What particular processes would an evaluator put in place to manage risks related to communication?

Student Challenges

1. **Evaluation Plan Critique**
   a. Review the evaluation plans provided below or one that you locate. Select an evaluation plan you would like to critique.
      i **Tuberculosis (TB) Support Program**
         Garcia, A. (2003). *TB support program. Evaluation plan for January–March 2004.* Centers for Disease Control and Prevention. Division of TB Control and Prevention Lull County. https://www.cdc.gov/tb/programs/Evaluation/Guide/PDF/Complete_guide_Developing_eval_plan.pdf

      ii **Nutrition Education and Obesity Prevention**
         California Department of Public Health. (2017). *Evaluation of the champions for change 2017 be better media campaign.* Nutrition Education and Obesity Prevention Branch. https://www.cdph.ca.gov/Programs/CCDPHP/DCDIC/NEOPB/CDPH%20Document%20Library/RES_Media-Evaluation2017.pdf

      iii **Policing and Community Outreach with the Homeless**
         Worwood, E. Seawright, J., & Butters, R. (2016). *Evaluation of the homeless outreach serve team (HOST) program.* Community Outreach Policing Services (COPS). U.S. Department of Justice. https://cops.usdoj.gov/ric/ric.php?page=detail&id=COPS-W0814

      iv **Case Management for Aboriginal Youth**
         Social Ventures Australia. (2014). *Forecast social return on investment – report.* https://www.niaa.gov.au/sites/default/files/publications/indigenous/Helping-Hand-and-Linking-Youth/pdf/Helping_Hand_and_Linking_Youth_SROI_Report_PDF.pdf

      v **Healthy Marriage**
         Bir, A., Corwin, E., MacIlvain, B., Beard, A., Richburg, K., Smith, K., & Lerman, R. (2012). *The community healthy marriage initiative evaluation impacts of a community approach to strengthening families.* Office of Planning, Research and Evaluation, Administration for Children and Families, U.S. Department of Health and Human Services. https://www.healthymarriageinfo.org/wp-content/uploads/2017/12/chmi_impactreport.pdf

   b. After reviewing your selected evaluation plan, use the rubric in the following reference to score the plan. See Appendix A for the rubric. Urban, J., Burgermaster, M., Archibald, T., & Byrne, A. (2014). Relationships between quantitative measures of evaluation plan and program model quality and a qualitative measure of participant perceptions of an evaluation capacity building approach. *Journal of Mixed Methods Research, 9*(2), 154-177.

   c. After using the rubric to judge the plan, use this checklist to assess the evaluation questions in the plan.

Centers for Disease Control and Prevention. (2013). *Checklist for assessing your evaluation questions.* National Asthma Control Program. https://www.cdc.gov/asthma/program_eval/assessingevaluationquestionchecklist.pdf

d. Answer the following questions after use of the rubric and checklist.

  1. What were your overall impressions of the evaluation plan before reviewing the rubric and checklist?

  2. What are the overall strengths and weaknesses of this plan based on

recommendations in the rubric and checklist?

3. Where are the strengths and weaknesses of the evaluation questions?

4. Are there any sections or other information you would add to provide more detail?

5. Do you have any recommendations for the evaluators?

6. What did you learn from this process?

Additional Readings and Resources

1. Saunders, M. (2000). Beginning an evaluation with RUFDATA: Theorizing a practical approach to evaluation planning. *Evaluation, 6*(1), 7–21. Saunders (2000) provides a framework for initiating new evaluators into evaluation practice and planning. RUFDATA is short for Reasons and purposes, Uses, Focus, Data and evidence, Audience, Timing, and Agency. The authors created the RUFDATA framework for novice evaluators introduced into a community of practice.

2. Scheirer, M. A. (1998). Commentary: Evaluation planning is the heart of the matter. *American Journal of Evaluation, 19*(3), 385–391. This commentary on evaluation planning uses a case study example related to proposed support services for former welfare recipients to maintain their employment status and develop new employment skills. The author examines various ethical, methodological, and practical challenges as the case study evaluator proposes a randomized treatment and control group with this population of interest.

3. Tolma, E., Cheney, M., Troup, P., & Hann, N. (2009). Designing the process evaluation for the collaborative planning of a Local Turning Point Partnership. *Health Promotion Practice, 10*(4), 537–548.

Tolma et al. (2009) discussed the process evaluation of a collaborative effort with community partners to address health issues in central Oklahoma. They introduce a planning framework that includes context, reach, dose delivered, dose received, fidelity, implementation, recruitment, barriers, and maintenance. The planning phase for this project includes developing an evaluation plan and measurements to answer KEQs. In addition, the authors employed the participatory evaluation method to engage stakeholders in the evaluation process.

4. The Productivity Commission. (2020). *A guide to evaluation under the Indigenous evaluation strategy.* Commonwealth of Australia. https://www.pc.gov.au/inquiries/completed/indigenous-evaluation/strategy/indigenous-evaluation-guide.pdf The authors of this toolkit provide guidance on building evaluation into policy and program design for Indigenous contexts. A major principle of the approach is the centering of Aboriginal and Torres Strait Islander people, perspectives, priorities and knowledge. Supporting principles include conducting evaluations that are credible, useful, ethical, and transparent.

COMMUNICATION, REPORTING, AND USE

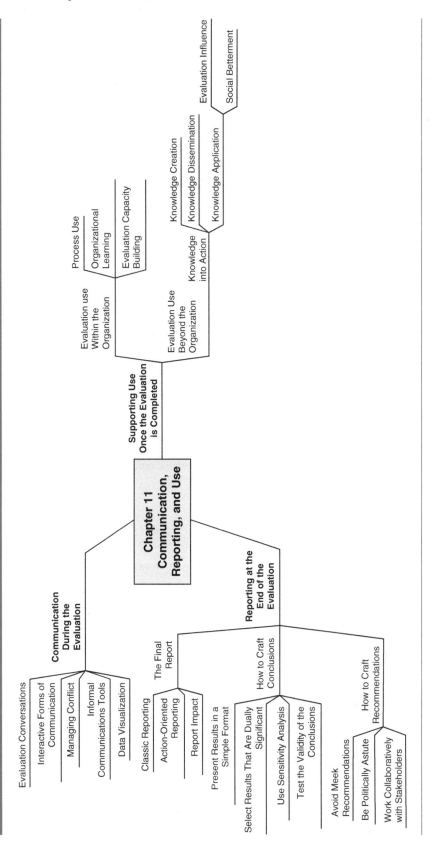

Chapter 11
Communication,
Reporting, and Use

Supporting Use
Once the Evaluation
is Completed

Evaluation use
Within the
Organization

Process Use

Organizational
Learning

Evaluation Capacity
Building

Evaluation Use
Beyond the
Organization

Knowledge Creation

Knowledge Dissemination

Knowledge
into Action

Knowledge Application

Evaluation Influence

Social Betterment

Communication
During the
Evaluation

Evaluation Conversations

Interactive Forms of
Communication

Managing Conflict

Informal
Communications Tools

Data Visualization

Reporting at the
End of the
Evaluation

The Final
Report

Classic Reporting

Action-Oriented
Reporting

Report Impact

Present Results in a
Simple Format

How to Craft
Conclusions

Select Results That Are Dually
Significant

Use Sensitivity Analysis

Test the Validity of the
Conclusions

How to Craft
Recommendations

Avoid Meek
Recommendations

Be Politically Astute

Work Collaboratively
with Stakeholders

EMERGENCY ON HALLOWE'EN

Source: istockphoto.com/MJ Felt

Atul Gawande, a well-known American surgeon and writer, tells the tale his friend told him of a patient with a stab wound who came into a San Francisco emergency room on Hallowe'en night. He had been to a costume party and this injury was the result. The trauma team thought it was "no big deal," just another busy night in the big city, and that they could take their time stitching him up. The patient lay on his stretcher while they readied the operating room, and it was only then that they noticed his heart rate had sky-rocketed and he was unresponsive. Now the team swung into action.

When they opened his belly, blood poured out. The weapon had passed more than a foot through his body, piercing his aorta. It was as bad an injury as anything his friend had ever seen in Vietnam. The team had done almost all the right things, but no one had thought to ask the patient about the weapon. Instead, they assumed the weapon was a knife. Later, they learned that the assailant, dressed as a soldier, had stabbed him with a bayonet. Fortunately, the patient did survive. Gawande thought deeply about the reasons for avoidable failures like this and what strategies could be used to overcome them. He went on to write his classic book, *The Checklist Manifesto: How to Get Things Right*. The team learned a valuable lesson that night about the importance of communication (Gawande, 2011).

INTRODUCTION

Chapter 11 focuses on three communication processes that span the evaluation study. First is communication during the evaluation. We look at different types of evaluation conversations including interactive processes, managing conflict, using informal communication tools, and data visualization. Second, we look at reporting at the end of the evaluation. Two types of final reporting are described, the classic final report and action-oriented reporting, and the core elements of each are presented. A brief discussion explores some of the reasons why evaluation reports may have limited impact and how evaluators need to attend to the original policy question. Suggestions are offered about how to craft conclusions and recommendations. Third, we consider communication processes to support evaluation use once the evaluation study is completed. We look at use within the organization, including process use, organizational learning, and capacity building; beyond the organization in terms of turning knowledge into action, knowledge dissemination, and knowledge application; and finally, look more broadly at evaluation influence, remembering that the ultimate purpose of evaluation is social betterment.

You will enjoy the resources in this chapter including our Spotlight on Equity on the Child360 Program which works with under-served communities, our experts, Dr. Stephanie Evergreen and Ann-Murray Brown, Key Terms, Main Ideas, Critical Thinking Questions, Student Challenges, and Additional Readings and Resources.

As Alkin et al. state (2006, p. 384), "it is probably not an exaggeration to say that evaluation without communication would not be possible." Therefore, in this chapter, we take a closer look at three critical processes that span the trajectory of the evaluation study:

- Communicating during the evaluation

- Reporting at the end of the evaluation

- Supporting evaluation use once the evaluation is completed.

COMMUNICATION DURING THE EVALUATION

To start with, we need to understand the difference between communication and communications. Mazur (2013) explains, "There is a HUGE divide between communication and communications. Saying there is not, is like saying PEZ candy and dark chocolate are the same thing – they're both candy, right (para. 2)?"

- **Communication** is the human element. It is how individuals exchange messages.

- **Communications** is how evaluators distribute messages, that is, the systems or technologies used to transmit the information.

Mazur (2013) concludes, "There is no 'S' in human communication" (para. 2).

Communication throughout the evaluation process helps shape what the evaluation will eventually produce and how stakeholders will use findings. This section describes the importance of evaluation conversations, looks at interactive forms of communication, and considers how conflict may arise and how to manage it. Then we explore some informal communications tools and look briefly at data visualization. Finally, we see how one evaluation team is adapting their tools to the needs of their stakeholders.

Evaluation Conversations

Communication involves talking to people and, as King and Stevahn (2013, pp. 66–67) point out, it is a skill that an evaluator can actively pursue and shape—throughout the evaluation. Therefore, it is essential to engage clients in what they call "substantive conversations (p. 67)." These conversations generally address the following topics:

1. To find out what clients want the evaluator to do

2. To facilitate the evaluation process

3. To monitor how well the evaluation is going.

They believe so strongly in the importance of these conversations that they say:

> *An evaluator's ability to converse effectively with people in an evaluation setting may well be a predictor of the eventual quality of the study that results. An inability to do so…may result in an evaluation that, while in some sense technically adequate, fails to provide intended users accurate information they can act on.* (p. 68)

Like Patton (2008), these authors focus on the primary intended user; however, when considering the dynamic, multidirectional, and interactive world of social media today, the options and audiences multiply with dizzying speed (see Figure 11.1).

FIGURE 11.1 ● HOW WE COMMUNICATE

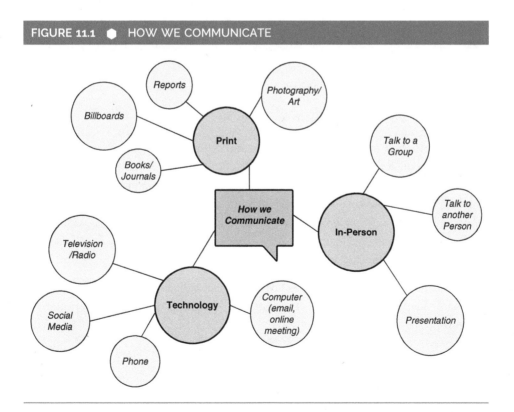

Keeping in mind our communication context, we need to think about how to craft conversations according to the evaluation's stage of development, including design, implementation, and conclusion. King and Stevahn (2013, pp. 76–77) discuss substantive conversations with stakeholders, ones that are continuous and deep. Their text offers many valuable examples of conversation starters and sample questions. However, above all, they caution that evaluators must take the time to plan and conduct substantive conversations at every stage of a study (see Figure 11.2).

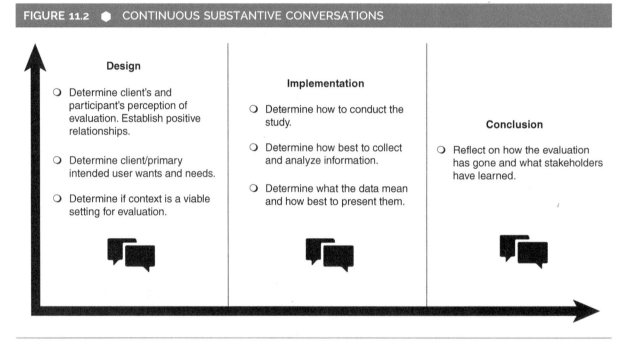

FIGURE 11.2 ● CONTINUOUS SUBSTANTIVE CONVERSATIONS

Design
- Determine client's and participant's perception of evaluation. Establish positive relationships.
- Determine client/primary intended user wants and needs.
- Determine if context is a viable setting for evaluation.

Implementation
- Determine how to conduct the study.
- Determine how best to collect and analyze information.
- Determine what the data mean and how best to present them.

Conclusion
- Reflect on how the evaluation has gone and what stakeholders have learned.

Source: King, J. A., & Stevahn, L. (2013). *Interactive evaluation practice: Mastering the interpersonal dynamics of program evaluation.* SAGE Publications.

Interactive Forms of Communication

Evaluation decision making often occurs in a social context, so small group facilitation is an essential skill for evaluators. Torres et al. (2005) maintain that group learning can support evaluation use. In addition, evaluators can provide opportunities for understanding, learning, and collaboration through interactive forms of communication (p. 5). Working sessions and synchronous electronic communications, including videoconferences, teleconferences, and synchronous web-based activities, occur in real time and allow participants from different locations to interact successfully.

Torres et al. (pp. 187–197) suggest ways for the evaluator to design and conduct successful interactions. See the checklist for designing successful interactions in Figure 11.3, p. 427.

Managing Conflict

Given the nature of human beings, conversations are often more complex than they appear, and communication barriers can arise unexpectedly. To avoid getting mired in

FIGURE 11.3 ● DESIGNING SUCCESSFUL INTERACTIONS

Designing Successful Interactions

1. Rate your skills for facilitating working sessions.

☐ 1   ☐ 2   ☐ 3   ☐ 4   ☐ 5

Poor   Exceptional

2. Identify ways you can build support for participation in these sessions and ensure vital stakeholders attend.

_____

_____

_____

_____

_____

3. How tailored is each session with clear objectives?

☐ 1   ☐ 2   ☐ 3   ☐ 4   ☐ 5

Not Tailored   Well Tailored

4. Did you...

- Add an interactive activity?   ☐ Yes | ☐ No
- Follow-up with stakeholders?   ☐ Yes | ☐ No
- Start with evaluation's purpose?   ☐ Yes | ☐ No
- Design consensus building activity?   ☐ Yes | ☐ No
- Start on time and work efficiently?   ☐ Yes | ☐ No
- Follow-up with stakeholders?   ☐ Yes | ☐ No
- List ground rules for confidentiality?   ☐ Yes | ☐ No
- Design worksheets to aid structure?   ☐ Yes | ☐ No
- Close the session with next steps?   ☐ Yes | ☐ No
- Follow up with no-show stakeholders?   ☐ Yes | ☐ No

Source: Torres, R. T., Preskill, H., & Piontek, M. E. (2005). *Evaluation strategies for communicating and reporting.* SAGE Publications.

opinion and self-interest, the evaluator needs to orchestrate group conversations to uncover the deeper meaning and workable solutions.

One small-group approach is the Focused Conversation Method (Stanfield, 1997, p. 2), enabling an evaluator to facilitate a conversation that leads participants from surface topics through to deeper levels, from questions that are objective, to reflective, to more interpretive, and finally to an eventual decision, as shown in Box 11.1, p. 428.

Once the intent of a conversation is clear, the evaluator can prepare for the interaction by brainstorming questions, writing them on post-it notes, and shuffling them into these four levels. It is then possible to rehearse the questions and imagine possible responses. This preparation is paramount when the evaluator expects that conflict or unexpected twists and turns may arise in a group's interaction.

Conflict is most likely to emerge at the second level when reflective questions are asked. If underlying emotions are not dealt with, the evaluation may be blocked, delayed, or terminated. Typically, evaluators are trained in research skills, not in interpersonal skills, so this is treacherous terrain.

Conflict Strategies Theory describes five responses to conflict (Johnson & Johnson, 2009):

1. Forcing, or achieving one's own goals at the expense of others

2. Withdrawing, or giving up one's personal goals and positive relationships with others

3. Smoothing, or appeasing others at the sacrifice of self-interest

4. Compromising, or using give-and-take to create partial gains for each

5. Problem-solving or using cooperative negotiation to maximize joint outcomes.

No doubt, we have all used each of these strategies at one time or another but problem solving is the best choice if cooperation and effective evaluation are the desired outcomes.

No one has tackled conflict management more successfully than Fisher et al. (1991), who wrote the classic, *Getting to Yes: Negotiating agreement without giving in*. The authors based the book on their experiences with the *Harvard Negotiation Project* working with world-sized conflict situations such as negotiating with airplane hijackers. They suggest that four obstacles typically inhibit the development of workable options.

- Premature judgment—being critical too soon can stifle imagination

- Searching for the single answer—thereby ignoring many other possible options

- The assumption of a fixed pie—a belief in a win-lose or fixed-sum scenario

- The belief that solving the problem is the problem—a focus only on immediate interests.

In order to solve problems, the evaluator should:

- Separate the act of inventing options from the act of judging them

- Broaden the number of options on the table rather than looking for a single answer

- Search for mutual gains by making the pie larger (e.g., adding more value) so that everyone gets a bigger piece

- Invent ways of making the decision easy by considering the outcome of the decision from the other's point of view and then reframing the options to make them more palatable.

Fisher and Ury's Circle Chart (see Figure 11.4, p. 430) shows the four basic steps to generating creative solutions (Ury, 2013). It presents four steps in a clockwise circle: identify the problem, analyze it, generate possible approaches to solving it, and finally select specific steps to deal with the problem.

The sequential, cyclical nature of the Circle Chart shows how easy it is to solve problems when participants are focused on the issue at hand rather than simply proving themselves right—and how approaching problems in this way is applicable in many circumstances (Jennings, 2020).

Informal Communications Tools

In addition to the communication skills required for client conversations, many informal communications tools and mechanisms are available to support them. As Torres et al. (2005, pp. 187–197) comment, brief and frequent communications about the evaluation can reach a wide range of individuals, elicit responses to various evaluation activities, and build rapport.

Today, evaluators use emails, meeting minutes, infographics, newsletters, blogs, dashboards, minireports, and media feeds on YouTube, Facebook, LinkedIn, Instagram, and Twitter, to name a few. These short messages act as a record of evaluation events,

FIGURE 11.4 ● FISHER & URY'S CIRCLE CHART: INVENTING OPTIONS FOR MUTUAL GAIN

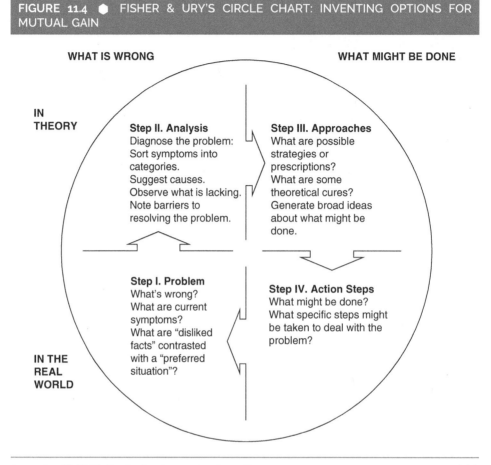

WHAT IS WRONG

WHAT MIGHT BE DONE

IN THEORY

Step II. Analysis
Diagnose the problem:
Sort symptoms into categories.
Suggest causes.
Observe what is lacking.
Note barriers to resolving the problem.

Step III. Approaches
What are possible strategies or prescriptions?
What are some theoretical cures?
Generate broad ideas about what might be done.

Step I. Problem
What's wrong?
What are current symptoms?
What are "disliked facts" contrasted with a "preferred situation"?

Step IV. Action Steps
What might be done?
What specific steps might be taken to deal with the problem?

IN THE REAL WORLD

Source: Ury, W. (2013). The five Ps of persuasion: Roger Fisher's approach to influence. *Negotiation Journal, 29*(2), 133–140.

activities, and decisions. They can create a trail of evidence that may prove helpful later when preparing the final report, offering a deep dive into the day-to-day operations of the evaluation.

Timing is another critical factor. Figure 11.5, p. 431 shows how different communications tools can support the evaluation process at different points in the journey (Corley, 2018).

Data Visualization

Data visualization has become an important way of connecting with readers. One of the most significant innovations in evaluation reporting comes from an enhanced understanding of how clients process information, mainly related to visual perception or how the brain interprets what the eyes see. The American Psychological Association (2020) states that "Cognitive psychologists, sometimes called brain scientists, study how the human brain works–how we think, remember, and learn" (para. 1). Reports should be a learning experience for clients and stakeholders. How the information is presented should support and promote the uptake of new knowledge so those invested can judge the worth

FIGURE 11.5 ● COMMUNICATIONS THROUGHOUT THE EVALUATION JOURNEY

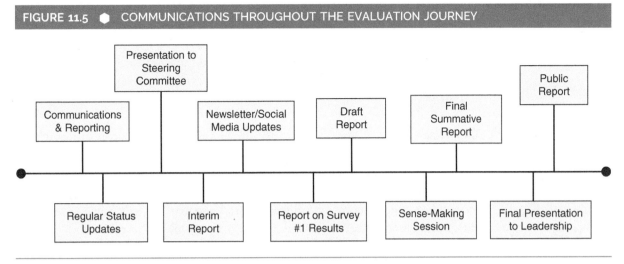

Source: Corley, S. (2018, May). *Doing reporting better.* Workshop presented to the Alberta Northwest Territories Chapter of the Canadian Evaluation Society, Edmonton, AB.

of the program. Thus, evaluators can use the concepts or best practices of brain science to design reports that are visually accessible and promote learning. **Data visualization** has become an important way to connect with readers.

Visual Processing

Evergreen (2011, p. 42) explains that processing information involves three phases: pre-attention, working memory, and long-term memory.

Preattention, or grabbing the reader's attention, is best achieved by creating a hierarchy of information for the reader, by using graphic design techniques to point to the essential parts of the report through judicious use of headings, typeface and size, color, and paragraphing. Charts and graphs can also draw attention, if used sparingly, and can cue the reader to the most critical information.

Working memory is where we process information; however, as Evergreen points out, we can only hold three to five chunks of information in our working memory at a time. The evaluator can assist those readers who may be suffering from overload by synthesizing information into manageable pieces. For example, color coding, clustering, visual clues, or other ways of differentiating topics can help readers understand which pieces fit together.

When messages make it into long-term memory, comprehension and cognition occur, and the brain incorporates new information into existing mental patterns. Formatting, spacing, color, graphics, and other design options can impact this interpretation function. For example, for textual data, evaluators can map key ideas, and present quotations and vignettes in boxes (Rogers, 2014b). Numeric data can be summarized and simplified into visually pleasing charts that remove unnecessary lines, text, and distracting backgrounds to engage the reader (Evergreen, 2011, p. 44). Photographs also offer a rich vicarious experience.

This growth in the understanding of cognitive processes has gone hand-in-hand with the now universal reliance on the Internet, which has (Azzam et al., 2013):

> *forced both public and private entities to be more transparent about their work, to share their data, and to make that data available in ways that an informed citizen can make sense of it.* (pp. 12–13)

Data visualization and study transparency are now essential components of report preparation. Many valuable resources, tutorials, websites, and training programs are available to help evaluators make information more interesting and accessible for stakeholders. For example, the American Evaluation Association's Data Visualization and Reporting Topical Interest Group provides training, discussion, and resources. In addition, the Data Visualization Checklist, created by Evergreen and Emery (2016), is a helpful tool to guide the creation of high-impact visuals.

The evaluator needs to consider both communication processes and communications tools to determine how the client will receive their messages. It takes time to match the language, style, message, and method with the recipient or audience. Brief, flexible, and accessible formats, color, interesting layouts, charts, graphics, and photographs increase the likelihood of making the information memorable.

A quick list of best practices is included as follows:

- Know the report audience.
- Avoid cluttered charts.
- Consider chart titles that explain the findings.
- Consider the type of chart that is best for the data (e.g, pie, line, bar, histogram, radar).
- Use a single font that is easy to read.
- Avoid over formatting (e.g., too many lines and variables).
- Limit pie chart to three slices.
- Enlarge values to highlight significance.
- Choose consistency with color categories, sequential, or diverging designs.
- Be sensitive to color selection when providing data for various races and ethnicities.
- Tell a story.

REPORTING AT THE END OF THE EVALUATION

While reporting occurs throughout an evaluation study, communications tools such as status reports, field reports, and interim reports relate to process issues, but, the key product of most evaluations is the final report. The Centers for Disease Control and Prevention (2013b) defines a final report as a "written document that describes how you monitored and evaluated your program. It presents the findings, conclusions, and recommendations from a thorough evaluation, including recommendations for how evaluation results can be used to guide program improvement and decision making" (p. 1).

This section examines two types of final reports: the classic final report and the action-oriented report. Then we consider some of the reasons why many evaluation reports have little impact and do not produce the changes envisioned by the evaluator. Finally, we look at how to craft effective conclusions and recommendations.

Source: Chris Lysy/FreshSpectrum.com

The Final Report

Evaluators structure final reports in two main ways: (1) the classic final report, a not-too-distant relative of the typical research report; and (2) the action-oriented report, the classic report's accessible modern cousin, influenced by design principles and stakeholder needs. The evaluator must determine the type of report the client prefers and then act accordingly—or produce compelling and persuasive evidence to change their expectations. This section explores both types of reports.

Classic Reporting

While details vary, the outline for a classic final report mirrors the topics in the evaluation plan, except now, the plans have become a reality and often differ in many respects from the original blueprint. In general terms, the core elements of a final report fulfill the following needs (Treasury Board of Canada Secretariat, 2004, p. 3):

- The evaluation covers outcomes and issues undertaken by the evaluator as represented in the evaluation plan.

- The methodology used is appropriate for the intended objectives of the study.

- Evidence drawn from the evaluation research is the basis for the findings and conclusions.

- The recommendations are built on the conclusions and suggest improved program performance based on the study's findings.

Table 11.1, p. 434 illustrates these core elements (Centers for Disease Control and Prevention, 2013b; Miron, 2004; Montrosse-Moorehead & Griffith, 2017; TBS, 2004).

TABLE 11.1 ⬢ CORE ELEMENTS OF A CLASSIC FINAL REPORT	
Element	**Report Topics**
1. Title page	• Name of the evaluation • Organizations involved in the evaluation with logos • Date • Evaluator's name and contact information.
2. Executive summary	• Brief synopsis of the report. • Description of the evaluand, evaluation questions, purpose, intended audience, and methodology • Summary of main findings, conclusions, and recommendations. • Can be a stand-alone document • 1–3 pages in length
3. Program description	• Brief narrative of the program and its context • Program setting and context • Description of program beneficiaries • Description of program resources, staffing, location(s)
4. Evaluation focus	• Purpose of the evaluation and issues or questions to be addressed • Client, audience, and key stakeholders • Evaluation philosophy, orientation, and approach • Evaluation objectives and scope • Evaluation questions and how they were prioritized • Theory of change or logic model • Timing of evaluation activities • Evaluation funding source, amount, and expected deliverables • Evaluation team characteristics • How results will be used
5. Evaluation design, data sources, and methods	• Methodological orientation (i.e., qualitative, quantitative, or mixed) • Epistemological orientation • Review of related research • Research design • Evaluation approach/model/theory • Demographics of sample • Links between evaluation questions, indicators, performance measures, data sources, methods used, and data collection instruments • Limitations, including bias, mitigating strategies to deal with limitations, and the strengths of this evaluation • Brief narrative of the evaluation process • How data were analyzed and synthesized
6. Key findings	• How findings were interpreted (who was involved, level of collaboration with stakeholders) • Plausible alternative interpretations or proof they were considered • Evidence to substantiate findings • Charts, tables, graphs, and other visual representations that are understandable and appropriately labeled • Plain language, minimal technical jargon • Parsimonious, not overly detailed • Sufficiently clear to allow readers to draw substantiated inferences • Reflections on lessons learned

Table 11.1 *(Continued)*

Element	Report Topics
7. Conclusions	• Address evaluation questions supported by the findings • Are valid and appropriate for the methods used • Judgment of merit or worth is based on study findings
8. Recommendations	• Supported by and flow logically from the findings and conclusions • Address significant issues and are prioritized (i.e., not a shopping list) • Provide pathways to program improvement • Are practical and can be realistically implemented • Address timeframe, cost, and degree of change recommended • Consider the potential impact of implementation • Where possible, identify specific groups likely to be involved in the implementation

Source: Montrosse-Moorhead, B., & Griffith, J. C. (2017). Toward the development of reporting standards for evaluations. *American Journal of Evaluation, 38*(4), 577–602; Centers for Disease Control and Prevention. (2013b). *Developing an effective evaluation report: Setting the course for effective program evaluation.* Centers for Disease Control and Prevention.

While this list of core elements for a final report may be comprehensive, it may not suit the needs of the primary intended users. For example, Evergreen (2011, p. 41) found that the average length of an evaluation report in the Western Michigan University Evaluation Center's library was 175 pages. Davidson (2007) comments that as many evaluators had their primary training in the social sciences, they need to "unlearn" some of the baggage acquired there. In particular, organizing evaluation reports like a Masters' thesis can make clients feel like they are "wading through mud" (p. vi) with page after page of graphs and quotations without any reference to the evaluation questions. The client is left gasping, "When, oh when, are they going to get to the point?" Luckily, if a traditional final report does not meet client needs, newer and more exciting options are available.

Action-Oriented Reporting

The **1:3:25 model** offers a valuable formula for reporting evaluation findings. It has a reader-friendly format and presents information in layers of increasing detail. The Canadian Health Services Research Foundation (2008) designed the model and practitioners have used it in health research and health technology assessment for over 20 years. It includes one page for critical messages, three pages for the executive summary, and 25 pages for full unabridged content. Evergreen (2017) depicts the model as follows, with appendices for more technical information such as the logic model, methods, and findings (see Figure 11.6, p. 436).

As Evergreen (2017) suggests:

> *In each of these layers, readers gain more and more detail. Of course, they can stop anytime, having already gotten the high points from us. But it provides a scaffolding toward learning, in which each step helps the reader learn a bit more without being completely overwhelm[ed].* (para. 4)

FIGURE 11.6 ● THE 1:3:25 REPORTING MODEL

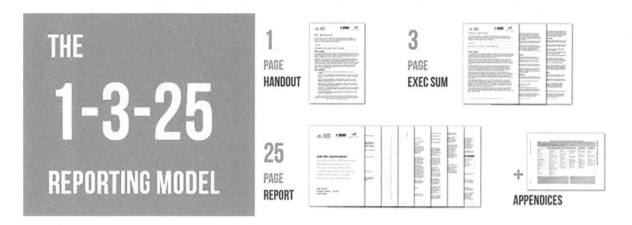

Source: Evergreen, S. (2017). The 1-3-25 reporting model. *Stephanie Evergreen Consulting.* https://stephanieevergreen.com/the-1-3-25-reporting-model/

The model focuses on decision makers, staff, and other audiences who need to use the data to take action and are less interested in reading about the research process.

At the request of the Ewing Marion Kauffman Foundation, Evergreen outlined the elements of what she terms the Action-Oriented Report. Table 11.2 provides key topics.

TABLE 11.2 ● CORE ELEMENTS OF THE ACTION-ORIENTED REPORT

Element	Report Topics
1. The cover (1 page)	• Title • Report Author Names • Author Organization • Organization Logo • Date • Image
2. The Executive Summary (1–2 pages)	• Most relevant key findings that are actionable • Visualized information • Brief interpretation of findings • 1–2 sentences on methods and rigor (could be in a sidebar)
3. Condensed Front Matter (1–2 pages)	• Table of Contents • List of Figures and Tables • Acknowledgments • Other essential information (e.g., Steering Committee members, client/evaluation manager, with photos)

Table 11.2 *(Continued)*

Element	Report Topics
4. Findings & Interpretation (<20 pages)	• Actionable findings reported first (based mainly on conclusions & recommendations) • Significant attention to formatting • Use of data visualization
5. Appendices (as needed)	• Methods and analysis • Design • Background • Key findings

Source: Ewing Marion Kauffman Foundation. (2017, November). Evaluation report guidance. https://www.kauffman.org/wp-content/uploads/2019/09/EMKF-Evaluation-Report-Guide-2017.pdf

Rakesh Mohan, Director of the Office of Performance Evaluations at the Idaho State Legislature in Boise, Idaho, has worked with his team for many years presenting evaluation findings to both policymakers and public audiences. To gain the attention of busy policymakers, he has learned that effective reports involve logic, organization and messaging, and a clear writing style. He comments (Mohan & Campbell, 2012), "If your writing doesn't have clarity, the report will not be used." While he is not suggesting to "dumb down" the report, he does feel that an academic writing style is not appropriate. Policymakers, who are certainly well able to interpret technical information, are simply too pressed by competing issues to take the time to do so. Therefore, the evaluator must write the report clearly to gain and hold their attention. Mohan and Campbell (2012) offer many tips to enhance report clarity in Figure 11.7.

FIGURE 11.7 ● EVALUATOR'S CHECKLIST FOR REPORT CLARITY

☐ Have a non-evaluator read your report.

☐ Use a brief executive summary to highlight report's central message.

☐ Use simple active verbs.

☐ Avoid long strings of prepositional phrases.

☐ Pay attention to the rhythm of sentences. Vary length

☐ Write key points first and follow with need-to-know details.

☐ Move technical details and other nonessential information to appendices.

☐ Minimize jargon and acronyms.

☐ Use numbered and bulleted lists mixed with images.

☐ Use headings and subheadings to guide the reader through the report.

☐ Use sidebars to highlight critical points.

☐ Use word economy; less is more.

☐ Use color to help reader focus on different parts of the results.

☐ Use headings and subheadings to guide the reader, sidebars for critical points.

Source: Adapted from Mohan, R., & Campbell, M. (2012, February 24). *DVR week: Rakesh Mohan and Margaret Campbell on making evaluation reports reader friendly.* American Evaluation Association. https://aea365.org/blog/dvr-week-rakesh-mohan-and-margaret-campbell-on-making-evaluation-reports-reader-friendly/

An example is the one-page summary of a 2018 evaluation produced by the Office of Performance Evaluations in the Idaho Legislature (2018), entitled Child Welfare System: Reducing the Risk of Adverse Outcomes. See Figure 11.8, p. 439.

Report Impact

Every evaluator believes that their study findings can lead to improved performance. Many share a social justice perspective and want to make the world a better place, one step at a time. However, for the past 50 years, theorists have worried that evaluations have limited impact.

As early as 1973, in her paper, *Where Politics and Evaluation Meet*, (as reprinted in Evaluation Practice in 1993), Weiss stated that, "only with sensitivity to the politics of evaluation research—can the evaluator be as creative and strategically useful as he should be" (p. 94). Further, she admitted, "As a matter of record, relatively few evaluation studies have had a noticeable effect on the making and remaking of public policy" (p. 98).

Perhaps, as Chelimsky (1987a) suggests, the lack of realistic solutions might be because evaluators do not understand the policy domain which influences evaluations. For example, when she chaired a symposium for evaluators, policymakers, sponsors, and other users, the evaluators were shocked to learn that users were dissatisfied with their evaluations. Some of the reasons included (p. 201):

- Bureaucratic relationships and conflicts can override the use of findings.

- Some program managers prefer to ignore the findings.

- Evaluations are only used if management wants them to be.

- Evaluation is an ivory tower process.

- Evaluations are too late to be helpful, too full of jargon to be understood, too lengthy for the user to read, and answer the wrong question.

If, as these theorists believe, reporting occurs in a political context, the ultimate credibility of the evaluation's final report is its responsiveness to the specific policy question and information needs of the decision maker. For Chelimsky, the policy question is the one that keeps decision makers awake at night, the question they posed to evaluators in the first place. Evaluators then turn around, translate the policy question into a research-worthy question, and build the study around it. Eventually, at the end of the study, the evaluator must translate the findings back into language that answers that policy question. Unfortunately, much can be lost in this two-way translation process.

When readers receive a final report, they often flip directly to its last few pages to find the answers to these two questions:

- *What did we find out?* (i.e., conclusions).

- *What should we do about it?* (i.e., recommendations).

FIGURE 11.8 ● IDAHO'S OFFICE OF PERFORMANCE EVALUATION INFOGRAPHIC

Child Welfare System: Reducing the Risk of Adverse Outcomes

Report highlights   **March 2018**

The report offers the Legislature and all child welfare partners a roadmap for reducing the risk of adverse outcomes for children and youth who have been maltreated or involved with juvenile justice.

Findings

The evaluation addressed three aspects of Idaho's child welfare system.

1. Diverting maltreated children from foster care when possible

Child and Family Services' data systems did not support the collection practices necessary for systematic analysis of foster care diversion.

Child protection partners (law enforcement, prosecutors, medical professionals, schools, and families) affected the use of foster care diversion.

Social workers inconsistently applied the child safety assessment model.

2. Preventing youth from crossing between the child protection and juvenile justice systems

Data sharing obstacles have hindered stakeholders' understanding of youth who have had contact with both the child protection and juvenile justice systems.

The system lacked a clear legal and policy framework that supports data sharing and coordinated approaches to treating dual system youth.

3. Preparing youth who are exiting the child welfare system for independent living as adults

Managing crises took precedence over providing independent living services.

Youth and staff showed inconsistent knowledge of benefits and services.

Unstable caregiver relationships or lack of community connections caused youth to have a false sense of support.

Recommendations

When used in conjunction with our 2017 recommendation to establish system-wide oversight, recommendations in this report will enable child protection partners to further improve collaboration and ensure that responsibility for child protection outcomes is shared.

25% of child maltreatment cases received safety services that diverted children from foster care in fiscal year 2016

19% of diversions escalated to foster care

70% of diversion cases relied on extended family or friends to ensure the safety of children

34% of youth involved with the juvenile justice system in 2014 or 2015 had previous contact with Idaho's child protection system

The evaluation builds on two of our previous studies:
1. *Child Welfare System*, February 2017
2. *Representation for Children and Youth in Child Protection Cases*, February 2018

View the report:
www.legislature.idaho.gov/ope/

Promoting confidence and accountability in state government

Source: Idaho Legislature. (2018, March). *Child welfare system: Reducing the risk of adverse outcomes*. Office of Performance Evaluations. https://legislature.idaho.gov/ope/reports/r1803/

For many readers, then, it seems that the final report is a vehicle for the conclusions and recommendations. As a result, preparing impactful conclusions and recommendations can make all the difference.

How to Craft Conclusions

According to Majchrzak (1984), the evaluator exerts substantial control when drawing conclusions. Evaluators usually collect more information than can be communicated to decision makers. Therefore, they must decide what data to report and how to present them. It is important to proceed cautiously to maintain both study validity and relevance while meeting this challenge. Here are some suggestions (Barrington, 2017b; Majchrzak, 1984, pp. 68–70).

Present Results in a Simple Format

Prepare the report for a lay audience. For example, assume stakeholders do not have a statistical background. It is also likely that their mathematical skills will vary considerably.

To present quantitative findings: (1) select findings that are credible and robust, (2) use simple analyses and brief tables, (3) move complex analyses to the appendix, (4) develop simple summary tables. Also, as evaluation questions tend to interact with each other, it may be useful to establish more flexible significance levels that the traditional .05 alpha level. In some studies, 85% or 90% may be robust enough. Report confidence intervals, especially if you are comparing alternative options. Specify how much better one option is than another.

To present qualitative findings consider a thematic description, select representative quotations, tell brief stories, provide mini-cases, or use photographs.

Select Results That Are Dually Significant

Study results must be significant from both the research and the program perspectives. As Majchrzak comments, "Unless the finding is both politically and statistically significant, it is probably not worth noting" (1984, p. 69). Chelimsky (1987b, p. 19) agrees, saying:

> *Prioritization of the evaluation findings is also a condition for use. Telling all is tantamount to telling nothing. The important thing is to answer the policy question as clearly and simply as possible, to emphasize a few critical and striking numbers, and to do all that in such a way as to highlight those findings that give rise to policy action.*

Because evaluation is conducted in a political context, the significance of findings must be considered carefully. If a policy or program change is warranted, the wording of the conclusions must be crafted so that they are acceptable to stakeholders and decision makers. A stakeholder meeting at this important juncture is essential to allow them to review draft conclusions alongside the supporting data and then to provide advice on wording. That is not to say that stakeholders can influence the research findings in any way, but often their knowledge of the organizational context is critical to the successful framing of them.

Use Sensitivity Analysis

Evaluators can use sensitivity analysis to test tentative conclusions. First, the evaluator should assess the significance of the study's limitations and the lack of generalizability of the findings. Next, the evaluator should consider how the conclusions might change if the team has made various changes to the data, values, assumptions, measurements, sampling, or analysis techniques. This allows the evaluator to ask, "If we had done this, instead of that, what would have happened?" Finally, as the evaluator identifies critical factors, the strength of the conclusion will become evident.

We must also consider the ethical implications of the draft conclusions. Who will be impacted and in what ways? Key stakeholders must help answer these thorny questions by sharing and discussing their varying interpretations of findings. In the final report, the evaluator should briefly mention how stakeholders were involved in crafting the conclusions. In itself, this strengthens conclusion credibility.

Test the Validity of the Conclusions

Typically, the evaluator addresses validity threats during the research process and then revisits them when drawing conclusions. However, validity is not inherent in the selected methods and the evaluator cannot take it for granted. We must base all conclusions on inference relative to the evaluation's purpose, circumstances, and context. Maxwell (2013, pp. 126–129) suggests some strategies for testing their validity:

- Intensive, long-term involvement in the research provides an opportunity to develop and test alternative hypotheses.

- Rich and varied data can counteract incorrect responses and observer bias.

- Both discrepant evidence and negative cases as well as supportive data and positive cases can help to identify flaws and assess plausibility.

- Comparisons in multicase, multisite, or time-series studies can highlight errors, as can a brief literature review on a relevant study topic.

Stakeholders are the final judge of the accuracy of study data and conclusions. Table 11.3, p. 442 provides an example of an administrative survey used to validate a draft final report (Barrington, 2017).

How to Craft Recommendations

As Patton (2008) so astutely comments: "Recommendations … draw readers' attention like bees to a flower's nectar" (p. 502). Well-written recommendations act like a magnet, pulling all the pieces of an evaluation together; done poorly, they are a lightning rod for an attack. We have three suggestions for crafting recommendations.

Avoid Meek Recommendations

Patton (2008, p. 504) suggests that the evaluator be courageous and avoid meek recommendations. Read the two statements below. Which sounds like a stronger recommendation and why?

Report Validation Survey (Using a 5-Point Scale, Consider to What Extent This Draft Report Meets the Following Criteria) The Report...	1 Not at All	2 Very Little	3 Somewhat	4 To a Considerable Extent	5 To a Great Extent
TABLE 11.3 ◆ GENERIC ADMINISTRATOR FEEDBACK SURVEY FOR DRAFT REPORT VALIDATION					
Validity					
• Accurately reflects the issues and concerns related to the goals of this evaluation.					
• Accurately reflects workplace factors that facilitate or inhibit the achievement of program objectives.					
Relevance					
• Is useful to your workplace.					
Utility					
• Is balanced in terms of the multiple perspectives of the staff concerned.					
• Is clear and concise.					
• Accurately describes your site.					
• Has an appropriate tone.					
Value or Worth					
• Relates directly to desired study components					
Write any additional comments about your impressions of the report below:					

Source: Barrington, G. V. (2014). *After data analysis: From report writing to knowledge translation.* Workshop presented at the National Capital Chapter, Canadian Evaluation Society. Ottawa, ON. November 27, 2014. pp. 22–23.

    a. Consider whether current staffing competencies meet program needs and professional standards in light of changing knowledge and skill expectations.

    b. Increase the amount and quality of staff development to meet accreditation standards.

The second option is a stronger recommendation because it specifies what to expect, namely more and better staff development. There also is a clear link to an organizational benchmark, the relevant accreditation standards. This connects the day-to-day work to recognized standards.

Be Politically Astute

Ask yourself critical questions about the relationship of the proposed recommendations to the organizational context (Chelimsky, 1987b; Majchrzak, 1984). Evaluation always occurs in a political context. Therefore, a number of issues must be considered, including the organization's power structure, the parameters and internal functioning of the organization, the consequences that may occur if the recommendations are implemented, and the probability that the recommendations will be adopted at all. See Figure 11.9 for considerations when crafting strong recommendations in the specific organization's context.

FIGURE 11.9 ● ORGANIZATIONAL CONSIDERATIONS WHEN CRAFTING RECOMMENDATIONS

Power Structure

1. Will recommendation have political support?
2. Which stakeholders have similar attitudes?
3. Which stakeholders have an interest in the outcome?
4. Who has final decision?
5. Who wants to influence the decision?
6. Who has time to address the issue?
7. What are the resources from stakeholders and can they mobilize and organize for action?
8. Who has access to decision makers?
9. Can evaluator share information without influence?
10. How many gatekeepers are between decision makers and stakeholders?
11. How interested is the decision maker in the study findings?

Organizational Parameters

1. What is the organizational structure for carrying out the recommendation (hierarchy, autonomy, control)?
2. How will partners be involved and affected?
3. What resources are needed to implement the recommendation (budget, personnel, capital, materials, time)?
4. What mechanism is needed to implement (communications, regulatory measures, professional development requirements, and required behavior change)?

Consequences

1. What are the intended and unintended effects or consequences of the recommendations?
2. How will the effects influence policies and programs?
3. What if the client ignores the recommendation?
4. What are my "if... then..." questions?
5. Are stakeholders involved in this process?

Probability

1. Is the recommendation feasible and acceptable to implement?
2. What is the likelihood, (between 20% and 80%) that this recommendation will be implemented?
3. If the likelihood of implementation is less than 60%, what are some alternative, or more modest, recommendations?
4. Are there incremental changes, half measures, a continuum of change, or changes to existing policies that might evoke less resistance?

Source: Majchrzak, A. (1984). *Methods for policy research.* SAGE Publications; Chelimsky, E. (1987b). What have we learned about the politics of program evaluation? *Evaluation Practice, 8*(1), 5–21.

Work Collaboratively With Stakeholders

Strong and memorable recommendations must be developed with stakeholders in a scheduled meeting that is planned well in advance so that all can attend. During that meeting:

- Review the recommendations for clarity, understandability, practicality, utility, and meaningfulness
- Discuss the costs, benefits, and challenges of implementing the recommendations
- Check language for political correctness and accuracy.

Of course, preparing good recommendations takes time, so enough time must be budgeted from the study outset to allow for the negotiations, communications, and revisions that these changes will entail. Finally, the revised draft recommendations should be circulated to the stakeholders accompanied by a quick survey to confirm the acceptability of the final wording. These editing activities may sound daunting to an already exhausted evaluator who is anxious to get on to the next project, but they are essential if the goal is organizational change.

Next, in our Spotlight on Equity, we invite you to read about working with community partnerships in Los Angeles County.

SPOTLIGHT ON EQUITY

Child360: Working With Community Partnerships in Los Angeles County

Child360 is a Los Angeles County nonprofit organization that supports a future where every child has the educational opportunities to succeed in school and life. The name reflects a 360-degree approach, improving and expanding the vital early learning opportunities young children need, working alongside educators, families, partner organizations, policymakers, and communities. For over a dozen years, Child360 has helped stakeholders deliver support for the whole child and has reached over 1,000 early learning programs.

Evaluators Dr. Donna Escalante and Alejandra Portillo are working on a place-based initiative to create community partnerships that share a common vision for children and families to thrive. Their evaluation team works with four of the 14 Best Start communities of color in the project, specifically those with a history of disenfranchisement and oppression contributing to chronic family stressors such as violence and poverty. The goal of the project is to support community partnerships in their systems change efforts.

Historically, these communities are underfunded and underserved by systems such as education, housing, transportation, and health. The communities include Spanish-speaking immigrants, individuals with low literacy levels, and those who have emotional or cognitive disorders, or are disadvantaged economically. Each partnership consists of 40–50 members and includes parents, community members, community-based organizations, advocacy groups, political representatives, and other key stakeholders. The evaluators based their approach on empowerment evaluation (Fetterman, 2001) to foster community self-determination, sustainability, and popular education (Friere, 1970), to value people's knowledge, experience, and struggles. They believe that these concepts can empower communities of color to challenge the status quo, be change agents in their communities, and take action.

Each Best Start community has determined their priority social issue through community led discussions and decision making processes and has begun developing anchor strategies, short-term outcomes, long-term outcomes, and action plans.

Escalante and Portillo have created evaluation processes that are transparent and foster trust. They use mapping techniques such as bubble maps, data sense-making activities such as Data Cafés or Data Tea Webinars (the online version of data cafés), Data Parties, and small group guided discussions. When planning these activities, they ensure that the tools and activities include the voices of community members. Each planned data collection activity begins by meeting partnership leaders and local organizations to cocreate the content. Staff modify visuals, tools, graphic organizers, and facilitation processes according to the feedback they receive.

This collaboration has made it clear that evaluation concepts tend to be described in abstract language and need to be "scaffolded" or made more accessible by building on prior knowledge and community expertise. For example, they initially used a logic model to represent the long-term outcomes of systems change for the project but quickly realized that the logic model visual did not resonate with community members. Instead, they used a mountain analogy. See Figure 11.10, p. 445.

The Outcomes Mountain

The Outcomes Mountain activity walks community members through developing long-term and short-term outcomes. Using the analogy of a mountain, the activity uses guiding questions, small group work, and a constructivist approach to demystify the creation of outcomes. First, participants "build" a mountain, and at the peak of the mountain, they write a long-term outcome. Then, they use footprints to symbolize the short-term outcomes. This activity

FIGURE 11.10 ⬡ USING AN OUTCOMES MOUNTAIN TO DEVELOP SHORT-TERM AND LONG-TERM OUTCOMES

Source: Child360

takes anywhere from 2 to 4 days to complete. Next, community residents work in small groups, move through a series of questions, and work with a trained small group facilitator to further develop the long-term and short-term outcomes. After this process, the community members vote to prioritize them. Sample questions to guide thinking include:

- In what time frame do we want to accomplish our long-term outcome?

- Whom do we want to impact?

- What systems do we want to change? Why is this important?

- What do we hope to see as a result of our work?

- What will be different if we are successful?

Examples of systems change that the communities are working toward include affordable housing units, childcare for infants and toddlers, and electronic devices and internet access for school-aged children. In the work the evaluators and communities have completed together so far, they have developed long-term outcomes that support these system changes and have identified short-term outcomes that they plan to select by vote. The communities are also drafting a bill of rights to present to elected officials at an upcoming town hall meeting.

This Spotlight on Equity is based on the contributions of Dr. Donna Escalante and Alejandra Portillo.

SUPPORTING USE ONCE THE EVALUATION IS COMPLETED

Finally, we return to the purpose of evaluation, namely, to assess social programs so they can use that information to have a positive effect on social conditions (Rossi et al., 2019, p. 1). You will note the indirect link between assessment and improvement. This may be the reason why evaluation use remains a topic of considerable concern.

As Christie (2007) laments, while "evaluation utilization is arguably the most researched area of evaluation and [has] received substantial attention in the theoretical literature" (p. 8), there is little agreement about how to ensure that it happens. Perhaps the most well-known advocate of use is Patton (2008, p. 37), who has defined utilization-focused evaluation as "evaluation done for and with specific intended primary users for specific, intended uses." In his view, evaluations should be judged "by their utility and actual use." While he offers many valuable suggestions on how to do this, he concedes that targeting an evaluation at intended use only "increases the odds of hitting the target" (p. 536).

Of Patton's three basic questions: What? So what? Now what? (2008, p. 5), it is the "now what" component that offers evaluators the greatest challenge, and perhaps is the reason why this topic is often neglected. At the end of a study, the evaluator and the client often part ways, at least until the next time the client needs an evaluation. Implementing recommendations and making changes are, for the most part, beyond the evaluator's control. Why, then, should we worry about it? The answer is straightforward. Our evaluations will not achieve their ultimate purpose of social betterment unless they influence change based on the evidence we obtained. Therefore, we need to take the "now what" piece very seriously.

It is not by accident that Utility is the first standard in The Program Evaluation Standards (Yarbrough et al., 2011). It is "due to its significance in determining the worth of evaluation process, findings, and products" (Donnelly & Searle, 2017, p. 307). This is why we evaluate in the first place.

In the following sections, we explore evaluation use within the organization, then move to evaluation use beyond the organization, and finally, consider the ultimate purpose of evaluation, namely social betterment.

Evaluation Use Within the Organization

Preskill and Torres (1999, p. 45) describe how learning can occur at each phase of an evaluation, including (1) focusing the inquiry, (2) carrying out the inquiry, and (3) applying learning. Their helpful model (see Figure 11.11, p. 447) outlines these activities.

In the model's inner circle are four activities that occur throughout this process:

1. Dialogue—talking back and forth in deep conversations

2. Reflection—using retrospection and critical assessment to develop insight

FIGURE 11.11 ● EVALUATIVE INQUIRY FRAMEWORK

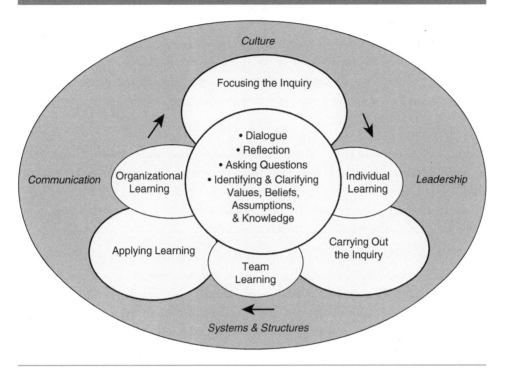

FIGURE 11.11 ● EVALUATIVE INQUIRY FRAMEWORK

Source: Preskill, H., & Torres, R. T. (1999). Building capacity for organizational learning through evaluative inquiry. *Evaluation, 5*(1), 42–60.

3. Asking questions—focusing on the relation between evaluation purpose and findings

4. Values clarification—identifying underlying beliefs, assumptions, and knowledge.

These iterative, incremental, and internal processes occur over time, from the beginning of an evaluation's design to several months or years after the evaluator completes the study (Preskill & Torres, 2000, p. 30). As a result, these processes can be complex, overlapping, and poorly identified.

However, it does appear that evaluation has three expanding rings of impact within an organization.

1. Process use occurs at the individual and team level but can have a lasting effect on attitudes about the value of evaluation.

2. Organizational learning can impact future decisions by management.

3. Evaluation capacity building can lead to the sustainability of an evaluation culture within the organization.

Process Use

Process use is defined by Patton (2008) as follows:

> *Process use occurs when those involved in the evaluation learn from the evaluation process itself or make program changes based on the evaluation process rather than findings—as, for example, when those involved in the evaluation later say, "the impact on our program came not just from the findings but also from going through the thinking process that the evaluation required.* (p. 109)

Patton provides many examples of the cognitive, attitudinal, and behavior changes that can result directly or indirectly from involvement in the evaluation process (p. 156). They include, for example, thinking more evaluatively, integrating evaluation into program activities, clarifying program goals, conceptualizing a program logic model, setting evaluation priorities, and improving outcomes measurement.

Process use is a central feature in many types of evaluation, including collaborative, participatory, empowerment, utilization-focused, and developmental approaches. As King and Stevahn (2013) comment, if the evaluator wants to increase the likelihood of use, "then working closely with specific individuals or groups of people who are interested in the evaluation process and its results is of paramount importance…" (p. 5). Therefore, the evaluator must take the **personal factor** into account.

> *The personal factor is the presence of an identifiable individual or group of people who personally care about the evaluation and the findings it generates. Where such a person or group is present, evaluations are more likely to be used; where the personal factor is absent, there is a correspondingly lower probability of evaluation impact.* (Patton, 2008, p. 69)

The evaluator must model good skills in interpersonal communication, relationship building, and small group management, acting as a guide and mentor by teaching clients and stakeholders the evaluation skills and processes they need so they can continue to use them after the evaluation is over (Preskill & Torres, 1999, p. 55).

Patton (2008, pp. 157–182) offers six ways to encourage process use:

1. Infuse evaluative thinking into the organization's culture

2. Enhance shared understandings about evaluation

3. Make evaluation integral to the program intervention

4. Attend to the potential impact of data collection

5. Increase participants' engagement, sense of ownership, and self-determination

6. Use evaluation as a component of organization and program development.

Since 1996, the Bruner Foundation has encouraged staff to use **evaluative thinking** to serve their clients better. They see it as "a type of reflective practice that incorporates use of systematically collected data to inform organizational decisions and other actions" (Bruner Foundation, 2007, p. 3) The Foundation has designed a tool to capture leader perceptions about evaluative thinking in 15 different areas such as mission, strategic planning, governance, finance, and leadership. They believe evaluative thinking goes beyond programs to the broader organizational context, building a culture where leadership and staff fully integrate systematic questioning, data collection, and analysis into everyday work practices.

Organizational Learning

Organizational Learning is the process by which an organization improves itself over time by gaining experience and using it to create, retain, and transfer knowledge. Once an evaluation is completed, the findings become part of the decision making mix along with other political, logistical, and cost considerations (Preskill & Torres, 1999, p. 51). In the view of Cousins et al. (2014, p. 11), organizational decision makers need to "experience the benefits of evaluation firsthand before they willingly embrace it as leverage for change." As they say, "data use leads to data valuing," and so the more positive experiences leaders have implementing evaluation results, the more likely they will continue to attend to them.

To be a learning organization, certain building blocks need to be in place (Cousins et al., 2014, p. 18) as shown in Figure 11.12.

FIGURE 11.12 ● BUILDING BLOCKS OF A LEARNING ORGANIZATION

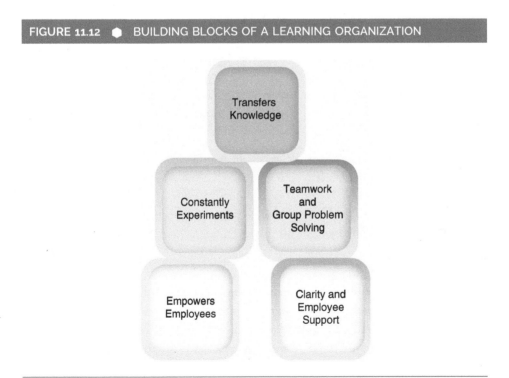

Source: Adapted from Cousins, J. B., Goh, S. C., Elliott, C. J., & Bourgeois, I. (2014). Framing the capacity to do and use evaluation. In J. B. Cousins, & I. Bourgeois (Eds.), *Special issue: Organizational capacity to do and use evaluation. New Directions for Evaluation, 2014*(141), 7–23.

Senge (2006, p. 1), popularized learning organizations in his book *The Fifth Discipline*. He described them as places where "people continually expand their capacity to create the results they truly desire, where new and expansive patterns of thinking are nurtured, where collective aspiration is set free, and where people are continually learning how to learn together."

The World Health Organization (n.d.) reviewed their evaluation function and determined that:

> *All too often evaluation has been an afterthought in planning, viewed as an optional luxury for well-funded programmes, or carried out only upon donor request. Furthermore, the utilization and follow-up of evaluation findings and recommendations, especially in relation to organizational learning, has not been optimal.* (p. 1)

The organization strengthened their evaluation function by making it a separate unit within the Office of the Director-General. Through consultation with stakeholders, they determined ways to strengthen evaluation and organizational learning:

1. Build a culture of evaluation by determining what it means to the organization and how it is being achieved

2. Establish an enabling environment in which policies, resources, organizational arrangements, and coordination/oversight support evaluation activities

3. Identify the types and scope of evaluation processes including quality assurance and outsourcing as appropriate

4. Facilitate organizational learning to inform strategic planning and policy decisions

5. Create interrelationships between evaluation and other types of assessment: internal ones such as audits, program budget assessments, and regular progress reports; organization–wide assessments; and external donor-initiated assessments

6. Communicate evaluation work and findings to both internal and external stakeholders and audiences.

An organizational learning framework was developed, and further avenues of organizational learning were defined (see Figure 11.13, p. 451).

Evaluation Capacity Building

Evaluation capacity building (ECB), a third form of learning in organizations, incorporates and builds on both process use and organizational learning but zeros in on the relationship between the evaluator and the organization in which the study occurs. As King and Stevahn (2013, p. 35) explain, ECB "examines the evaluator's commitment to building the continuing capacity of organization members to conduct evaluation studies within their organization," thus creating evaluation sustainability and an evaluation culture.

Cousins and Bourgeois (as reported in Cousins et al., 2014, p. 19) conducted case study research in eight organizations, including government, the voluntary sector, and

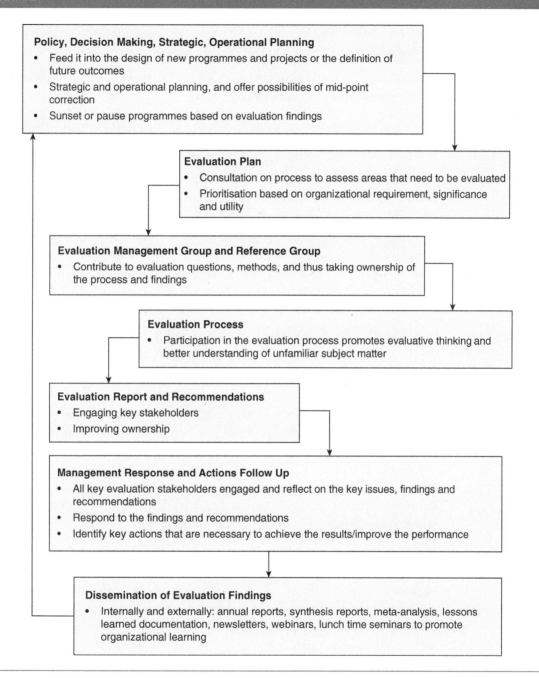

FIGURE 11.13 ● WORLD HEALTH ORGANIZATION'S FURTHER AVENUES FOR ORGANIZATIONAL LEARNING

Policy, Decision Making, Strategic, Operational Planning
- Feed it into the design of new programmes and projects or the definition of future outcomes
- Strategic and operational planning, and offer possibilities of mid-point correction
- Sunset or pause programmes based on evaluation findings

Evaluation Plan
- Consultation on process to assess areas that need to be evaluated
- Prioritisation based on organizational requirement, significance and utility

Evaluation Management Group and Reference Group
- Contribute to evaluation questions, methods, and thus taking ownership of the process and findings

Evaluation Process
- Participation in the evaluation process promotes evaluative thinking and better understanding of unfamiliar subject matter

Evaluation Report and Recommendations
- Engaging key stakeholders
- Improving ownership

Management Response and Actions Follow Up
- All key evaluation stakeholders engaged and reflect on the key issues, findings and recommendations
- Respond to the findings and recommendations
- Identify key actions that are necessary to achieve the results/improve the performance

Dissemination of Evaluation Findings
- Internally and externally: annual reports, synthesis reports, meta-analysis, lessons learned documentation, newsletters, webinars, lunch time seminars to promote organizational learning

Source: World Health Organization. (n.d.). *A framework for strengthening evaluation and organizational learning in WHO.* https://www.who.int/about/who_reform/documents/framework-strengthening-evaluation-organizational-learning.pdf

educational institutions, to understand their capacity to do and use evaluation. Their findings revealed that the organizations varied in the amount of internal support they had to conduct evaluation, the degree to which leadership and staff use evaluation findings for decision making, and how seriously senior management accepted the evidence.

The organizations with higher levels of ECB shared some essential characteristics (Cousins & Bourgeios, 2014, pp. 108–111):

- An administrative commitment to evaluation and leaders who promotes and models the use of evidence for decision making

- An organizational culture of learning that provides opportunities to learn from both data and evaluation processes

- Staff expertise in research disciplines, an inquiry-oriented mindset, and a belief in the power of evidence.

These high-functioning organizations used several strategies to enhance their evaluation function, such as well-established evaluation units and dedicated staff, resources to raise the profile of evaluation, external stakeholder involvement such as the use of advisory committees, and training opportunities on evaluation topics for staff. When organizations are at an early stage of ECB development, they can benefit from the support of external agencies, consulting firms, or university research programs when conducting evaluation activities.

Evaluation Use Beyond the Organization

What happens after the evaluation is completed is beyond the evaluator's control. However, the topic continues to fascinate us. We want to know:

how knowledge, in the form of ideas, innovation, or skills, moves in some direction among a group of stakeholders as they are situated within their specified contexts. (Donnelly & Searle, 2017, pp. 306–307)

One of the issues that hinders this process is that the terminology has splintered, and sometimes shattered, among the various disciplines that explore it, thus impeding effective interprofessional communication and theory development.

In the social sciences, "use" is known as knowledge mobilization (KMb), which describes researchers' attempts to maximize their work's cultural, intellectual, social, and economic impacts (Donnelly & Searle, 2017). In other fields, the term "use" is referred to by scholars as implementation science, a relatively new field that facilitates the uptake of evidence-based practice, such as in health care. Another term, knowledge translation (KT), has a long history in health care.

However, scholars have replaced KT with many other terms, such as knowledge utilization, knowledge diffusion, knowledge dissemination, knowledge exchange, knowledge brokering, knowledge transfer, and research utilization. According to McKibbon et al. (2010), it is a veritable Tower of Babel. They analyzed over 2,500 articles indexed in Medline and identified 100 individual terms related to KT. Not surprisingly, they recommended building a standardized vocabulary to streamline communication about this critical topic.

Not only is conceptual clarity lacking, but as Wensing and Grol (2019) explain:

> *A fundamental challenge is to overcome the misconceptions, silo-thinking, and self-interests among stakeholders. These stakeholders include politicians and managers who prefer to act on the basis of conviction rather than research evidence, healthcare providers who deny that research findings apply to them, and researchers who prefer to focus on concepts and approaches that fit their particular academic background.* (p. 5)

High-quality evidence is not the norm and policymakers rarely adopt it. Moreover, among the over 100 identified barriers to change, decision makers face a lack of skills in knowledge management and infrastructure; in other words, they are daunted by "the sheer volume of research evidence produced, access to research evidence, time to read, and the skills to appraise, understand and apply research evidence" (Straus et al., 2009, p. 166).

In fact, after several decades of discussion, we are still far from understanding how practice can be improved "rapidly, comprehensively, at large scale, and sustainably" (Wensing & Grol, 2019, p. 2).

Knowledge Into Action

Evaluators need to be aware of "methods for closing the gaps from knowledge to practice" or getting knowledge used by stakeholders (Straus et al., 2009, p. 3). One area where KT has become prominent is in the health disciplines which can serve as a potential model for the social sciences. In healthcare, KT is essential there because failure to use research evidence to make informed decisions, quite simply, costs lives. As an example, Morgan et al. (2020) state that "Oncology is an important and fast-growing field for KT. In the oncologic world, practitioners know the translation of cancer research as bench-to-bedside. If doctors apply lessons from high-quality research to patients, their lives could be improved tremendously by using all the output from well-designed research projects and applying that to patients using a personalized approach" (p. 6).

Health research consumes billions of dollars each year. Ciliska (2012) suggests that the impact is muted:

- To create a policy from research findings, it takes about 15 years (Antman et al., 2001).
- Only 40% of those findings become part of practice (Antman et al., 2001).
- Recommended care is only received by up to 50% of people (Schuster et al., 1998).

Needless to say, program recipients bear the brunt of these health program failures. They continue to suffer from incomplete or inadequate services or lack of attention to their social, cultural, and emotional needs. Evaluators have much to learn from these healthcare lessons.

A useful model developed by Graham and Tetroe (2010) is the **knowledge-to-action framework**. It depicts the process of translating knowledge to action as a complex and iterative set of interactions between researchers and knowledge users (see Figure 11.14).

FIGURE 11.14 ● THE KNOWLEDGE-TO-ACTION FRAMEWORK

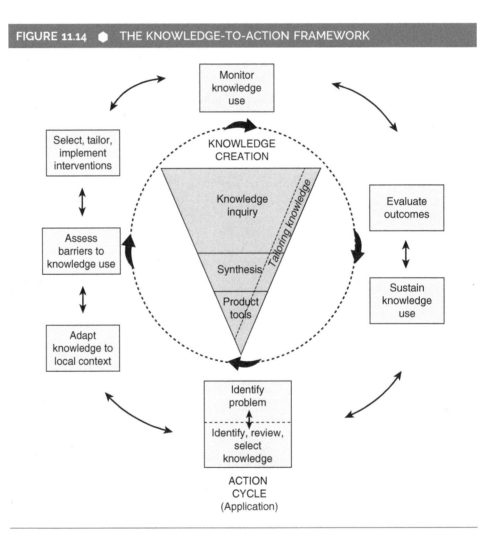

Source: Graham, I. D., & Tetroe, J. (2010). The knowledge to action framework. In J. Rycroft-Malone, & T. Bucknall (Eds.), *Models and frameworks for implementing evidence-based practice: Linking evidence to action* (pp. 207–214). John Wiley & Sons.

In an evaluation context, there are several ways that evaluators can work with stakeholders in their journey to translate knowledge into action including knowledge creation, dissemination, and application. In this way they can exert influence in multidirectional ways so that social betterment is the ultimate result. In this model, the funnel symbolizes knowledge creation. The cycle represents the activities and processes related to applying that knowledge (Graham & Tetroe, 2010). While knowledge is empirically derived (i.e., research-based), it can also encompass other forms of knowing, such as experiential or cultural knowledge.

Knowledge Creation

Knowledge creation is the evaluator's job. This book has already explored the parameters of an evaluation study at length. First, we collect data and interpret its meaning. Then, as our work progresses through the funnel, our findings become more distilled until we, at last, arrive at our conclusions and recommendations, the products of our data synthesis process—the knowledge we have created through our efforts. Many evaluators stop here, figuring that their job is concluded and now it is up to the client to do something about the findings. Others, who are more aware, develop tools or products that can present findings in clear, concise, and user friendly formats to facilitate the uptake of that knowledge.

Knowledge Dissemination

Barwick (2008) explored different ways to dissemination research findings. Based on a meta-review of systematic reviews, she explored the uptake effectiveness of different KT communications tools. Some of the more effective methods included:

- Interactive small groups
- Educational outreach
- Multi-professional collaboration
- Mass media campaigns
- Reminder systems
- Financial interventions and incentives
- Combined interventions.

KT tools with mixed effects included:

- Conferences and courses
- Use of opinion leaders and champions
- Educational strategies and materials
- Performance feedback.

There was limited effectiveness when total quality management and continuous quality improvement methods were used for KT.

Carpenter et al. (2005) developed a Dissemination Planning Tool to assist grant recipients from the Agency for Healthcare Research and Quality (AHRQ) Patient Safety to disseminate their research results beyond the traditional peer-reviewed publications and conference presentations. They reviewed literature from health care, sociology, organizational development, psychology, and the social sciences, to get a sense of dissemination theory and practices. The tool moves the researcher from being research-centric (or evaluation-centric in our case) to user-centric, considering the needs of the end user. It asks six questions:

1. What is going to be disseminated?
   Researchers determine specifically what they want to disseminate, creating a value statement for the user. In traditional marketing terms, this is the "product" that the research wishes to share. They also consider ways to bundle or package their research.

2. Who will apply it in practice?
   Understanding the behavior of end users and the systems they work in will help the researcher clarify end users' needs and values and why the research is important to them. Barriers to use are also considered.

3. How can you reach end users?
   Dissemination is not linear but is fluid like a storytelling process. The informal spread of innovation through networking, between users, or through existing networks is powerful. Researchers are prompted to identify organizations which can influence intended users through their credibility, expertise, and networking capacity. An important strategy is to align the information with organizational goals and values.

4. How can the research outcomes be conveyed?
   Multiple strategies and frequency of exposure are important considerations. The complexity of the information must be matched to the right medium. Channels such as websites and newsletters are potential connectors.

5. How do you determine what worked?
   Continuous feedback helps the researchers judge the effectiveness of their messages and communications methods. Interim measures of success such as numbers of users requesting additional information can help the research adjust the dissemination plan. Cost-effectiveness can also be considered.

6. Where do you start?
   Dissemination plans often fail because they can be an unrealistic shopping list of every possible use or user with no realistic time, resource, or accountability requirements. The plan helps the researcher outline immediate and long-term actions along with timeframes, costs, and those responsible.

Once the dissemination plan is prepared, a checklist such as the one presented in Box 11.2, p. 457 could provide useful feedback on its potential effectiveness.

BOX 11.2 ● CHECK YOUR DISSEMINATION PLAN

1. After preparing your dissemination plan, complete the following statements.

    a. My research finding or product is: *(Description).*

    b. It can be used to: *(Value statement of advantages over current practice).*

    c. My primary end users are: *(List those in a position to use the information).*

    d. I plan to involve users in my dissemination efforts by: *(Strategies to involve users).*

    e. I can use the following individuals, organizations, and networks to help: *(List those who influence intended users).*

    f. The ways that I will communicate the results include: *(Communication mechanisms).*

    g. Potential obstacles that I may face in disseminating my research include: *(List potential difficulties).*

    h. I can mitigate these obstacles by: *(Plans to overcome the difficulties).*

    i. I plan to evaluate the dissemination plan by: *(Indicators to be used; plans for involving end users and partners).*

2. I plan to encourage feedback from end users and dissemination partners by *(date)* and provide feedback to them by *(date)* *(List strategies to provide and obtain feedback).*

Source: Adapted from Agency for Healthcare Research and Quality. (2010). *Health care systems for tracking colorectal cancer screening tests* (HHSA290200600014 Task Number 290-06-0014-1). U.S. Government Printing Office. https://www.ahrq.gov/research/findings/final-reports/crcscreeningrpt/index.html

Knowledge Application

In the Graham and Tetroe (2010) model, the action cycle consists of dynamic, iterative, and interactive activities that reflect how the knowledge will be used. The phases described by Graham and Tetroe (2006, pp. 20–21) are visualized in Figure 11.15, p. 458.

Evaluators have conducted several reviews of the literature on evaluation use. For example, Cousins and Leithwood (1986) reviewed 65 empirical studies in education, mental health, and social services. They found that evaluation use seemed to be most strongly evident when the evaluations matched the sophistication of users, when recommendations were meaningful and relevant to them, when findings were consistent with users' beliefs and expectations, when they were involved in the evaluation process and were already committed to the benefits of evaluation, and when findings did not conflict with information from other sources (p. 360). Johnson et al. (2009) updated the study and found that "engagement, interaction, and communication between evaluation clients and evaluators is critical to the meaningful use of evaluations" (p. 389).

FIGURE 11.15 ● STEPS TO KNOWLEDGE USE

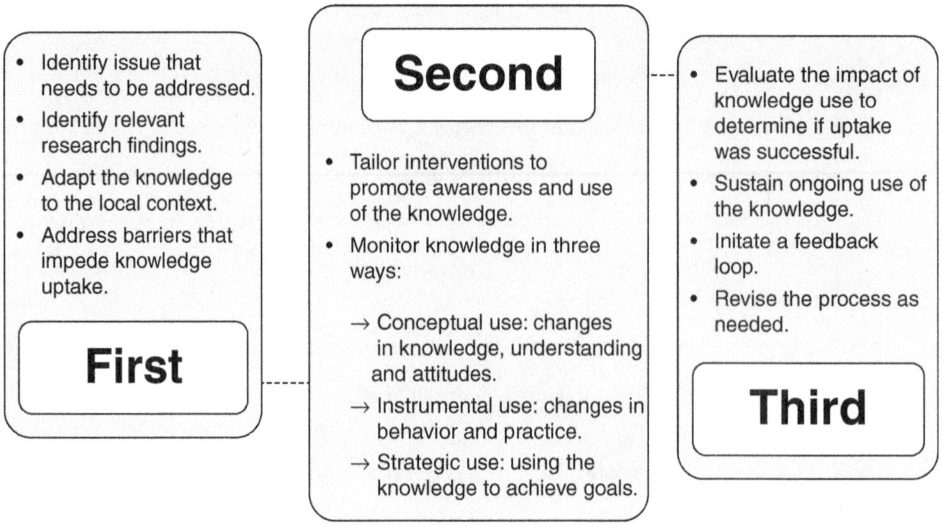

First

- Identify issue that needs to be addressed.
- Identify relevant research findings.
- Adapt the knowledge to the local context.
- Address barriers that impede knowledge uptake.

Second

- Tailor interventions to promote awareness and use of the knowledge.
- Monitor knowledge in three ways:
  → Conceptual use: changes in knowledge, understanding and attitudes.
  → Instrumental use: changes in behavior and practice.
  → Strategic use: using the knowledge to achieve goals.

Third

- Evaluate the impact of knowledge use to determine if uptake was successful.
- Sustain ongoing use of the knowledge.
- Initate a feedback loop.
- Revise the process as needed.

Source: Adapted from Graham, I. D., & Tetroe, J. (2010). The knowledge to action framework. In J. Rycroft-Malone, & T. Bucknall (Eds.), *Models and frameworks for implementing evidence-based practice: Linking evidence to action* (pp. 207–214). John Wiley & Sons.

Evaluation Influence. Kirkhart (2000) suggests that in order to answer the question, "How and to what extent does evaluation shape, affect, support, and change persons and systems?" (p. 7), we need to use a broader construct than the term "use." Instead, she recommends looking at **evaluation influence**, defined as "the capacity or power of persons or things to produce effects on others by intangible or indirect means" (p. 7). For Kirkhart, looking at use resulted in finding effects that were unidirectional, episodic, intentional, and instrumental—or in other words, finding the outcomes that evaluators were expecting. Instead, by looking at influence, she found indirect effects of an evaluation that were multidirectional, incremental, unintentional, and noninstrumental. She combined three dimensions of influence into an integrated model, which she felt was a more expansive canvas against which to map evaluation influence (p. 18). The dimensions include:

- Sources of influence—process use and evaluation results

- Intention—intended and unintended influences

- Time—the periods in which evaluation influence emerges, exists, or continues (i.e., immediate, end-of-cycle, and long-term).

As Mark and Henry (2004) comment, "evaluation influence explicitly includes both changes that take place at the location and general time frame of the evaluation and changes that take place elsewhere and later" (p. 40). They found that most evaluation theorists had ignored how evaluation influenced attitudes, motivations, and action (p. 45). Looking at influence pathways, they noted that there are complex and sometimes circuitous linkages between individual, interpersonal, and collective or organizational actions. They commented, "the more complete and coherent story a pathway provides about how influence unfold[s], the claim that 'evaluation influence has occurred' becomes more credible" (p. 49). At the end of the pathways, they suggest, the search for influence should focus on the outcomes of evaluation, "such as changes in attitudes about service delivery practices or changes in policy" (p. 40), leading eventually toward social betterment, the outcome by which evaluators, stakeholders, and society should judge an evaluation.

Social Betterment. As we stated in Chapter 1, Henry (2000, pp. 86–87) maintains that the goal of evaluation is not use but is, in fact, **social betterment**, meaning "improved social conditions, the reduction of social problems, or the alleviation of human distress." He comments, the goal of evaluation is "to promote social betterment, albeit indirectly, by providing information to those charged with setting social policies, to those charged with carrying them out, to stakeholders, including service consumers, and to citizens." Whether social conditions improve due to evaluation depends on the quality of the information, how clients use the information, and possibly a little luck. Henry suggests that social betterment requires three functions:

- Determine what constitutes "social betterment" in the specific context
- Choose a course of action that leads to the common good
- Adapt the chosen course to specific circumstances.

However, resources to conduct an evaluation are limited. It is often more expedient to focus on adapting the preconceived course of action than moving into the broader policy space where change may be required. If an evaluation is to respond to our defining purpose (i.e., to improve social conditions), our data collection and reporting efforts must be motivated by the possibility of making things better. Henry (2000) posits that evaluation can contribute to

the public understanding of an issue and influence the competition for framing the relevant issues of the day in very important ways by answering such questions as, Is the program working? How/ For whom? In what circumstances? Providing a basis of facts that relate to valued effects of outcomes for public deliberations is no mean feat. (p. 94)

Evaluators can enhance their relevance by supporting unbiased representation and the complete disclosure of information, including use of the media and the Internet; by debunking bad ideas or false science; by raising the salience of issues; by providing complete information to influence the judgment of social policies; and by participating in policy discourse (Henry, 2000, pp. 94–95). In our efforts to be impartial, we may have lost our voice, and yet now, more than ever before, as evaluators, we need to step up and be heard.

Now it's time for our Expert Corner with data visualization experts, Dr. Stephanie Evergreen and Ann-Murray Brown.

EXPERT CORNER

A Conversation With Dr. Stephanie Evergreen and Ann-Murray Brown

Dr. Stephanie Evergreen is an internationally recognized speaker, designer, trainer, and researcher who helps people communicate their work through more effective graphs, slides, and reports. She applies design techniques that make data more aesthetically appealing and support the ability of audiences to comprehend and remember the findings. She has trained researchers and evaluators from Fortune 500 clients to mission-based agencies like the Alaska Native Tribal Health Consortium. She writes a popular blog on data presentation and has written two bestsellers on high-impact design.

Ann Murray-Brown was born in Jamaica, studied in South Korea, and lives in the Netherlands. With degrees in international development and cooperation and nearly two decades of experience as a Monitoring and Evaluation (M&E) expert, she has been involved in evaluations in over 20 countries. She specializes in gender equality, diversity, child protection, social inclusion, and governance. She offers training in evaluation capacity building, produces videos and resources, and helps organizations turn "dry" data into powerful and compelling human stories.

1. *Recent civil unrest has heightened our awareness about the institutionalization of racism and how the messages we send can perpetuate discrimination and inequality. How can data visualization be used to break down racial divisions, intolerance, and discrimination?*

Ann: Data visualization is a powerful tool for social commentary. It can be used to facilitate discourse on injustice, racism, inequality and the spectrum of human rights abuses. How we visualize and present data can be a tool for social change by presenting the facts in an aesthetically appealing way to educate and inform.

The first step to responsibly visualize data is to be aware of the ways data can be manipulated and presented to reinforce certain narratives that support a status quo. At all times be mindful to disaggregate data to uncover trends and patterns to highlight how certain sub-sections of the population may be impacted differently. Use of color, images, and the like are also considerations to ensure the visualizations do not reinforce negative stereotypes.

Stephanie: In addition to Ann's comments, I have found that certain chart types highlight concepts like disparity and inequality better than others. But beyond just the chart types we choose or the colors we apply, data visualization makes people look, think, and remember. While that works with just about any topic, when it comes to social justice, we have a duty to bring well-designed data visualizations to the forefront. We have seen research showing how graphs can cause behavior change, even among those who are oppositional. I'd add that social justice benefits from both qualitative and quantitative data visualization.

(Continued)

(Continued)

2. *How can our readers, who may just be starting to explore the field of evaluation, actively develop their ability to use visual elements in their content?*

Ann: Read. Read. Read. There are several great books that cover the steps to create data visualizations, graphs psychology, how to select charts and storytelling techniques in data analysis.

Stephanie: Start by telling people your point, the insight that you see in the data. Everything will stem from the takeaway ideas that you discover during your data analysis and exploration. Then, don't use the default charts provided in any software program. Learn how to work from them to create something that tells your story. Because the software doesn't know your insights.

I have found that people who are really new to data visualization tend to give too much credit to the graphing software. Ask Excel to insert a chart and often it will throw a bar chart at you—even if you know that your story is about the gap between two of your respondent groups and a slope graph would be a better choice.

Ann: At the end of the day, data visualization software is just a tool, a means to communicate your message. Your starting point should always be the story that you wish to tell. Be clear on what you wish for your audience to know and then choose the appropriate medium to bring that narrative alive. As human beings we had an oral tradition long before we could write. As such, we may not all be tech savvy, but we are all storytellers.

Key Terms

1:3:25 model 435

Communication 424

Communications 424

Data visualization 430

Evaluation capacity building 450

Evaluation influence 458

Evaluative thinking 449

Knowledge-to-action framework 454

Organizational learning 449

Personal factor 448

Process use 448

Social betterment 459

The Main Ideas

1. Three critical processes span the trajectory of the evaluation study: (a) communicating during the evaluation, (b) reporting at the end of the evaluation, and (c) and supporting evaluation use once the evaluation is completed.

2. Evaluation conversations, occurring during the evaluation, allow the evaluator to determine what the client wants them to do, connect the client and evaluator during the evaluation, and provide a space for monitoring how the evaluation is proceeding. Other notable skills during evaluation include interactive forms of communication, managing conflict, informal communication tools, and data visualization.

3. Reporting at the end of the evaluation considers the final report, crafting conclusions, and how to craft recommendations.

4. There are two main evaluation report styles, including the classic report (similar to a research report) and the action-oriented report. This newer format includes a one-page summary of the main ideas, three pages for an executive summary, and a more detailed 25-page report. Additional material, tools, and data can be provided in an appendix.

5. Crafting conclusions well depends on the simplicity of the format, presentation of dually significant findings, and prediction of use of results.

6. Evaluators should avoid meek recommendations, be politically astute considering the context of the evaluation, and work collaboratively with stakeholders in the development of the recommendations.

7. Learning can occur within the organization at each phase in an evaluation and may include a) process use by learning more about evaluation and its purpose; b) organizational learning by implementing evaluation findings and building a culture of evaluation; and c) evaluation capacity building by building the ability of the organization to conduct further evaluation and to think evaluatively (Preskill & Torres, 2000, p. 30).

8. Knowledge creation can lead to an action cycle that includes knowledge dissemination and knowledge application, either directly or indirectly. Ultimately, the goal of evaluation is social betterment.

Critical Thinking Questions

1. King and Stevahn (2013) describe "substantive conversations" (p. 67) as they occur along the path of an evaluation. What typed of conversations and questions are likely to occur at different phases of the evaluation?

2. What should evaluators consider when deciding how to report their findings? How does the report structure increase the client's understanding of the evaluation?

3. How can an evaluator craft more effective conclusions?

4. What are the hallmarks of a good evaluation recommendation?

5. What are the characteristics of organizations that learn?

Student Challenge

1. **Quality of an Evaluation Report**. There are many ways you can write an evaluation report, but some key elements are always needed. Approach the challenge as if you were a stakeholder needing the information to make decisions about a program. This challenge asks you to do the following:

   a. Locate an evaluation report of interest.

   b. Read the report first without reviewing the Report Rubric provided in this section.

   c. Review the Report Rubric noting the recommended details of a good report.

   d. Score the report you read, identifying elements that were well presented, needed more or different information, or were missing.

   Did using the Report Rubric make it easier to determine where the report could be improved?

TABLE 11.4 ● FINAL REPORT RUBRIC

Score Each Statement With a: 0 for Not Present or a 1 for Present

Attribute	Score	Rationale/ Evidence/ Comments
Evaluation Issues		
a. Identifies program issues to be addressed by the evaluation.		
b. Identifies evaluation objectives.		
Methods		
a. Methods clearly explained.		
b. Clear evaluation questions asked.		
c. Limitations provided.		
d. Data sources presented.		
e. Quantitative, qualitative or mixed methods strategies used appropriately.		
Findings		
a. Presents findings that relate to the identified evaluation issues.		
b. Data were systematically collected and analyzed.		
c. Findings are supported by the data.		
d. Negative data are reported and discussed.		

(Continued)

Table 11.4 *(Continued)*

Score Each Statement With a: 0 for Not Present or a 1 for Present		
Attribute	Score	Rationale/ Evidence/ Comments
Conclusions		
a. Conclusions address the evaluation issues.		
b. Conclusions are based on the evaluation findings.		
c. The report considers the future implications of the findings.		
Recommendations		
a. Recommendations are evidenced-based and linked to the evaluation findings.		
b. Recommendations are realistic, practical and include timelines.		
Quality		
a. Adheres to evaluation standards: utility, feasibility, propriety, accuracy, accountability as appropriate.		
b. Considers organizational readiness issues.		
c. Demonstrates evaluator competence and appropriateness for this evaluation.		
d. Considers the needs of the primary end users.		
e. Uses culturally responsive methods.		
f. Includes stakeholders who have an interest, whether or not they have power.		
g. Includes stories and narratives.		
h. Includes quantitative data.		
i. Includes a logic model with relationships among resources needed, activities planned, evidence of implementation, and the changes or results anticipated.		
j. Asks questions at the appropriate level of abstraction.		
k. Is visually pleasing and informative.		
l. Data is visualized in accessible ways.		
m. Report is brief.		
n. Report is clearly written & well edited.		
o. Communication of results shows dignity/worth to stakeholders.		
p. References are provided.		

Source: Adapted from Centre of Excellence for Evaluation. (2004). *Guide for the review of evaluation reports.* Treasury Board of Canada. https://www.tbs-sct.gc.ca/cee/tools-outils/grer-gere-eng.pdf

Additional Readings and Resources

1. Berinato, S. (2016). *Good charts: The HBR guide to making smarter, more persuasive data visualizations.* Boston, MA: Harvard Business School Publishing Corporation.
Berinato focuses on visual perception, neuroscience, and visualization science in his book. He helps you review your current charts and images and gives recommendations on making them more effective visualizations.

2. Bruner Foundation. (2015). *Evaluative thinking assessment tool.* http://www.evaluativethinking.org/evalthink.html
This tool in an Excel spreadsheet is designed to delineate the various areas where evaluative thinking can take place within an organization. Each organizational capacity area has numerous statements, which include specific evaluation activities or documents. These statements are scored by the individual or team in the organization as either not existing (scored a 0) or existing (scored a 1). A summary score report is provided on the last table after the assessment is completed.

3. Davidson, E. J. (2007). Editorial: Unlearning some of our social scientist habits. *Journal of MultiDisciplinary Evaluation*, 4(8), iii–vi. https://journals.sfu.ca/jmde/index.php/jmde_1/article/view/68/71
This editorial, written by E. Jane Davidson, provides a push back to the standard ways of report writing. Her criticisms include (a) not using theories evaluatively, (b) too quick to focus on measurement, (c) providing the client the results separated by data type, and (d) using the Master's thesis outline.

4. D'Ignazio, C., & Klein, L. (2020). Seven intersectional feminist principles for equitable and actionable COVID-19 data. *Big Data & Society, 7*(2), 1–6. https://doi.org/10.1177/2053951720942544
D'Ignazio and Klein (2020) offer seven principles for guiding the data collected and disseminated during the COVID-19 pandemic. These principles assist us in "identifying existing power imbalances with respect to the impact of the novel coronavirus and its response, and for beginning the work of change" (p. 1). The principles are to examine power, challenge power, elevate emotion and embodiment, rethink binaries and hierarchies, embrace pluralism, consider context, and make labor visible.

5. Evergreen, S., & Emery, A. K. (2016). *Data visualization checklist.* https://stephanieevergreen.com/wp-content/uploads/2016/10/DataVizChecklist_May2016.pdf
Evergreen and Emery created a checklist to guide the creation of high-impact data visualizations. The Checklist is in the form of statements that act as guidelines. The user scores each guideline on a scale of 2, 1, 0, or not applicable. The higher the score, the better the document conforms to best practices.

6. Gawande, A. (2011). *The checklist manifesto: How to get things right.* Henry Holt and Company.
Gawande provides a simple tool, the checklist, and discusses how it can elevate your work and make it more efficient and effective.

7. Montrosse-Moorhead, B., & Griffith, J. (2017). Toward the development of reporting standards for evaluations. *American Journal of Evaluation, 38*(4), 577–602.
The authors make a case for the establishment of Evaluation Reporting guidelines. In addition, they set forth a series of recommendations about the contents of an evaluation report to ensure rigor in the evaluation field.

8. Office on Smoking and Health and the Division of Nutrition, Physical Activity and Obesity and the ICF International. (2013). *Setting the course for effective program evaluation.* Centers for Disease Control and Prevention. https://www.cdc.gov/eval/materials/developing-an-effective-evaluation-report_tag508.pdf
The authors of this workbook provide ample detail on the elements of an evaluation report. They define a report, why you want one, and the steps for writing one.

EVALUATION CONTEXT AND THE EVALUATOR'S NEW STANCE

LEARNING OBJECTIVES

1. List the dimensions of context that may be encountered in any evaluation.

2. Explain the statement, "evaluators have more power than they realize."

3. Describe why a microenvironment viewpoint can limit evaluation effectiveness.

4. Explain why big picture thinking is needed in the evaluation of systems change.

5. Identify the UN Sustainable Development Goal most relevant to your field of study.

6. Describe reasons why evaluators' interpretation of program "truth" may be compromised when considering racial equity.

7. Explain why Indigenous peoples may not trust the research process.

8. Explain why understanding cultural values among Hispanic communities is important for evaluation work.

9. Provide reasons why organizations may fail to use evaluation findings.

10. Identify several actions in the evaluator's new stance that can be implemented immediately.

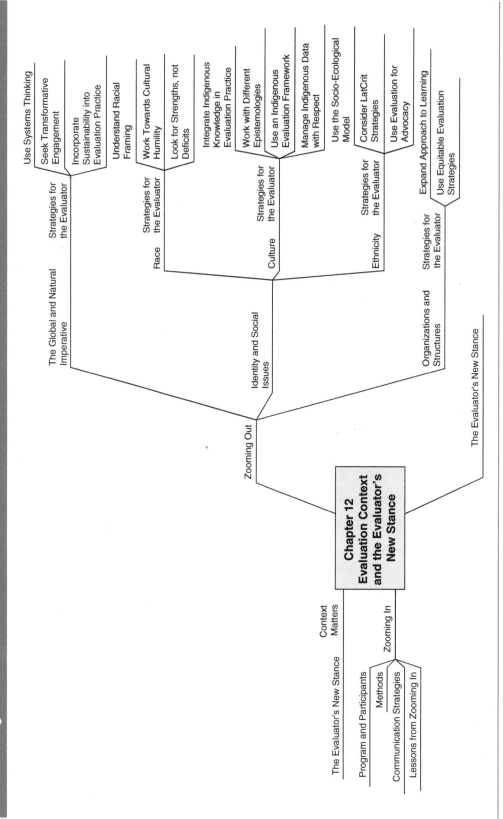

THE CREATION OF TURTLE ISLAND, AN OJIBWE LEGEND

Many Ojibwe refer to themselves as Anishinaabe, which means original man. Their legend tells that long ago, the Anishinaabe gave up their peaceful ways and began to fight against each other, brother against brother, sister against sister. Discord, jealousy, and bitterness grew. Seeing that they no longer respected each other or all living things, Creator decided to cleanse the Earth by flooding it. The Anishinaabe people and most of the animals drowned. The only survivor was Nanabush and a few animals that could swim or fly. Nanabush floated on a log in the water, and he allowed the animals to take turns resting with him.

Source: Katalinks/Dreamstime

Then he had an amazing idea. "I'm going to dive to the bottom of the water and grab a handful of earth. We can use it to make a new land on which to live." He dived into the water and disappeared for a long time. The animals became worried and thought he had drowned. Finally, he surfaced, gasping for air. "It's too deep," he said. "I can't reach the bottom."

Then Loon offered to try. "I'm used to swimming and I dive deeply to catch my food." He was gone a long time and came back weak and out of breath. "I couldn't make it," he said. "I don't think there is a bottom."

After that, many more animals tried to reach the bottom, but no one succeeded. Finally, when it seemed like their plan had failed, a soft voice said, "I can do it." Everyone looked around to see who had spoken. It was Muskrat. The larger animals laughed and mocked him because he was small and did not know how to dive. But Muskrat was undeterred. He took a deep breath, dove into the water, and disappeared. He stayed down for the longest time but eventually did manage to reach the bottom. He was exhausted and his lungs were burning, so he grabbed some earth in his paw and swam back to the top using all his strength. The other animals had nearly given up when at last, they saw him. They rushed to help him, but sadly he was already dead. They sang a song of mourning and praise as the muskrat's spirit passed into the spirit world. Suddenly Nanabush noticed that Muskrat's paw was still tightly clenched, holding a small ball of earth. The animals cheered. Muskrat had sacrificed his life so that life on Earth could begin again.

Then Turtle said, "If Muskrat was willing to give up his life, then I can do something too. Use my shell to bear the weight of this new world." So Nanbush and the animals put the earth that the Muskrat had brought on Turtle's back, and he began to carry it for them. The winds blew from four directions and the tiny ball of earth began to grow. The island grew heavier and heavier, but Turtle never wavered. Finally, the winds stopped, and the water became still. A vast island had appeared. It became known as Turtle Island and is what we now call North America.

INTRODUCTION

We were halfway through writing this book when the COVID-19 pandemic struck. Over two years later, as the virus persists, we begin to see a new normal and realize that we are not going back to "the way we were." We have learned so much and are intensely aware of new realities—how fragile our world, how tenuous our health, how easily our systems are shattered, and how important the context in which we find ourselves.

This chapter has always been about the context of evaluation but now we look at it in a new way. We have broadened our reach, acknowledged our unique power, and clarified the role that evaluators can play. Using our telephoto lens, we zoom in to look at local or micro systems and zoom out to see the global or macro systems that impact our work. Each system is discussed in terms of where we are, the possibilities and problems that lie ahead, and some strategies for a way forward. We provide a model to illustrate a new stance for evaluators and a checklist is presented.

You will enjoy the resources in this chapter including the Spotlight on Equity, which presents the work of the Global Data and Insights team at the Wikimedia Foundation, our expert Dr. Nicole Bowman/Waapalaneexkweew (Lunaape/Mohican), Key Terms, Main Ideas, Critical Thinking Questions, Student Challenges, and Additional Readings and Resources.

Source: Christoph Vorlet/https://vorlet.com/about

CONTEXT MATTERS

"**Context** matters," Debra Rog declared unequivocally at her presidential address to AEA in 2009. It shapes "the questions we address, the designs and methods we choose, the ways in which we report our findings," (Rog, 2012, p. 25) and affects the implementation and outcomes of the programs we study. Context matters now more than ever. Greene (2005b) states, "All evaluators also agree that good evaluation is responsive to, respectful of, and tailored to its contexts in important ways." (p. 84)

In broad terms, context refers to the setting in which the program is situated, where a wide variety of dimensions intersect. In Figure 12.1, p. 471, we exhibit a range of context descriptors based on a variety of sources (Coldwell, 2019; Greene, 2005; Patton, 2020; Rog, 2012; Thomas & Parsons, 2017).

FIGURE 12.1 ● CHECKLIST FOR DIMENSIONS OF CONTEXT

- ❑ Environment and Global Issues
- ❑ Location and Demographics
- ❑ Political Structures and Regulatory Frameworks
- ❑ Tradition and History
- ❑ Culture, Race, Gender, and Social Norms
- ❑ Attitudes, Expectations, and the Perception of Self
- ❑ Interpersonal Relations
- ❑ Social Media and Civil Society
- ❑ Organizational Climate, Capacity, Behavior, and Leadership
- ❑ Stakeholders and Inter-Organizational Linkages
- ❑ Material, Financial, Human Resources, and Time

We are immersed in evaluation perspectives, theories, and methods that influence the work and conduct of our work but context is central because it affects the systems in which our program is embedded. Change and interconnectedness are now part of our worldview.

In this chapter, we will look briefly at some of the intractable issues and **wicked problems** we face. While we have neither the time nor the space to dive into them, we cannot ignore their critical nature and the need for action on our part. We hope to raise awareness, open the discussion, and look at strategies that offer a way to see:

> the interconnections between the global and the local, the macro and the micro, and the relationships between world-wide patterns and area-specific challenges. (Patton, 2020, p. 3)

As evaluators we have more power than we realize. We stand at the nexus of environmental and large-scale political problems, racism and other identity issues, and organizations and structures which fail to respond to the need for change. At the same time, however, we have "the awesome responsibility of speaking for those who cannot speak for themselves to, in essence, define their reality" (Thomas et al., 2018, p. 516).

As McBride et al. (2020) so wisely state:

> We have a rare skillset of critical thinking, analysis, synthesis, and communication that we can use to develop and share deeper insights on structural racism and connect them to practices on the ground. On the one hand, we are often connected to leaders within organizations, corporations, academic settings or communities, and on the other, have access to those most affected by the programs or policies those leaders put in place.

Additionally, we have an explicit charge to aid decision-makers in guiding programs, services, and organizations. Given these strengths, we can use our leverage to make large shifts towards structural equity…. (p. 120)

Let us take our power and our specialized skill set to explore the new stance that is offered to evaluators.

The Evaluator's Power and Responsibility

Change can be incremental at times, moving so slowly we hardly notice it, but other times it is swift and inexorable. Either way, it is happening now, and we must begin to acknowledge it from exactly where we stand. We must position ourselves to see the impact change has on program contexts. We have both the power and the responsibility to influence positive change because we can access both decision makers and program participants. We understand the issues and barriers they face and we have the skills to work with them. We can be a bridge to change. The evaluator's new stance is envisioned in Figure 12.2.

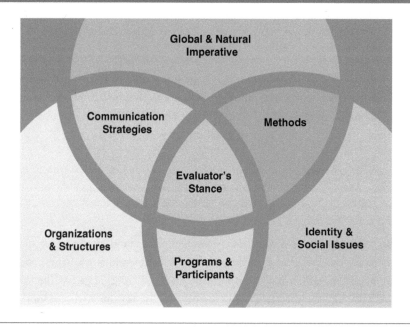

FIGURE 12.2 ◆ THE EVALUATOR'S NEW STANCE: A BRIDGE TO CHANGE

In this chapter, we use our telephoto lens, first to zoom in on the context of programs and the micro systems most familiar to evaluators—programs and participants, methods, and communication strategies. Then we zoom out to explore the big picture, the macro systems that surround the evaluator, the program, and the organization—including global and natural systems, identity and social issues, and organizations and structures. Finally, we consider the evaluator's role and begin a discussion on some strategies for change.

ZOOMING IN

We start on familiar territory, looking at where the evaluator is situated in terms of the **micro systems** of programs and their participants, the evaluation methods we employ, and communication strategies we use, all topics which have been discussed at length in this book. Figure 12.3 depicts this micro view.

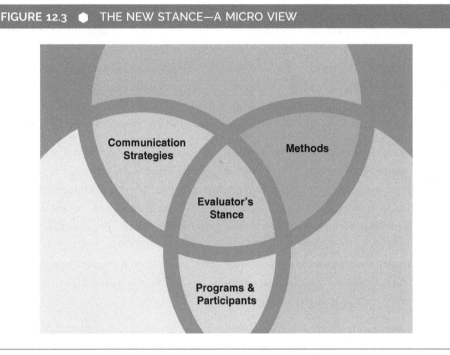

Program and Participants

The evaluation process begins when a client or organization asks the evaluator to conduct an evaluation. This initial request sets in motion a cascade of activities with which we are very familiar. Depending on the stage of program development, the evaluator determines the best evaluation approach for both the context and client needs. A series of pre- and early, midcycle, or end-of-cycle evaluation activities ensues. During this process we become familiar with the program, its decision makers, and its organizational context. At the same time, our evaluation allows us to work with and get to know program participants, sometimes regarding very personal topics. In this relationship, we come to understand the complexities of participants' lives in terms of roles, resources, positions, settings, identities, and the social issues they may face.

Throughout this process, our goal is program improvement so that the lives of program participants can be improved and so that the structures and systems that support them can be streamlined or enhanced. Chapters 4, 5, and 6 provide many examples of evaluation types, data collection methods and measures, and key questions that can be used during this intense but time-bound relationship. Once the evaluation is completed, external evaluators may no longer have a connection to the program. Typically, their gaze moves on to their next project. Internal evaluators may be more aware of ongoing program developments but again, are likely working on other projects and are not directly involved. For any evaluator, the evaluation period offers a unique opportunity for learning and growth for all involved.

Methods

The methods selected for an evaluation are connected to the paradigm or framework we use to view reality. Chapter 2 provides an overview of four paradigms commonly used in the social sciences, namely: positivism/postpositivism, constructivism, subjectivism/ transformative, and pragmatism. Typically, as evaluators, we feel more comfortable in one paradigm than another. These preconditions and assumptions shape our research approach, but we can shift our view from one paradigm to another if needed by the project.

Whether the perspective is overt or intuitive, our choices are bound by our worldview. If we view meaning as a truth that is external to the object under study, we tend to be positivists or empiricists, and, relying on the scientific method, choose quantitative methods such as surveys and statistical analysis to produce definitive answers to the research questions. Many modern positivists, or postpositivists as they are called, may also include some qualitative methods, adding open-ended questions to their surveys or filling in their research with focus groups or interviews, but the goal remains the desire for a singular truth. Chapter 7 provides an overview of some of the quantitative methods that are frequently employed in evaluation.

On the other hand, if we are a constructivist, we try to understand reality from the multiple perspectives and lived experiences of program participants and stakeholders. Reality is contextual, not absolute. Qualitative methods are usually employed to uncover multiple meanings. Chapter 8 provides an overview of the typical qualitative methods used in evaluation.

A third option is the transformative paradigm. Subjectivists tend to work with marginalized groups where values, culture, power dynamics, and social justice issues hold sway. As a subjectivist, we try to bring these perspectives forward so that issues of inequality can be revealed. We often use mixed methods to capture and reflect on our emergent understanding.

Finally, if we are pragmatists, we also use mixed methods, but unlike the other three paradigms, we say, "It depends. Whatever works." We focus on the consequences of a specific problem or issue, and working backwards, ask, "Which methods will produce the most useful information?" Chapter 9 provides an overview of the mixed methods approach.

When thinking about evaluation methods, no one paradigm is more important than another. The task is to find the most effective way to answer the research question and to respond to the information needs of the evaluation. This paradigmatic choice give us a great deal of power because we are probably the most aware of how our methods decisions will affect the final outcomes of the study.

Communication Strategies

Communication begins even before the evaluation study gets under way and often continues well after the final report is submitted. A great deal of planning is required from

> generating evaluation questions; incorporating diverse perspectives; understanding context; setting boundaries around the evaluation; identifying important system interrelationships; and interpreting, reporting, and facilitating engagement in the findings. (Patton, 2020, p. 126)

Starting with the evaluation plan, outlined in Chapter 10, and including the development of the logic model, which often guides the evaluator's thought processes (Chapter 2), communication shapes what the study will produce and how stakeholders will use the findings. Chapter 11 explores methods of communication throughout the evaluation process, how results are shared, and how new knowledge can be disseminated once the study is completed.

Lessons From Zooming In

What becomes clear from this review is how central the evaluator's role is to each of these areas. Evaluation processes, research methods, and communication strategies shape the both the study and its findings and may influence future policy decisions and their effect of program participants. These are the topics most frequently covered in evaluation curriculums. They also form the basis of most conference discussions and journal articles in the discipline of evaluation. However, danger lies here. We may suffer from myopia as we peer inward, assessing our work against other similar work, looking in an endlessly reflecting set of mirrors. Invisible barriers can be ignored, questions left unasked, and context limited to the known, the familiar, and the predictable. It is a larger world, and we must be aware of and assess the connections between the micro and the macro systems as well. This requires our telephoto lens to zoom out.

ZOOMING OUT

We begin again where we stand as evaluators, at the center, but now we look outward at three overlapping **macro systems** that influence the potential success of any program evaluation (See Figure 12.4, p. 476).

A macro view reveals how the evaluator stands at the intersection of three large-scale systems, all of which influence the programs[1] we work with, often in unacknowledged ways. We cannot simply carve out a bubble of interest or a silo of responsibility and exert a

---

[1]Note that throughout this discussion, we refer to 'program' as a generic term that also encompasses projects, policies, products, and other outcomes related to the professional practice of evaluators.

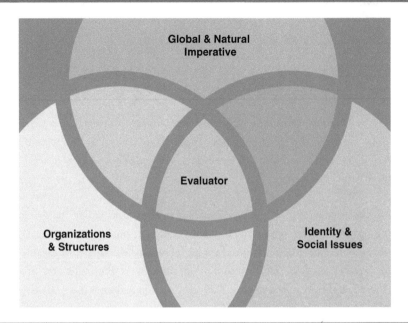

FIGURE 12.4 ⬢ THE NEW STANCE—A MACRO VIEW

laser focus on a specific program while ignoring the larger forces at play. Program interventions that target narrow outcomes will fail in the long run if they do not also in some way address the scale and scope of what must change in our global and natural world. It is not a choice, it is an imperative (Patton, 2020, pp. 21–22).

For example, in 2019, COVID-19 convulsed the world and became a pandemic. At the time of this writing, COVID-19 has infected 524,339,768 world citizens and claimed 6,281,260 lives worldwide (World Health Organization, 2022). No person and no program is unscathed. Millions have suffered or died, and the impact is likely to be generational. The pandemic is a global issue, and it fits in the top circle of our model, the global and natural imperative, where dynamic and entangled systems affect the whole Earth. An example of a natural issue is **climate change** which has affected all our natural systems and put us on a disastrous trajectory.

The second overlapping circle (to the right) embodies the many long-standing identity issues such as race, culture, gender, class, religion, and political affiliation, all of which continue to cause worldwide unrest. The uneven distribution of wealth, unequal access to food, water, and other resources, educational and health disparities, and the rise of special interest groups have resulted in increasing cycles of disaffection, unhappiness, conflict, grief, and death.

The third circle (to the left) corresponds to the organizations and structures within which evaluators function. At the most basic level, an evaluation represents a financial transaction between an evaluator and a client or commissioner. This transactional mindset can shrink the scope of the evaluation and constrain its impact or stifle it altogether. On the other hand, a transformative perspective can shed light on opportunities and perspectives across sectors, silos, and structures. As evaluators we must understand how organizations function and can look beyond the parameters of our evaluation work at capacity building, growth, and regeneration.

The evaluator stands at the nexus of these three large-scale systems. Let us follow some of these pathways to see how evaluation and evaluators are affected by them and how evaluation can be better positioned to support real change.

The Global and Natural Imperative

We begin by thinking about global and natural systems. A key question we need to ask is, "With what systems is my program engaged and what do I need to measure?" Patton advises that his Blue Marble perspective connects the global to the local and the local to the global. He offers four principles (Patton, 2020, p. 4 and p. 29):

1. **Global Thinking**. Apply whole-Earth, big-picture thinking to all aspects of systems change. It can be applied to programs and initiatives that may be local in perspective but are affected by global trends.

2. **Anthropocene** as Context. Scientists call our current geological era the Anthropocene era, "the period during which human activity is considered to be the dominant influence on the environment, climate, and ecology of the earth" (Oxford English Dictionary, 2014).

3. **Transformative Engagement**. We must respond to the changes required with the magnitude, speed, and direction needed for dramatic, radical change on a global scale.

4. **Integration**. The global problems are not created by one source; there is a web of causation with numerous causes, solutions, and players which must all coalesce to solve these problems.

This is not a "pick and choose" menu of options. It is a comprehensive and integrated package (Patton, 2020, p. 28) and traditional approaches to evaluation will not address the systems change required.

Part of the natural imperative we face is the result of climate change and global warming. While these terms are often used interchangeably, they have different meanings. Climate change is the umbrella term for all the various changes occurring on our planet, such as the quickly melting ice in Greenland, Antarctica, and the Arctic (National Aeronautics and Space Administration, 2021b). Global warming relates to only one type of climate change, namely a rise in temperature. Lindsey and Dahlman (2021) state the "earth's temperature has risen by 0.14 °F (0.08°) per decade since 1880, and the rate of warming over the past 40 years is more than twice that" 0.32 °F (0.18 °C) per decade since 1981" (para. 1).

Figure 12.5 provides a listing of the causes and indicators of global climate change. Also provided are the various human, animal, and planet effects of the climate change (Centers for Disease Control and Prevention, 2022; Environmental Protection Agency, 2022; European Commission, 2022; IBERDROLA, 2022; World Meterological Organization, 2022).

FIGURE 12.5 ● CLIMATE CHANGE INDICATORS

Causes
Generating electricity and heat for residential and commercial buildings • Use of petrochemical products (plastics, rubber, adhesives, dyes, detergents, pesticides, paint) • Manufacturing (cement, iron, steel, electronics, clothes) • Deforestation • Transportation • Livestock • Machinery • Consumer culture

Outputs
Greenhouse gases (carbon dioxide, fluorinated gases, nitrous oxide, and methane) trapped in the atmosphere.

Indicators
- Greenhouse gas concentrations
- Sea level rise
- Ocean heat
- Ocean acidification
- Extreme weather
- Global annual mean temperature

- Glacier thinning
- Heatwaves
- Flooding
- Drought
- Hurricane
- Wildfires

Human, Animal, and Planet Outcomes and Impact
Poor air • Food chain contamination • Extreme weather events • Unsafe drinking water Loss of nature and biodiversity • Food insecurity • Loss of cities and coastal areas Climate refugees • Trauma • Microplastics entering bloodstream • Mental health disorders • Animal and human diseases • Death

---

Source: Canada Energy. (2018). *Market snapshot: Petrochemical products in everyday life.* United Nations. (2022). *Climate action fast facts.* https://www.un.org/en/climatechange/science/key-findings#physical-science United Nations Foundation. (2022, April 6). *7 ways climate change harms our health.* iStockphoto.com/janrsavy

Extreme events such as floods, droughts, heatwaves, and fires are changing in frequency, intensity, and timing and have devastating costs. Since 1980, the United States, has sustained over 308 weather and climate disasters. The total cost of these events exceeds $2.085 trillion (National Oceanic Atmospheric Administration National Centers for Environmental Information, 2021). In global terms, in 2020 alone, extreme events caused $210 billion in damages (Jeworrek, 2021).

Sustainability is a concept that was developed in the 1970s (Kidd, 1992). By the late 1980s, advocates were making a concerted effort to reconcile economic growth with social and ecological perspectives. The United Nations (UN) defined sustainable development as "development that meets the needs of the present without compromising the ability of future generations to meet their own needs" (Brundtland, 1987, p. 41).

In 2015, a UN working group representing 70 countries set an agenda for sustainable development. They produced the **17 Sustainable Development Goals** (SDGs) with 169 targets (United Nations, n.d.) and 193 member states agreed to work toward achieving them by 2030. The Goals emphasize a holistic approach to sustainable development and define the world we want. They apply to all nations and are based on the idea that no one is left behind (Smale, n.d.). See Figure 12.6.

FIGURE 12.6 ⬡ THE UNITED NATION'S SUSTAINABLE DEVELOPMENT GOALS

Source: United Nations. (n.d.). *The 17 goals.* Department of Economic and Social Affairs: Sustainable Development. https://www.un.org/sustainabledevelopment/. *Note:* The content of this publication has not been approved by the United Nations and does not reflect the views of the United Nations or its officials or Member States.

On the world stage, sustainable development has come to the forefront as global challenges deepen, particularly in the areas of environment, climate, poverty, and inequality. Evaluators are beginning to consider both human and natural systems in their work. Rowe (2019, p. 32) stresses that sustainability intersects with the many disruptions and adaptations that emerge as man and nature collide. Instead of working around issues as we conduct our evaluations, we should incorporate them into our evaluation designs. Table 12.1, p. 480 provides a few examples of sustainability issues facing evaluators.

Evaluating from a sustainability perspective is complex and challenging. However, it offers a leadership opportunity and lets us organize our thoughts around activities needed to sustain organizations and programs. It also makes room for deep conversations about institutionalizing this perspective as funders and decision makers may not be aware of them or willing to broaden their scope. Julnes (2019) comments that by viewing sustainability as a process rather than an end state, we can continue to incorporate sustainability questions in all our work.

TABLE 12.1 ● SUSTAINABILITY ISSUES FACING EVALUATORS	
Major Issue	**Description**
1. Public health	• Adapting public health systems to address highly contagious infections shared between humans and animals; outbreaks of diseases such as cholera associated with frequent storms and flooding, health effects of extreme temperatures
2. Education	• Educating in the context of more frequent disruptions from extreme weather, increasing share of budgets allocated to addressing costs of sustainability issues, more frequent school closures; adapting curricula to changed realities, addressing political influences
3. Disabilities, mental health, homelessness	• Providing safety, mobility, and services to already vulnerable and heavily urban populations made more vulnerable by climate change
4. Transportation, urban governance, infrastructure, and environmental services	• Disruptions and physical instability of current transport, sewage and water, food storage and distribution systems, responding to extreme weather and natural disasters
5. Public safety and climate risk	• Destabilizing dynamics from extreme weather events, wildfires, and flooding; insurance and recovery programs
6. Economic and community development	• Incorporating ecosystem services, waste, recycling

Source: Adapted from Rowe, A. (2019). Sustainability-Ready evaluation: A call to action. In G. Julnes (Ed.), *Evaluating sustainability: Evaluative support for managing processes in the public interest* (pp. 29–48). Wiley.

Strategies for Evaluators

We must broaden our assumptions, theories, and methods to incorporate global equity and sustainability. Some strategies include using systems thinking, seeking transformative engagement, and incorporating sustainability practices in everything we do.

Use Systems Thinking. When working in a complex and rapidly changing context, the systems perspective provides a relational worldview that can uncover hidden connections, political structures, and intangibles. Norms, stereotypes, and attitudes, as well as the more traditional and readily observable evaluation results, are revealed (Thomas & Parsons, 2017, p. 7). Systems concepts help to address and resolve situations that are "wicked, messy, and horribly tangled," or seem "impossible to sort out" (Williams & Hummelbrunner, 2010, p. 1).

Systems thinking includes (p. 3):

- An understanding of interrelationships—how things are connected and the consequences that result from those connections.

- A commitment to multiple perspectives—the different mental models that affect the way people understand an endeavor and judge its success.

- An awareness of boundaries—or what is considered "in" or "out" of the frame.

Many of the problems we face as evaluators today are wicked problems (Schwandt et al., 2016, p. 3) especially in the context of large-scale programs such as those linked to the SDGs. Because multiple stakeholders are involved and contexts continue to change, any solution is only temporary. An adaptive management approach is needed to allow solutions to evolve as conditions change.

These complex relationships mean that links between a policy or program and goal achievement cannot be captured in a linear way. Evaluators are increasingly drawn to systems thinking and approaches that provide tools to describe and analyze the boundaries, interrelationships and perspectives involved. Examples of these tools include causal loop diagrams, system dynamics, and outcome mapping. Techniques such as soft systems methodology and critical system heuristics also provide ways to bring together perspectives and frame value judgments (Schwandt et al., 2016, p. 3).

Evaluation is coupled with learning, strategic planning and knowledge development. Building stakeholders' capacity to understand these complex processes is essential if transformative change is to occur at the global and national levels.

Seek Transformative Engagement. "Business as usual will not suffice," warns Patton (2020, p. 22). He urges us to engage and evaluate consistently with the magnitude, direction, and speed needed for transformation to occur. Unfortunately, in many cases, evaluation has fallen into a mechanistic state, becoming a regulator of the status quo. Hummelbrunner (2007) states:

> *An objective is set and a measure (e.g., indicator) established, which allows to observe whether actions achieve the objective. When this measure shows a deviation...evaluation functions as a regulator and proposes adaptations with the intention of modifying the action so the original objective can be met.* (p. 167)

Differences from the original target are regarded as negative and in need of corrective action.

Rigid strategies like these cannot support the fundamental and transformative change needed in today's context. Instead, we must rise to the moment, look for the levers of change, and bring our attention to global trends and local connections (Neubauer & Hall, 2020, p. 131; Patton, 2020, p. 189). It is not just knowledge, attitudes, and behavior that need to change but also paradigms and mindsets. We must start a global conversation with every client in every project. We must collect data with a longer trajectory; pin the program's objectives to the larger context (e.g., the SDGs); make connections with contacts, colleagues, and networks; share data internationally; and ensure that findings make it to the larger stage. A transformative mindset "incorporates and integrates multiple theories of change operating at many levels that knitted together, explain how major systems transformation occurs" (Patton, 2020, p. 154).

Incorporate Sustainability Into Evaluation Practice. We need to model positive attitudes and behaviors about sustainability and environmental stewardship in our work. Rowe (2021) suggests that we should include both natural science and social science expertise on our evaluation teams, use mixed methods, and consult with a broader range of stakeholders.

Through our professional organizations, we can put sustainability on the agenda and begin to incorporate it into evaluation culture and practice. For example, the Canadian Evaluation Society (2018) states in the third domain (Situational Practice) of their Competencies for Canadian Evaluation Practice that evaluators focus on "understanding, analyzing, and attending to the many circumstances that make every evaluation unique, including culture, stakeholders, and context" (p. 6). In particular, the first sub-competency reads:

Examines and responds to the multiple human and natural contexts within which the program is embedded (p. 6).

In every evaluation, we need to report on program contributions to sustainability, whether the findings are positive or negative, using:

- A "do no harm" perspective—include a standard for program performance that acts as a placeholder while the program transitions to a positive environmental contribution.

- A restorative contribution—include a recommendation for how the program can address sustainability.

- A commitment to knowledge dissemination—contribute valuable evaluation processes and findings to the related body of knowledge and best practices.

Davidson and Rowe (2022) have crafted some Key Evaluation Questions (KEQ) as part of the Footprint Evaluation project to illustrate how sustainability can be embedded in an evaluation. See Box 12.1. The questions are generic in nature and can be selected and revised to fit the context of any specific evaluation. Remember that "evaluand" is the term

---

BOX 12.1 ● KEY EVALUATION QUESTIONS (KEQS) INCORPORATING SUSTAINABILITY

1: Relevance & Coherence
How relevant is the evaluand to the issues facing the population/sector and the natural environment — and how well does it complement other related efforts in the context?

2: Design & Adaptation
How well does the design address the strengths, needs, and aspirations of both human and natural systems — in ways that are equitable, restorative, and enable both to thrive?

3: Implementation
How well has the evaluand been implemented so that the right people and natural system elements receive what is most needed at the right times and places and in the right ways?

(Continued)

(Continued)

4: Outcomes & Impacts
How good, valuable, and important are the outcomes and impacts on both human and natural systems, particularly where equity and/or previous harm needed to be addressed?

5: Patterns, Outliers, and Links
How did the evaluand influence change – and then how did that change continue to unfold – in the relevant coupled human and natural systems? Where, when, for whom, and under what conditions did we see the most and least valuable outcomes? Why?

6: Durability
How resilient and durable are the changes that the evaluand has contributed to, and how well are they likely to last in the face of emerging environmental and other changes?

7: Overall Value
How good, valuable, or worthwhile is the evaluand overall, given its relevance and coherence, its design and implementation, the value of its outcomes and impacts, their durability, and what it cost to achieve them?

Source: Davidson, E. J., & Rowe, A. (2022, May). *Key evaluation questions (KEQs) to guide Footprint Evaluations (v. 5).* BetterEvaluation. https://www.betterevaluation.org/resources/key-evaluation-questions-keqs-guide-footprint-evaluations

used to describe whatever is being evaluated, such as a policy, strategy, program, project, initiative). Sub-questions can also be found in their document.

Now let's take a look at some of the challenges that are involved in preparing global surveys. The Global Data and Insights Team at the Wikimedia Foundation describe their recent experience.

SPOTLIGHT ON EQUITY

Preparing Global Surveys: The Wikimedia Challenge

The Wikimedia Foundation is a nonprofit organization that supports 13 open-source Wikimedia projects. The most well-known is Wikipedia, a free, collaborative encyclopedia written in over 300 languages. At the core of these projects is MediaWiki, the free, open-source software that supports the collaborative development process and the collective ownership of all projects. The protection of collaborator and user privacy is essential to Wikimedia, and it requires careful attention to survey processes.

The Wikimedia movement is a global, volunteer-driven network of individuals, affiliates, partners, and organizations working to foster open knowledge. They share the belief that universal access to reliable and verifiable knowledge is a basic human right, and that a globally inclusive, consensus-based dialogue enables the collective generation of that knowledge. Figure 12.7, p. 484 provides an illustration of the Wikimedia movement's ecosystem and actors and offers us some idea of the vast scope of their work.

To learn more about the political, social, and economic barriers that contributors may face due to their

FIGURE 12.7 ◆ WIKIMEDIA MOVEMENT ECOSYSTEM AND ACTORS

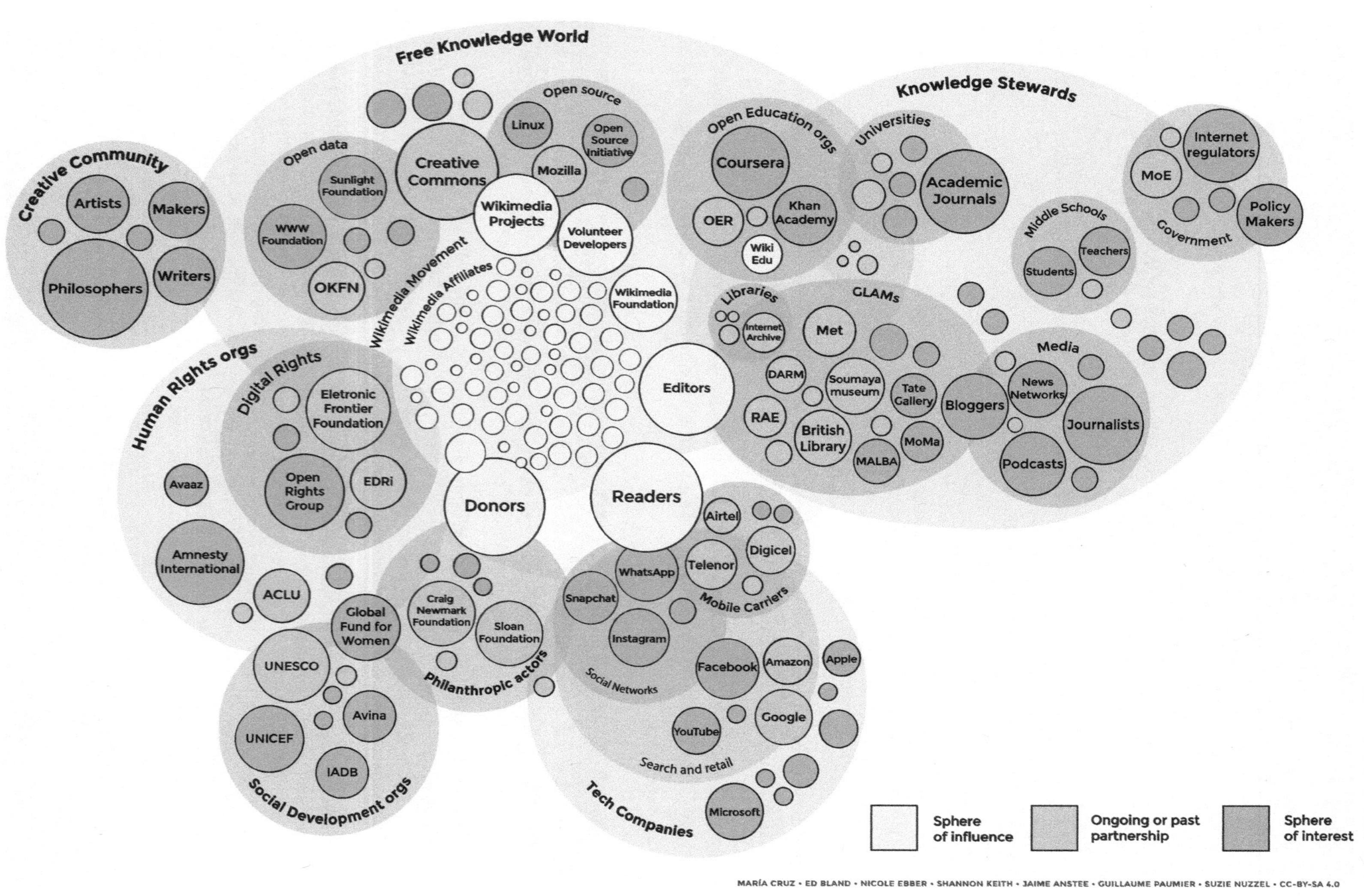

Source: María Cruz, Ed Bland, Nicole Ebber, Shannon Keith, Dr. Jaime Anstee, Guillaume Paumier, Suzie Nuzzel. Wikimedia Foundation, CC BY -SA 4.0. https://creativecommons.org/licenses/by-sa/4.0, available via Wikimedia Commons: https://upload.wikimedia.org/Wikipedia/commons/0/00/Strategy_Graphic_-_For_collaborative_editing.svg

engagement with Wikimedia, more information is needed about communities left out of their projects by structures of power and privilege. Dr. Jaime Anstee and the Global Data and Insights team have been working for the past three years to improve the validity of their survey design strategies, the representativeness of their samples, and the depth of their data. While the process is ongoing, several lessons have been learned that are useful for any evaluator.

Source: Dr. Jaime Anstee

1. **Giving communities a voice**

   Affiliates are a primary organizing body for Wikimedia, giving their movement a consistent presence in 85 countries and a reach to over 100 countries through international programs. However, reaching affiliates' members has been challenging. A previous survey attempt yielded a 16% response of the intended affiliate member sample. The team experimented with a participatory randomized sampling approach and developed a sampling toolkit to teach affiliates about the sampling process. Still, some of these volunteers were confused or overwhelmed by the idea of multiple sampling groups tailored to different affiliate sizes but some progress has been made, and the 2021 response rate increased to 48%.

2. **Aligning data across naming conventions**

   To develop an exhaustive global database, data must be aligned across various sources despite divergent country and territory naming conventions. For instance, recent changes to English versions of country names, such as the change from Macedonia to North Macedonia, or from Czech Republic to Czechia, cause database errors. Further, no matter what set of databases are used, e.g., United Nation (UN), United Nations Educational, Scientific, and Cultural Organization (UNESCO), Groupe Speciale Mobile Association (GSMA), or the World Bank, there are inconsistencies in country/area labels and regional groupings. The team has now developed a relational database with built-in redundancies that functions as a central lookup table and is also aligned to the ISO 3116 country codes. They continuously enlist data stewards to review data and submit updates directly to open repositories.

3. **Translating into user languages**

   To ensure that all participants have a voice in cocreating Wikimedia data, surveys need to be in user languages. The Community Insights survey is currently translated into 19 languages, but ensuring that translations are accurate and culturally appropriate is tricky when no team member speaks the language. The team first attempted community-based translations, but they found that volunteers might not capture the nuances of survey questions and could introduce regional language variations. Then they worked with professional translators, but in some cases the results were politically biased. Their third option has been to use an iterative approach, starting with professional translations, getting community verification, and then piloting the revised survey in each language. Overall, their lesson for this painstaking process is to take it slowly, one step at a time.

4. **Measuring race and ethnicity**
Understanding the racial and ethnic diversity of both primary and secondary contacts has been a struggle, as these socially based constructs vary geographically, culturally, and economically. The team used local census classifications where available but found that variations in definitions meant limited comparisons were possible. Using U.S.-centric race categories in other countries was not effective. An alternative has been to use a minority status question, which does not provide the demographic specifics but does safely surface experiences more generally. They decided to ask race/ethnicity questions only when the information is really needed, to focus on minority experiences, and to pilot the questions with potential participants from the local context,

being sure to communicate the reason for asking the question in the first place.

5. **Measuring gender**
Like race and ethnicity, "gender identity" is a social construct. While gender and sexuality information are needed to understand diversity, distinctions vary across languages. Further, diverse sexualities and gender categories are not safely accepted in all countries. The team has started by agreeing upon the need for this data and the language used and then developing shared meaning. They have decoupled gender from sex categories to ensure that translations say "man" and "woman" rather than "male" and "female," while acknowledging this is not possible in all languages. Finally, they treat each new data request with caution and accept the fact that gender fluidity and sexuality vary by region and demographic.

As Anstee commented, "By iteratively improving our data collection, we are slowly revealing a more complete picture of our communities and operating spaces so we can proactively focus on interventions to support healthier development, together, with our movement."

This Spotlight on Equity is based on the contribution of Dr. Jaime Anstee of the Wikimedia Foundation.

Identity and Social Issues

The second overlapping macro system in our model relates to long-standing identity issues and the resource disparities that accompany them. Identity is a critical driver of modern behavior and often stems from experiences of injustice shared by groups that desire greater self-determination and political freedom. Identity is associated with various social movements, including the women's movement, the African American civil rights movement, the gay and lesbian movement, the postcolonial movement, and nationalism.

Before we enter this discussion, however, as authors, we need to acknowledge our own positions of power and privilege as a second-generation Hispanic American (Triana-Tremain) and a fifth-generation White, English speaking Canadian (Barrington) and to record our very limited experience with systemic racism. Despite these notable limitations, or maybe because of them, we are compelled to highlight the importance of identity in the evaluation context.

Race, culture, and ethnic identity influence an individual's education, career path, wealth, and health. These are often invisible components of the context in which evaluators work and contribute significantly to world unrest. They are "social constructs used to categorize and characterize seemingly distinct populations" (Blakemore, 2019, para. 2) and can be described as follows:

- Race. Linked to physical characteristics like skin color or ancestry, although most genetic markers do not differ significantly enough by race to be helpful in medical research (Cosmides et al., 2003; Duster, 2009). Race reflects historical attitudes and beliefs imposed on different populations.

- Culture. Describes the unique characteristics, knowledge, social behaviors, and norms of a specific group.

- Ethnicity. Encompasses either geographic or learned traits such as language, nationality, culture, and religion.

Using demographics can be complicated because the terms race, culture, and ethnicity are often conflated or split into confusing categories. For example, as of July 1, 2019, the US Census Bureau (2019) offered population estimates, including Race and Hispanic Origin (reorganized into descending order of frequency), as follows (Table 12.2):

TABLE 12.2 ● RACE AND HISPANIC ORIGIN IN THE U.S. POPULATION

Race Category	% of Total
White alone	76.3
Black or African American alone	13.4
Asian alone	5.9
American Indian and Alaskan Native alone	1.3
Native Hawaiian/Other Pacific Islander alone	0.2
Two or more races	2.8
Population estimates, July 1, 2019 Ethnicity Category	**328,239,523**
Hispanic or Latino	18.5%
White alone, not Hispanic or Latino	60.1%

Source: U.S. Census Bureau. (2019). Population estimates. (Version 2019) [Data set]. U.S. Census Bureau.

Focusing on a single demographic category does not capture an individual's lived experience, but to assume we know enough about a group's identity without adequate preparation is itself an example of systemic racism (Thomas et al., 2018, p. 516). While the following discussion in no way reflects the full array of possible identities that can be at play in an evaluation, we have selected one demographic group for race (African Americans), culture (Indigenous peoples), and ethnicity (Hispanics). There can be overlap and confusion among these categories but the work we do in North America often relates to these populations.

Race

African American generally refers to individuals of the United States, usually raised there, of African ancestry, and whose ancestors were enslaved and brought to America against their will. Black is a more general term and can refer to anyone of African ancestry, including recent immigrants. Racism is defined as "discrimination or antagonism directed against a person or people on the basis of their membership in a particular racial or ethnic group, typically one that is a minority or marginalized" (Oxford Lexico, n.d.).

Racial disparities have a long and painful history in the United States. Ernest House (2017) commented that America has been racist since its inception, "much of its early wealth built on stolen lands and slave labor" (p. 175). Privilege and racism have been systematically institutionalized and perpetuated in areas such as housing, education, health, and criminal justice. In 2020, the death of George Floyd, while in police custody, sparked worldwide protests, raised significant support for the Black Lives Matter movement, and sensitized a world, already reeling from a global pandemic, to the persistent issues of power, racism, and oppression.

Despite significant advances made in the name of social justice, gaps in racial equity remain. Two quick measures, wealth and health, provide stark examples:

- Black Americans constitute 13.4% of the U.S. population, but they hold less than 3% of the country's wealth (Smith & Rosalsky, 2020).

- In 2017, Blacks between the ages of 18–49 years were nearly twice as likely to die from heart disease, stroke, and diabetes compared to Whites (Moss & Crewe, 2020).

While these data may make some of us uncomfortable, for many others, it is simply stating the obvious.

When we scrutinize the notion of equity, we are challenged to reexamine foundational concepts such as validity, rigor, and objectivity. As Madison (1992) reminds us:

> *The fundamental question is not whether the evaluation enterprise is capable of determining the truth about the outcomes of social programs in the lives of individuals designated as the beneficiaries of redistributive social policy; rather, the question is whether evaluators are willing to employ the greatest range of techniques in the discovery of truth.* (p. 1)

Our interpretation of program "truth" can have serious consequences for the lives of these individuals who depend on us to validate their perspectives. Scholars and theorists have long questioned the value of using traditional frameworks to evaluate cultural differences, and some have commented that evaluation has been complicit in perpetuating theories, methods, and practices that exclude diverse ways of knowing beyond the focus of the dominant culture (Caldwell & Bledsoe, 2019).

Hilliard (1989) and Stanfield (1999) both state that our field is neither race nor culture neutral because our epistemology, methods, and processes have foundations in a singular Eurocentric worldview, ignoring "culturally diverse questions, definitions of data, and interpretations of findings [and] thereby compromising the validity and credibility of the evaluations conducted" (Caldwell & Bledsoe, 2019, p. 8).

Critical Race Theory (CRT), originated by Derrick Bell and other legal scholars in the 1970s, is a theoretical framework that provides a critical lens to deconstruct oppressive policies and practices and construct more emancipatory systems for racial equity and justice. It places race or positionality in the center of analysis to identify ways that ideologies, structures, and institutions create and maintain inequality. The core objective of CRT is to challenge the pervasiveness and societal impact of White supremacy. Thus, "CRT has a fundamental commitment to a social justice agenda that struggles to eliminate all forms of racial, gender, language, generation, status, and class subordination" (Parker & Villalpando, 2007, p. 520). Other forms of critical theory have emerged that critique social injustice from a variety of perspectives including LatCrit, Indigenous, critical feminism, ableism, and others.

Hall (2020, p. 16) comments that as evaluators we have had many opportunities to insulate ourselves from social justice issues for many reasons, including a limited interest in or knowledge about racial issues, a paucity of strategies to accommodate cultural needs, a desire to promote the legitimacy of a detached and neutral perspective (i.e., our heritage), or a fear of confronting funders with uncomfortable truths and thus increasing the potential for the evaluator to lose income.

Since 2000, the field of evaluation has become more sensitized to racial bias and inequality. There has been significant growth in the number of evaluators of diverse backgrounds and self-identities. Many organizations have developed statements affirming the importance of cultural competence and sensitivity (Hall, 2020, pp. 18–19). For example, in 2011, the AEA released a Public Statement on Cultural Competence in Evaluation which stresses that evaluation is not culture free, is context specific, and is an ongoing learning process. It urges evaluators to acknowledge the complexity of cultural identity, recognize power dynamics, eliminate bias in language, and employ culturally appropriate methods.

As a result of the Building Diversity initiative, AEA created the Graduate Education Diversity Internship (GEDI) Program in 2004 (see Chapter 1). Other diversity-focused initiatives in evaluation include, for example (Dean-Coffey, 2018, p. 533):

- The Evaluation Roundtable for foundation evaluation leaders to advance racial equity and justice in philanthropy

- The Robert Wood Johnson Foundation Evaluation Fellowship Program to provide fellowships for recent master's/doctoral graduates and midcareer professionals

- The Leaders in Equitable Evaluation and Diversity (LEEAD) Program to train diverse leaders in culturally responsive and equitable evaluation.

Strategies for Evaluators. To address racism in evaluation we can work to understand racial framing in our own context, adopt practices of cultural humility, and always look for strengths, not deficits. Many more strategies are available in the evaluation literature.

Understand Racial Framing. Racial framing leads to racial bias. Evaluators need to be prepared to "anticipate, discover, and deal with the biases, much as we deal with other threats to validity" (House, 2017, p. 168). Racial bias develops over a lifetime through our experiences and influences many of our decisions about race at the unconscious level (Caldwell & Bledsoe, 2019, p. 9). It acts as a screen to block facts and events inconsistent with the frame and accounts for why we may have preconceived ideas about someone from a different culture. In daily life, individuals draw selectively on parts of the frame, accepting or rejecting various aspects. Repetition, performance, collective memory, and collective forgetting (House, 2017, p. 171) are part of this process.

House (2017) offers three critical thoughts about racism:

1. If society sees itself as democratic yet is racist and does not recognize the extent or nature of that racism, it will promulgate programs and policies purported to help minorities that will damage them significantly (House, 2017, p. 168).

One such example is standardized testing, presumed to measure intelligence yet tending to winnow out Black, Hispanic, Indigenous, and students of Asian descent from opportunities throughout their educational careers (Rosales & Walker, 2021). Often, test creators frame questions around familiar experiences for children who speak American English and come from advantaged backgrounds (Hilliard, 1997). Moreover, because the tests have face validity, their underlying assumptions are seldom examined.

2. If racism is not a vestige of the past but is created and recreated in the present, what social entities, mechanisms, processes, and structures generate racist beliefs and behaviors (House, 2017, p. 168)?

In a recent paper on the psychology of American racism, psychologists Roberts and Rizzo (2021) identified seven contributing factors:

- Categories, which organize people into distinct groups

- Factions, which trigger group loyalty and intergroup competition

- Segregation, which hardens racial perceptions, preferences, and beliefs

- Hierarchy, which emboldens people to think, feel, and behave in racist ways

- Power, which legislates racism on both micro and macro levels

- Media, which legitimizes idealized overrepresentations of White Americans while marginalizing or minimizing people of color

- Passivism, which enables people to overlook or deny the existence of racism.

And perhaps most important for evaluators, House asks:

3. As evaluation plays a vital role in these social processes that generate racism, while not a cause of racism itself, can the evaluation function be distorted, coopted, or corrupted (House, 2017, p. 168)?

A number of theorists believe this is the case. While individual evaluators may not hold strong and personal beliefs about racism, "we often participate in systems and institutions that perpetuate it as well as other forms of oppression" (Caldwell & Bledsoe, 2019, p. 9). Thomas and Parsons (2017) consider the importance of hidden elements and intangibles, such as social norms, political structures, relationships, stereotypes, attitudes, and expectations, as all part of structural racism. Ignoring the impact of these complexities on the behavior of a marginalized population can render the findings inaccurate, incomplete, or seriously flawed, with potentially devastating consequences (Thompson & Parsons, 2017, p. 9).

Work Toward Cultural Humility. Cultural humility as Lekas et al. (2020) explains "means admitting that one does not know and is willing to learn…about [others] experiences, while being aware of one's own embeddedness in culture(s)." While competence suggests mastery, humility refers to an intrapersonal and interpersonal approach (p. 2).

Culturally Responsive Evaluation (CRE) has gained a foothold in evaluation. It recognizes that culturally defined values and beliefs lie at the heart of any evaluation effort (Frierson et al., 2002, p. 63; Hood et al., 2015, p. 283). It is a holistic approach that promotes social justice, attends to culture and context, and grounds evaluation practice in evaluation approaches that attend to democracy, social change, inclusion, and power relationships (Thomas & Parsons, 2017, pp. 9–10).

Key recommendations for evaluators that address cultural humility include how to conduct the study, handle data and findings, and communicate (Frierson et al., 2002, pp. 63–73; Thomas & Parsons, 2017, pp. 18–19):

Conduct the Study:

- Understand that instruments normed on a different cultural group cannot be assumed to be effective.

- Train data collectors in culturally responsive processes.

- Use multiethnic teams to increase the chances of hearing the voices of the underrepresented.

Handle Data and Findings:

- Discuss what constitutes acceptable evidence before conducting the evaluation.

- Disaggregate data and explore outliers.

- Present findings to relevant audiences in meaningful ways to improve validity, utility, and truth.

Communicate:

- Ask the questions that stakeholders care about the most and that support sound decision making.

- Illuminate the benefits of the evaluation to targeted individuals and communities, particularly those most under-served.

- Attend to nonverbal behavior.

- Ensure ongoing feedback to stakeholders using culturally appropriate channels of communication.

- Share lived experiences between the evaluation team and evaluation participants.

Look for Strengths, Not Deficits. Strengths-based practice evolved from the field of social work and is now in the human service field. Instead of focusing on risks, deficits, blaming, and judgment, it focuses on what is going well, how to do more of it, and how to build on it (Barwick, 2004).

Dhaliwal et al. (2020) describe a strength-based evaluation culture that emerged at the RYSE Youth Center in Richmond, California, a safe space created specifically for young people living in an atmosphere of trauma and violence. In their view, conventional research and evaluation can replicate unjust narratives and assumptions about young people of color's capacities, abilities, and needs, treating them as risk, problem, or disease. As they so eloquently describe:

> *RYSEs Members live, die, navigate, hustle, struggle, and succeed within a context of persistent danger, distress, and dehumanization…. Daily we see the burdens of inequity, pain, and insidious racial trauma young people of color bear. We also see the fortitude, tenacity, resilience, and resistance it takes to survive when living with persistent stress of social identity threat and racial trauma. This knowledge necessitates foundational shifts in how we frame, design, implement, analyze, and act on young people of color's priorities, needs and interests.* (p. 59)

By becoming advocates for democratic ideals, we can ask, "Why does this problem occur?" Rather than simply focusing on how well a particular program is achieving its goals, we can illuminate the potential impact of race and racism on the programs we evaluate and the contexts with which we engage (Thomas et al., 2018, p. 524).

Culture[2]

American Indians and Alaskan Natives (described in our text as Indigenous Peoples) represent 1.3% of the population but come from 574 different federally recognized tribal nations, including tribes, nations, bands, pueblos, communities, and native villages in the United States. While considered a race, their historical traditions and values constitute a culture, despite the significant variation found among specific subgroups.

In 1997, Marlene Brant Castellano (Mohawk) told evaluators that "Aboriginal people have been 'researched to death,' with little benefit deriving from the numerous studies that have been carried out" (1997, p. 1). Linda Tuhiwai Smith, a well-known Maori researcher from New Zealand, went even further, beginning her seminal book, *Decolonizing Methodologies: Research and Indigenous Peoples* (2012), by stating:

> *The word itself, 'research,' is probably one of the dirtiest words in the Indigenous world's vocabulary..... The ways in which scientific research is implicated in the worst excesses of colonialism remains a powerful remembered history for many of the world's colonized peoples.* (p. 1)

Gathering information is viewed as an inherently political process (Government of Canada, 1991).

> *In the past, Aboriginal people have not been consulted about what information should be collected, who should gather that information, who should maintain it, and who should have access to it. The information gathered may or may not have been relevant to the questions, priorities and concerns of Aboriginal peoples. Because data gathering has frequently been imposed by outside authorities, it has met with resistance in many quarters.* (p. 4)

According to Schnarch (2004), there is a mistaken assumption that data are value neutral, ready to be collected or interpreted by anyone on an equal basis. Instead, he comments, data are constructed through a series of choices involving questions, frameworks, methods, and instruments, all situated in a specific research (and social) context. Researchers unfamiliar with Indigenous knowledge may not follow proper protocols or honor traditional laws when accessing, using, or interpreting information. This is viewed as a form of theft by many Indigenous peoples.

Colonization in America involved the appropriation of property and the establishment of control over American Indians out of fear, greed, perceived superiority, and a general lack

---

[2]In the following discussion, we have selected the term Indigenous Peoples to describe Native Indians and Alaskan Natives (American) and First Nations, Inuit, and Metis (Canada) as described by the United Nations Declaration of the Rights of Indigenous Peoples (2007) except when using direct quotations from other authors.

of understanding about the importance of tradition and culture. History reminds us of heart-wrenching stories of warfare and bloodshed. Among others:

- The Trail of Tears (1830–1850) forced the removal of approximately 60,000 Native Americans from their ancestral homes.

- The "Termination" period (1946–1964) occurred when 109 tribes were terminated, approximately 2.5 million acres of tribal land were removed, and 12,000 American Indians lost tribal affiliation (Pacheco et al., 2013, pp. 2152–2153).

- The involuntary sterilization of at least 3,406 American Indian women (1973–1976) aged 15–44 years (Pacheco et al., 2013, p. 2153).

- The stripping away of language, culture, and self-hood, in the removal of thousands of Indigenous children to residential or boarding schools (Kao, 2020) and the undocumented deaths of hundreds of children at residential schools, such as in Kamloops, British Columbia (Dickson & Watson, 2021).

A striking example was the 1989 Havasupai Diabetes Project, a research project conducted by Arizona State University (ASU). Researchers assisted the Havasupai Tribe with an epidemic of type 2 diabetes but, unknown to the Tribe, some researchers also used the blood samples collected for this research for other genetic studies to examine causes of schizophrenia and inbreeding, and to test theories of population migration (Pacheco et al., 2013; Morton et al., 2013; Kelley et al., 2013, Garrison, 2017). Researchers at several academic institutions benefited from the information, writing articles and theses referencing the Havasupai samples; none had permission from the Tribe. Tribal members suffered stigma, loss of privacy, mental anguish, and intrusion on their spiritual beliefs. In 2004, the Havasupai Tribe filed a lawsuit against the Arizona Board of Regents and ASU researchers. It was settled in 2010 with monetary compensation, scholarships, and the return of the DNA samples but it left no legal precedent as it was never tried in court due to a procedural error.

As Garrison (2017) states:

> *The case raised issues of just and respectful research practices involving indigenous people. In particular, it highlighted the effects of research harms on the community, challenged the appropriateness of certain types of research, and questioned the adequacy of informed consent…. Until now, however, very little work has been done to examine whether and how researchers and IRBs understand that their expertise has been challenged and, further, whether this challenge has altered their notions of human subjects' protection and their practices of implementing just research practices. The specific implications of this case on the conduct of genetic researchers and IRBs in the United States have not been thoroughly explored.* (p. 4)

Over time, consent practices and the way researchers think about interacting with research participants have evolved but whether the Havasupai case had an impact on informed consent is debatable. Garrison concludes: "We must remain mindful of the diverse views of research participants and work harder to ensure that just and equitable research practices encourage communication and inclusion of minorities in research in order to breakdown the barriers of distrust" (p. 15).

As evaluators, we may rely on the history that was taught to us in school to judge Indigenous peoples, or we may use the shorthand of the stereotypes promulgated by the media and entertainment industries. This information is typically oversimplified, incomplete, or wrong (Kao, 2020). We may be unaware of "the extent to which federal government agencies and affiliated institutions have oppressed, discriminated against, and engaged in culturally biased practices with these communities" (Kelley et al., 2013, p. 2146).

The dispossession of land and property and the denial of personal agency has resulted in impoverishment, intergenerational trauma, and poor mental and physical health for many Indigenous people. For example, researchers link their frequent dependence on poor food sources due to location and lack of access to high rates of Type 2 diabetes, the highest in the world.

Indigenous people in America also suffer from high rates of homicide, suicide, substance use disorders, accidental deaths, community/domestic violence, child abuse/neglect, poverty, poor education, and lack of employment opportunities. In addition, the legacy of transgenerational trauma, loss, grief, and anger continues.

In 2007, 144 states adopted the United Nations Declaration on the Rights of Indigenous Peoples (UNDRIP). It establishes "a universal framework of minimum standards for the survival, dignity and well-being of the Indigenous peoples of the world and it elaborates on existing human rights standards and fundamental freedoms as they apply to the specific situation of Indigenous peoples" (United Nations, 2007). However, in both the United States and Canada, moral and political support was hampered by existing laws and policies. UNDRIP was adopted in Canada in 2021, and while the United States has not yet endorsed it, there is agreement to support the Declaration (Organization of American States, 2020).

Changes are required at all levels (i.e., systems, organizations, individuals). The field of evaluation needs to know about and to embrace these human rights standards. As Bowman (2019) suggests:

> *Evaluators can be facilitators to the critical levers of change that are needed to make policies, principles, and declarations operational and impactful. Through research on evaluation, evaluation policy, evaluation technical assistance, and development activities, and as co-leaders with Indigenous scholars and Tribal/First Nations designing and implementing evaluations, the field of evaluation can be the catalyst for needed changes that should have happened centuries ago.* (p. 349)

Strategies for the Evaluator. If we wish to promote social justice in our work with Indigenous peoples, we need to search for ways to integrate Indigenous knowledge in our evaluation practice, work with different epistemologies, use an Indigenous evaluation framework when appropriate, and manage Indigenous data with respect.

Integrate Indigenous Knowledge in Evaluation Practice. Bowman (2021) suggests that a change in evaluation education, professional practice, and individual behavior is needed. The way evaluation is theorized, transmitted, and taught needs to address privilege directly. Curriculum, texts, and syllabi should incorporate decolonized content as core material, not as add-ons or options. Bowman (2021) comments:

> *Knowing origin stories of oppression will reveal to evaluation students how we participate in these systems so that we can begin to deconstruct and dismantle them. To ignore or exclude this from academic instruction about evaluation simply makes the modern-day academic, policymaker, or practitioner commit the same trauma and injustice ....* (p. 322)

We need to understand that colonization still exists in procurement policies, monetary awards, data access, and peer review processes and that that some professional networks still deny Indigenous evaluators, scholars, and governments a place at the evaluation table. When the opportunity arises, such as through committee work, conducting peer reviews, or writing our own proposals and designs, we can exert influence to diminish these barriers. The good news is that things are starting to change. The American Evaluation Association has an Indigenous People's Group (IPG) Topical Interest Group (TIG). Additionally, the Canadian Evaluation Society has a Diversity, Equity, and Inclusion Working Group as well as an Equity, Diversity, Inclusion, and Environmental Sustainability Committee.

Bowman (2021) comments:

> *Privileged evaluators need to hold space for, and value, the intellectual and practical strengths that Indigenous evaluators have to offer through invitations to "thought-leader gatherings" and memberships in professional organizations; open discussions with colleagues at book clubs, brown bag lunches, panels, and plenaries; joint presentations and publications; and the routine practice of including topics of power and privilege in professional discourse* (p. 323).

Work With Different Epistemologies. Western Thought and Indigenous Knowledge are two fundamentally different epistemologies. While Western Thought has been viewed as "an empirical, intellectual tradition which satisfied western culture standards of validity, but which perpetuated the dominating structures of the past" (Brandt-Castellano, 1997, p. 2), Indigenous Knowledge encompasses three processes: observation, traditional teachings, and revelation (Brandt-Castellano, 2000, p. 24). Traditional teachings rest on knowledge passed from generation to generation by Elders and knowledge keepers. Before colonization, Indigenous peoples already had a body of knowledge that encompassed survival skills, environmental skills, and philosophies about meaning, purpose, and values. They acquired knowledge through revelation, dreams, visions, and intuition and gained spiritual knowledge through ancestors and the spirit world (Lavallée, 2009, p. 22). These sources of knowledge remain valid today.

Two-Eyed Seeing, (a Mi'kmaw saying translated from Etuaptmumk), provides one way to view the two epistemologies simultaneously. Mi'kmaw Elder Albert Marshall developed the idea in 2004, to encourage science students to benefit from cross-cultural dialogue, understanding, and healing (Bartlett et al., 2012, p. 2). It allowed them to weave Indigenous and mainstream knowledge together, as Elder Albert indicates:

> …*learning to see from one eye with the strengths of Indigenous knowledges and ways of knowing, and from the other eye with the strengths of Western knowledges and ways of knowing, and to using both these eyes together, for the benefit of all.* (p. 5)

The Seventh Generation Principle is an ancient Haudenosaunee (Iroquois) philosophy that maintains that today's decisions should result in a sustainable world seven generations into the future (Indigenous Corporate Training, 2020). Families use it to hold close the lives, memories, and hopes of seven generations. Each generation is responsible for learning from the three generations that have come before and teaching and protecting the next three while interacting responsibly with their own generation (Wilkins, 2018).

Use an Indigenous Evaluation Framework. LaFrance and Nichols (2010) developed an indigenous evaluation framework that "synthesizes Indigenous ways of knowing and Western evaluation practice" (p. 13). See Table 12.3.

TABLE 12.3 ● CORE VALUES AND EVALUATION PRACTICE

Core Values	Indigenous Evaluation Practice
Indigenous knowledge creation context is critical	• Evaluation itself becomes part of the context; it is not an "external" function • Evaluators need to attend to the relationships between the program and community • If specific variables are to be analyzed, care must be taken to do so without ignoring the contextual situation
People of a place	• Honor the place-based nature of many of our programs • Situate the program by describing its relationship to the community, including its history, current situation, and the individuals affected • Respect that what occurs in one place may not be easily transferred to other situations or places
Recognizing our gifts—personal sovereignty	• Consider the whole person when assessing merit • Allow for creativity and self-expression • Use multiple ways to measure accomplishment • Make connections to accomplishment and responsibility

(Continued)

Table 12.3 *(Continued)*

Core Values	Indigenous Evaluation Practice
Centrality of community and family	• Engage the community, not only the program, when planning and implementing an evaluation • Use participatory practices that engage stakeholders • Make evaluation processes transparent • Understand that programs may focus not only on individual achievement, but also on restoring community health and well-being
Tribal sovereignty	• Ensure tribal ownership and control of data • Follow tribal Institutional Review Board processes • Build capacity in the community • Secure proper permission if future publishing is expected • Report in ways meaningful to tribal audiences as well as to funders

Source: LaFrance, J., & Nichols, R. (2010). Reframing evaluation: Defining an indigenous evaluation framework. *The Canadian Journal of Program Evaluation, 23*(2), 13–31.

Manage Indigenous Data With Respect. An important response to Indigenous mistrust of both research and researchers has been the development of a set of principles to guide the collection and management of Indigenous data while honoring Indigenous knowledge. The standards of ownership, control, access, and possession, or OCAP® (Neglia, 2021), address government and academic self-regulation and provide guidelines for research that are endorsed by Indigenous communities and protect Indigenous peoples' rights and interests (Drawson et al., 2017).

The lawsuit between the Havasupai Tribe and Arizona State University illustrated the need for tribally based IRBs (Morton et al., 2013). By 2013, there were over 20 tribal and regional Indian Health Service IRBs or Institutional Review Boards (Indian Health Service, 2021) to encourage successful collaboration and shared responsibility between academia and Indigenous peoples.

In addition to federal requirements, the Boards reflect other community needs such as:

> *community-level protections, protocol reviews by cultural committees or elders, publication and dissemination agreements, agreements related to monetary benefits, and Tribal consideration of the meaning of research questions.* (p. 2147)

Many researchers now ensure that Indigenous research is respectful and in keeping with Indigenous values and traditions. "This change has been a powerful and positive step toward the establishment of principles and guidelines for academics, universities, governmental institutions, partners in research, and communities doing research with Aboriginal peoples" (Marsh et al., 2015, p. 3).

The Truth and Reconciliation Commission (TRC) was established by the Government of Canada in response to a class-action settlement with Indian Residential School survivors.

Its goal was to facilitate reconciliation among former students, their families, their communities, and all Canadians (Government of Canada, 2021). In 2015, the final report was released and included 94 Calls to Action. As of June 30, 2021, 14 had been completed (BC Treaty Commission, 2021). One priority is to codevelop a national interdisciplinary research and training model with Indigenous communities. The three federal research granting agencies, known as the Tri-Council, have committed to supporting new research models based on the following key principles (Government of Canada, 2019):

1. **Self-determination**: fostering the right for First Nations, Inuit and Métis peoples to set their own research priorities

2. **Decolonization of research**: respecting Indigenous ways of knowing and supporting community-led research

3. **Accountability**: strengthening accountability in respecting Indigenous ethics and protocols in research and identifying the benefits and impacts of research in Indigenous communities

4. **Equitable access**: facilitating and promoting equitable access and support for Indigenous students and researchers.

Ethnicity

Hispanics and Latinos are the largest racial minority in the United States, making up 18.5% of the population (2019 U.S. Census) which is comprised of people of "Cuban, Mexican, Puerto Rican, South or Central American, or other Spanish culture or origin, regardless of race" (U.S. Census Bureau, 2020, para. 1). Hispanics are people from Spain or Spanish-speaking countries in Latin America (excluding Brazil, where Portuguese is the official language), while Latinos are people from Latin America regardless of language (including Brazil but excluding Spain). People of Mexican ancestry constitute the most significant (63%) and fastest-growing Latino subgroup (Buriel, 2012). Passel and Cohn (2008) indicate that "by 2050, the nation's racial and ethnic mix will look quite different than it does now. Non-Hispanic whites, who made up 67% of the population in 2005, will be 47% in 2050. Hispanics will rise from 14% of the population in 2005 to 29% in 2050 (p. 1).

Terminology is important in this discussion. The term Latinx term came into use in 2004 as a new, gender-neutral label and was adopted by news and entertainment outlets, corporations, local governments, and universities. However, only 23% of U.S. adults who self-identify as Hispanic or Latino have heard of the term, and only 3% say they use it. Since Spanish is a gendered language, people debated the use of the term and support is moving away from it. In 2021, the League of United Latin American Citizens, the oldest Latino civil rights organization, decided to remove Latinx from their official communication (Gamboa, 2021). When researchers examine the preference between the Hispanic and Latino labels, Hispanic has a marginal lead (Noe-Bustamante et al., 2020). Therefore, we will retain the term Hispanic in this brief section unless using a direct quotation from another author.

The Hispanic population has a complex history and is the result of conquest and absorption. For example, 500 years ago, there were no Mexicans in Mexico, (Buriel, 2012, p. 292). The area was populated by various tribes of American Indians. After the arrival of Cortes in 1519,

European diseases decimated the population. At the same time, the Spaniard colonizers were absorbed into the Indian and mestizo populations, as were many of the African slaves brought to replace a vanishing Indigenous labor pool. This makes Mexicans a uniquely mixed-race people but ironically, the U.S. Census Bureau does not consider them to be a distinct "race." They are an "ethnic" group that is racially White for census purposes.

While Spaniards as a subgroup generally disappeared from the Mexican population, their cultural imprint was profound. Spanish replaced many Indigenous languages and Spanish Catholicism was forcefully imposed. With time, the religion was infused with many Indigenous practices and symbols (e.g., the Virgin of Guadalupe). Mexican Catholicism remains an essential component of Mexican identity.

As Hispanic immigration to the United States continues, values vary and shift, dependent on different generational and regional subgroups, and country of origin, level of education, and class, but there are four cultural values that evaluators need to keep in mind when working with Hispanic communities (Buriel, 2012, p. 297; Galanti, 2003, p. 181; Guajardo et al., 2020). See Table 12.4.

TABLE 12.4 ● FOUR VALUES FOUND IN U.S. HISPANIC COMMUNITIES	
Term	**Description**
Familismo	• Perceived obligation to provide material and emotional support to the members of the extended family • Reliance on relatives for decision making support • Perception of relatives as the behavioral and attitudinal referents • Importance of milestone events such as birthdays, baptisms, quinceañeras, weddings, and funerals.
Respeto	• Highlights appropriate communication processes • Use of titles, formal communication styles, manners of dress and presentation, and ways of interacting with those in positions of power • Respect and obedience toward elders, males, and other authority figures • Values obedience, deference, decorum, self-monitoring of public behavior, good manners, and being *bien educado,* or well-educated
Simpatía	• Avoidance of interpersonal conflict. • Downplaying or covering up personal and family difficulties to present oneself and one's family in the best possible light. • Emphasizes the need to lessen emotional distress • Importance of relationship building
Marianismo/Machismo	• A dichotomy in gender roles and expectations. • Marianismo defines feminine attributes and roles related to purity, motherhood, virginity, reverence for the Virgin Mary, submissiveness of women, and the unquestioned authority of the father • Machismo reflects expectations for male behavior as a strong sense of masculine pride and dominance. On the positive side, dictates protecting the honor and welfare of their families, on the other, may refer to excessive alcohol use, risky behaviors, and the subjugation of women.

These values have significant implications not only for evaluators but for the uptake, engagement, and retention of the Hispanic population in health, education, and social services. The degree to which the individual has taken on American culture (i.e., acculturation) plays a significant role in the health of Hispanics, "particularly in terms of alcohol and/or drug use, sexual mores, domestic violence, and HIV risk behaviors, especially among women" (Galanti, 2003, p. 181). As Guajardo et al. (2020) stress, "In evaluation, attention to gender identity, roles, stereotypes, and power dynamics and interplay across multiple levels are critical" (p. 73).

Evaluators also need to understand the impact of national immigration policies and procedures on Hispanic families and children. Overall, current policies can create vulnerabilities, poor mental health outcomes, mistrust and fear, limited access to services, separated parents and children, and exacerbated poverty and discrimination.

Immigrants fall into distinct categories that carry different entitlements to benefits, services, and legal rights, including:

- Legal Permanent Resident (LPR)
- Naturalized Citizen
- Legal Temporary Resident (LTR)
- Refugee/Asylee
- Undocumented Immigrant.

Heightened enforcement measures in recent years, family separation, serial migration, forced removal or fear of deportation, and restricted access to federal public benefits have significantly increased fear and mistrust that transcend entire families and communities.

Inevitably, like other minority groups we have discussed, Hispanics experience acculturation pressures, discrimination, and persecution. A story Bev recalls goes as follows:

The setting was Marfa, Texas in the 1950s. Hispanic schools were segregated. Maggie, aged 73 and Jessi, 69, remember very well the burial of Mr. Spanish when they were six years old. The students were told to write on a piece of paper, "I will not speak Spanish in school." The teacher used a little cigar box to collect the children's papers. A hole was dug near the flagpole and the whole school was marched outside to watch the burial process. The children had been to funerals before, but they were not sure exactly what was going on. They went back to class and were told not to speak Spanish again.

Maggie continued, "So I told my friends, 'Nadie me va a parar que yo no hable el español. Nobody's gonna stop me from speaking Spanish.' And I didn't know the teacher was right behind me." She was taken to the principal who hit her with a paddle three times. She ran home, bruised and hurting but while her parents weren't happy about it, they told her to follow instructions. Jessi added, "Our parents always supported the teachers. And I remember my dad said, 'If you're in school, you just be obedient. Don't stir the waters.'"

*The children felt like something had been ripped away from them. Language is one of the
things that defines you; take that away and you are left with emptiness and a sense of loss.*
(Warren & Glenn, 2017)

Strategies for the Evaluator. Evaluators need to be aware of the issues affecting the
growing Hispanic community in the United States. Our designs and data collection
methods must be culturally sensitive and relevant to the specific context. Sample strategies
include the use of the Socio-Ecological Model, approaches outlined in LitCrit theory, and
evaluation for advocacy.

Use the Socio-Ecological Model (SEM). Barriers such as the lack of quality education, inadequate health insurance coverage, lack of culturally responsive healthcare systems, poverty,
and limited political power hinder the success of many Hispanic immigrants. The SEM
model (see Chapter 2) allows the evaluator to consider a broader socio-ecological perspective
beyond the interpersonal and intrapersonal factors usually addressed by evaluation (Lemos
& Garcia, 2020, p. 92). The evaluator can obtain evidence at the multiple levels of influence
that impact uptake and engagement in social and health services. For example, an evaluator
can use SEM to assess the presence of immigration-related stressors and resulting mental
health issues (Torres et al., 2018, p. 849).

Lemos and Garcia (2020, pp. 92–93) comment that evaluators need to be aware that
immigration status is not protected information and can potentially be subpoenaed.
Therefore, this information must be kept confidential and deidentified. Where possible
proxy indicators such as primary language, country of origin, years lived in the United
States, and receipt of Emergency Medicaid services can be used.

They also recommend that evaluation tools are translated into Spanish and piloted by
those fluent in Spanish in various countries of origin. Castillo (2019), a evaluator of
Mexican descent, experienced some mortification when collecting data from Salvadoran
American teenaged gang members. As he found out, "cultures and languages are not
monolithic" (p. 100). He described several blunders he made in his use of Spanish,
causing members of a gang to question his credibility. As he said, "There are frequently
differences in regional cultures or dialects that can lead even experienced evaluators into
embarrassment, scorn, or the worst outcome of all: inaccurate data." He learned to
translate with the local context and population in mind and was reminded that the
evaluator's response to the situation is important: "you must be respectful, you should
learn why what you did is problematic so that you will not repeat the offense, and (if
appropriate) don't forget to laugh at yourself" (p. 103).

Consider LatCrit Strategies. LatCrit is an evaluation theory that moves beyond the Black/
White dichotomy of Critical Race Theory to attend to Hispanic ethnicity, identity,
migration, cultures, values, and language and their relationship to White privilege. It offers
"a unique interplay among race, ethnicity, coalition-building, and action" (Guajardo et al.,
2020, p. 69), similar in many ways to Culturally Responsive Evaluation (Frierson et al.,
2002).

Four strategies foster culturally relevant practice (Guajardo et al., 2020, pp. 69–71), including:

1. View the Hispanic experience through a historical lens that acknowledges ethno-racial identity, language, cultural values, traditional gender roles and experiences; the impact of immigration; and the impact of these influences on Hispanic communities.

2. Identify how evaluation explicitly links with activism, organizing, and political or social discourse.

3. Commit to expansion and interconnectedness; engage in critical individual and collective reflective processes, and work toward social justice for all Hispanic identities.

4. Cultivate community, coalition-building, and equity in all phases of the evaluation process.

The Child360 project described in the Chapter 11 Spotlight on Equity provides a good example of this approach.

Using LatCrit allows evaluators explore how Hispanic identity shapes the work of evaluators. For example, Guajardo et al. (2020) state that "It offers social justice and equity-oriented evaluators an intersectional framework for responsive, values-aligned practice and social change" (p. 73).

Use Evaluation for Advocacy. Greene (1997) comments, "evaluators are inevitably on somebody's side and not on somebody else's side" (p. 25). However, the idea of advocacy "immediately raises the many specters of bias, cooptation, and contamination that haunt the corners and byways of evaluation design and implementation" (p. 26). In the context of social justice, if evaluators believe that their work can support positive social change, then they are already advocating. Neubauer and Hall (2020) suggest:

> *the role of evaluator is one of power, because as a knowledge worker, evaluators are able to utilize their inquiry skills to aid and abet the process of seeking change. As advocates, evaluators can use the knowledge they glean from inquiry to promote change.* (p. 133)

When evaluators advocate for disenfranchised groups such as Hispanic immigrants, we can use these strategies (Lemos & Garcia, 2020; McBride et al., 2020):

*   Build evaluation capacity in community members, grassroots groups, leaders, and other stakeholders.

*   Educate stakeholders about the impact of restrictive or biased policies.

*   Use strengths-based and equity-focused evaluation approaches to measure change.

*   Teach stakeholders how to find their voices and exercise their rights.

Organizations and Structures

The third and final macro system in our model represents the organizations and structures in which evaluators work. While an evaluation is supposed to shed light on successes and failures, facilitate informed decision making, support corrective action, and foster better results (Heider, 2016), the reality is more complex. Too often, evaluations do not lead to positive change. We need to ask ourselves why our findings may remain disconnected from organizational decision making and improvement strategies.

Evaluation effectiveness can be undercut by these responses from management (Porter & Hawkins, 2019, pp. 89–91):

- **Aversion to reality**. Evaluation evidence can identify the mismatch between deeply held values and assumptions and day-to-day reality. This dissonance can result in resistance to the evidence, and so management may avoid taking appropriate action.

- **Disfigured accountability**. When the evaluation serves the agendas of donors and funders, it becomes a tool of compliance to maintain the status quo or to tell people what they want to hear.

- **Ritualization**. When managers do not include evaluation findings in the decision making process, they become tick-box exercises, valuing other sources of information and influences instead of the evaluation evidence.

- **Empty rhetoric**. Managers may be aware that a specific funder or champion favors evidence-based decision making and so give lip service to the importance of evaluation but are unwilling to allocate resources for proposed changes or to use the evidence in their own work.

- **Censorship**. Many organizations are leery of transparency and making performance information publicly available. They fear media attention or a negative public response. Instead, they may encourage the release of brief evaluation summaries that are edited for political expediency.

Another potential reason for failure relates to nature of the client-evaluator relationship. Is it transactional or transformational? A transaction involves "an instance of buying or selling something; a business deal (Oxford Lexico, 2021b, para. 1). A transactional conversation about evaluation might go something like this: "We will pay you this amount (as stated in the contract) to conduct an evaluation of our program and you will produce a final report describing the program's impact." A "this for that" mentality can shrink the scope of an evaluation and constrain its potential for change. It can become a reductionist exercise that diminishes understanding, eliminates complexity, and reduces the quality of decisions (Tester, n.d.).

As an alternative, transformation can offer a "thorough or dramatic change in form or appearance (Oxford Lexico, 2021, para. 1). In evaluation terms, the transformational conversation might be: "We all come to this evaluation thinking one way. As a result of our learning and work together, we are changed—reordered, reshaped, and reeducated by the shared experience" (Frazier, 2019). Like opening the lens in a camera, the transformational mindset lets more light enter and floods the mind with new possibilities (Tester, n.d.). The evaluator can envision the responsibilities, opportunities, perspectives, and problems to be solved.

Table 12.5 compares the transactional and transformational mindset in response to components of the evaluation process.

TABLE 12.5 ● COMPARISON OF TRANSACTIONAL AND TRANSFORMATIONAL MINDSETS		
Evaluation Component	**Transactional Mindset**	**Transformational Mindset**
Focus	• Continuity	• Opportunity
Scope	• Within program	• Across systems
Thought process	• Standardized, reductionist, mechanical	• Eclectic, expansive, aspirational
Goal	• Process-oriented	• Outcomes-oriented
Time horizon	• Short term	• Long term
Risk tolerance	• Minimize risk	• Embrace risk as part of growth
Motivation	• Time and tactics	• Purpose and vision
Attitude to change	• Maintain status quo	• Foster meaningful innovation
Accountability	• Contain and control	• Share ownership and authority

Source: Adapted from Tester, T. (n.d.). *Move beyond the transactional mindset. Beyond the deal.* https://btd.consulting/manage-the-ma-process/move-beyond-the-transactional-mindset/

Throughout this book, we have discussed the importance of understanding systems. Kania et al. (2018) tell the following story:

> *A fish is swimming along one day when another fish comes up and says "Hey, how's the water?" The first fish stares back blankly at the second fish and then says, "What's water?"* (p. 2)

Organizations may not even see the water or recognize the environment in which they have been swimming all along. The authors cite the many complex problems found in a program's macro environment, such as environmental degradation, government policies, societal norms, market forces, incentives, power imbalances, knowledge gaps, and embedded social narratives. Thus, the evaluator must recognize the "messy kaleidoscope of factors" (p. 2) surrounding the program.

To understand how change is influenced and "to enhance the wellbeing of communities and support people to thrive—to take on our systemic problems—we need to shift the systems holding a problem in place. We need systemic solutions" (Social Innovation Generation, 2021, para. 2). Thus, it is essential to determine what these conditions are and how evaluators, stakeholders, and communities can shift them.

The model by Kania et al. (2018) outlines six conditions of systems change (pp. 4-5). The six conditions are grouped by types of change, including structural, relational, and transformative. See Figure 12.8, p. 506.

FIGURE 12.8 ◆ SIX CONDITIONS OF SYSTEMS CHANGE

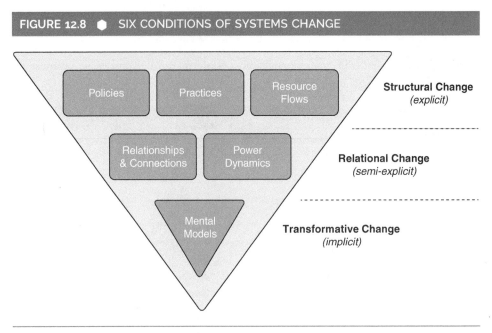

Source: Kania, J., Kramer, M., & Senge, P. (2018). *The water of systems change*. FSG. Reprinted with permission from FSG.

Kania et al. (2018, pp. 4–5) further describe these conditions in describe these condition Figure 12.9.

FIGURE 12.9 ◆ TYPES OF CHANGES FOR SYSTEMS

Structural Change (explicit)

- Policies: Government, institutional and organizational rules, regulations, and priorities that guide the actions of organizations and other stakeholders.

- Practices: Espoused activities of institutions, coalitions, networks, and other entities targeted to improving social and environmental progress. Also, within the entity, the procedures, guidelines, or informally shared habits that comprise their work.

- Resource Flows: How money, people, knowledge, information, and other assets such as infrastructure are allocated and distributed.

Relational Change (semi-explicit)

- Relationships & Connections: Quality of connections and communication occurring among actors in the system, especially among those with differing histories and viewpoints.

- Power Dynamics: The distribution of decision-making power, authority, and formal and informal influence among individuals and organizations.

Transformative Change (implicit)

- Mental Models: Habits of thought—deeply held beliefs and assumptions and taken-for-granted ways of operating that influence how we think, what we do, and how we talk.

Source: Kania, J., Kramer, M., & Senge, P. (2018). *The water of systems change*. FSG. Reprinted with permission from FSG.

Abercrombie et al. (2015) state, system change "is about addressing the root causes of social problems, which are often intractable and embedded in networks of cause and effect. It is an intentional process designed to fundamentally alter the components and structures that cause the system to behave in a certain way" (p. 3).

As organizations consider the macro forces at play, they also need to understand that these conditions also flow within the organization. An organization can inhibit change through its "internal policies, practices, and resources, its relationships and power imbalances, and the tacit assumptions of its board and staff" (Kania et al., 2018, p. 5). For example, unrealistic time horizons and traditional power dynamics can limit an ability to examine conditions in any deep and meaningful way.

Structural change involves examining policies, practices, and resource flows for needed change. Evaluators have collected data, written reports, and produced recommendations on these topics for many years, yet Kania et al. (2018) contend that by excluding the relational and transformative levels, conditions will not shift. For example, the Affordable Care Act (ACA) created a significant change in policy and resource flows, allowing millions of Americans access to health care. At the level of relational change, the ACA catalyzed stronger relationships between the community and health providers. Unfortunately, the relationships among other key players such as providers, insurers, pharmaceutical companies, and patients did not change, and power did not shift away from lobbyists, political parties, or legislators. Additionally, at the level of transformative change, a new narrative was not instilled about why the uninsured deserve access to health care. Without shifting the mental models of a critical mass of lawmakers, corporate leaders, and the public, the ACA has remained at risk.

Relational change involves dislodging power dynamics and entrenched relationships. To do so, organizations must strengthen cross-sector coalitions and community connections. All stakeholders must openly discuss equity and power-sharing issues if systems change is to occur. For example, in Los Angeles, supportive housing seemed a promising solution to end chronic homelessness, but the two participating levels of government, city administration and social services, had never worked together, and each blamed the other for the growing homeless problem. By building relationships across these departments, they developed a joint plan and each partner contributed significant resources (Kania et al., 2018, p. 8).

Transformative change involves a change to mental models. It presents the greatest challenge but if it is not confronted, change at the other two levels will be temporary. Our mental models shape the meaning we assign to external events, media reports, and the public discourse we find on Facebook and Twitter. These, in turn, can strengthen our mental models. For example, a fear of needles may shape an individual's mental model about avoiding injections, so they may not want a COVID-19 vaccination. Social media stories and online disinformation about the lack of vaccine safety can reinforce this perception, and the resulting behavior is a refusal to get vaccinated. Unless that mental model is changed, the individual will not support the desired public health outcome of curtailing the spread of the virus regardless of the structural and relational changes made to that end. Thus, if the conditions that hold a problem in place are to be changed, strategies must be constructed to attend to all three levels of change.

Strategies for the Evaluator

When using a macro systems perspective in an organizational or structural context, we can work with organizations to expand the approach to learning and use equitable evaluation strategies to raise organizational awareness.

Expand Approach to Learning. Decision making in organizations tends to follow a predictable path. Typically, people define the scope of the problem, seek a potential solution, plan a path forward, and then test the outcome for effectiveness.

Schön and Argyris researched organizational learning (Argyris, 1977) and found that people tend to advocate for a position while simultaneously controlling others so that they can win their position and control the tasks to be done, "secretly deciding how much to tell people and how much is to be distorted, usually to save somebody's face" (Argyris, 1977, para. 29).

The predisposition to polarize and ignore or suppress dilemmas and paradoxes is a crucial problem for organizations wishing to shift mental models and to initiate real systems change. For deep learning to occur, double-loop learning is required. See Figure 12.10 (McKinney, 2008, p. 1).

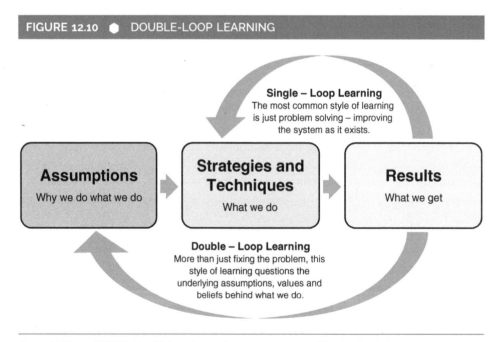

FIGURE 12.10 ◆ DOUBLE-LOOP LEARNING

Source: McKinney, M. (2008, May 13). Learning requires personal responsibility. *Leadership Now.*

Double-Loop Learning used reflection to achieve transformative change. The process is powerful and potentially unsettling but may lead to a fundamental change in understanding. Using our intuition, emotional intelligence, and critical self-reflection, we can confront our technical errors, mistakes in judgment, and conflicted interactions. We can shift our frames of reference and mental models, deepening our understanding of the substance, forms, and patterns of our experience (Barrington, 2021a).

Garvin (1993) suggests that organizational change has three stages.

1. Cognitive change. By exposing employees and stakeholders to new ideas, expanding their knowledge, and encouraging shifts in mental models, changes to thinking begin to occur. The organization can foster learning by allowing time for reflection and analysis, strategic planning, assessment, and innovation.

2. Behavioral change. To overcome silos and boundaries, information must be shared, and cross-team collaborations created through joint conferences, meetings, and projects.

3. Performance improvement. This is familiar territory for the evaluator. Changes can be observed, measured, reported, discussed, and plans for further change developed.

Use Equitable Evaluation Strategies. Dean-Coffey et al. (2014) offer an approach that combines individual and organizational learning to foster change. It weaves the AEAs Statement on Cultural Competence (2011) and equitable evaluation concepts into the **Equitable Evaluation Framework™** shown in Figure 12.11.

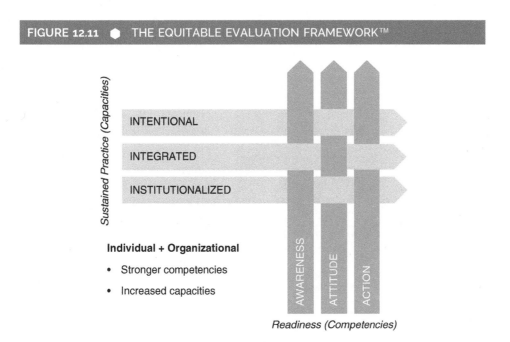

FIGURE 12.11 ● THE EQUITABLE EVALUATION FRAMEWORK™

Source: From "Raising the Bar—Integrating Cultural Competence and Equity: Equitable Evaluation" by J. Dean-Coffey, J. Casey, & L. D. Caldwell, 2014, *The Foundation Review*, 6(2), 84. Reprinted with permission.

This integrated framework reflects a dynamic continuum, a continual threading and weaving together of intentional reflecting, thinking, and realigning to create a tapestry of greater understanding. Thus, systems must attend to both individual competencies (awareness, attitude, and action) and organizational capacities (intentionality, integration, and institutionalization). In particular, the framework offers us a way to consider the intersectionality of race, ethnicity, and other socially defined characteristics such as gender, ability, culture, class, nationality, and age, with issues of equity and diversity.

For organizations to achieve breakthroughs for transformation and sustained change, they must face the pain. It is not easy to change predictable ways of being. It is no small challenge to hold to account both ourselves and the organizations we work with. To do this, we need a deep understanding of the context, or water, in which we swim.

THE EVALUATOR'S NEW STANCE

Having considered the nature of program context and the dimensions that affect it, the evaluator can understand the underlying forces that have made a program the way it is. By linking local program issues with global trends, we can see connections, patterns, and discrepancies and can adapt the evaluation design and methods to be more responsive. Moving beyond narrow assumptions and expectations, we can commit to our role as global citizens, at the same time, asking the questions that will illuminate the local experience. We return then to the evaluator's new stance to consider both our power and our responsibility.

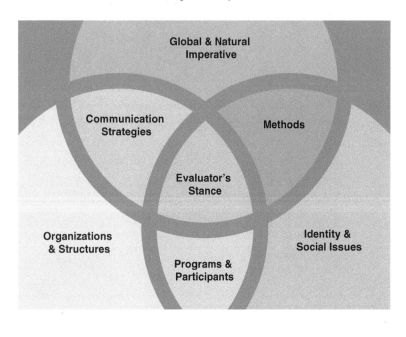

In this swirling mix of local and global factors stands the evaluator, cognizant of our rare skill set, described so well by McBride et al. (2020). We can think critically, design, conduct, analyze, synthesize, interpret, and communicate what we observe to the decision makers and leaders who set the policies that affect the participants in our studies. We can use our connection with program participants to explain organizational intentions and work collaboratively with them to identify gaps in program logic and implementation. No one else has this two-way interaction. This gives us the power to influence positive change. At the same time, it burdens us with the responsibility to speak up, not to remain passive passive, silent, or bound by a mistaken view of our impartiality. We are not impartial. No one is impartial. We simply must declare our biases, report what we have found, and share what can happen if change is embraced, if stakeholders are willing to shift their mental models, and if we are willing to shift our own.

We need to share our experiences and exchange best practices about zooming out and zooming in. Having a sense of purpose, balance, and connectedness will lead to the transformation that is needed to meet our goal of social betterment.

In this new interconnected world, we must use our unique skills to understand systemic threats and barriers and to access decision makers and program participants to reform systems and contribute to global sustainability and social equity. Each of the issues discussed in this chapter presses upon us. In the past, evaluators have chosen to address one issue or another, and their contributions have enriched the literature. However, only a few have taken up the challenge of true intersectionality (i.e., The Evaluator's New Stance). How can we do otherwise?

We must see how complex systems continually interact, adapting in self-organizing ways. Things change before our eyes, and each of us must deal with uncertainty. We must learn that the unexpected is more likely than the planned. Furthermore, we must believe that evaluators can make a difference, working with these messy and intractable problems and finding solutions—not on our own, but collaboratively, across silos, boundaries, and barriers. As we stand at the intersection of this global-local mix, we can link decision makers and program participants, apply new paradigms and tools, reflect on the conditions of systems change, and work with organizations to stimulate transformative change.

To do this, we need survival skills. We must strengthen and nurture ourselves because evaluation is a taxing endeavor and our energy and passion need to be continually replenished. For example, we need to think about ourselves as individuals to combat the fatigue and burnout that this new stance may generate. We must practice active self-care, conduct ongoing self-reflection, maintain loving relationships, discover creative outlets, and get involved with our communities. By continually strengthening ourselves, we can contribute our skills, wisdom, and common sense to the challenges ahead.

In closing, we offer a checklist that distills our learning from the literature and our own practice-based wisdom to support evaluators in the transition to this new stance. Incorporating both macro or worldwide challenges and micro or program-specific issues we can open the discussion and work together to support positive change. We welcome your input.

The checklist in Table 12.6, p. 512, focuses on strategies related to the macro systems discussed in this chapter. Many strategies for micro systems have been discussed throughout the book. The Macro Systems Checklist is divided into issues and suggested actions for the three overlapping macro systems and lists some strategies to consider when adapting your evaluation practice to this new intersectional stance.

TABLE 12.6 ⬡ MACRO SYSTEMS CHECKLIST FOR THE EVALUATOR'S NEW STANCE		
Systems	Issues	Actions
Global and Natural Imperative • Global Issues	Inequitable distribution of wealth, escalating poverty, disruption, migration, social unrest, educational and health disparities, violence	• Commit to your role and responsibility as a global citizen. • Use mixed methods to obtain multiple perspectives. • Use the transformative paradigm when addressing issues of power and justice. • Understand the needs of marginalized groups and choose responsive methods. • Become familiar with the SDGs and seek linkages to your projects. • Break down country barriers and organizational silos to find development evaluators working on similar topics. Invite one to speak at your next stakeholder meeting. • Find an evaluator in the Global South to work with on an upcoming project. • Develop and contribute to local and global databases on methods, findings, and lessons learned. • Share your stories at professional events and build the capacity of your colleagues.
• Natural Systems	In the Anthropocene, human impact on the Earth is irreversible. It affects climate change, environmental degradation, and the unsustainable use of resources.	• Make changes in your own life to support global sustainability. • Use a systems perspective. • Understand interrelationships, connections and their consequences. • Identify boundaries and how they relate to your evaluation. • Use developmental evaluation and emergent designs. • Be comfortable with complexity and uncertain timeframes. • Incorporate sustainability and stewardship into every evaluation. • Focus on regenerative practices; build on strengths. • Incorporate the Footprint Evaluation KEQs as appropriate. • Work with stakeholders on your current evaluation to identify two positive changes the program can make. • Include consideration of global and natural systems in professional competency criteria. • Incorporate global and natural systems in professional competencies criteria.
Identity and Social Issues • Race	Privilege and power are linked to racism and oppression; social and economic equity remains a distant goal for many African Americans.	• Explore your own biases and surface the racial frames and historical beliefs you hold; work to expand your perspective. • Understand how evaluation methods have been influenced by structural racism. Use evaluation theories and methods that counteract this worldview.

Table 12.6 *(Continued)*

Systems	Issues	Actions
		• Look for hidden factors such as social norms, political structures, relationships, stereotypes, attitudes, and expectations that may influence your evaluation. • Promote social justice by using methods that are culturally responsive and strengths based. • Include members of the target group in the program and instrument design and the interpretation of findings. • Hear their stories of survival, fortitude and positive change. • Participate in initiatives that support racial equity. • Read fiction written by the racial or cultural group you are working with. It is a great way to enhance your understanding.
• Culture	A history of oppression and dispossession has led Indigenous people to impoverishment, intergenerational trauma, and mental and physical health concerns.	• Learn about the Indigenous history of the land on which you stand. • Understand that Indigenous people have a unique legal and political status. • Become familiar with past actions by governments and institutions to exterminate and acculturate Indigenous peoples. What vestiges of these attitudes remain? • Explore the concept of tribal sovereignty at the systems level and how it can impact an evaluation. • Include Indigenous people as coleaders in relevant research, education, evaluation, and professional development initiatives. • Understand Indigenous ways of knowing and find ways to incorporate different epistemologies in your evaluation work. • Use methods that are flexible, collaborative, and reflexive. • Decolonize your methods by adhering to Indigenous standards of ownership, control, access, and possession. • Avoid cultural appropriation by giving credit for original sources. • Respect data shared by program participants and honor traditional values. • Expand your understanding of Indigenous stewardship of the environment, Indigenous philosophy and values, and Indigenous myths, stories and literature. • Take time. Build relationships. Drink tea.
• Ethnicity	Hispanics are the largest minority group in the United States, yet conditions persist in marginalizing them.	• Avoid stereotyping and understand that Hispanics do not share a homogenous identity. • View the Hispanic experience through a historical lens and how it has shaped the modern experience.

(Continued)

Table 12.6 *(Continued)*

Systems	Issues	Actions
		• Understand how oppression and marginalization affect study populations. • Use data collection methods that elicit trust and protect identifiable information. • Understand culturally significant values and how they can affect data quality; work collaboratively to develop methods that attend to them. • Involve stakeholders throughout the evaluation process, actively encourage community input, and seek the advice of community partners to interpret social and political concerns. • Use the SEM or other similar systems approaches to center the intended group within a nested set of family, organizational, community, and policy systems. • Understand the trauma associated with immigration and its impact on Hispanic children and families. Use methods such as trauma-informed interviewing to address associated mental stress, vulnerability, and protracted fear. • Make language choices for data collection which reflect the informal speech patterns of the target group. Consider using reverse translation (i.e., prepare the tool in Spanish first, pilot test it, then translate it into English.) • Find appropriate ways to advocate for change based on the results of your study.
• Organizations and Structures	Organizations are the critical link between evaluations and their use, yet many barriers hamper follow-up and transformative change.	• Understand your relationship with your client/commissioner. To what extent is it transactional? How much scope is there for transformational change? • What assumptions are embedded in the organization's view of the program and its participants? Do any organizational or program factors hold inequities in place? • Use a systems perspective to identify hidden factors which may constrain social justice or provide a faulty conceptualization of program purpose. • Work towards a learning culture. • Ensure that the evaluation design and conduct do not seek confirmation of faulty assumptions, nor do they promulgate inequity. • Discuss anticipated evaluation responses with organizational leaders at the planning phase; strategize to counter ways that evaluation findings can be discounted. • Explore ways to develop a transformational mindset within the organization.

Table 12.6 *(Continued)*

Systems	Issues	Actions
		• Incorporate professional development in your evaluation contract. Provide evaluation stakeholders with training on the conditions of systems change and double-loop learning. Discuss strategies for change. • Consider how Equitable Evaluation can be used to develop capacity at both the individual and organizational levels. Then, work with leaders to plan future professional development activities. • Work with a facilitator trained in conflict resolution and collaborative problem-solving to assist with difficult conversations that threaten deeply held values, assumptions and mental models. • Embrace the messiness and risk involved in transformative change and hold to the values of equity, inclusion, and stewardship.
• The Evaluator as Individual	Evaluators may have the evaluation methods and competencies required to meet the challenges of this new stance but may lack the survival skills needed to combat fatigue and burnout in this demanding context.	• Practice active self-care, using the discipline needed to ensure physical and mental health. This means good food, regular exercise and adequate sleep. No excuses! If you want to contribute over the long term, you will never be "too busy" for self-care. • Conduct daily reflection to stay alert; explore assumptions and mental models; assess successes and failures; and foster learning, curiosity, and courage. Continue to grow. • Maintain loving relationships and take the time for family, friends, and good colleagues. They give you strength. • Discover your creativity, intuition, and untapped talents. "Do what your heart draws you to, not what your mind decides" (Wagamese, 2016). • Get involved with the community. Volunteer—you will receive more than you give. • Be a mentor. Train others. Write about your own learning. • Read widely. Explore new genres. Join a book club. • Go for long walks and appreciate the natural world. Do not forget to breathe.

Finally, as we near the end of both this chapter and our book, we present our expert, Dr. Nicole Bowman//Waapalaneexkweew (Lunaape/Mohican).

EXPERT CORNER

Dr. Nicole Bowman/Waapalaneexkweew (Lunaape/Mohican)

Nicole Bowman/Waapalaneexkweew (Lunaape/Mohican), PhD, is a traditional Ndulunaapeewi Kwe (Lunaape woman) and an evaluation innovator whose academic lodge sits at the intersection of traditional knowledge, Tribal sovereignty, and evaluation. She is the President of Bowman Performance Consulting and an Associate Scientist with the University of Wisconsin-Madison. Dr. Bowman is a subject matter expert in systems (Nation to Nation) and culturally responsive and Indigenous research, policy, and evaluation. She was named the American Evaluation Association's (AEA) 2018 Robert Ingle Service Award winner (first Indigenous awardee). She is the coeditor for the Roots and Relations permanent publication section within the Canadian Journal of Program Evaluation and serves on numerous global evaluations, Indigenous, and educational journals or scientific/technical review boards. For decades she has served as chair or cochair of AEA's Indigenous Peoples in Evaluation Topical Interest Group and is a Global Member of EvalPartner's EvalIndigenous and of AEAs International Work Group.

1. *Based on your work as an evaluator and international thought leader, how can an evaluator be responsive to both environmental and global imperatives and cultural issues? Can you provide an example?*

For Indigenous people, these are all interrelated. We do not separate culture from environment or the globe because Nii Eelaangoomaatiit (we are all related). Kukuna Ahkuy (Mother Earth) and all the nonhuman aspects of the ecosystem are our relatives, as are the air, water, mountains, rocks, sun, moon, and stars. As traditional people we care for all our relatives. When you have a relational ethic and lifestyle coupled with humility, love, and respect, then it is clear how to live responsibly and sustainably. But not all humans think or live this way. The colonial mindset and behavior pattern are disconnected from the environment, and Indigenous ways make those in power and privilege uncomfortable. But that disconnection, which is the settler state origin story and the current legacy of colonization, is the root cause of the global crisis that threatens life. It is why we need sustainability frameworks, climate and environmental justice initiatives, and advocacy activities. We must also defund the capitalist practices that continue to conquer the earth, natural resources, and humanity.

2. *What wisdom can elders offer evaluators on how to expand their self-awareness in a complex world?*

I am not an elder, but I hope that I am living as an elder in training. With that awareness, I would offer that the world does not have to be as complex as society often makes it. Many of the teachings of traditional ecological knowledge and ancestral wisdom quite simple. But elder wisdom is one of the most effective bases for practical living that sustains all of life: mine, yours, and everything on the planet and in the Milky Way. Elder wisdom teaches that by knowing your origin story, you may gain access to a deeper understanding about your sacred relationship to the past, present, and future (seven generations ahead). When you seek to know yourself deeply this way, your life choices become more in tune with what the world needs from you. Self-awareness becomes an important transformational pathway to understanding, but only if you can be self-aware in context, with humility, and in an intentional and respectful relationship with all other beings, human and nonhuman. Having an awareness and living beyond the self in contexts of practice is where wisdom can happen.

(Continued)

(Continued)

3. *What advice can you offer those of our readers who are just beginning to explore the field of evaluation?*

Be in kinship with each other. Do not listen with your mind or ego. Close your eyes and listen with your spirit and heart. What gives you a sense of community? Where do you feel passion? Are you ever moved to tears or high levels of inspired behaviors? These are the people and initiatives you want to be part of and in service to. The seen and unseen should be guiding you not just frontal lobes, footnotes, and keynotes. This is a lifelong journey so you should look all around you, not just on pages of publications or who is being projected on the big screen. If you walk in academic and cultural humility, you will be open to so much more, and many opportunities you have never even dreamed of will become your reality. It is about your sense of identity and development, self-actualization as a contributing community member, and using wisdom to create an impactful practice that is a sustainable legacy that others can learn from.

Key Terms

17 Sustainable Development Goals
478

Climate change 476

Context 470

Equitable Evaluation Framework™
509

Macro systems 475

Micro systems 473

The Seventh Generation Principle 497

Systems thinking 480

Two-eyed seeing 497

Wicked problems 471

The Main Ideas

1. Context is the setting in which a program is situated.

2. Wicked problems have many causes, and the solutions are not readily apparent.

3. The Evaluator's New Stance includes the micro-view and the macroview. The microview includes communication strategies, program and participants, and methods. The macroview includes the global and natural imperative, organizations and structures, and identity and social issues.

4. While Zooming In (the microview), we come to understand the complexities of participants' lives in terms of roles, resources, positions, settings, identities, and the social issues they may face. Our goal is program improvement so that the lives of program participants can be improved and so that the structures and systems that support them can be streamlined or enhanced.

5. In the microview, our methods are influenced by our worldview.
   - If we view truth as external to our study, then we are positivists.
   - If we think truth is found through multiple perspectives, we are constructivists.
   - If we connect with marginalized groups where power, culture, and social issues are important, we use the transformative paradigm.
   - Lastly, if we say, 'It depends,' we are pragmatists.

6. Communication Strategies, the third element of the microview, is paramount to the role of the evaluator.

From developing the logic model, to writing the evaluation plan, to disseminating the results, continual communication with clients and stakeholders is essential.

7. While Zooming out (the macroview), the global and natural imperative encourages us to ask how our program and participants are connected to the larger system and how it will that affect evaluation processes. Guiding this perspective are four principles (Patton, 2020): global thinking, the Anthropocene, transformative engagement, and integration (p. 29).

8. Systems thinking is an important concept for the evaluator because it supports the understanding of interrelationships, multiple perspectives, and the scope of the problem.

9. Identity and social issues, the second overlapping macro system, relate to long-standing identity issues and disparities. Race, culture, and ethnicity are influential not only in a person's life, but they also influence the choices that evaluators make.

10. We must examine the way we work and include the lived experience of others. Indigenous knowledge helps us understand the many "ways of knowing" that can yield truth for the communities with whichwe work. Two-Eyed Seeing suggests that Indigenous and Western ways of knowing can coexist. Both can strengthen an evaluation context.

11. The socio-ecological model sets the individuals under study in a nest of multiple levels and includes family, organization, institution, and public policy levels. This model promotes a broad systems approach.

12. The organizations and structures in which an evaluator works can pose challenges. Our hope is that evaluation will lead to change in individual and group behavior, decision making, policy change and organizational transformation. Organizations that are more transformational in mindset see opportunity, look across systems, are eclectic, work long-term, and foster meaningful innovation (Tester, n.d.). Kania et al. (2018) created the six conditions of system change as policies, practices, resource flows, relationships and connections, power dynamics, and mental models.

Critical Thinking Questions

1. What is a wicked problem that interests you? Why are some problems described as wicked? What makes them different from ordinary problems? Refer to the Additional Readings and Resource Section for an article by McGrail (2014) on wicked problems.

2. What is evidence that we are in the Anthropocene era? Give examples from your daily life.

3. What is the difference between racism and structural racism? Give two examples.

4. What is one example of a problem that has multiple root causes (i.e., web of causation)? How does this affect the solution to this problem?

5. Why is gathering information during an evaluation inherently a political process?

6. Given the causes of climate change, what are five changes you could personally make to conserve resources? As a professional evaluator, what five changes could you make to apply the concepts learned in this chapter?

7. What are the characteristics of an evaluator who serves as an advocate? How might their role be different that another evaluator who is taking a more objective stance?

8. What does OCAP® stand for? Why are these concepts important for evaluators working in an Indigenous context?

9. How would you describe an evaluator who works with a transformational mindset? Are you a transactional or transformational thinker, or, a little of both?

10. Give an example of how mental models shape and support ongoing problems in our world.

Student Challenge

1. **The Sustainable Development Goals (SDGs).** In 2015, a United Nations working group representing 70 countries produced the 17 Sustainable Development Goals (SDGs) with 169 targets (United Nations, n.d.). The member states, 193 of them, agreed to work toward achieving them by the year 2030. The Goals define the world we want, apply to all nations, and decide that no one is left behind (Smale, n.d.). Regardless of your evaluation topic, it aligns with these broad global categories. Each evaluator, in their small way, can contribute to a related body of knowledge and best practices. As Rowe (2019) stresses, "Sustainability is an evaluation issue that potentially intersects with and affects all aspects of human and natural systems. Incorporating sustainability into evaluation is no longer a choice or moral issue, but an imperative".

Your tasks are:

a. Review the UN website on the 17 Sustainable Development Goals at https://sdgs.un.org/goals.

b. Explore the goal that best fits with your work area (e.g., #2 Zero Hunger, #3 Good Health and Well-being, #4 Quality Education).

c. Review some of the publications and other documents in your area of interest and zero in on one document or study. Summarize its key points.

d. Investigate best practices or partnerships in this area and see if there is any way you and/or your organization can become more involved.

e. Share your summary, reflections, and other thoughts with your classmates.

Additional Readings and Resources

1. Barlett, C. [Cheryl Barlett]. (2012, November 8). Two-eyed Seeing [Video]. *YouTube.* https://www.youtube.com/watch?v=_CY-iGduw5c This YouTube video shows the concept of "Two-Eyed Seeing." Mi'kmaq Elder Albert Marshall from the Eskasoni First Nation in Atlantic Canada explains that this way of seeing merges current knowledge and practices with the Indigenous ways of knowing. Elder Albert reminds us that "we need to learn to see from one eye with the strengths (or best) in the Indigenous knowledges and ways of knowing and learn to see from the other eye with the strengths (or best) in the mainstream" (para. 1).

2. Krause, H. [DataVizDC]. (2020, July 2020). DVDC: How not to use data like a racist [Video]. *YouTube.* https://www.youtube.com/watch?v=1ymCmauANUc This YouTube Video with Heather Krause illustrates the seven steps to find sources of bias in the data life cycle. Sources of bias can be found in funding, motivation, project design, data collection and sourcing, analysis, interpretation, and communication and distribution.

3. Lee, K. (n.d.). *The Importance of culture in evaluation: A practical guide for evaluators.* The Colorado Trust. https://communityscience.com/wp-content/uploads/2021/01/CrossCulturalGuide.r3-1.pdf This practical guide offers many suggestions on how to integrate culture and evaluation. The guide is an excellent primer for all evaluators, new and seasoned. The author says that culture, social identity, group membership, privilege, and power influence how people intermingle. The guidance document offers characteristics of cross-culturally competent evaluators. Lee provides wise advice in that "nobody can ever know everything about a culture, therefore, one must develop the capacity to not make assumptions and respectfully ask the right questions" (p. 4).

4. McGrail, S. (2014). Rethinking the roles of evaluation in learning how to solve "wicked" problems: The case of anticipatory techniques used to support climate change mitigation and adaption. *Evaluation Journal of Australasia, 14*(2), 4–16.
McGrail (2014) defines wicked problems and why they are essential to evaluators. He compares them to tame problems. The article provides the difficulties evaluators may face when evaluating climate change issues. He provides four roles for an evaluator working with wicked problems.

5. Race Forward. (2021). *Clockin-In: Making work that works for all of us*. The Center for Racial Justice Innovation. https://clockingin.raceforward.org/
This interactive tool educates the user on the fastest growing sectors of our economy, people of color and women. As you click through the quizzes, you will receive data, resources, and action ideas for how to prevent and fight low wages, inadequate benefits, lack of advancement, and prejudice in scheduling.

6. Schwandt, T., Ofir, Z. Lucks, D., El-Saddick, K., & D'Errico, S. (2016, April). *Evaluation: A crucial ingredient for SDG success.* International Institute for Environment and Development (IIED). https://pubs.iied.org/sites/default/files/pdfs/migrate/17357IIED.pdf
Schwandt et al. (2016) state that evaluation is critical to ensure the SDGs complete their goals. The authors provide a definition for evaluation and give several ways evaluation should be part of the SDGs: (a) measurement is not sufficient; (b) evaluation focuses on the complexity of the SDG movement; (c) evaluative thinking can help stakeholders answer, "Are we doing things right? Are these the right things to do?" (p. 3); (d) evaluation of policies is essential; (e) data from evaluation helps to support the conclusions and recommendations; and (f) evaluators must help build the evaluation capacity of communities.

GLOSSARY

1:3:25 Model provides a formula for the reporting of evaluation findings and was created by the Canadian Health Services Research Foundation. It translates to one page, three pages, or 25 pages of content dependent upon the audience and dissemination need.

17 Sustainable Development Goals were created by the United Nations Workgroup Group to focus on environmental challenges, poverty, and inequality.

Accreditation is a set of standards set for an industry or type of practice to judge their quality of operation and effectiveness. Accreditation is managed by an independent body.

Activities are what the program does to bring about change in the target population.

Assumptions are the beliefs we have without necessarily having any proof.

Bloom's Taxonomy classifies learning objectives into three domains: cognitive, affective, and psychomotor.

Chaos Theory is a branch of mathematics that looks at the behavior of dynamical systems that are highly sensitive to initial conditions.

Climate Change is an umbrella term that considers all the changes in climate patterns that have occurred on our planet.

Coherence means that the parts of something fit together in a reasonable way.

Communication is an integral part of the evaluation process and involves the exchange of ideas, concepts, and findings.

Communications is an integral part of the evaluation process and includes how messages about evaluation processes and findings are delivered to stakeholders and clients.

Community Health Needs Assessment identifies vital community health needs and issues (e.g., chronic disease, infectious disease, crime, mental health, poverty) through systematic, comprehensive data collection and analysis.

Comparison Group receives a different type of intervention from the main (or treatment) group, and its outcomes are compared to those of the main group.

Complexity Theory has evolved from chaos theory to help us understand highly unpredictable and nonlinear situations.

Confirmability is the ability to corroborate or repeat the research.

Constructivism is the belief that we find meaning in our interaction and engagement with the world.

Context is the environmental, physical, political, and organizational setting in which a program is found.

Contextual Factors are a set of characteristics surrounding the program and participants that can influence how they respond.

Contribution Analysis is a method used to assess causality in a program.

Control Group participants do not receive the intervention or treatment.

Cost–Benefit Analysis compares the costs and benefits of a service or program as expressed in a ratio of dollar costs to dollar benefits, thus representing the net benefit (or loss) of one program over another.

Cost-Effectiveness Analysis compares the costs and effects of alternative programs with similar goals even when the outcomes are not monetary.

Coverage refers to the proportion of people reached by a specific program within its broader service category.

Convergent is a design used when qualitative and quantitative methods explore the same evaluation questions, and the evaluator merges the results at the end of the study to compare or combine.

Critical Thinking is a way to reflect on one's own thinking to assess information, inferences, assumptions, implications, main concepts, and point of view.

Cross-Over Tracks Analysis in a mixed-methods design it provides for concurrent analysis, comparison, and integration of the qualitative and quantitative strands of a study.

Data Analysis is a process of inspecting, cleaning, transforming, and modeling data in order to discover their meaning.

Data Collection Matrix (DCM) is a document that contains the evaluation questions, indicators, and data sources which will be used to craft the data collection tools.

Data Management Plan identifies how data will be handled at each stage of the evaluation project, providing information on storing, sharing, and disposing of data.

Data Preparation includes transcribing, cleaning, combining, and transforming raw data into curated data sets for further analysis.

Data Reduction is the process for combining, summarizing, and simplifying data using a three-step coding process: initial coding, categorizing, and theming.

Data Visualization is the representation of either quantitative or qualitative data in the form of a chart, diagram, picture, or other image to provide an accessible interpretation of trends and patterns in the data.

Dependability is the accuracy and completeness of data obtained in an evaluation.

Dependent Variable is a variable whose value depends on that of another (i.e., the independent variable). In a cause–effect relationship, it is the effect.

Descriptive Evaluation is a type of formative evaluation that provides detailed information about what happens in the implementation and operation of a program.

Descriptive Statistics describe, show, and summarize the basic features of a study dataset in an evaluation study. No inferences, probabilities, or conclusions are included.

Developmental Evaluation is a type of formative evaluation used in complex and dynamic environments where ongoing adaptation is needed to track emergent developments. It is used in evaluations that support social innovation.

Dewey's Five-Step Model of Inquiry provides the evaluator with a way to think through what kinds of research questions to ask and what methods will best address these questions.

Economic Evaluation refers to a comparison of the costs and outcomes on an intervention.

Empowerment Evaluation involves stakeholders in designing the tools and knowledge they need to monitor and evaluate their own performance.

Epistemology is concerned with the nature, sources, and limits of knowledge. It describes an evaluator's understanding of what constitutes their own knowledge.

Equality is the state of being equal especially in terms of status, rights, and opportunities.

Equitable Evaluation Framework™ generates understanding through developing the readiness for enhanced awareness, attitude, and action and involves a sustained practice of intentional reflection, thinking, and realignment.

Equity refers to fairness and justice and recognizes that all people do not start from the same place. Adjustments must be made to address imbalance in social systems.

Ethics are moral principles that govern our behavior including the conduct of an evaluation.

Ethnography is the study in the culture of a group of people.

Evaluability Assessment is an assessment to determine if a program is ready to be evaluated.

Evaluand is the person, program, idea, policy, product, object, performance, or any other entity that is being evaluated.

Evaluation Capacity Building is focused on increasing the knowledge and skills of organizational members to engage in and sustain evaluation activities in the future.

Evaluation Influence is the ability of the evaluation to directly or indirectly affect changes that take place either internally or externally after the evaluation is completed.

Evaluation Management is the planning element that details how the evaluator will manage people, resources, and time to complete the evaluation as proposed.

Evaluation Plan is a written document that outlines how the evaluation will be conducted and how results will be used.

Evaluation Questions are high-level questions that the evaluation is designed to answer.

Evaluative Thinking is the critical thinking applied by the evaluator to question, reflect on, learn, and modify thoughts about the evaluation to make better informed decisions about its conduct.

Evaluation Working Group is a group of stakeholders who help guide the evaluation's processes. They provide useful feedback to the evaluator to help guide the evaluation.

Evaluator Competencies are the knowledge, skills, attitudes, behaviors, and practices of evaluators that can be measured against accepted standards.

Experimental Design is a measurement and data collection method that maintains an intervention in a controlled environment to examine the relationship between an independent and dependent variable.

Explanatory Sequential is a mixed-methods design where the quantitative aspect is followed up by a qualitative component to clarify and expand initial results.

Exploratory Sequential is a mixed-methods design where the qualitative findings are followed up with quantitative measures and analysis to further investigate the phenomenon.

External Evaluations are conducted by an evaluator who is not employed by the organization that has commissioned the evaluation. An external perspective brings credibility to the process because it is perceived as more objective and accountable than an evaluation conducted by internal staff.

Focus Group is a group of individuals who are assembled to participate in a guided discussion about a topic related to an evaluation.

Formative Evaluation is usually undertaken early in the program implementation phase to inform program staff and stakeholders about whether the program is unfolding as planned and what obstacles or opportunities are affecting the likelihood of program success.

Gantt Chart is a display of horizontal lines that illustrates a project schedule and the relationship of project activities to planned timelines.

Generic Literature Review is a brief review of published materials from recent or current literature on topics related to the research question.

Golden Thread is the research question posed at the beginning of an evaluation and is the program logic that guides the evaluation process, linking purpose to strategy and outcomes.

Grounded Theory is a set of qualitative research methods that are systematic, flexible, comparative, and iterative. They are used to collect and analyze qualitative data to construct theories or meaning that is "grounded" in the data themselves.

Guiding Principles for Evaluators reflect the core values of the American Evaluation Association and are intended to guide the professional and ethical conduct of evaluators. They include systematic inquiry, competence, integrity, respect for people, and common good and equity.

Hypothesis is a statement or supposition indicating the evaluator's idea about the relationship between an independent and dependent variable that will be tested in the evaluation to determine if it is true.

IF-THEN Statement is a simple way to show the relationship between cause and effect in a program theory.

Impact Evaluation assesses how the program being evaluated affects the outcomes of a program and whether these changes are intended or unintended.

Implementation Evaluation assesses whether program activities have been implemented as intended.

Independent Variable is the variable whose value does not depend on other variables in a study. In a cause–effect relationship, it is the cause.

Indicators of Success measure the implementation and effectiveness of the initiative.

Inferential Statistics are calculations that allow us to make generalizations to a larger population. There are two types of inferential statistics: parametric and nonparametric. Parametric statistics have specific assumptions that the researcher makes about the data, such as if they are normally distributed. Nonparametric statistics make no assumptions about the data.

Inputs are the human, financial, physical, and philosophical resources needed for the program to take place.

Integration in a mixed-methods design it includes decisions about how and when the quantitative and qualitative aspects of the study will be combined.

Intended Users are people who will, when the evaluation is conducted and finished, use the results of the evaluation to inform policy or change organizational practices. They are more likely to use the evaluation results if they understand and feel ownership for the evaluation.

Internal Evaluations are conducted by an employee of an organization to evaluate the organization's own programs.

Intervention are the activities within a program that are designed to produce specific outcomes such as changes in attitudes, skills, and behaviors.

Interview is a formal data collection activity used when a program participant is asked questions by an evaluator about the topics under review.

Key Informants are those individuals in an evaluation who by their position or representation hold special background knowledge and experience on a relevant topic. They can help to inform the evaluation design or to interpret study findings.

Knowledge-to-Action Framework is a useful way to express the time from learning new knowledge and taking action on that knowledge to making changes in the organization or community. Use of the knowledge, or resulting action, is the key.

Literature Review is a systematized review of existing studies about an evaluation topic, mainly in the scholarly literature.

Logic Model is a visual way to show the linkages between inputs, activities, and outputs of a program with its short-term, mid-term, and long-term outcomes.

Long-term Outcomes identified in a logic model they tend to be broader changes to a population's state or condition, such as changes in environmental, social, health, or economic conditions. They are sometimes called impacts. It can take decades for changes to occur.

Macro Systems are the large-scale cultural, societal, political, physical, and environmental systems that affect or frame the smaller micro systems within them.

Memorandum of Understanding is a document that outlines the purpose of a stakeholder group. It provides details of roles, expectations, time commitment, schedules, communications strategies, and the decision-making process to be used.

Merit refers to the intrinsic, context-free attributes and properties of an evaluand.

Meta-Analysis is a statistical analysis process that combines the results of multiple studies to assess findings in order to develop a single conclusion.

Micro Systems are aspects of the environment that sit at the individual, group, organizational, and community levels.

Mid-Cycle Program Evaluation focuses on how the program or intervention is implemented and carried out. Also called implementation evaluation.

Mid-Term Outcomes identified in a logic model to reflect the causal sequence of events occurring as a result of the program intervention and can be precursors of long-term outcomes or impacts.

Mixed Methods combine both quantitative and qualitative data in the same study and integrate them to reach conclusions.

Mixed-Methods Thinking requires a mental model that invites dialogue about multiple ways of making sense of the social world and with an emphasis on what is valued.

Monitoring and Evaluation is the two elements required to provide feedback on a program's progress toward the achievement of results. Monitoring occurs regularly to ensure that delivery of the services planned is occurring and are implemented with fidelity. This is coupled with evaluation activities to compare the objectives of the program or service and the intended outcomes.

Needs Assessment is a systematic process to collect data and set priorities about a proposed program based on the gap between identified needs and current service provision.

Normal Distribution shows the systemic distribution of the scores in a data set around the mean of that same dataset.

Notation in quantitative methods provides a visual model to illustrate if randomization will occur, when participants are observed (data collected), and when the intervention occurs. In qualitative methods the notation also provides a visual model to describe the timing and emphasis of the qualitative and quantitative strands of a mixed-methods study.

Null Hypothesis is stated in the negative in that there is no significant relationship or difference between the variables or groups under study.

Objectivity is an idea that stems from the realist ontology and the scientific method, that truth can be discovered through observation and measurement and exists independently in the external world, regardless of who is measuring the data.

Ontology underscores an evaluator's approach to the interpretation of existence, and deals with our understanding about the fundamental properties of reality.

Organizational Learning is the process by which an organization improves itself over time by gaining experience and using it to create, retain, and transfer knowledge. Learning organizations seek opportunities to learn from failure, and place an emphasis on building teams, innovation, and problem-solving.

Outcome Evaluation is the type of evaluation that measures program effects in the target population by assessing outcomes.

Outcome Harvesting works retrospectively and harvests changes in outcomes and works backwards to uncover how the program contributed to these changes.

Outcome Mapping works prospectively to offer evaluators and stakeholders methods for focusing on overall intentions and strategies of the program in focused evaluation studies.

Outcomes are what we hope to achieve as a result of the service or program, such as short-, mid-, and long-term outcomes.

Outputs identified in a logic model connect directly to program activities and provide concrete evidence that the activities have occurred.

Paradigm Shift is the point at which a thought revolution takes place, and a new theory emerges that appears to be more relevant than the old one.

Paradigm is a set of assumptions, concepts, values, and practices that reflect a way of viewing reality.

Parallel Tracks Analysis occurs when two different strands of data analysis, one quantitative (e.g., survey) and qualitative (e.g., interviews), proceed separately until they are synthesized to allow for comparisons.

Participatory Evaluation is an overarching term for any evaluation approach that involves program staff, stakeholders, and sometimes participants, in decision-making and other activities related to the planning and implementation of an evaluation.

Performance Management is an umbrella term that describes a systematic process to measure, monitor, and report on an organization's progress toward strategic and program goals.

Personal Factor is the presence of an identifiable person or group of people who deeply care about the organization, the program, the evaluation, and the findings it generates. Their involvement influences the likelihood of the use of the evaluation by the organization.

Phenomenon is the program under study by the evaluator and stakeholders.

Positivism posits that there is only one reality.

Pragmatism focuses on the practical application of ideas and problem-solving in the real world. It is a "whatever works" philosophy.

Pre- and Early Program Evaluation is a first, critical phase that lays the foundation for program development.

Preexperimental Designs have no randomization and only involve studying one group. They are convenient and low cost to implement.

Problem is something that needs to be solved, such as a community health issue, transportation challenge, educational gap, or housing access.

Process Evaluation determines whether the program activities have been implemented as intended.

Process Use is the cognitive, behavioral, program, and organizational changes that result from stakeholders' involvement in the evaluation process.

Professional Competencies are the capacities that an evaluator has to plan and implement an evaluation.

Program Evaluation is the systematic use of different methods to collect, analyze, and interpret information to answer questions about whether projects, policies, and programs have achieved their desired outcomes and whether the intervention has improved the initial conditions.

Program Evaluation Standards identify how the quality of an evaluation will be judged. Prepared by the Joint Committee on Standards for Educational Evaluation (JCSEE), they include standards related to utility, feasibility, propriety, accuracy, and accountability.

Program Life Cycle is a chronological model of the program where evaluation methods are matched to the stage of program development.

Program Theory defines how the program or intervention is designed to work and links program activities with expected outcomes.

Qualitative data are nonnumerical data such as text, photographs, video, and audio recordings.

Qualitative Design is used in an evaluation that employs qualitative methods to collect data.

Qualitative Traditions are philosophical perspectives adopted from general social science theory for use in evaluation, such as ethnography and phenomenology, for example.

Qualitizing occurs when the evaluator takes quantitative data and describes them in a qualitative fashion to enrich their presentation and evoke more meaning.

Quality implies that a standard has been used against which to measure the totality of the features and characteristics of whatever is under review.

Quality of Life is an individual's thoughts and beliefs about their health, comfort, and happiness.

Quantitative data are numerical data.

Quantitizing is the act of transforming qualitative data into categorical or ordinal values to help the evaluator comprehend trends or themes.

Quasi-Experimental Designs have no randomization of the subjects to the two groups to be studied.

Randomization means that the individuals in the population under study have an equal chance of being selected or not selected as a subject in either the treatment or control group.

Reach is the extent to which a program attracts its intended audience.

Realism means that only one reality exists and that humans experience it as the truth.

Relativism means that reality exists in the mind of the individual and that each of us creates our own version of reality.

Reliability describes the ability of an instrument to yield the same results when used repeatedly.

Research is the systematic investigation of phenomena to establish facts and reach new conclusions. Its goal is to gain a better understanding of how the world works

Research Methods consists of quantitative, qualitative, and mixed methods.

Review of Program Documents is a process designed to gain a deeper understanding of the evaluation questions, the organization with the program, and its culture. It also provides the historical context for the program and its history.

Scientific Method is grounded in observation, experimentation, and replication and is based on studying cause–effect relationships in the natural world.

Sensitivity indicates an instrument can determine changes or differences in outcomes that can be considered program effects.

Seventh Generation Principle is an ancient Iroquois philosophy that encourages behavior that benefits the next seven generations.

Short-term outcomes identified in a logic model and are observable immediately after participation in the program under study.

Significance relates to the values and meanings ascribed to an evaluand and have great symbolic value.

Situation is a problem statement with supporting data or some other statement providing justification for an intervention and subsequent evaluation of the program or service.

Social Betterment is arguably the goal of evaluation, that is, to improve the lives of individuals in communities with better health and social outcomes.

Social Justice is achieved when wealth, opportunity, and privilege are distributed fairly.

Social Network Analysis identifies social structures, such as individual actors, groups of people, or organizations and links them based on their relationships.

Social Science Theory is focused on testable knowledge and what shapes human behavior in social settings.

Stakeholder Identification occurs in the planning phase and includes listing stakeholders, identifying their interests, diagramming their interrelationships and influence, and identifying their sources of power.

Stakeholder Mapping is the creation of a diagram of all potential stakeholders who are then prioritized by important factors such as power and influence.

Stakeholders are those individuals who have an interest in the process and outcomes of the program under review.

Subjectivism is a research approach that finds meaning within the individuals being studied and then interprets the phenomena being studied using their perspective.

Subjects are individuals who are studied in an evaluation.

Summative Evaluation is used to judge whether a program should be continued, changed, or terminated.

Surveys is a list of questions used to collect evaluation information from program participants. They can be conducted by printed text, phone, mail, email, internet, or in person.

Sustainability Evaluation in terms of a program refers to the likelihood that the program can be sustained over time, especially once supplementary funding is removed. Sustainability evaluation is also being used more frequently to assess the status of global or macro systems.

Synthesis Stage occurs when data are being recombining to produce overarching themes and conclusions.

Systematic Review is a literature review which is narrow in scope and has a specific research question as its focus.

Systems Theory looks at the interrelated, interdependent parts of either a natural or man-made entity.

Systems Thinking is a way of making sense of complexity in the world by looking at the interrelationships of a whole and its parts.

Theory of Change is the organization's story about how their proposed program will make observable changes in a population. It starts with long-term goals and maps backwards to necessary preconditions.

Three Evaluation Pillars are the Guiding Principles, the Evaluation Standards, and the Competencies for Evaluation Practice.

TransScientific or TransScience is a term developed by Michael Scriven and presents evaluation as a driver of logic for disciplines outside of the realm of science.

Trustworthiness in qualitative research means that the results are credible based on the opinion of the research participant and are not influenced by bias or personal motivation on the part of the researcher.

Two-Eyed Seeing is holding the Indigenous and mainstream ways of knowing simultaneously and generating better solutions to problems.

Types of Data include nominal, ordinal, interval, and ratio.

Utilization-Focused Evaluation is evaluation done for and with specific users in mind for specific intended uses. It is based on the premise that evaluations should be judged by their utility and actual use.

Validity occurs when the instrument measures what it is supposed to measure.

Variable is a characteristic or attribute of an individual or organization that can be measured or observed and is likely to vary among study participants.

Wicked Problems are problems that are caused by many different factors and do not seem to have easy solutions.

Worth is the extrinsic value attached to an evaluand in a specific context.

REFERENCES

Abercrombie, R., Harries, E., & Wharton, R. (2015). *Systems change: A guide to what it is and how to do it*. LankellyChase Foundation. https://www.thinknpc.org/resource-hub/systems-change-a-guide-to-what-it-is-and-how-to-do-it/

Adams, R. (1975). *Watership down*. Avon Books.

African-Canadian Civic Engagement Council and Innovative Research Group. (2020). *Impact of COVID-19: Black Canadian perspectives*. https://innovativeresearch.ca/wp-content/uploads/2020/09/ACCEC01-Release-Deck.pdf

Agar, M. H., & Kozel, N. J. (1999). Ethnography and substance use: Talking numbers. Introduction. *Substance Use & Misuse*, 34(14), 1935–1949. https://doi.org/10.3109/10826089909039433

Agency for Healthcare Research and Quality. (2010). *Health care systems for tracking colorectal cancer screening tests* (HHSA290200600014 Task Number 290-06-0014-1). U.S. Government Printing Office. https://www.ahrq.gov/research/findings/final-reports/crcscreeningrpt/index.html

Agency for Toxic Substances and Disease Registry. (2015). *Social vulnerability index (SVI)*. Centers for Disease Control and Prevention. https://www.atsdr.cdc.gov/placeandhealth/svi/index.html

Ali, A.S., & Backlund, C. (2018). *Pathways evaluation: Year four summary report*. https://lawsocietyontario.azureedge.net/media/lso/media/about/convocation/2018/convocation-dec-2018-professional-regulation-committee-report_1.pdf

Ali, A. S., Bridgmohan, A., & Harduwar, R. (2016). *Pathways evaluation: Interim results – years one and two*. https://lawsociety-ontario.azureedge.net/media/lso/media/legacy/pdf/p/pd/pdc-pathways-pilot-project-evaluation-and-enhancements-to-licensing-report-sept-2016.pdf

Alkin, M. C. (2004). *Evaluation roots: Tracing theorists' views and influences*. SAGE Publications.

Alkin, M. C. (2012). *Evaluation roots: A wider perspective of theorists' views and influences* (2nd ed.). SAGE Publications.

Alkin, M. C., & Christie, C. A. (2004). An evaluation theory tree. In M. C. Alkin (Ed.), *Evaluation roots: Tracing theorists' views and influences*. SAGE Publications.

Alkin, M. C., Christie, C., & Rose, M. (2006). Communicating evaluation. In I. Shaw, J. Greene, & M. Mark (Eds.), *Handbook of evaluation: Policies, programs and practices* (pp. 384–403). SAGE Publications.

Alkin, M. C., & Vo, A. T. (2018). *Evaluation essentials: From A to Z* (2nd ed.). Guilford.

Allen, K., Kaestle, C., & Goldberg, A. (2010). More than just a punctuation mark: How boys and young men learn about menstruation. *Journal of Family Issues*, 32(2), 129–156.

Almutairi, A. F., Gardner, G. E., & McCarthy, A. (2014). Practical guidance for the use of a pattern-matching technique in case-study research: A case presentation. *Nursing & Health Sciences*, 16, 239–244.

Altschuld, J. W. (2012, April 9). *James Altschuld on lessons learned: Use the 3 phase Roholtmodel*. American Evaluation Association. https://aea365.org/blog/na-week-james-altschuld-on-lessons-learned-use-the-3-phase-model/

Altschuld, J. W. (2014). *Bridging the gap between asset/capacity building and needs assessment*. SAGE Publications.

Altschuld, J. W. (2015, May 10). *The 10 commandments of needs assessors*. https://aea365.org/blog/na-tig-week-james-w-altschuld-the-10-commandments-of-needs-assessors/

Altschuld, J. W., Hung, H. L., & Lee, Y. F. (2014). Needs assessment and asset/capacity building: A promising development in practice. In J. W. Altschuld & R. Watkins (Eds.), *Needs assessment: Trends and a view toward the future. New directions for evaluation*, 2014(144), 89–103. https://doi.org/10.1002/ev.20105

Altschuld, J. W., & Kumar, D. D. (2010). *Needs assessment: An overview*. SAGE Publications.

Altschuld, J. W., & Witkin, B. R. (2000). *From needs assessment to action: Transforming needs into solution strategies*. SAGE Publications.

American Evaluation Association. (2011). *Public statement on cultural competence in evaluation*. https://www.eval.org/Portals/0/Docs/aea.cultural.competence.statement.pdf

American Evaluation Association. (2018a). *Guiding principles for evaluators and code of ethics.* https://www.eval.org/About/Guiding-Principles

American Evaluation Association. (2018b). *About us.* https://www.eval.org/Events/Conference-History

American Evaluation Association. (2018c). *The 2018 AEA evaluator competencies.* https://www.eval.org/Portals/0/Docs/AEA%20Evaluator%20Competencies.pdf

American Journal of Managed Care Staff. (2021, December). *A timeline of COVID-19 vaccine developments for the second half of 2021.* https://www.ajmc.com/view/a-timeline-of-covid-19-vaccine-developments-for-the-second-half-of-2021

American Psychological Association. (2014). *Cognitive psychology explores our mental processes.* https://www.apa.org/education-career/guide/subfields/brain-science#:~:text=Cognitive%20psychologists%20study%20how%20people,interplay%20between%20cognition%20and%20emotion

American Psychological Association. (2020). *Understanding brain science and cognitive psychology.* https://www.apa.org/action/science/brain-science

American Veterinary Medical Association. (2018). *Human-animal bond.* AVMA Policy. https://www.avma.org/one-health/human-animal-bond#:~:text=The%20human%2Danimal%20bond%20is,%2C%20animals%2C%20and%20the%20environment

Ammenwerth, E., Iller, C., & Mansmann, U. (2003). Can evaluation studies benefit from triangulation? A case study. *International Journal of Medical Informatics*, 70(2), 237–248.

Anderson, A. (2004). *Theory of change as a tool for strategic planning: A report on early experiences* (pp. 1–36). The Aspen Institute, Roundtable on Community Change. https://www.wallacefoundation.org/knowledge-center/Documents/Theory-of-Change-Tool-for-Strategic-Planning-Report-on-Early-Experiences.pdf

Anderson, C. (2010). Presenting and evaluating qualitative research. *American Journal of Pharmaceutical Education*, 74(8), 1–7. https://doi.org/10.5688/aj7408141

Antman, E. M., Lau, J., Kupelnick, B., Mosteller, F., & Chalmers, T. C. (1992). A comparison of results of meta-analyses of randomized control trials and recommendations of clinical experts. Treatments for myocardial infarction. *Journal of the American Medical Association*, 268(2), 240–248.

Aotearoa New Zealand Evaluation Association. (2015). *Evaluation standards for Aotearoa New Zealand.* https://anzea.org.nz/assets/Key-ANZEA-Files/ANZEA-Superu-Evaluation-standards-final-020415.pdf

Aponte-Soto, L., Ling Grant, D. S., Carter-Johnson, F., Colomer, S. E., Campbell, J. E., & Anderson, K. G. (2014). Championing culturally responsive leadership for evaluation practice. In P. M. Collins & R. Hopson (Eds.), *Building a new generation of culturally responsive evaluators through AEA's Graduate Education Diversity Internship program. New directions for evaluation*, 2014(143), 37–47. https://doi.org/10.1002/ev.20092

Argyris, C. (1977, September). Double loop learning in organizations. *Harvard Business Review.* https://hbr.org/1977/09/double-loop-learning-in-organizations

Artiga, S., & Hinton, E. (2018, May 10). *Beyond health care: The role of social determinants in promoting health and health equity.* KFF. https://www.kff.org/racial-equity-and-health-policy/issue-brief/beyond-health-care-the-role-of-social-determinants-in-promoting-health-and-health-equity/

Association of Family Health Teams of Ontario. (2016). *Program planning and evaluation: Framework for FHTs and NPLCs.* https://www.afhto.ca/wp-content/uploads/Program-Planning-and-Evaluation-Framework-February-2016.pdf

Avellar, S. A., Thomas, J., Kleinman, R., Sama-Miller, E., Woodruff, S., Coughlin, R., & Westbrook, T. (2017). External validity: The next step for systematic reviews? *Evaluation Review*, 41(4), 283–325. https://doi.org/10.1177/0193841X16665199

Azzam, T., Evergreen, S., Germuth, A. A., & Kistler, S. J. (2013). Data visualization and evaluation. In T. Azzam & S. Evergreen (Eds.), *Data visualization, part 1. New directions for evaluation*, 2013(139), 7–32. https://doi.org/10.1002/ev.20065

Baldwin, S., & Shadish, W. (2011). A primer on meta-analysis in clinical psychology. *Journal of Experimental Psychopathology*, 2(2), 294–317.

Banyard, F. L., & Williams, L. M. (2007). Women's voices on recovery: A multi-method study of the complexity of recovery from child sexual abuse. *Child Abuse & Neglect*, 31(3), 275–290. https://www.ncbi.nlm.nih.gov/pubmed/17395261

Barker, S. B., & Wolen, A. R. (2008). The benefits of human-companion animal interaction: A review. *Journal of Veterinary Medical Education*, 35(4), 487–495. https://doi.org/10.3138/jvme.35.4.487

Barnes, P., Mayo-Gamble, T., Harris, D., & Townsend, D. (2018). Correlation between personal health history and depression self-care practices and depression screening among African Americans with chronic conditions. *Preventing Chronic Disease*, 15, 1–7.

Barnett, C., & Camfield, L. (2016). Ethics in evaluation. *Journal of Development Effectiveness*, 8(4), 528–534. https://doi.org/10.1080/19439342.2016.1244554

Barrington, G. V. (2010, May 3). Running alongside: Developmental evaluation proves its worth in an early childhood distance education program. [Conference session]. *Canadian Evaluation Society 2010 Conference, Victoria, British Columbia.*

Barrington, G. V. (2012a). *Consulting start-up and management: A guide for evaluators and applied researchers.* SAGE Publications.

Barrington, G. V. (2012b, June). Handling data: From logic model to final report. The Summer Institute. *Presentation conducted at the meeting of the American Evaluation Association and The Centers for Disease Control and Prevention, Atlanta, GA.*

Barrington, G. V. (2012c, October 10). *Ethics on the go: Which lens should we use?* Barrington Research Group. https://www.barringtonresearchgrp.com/blog/34-6-ethics-on-the-go-which-lens-should-we-use.html

Barrington, G. V. (2014, June 15). Handling data: From logic model to final report [conference presentation]. *Canadian Society annual conference, Ottawa, ON, Canada.*

Barrington, G. V. (2014, November 27). After data analysis: From report writing to knowledge translation. *Workshop presented at the National Capital Chapter, Canadian Evaluation Society, Ottawa, ON.* pp. 22–23.

Barrington, G. V. (2015, November). The one-question focus group: An AI evaluation strategy in long-term care. *Presentation at the American Evaluation Association, Chicago, IL.*

Barrington, G. V. (2017a, November). *Staying power: Strategies to handle consulting issues* [Workshop]. American Evaluation Association from Learning to Action.

Barrington, G. V. (2017b, November 11). *Using a policy framework to develop astute recommendations: A checklist and case study* [Workshop]. From learning to action 2017 American Evaluation Association Conference, Washington, DC, United States.

Barrington, G. V. (2021a, May 6). Reflective practice and innovation: Making creativity part of your life. *Workshop presented at the Canadian Evaluation Society annual conference, virtual.*

Barrington, G. V. (2021b, July 21). *Teaching you, teaching me: The power of photovoice during the pandemic* [Conference presentation]. AEA TOE TIG Week AEA 365, online. https://aea365.org/blog/toe-tig-week-teaching-you-teaching-me-the-power-of-photovoice-during-the-pandemic-by-gail-vallance-barrington/

Barry, P., & DeFriese, G. (1990). Cost-benefit and cost-effectiveness analysis for health promotion programs. *American Journal of Health Promotion*, 4(6), 458–451.

Bartlett, C., Marshall, M., & Marshall, A. (2012) Two-eyed seeing and other lessons learned within a co-learning journey of bringing together Indigenous and mainstream knowledges and ways of knowing. *Journal of Environmental Studies and Sciences*, 2(4), 331–340. https://doi.org/10.1007/s13412-012-0086-8

Barwick, H. (2004). *Young males: Strength-based and male-focused approaches, a review of the research and best evidence.* New Zealand Ministry of Youth Development. www.myd.govt.nz

Barwick, M. (2008). *Knowledge translation research plan template.* The Hospital for Sick Children. https://www.sickkids.ca/contentassets/4ba06697e24946439d1d6187ddcb7def/79482-ktplanningtemplate.pdf

Bazeley, P. (2010). Computer assisted integration of mixed methods data sources and analyses. In C. Teddlie, & A. Tashakkori (Eds.), *Handbook of mixed methods research for the social and behavioral sciences.* SAGE Publications.

Bazeley, P. (2012). Integrative analysis strategies for mixed data sources. *American Behavioral Scientist*, 56(6), 814–828.

Bazeley, P. (2013). *Qualitative data analysis: Practical strategies.* SAGE Publications.

Bazeley, P. (2018). *Integrating analyses in mixed methods research.* SAGE Publications.

BC Treaty Commission. (2021, June 30). *Truth and reconciliation commission of Canada: 94 calls to action.* https://www.bctreaty.ca/94-calls-action#:~:text=Implementing%20the%2094%20Calls%20to%20Action&text=Important%20work%20is%20still%20needed,have%20yet%20to%20be%20started

Bean, C. N., Kendellen, K., Halsall, T., & Forneris, T. (2015). Putting program evaluation into practice: Enhancing the girls just wanna have fun program. *Evaluation and Program Planning*, 49, 31–40.

Beaton, S. (2016). BUZZING-A theory-based impact evaluation design. *Evaluation Journal of Australasia*, 16(4), 21–29. https://doi.org/10.1177/1035719X1601600404

Bélisle, P., & Joseph, L. (n.d.). *Codebook cookbook: A guide to writing a good codebook for data analysis projects in medicine.* McGill University Health Centre. http://www.medicine.mcgill.ca/epidemiology/joseph/pbelisle/CodebookCookbook/CodebookCookbook.pdf

Belza, B., Toobert, D., & Glasgow, R. (2013). *RE-AIM for program planning: Overview and applications.* National Council on Aging's Center for Health Aging. https://fromhungertohealth.files.wordpress.com/2013/02/re-aim_issue_brief.pdf

Berkin, C. (2011). *Making America: A history of the United States: Since 1865.* Cengage Learning.

Berman, E. A. (2017). An exploratory sequential mixed methods approach to understanding researchers' data management practices at UVM: Integrated findings to develop research data services. *Journal of eScience Librarianship*, 6(1), e1104. https://doi.org/10.7191/jeslib.2017.1104

Bernal, J., Cummins, S., & Gasparrini, A. (2017). Interrupted time series regression for the evaluation of public health interventions: A tutorial. *International Journal of Epidemiology*, 46(1), 348–355.

Berry, A. (2016). *Is the amoeba a friend or a foe? Or is it both?* Prezi. https://prezi.com/bxsomiczjtst/is-the-amoeba-a-friend-or-a-foe/

Best, E. (n.d.). *The 5-hour rule that turns ordinary people into successful ones*. Lifehack. https://www.lifehack.org/538067/the-5-hour-rule-that-turns-ordinary-people-into-successful-ones

Betancourt, T., Meyers-Ohki, S. E., Stevenson, A., Ingabire, C., Kenyanganzi, R., & Munyana, M. (2011). Using mixed-methods research to adapt and evaluate a family strengthening intervention in Rwanda. *African Journal of Traumatic Stress*, 2(1), 32–45. https://www.ncbi.nlm.nih.gov/pmc/articles/PMC4189126/

Bethany Care Society. (2014). *Learning circles pilot project final evaluation report*. Gail V. Barrington.

BetterEvaluation. (n.d. a). *Approaches*. https://www.better-evaluation.org/en/approaches

BetterEvaluation. (n.d. b). *Case study*. https://www.better-evaluation.org/en/plan/approach/case_study

BetterEvaluation. (n.d. c). *Define*. https://www.betterevaluation.org/en/rainbow_framework/define

BetterEvaluation. (n.d. d). *Identify primary intended users*. https://www.betterevaluation.org/en/rainbow_framework/frame/identify_primary_intended_users

BetterEvaluation. (2016a). *Specify the key evaluation questions*. https://www.betterevaluation.org/en/rainbow_framework/frame/specify_key_evaluation_questions

BetterEvaluation. (2016b). *Step 7: Manage implementation of the evaluation in the managers guide to evaluation*. https://www.betterevaluation.org/en/commissioners_guide/step7

Bhat, A. (2020). *What is a survey?* Question Pro. https://www.questionpro.com/blog/surveys/

Bickman, L. (1987). The functions of program theory. In L. Bickman (Ed.), *Special issue: Using a program theory in evaluation. New directions for program evaluation*, 1987(33), 5–18. https://doi.org/10.1002/ev.1443

Biggs, J., Farrell, L., Lawrence, G., & Johnson, J. (2014). A practical example of contribution analysis to a public health intervention. *Evaluation*, 20(2), 214–229.

Black Public Health Collective. (2020). *Race-Based data is not racial justice*. https://blackpublichealth.ca/wp-content/uploads/2020/06/BPHC-Statement-on-Race-Based-Data_COVID-19_Policing.pdf

Blackburn, S., Harrington, T., Vidler, A., & Weddle, B. (2021, August 3). *Government transformations in times of extraordinary change: Key considerations for public-sector leaders*. McKinsey & Company. https://www.mckinsey.com/industries/public-and-social-sector/our-insights/government-transformations-in-times-of-extraordinary-change-key-considerations-for-public-sector-leaders

Blakemore, E. (2019, February 22). *Race and ethnicity: How are they different?* National Geographic Society. https://www.nationalgeographic.com/culture/article/race-ethnicity

Bloom, B. S. (1956). *Taxonomy of educational objectives: The classification of educational goals*. David McKay.

Bloom, M. (2010). Client-centered evaluation: Ethics for the 21st century practitioners. *Journal of Social Work Values and Ethics*, 7(1), 1–7.

Bonino, F., Jean, I., & Clarke, P. (2014). *Effective feedback in humanitarian contexts: Practitioner guidance*. ALNAP-CDA. https://www.alnap.org/system/files/content/resource/files/main/closing-the-loop-alnap-cda-guidance.pdf

Bonnefoy, J., Morgan, A., Kelly, M. P., Butt, J., & Bergman, V. (2007). Constructing the evidence base on the social determinants of health: A guide. World Health Organization: The Measurement and Evidence Knowledge Network (MEKN) of the WHO Commission on Social Determinants of Health. World Health Organization. https://www.who.int/social_determinants/knowledge_networks/add_documents/mekn_final_guide_112007.pdf?ua=1

Bowman, N. (Waapalaneexkweew). (2019). Nation-to-Nation evaluation: Governance, tribal sovereignty, and systems thinking through culturally responsive Indigenous evaluations. *Canadian Journal of Program Evaluation/La Revue canadienne d'évaluation de programme*, 34(2), 343–356. https://doi.org/10.3138/cjpe.67977

Bowman, N. (Waapalaneexkweew). (2021). Praxis makes perfect? Transcending textbooks to learning evaluation experientially and in cultural contexts. *Canadian Journal of Program Evaluation/La Revue canadienne d'évaluation de programme*, 35(3), 320–329. https://doi.org/10.3138/cjpe.69698

Brant-Castellano, M. (1997, May 7). Partnership: The key to ethical cross-cultural research. *The Canadian Evaluation Society Conference, Ottawa, ON*.

Brant-Castellano, M. (2000). Updating aboriginal traditions of knowledge. In G. Dei, B. Hall, & D. Rosenberg (Eds.), *Indigenous knowledges in global contexts* (pp. 21–36). University of Toronto Press.

Braverman, M. T., & Arnold, M. E. (2008). An evaluator's balancing act: Making decisions about methodological rigor. In M. T. Braverman, M. Engle, M. E. Arnold, & R. A. Rennekamp (Eds.), *Program evaluation in a complex organizational system: Lessons from cooperative extension. New directions for evaluation*, 2008(120), 71–86. https://doi.org/10.1002/ev.277

Braverman, M. T., & Engle, M. (2009). Theory and rigor in extension program evaluation planning. *Journal of Extension*, 47(3), 1–10.

Braverman, P., Kumanyika, S., Fielding, J., Laveist, T., Borrell, L. N., Manderscheid, R., & Troutman, A. (2011). Health disparities and health equity: The issue is justice. *American Journal of Public Health*, 101(S1), S149–S155.

Brechter, C., Silver, D., Searcy, C., Weitzman, B. (2005). Following the money: Using expenditures as an evaluation tool. *American Journal of Evaluation*, 26(2), 166–188.

Bretschneider, P. J., Cirilli, S., Jones, T., Lynch, S., & Wilson, N. A. (2016). *Document review as a qualitative research data collection method for teacher research*. SAGE Publications.

British Columbia's Office of the Human Rights Commissioner. (2020, September). *Disaggregated demographic data collection in British Columbia: The grandmother perspective*. https://bchumanrights.ca/wp-content/uploads/BCOHRC_Sept2020_Disaggregated-Data-Report_FINAL.pdf

Britt, H. (2020). *Evaluation costing*. BetterEvaluation. https://www.betterevaluation.org/en/evaluation-options/calculate_evaluation_costs

Bronfenbrenner, U. (1977). Toward an experimental ecology of human development. *American Psychologist*, 32(7), 513–531. https://doi.org/10.1037/0003-066X.32.7.513

Brundtland, G. (1987). *Report of the world commission on environment and development: Our common future*. United Nations General Assembly. https://sustainabledevelopment.un.org/content/documents/5987our-common-future.pdf

Bruner Foundation. (2007). *Evaluative thinking assessment tool: Sample report*. http://www.evaluativethinking.org/docs/sample.report.pdf

Bryson J. M. (2004) What to do when stakeholders matter: Stakeholder identification and analysis techniques. *Public Management Review*, 6(1), 21–53.

Bryson, J. M., Patton, M. Q., & Bowman, R. A. (2011). Working with evaluation stakeholders: A rationale, step-wise approach and toolkit. *Evaluation and Program Planning*, 34, 1–12.

Buchanan, A., & O'Neill, M. (2001). *Inclusion and diversity: Finding common ground for organizational action*. Canadian Council for International Co-Operation. http://www.racialequitytools.org/resourcefiles/buchanan2.pdf

Buckley, J., Archibald, T., Hargraves, M., & Trochim, W. (2015). Defining and teaching evaluative thinking: Insights from research on critical thinking. *American Journal of Evaluation*, 36(3), 375–388.

Buffalo Center for Social Research. (2015). *What is trauma-informed care?* http://socialwork.buffalo.edu/social-research/institutes-centers/institute-on-trauma-and-trauma-informed-care/what-is-trauma-informed-care.html

Burch, P., & Heinrich, C. J. (2016). *Mixed methods for policy research and program evaluation*. SAGE Publications.

Buriel, R. (2012). Historical, socio-cultural, and conceptual issues to consider when researching Mexican American children and families, and other Latino subgroups. *Psychosocial Intervention*, 21(3), 291–303.

Burns, J. (2002). Chaos theory and leadership studies: Exploring unchartered seas. *Journal of Leadership and Organizational Studies*, 9(2), 42–56.

Butterfoss, F. D., & Francisco, V. T. (2004). Evaluating community partnerships and coalitions with practitioners in mind. *Health Promotion Practice*, 5(2), 108–114. http://citeseerx.ist.psu.edu/viewdoc/download?doi=10.1.1.1030.3764&rep=rep1&type=pdf

Butterfoss, F. D., & Kegler, M. C. (2002). Toward a comprehensive understanding of community coalitions: Moving from practice to theory. In R. J. DiClemente, R. A. Crosby, & M. C. Kegler (Eds.), *Emerging theories in health promotion practice and research* (pp. 157–193). Jossey-Bass.

Caldwell, L. D., & Bledsoe, K. L. (2019). Can social justice live in a house of structural racism? A question for the field of evaluation. *American Journal of Evaluation*, 40(1), 6–18.

Calhoun, A. (2012, December 17). *Annaliese Calhoun on measuring sustainability capacity and planning for long term success*. American Evaluation Association. https://aea365.org/blog/annaliese-calhoun-on-measuring-sustainability-capacity-and-planning-for-long-term-success/

Callejas, L. M. (2021). *Addressing disparities in behavioral health for communities of color: The community defined evidence project (CDEP)*. National Latino Behavioral Health Association. http://www.nlbha.org/index.php/projects/other-projects/cdep

Calvello, M. (2020). *Data mining: Uncover the valuable business insights you need: Learning hub G2*. G2 Learning Hub. https://learn.g2.com/data-mining?__hstc=171774463.8bd4d8b00b69225ed2a317c4aa271fe5.1592497882869.1592497882869.1592497882869.1&__hssc=171774463.1.1592497882869&__hsfp=2580237459

Cambridge Dictionary Online. (n.d. a). *Assumption*. In Cambridge Dictionary Online. https://dictionary.cambridge.org/us/dictionary/english/assumption

Cambridge Dictionary Online. (n.d. b). *Coherence*. In Cambridge Dictionary Online. https://dictionary.cambridge.org/us/dictionary/english/coherence

Cameron, W. B. (1963). *Informal sociology: A casual introduction to sociological thinking*. Random House.

Campbell, D., & Stanley, J. (1963). Experimental and quasi-experimental designs for research on teaching. In N. L. Gage (Ed.), *Handbook of research on teaching* (pp. 1–76). Houghton Mifflin Company. https://www.sfu.ca/~palys/Campbell&Stanley-1959-Exptl&QuasiExptlDesignsForResearch.pdf

Canada Energy. (2018). *Market snapshot: Petrochemical products in everyday life*. https://www.cer-rec.gc.ca/en/data-analysis/energy-markets/market-snapshots/2018/market-snapshot-petrochemical-products-in-everyday-life.html#:~:text=Petrochemical%20products%20include%20plastics%2C%20rubbers,petroleum%2Dderived%20paints%20and%20coatings

Canadian Evaluation Society. (2018). *Competencies for Canadian Evaluators*. https://evaluationcanada.ca/txt/2_competencies_cdn_evaluation_practice_2018.pdf

Canadian Evaluation Society. (2018). *About the CE designation*. https://evaluationcanada.ca/about-us

Canadian Institutes of Health Research. (2014). *Tri-council policy statement: Ethical conduct for research involving humans*. Providence Research. http://www.providenceresearch.ca/sites/default/files/documents/TCPS_2_2014.pdf

Canadian Public Health Association. (n.d.). *What are the social determinants of health?* https://www.cpha.ca/what-are-social-determinants-health

Carden, F., & Alkin, M. C. (2012). Evaluation roots: An international perspective. *Journal of MultiDisciplinary Evaluation*, 8(17), 102–118.

Carlson, J., Fossmire, M., Miller, C. C., & Nelson, M. S. (2011). Determining data information literacy needs: A study of students and research faculty. *Portal: Libraries and the Academy*, 11(2), 629–657.

Carpenter, D., Nieva, V., Albaghal, T., & Sorra, J. (2005). Development of a planning tool to guide research dissemination. In K. Henriksen, J. Battles, & E. Marks (Eds.), *Advances in patient safety: From research to implementation* (pp. 83–91). Agency for Healthcare Research and Quality. https://www.ncbi.nlm.nih.gov/books/NBK20603/

Carr, M., & Evergreen, S. (2017, November). *Evaluation report guidance*. Ewing Marion Kauffman Foundation. https://stephanieevergreen.com/kauffman-report-guidance/

Carr, A. J., Thompson, P. W., & Kirwan, J. R. (1996). Quality of life measures. *British Journal of Rheumatology*, 35, 275–281.

Castillo, I. D. (2019). Are you my amigo, or my chero? The importance of cultural competence in data collection and evaluation. In K. Hutchinson (Ed.), *Evaluation failures: 22 tales of mistakes made and lessons learned* (pp. 99–104). SAGE Publications.

Catchpole, K., Neyens, D., Abernathy, J., Allison, D., Joseph, A., & Reeves, S. (2016). Framework for direct observation of performance and safety in healthcare. *British Medical Journal Quality and Safety*, 26(12), 1015–1021.

Caudle, S. L. (2004). Qualitative data analysis. In J. S. Wholey, H. P. Hatry, & K. E. Newcomer (Eds.), *Handbook of practical program evaluation* (pp. 417–438). Jossey-Bass.

Celestine, N. (2021, January 30). *5 Quality of life questionnaires and assessments*. Positive Psychology. https://positivepsychology.com/quality-of-life-questionnaires-assessments/

Centers for Disease Control and Prevention. (n.d.). *Evaluation guide: Developing and using a logic model*. U.S. Department of Health and Human Services. https://www.cdc.gov/dhdsp/docs/logic_model.pdf

Centers for Disease Control and Prevention. (2008). *Introduction to process evaluation in tobacco use prevention and control*. Office on Smoking and Health, U.S. Department of Health and Human Services. https://www.cdc.gov/tobacco/stateandcommunity/tobacco-control/guidelines-resources.htm

Centers for Disease Control and Prevention. (2011a). *Developing an effective evaluation plan*. U.S. Department of Health and Human Services. https://www.cdc.gov/obesity/downloads/cdc-evaluation-workbook-508.pdf

Centers for Disease Control and Prevention. (2011b). *Program evaluation tip sheet: Reach and impact*. U.S. Department of Health and Human Services. https://www.cdc.gov/dhdsp/programs/spha/docs/reach_impact_tip_sheet.pdf

Centers for Disease Control and Prevention. (2013a). *Roadmap for state program planning: Develop plans*. U.S. Department of Health and Human Services. https://www.cdc.gov/dhdsp/programs/spha/roadmap/develop_state_plan.htm

Centers for Disease Control and Prevention. (2013b). *Developing an effective evaluation report: Setting the course for effective program evaluation.* U.S. Department of Health and Human Services. https://www.cdc.gov/eval/materials/Developing-An-Effective-Evaluation-Report_TAG508.pdf

Centers for Disease Control and Prevention. (2018a). *Data collection methods for evaluation: Document review* (p. 18). Evaluation Briefs. https://www.cdc.gov/healthyyouth/evaluation/pdf/brief18.pdf

Centers for Disease Control and Prevention. (2018b, November 29). *CDC director's media statement on U.S. life expectancy, Robert R. Redfield.* U.S. Department of Health and Human Services. https://www.cdc.gov/media/releases/2018/s1129-US-life-expectancy.html

Centers for Disease Control and Prevention. (2019). *Community health assessments and health improvement plans: What is a community health assessment?* U.S. Department of Health and Human Services. https://www.cdc.gov/stltpublichealth/cha/plan.html

Centers for Disease Control and Prevention. (2020). *Original essential public health services framework: The public health system.* U.S. Department of Health and Human Services. https://www.cdc.gov/publichealthgateway/publichealthservices/originalessentialhealthservices.html

Centers for Disease Control and Prevention. (2021). *Community health assessment and Group Evaluation (CHANGE) tool.* https://www.cdc.gov/nccdphp/dnpao/state-local-programs/change-tool/index.html

Center for Disease Control and Prevention. (2021). *Monitor and evaluate.* U.S. Department of Health and Human Services. https://www.cdc.gov/nutrition/food-service-guidelines/monitor-and-evaluate/index.html

Centers for Disease Control and Prevention. (2021, March 18). *The public health system and the 10 essential public health services.* U.S. Department of Health and Human Services. https://www.cdc.gov/publichealthgateway/publichealthservices/essentialhealthservices.html

Centers for Disease Control and Prevention. (2022). *Climate effects on health.* https://www.cdc.gov/climateandhealth/effects/default.htm

Center for Theory of Change. (2019a). *What is theory of change?* https://www.theoryofchange.org/what-is-theory-of-change/

Center for Theory of Change. (2019b). *How does theory of change work? TOC maps out your initiative through 6 stages.* https://www.theoryofchange.org/what-is-theory-of-change/how-does-theory-of-change-work/

Centre of Excellence for Evaluation. (2004). *Guide for the review of evaluation reports.* Treasury Board of Canada. https://www.tbs-sct.gc.ca/cee/tools-outils/grer-gere-eng.pdf

Chamorro-Premuzic, T. (2015, March 25). Why group brainstorming is a waste of time. *Harvard Business Review.* https://hbr.org/2015/03/why-group-brainstorming-is-a-waste-of-time

Chapel, T. J. (2012, January 5). *Coffee break: 5 hints to make your logic models worth the time and effort* [PowerPoint slides]. American Evaluation Association.

Charmaz, K. (2014). *Constructing grounded theory.* SAGE Publications.

Chawla, D., & Deorari, A. (2005). Inferential statistics: Introduction to hypothesis testing. *Journal of Neonatology, 19*(3), 259–264.

Chelimsky, E. (1987a). What have we learned about the politics of program evaluation? *Educational Evaluation and Policy Analysis, 9*(3), 199–213.

Chelimsky, E. (1987b). What have we learned about the politics of program evaluation? *Evaluation Practice, 8*(1), 5–21.

Chen, H. (1990). *Theory-driven evaluations.* SAGE Publications.

Chick, N. (2013). *Metacognition: Thinking about one's thinking.* Vanderbilt University Center for Teaching. https://cft.vanderbilt.edu/guides-sub-pages/metacognition/

Chodos, A., & Ouellette, J. (2003). This month in physics history circa January 1961: Lorenz and the butterfly effect. *American Physical Society News, 12*(1), 2.

Christensen, E. W. (1983) Study circles: Learning in small groups. *The Journal for Specialists in Group Work, 8*(4), 211–217.

Christie, C. A. (2003). What guides evaluation? A study of how evaluation practice maps onto evaluation theory. In C. A. Christie (Ed.), *Special issue: The practice-theory relationship in evaluation. New directions for evaluation, 97,* 7–36. https://doi.org/10.1002/ev.72

Christie, C. A. (2007). Reported influence of evaluation data on decision makers' actions: An empirical examination. *American Journal of Evaluation, 28*(1), 8–15.

Christou, P., & Papastamatis, K. (2008). *Greek mythology: The Trojan war, the Odyssey, and the Aeneid.* Bonechi.

Ciliska, D. (2012). *Introduction to evidence-informed decision making.* Canadian Institutes of Health Research. https://cihr-irsc.gc.ca/e/45245.html

Čirjak, A. (2020, February 2). *How did Rosa Parks change the world?* https://www.worldatlas.com/articles/how-did-rosa-parks-change-the-world.html

Classen, S., Lopez, D., Winter, S., Awadzi, K. K., Ferree, N., & Garvan, C. W. (2007). Population-based health promotion perspective for older driver safety: Conceptual framework to intervention plan. *Clinical Interventions in Aging, 2*(4), 677–693. https://www.ncbi.nlm.nih.gov/pmc/articles/PMC2686324/

Clear Impact. (n.d.). *Example performance measures you can use for your program or service: Designing effective performance measures.* https://clearimpact.com/results-based-accountability/example-performance-measures-can-use-program-service/#

Cohn, B. J., Brenman, J., & Vasquez, V. (2004). Trained observer ratings. In J. S. Wholey, H. P. Hatry, & K. E. Newcomer (Eds.), *Handbook of practical program evaluation* (pp. 298–320). Jossey-Bass.

Coldwell, M. (2019). Reconsidering context: Six underlying features of context to improve learning from evaluation. *Evaluation*, 25(1), 99–117.

College of Physicians and Surgeons of Alberta. (2006). *Let's talk about prescribing opioids.* https://cpsa.ca/wp-content/uploads/2020/06/aa_safe-prescribing-oud.PDF

Collin College. (n.d.). *APA literature review template.* https://www.collin.edu/studentresources/writingcenter/pdfs/PRCHandouts/APA%20Literature%20Review.pdf

Collins, P. M., Kirkhart, K. E., & Brown, T. (2014). Envisioning an evaluation curriculum to develop culturally responsive evaluators and support social justice. In P. M. Collins & T. Brown (Eds.), *Building a new generation of culturally responsive evaluators through AEA's graduate education diversity internship program. New directions for evaluation*, 2014(143), 23–36. https://doi.org/10.1002/ev.20091

Community Solutions. (2010). *Logic model assessment rubric.* https://communitysolutions.ca/web/wp-content/uploads/2013/07/Logic-Model-Rubric.pdf

Cooper, C. W., & Christie, C. A. (2005). Evaluating parent empowerment: A look at the potential of social justice evaluation in education. *Teachers College Record*, 107(10), 2248–2274.

Corley, S. (2018, May). Doing reporting better. *Workshop presented to the Alberta northwest territories chapter of the Canadian Evaluation Society, Edmonton, AB.*

Coryn, C. L. S. (2007). The holy trinity of methodological rigor: A skeptical view. *Journal of MultiDisciplinary Evaluation*, 4(7), 26–31.

Cosmides, L., Tooby, J., & Kurzban, R. (2003). Perceptions of race. *Trends in Cognitive Science*, 4(7), 173–179. https://doi.org/10.1016/s1364-6613(03)00057-3

Cousins, J. B., & Bourgeois, I. (2014). Cross-case analysis and implications for research, theory, and practice. In J. B. Cousins, & I. Bourgeois (Eds.), *Special issue: Organizational capacity to do and use evaluation. New directions for evaluation*, 2014(141), 101–119. https://doi.org/10.1002/ev.20078

Cousins, J. B., & Earl, L. (1995). The case for participatory evaluation: Theory, research, practice. In J. B. Cousins, & L. Earl (Eds.), *Participatory evaluation in education: Studies in evaluation use and organizational learning* (pp. 3–18).

Cousins, J. B., Goh, S. C., Elliott, C. J., & Bourgeois, I. (2014). Framing the capacity to do and use evaluation. In J. B. Cousins, & I. Bourgeois (Eds.), *Special issue: Organizational capacity to do and use evaluation. New directions for evaluation*, 2014(141), 7–23. https://doi.org/10.1002/ev.20076

Cousins, J. B., & Leithwood, K. A. (1986). Current empirical research on evaluation utilization. *Review of Educational Research*, 56(3), 331–364.

Creswell, J. W. (2015). *A concise introduction to mixed methods research.* SAGE Publications.

Creswell, J. W., & Creswell, J. (2018). *Research design: Qualitative, quantitative, and mixed methods approaches.* SAGE Publications.

Creswell, J. W., & Plano Clark, V. L. (2018). *Designing and conducting mixed methods research* (3rd ed.). SAGE Publications.

Cronbach, J. L., Ambron, S. R., Dornbusch, S. M., Hess, R. D., Hornik, R. C., Phillips, D. C., Walker, D. F., & Weiner, S. S. (1980). *Toward reform of program evaluation.* Jossey-Bass.

Croskerry, P. (2018). Adaptive expertise in medical decision making. *Medical Teacher*, 40(8), 803–808. https://doi.org/10.1080/0142159X.2018.1484898

Crotty, M. (1998). *The foundations of social research: Meaning and perspectives in the research process.* SAGE Publications.

Cullen, P., Clapham, K., Byrne, J., Hunter, K., Senserrick, T., Keay, L., & Ivers, R. (2016). The importance of context in logic model construction for a multi-site community-based Aboriginal driver licensing program. *Evaluation and Program Planning*, 57(Suppl. C), 8–15.

Curry, D. W. (2018). Perspectives on monitoring and evaluation. *American Journal of Evaluation*, 40(1), 147–150.

Czechowski, K., Sylvestre, J., & Moreau, K. (2019, Spring). Secure data handling: An essential competence for evaluators. *The Canadian Journal of Program Evaluation*, 34(1), 139–151.

Damschroder, L. J., Aron, D. C., Keith, R. E., Kirsch, S. R., Alexander, J. A., & Lowery, J. C. (2009). Fostering implementation of health services research findings into practice: A consolidated framework for advancing implementation science. *Implementation Science*, 50, 1–15.

Datta, L. (2001). Mixed methods evaluation: The wheelbarrow, the mosaic and the double helix. *Evaluation Journal of Australasia*, 1(2), 33–40.

Davenport, S. (2013, July 23). Prioritise citizen feedback to improve aid effectiveness. *The Guardian.* https://www.theguardian.com/global-development-professionals-network/2013/jul/22/feedback-loops-citizen-development

Davidson, E. J. (2000) Ascertaining causality in theory-based evaluation. In A. Petrosino, P. J. Rogers, T. A. Huebner, & T. A. Hacsi (Eds.), *Special issue: Program theory in evaluation: Challenges and opportunities. New directions for evaluation*, 2000(87), 17–26. https://doi.org/10.1002/ev.1178

Davidson, E. J. (2007). Editorial: Unlearning some of our social scientist habits. *Journal of MultiDisciplinary Evaluation*, 4(8), iii–v1.

Davidson, E. J. (2009, November 12). *Improving evaluation questions and answers: Getting actionable answers for real-world decision makers* [Presentation]. Context and Evaluation American Evaluation Association Conference, Orlando, FL, United States.

Davidson, E. J., & Rowe, A. (2022, May). *Key evaluation questions (KEQs) to guide Footprint Evaluations (v. 5)*. BetterEvaluation. https://www.betterevaluation.org/resources/key-evaluation-questions-keqs-guide-footprint-evaluations

Davies, R. (2013). *Planning evaluability assessments: A synthesis of the literature and recommendations* (Working Paper 40). UK Department for International Development.

Davison, J. (2020, February 20). *Artifacts recovered from HMS Erebus offer tantalizing links to sailors on doomed Franklin Expedition*. Canadian Broadcasting Corporation. https://www.cbc.ca/news/canada/erebus-wreck-exploration-franklin-expedition-mystery-artifacts-1.5469843

Dean-Coffey, J. (2018). What's race got to do with it? Equity and philanthropic evaluation practice. *American Journal of Evaluation*, 39(4), 527–542.

Dean-Coffey, J., Casey, J., & Caldwell, L. D. (2014). Raising the bar—Integrating cultural competence and equity: Equitable evaluation. *The Foundation Review*, 6(2), 81–94.

Delbecq, A. L., & Van de Ven, A. H. (1971). A group process model for problem identification and program planning. *Journal of Applied Behavioral Science*, 7, 466–491.

Desch, H. (2007). *Night of the grizzlies-40 years later*. White Fish Pilot. https://hungryhorsenews.com/news/2007/aug/09/night-of-the-grizzlies-40-years-later-10/

Dettmer, S. (2017). *Night of the grizzlies: Lessons learned in 50 years since attacks*. https://www.greatfallstribune.com/story/news/2017/08/03/night-grizzlies-lessons-learned-50-years-since-attacks/525884001/

Dhaliwal, K., Casey, J., Aceves-Iñiguez, K., & Dean-Coffey, J. (2020). Radical inquiry—Liberatory praxis for research and evaluation. In L. C. Neubauer, D. McBride, A. Guajardo, W. Casillas, & M. Hall (Eds.), *Special issue: Examining issues facing communities of color today: The role of evaluation to incite change. New directions for evaluation*, 2020(166), 49–64. https://doi.org/10.1002/ev.20415

Dickson, C., & Watson, B. (2021, May 27). *Remains of 215 children found buried at former B.C. residential school, First Nation says*. https://www.cbc.ca/news/canada/british-columbia/tk-eml%C3%BAps-te-secw%C3%A9pemc-215-children-former-kamloops-indian-residential-school-1.6043778

Dillman, D. A. (1978). *Mail and telephone surveys: The total design method*. Wiley.

Dillman, D. A. (2014, July). *The tailored design method*. Washington State University. https://sesrc.wsu.edu/about/total-design-method/

Dizikes, P. (2011, February 22). *When the butterfly effect took flight*. MIT News Magazine. https://www.technologyreview.com/2011/02/22/196987/when-the-butterfly-effect-took-flight/

DME for Peace. (2014, December 3). *Using feedback effectively in peacebuilding contexts*. https://www.dmeforpeace.org/resource/using-feedback-effectively-in-peacebuilding-contexts/

Donaldson, S. I. (2005). Using program theory-drive evaluation science to crack the Da Vinci Code. In M. C. Alkin, & C. A. Christie (Eds.), *Special issue: Theorists' models in action. New directions for evaluation*, 2005(106), 65–84. https://doi.org/10.1002/ev.152

Donaldson, S. I., & Christie, C. A. (2006). Emerging career opportunities in the transdiscipline of evaluation science. In S. I. Donaldson, D. E. Berger, & K. Pezdek (Eds.), *Applied psychology: New frontiers and rewarding careers* (pp. 243–259). Lawrence Erlbaum Associates.

Donaldson, S. I., & Lipsey, M. W. (2006). Roles for theory in contemporary evaluation practice: Developing practical knowledge. In I. Shaw, J. Greene, & M. Mark (Eds.), *The handbook of evaluation: Policies, programs, and practices* (pp. 56–75). SAGE Publications.

Donnelly, C., & Searle, M. (2017). Optimizing use in the field of program evaluation by integrating learning from the knowledge field. Canadian Journal of Program Evaluation, 31 2(Special Issue), 305–327.

Doyle, A. C. (1894). *The memoirs of Sherlock Holmes*. George Newnes.

Dozois, E., Langlois, M., & Blanchet-Cohen, N. (2010). *DE 201: A practitioner's guide to developmental evaluation*. The J.W. McConnell Family Foundation and the International Institute for Child Rights and Development. https://mcconnellfoundation.ca/wp-content/uploads/2017/07/DE-201-EN.pdf

Drawson, A. S., Toombs, E., & Mushquash, C. J. (2017). Indigenous research methods: A systematic review. *The*

International Indigenous Policy Journal, 8(2), 1–25. https://doi.org/10.18584/iipj.2017.8.2.5

Drucker, A., Fleming, P., & Chan, A. W. (2016). Research techniques made simple: Assessing risk of bias in systematic reviews. *Journal of Investigative Dermatology*, 136, e109–e114.

Drummond, M. F., Stoddart, G. L., & Torrance, G. W. (1987). *Methods for the economic evaluation of health care programmes.* Oxford University Press.

Duster, T. (2009). Debating reality and relevance. *Science*, 324(5931), 1144–1145.

Earl, S., Carden, F., & Smutylo, T. (2001). *Outcome mapping: Building learning and reflection into development programs.* International Development Research Centre. https://www.idrc.ca/en/book/outcome-mapping-building-learning-and-reflection-development-programs

Eberhardt, N., Hawks, S., Mendoza, W., & Mendoza, M. (2004). Participatory evaluation on the Volivian Altiplano: Collaboration and empowerment. *IUHPE-Promotion and Education*, 10(1), 6–10.

Ebers, M. (2015). *International encyclopedia of the social & behavioral sciences.* Elsevier.

Eddy, D. M. (1990). Practice policies: Guidelines for methods. *Journal of the American Medical Association*, 263(13), 1839–1841.

Eden, C., & Ackerman, F. (1998). *Making strategy.* SAGE Publications.

Elrod, H. (2017). *Miracle morning.* Hal Elrod International.

Elvik, R. (2005). Can we trust the results of meta-analysis? A systematic approach to sensitivity analysis in meta-analyses. *Transportation Research Record: Journal of the Transportation Research Board*, 1908, 221–229.

Eoyang, G., & Oakden, J. (2016). Adaptive evaluation: A synergy between complexity theory and evaluation practice. *Emergence: Complexity and Organization*, 18(3–4), 1–16. https://doi.org/10.emerg/10.17357.e5389f5715a734817dfbeaf25ab335e5

Estrella, M., & Gaventa, J. (Eds.). (1998). *Who counts reality? Participatory monitoring and evaluation: A literature review.* Institute of Development Studies. https://www.ids.ac.uk/publications/who-counts-reality-participatory-monitoring-and-evaluation-a-literature-review/

Environmental Protection Agency. (2022). *Causes of climate change.* https://www.epa.gov/climatechange-science/causes-climate-change

European Commission. (2022). *Causes of climate change.* https://ec.europa.eu/clima/climate-change/causes-climate-change_en

Evergreen, S. (2011). Eval + Com. In S. Mathison (Ed.), *Really new directions in evaluation: Young evaluators' perspectives. New directions for evaluation*, 2011(131), 41–45. https://doi.org/10.1002/ev.376

Evergreen, S. (2017). *The 1-3-25 reporting model.* Stephanie Evergreen Consulting. https://stephanieevergreen.com/the-1-3-25-reporting-model/

Evergreen, S., & Emery, A. K. (2016). *Data visualization checklist.* Stephanie Evergreen Consulting. https://stephanieevergreen.com/wp-content/uploads/2016/10/DataVizChecklist_May2016.pdf

Ewert, A., & Sibthorp, J. (2009). Creating outcomes through experiential education: The challenge of confounding variables. *Journal of Experiential Education*, 31(3), 376–389.

Fawcett, S., Boothroyd, R., Schultz, J., Francisco, V., Carson, V., & Bremby R. (2003). Building capacity for participatory evaluation within community initiatives. *Journal of Prevention and Intervention in the Community*, 26, 21–26.

Fetterman, D. M. (1994). Empowerment evaluation. *Evaluation Practice*, 15(1), 1–15.

Fetterman, D. M. (2001). *Foundations of empowerment evaluation.* SAGE Publications.

Fetterman, D. M., Delaney, L., Triana-Tremain, B., & Evans-Lee, M. (2015). Empowerment evaluation and evaluation capacity building in a 10-year tobacco prevention initiative. In D. Fetterman, S. Kaftarian, & A. Wandersman (Eds.), *Empowerment evaluation* (pp. 295–314). SAGE Publications.

Fetterman, D. M., Kaftarian, S. J., & Wandersman, A. (Eds.). (1995). *Empowerment evaluation: Knowledge and tools for self-assessment and accountability.* SAGE Publications.

Fetterman, D. M., Rodriguez-Campos, L., & Zukoski, A. P. (2017). An introduction to collaborative, participatory, and empowerment evaluation approaches. In D. Fetterman, L. Rodriguez-Campos, A. Wandersman, R. O'Sullivan, & A. Zukoski (Eds.), *Collaborative, participatory, and empowerment evaluation: Stakeholder involvement approaches* (pp. 1–9). Guilford Press.

Fetterman, D. M., & Wandersman, A. (2005). *Empowerment evaluation principles in practice.* Guilford Publications.

Fetters, M. D., Curry, L. A., & Creswell, J. W. (2013). Achieving integration in mixed methods designs-principles and practices. *Health Services Research*, 48(6), 2134–2156. https://doi.org/10.1111/1475-6773.12117

Fisher, R., Ury, W., & Patton, B. (1991). *Getting to yes: Negotiating agreement without giving* (2nd ed.). Houghton Mifflin.

Fiver Children's Foundation. (n.d. a). *Learn about us*. https://www.fiver.org/#:~:text=Our%20Mission&text=Through%20character%2Dbuilding%20summer%20and,school%2C%20careers%2C%20and%20life

Fiver Children's Foundation. (n.d. b). *Fiver children's foundation theory of change*. https://www.theoryofchange.org/wp-content/uploads/toco_library/pdf/FiverChildrensFoundationTheoryofChangeandNarrative.pdf

Foley, G., & Tinonen, V. (2015). Using grounded theory method to capture and analyze health care experiences. *HSR Health Services Research*, 50(4), 1195–1210. https://www.ncbi.nlm.nih.gov/pmc/articles/PMC4545354/

Fournier, D. M. (2005). Evaluation. In S. Mathison (Ed.), *Encyclopedia of evaluation* (pp. 139–140). SAGE Publications.

Francisco, V., Capwell, E., & Butterfoss, F. (2000). Getting off to a good start with your evaluation. *Health Promotion Practice*, 1(2), 126–131.

Frankel, N., & Gage, A. (2016). *M & E fundamentals: A self-guided mini-course*. MEASURE Evaluation for the U.S. Agency for International Development's Global Health Learning. https://www.measureevaluation.org/resources/publications/ms-07-20-en/at_download/document

Frazier, K. H. (2019, April 29). *Transactions vs. transformations*. Medium. https://medium.com/@kenthfrazier/transactions-vs-transformations-e2c482b82801

Fredericks, K., & Carman, J. (2013). *Using social network analysis in evaluation*. Robert Wood Johnson Foundation. https://www.rwjf.org/en/library/research/2013/12/using-social-network-analysis-in-evaluation.html

Fredericks, K. A., & Durland, M. (2005). The historical evolution and basic concepts of social network analysis. In M. M. Durland & K. A. Fredericks (Eds.), *Special issue: Social network analysis in program evaluation. New directions for evaluation*, 2005(107), 15–23. https://doi.org/10.1002/ev.158

Freishtat, R., & Leipzig, A. (2019). *Information acrobat: Climbing the ladder of abstraction*. https://go.executive.berkeley.edu/hubfs/PDFs_Faculty%20White%20Papers/Climbing%20the%20Ladder%20of%20Abstraction_Richard%20Freishtat%20and%20Adam%20Leipzig%20.pdf

Frey, B., Lohmeier, J., Lee, S., & Tollefson, N. (2006). Measuring collaboration among grant partners. *American Journal of Evaluation*, 27(3), 383–392.

Friere, P. (1970). *Pedagogy of the oppressed* (M. Ramos, Trans.). Seabury Press. (Original work published in 1968).

Frierson, H. T., Hood, S., & Hughes, G. H. (2002). A guide to conducting culturally responsive evaluation. In J. Frechtling (Ed.), *The 2002 user-friendly handbook for project evaluation*. National Science Foundation. https://www.nsf.gov/pubs/2002/nsf02057/nsf02057.pdf

Frye, A. W., & Hemmer, P. A. (2012). Program evaluation models and related theories: AMEE guide. *Medical Teacher*, 34(5), 288–299. https://www.tandfonline.com/doi/full/10.3109/0142159X.2012.668637

Fuscaldi, D., Kaye, J., & Philliber, S. (1998). Evaluation of a program for parenting. *Families in Society: The Journal of Contemporary Human Services*, 79(1), 53–61.

Gaille, B. (2018, February). *Advantages and disadvantages of qualitative research*. Brandon Gaille Small Business and Marketing Advice. https://brandongaille.com/25-advantages-disadvantages-qualitative-research/

Galanti, G. (2003). The Hispanic family and male-female relationships: An overview. *Journal of Transcultural Nursing*, 14(3), 180–185. https://www.rit.edu/liberalarts/sites/rit.edu.liberalarts/files/documents/our-work/2009-12.pdf

Gamboa, S. (2021). *Latino civil rights organization drops 'Latinx' from official communication*. NBC News. https://www.nbcnews.com/news/latino/latino-civil-rights-organization-drops-latinx-official-communication-rcna8203

Garrison, A. (2013). Genomic justice for Native Americans: Impact of the Havasupai case on genetic research. *Science, Technology & Human Values*, 38(2), 1–17. https://www.ncbi.nlm.nih.gov/pmc/articles/PMC5310710/pdf/nihms843786.pdf

Garvin, D. A. (1993, July–August). Building a learning organization. *Harvard Business Review*. https://hbr.org/1993/07/building-a-learning-organization

Gawande, A. (2011). *The checklist manifesto: How to get things right*. Henry Holt and Company.

Gersten, R., & Hitchcock, J. (2009). What is credible evidence in education? The role of the What Works Clearinghouse in informing the process. In S. I. Donaldson, C. A. Christie, & M. M. Mark (Eds.), *What counts as credible evidence in applied research and evaluation practice?* (pp. 78–95). SAGE Publications. https://dx.doi.org/10.4135/9781412995634.d11

Girls not Brides. (2017). *Design for success! A guide to developing end child marriage projects and how to fundraise for them*. The Global Partnership to End Child Marriage. https://www.girlsnotbrides.org/documents/850/Girls-Not-Brides-Design-for-Success-Toolkit_Final-ENG-high-res.pdf

Glasser, B. G., & Strauss, A. L. (1967). *The discovery of grounded theory: Strategies for qualitative research.* Aldine Transaction.

Goodyear, L., Jewiss, J., Usinger, J., & Barela, E. (Eds.). (2014). *Qualitative inquiry in evaluation: From theory to practice.* Jossey-Bass.

Government Accountability Office. (2018). *Performance and accountability report* (GAO Publication No. 19-1SP). U.S. Government Printing Office. https://www.gao.gov/assets/700/695501.pdf

Government of Canada. (1991). *Report of the royal commission on Aboriginal Peoples.* Royal Commission on Aboriginal Peoples. https://www.bac-lac.gc.ca/eng/discover/aboriginal-heritage/royal-commission-aboriginal-peoples/Pages/final-report.aspx

Government of Canada. (2016). *Policy on results.* Treasury Board. https://www.tbs-sct.gc.ca/pol/doc-eng.aspx?id=31300

Government of Canada. (2018a). *CSPS strategic directions initiative integrated summative evaluation.* Canadian School of Public Service. https://www.csps-efpc.gc.ca/About_Us/currentreport/sdi-ise/index-eng.aspx

Government of Canada. (2018b). *Research involving the first nations, inuit and métis peoples of Canada.* https://ethics.gc.ca/eng/tcps2-eptc2_2018_chapter9-chapitre9.html

Government of Canada. (2019, December). *Setting new directions to support Indigenous research and research training in Canada.* https://www.canada.ca/content/dam/crcc-ccrc/documents/strategic-plan-2019-2022/sirc_strategic_plan-eng.pdf

Government of Canada. (2021). *Truth and reconciliation commission of Canada.* https://www.rcaanc-cirnac.gc.ca/eng/1450124405592/1529106060525#chp2

Graham, I. D., & Tetroe, J. (2010). The knowledge to action framework. In J. Rycroft-Malone, & T. Bucknall (Eds.), *Models and frameworks for implementing evidence-based practice: Linking evidence to action* (pp. 207–214). Wiley.

Grand Rapids African American Health Institute. (2020). *Logic models.* Health Equity Index of the Grand Rapids African American Health Institute. https://hei.graahi.org/Logic-Model

Granner, M., & Sharpe, P. (2004). Evaluating community coalition characteristics and functioning: A summary of measurement tools. *Health Education Research*, 19(5), 514–532.

Grant, M., & Booth, A. (2009). A typology of reviews: An analysis of 14 review types and associated methodologies. *Health Information and Libraries Journal*, 26, 91–108.

Greene, J. C. (1997). Evaluation as advocacy. *Evaluation Practice*, 18(1), 25–35.

Greene, J. C. (2005a). Mixed methods. In S. Mathison (Ed.), *Encyclopedia of evaluation* (pp. 255–256). SAGE Publications.

Greene, J. C. (2005b). Context. In S. Mathison (Ed.), *Encyclopedia of evaluation* (pp. 82–84). SAGE Publications.

Greene, J. C. (2005c). Stakeholders. In S. Mathison (Ed.), *Encyclopedia of evaluation* (pp. 397–398). SAGE Publications.

Greene, J. C. (2007). *Mixed methods in social inquiry.* Jossey-Bass.

Greene, J. C., Caracelli, V. J., & Graham, W. J. (1989). Toward a conceptual framework for mixed-method evaluation designs. *Educational Evaluation and Policy Analysis*, 11(3), 255–274.

Greenfieldboyce, N. (2019, April 29). *This week, NASA is pretending an asteroid is on it way to smack the Earth.* National Public Radio. https://www.npr.org/2019/04/29/718296681/this-week-nasa-is-pretending-an-asteroid-is-on-its-way-to-smack-the-earth

Greiner, J. (2004). Trained observer ratings. In J. S. Wholey, H. Hatry, & K. Newcomer (Eds.), *Handbook of practical program evaluation* (2nd ed., pp. 211–256). Jossey-Bass.

Grol, R. (2001). Successes and failures in the implementation of evidence-based guidelines for clinical practice. *Medical Care*, 39(8 Supplement 2), II46–II54.

Guajardo, A., Robles-Schrader, G. M., Aponte-Soto, L., & Neubauer, L. C. (2020). LatCrit theory as a framework for social justice evaluation: Considerations for evaluation and evaluators. In L. C. Neubauer, D. McBride, A. Guajardo, W. D. Casillas, & M. E. Hall (Eds.), *Special issue: Examining issues facing communities of color today: The role of evaluation to incite change*, 2020(166), 1–135.

Guba, E. G., & Lincoln, Y. S. (1989). *Fourth generation evaluation.* SAGE Publications.

Guetterman, T. C., Fetters, M. D., & Creswell, J. W. (2015). Integrating quantitative and qualitative results in health science mixed methods research through joint displays. *Annals of Family Medicine*, 13(6), 554–561.

Guichard, A., Tardieu, E., Dagenais, C., Nour, K., Lafontaine, G., & Ridde, V. (2017). Use of concurrent mixed methods combining concept mapping and focus groups to adapt a health equity tool in Canada. *Evaluation and Program Planning*, 61, 169–177.

Guijt, I. (2014, December 15). *Week 50: Feedback loops-new buzzword, old practice?* Better Evaluation. https://www.better-evaluation.org/en/blog/feedback_loops_new_buzzword_old_practice

Hall, M. E. (2020). Blest be the tie that binds. In L. Neubauer, D. McBride, A. Guajardo, W. Casillas, & M. Hall (Eds.), *Special issue: Examining issues facing communities of color today: The role of evaluation to incite change. New directions for evaluation*, 2020(166), 7–11. https://doi.org/10.1002/ev.20414

Halwes, T. (1998). *Deming's philosophy of quality management*. Dharma-Haven. http://www.dharma-haven.org/five-havens/deming.htm

Hammersley, M. (1987). Some notes on the terms 'validity' and 'reliability'. *British Educational Research Journal*, 13(1), 73–81.

Hammersley M., & Atkinson P. (1983). *Ethnography: Principles in practice*. Tavistock.

Hardy, C. (2015). *International encyclopedia of the social and behavioral sciences*. Elsevier Publications.

Harkreader, S. A., & Henry, G. T. (2000). Using performance measurement systems for assessing the merit and worth of reforms. *American Journal of Evaluation*, 21(2), 151–170. https://doi.org/10.1177/109821400002100203

Harvard University. (2019). *Research data ownership policy*. https://vpr.harvard.edu/data-ownership

Hayakawa, S. I. (1939). *Language in thought and action*. Harcourt Publishers.

Heider, C. (2016, February 29). *Influencing change through evaluation: What is the theory of change?* World Bank Group. https://ieg.worldbankgroup.org/blog/influencing-change-through-evaluation-what-theory-change

Henry, G. T. (2000). Why not use? In V. Caracelli, & H. Preskill (Eds.), *The expanding scope of evaluation use. New directions for evaluation*, 2000(88), 85–98. https://doi.org/10.1002/ev.1193

Henry, H. (2014). *Complexity theory in nursing*. Independent Nurse. http://www.independentnurse.co.uk/professional-article/complexity-theory-in-nursing/65669/

Hilliard, A. G. (1989). Kemetic (Egyptian) historical revision: Implications for cross-cultural evaluation and research in education. *Evaluation Practice*, 10(2), 5–99.

Hilliard, A. G. (1997). Language, culture, and the assessment of African American children. In A. Lin Goodwin (Ed.), *Assessment for equity and inclusion: Embracing all our children* (pp. 229–240). Routledge.

HM Treasury. (2020). *Magenta book: Central government guidance on evaluation*. https://assets.publishing.service.gov.uk/government/uploads/system/uploads/attachment_data/file/879438/HMT_Magenta_Book.pdf

Hodgkin, S. (2008). Telling it all: A story of women's social capital using a mixed methods approach. *Journal of Mixed Methods Research*, 2, 296–316.

Hogan, R. L. (2007). The historical development of program evaluation: Exploring the past and present. *Online Journal of Workforce Education and Development*, 2(4). https://pdfs.semanticscholar.org/ee2f/dbbe116a30ab7a79b19e1033a7cab434feec.pdf

Hogue, T. (1993). *Community-based collaboration: Community wellness multiplied*. Chandler Center for Community Leadership. https://www.ojp.gov/ncjrs/virtual-library/abstracts/community-based-collaboration-community-wellness-multiplied

Holden, D. J., & Zimmerman, M. A. (2012). Evaluation planning: Here and now. In M. A. Zimmerman, & D. J. Holden (Eds.), *A practical guide to program evaluation planning: Theory and case examples* (pp. 1–22). SAGE Publications.

Hood, S. (2014). How will we know it when we see it? A critical friend perspective of the graduate education diversity internship (GEDI) program and its legacy in evaluation. In P. M. Collins, & R. Hopson (Eds.), *Building a new generation of culturally responsive evaluators through AEA's graduate education diversity internship program. New directions for evaluation*, 2014(143), 109–121. https://doi.org/10.1002/ev.20097

Hood, S., Hopson, R. K., & Kirkhart, K. E. (2015). Culturally responsive evaluation. In K. E. Newcomer, H. P. Hatry, & J. S. Wholey (Eds.), *Handbook of practical program evaluation* (pp. 281–317), Jossey-Bass.

Hoskins, K. (1968). The examination, disciplinary power and rational schooling. *History of Education*, 8(1), 135–146.

House, E. (1991). Evaluation and social justice. Where are we? In M. McLaughlin, & D. Phillips (Eds.), *Evaluation and education at quarter century* (pp. 233–247). University of Chicago Press.

House, E. R. (2005). Social justice. In S. Mathison (Ed.), *Encyclopedia of evaluation* (pp. 393–396). SAGE Publications.

House, E. R. (2017). Evaluation and the framing of race. *American Journal of Evaluation*, 38(2), 167–189.

Howell, D. (1997). *Statistical methods for psychology* (4th ed.). Wadsworth Publishing Company.

Howell, E., & Yemane, A. (2006). An assessment of evaluation designs: Case studies of 12 large federal evaluations. *American Journal of Evaluation*, 27(2), 219–236.

Hoyle, R., Harris, M., & Judd, C. (2001). *Research methods in social relations* (7th ed.). Wadsworth Publishing.

Hseih, H., & Shannon, S. (2005). Three approaches to qualitative content analysis. *Qualitative Health Research*, 15(9), 1277–1288.

Huhman, M., Heitzler, C., & Wong, F. (2004). The VERB™ campaign logic model: A tool for planning and evaluation. *Prevention in Chronic Disease*, 1(3), 1–6. https://www.ncbi.nlm.nih.gov/pmc/articles/PMC1253476/pdf/PCD13A11.pdf

Hummelbrunner, R. (2007). Systemic evaluation in the field of regional development. In B. Williams, & I. Imam (Eds.), *Systems concepts in evaluation: An expert anthology* (pp. 161–180). American Evaluation Association.

Hunter, M. T., & McDavid, J. C. (2019). Comparison of Canadian and American graduate evaluation education programs. *Canadian Journal of Program Evaluation/La Revue canadienne d'évaluation de program*, 34(2), 207–234. https://doi.org/10.3138/cjpe.56989

Hurworth, R. (2008). Program clarification: An overview and resources for evaluability assessment program theory and program logic. *Evaluation Journal of Australasia*, 8(2), 42–48.

Hutchinson, K. (2010). *Literature review of program sustainability assessment tools*. Community Solutions. http://communitysolutions.ca/web/wp-content/uploads/2013/07/Review-of-Sustainability-Tools-2010.pdf

Hyland, M. E. (2003). A brief guide to the selection of quality of life instrument. *Health and Quality of Life Outcomes*, 1(24), 1–5.

Iasemidis, L., & Sackellares, C. (1996). Chaos theory and epilepsy. *The Neuroscientist*, 2, 118–126.

IBERDROLA. (2022). *How is climate change affecting the economy and society?* https://www.iberdrola.com/sustainability/impacts-of-climate-change

Idaho Legislature. (2018, March). *Child welfare system: Reducing the risk of adverse outcomes*. Office of Performance Evaluations. https://legislature.idaho.gov/ope/reports/r1803/

Ihrig, L., Lane, E., Mahatmya, D., & Assouline, S. G. (2018). STEM excellence and leadership program: Increasing the level of STEM challenge and engagement for high-achieving students in economically disadvantaged rural communities. *Journal for the Education of the Gifted*, 41(1), 24–42.

Indian Health Service. (2021). *Indian health service institutional review boards (IRB)*. https://www.ihs.gov/dper/research/hsrp/instreviewboards/

Indigenous Corporate Training. (2020, May 30). *What is the seventh generation principle?* Indigenous Corporate Training. https://www.ictinc.ca/blog/seventh-generation-principle

Ingoldsby, E., Morrison, C., Ruben, J., Melz, H., & Cairone, K. (2020). *Using logic models grounded in theory of change to support trauma-informed initiatives. Trauma-informed approaches: Connecting research, policy, and practice to build resilience in children and families (ASPE Issue Brief)*. Office of the Assistant Secretary for Planning and Evaluation (ASPE), U.S. Department of Health and Human Services (HHS).

Internal Revenue Service. (2018). *Requirements for 501©(3) hospitals under the Affordable Care Act – Section 501(r)*. U.S. Treasury. https://www.irs.gov/charities-non-profits/charitable-organizations/new-requirements-for-501c3-hospitals-under-the-affordable-care-act

International Organization for Cooperation in Evaluation. (2018). *About us*. https://www.ioce.net/about-us

International Organization for Standardization. (n.d.). *ISO standards are internationally agreed by experts*. https://www.iso.org/standards.html

Iofciu, F., Miron, C., & Antoh, S. (2012). Constructivist approach of evaluation strategies in science education. *Procedia, Social and Behavioral Sciences*, 31, 292–296.

Isaacs, M. R., Huang, L. N., Hernandez, M., & Echo-Hawk, H. (2005). *The road to evidence: The intersection of evidence-based practices and cultural competence in children's mental health*. National Alliance of Multi-Ethnic Behavioral Health Associations. http://www.multiculturalmentalhealth.ca/wp-content/uploads/2013/10/Isaacs-RoadtoEvidence-93006.pdf

Ishikawa, K. (1968). *Guide to quality control*. JUSE.

Ithal, S. (2019, November 26). *12 Disturbing stories of bodies left on top of Mount Everest* [online article]. https://www.ranker.com/list/creepy-stories-mount-everest/sabrina-ithal

Jackson, K. M., Pukys, S., Castro, A., Hermosura, L., Mendez, J., Vophra-Gupta, S., Padilla, Y., & Morales, G. (2018). Using the transformative paradigm to conduct a mixed methods needs assessment of a marginalized community: Methodological lessons and implications. *Evaluation and Program Planning*, 66, 111–119. https://doi.org/10.1016/j.evalprogplan.2017.09.010

Janssens, M., & Seynaeve, K. (2000). Collaborating to desegregate a "Black" school: How can a low-power stakeholder gain voice? *The Journal of Applied Behavioral Science*, 36(1), 70–90.

Jenkinson, H., Leahy, P., Scanlon, M., Power, F., & Byrne, O. (2019). The value of groupwork knowledge and skills in focus group research: A focus group approach with marginalized teens regarding access to third-level education. *International Journal of Qualitative Methods*, 18, 1–11.

Jennings, A. (2004). *Models for developing trauma-informed behavioral health systems and trauma-specific services* [PDF file]. http://theannainstitute.org/MDT.pdf

Jennings, R. (2020, June 26). *Getting to yes Chapter 4: Invent options for mutual gain*. LitCharts LLC. https://www.litcharts.com/lit/getting-to-yes/chapter-4-invent-options-for-mutual-gain

Jeworrek, T. (2021, January 7). *Record hurricane season and major wildfires – The natural disaster figures for 2020*. Munich RE. https://www.munichre.com/en/company/media-relations/media-information-and-corporate-news/media-information/2021/2020-natural-disasters-balance.html

Johnson, D. W., & Johnson, F. P. (2009). *Joining together: Group theory and group skills*. Pearson Education.

Johnson, K., Greenseid, L. O., Toal, S. A., King, J. A., Lawrenz, F., & Volkov, B. (2009). Research on evaluation use: A review of the empirical literature from 1986 to 2005. *American Journal of Evaluation*, 30(3), 377–410.

Johnson, R. B., & Christensen, L. (2020). *Educational research: Quantitative, qualitative, and mixed approaches* (7th ed.). SAGE Publications. https://www.sagepub.com/sites/default/files/upm-binaries/26101_7.pdf

Johnson, R. B., & Onwuegbuzie, A. J. (2004) Mixed methods research: A research paradigm whose time has come. *Educational Researcher*, 33, 14–26.

Joint Committee on Standards for Educational Evaluation. (2018). *Program evaluation standards statements*. http://www.jcsee.org/program-evaluation-standards-statements

Jones, J., Salazar, L., & Crosby, R. (2015). Contextual factors and sexual risk behaviors among young, black men. *American Journal of Men's Health*, 11(3), 508–517.

Julnes, G. (2019). Evaluating sustainability: Controversies, challenges, and opportunities. In G. Julnes (Ed.), *Special issue: Evaluating sustainability: Evaluative support for managing processes in the public interest. New directions for evaluation*, 2019(162), 13–28. https://doi.org/10.1002/ev.20361

J. W. McConnel Foundation. (2020). *Tamarack Institute for community engagement: Cities reducing poverty*. Tamarack Institute for Community Engagement. https://mcconnellfoundation.ca/grant/tamarack-institute-for-community-engagement-cities-reducing-poverty/

Kahneman, D. (2011). *Thinking, fast and slow*. Farrar, Straus and Giroux.

Kania, J., Kramer, M., & Senge, P. (2018). *The water of systems change*. FSG. https://www.fsg.org/publications/water_of_systems_change

Kao, A. C. (2020). Health of the first Americans. *American Medical Association Journal of Ethics*, 22(10), E833–E836. https://doi.org/10.1001/amajethics.2020.833

Kaplan, R., & Norton, D. P. (1996). *The balanced scorecard: Translating strategy into action*. Harvard Business School Press.

Kaplan, R. S., & Norton, D. P. (2007, September–October). Using the balanced scorecard as a strategic management system. *Harvard Business Review*, Product No. 4118, 1–7.

Kass, N. E. (2001). An ethics framework for public health. *American Journal of Public Health*, 91(11), 1776–1782.

Kekahio, W., Cicchinelli, L., Lawton, B., & Brandon, P. R. (2014). *Logic models: A tool for effective program planning, collaboration, and monitoring* (REL 2014–025). U.S. Department of Education, Institute of Education Sciences, National Center for Education Evaluation and Regional Assistance, Regional Educational Laboratory Pacific. https://www2.ed.gov/about/offices/list/oese/oss/technicalassistance/easnlogicmodelstoolmonitoring.pdf

Kelley, A., Belcourt-Dittloff, A., Belcourt, C., & Belcourt, G. (2013). Research ethics and Indigenous communities. *American Journal of Public Health*, 103(12), 2146–2152. https://doi.org/10.2105/AJPH.2013.301522

Kidd, C. V. (1992). The evolution of sustainability. *Journal of Agricultural Environmental Ethics*, 5, 1–26. https://doi.org/10.1007/BF01965413

Kidd, S. (2006). Factors precipitating suicidality among homeless youth: A quantitative follow-up. *Youth and Society*, 37(4), 393–422.

Kilanowski, J. F. (2017). Breadth of the socio ecological model. *Journal of Agromedicine*, 22(4), 295–297. https://doi.org/10.1080/1059924X.2017.1358971

Kim, S., & Crutchfield, C. (2004). An evaluation of substance abuse aftercare program for homeless women with children using confounding variable-control design. *Journal of Drug Education*, 34(3), 213–233.

King, J. A. (2020). Editor's notes. In J. A. King (Ed.), *Special issue: The American Evaluation Association's program evaluator competencies. New directions for evaluation*, 2020(168), 7–11. https://doi.org/10.1002/ev.20441

King, J. A., Morris, L. L., & Fits-Gibbon, C. T. (1987). *How to assess program implementation*. SAGE Publications.

King, J. A., & Stevahn, L. (2013). *Interactive evaluation practice: Mastering the interpersonal dynamics of program evaluation.* SAGE Publications.

King, J. A., Stevahn, L., Ghere, G., & Minnema, J. (2001). Toward a taxonomy of essential evaluator competencies. *American Journal of Evaluation, 22*(2), 229–247.

Kirkhart, K. (2000). Reconceptualizing evaluation use: An integrated theory of influence. In V. Caracelli, & H. Preskill (Eds.), *Special issue: The expanding scope of evaluation use. New directions for evaluation, 2000*(88), 5–23. https://doi.org/10.1002/ev.1188

Kirkpatrick, J., & Kirkpatrick, W. (2016). *Kirkpatrick's four levels of training evaluation.* ATD Press.

Klugman, B. (2021). *How has work funded by Comic Relief's power up programme contributed to shifts in women and girls' power?* https://assets.ctfassets.net/zsfivwzfgl3t/37b92Qfj8fnipl VyHRjfyd/26b378fdc558c6fea0076dbdd7b213c5/Power_Up_Outcome_Harvesting_Report_2021.pdf

Kranias, G. (2017, March). *Participatory evaluation toolkit.* HC Link. https://en.healthnexus.ca/sites/en.healthnexus.ca/files/resources/participatoryevaltoolkit.pdf

Kreuger, R., & Casey, M. (2009). *Focus groups: A practical guide for applied research.* SAGE Publications.

Krippendorf, K. (1980). *Content analysis: An introduction to its methodology.* SAGE Publications.

Kubiak, S., Shamrova, D., & Comartin, E. (2019). Enhancing knowledge of adolescent mental health among law enforcement: Implementing youth-focused crisis intervention team training. *Evaluation and Program Planning, 73,* 44–52.

Kuhn, T. S. (1962). *The structure of scientific revolutions.* University of Chicago Press.

Kuhn, T. S. (1996). *The structure of scientific revolution.* University of Chicago Press.

Kumar, A., & Hegde, B. (2012). Chaos theory: Impact on and applications in medicine. *Nitte University Journal of Health Sciences, 2*(4), 93–99.

LaFrance, J., & Nichols, R. (2010). Reframing evaluation: Defining an indigenous evaluation framework. *The Canadian Journal of Program Evaluation, 23*(2), 13–31.

Lam, C. Y. (2013, November 11). *Merit/worth/significance explained in plain language.* Dr. Chi Yan Lam 5X52. https://chiyanlam.com/2013/11/11/meritworthsignificance-explained-in-plain-language/

Lauterborn, W. (2003). Acoustic chaos. In R. A. Meyers (Ed.), *Encyclopedia of physical science and technology* (pp. 117–127). Elsevier.

Lavallée, L. F. (2009). Practical application of an Indigenous research framework and two qualitative Indigenous research methods: Sharing circles and Anishnaabe symbol-based reflection. *International Journal of Qualitative Methods, 8*(1), 21–40.

LaVelle, J. M. (2014). *An analysis of evaluation education programs and evaluator skills across the world (Publication No. 3617417)* [Doctoral dissertation, Claremont Graduate University]. ProQuest Dissertations Publishing. https://www.proquest.com/openview/0396ddb4270c11e845ea80f92729af5f/1?pq-origsite=gscholar&cbl=18750

LaVelle, J. M. (2018). *2018 Directory of evaluator education programs in the United States.* University of Minnesota Libraries Publishing.

LaVelle, J. M., Donaldson, S. I. (2015). The state of preparing evaluators. In J. Altschuld & M. Engle (Eds.), *Special issue: Accreditation, certification, and credentialing: Relevant concerns for U.S. evaluators. New directions for evaluation, 2015*(145), 39–52. https://doi.org/10.1002/ev.20110

Lavinghouze, S. R., & Snyder, K. (2013). Developing your evaluation plans: A critical component of public health program infrastructure. *American Journal of Health Education, 44,* 237–243.

Law, A., Amundson, N., & Alden L. (2014). Helping highly anxious clients embrace chaos and career uncertainty using cognitive behavioral techniques. *Australian Journal of Career Development, 23*(1), 29–36.

Lee, J. (2020). Statistics, descriptive. In A. Kobayashi (Ed.), *International encyclopedia of human geography* (2nd ed.). Elsevier. https://www.sciencedirect.com/science/article/pii/B9780081022955104287

Leeuw, F. L., & Donaldson, S. I. (2015). Theory in evaluation, reducing confusion and encouraging debate. *Evaluation, 21*(4), 467–480.

Lekas, H., Pahl, K., Lewis, C. (2020). Rethinking cultural competence: Shifting to cultural humility. *Health Services Insights, 13,* 1–4.

Lemos, D., & Garcia, D. (2020). Promoting culturally responsive and equitable evaluation with Latinx immigrants. In L. C. Neubauer, D. McBride, A. D. Guarjardo, W. E. Casillas, & M. E. Hall (Eds.), *Examining issues facing communities of color today: The role of evaluation to incite change. New directions for evaluation, 2020*(166), 89–100. https://doi.org/10.1002/ev.20410

Levin, H. M. (1983). *Cost effectiveness: A primer*. SAGE.

Leviton, L. C. (2015). Evaluation practice and theory: Up and down the ladder of abstraction. *American Journal of Evaluation*, 36(2), 238–242.

Levy, R. (2018). *Canada's cold war purge of LGBTQ from public service*. The Canadian Encyclopedia. https://thecanadianencyclopedia.ca/en/article/lgbtq-purge-in-canada

Li, S., Marquart, J. M., & Zercher, C. (2000). Conceptual issues and analytic strategies in mixed-methods studies of preschool inclusion. *Journal of Early Intervention*, 23(2), 116–132.

Lincoln, Y., & Guba, E. (1980). The distinction between merit and worth in evaluation. *Educational Evaluation and Policy Analysis*, 2(4), 61–71.

Lincoln, Y. S., & Guba, E. G. (1985). *Naturalistic inquiry*. SAGE Publications.

Lincoln, Y. S., & Guba, E. G. (2013). *The constructivist credo*. Left Coast Press.

Lindqvist, G., Hakansson, A., & Petersson, K. (2004). Informal home caregiving in a gender perspective: A selected literature review. *Nursing Science*, 24(74), 26–30.

Lindsey, R., & Dahlman, L. (2021, August 12). *Climate change: Global temperature*. Climate.gov. https://www.climate.gov/news-features/understanding-climate/climate-change-global-temperature#:~:text=August%2012%2C%202021-,Highlights,land%20areas%20were%20record%20warm

Lipsey, M. W., & Cordray, D. S. (2000). Evaluation methods for social intervention. *Annual Review of Psychology*, 51, 345–375.

Lopez, J. (2021). *K9s for Camo*. https://k9sforcamo.org/

Love, A. (1991). *Internal evaluation: Building organizations from within*. SAGE Publications.

Love, A. (2004). Implementation evaluation. In J. S. Wholey, H. P. Hatry, & K. E. Newcomer (Eds.), *Handbook of practical program evaluation* (pp. 63–97). Jossey-Bass.

Lub, V. (2015). Validity in qualitative evaluation: Linking purposes, paradigms, and perspectives. *International Journal of Qualitative Methods*, 14(5), 1–8.

Lundquist, E., Hsueh, J., Lowenstein, A., Faucetta, K., Gubits, D., Michalopoulos, C., & Knox, V. (2014). *A family-strengthening program for low-income families: Final impacts from the supporting healthy marriage evaluation*. OPRE Report 2014-09A. Office of Planning, Research and Evaluation, Administration for Children and Families, U.S. Department of Health and Human Services. https://www.acf.hhs.gov/sites/default/files/documents/opre/shm2013_30_month_impact_reportrev2.pdf

Lynch, L., Lynch, N., Richards, E. (2021). Case Study: Central Iowa shows reducing poverty is possible. https://www.tamarackcommunity.ca/hubfs/Resources/Case%20Studies/Case%20Study%20-%20Central%20Iowa%20Shows%20Reducing%20Poverty%20is%20Possible.pdf?hsCtaTracking=66d02d24-e7ce-4f40-ad0a-c7b7195d136e%7C5b669653-52b1-416f-bd0e-e2aff400069f

MacDonald, G. (2018). *Checklist of key considerations for development of program logic models*. The Checklist Project. https://wmich.edu/evaluation/checklists

Madison, A. M. (1992). Editor's notes. In A. M. Madison (Ed.), *Special issue: Minority issues in program evaluation. New directions for program evaluation*, 1992(53), 1–4. https://doi.org/10.1002/ev.1596

Magana, A. (n.d.). *Variety in qualitative inquiry: Theoretical orientations* [PDF file]. web.ics.purdue.edu/~admagana/CMaps/ResearchMethods/3theoretical_orientations.pdf

Majchrzak, A. (1984). *Methods for policy research*. SAGE Publications.

Mallen, M., Vogel, D., Rochlen, A., & Day, S. (2005). Online counseling: Reviewing the literature from a counseling psychology framework. *The Counseling Psychologist*, 33(6), 819–871.

Mark, J. M. (2011, February 18). *Theseus & the Minotaur: More than a myth?* World History Encyclopedia. https://www.worldhistory.org/article/209/theseus–the-minotaur-more-than-a-myth/

Mark, M. M., & Henry, G. T. (2004). The mechanisms and outcomes of evaluation influence. *Evaluation*, 10(1), 35–57.

Mark, M. M. (2009). Credible evidence: Changing the terms of the debate. In S. I. Donaldson, C. A. Christie, & M. M. Mark (Eds.), *What counts as credible evidence in applied research and evaluation practice?* (p. 214). SAGE Publications.

Marras, W., & Kroemer, K. (1980). A method to evaluate human factors/ergonomics design variables of distress signals. *Human Factors*, 22(4), 389–399.

Marsh, T. N., Cote-Meek, S. C., Toulouse, P., Najavits, L. M., & Young, N. L. (2015). The application of two-eyed seeing decolonizing methodology in qualitative and quantitative research for the treatment of intergenerational trauma and substance use disorders. *International Journal of Qualitative Methods*, 14(5), 1–13. https://doi.org/10.1177/1609406915618046

Martens, K. S. R. (2018). Rubrics in program evaluation. *Evaluation Journal of Australasia*, 18(1), 21–44. https://doi.org/10.1177/1035719X17753961

Massoud, R., Askov, K., Reinke, J., Franco, L., Borstein, T., Knebel, E., & MacAulay, C. (2001). *A Modern paradigm for improving healthcare quality*. U.S. Agency for International Development (USAID) for the Quality Assurance Project. https://www.usaidassist.org/resources/modern-paradigm-improving-healthcare-quality-0

Mathison, S. (2005). *Encyclopedia of evaluation*. SAGE Publications.

Maviglia, S., Yoo, J., Franz, C., Featherstone, E., Churchill, W., Bates, D., Gandhi, T., & Poon, E. (2007). Cost-benefit analysis of a hospital pharmacy bar code solution. *JAMA Internal Medicine*, 167(8), 788–794. https://doi.org/10.1001/archinte.167.8.788

Maxwell, J. A. (2013). *Qualitative research design: An interactive approach*. SAGE Publications.

Mayan, M. J. (2009). *Essentials of qualitative inquiry*. Left Coast Press.

Mayne, J. (2008) *Contribution analysis: An approach to exploring cause and effect*. Institutional Learning and Change Initiative. https://cgspace.cgiar.org/handle/10568/70124

Mayne, J. (2012). Contribution analysis: Coming of age? *Evaluation*, *18*, 270–280.

Mayne, J. (2017). Theory of change analysis: Building robust theories of change. *Canadian Journal of Program Evaluation/LaRevue canadienne d'évaluation de programme*, 32(2), 155–173.

Mazur, M. (Host). (2013 to present). *The huge difference between communication and communications*. Communication Rebel: Rebel Uprising Podcast. Dr. Michelle Mazur. https://drmichellemazur.com/2013/03/difference-between-communication-communications.html

McBride, D., Casillas, W., & LoPiccolo, J. (2020). Inciting social change through evaluation. In L. D. Neubauer, D. McBride, A. D. Guarjardo, W. E., Casillas, & M. E. Hall (Eds.), *Special issue: Examining issues facing communities of color today: The role of evaluation to incite change. New directions for evaluation*, 2020(166), 119–127. https://doi.org/10.1002/ev.20405

McCombs, J., Whitaker, A., & Yoo, P. (2017). *The value of out-of-school time programs*. Rand Corporation. https://www.rand.org/pubs/perspectives/PE267.html

McDaniel, R. R., & Driebe, D. J. (2001). Complexity science and health care management. In L. H. Friedman, J. Goes, & G. T. Savage (Eds.), *Advances in health care management* (pp. 11–36). Emerald Group Publishing.

McDavid, J. C., Huse, I., & Hawthorn, L. R. L. (2013). *Program evaluation and performance measurement: An introduction to practice* (2nd ed.). SAGE Publications.

McDowell, M. (2017). *Rigorous PBL by design: Three shifts for developing confident and competent learners*. Corwin Press.

McGrail, S. (2014). Rethinking the roles of evaluation in learning how to solve 'wicked' problems: The case of anticipatory techniques used to support climate change mitigation and adaption. *Evaluation Journal of Australasia*, 14(2), 4–16.

McKibbon, K. A., Lokker, C., Wilczynski, N. L., Ciliska, D., Dobbins, M., Davis, D., Haynes, R. B., & Straus, S. (2010). A cross-sectional study of the number and frequency of terms used to refer to knowledge translation in a body of health literature in 2006: A tower of Babel? *Implementation Science*, 5(16), 1–11. https://doi.org/10.1186/1748-5908-5-16

McKinney, M. (2008, May 13). *Learning requires personal responsibility*. Leadership Now. https://www.leadershipnow.com/leadingblog/2008/05/

McLeroy, K. R., Bibeau, D., Steckler, A., & Glanz, K. (1988). An ecological perspective on health promotion programs. *Health Education Quarterly*, 15(4), 351–377.

Meijering, L., & Weitkamp, G. (2016). Numbers and narratives: Developing a mixed-methods approach to understand mobility in later life. *Social Science & Medicine*, 168, 200–206.

Mendelow, A. L. (1987). Stakeholder analysis for strategic planning and implementation. In W. R. King & D. I. Cleland (Eds.), *Strategic planning and management handbook* (pp. 176–191). Van Nostrand Reinhold.

Mensing, J. F. (2017). The challenges of defining and measuring outcomes in nonprofit human service organizations. *Human Service Organizations: Management, Leadership & Governance*, 41(3), 207–212.

Mertens, D. M. (1999). Inclusive evaluation: Implications of transformative theory for evaluation. *American Journal of Evaluation*, 20(1), 1–14.

Mertens, D. M. (2009). *Transformative research and evaluation*. Guilford Press.

Mertens, D. M. (2015a). *Mixed methods design in evaluation*. SAGE Publications.

Mertens, D. M. (2018). *Mixed methods design in evaluation*. SAGE Publications.

Mertens, D. M. (2020). *Research and evaluation in education and psychology*. SAGE Publications.

Mertens, D. M., & Wilson, A. (2019). *Program evaluation theory and practice: A comprehensive guide* (2nd ed.). Guilford Press.

Mezirow, J. (1990). *Fostering critical reflection in adulthood: A guide to transformative and emancipatory learning*. Jossey-Bass.

Michael, R. S. (n.d.). *Threats to internal and external validity* [PowerPoint slides]. Indiana University. http://www.indiana.edu/~educy520/sec5982/week_9/520in_ex_validity.pdf

Michelin Group. (n.d.). *What the MICHELIN guide's symbols mean*. https://guide.michelin.com/th/en/to-the-stars-and-beyond-th

Mikkonen, J., & Raphael, D. (2010). *Social determinants of health: The Canadian facts*. York University School of Health Policy and Management.

Miles, M. G., & Huberman, A. M. (1984). *Qualitative data analysis: A sourcebook of new methods*. SAGE Publications.

Miles, M. B., Huberman, A. M., & Saldaña, J. (2020). *Qualitative data analysis: A methods sourcebook* (4th ed.). SAGE Publications.

Milkie, M., & Warner, C. (2011). Classroom learning environments and the mental health of first grade children, *Journal of Health and Social Behavior*, 52(1), 4–22. https://doi.org/10.1177/0022146510394952

Miller, J. (2015, January 26). *VA begins biggest transformation in history*. Federal News Network. https://federalnewsnetwork.com/defense/2015/01/va-begins-biggest-transformation-in-history/

Mind Tools Content Team. (n.d.). *Kirkpatrick's four level training evaluation model: Analyzing learning effectiveness*. https://www.mindtools.com/pages/article/kirkpatrick.htm

Miron, G. (2004). *Evaluation report checklist* [online tool]. https://wmich.edu/sites/default/files/attachments/u350/2014/evaluation-reports.pdf

Moen, R., & Norman, C. (2009). *Evolution of the PDCA cycle*. [web article]. https://rauterberg.employee.id.tue.nl/lecturenotes/DG000%20DRP-R/references/Moen-Norman-2009.pdf

Mogalakwe, M. (2006). The use of documentary research methods in social research. *African Sociological Review*, 10(1), 221–230.

Mohan, R., & Campbell, M. (2012, February 24). *DVR week: Rakesh Mohan and Margaret Campbell on making evaluation reports reader friendly*. American Evaluation Association. https://aea365.org/blog/dvr-week-rakesh-mohan-and-margaret-campbell-on-making-evaluation-reports-reader-friendly/

Mohan, R., & Sullivan, K. (2006, Winter). Managing the politics of evaluation to achieve impact. In R. Mohan, & K. Sullivan (Eds.), *Special issue: Promoting the use of government evaluations in policymaking. New directions for evaluation*, 2006(112), 7–23. https://doi.org/10.1002/ev.204

Montague, S. (1998). *Build reach into your logic model*. Performance Management Network, Inc. http://www.pmn.net/wp-content/uploads/Build-Reach-into-Your-Logic-Model.pdf

Montrosse-Moorhead, B., & Griffith, J. C. (2017). Toward the development of reporting standards for evaluations. *American Journal of Evaluation*, 38(4), 577–602.

Moon, K., & Blackman, D. (2014). A guide to understanding social science research for natural scientists. *Conservation Biology*, 28, 1167–1177.

Moore, C. (1987). *Group techniques for idea building*. SAGE Publications.

Morgan, D. L. (2014). *Integrating qualitative & quantitative methods: A pragmatic approach*. SAGE Publications.

Morgan, D. L. (2018a, August). Planning for successful focus groups [Conference presentation]. *International institute for qualitative methodology (IIQM) 2020 conference, Edmonton, AB*.

Morgan, D. L. (2018b, August). Focus groups: Planning for success [Conference presentation]. *Qualitative health research 2018 conference, Banff, AB*.

Morgan-Trimmer, S., & Wood, F. (2016). Ethnographic methods for process evaluations of complex health behaviour interventions. *Trials*, 17, 232. https://trialsjournal.biomedcentral.com/articles/10.1186/s13063-016-1340-2

Morgan, S., Hanna, J., & Yousef, G. M. (2020). Knowledge translation in oncology: The bumpy ride from bench to bedside. *American Journal of Clinical Pathology*, 153(1), 5–13. https://doi.org/10.1093/ajcp/aqz099

Morra, L. G., & Friedlander, A. C. (1999). *Case study evaluations (English) operations evaluation department (OED) working paper series number 2*. The World Bank. http://documents.worldbank.org/curated/en/323981468753297361/Case-study-evaluations

Morris, M. (2008). Ethics. In S. Mathison (Ed.), *Evaluation encyclopedia* (pp. 131–134). SAGE Publications.

Morse, J. M. (1991). Approaches to qualitative-quantitative methodological triangulation. *Nursing Research*, 40, 120–123.

Morse, J. M. (1999). The armchair walkthrough. *Qualitative Health Research*, 9, 5–6.

Morse, J. M., Barrett, M., Mayan, M., Olson, K., & Spiers, J. (2002). Verification strategies for establishing reliability and validity in qualitative research. *International Journal of Qualitative Methods*, 1(2), 6.

Morton, D. J., Proudfit, J., Calac, D., Portillo, M., Lofton-Fitzsimmons, G., Molina, T., Flores, R., Lawson-Risso, B., & Majel-McCauley, R. (2013). Creating research capacity through a tribally based institutional review board. *American Journal of Public Health*, 103(12), 2160–2164. https://doi.org/10.2105/AJPH.2013.301473

Moss, T., & Crewe, S. E. (2020). The black perspective: A framework for culturally competent health related evaluations for African Americans. In L. C. Neubauer, D. McBride, A. D. Guarjardo, W. E. Casillas, & M. E. Hall (Eds.), *Examining issues facing communities of color today: The role of evaluation to incite change. New directions for evaluation*, 2020(166), 77–87. https://doi.org/10.1002/ev.20406

Mowbray, C., Holter, M., Teague, G., & Bybee, D. (2003). Fidelity criteria: Development, measurement, and validation. *American Journal of Evaluation*, 24(3), 315–340.

Mullen, B., Johnson, C., & Salas, E. (1991). Productivity loss in brainstorming groups: A meta-analytic integration. *Basic and Applied Social Psychology*, 12(1), 3–23.

Mustard, D., Skivington, K., Lay, M., Lifshen, M., Etches, J., & Chambers, A. (2017). Implementation of a disability management policy in a large healthcare employer: A quasi-experimental, mixed-methods evaluation. *British Medical Journal Open*, 7(6), 1–7.

National Aeronautics and Space Administration. (2018). *Sputnik and the dawn of the space age*. NASA History Division. https://history.nasa.gov/sputnik/

National Aeronautics and Space Administration. (2021a, July 27). *Climate change: How do we know?* Global Climate Change: Vital Signs of the Planet. https://climate.nasa.gov/evidence/

National Aeronautics and Space Administration. (2021b, July 27). *What's the difference between climate change and global warming?* Global Climate Change: Vital Signs of the Planet. https://climate.nasa.gov/faq/12/whats-the-difference-between-climate-change-and-global-warming/

National Association of County and City Health Officials. (2018). *Performance management: Measuring what matters in public health*. https://www.naccho.org/programs/public-health-infrastructure/performance-improvement/performance-management

National Center for Health Statistics. (2017). *Wide-ranging online data for epidemiologic research (WONDER)* [Data file]. http://wonder.cdc.gov

National Community Anti-Drug Coalition Institute. (2009). *Evaluation primer: Setting the context for a community anti-drug coalition evaluation*. Community Anti-Drug Coalitions of America. https://www.cadca.org/sites/default/files/resource/files/evaluationprimer.pdf

National Indian Child Welfare Association. (n.d.). *Positive Indian parenting*. https://www.nicwa.org/about-pip/

National Institutes of Health Office of Behavioral and Social Sciences. (2018). *Best practices for mixed methods research in the health sciences* (2nd ed.). https://implementationscience-gacd.org/wp-content/uploads/2020/11/Best-Practices-for-Mixed-Methods-Research-in-the-Health-Sciences-2018-01-25-1.pdf

National Oceanic Atmospheric Administration National Centers for Environmental Information (NCEI). (2021). *U.S. billion-dollar weather and climate disasters*. https://www.ncdc.noaa.gov/billions/

National Science and Technology Council. (2018, June). *National Near-Earth object preparedness strategy and action plan*. Interagency Working Group for Detecting and Mitigating the Impact of Earth-Bound Near-Earth Objects. https://www.nasa.gov/sites/default/files/atoms/files/ostp-neo-strategy-action-plan-jun18.pdf

Neades, B. L., Lawson, B., Watson, W., & Montgomery, S. (2017). *The use of phenomenological approach in evaluating mentorship preparation program in South East Scotland*. SAGE Publications. https://pdfs.semanticscholar.org/1fc6/ef52646248eae1f15ff13883e3b2d848487f.pdf

Neal, N. (n.d.). *What is stakeholder analysis and why it helps six sigma projects?* Master of Project. https://blog.masterofproject.com/stakeholder-analysis/

Neglia, K. (2021). *The first nations principles of OCAP®: Understanding OCAP®*. First Nations Information Governance Centre/Le Centre de gouvernance de l'information des Premiéres Nations. https://fnigc.ca/ocap-training/ OCAP® is a registered trademark of the First Nations Information Governance Centre (FNIGC).

Neubauer, L. C., & Hall, M. E. (2020). Is inciting social change something evaluators can do? Should do? In L. C. Neubauer, D. McBride, A. D. Guarjardo, W. D. Casills, & M. E. Hall (Eds.), *Examining issues facing communities of color today: The Role of evaluation to incite change. New directions for evaluation*, 2020(166), 129–135. https://doi.org/10.1002/ev.20406

Newcomer, K. E., & Triplett, T. (2004). Using surveys. In J. S. Wholey, H. P. Hatry, & K. E. Newcomer (Eds.), *Handbook of practical program evaluation* (pp. 257–291). Jossey-Bass.

Noe-Bustamante, L., Mora, L., & Lopez, M. H. (2020, August 11). *About one-in-four U.S. Hispanics have heard of Latinx, but just 3% use it.* Pew Research Center. https://www.pewresearch.org/hispanic/2020/08/11/about-one-in-four-u-s-hispanics-have-heard-of-latinx-but-just-3-use-it/

NORC at the University of Chicago. (2016, December). *Final report: Initial evaluation of the public health accreditation program.* University of Chicago. https://www.norc.org/Research/Projects/Pages/evaluation-of-the-public-health-accreditation-program.aspx

Nyumba, T. O., Wilson, K., Derrick, C., & Mukherjee, N. (2017). The use of focus group discussion methodology: Insights from two decades of application in conservation. *Methods in Ecology and Evolution*, 9, 20–32. https://besjournals.onlinelibrary.wiley.com/doi/full/10.1111/2041-210X.12860

Nzabonimpa, J. P. (2018). Quantitizing and qualitizing (im-) possibilities in mixed methods research. *Methodological Innovations*, 11(2), 443–449.

Office on Drugs and Crime. (2006). *Monitoring and evaluating: Youth substance abuse prevention programmes.* United Nations. https://www.unodc.org/pdf/youthnet/action/planning/m&e_E.pdf

Office for Victims of Crime Training and Technical Assistance Centre. (n.d.). *Human trafficking task force e-guide* [online article]. https://www.ovcttac.gov/taskforceguide/eguide/5-building-strong-cases/53-victim-interview-preparation/trauma-informed-victim-interviewing/

Olney, C., & Barnes, S. (2013). Collecting and analyzing evaluation data: Planning and evaluating health information outreach projects. *National Network of Libraries of Medicine* https://nnlm.gov/sites/default/files/2021-08/booklet-three.pdf

Olsen, J. (1996). *Night of the grizzlies.* Homestead Publishing.

Omolo, A. (2010). *Our experience with the balanced scorecard strategy development process* [online article]. https://balancedscorecard.org/wp-content/uploads/pdfs/KenyaRed%20Cross-ScorecardPoster.pdf

One Sky Center. (n.d.). *Evidence-based practices and best practices.* http://www.oneskycenter.org/osc/health-care-issues/evidence-based-practices-and-best-practices/

Onkka, A. (2018, March 13). *What is Bennett's hierarchy logic model?* Aurora Consulting. https://www.auroraconsult.com/what-is-bennetts-hierarchy-logic-model/

Onwuegbuzie, A. J., & Leech, N. L. (2019). On qualitizing. *International Journal of Multiple Research Approaches*, 11(2), 98–131.

Organization of American States. (2020). *American declaration on the rights of Indigenous peoples.* http://www.narf.org/wordpress/wp-content/uploads/2015/09/2016oas-declaration-indigenous-people.pdf

Osborn, A. (1953). Applied imagination: Principles and procedures of creative problem solving. Charles Scribner's Sons.

Ottenbacher, M., & Harrington, R. (2008). Institutional, cultural and contextual factors: Potential drivers of the culinary innovation process. *Tourism and Hospitality Research*, 9(3), 235–249.

Oxford Lexico. (2021a). *Anthropocene.* In Oxford Lexico.com Dictionary. https://www.lexico.com/en/definition/anthropocene

Oxford Lexico. (2021b). *Transaction.* In Oxford Lexico.com Dictionary. https://www.lexico.com/en/definition/transaction

Oxford Lexico. (2021c). *Transformation.* In Oxford Lexico.com Dictionary. https://www.lexico.com/en/definition/transformation

Oxford Lexico. (n.d.). *Racism.* In Oxford Lexico.com Dictionary. https://www.lexico.com/en/definition/racism

Pacheco, C. M., Daley, S. M., Brown, T., Fillippi, M., Greiner, K. A., & Daley, C. M. (2013). Moving forward: Breaking the cycle of mistrust between American Indians and researchers. *American Journal of Public Health*, 103(12), 2162–2159.

Palihapitiya, M. (2019, June 21). *Saying it visually! Participatory photography for needs assessment and asset mapping.* American Evaluation Association. https://aea365.org/blog/na-tig-week-saying-it-visually-participatory-photography-for-needs-assessment-and-asset-mapping-by-madhawa-mads-palihapitiya/?utm_source=feedburner&utm_medium=email&utm_campaign=Feed%3A+aea365+%28AEA365%29

Parker, L., & Villalpando, O. (2007). A race(cialized) perspective on education leadership: Critical race theory in educational administration. *Educational Administration Quarterly*, 43(5), 519–524.

Parkhurst, M., Preskill, H., Lynn, J., & Moore, M. (2016, March 1). The case for developmental evaluation. *FSG*. https://www.fsg.org/blog/case-developmental-evaluation

Pascal, B. (2012). *The provincial letters.* Veritatis Splendor Publications.

Passel, J. S., & Cohn, D. (2008). *U.S. Population projections: 2005–2050.* Pew Research Center. https://www.pewresearch.org/hispanic/2008/02/11/us-population-projections-2005-2050/

Patton, M. Q. (1990). *Qualitative evaluation and research methods.* SAGE Publications.

Patton, M. Q. (1996). A world larger than formative and summative. *Evaluation Practice*, 17(2), 131–144.

Patton, M. Q. (2002). *Qualitative research & evaluation methods*. SAGE Publications.

Patton, M. Q. (2004). The roots of utilization-focused evaluation. In M. C. Alkin (Ed.), *Evaluation roots: Tracing theorists' views and influences* (pp. 276–292). SAGE Publications.

Patton, M. Q. (2008). *Utilization-focused evaluation*. SAGE Publications.

Patton, M. Q. (2010). *Developmental evaluation: Applying complexity concepts to enhance innovation and use*. Guilford Press.

Patton, M. Q. (2011). *Developmental evaluation: Applying complexity concepts to enhance innovation and use*. Guilford Press.

Patton, M. Q. (2012). *Essentials of utilization-focused evaluation*. SAGE Publications.

Patton, M. Q. (2013). *Utilization-Focused evaluation (U-FE) checklist* [online tool]. https://wmich.edu/sites/default/files/attachments/u350/2014/UFE_checklist_2013.pdf

Patton, M. Q. (2015). *Qualitative research and evaluation methods* (4th ed.). SAGE Publications.

Patton, M. Q. (2017). *Evaluation flash cards: Embedding evaluative thinking in organizational culture* (p. 7). Otto Bremer Foundation, ottobremer.org. https://ottobremer.org/wp-content/uploads/2017/12/OBT_flashcards_201712.pdf

Patton, M. Q. (2020). *Blue marble evaluation: Premises and principles*. Guilford.

Patton, M. Q. (2021). *Blue marble evaluation*. https://bluemarbleeval.org/principles/operating-principles/yin-yang-principle

Paul, R., & Elder, L. (2008). *The miniature guide to critical thinking: Concepts and tools* [online article]. https://www.criticalthinking.org/files/Concepts_Tools.pdf

Perrin, B. (2002, October 31). *Towards a new view of accountability*. https://evaluationcanada.ca/distribution/20021010_perrin_burt.pdf

Pfadenhauer, L., Rohwer, A., Burns, J., Booth, A., Lysdahl, K. B., Hofmann, B., Ansgar, G., Mozygemba, K., Tummers, M., Wahlster, P., & Rehfuess, E. (2016). *Guidance for the assessment of context and implementation in health technology assessments (HTA) and systematic reviews of complex interventions: The context and implementation of complex interventions (CICI) framework*. INTEGRATE-HTA. https://www.researchgate.net/publication/298340571_Guidance_for_the_Assessment_of_Context_and_Implementation_in_Health_Technology_Assessments_HTA_and_Systematic_Reviews_of_Complex_Interventions_The_Context_and_Implementation_of_Complex_Interventions_C

Pickell, D. (2019, March 6). *5 Steps of the data analysis process*. Learning Hub G2 [online article]. https://learn.g2.com/data-analysis-process

Porter, S., & Hawkins, P. (2019). Achieving sustainability through sustainable organizational evaluation systems. In G. Julnes (Ed.), *Evaluating sustainability: Evaluative support for managing processes in the public interest. New directions for evaluation*, 2019(162), 87–101. https://doi.org/10.1002/ev.20360

Powell, J., & Black, T. (2003). Questioning the assumptions of youth violence prevention programs: The role of reflexive evaluation in program development. *Journal of Applied Sociology*, 20(1), 37–63.

Preskill, H., & Boyle, S. (2008). Insights into evaluation capacity building: Motivations, strategies, outcomes, and lessons learned. *The Canadian Journal of Program Evaluation*, 23, 147–174.

Preskill, H., & Catsambas, T. T. (2006). *Reframing evaluation through appreciative inquiry*. SAGE Publications.

Preskill, H., & Torres, R. T. (1999). Building capacity for organizational learning through evaluative inquiry. *Evaluation*, 5(1), 42–60.

Preskill, H., & Torres, R. T. (2000). The learning dimension of evaluation use. In V. J. Caracelli, & H. Preskill (Eds.), *Special issue: The expanding scope of evaluation use. New directions for evaluation*, 2000(88), 25–37. https://doi.org/10.1002/ev.1189

Price, J. (2020). *The BC government and the dispossession of Japanese Canadians (1941–1949)*. Canadian Centre for Policy Alternatives.

Prochaska, J., & Velicer, W. (1997). The transtheoretical model of health behavior change. *American Journal of Health Promotion*, 12(1), 38–48.

Public Health Foundation. (n.d.). *About the performance management system framework*. http://www.phf.org/focusareas/performancemanagement/toolkit/Pages/PM_Toolkit_About_the_Performance_Management_Framework.aspx

Puddy, R. W., & Wilkins, N. (2011). *Understanding evidence part 1: Best available research evidence. A guide to the continuum of evidence of effectiveness*. Centers for Disease Control and Prevention.

Purcell, N., Zamora, K., Bertenthal, D., Abadjian, L., Tighe, J., & Seal, K. H. (2021). How VA whole health coaching can impact veterans' health and quality of life: A mixed-methods pilot program evaluation. *Global Advances in Health and Medicine*, (10), 1–13.

Rabinowitz, P. (n.d.). *Participatory evaluation*. Community Tool Box. https://ctb.ku.edu/en/table-of-contents/evaluate/evaluation/participatory-evaluation/main

Radhakrishna, R., & Bowen, C. F. (2010). Viewing Bennett's hierarchy from a different lens: Implications for extension program evaluation. *Journal of Extension*, 48(6), 1–5.

Raimondo, E., & Vaessen, J. (2019, November). Evaluation design and planning. *4th Eval Youth virtual conference. Presentation at the meeting of the UNEG Secretariat, New York, NY*.

Rajkumar, S. (2010). *Art of communication in project management*. Project Management Institute. https://www.pmi.org/learning/library/effective-communication-better-project-management-6480

Rawls, J. (1971). *A theory of justice*. Harvard University Press.

Razzetti, G. (2019, November 27). *What? So what? Now what?* Fearless Culture. https://www.fearlessculture.design/blog-posts/what-so-what-now-what

Reiser, R. A. (2001). A history of instructional design and technology (Part II). *Educational Technology, Research and Development*, 49(2), 57–68.

Reiss, J., & Sprenger, J. (2020). Scientific objectivity. In E. N. Zalta (Ed.), *The stanford encyclopedia of philosophy* (Winter ed.). Stanford University. https://plato.stanford.edu/entries/scientific-objectivity/

Renger, R. (2015). System evaluation theory (SET): A practical framework for evaluators to meet the challenges of system evaluation. *Evaluation Journal of Australia*, 15(4), 16–28.

Renger, R., Renger, J., Donaldson, S. I., Renger, J., Hart, G., & Hawkins, A. (2020). Comparing and contrasting a program versus system approach to evaluation: The example of a cardiac care system. *Canadian Journal of Program Evaluation/La Revue canadienne d'évaluation de programme*, 35(2), 240–257. https://doi.org/10.3138/cjpe.68127

Resnik, D. B. (2020). *What is ethics in research & why is it important?* National Institute of Environmental Health Sciences. https://www.niehs.nih.gov/research/resources/bioethics/whatis/index.cfm

Rettie, C. (2016, October 10). *The butterfly effect: Small actions big effects*. National Nurse Practitioner Residency and Fellowship Training Consortium. https://www.nppostgrad-training.com/2016/10/10/the-butterfly-effect-small-actions-big-effects/

Riley, W., Moran, J., Corso, L., Beitsch, L., Bialek, R., & Cofsky, A. (2010). Defining quality improvement in public health. *Journal of Public Health Management Practice*, 16(1), 5–7.

Robert Wood Johnson Foundation. (2017, June 30). *Visualizing health equity: One size does not fit all infographic*. https://www.rwjf.org/en/library/infographics/visualizing-health-equity.html

Roberts, S. O., & Rizzo, M. T. (2021). The psychology of American racism. *American Psychologist*, 76(3), 475–487. https://doi.org/10.1037/amp0000642

Rockwell, S. K., Albrecht, J. A., Nugent, G. C., & Kunz, G. M. (2012). Using targeting outcomes of programs as a framework to target photographic events in nonformal educational programs. *American Journal of Evaluation*, 33(2), 179–194. https://doi.org/10.1177/1098214011421522

Rog, D. J. (2012). When background becomes foreground: Toward context-sensitive evaluation practice. In D. J. Rog, J. L. Fitzpatrick, & R. F. Connor (Eds.), *Context: A framework for its influence on evaluation practice. New directions for evaluation*, 2012(135), 25–40. https://doi.org/10.1002/ev.20025

Rogers, E. (2003). *Diffusion of innovations*. Simon and Schuster.

Rogers, P. (2014a). *Contractual agreement*. https://www.better-evaluation.org/en/evaluation-optiSons/contractual_agreement

Rogers, P. (2014b, March 23). *Producing engaging and accessible evaluation reports*. Better Evaluation. https://www.betterevaluation.org/en/blog/producing_engaging_accessible_evaluation_reports

Rogers, P. (2014c, May 9). *Week 19: Ways of framing the difference between research and evaluation*. BetterEvaluation. https://www.betterevaluation.org/en/blog/framing_the_difference_between_research_and_evaluation

Roholt, R. V., & Baizerman, M. L. (Eds.). (2012). *Evaluation advisory groups: New directions for evaluation*. Wiley Publications.

Rosales, J., & Walker, T. (2021, March 20). *The racist beginnings of standardized testing*. National Education Association News. https://www.nea.org/advocating-for-change/new-from-nea/racist-beginnings-standardized-testing

Roser, M., Ochmann, S., Behrens, H., & Ritchie, H., Dadonaite, R. (2018, October). *Eradication of diseases*. Our World in Data. https://ourworldindata.org/eradication-of-diseases

Rossi, P. H., Lipsey, M. W., & Freeman, H. E. (2004). *Evaluation: A systematic approach*. (7th ed.). SAGE Publications.

Rossi, P. H., Lipsey, M. W., & Henry, G. T. (2019). *Evaluation: A systematic approach.* (8th ed.). SAGE Publications.

Rowe, A. (2019). Sustainability-ready evaluation: A call to action. In G. Julnes (Ed.), *Evaluating sustainability: Evaluative support for managing processes in the public interest* (pp. 29–48). Wiley.

Rowe, A. (2021, July 12). *Mainstreaming sustainability in evaluation: Canadian evaluation society stocktaking report.* European Evaluation Society. https://europeanevaluation.org/2021/07/12/mainstreaming-sustainability-in-evaluation-canadian-evaluation-society-stocktaking-report/

Rubin, H. J., & Rubin, I. S. (2005). *Qualitative interviewing: The art of hearing data.* SAGE Publications.

Sabarre, N. (2018). *Bridging the gap: Evaluation theory and practice.* American University. https://programs.online.american.edu/online-graduate-certificates/project-monitoring/resource/evaluation-theory-and-practice

Safonov, L., Tomer, E., Strygin, V., Ashkenazy, Y., & Havlin, S. (2002). Multifractal chaotic attractors in a system of delay-differential equations modeling road traffic. *Chaos: An Interdisciplinary Journal of Nonlinear Science*, 12 (4), 1006–1014.

Sahota, P. C., & Kastelic, S. (2012). Culturally appropriate evaluation of tribally based suicide prevention programs: A review of current approaches. *Wicazo Sa Review*, 27(2), 99–127.

Saldaña, J. (2016). *The coding manual for qualitative researchers.* SAGE Publications. https://www.researchgate.net/publication/320395322_Theoretical_Data_Collection_and_Data_Analysis_with_Gerunds_in_a_Constructivist_Grounded_Theory_Study/figures?lo=1

Salm, M., & Stevens, K. (2016, August 9). *Stories.* BetterEvaluation. https://www.betterevaluation.org/en/evaluation-options/stories

Sandelowski, M. (2000). Combining qualitative and quantitative sampling, data collection, and analysis techniques in mixed-method studies. *Research in Nursing & Health*, 23(3), 246–255.

Sandelowski, M., Voils, C. I., & Knafl, G. (2009). On quantitizing. *Journal of Mixed Methods Research*, 3(3), 208–222.

Saunders, R. P. (2016). *Implementation monitoring and process evaluation.* SAGE Publications.

Saunders, R. P., Evans, M., & Joshi, P. (2005). Developing a process-evaluation plan for assessing health promotion program implementation: A how-to guide. *Health Promotion Practice*, 6(2), 134–147.

Scales, R. Q., Wolsey, T. D., Lenski, S., Smetana, L., Yoder, K., Dobler, E., Grisham, D. L. & Young, J. R. (2018). Are we preparing or training teachers? Developing professional judgment in and beyond teacher preparation programs. *Journal of Teacher Education*, 69(1), 7–21. https://doi.org/10.1177/0022487117702584

Scassa, T. (2018). *Data ownership.* Centre for International Governance Innovation. https://www.cigionline.org/static/documents/documents/Paper%20no.187_2.pdf

Schaeffer, K. (2021, April 5). *The changing face of America's veteran population.* Pew Research Center. https://www.pewresearch.org/fact-tank/2021/04/05/the-changing-face-of-americas-veteran-population/

Scheirer, M. A. (2012). Planning evaluation through the program life cycle. *American Journal of Evaluation*, 33(2), 263–294.

Scheirer, M. A., & Dearing, J. W. (2011). An agenda for research on the sustainability of public health programs. *American Journal of Public Health*, 101(11), 2059–2067.

Schnarch, B. (2004). Ownership, control, access, and possession (OCAP) or self-determination applied to research: A critical analysis of contemporary first nations research and some options for first nations communities. *Journal of Aboriginal Health*, 1(1), 80–95. https://doi.org/10.3138/ijih.v1i1.28934

Schroeter, D. (2010). *Sustainability evaluation checklist.* https://www.researchgate.net/profile/Daniela-Schroeter/publication/282862008_Sustainability_Evaluation_Checklist/links/561fff4908ae70315b5526bd/Sustainability-Evaluation-Checklist.pdf

Schuster, M. A., McGlynn, E. A., & Brook, R. H. (1998). How good is the quality of health care in the United States? *Milbank Quarterly*, 76(4), 517–563.

Schwandt, T. A. (2000). Three epistemological stances for qualitative inquiry: Interpretivism, hermeneutics and social constructivism. In N. K. Denzin, & Y. S. Lincoln (Eds.), *Handbook of qualitative research* (pp. 189–214). SAGE Publications.

Schwandt, T. A. (2009). Toward a practical theory of evidence for evaluation. In S. I., Donaldson, C. Christie, & M. M. Mark (Eds.), *What counts as credible evidence in applied research and evaluation practice?* (pp. 197–212). SAGE Publications.

Schwandt, T., Ofir, Z., Lucks, D., El-Saddick, K., & D'Errico, S. (2016, April). *Evaluation: A crucial ingredient for SDG success.* Briefing. The International Institute for Environment and Development (IIED), EVLSDGs, Ministry of Foreign Affairs of Finland.

Scriven, M. (1991a). *Evaluation thesaurus* (4th ed.). SAGE Publications.

Scriven, M. (1991b). Beyond formative and summative evaluation. In G. W. McLaughlin, & D. C. Phillips (Eds.), *Evaluation and education: At quarter century* (pp. 19–64). University of Chicago Press.

Scriven, M. (1994). The final synthesis. *American Journal of Evaluation*, 15, 367–382.

Scriven, M. (1996). The theory behind practical evaluation. *Evaluation*, 2(4), 393–404.

Scriven, M. (2003). Evaluation theory and metatheory. In T. Kellaghan, & D. L. Stufflebeam (Eds.), *International handbook of educational evaluation* (pp. 15–30). Springer.

Scriven, M. (2006). *Can we infer causation from cross-sectional data?* National Academiess of Medicine. http://www7.nationalacademies.org/bota/School-Level Data_Michael ScrivenPaper.pdf

Scriven, M. (2021, November 12). *The transScientific evaluation* [Expert lecture]. American Evaluation Association Eval 21 Reimagined, Virtual.

Senge, P. (2006). *The fifth discipline: The art and practice of the learning organization*. Currency.

Sette, C. (n.d.). *Participatory evaluation*. BetterEvaluation. https://www.betterevaluation.org/en/plan/approach/participatory_evaluation

Severgnini, B. (2006). *La bella figura: A field guide to the Italian mind*. Broadway Books.

Shadish, W. R. (1998). Evaluation theory is who we are. *American Journal of Evaluation*, 19(1), 1–19.

Shadish, W., Cook, T. D., & Leviton, L. C. (1991). *Foundations of program evaluation*. SAGE Publications.

Shapton, L. (2016, March 8). Artifacts of a doomed expedition. *The New York Times Magazine*. https://www.nytimes.com/interactive/2016/03/20/magazine/franklin-expedition.html

Shaw, R. (1984). *The dripping faucet as a model chaotic system*. Aerial Press.

Siger, J. (2010). *Prey on patmos*. Poisoned Pen Press.

Silka, L. (2009). Partnership ethics. In D. M. Mertens, & P. E. Ginsberg (Eds.), *Handbook of social research ethics* (pp. 337–352). SAGE Publications.

Silverman, B., Mai, C., Boulet, S., & O'Leary, L. (n.d.). *Logic models for planning and evaluation*. Centers for Disease Control Division of Birth Defects and Developmental Disabilities. file:///C:/Users/btrem/Downloads/cdc_11569_DS1%20(2).pdf

Simmons, M., & Chew, I. (2016, June 20). *Why constant learners all embrace the 5-hour rule*. Inc. https://www.inc.com/empact/why-constant-learners-all-embrace-the-5-hour-rule.html

Singh, J. (2012, May). *Monitoring and evaluation (M&E) for community driven development (CDD) programs: Introduction to concepts and examples*. [Power Point Slides]. http://siteresources.worldbank.org/EXTCDD/Resources/430160-1361480685593/Session5_MonitoringEvaluation.pdf

Sirontnik, K., & Oakes, J. (1990). Evaluation as critical inquiry: School improvement as a case in point. *New Directions for Program Evaluation*, 45, 37–59.

Skelly, A., Dettori, J., & Brodt, E. (2012). Assessing bias: The importance of considering confounding. *Evidence-Based Spine-Care Journal*, 3(1), 9–12.

Smale, A. (n.d.). *What the SDGs mean*. UN Chronicle. https://www.un.org/en/chronicle/article/what-sdgs-mean

Smith, L. T. (2012). *Decolonizing methodologies* (2nd ed.). Zed Books.

Smith, S. V., & Rosalsky, G. (2020, June 3). *Black Americans bear the brunt of the COVID-19 pandemic's economic impact*. NPR News Morning Edition. https://www.npr.org/2020/06/03/868469779/black-americans-bear-the-brunt-of-the-covid-19-pandemics-economic-impact

Smith, M. C., Stallings, M. A., Mariner, S., & Burrall, M. (1999). Benefits of massage therapy for hospitalized patients: A descriptive and qualitative evaluation. *Alternative Therapeutic Health Medicine*, 5(4), 64–71. https://www.ncbi.nlm.nih.gov/pubmed/10394676

Social Innovation Generation. (2021). *Ecosystems for systems change*. https://mcconnellfoundation.ca/sig-10-years/

Social Ventures Australia. (2012). *Finding the golden thread: A new approach to articulating program logic*. https://www.socialventures.com.au/sva-quarterly/finding-the-golden-thread-a-new-approach-to-articulating-program-logic-statements/

Spiers, J. (2015). Qualitative research and data analysis. [Conference presentation]. *International institute of qualitative methods 2015 convention, Edmonton, AB*.

Srnka, K. J., & Koeszegi, S. T. (2007). From words to numbers: How to transform qualitative data into meaningful quantitative results. *Schmalenbach Business Review*, 59(1), 29–57. http://ezproxy.msu.edu/login?url=https://search-proquest-com.proxy1.cl.msu.edu/docview/219555984?accountid=12598

Stacy, S. T., Acevedo-Polakovich, I. D., & Rosewood, J. (2018). Youth GO: An approach to gathering youth perspectives in out-of-school time programs. *Afterschool Matters*, 28, 34–43.

Stacy, S. T., Castro, K. M., & Acevedo-Polakovich, I. D. (2020). The cost of youth voices: Comparing the feasibility of Youth GO against focus groups. *Journal of Participatory Research Methods*, 1(1), 13312.

Stanfield, B. (1997). Focused conversation. *Edges: New Planetary Patterns*, 9(1), 1–8. https://wedgeblade.net/files/archives_assets/10858.pdf

Stanfield, J. H. (1999). Slipping through the front door: Relevant social scientific evaluation in the people of color century. *The American Journal of Evaluation*, 20(3), 415–626.

Statistics How To. (2020a). *What is internal consistency reliability?* https://www.statisticshowto.com/internal-consistency/

Statistics How To. (2020b). *Test-retest reliability.* https://www.statisticshowto.com/test-retest-reliability/

Steneck, N. H. (2007). *Introduction to the responsible conduct of research.* U.S. Department of Health and Human Services and the Office of Research Integrity. https://ori.hhs.gov/sites/default/files/2018-04/rcrintro.pdf

Stevahn, L., King, J., Ghere, G., & Minnema, J. (2005). Establishing essential competencies for program evaluators. *American Journal of Evaluation*, 26(2), 43–59.

Stevens, S. S. (1946). On the theory of scales of measurement. *Science*, 103, 677–680.

Stone, J. C. (1975). What is phenomenological evaluation? *California Journal of Teacher Education*, 2(3), 62–69.

Straus, S. E., Tetroe, J., & Graham, I. (2009). Defining knowledge translation. *Canadian Medical Association Journal*, 181(3–4), 165–168. https://doi.org/10.1503/cmaj.081229

Stufflebeam, D. L. (1994). Empowerment evaluation, objectivist evaluation, and evaluation standards: Where the future of evaluation should not go and where it needs to go. *Evaluation Practice*, 15(3), 321–338.

Stufflebeam, D. L. (1999a). *Evaluation plans and operations checklist.* Evaluation Checklist Project. https://wmich.edu/sites/default/files/attachments/u350/2018/eval-plans-operations-stufflebeam.pdf

Stufflebeam, D. L. (1999b). *Evaluation contracts checklist.* Evaluation Checklist Project. https://wmich.edu/sites/default/files/attachments/u350/2014/contracts.pdf

Stufflebeam, D. L. (2001). Interdisciplinary PhD programming in evaluation. *American Journal of Evaluation*, 23(3), 445–455.

Stufflebeam, D. L., Madaus, G. F., & Kellaghan, T. (2000). *Evaluation models: Viewpoints on educational and human services evaluation.* Kluwer Academic Publishers.

Substance Abuse and Mental Health Administration. (2017, April). *A guide to GPRA data collection using trauma-informed interviewing skills.* U.S. Department of Health and Human Services. https://www.integration.samhsa.gov/about-us/Trauma-InformedInterviewingManual-508.pdf

Symonette, H., Mertens, D. M., & Hopson, R. (2014). The development of a diversity initiative: Framework for the graduate education diversity internship (GEDI) program. In P. M. Collins, & R. Hopson (Eds.), *Building a new generation of culturally responsive evaluators through AEA's graduate education diversity internship program. New directions for evaluation*, 2014(143), 9–22. https://doi.org/10.1002/ev.20090

Taplin, D., & Rasic, M. (2012). *Facilitator's source book: Leading theory of change development sessions.* ActKnoweldge. https://www.theoryofchange.org/wp-content/uploads/toco_library/pdf/ToCFacilitatorSourcebook.pdf

Tarsilla, M. (2010). Theorists theories of evaluation: A conversation with Jennifer Greene. *Journal of MultiDisciplinary Evaluation*, 6(13), 209–219.

Tausch, A. P., & Menold, N. (2016). Methodological aspects of focus groups in health research: Results of qualitative interviews with focus group moderators. *Global Qualitative Nursing Research*, 3, 1-12. https://www.ncbi.nlm.nih.gov/pmc/articles/PMC5342644/

Taylor, A. (2018, April 9). Travel monday: A photo trip to Meteora, Greece. *The Atlantic.* https://www.theatlantic.com/photo/2018/04/travel-monday-a-photo-trip-to-meteora-greece/557537/

Taylor-Powell, E., & Hermann, C. (2000). *Collecting evaluation data: Surveys.* University of Wisconsin-Extension. https://cdn.shopify.com/s/files/1/0145/8808/4272/files/G3658-10.pdf

Taylor-Powell, E., Steele, S., & Douglah, M. (1996). *Planning a program evaluation.* University of Wisconsin-Extension. https://sref.info/seeding-success/resources/G3658-01%20-1.pdf

Taylor, M. J., McNicholas, C., Nicolay, C., Darzi, A., Bell, D., & Reed, J. (2014). Systematic review of the application of the plan–do–study–act method to improve quality in healthcare. *British Medical Journal Quality & Safety*, 23(4), 290–298. https://doi.org/10.1136/bmjqs-2013-002703

Tenney, Y., & Pew, R. (2006). Situation awareness catches on: What? So what? Now what? *Reviews of Human Factors and Ergonomics*, 2(1), 1–34.

Tester, T. (n.d.). *Move beyond the transactional mindset*. Beyond The Deal. https://btd.consulting/manage-the-ma-process/move-beyond-the-transactional-mindset/

The Canadian Health Services Research Foundation. (2008, January). A handbook on knowledge sharing: Strategies and recommendations for researchers, policymakers, and service providers. *Insight and Action*, 28. https://www.westernsydney.edu.au/__data/assets/pdf_file/0018/405252/Knowledge_Sharing_Handbook.pdf

The Health Communication Unit. (2002). *Using focus groups: Version 2.0.* Centre for Health Promotion, University of Toronto. https://sswm.info/sites/default/files/reference_attachments/THCU%202002%20Using%20Focus%20Group.pdf

The Union of B.C. Indian Chiefs. (2020, June 19). *UN questionnaire: Impact of COVID-19 on Indigenous peoples*. https://d3n8a8pro7vhmx.cloudfront.net/ubcic/pages/4219/attachments/original/1592506810/2020June_UBCICSubmission_COVID19Impacts_Final.pdf?1592506810

The University of British Columbia. (n.d.). *Ownership of data*. Graduate School. https://www.grad.ubc.ca/intellectual-property-guide/ownership-data

The University of Vermont. (2021). *Vision, mission, and goals*. Department of Computer Science Within the College of Engineering and Mathematical Sciences. https://www.uvm.edu/cems/cs/vision_mission_and_goals

The University of Wisconsin Population Health Institute. (2022). *County health rankings & roadmaps*. www.countyhealthrankings.org

The W. Edwards Deming Institute. (2019). *Deming the man*. https://deming.org/deming/deming-the-man

Thomas, V. G., Madison, A., Rockcliff, F., De Lain, K., & Lowe, S. M. (2018). Racism, social programming and evaluation: Where do we go from here? *American Journal of Evaluation*, 39(4), 514–526.

Thomas, R. G., & Parsons, B. A. (2017). Culturally responsive evaluation meets systems-oriented evaluation. *American Journal of Evaluation*, 38(1), 7–28.

Thompson, W. (n.d.). *Big data: What it is and why it matters: SAS*. https://www.sas.com/en_ca/insights/big-data/what-is-big-data.html

Thurston, W. E., & Potvin, L. (2003). Evaluability assessment: A tool for incorporating evaluation in social change programmes. *Evaluation*, 9(4), 453–469.

Torres, R. T., Preskill, H., & Piontek, M. E. (2005). *Evaluation strategies for communicating and reporting*. SAGE Publications.

Torres, S. A., Santiago, C. D., Walts, K. K., & Richards, M. H. (2018). Immigration policy, practices, and procedures: The impact on the mental health of Mexican and Central American youth and families. *American Psychologist*, 73(7), 843–854. http://dx.doi.org.proxy1.cl.msu.edu/10.1037/amp0000184

Treasury Board of Canada Secretariat. (2004). *Guide for the review of evaluation reports*. Government of Canada. https://www.tbs-sct.gc.ca/cee/tools-outils/grer-gere-eng.pdf

Trevisan, M. S., & Walser, T. M. (2015). *Evaluability assessment: Improving evaluation quality and use*. SAGE Publications.

Trochim, W. (2002). *Qualitative validity*. Research Methods and Knowledge Base. http://www.socialresearchmethods.net/kb/qualval.html

Trochim, W. (2006). *Positivism & post-positivism*. Research Methods and Knowledge Base. https://socialresearchmethods.net/kb/positvsm.php

Trochim, W. (2020). *Internal validity*. Research Methods and Knowledge Base. https://socialresearchmethods.net/kb/internal-validity/

Trott, P., Hartmann, D., van der Duin, P., Scholten, V., & Ortt, R. (2016). *Managing technology entrepreneurship and innovation*. Routledge.

True Colors United. (2020). *Our issue*. https://truecolorsunited.org/our-issue/

Tucker, S. A., & King, J. A. (2020). Next steps for AEA the newly created AEA professionalization and competencies working group. In J. A. King (Ed.), *The American Evaluation Association's program evaluator competencies. New directions for evaluation*, 2020(168), 149–162. https://doi.org/10.1002/ev.20436

Tunguz, B. (2018, March 5). *6 Methods for dealing with missing data*. Zest. https://www.zest.ai/insights/6-methods-for-dealing-with-missing-data

United Nations. (2007). *United nations declaration on the rights of indigenous peoples*. https://www.un.org/development/desa/indigenouspeoples/wp-content/uploads/sites/19/2018/11/UNDRIP_E_web.pdf

United Nations. (2019). *The revised UNDP evaluation policy*. http://web.undp.org/evaluation/documents/policy/2019/DP_2019_29_E.pdf

United Nations. (2022). Climate action fast facts. https://www.un.org/en/climatechange/science/key-findings#physical-science

United Nations Educational, Scientific and Cultural Organization. (2015). *Who was Ibn al-Haytham?* 1001 Inventions and the

World of Ibn Al-Haytham. http://www.ibnalhaytham.com/discover/who-was-ibn-al-haytham/

United Nations Foundation. (2022, April 6). *7 ways climate change harms our health.* https://unfoundation.org/blog/post/seven-ways-climate-change-harms-our-health/?gclid=Cj0KCQjwzLCVBh-D3ARIsAPKYTcS2qFAvFfeoV2QQLOEnE1bx9-bT-wN2zKaTZ9tQ6Aun4DMSOAaDkI0aAqLXEALw_wcB

United Nations. (n.d.). *The 17 goals.* Department of Economic and Social Affairs: Sustainable development. https://sdgs.un.org/goals

United Nations Office on Drugs and Crime. (2019). *Evaluability assessment template.* https://www.unodc.org/unodc/en/evaluation/guidelines-and-templates.html

United States Interagency Council on Homelessness. (2018). *What does ending homelessness mean?* The White House. https://www.usich.gov/goals/what-does-ending-homelessness-mean/

Urban, J., Burgermaster, M., Archibald, T., & Byrne, A. (2015). Relationships between quantitative measures of evaluation plan and program model quality and a qualitative measure of participant perceptions of an evaluation capacity building approach. *Journal of Mixed Methods Research, 9*(2), 154–177. https://doi.org/10.1177/1558689813516388

Ury, W. (2013) The five Ps of persuasion: Roger Fisher's approach to influence. *Negotiation Journal, 29*(2), 133–140.

USAID. (1996). *Performance monitoring and evaluation TIPS: Conducting a participatory evaluation.* Center for Development Information and Evaluation. https://pdf.usaid.gov/pdf_docs/pnabs539.pdf

U.S. Census Bureau. (2019). *Population estimates.* (Version 2019) [Data set]. https://www.census.gov/newsroom/press-releases/2019/popest-nation.html#:~:text=The%20nation's%20population%20was%20328%2C239%2C523,multiyear%20slow-down%20since%20that%20period

U.S. Census Bureau. (2020). *About Hispanic origin.* https://www.census.gov/topics/population/hispanic-origin/about.html

U.S. Department of Health & Human Services. (2014a). *The supporting healthy marriage evaluation: A family-strengthening program for low-income families: Final impacts from the supporting healthy marriage evaluation, technical supplement.* https://www.acf.hhs.gov/opre/report/supporting-healthy-marriage-evaluation-family-strengthening-program-low-income-families

U.S. Department of Health and Human Services. (2014b). *Healthy people 2020: Leading health indicators progress update.* Office of Disease Prevention and Health Promotion. https://www.healthypeople.gov/2020/leading-health-indicators/Healthy-People-2020-Leading-Health-Indicators%3A-Progress-Update

U.S. Department of Health and Human Services. (2018). *IRBs and assurances.* https://www.hhs.gov/ohrp/irbs-and-assurances.html

U.S. Department of Veterans Affairs. (2016, November). *My VA: Putting veterans first. Transformation Update.* https://www.va.gov/myva/docs/myva-3-0-v9-digital-11816.pdf

U.S. Department of Veterans Affairs. (2021). *Cost-effectiveness analysis.* https://www.herc.research.va.gov/include/page.asp?id=cost-effectiveness-analysis.

Valente, T., & Rogers, E. (1995). The origins and development of the diffusion of innovations paradigm as an example of scientific growth. *Science Communication, 16* (3), 242–273.

van Manen, M. (1984). Practicing phenomenological writing. *Phenomenology + Pedagogy, 2*(1), 20–21.

van Manen, M. (1990). *Researching the lived experience: Human science for an action sensitive pedagogy.* Althouse Press.

Vibrant Communities. (2018). *Opportunity central Iowa reports reduction in poverty: A collective impact success story.* Tamarack Institute. https://www.tamarackcommunity.ca/latest/opportunity-central-iowa-reports-reduction-poverty

Vogel, I. (2012). *Review of the use of 'theory of change' in international development review report.* United Kingdom Department of International Development.

von Bertalanffy, L. (1968). *General system theory: Foundations, development, applications.* George Braziller.

Vuntut Gwitchin First Nation. (2022). *Rampart house.* http://www.oldcrow.ca/ramp1.htm

Wagamese, R. (2016). *Embers: One Ojibway's meditations.* Douglas and McIntyre.

Walker, B. (1989). The future of public health: *The Institute of Medicine's 1988 Report. Journal of Public Health Policy, 10*(1), 19–31.

Wallace, S. (2015). Addressing the rise in neonatal abstinence syndrome: A multifaceted approach. *Pennsylvania Patient Safety Authority, 12*(4), 125–131. http://patientsafety.pa.gov/ADVISORIES/Pages/201512_125.aspx

Wang, C., & Burris, M. A. (1997). Photovoice: Concept, methodology, and use for participatory needs assessment. *Health Education & Behavior*, 24(3), 369–387.

Wanzer, D. L. (2019, May 22). *AEA 365: What is evaluation? And how does it differ from research?* American Evaluation Association. https://aea365.org/blog/what-is-evaluation-and-how-does-it-differ-from-research-by-dana-wanzer/

Wanzer, D. L. (2021). What is evaluation? Perspectives of how evaluation differs (or not) from research. *American Journal of Evaluation*, 42(1), 28–46. https://doi.org/10.1177/1098214020920710

Warren, M., & Glenn, H. (2017, October 20). *The day a Texas school held a funeral for the Spanish language*. StoryCorps, National Public Radio. https://www.npr.org/2017/10/20/558739863/the-day-a-texas-school-held-a-funeral-for-the-spanish-language#:~:text=Music%20Of%202021-,The%20Day%20A%20Texas%20School%20Held%20A%20Funeral%20For%20The,Spanish.%22

Warwick, C., & Clevenger, J. (2011). *Help...I've been asked to synthesize!* Bowling Green State University. http://www.bgsu.edu/content/dam/BGSU/learning-commons/documents/writing/synthesis/asked-to-synthesize.pdf

Washington State Department of Health. (2009, November). *Local public health indicators* (PowerPoint slides). Public Health Improvement Partnership. https://www.doh.wa.gov/Portals/1/Documents/1200/PHI-presentation.pdf

Weave, L., Born, P., & Whaley, D. L. (2010). *Approaches to measuring community change indicators*. Tamarak Institute. https://www.tamarackcommunity.ca/hubfs/Resources/Publications/Approaches%20to%20Measuring%20Community%20Change%20Indicators.pdf

Weiss, C. H. (1972). *Evaluation research: Methods of assessing program effectiveness*. Prentice Hall.

Weiss, C. H. (1993). Where politics and evaluation research meet. *Evaluation Practice*, 14(1), 93–106.

Weiss, C. H. (1995). Nothing as practical as good theory: Exploring theory-based evaluation for comprehensive community initiatives for children and families. In J. Connell, A. Kubisch, L. Schorr, & C. Weiss (Eds.), *New approaches to evaluating community initiatives: Concepts, methods and contexts*. Aspen Institute.

Weiss, H. B., Kreider, H., Mayer, E., Hencke, R., & Vaughn, M. A. (2005). Working it out: The chronicle of a mixed-methods analysis. In T. S. Weisnere (Ed.), *Discovering successful pathways in children's development: Mixed methods in the study of childhood and family life* (pp. 47–64). University of Chicago Press.

Wenger, N. K., Mattson, M. E., Furberg, C. D., & Elinson, J. (1984). Assessment of quality of life in clinical trials of cardiovascular therapies. *American Journal of Cardiology*, 54, 908–913.

Wensing, M., & Grol, R. (2019). Knowledge translation in health: How implementation science could contribute more. *BMC Medicine*, 17(88), 1–6. https://doi.org/10.1186/s12916-019-1322-9

West, M., & Lyubovnikova, J. (2015). *International encyclopedia of the social & behavioral sciences*. Elsevier.

Wholey, J. S. (1979). *Evaluation: Promise and performance*. Urban Institute.

Wholey, J. S. (1996). Formative and summative evaluation: Related issues in performance measurement. *Evaluation Practice*, 17(2), 145–149.

Wholey, J. S. (2004). Evaluability assessment. In J. S. Wholey, H. P. Hatry, & K. E. Newcomer (Eds.), *Handbook of practical program evaluation* (pp. 33–62). Jossey-Bass.

Wholey, J., & Newcomer, K. (1997). Clarifying goals, reporting results. In K. E. Newcomer (Ed.), *Using performance measurement to improve public and nonprofit programs*. New directions for evaluation, 1997(75), 91–98. https://doi.org/10.1002/ev.1082

Whyte, W. F. (1943). *Street corner society: The social structure of an Italian slum*. University of Chicago Press.

Wilkins, D. E. (2018, September 12). *How to honor the seven generations*. Indian Country Today. https://indiancountrytoday.com/archive/how-to-honor-the-seven-generations

Williams, B. (2019). *Systematic evaluation design: A workbook*. https://gumroad.com/l/evaldesign

Williams, B., & Britt, H. (2014). *System thinking for monitoring: Attending to interrelationships, perspectives and boundaries*. USAID. https://usaidlearninglab.org/sites/default/files/resource/files/systemic_monitoring_ipb_2014-09-25_final-ak_1.pdf

Williams, B., & Hummelbrunner, R. (2010). *Systems concepts in action: A practitioner's toolkit*. Stanford University Press.

Wilson-Grau, R. (2015). *Outcome harvesting*. BetterEvaluation. https://www.betterevaluation.org/en/plan/approach/outcome_harvesting#OH_what_is_OutcomeHarvesting

Wilson-Grau, R., Wilson-Grau, C., Scheers, G., & Hoitink, C. (n.d.). *The essence*. Outcome Harvesting. https://outcomeharvesting.net/the-essence/

W. K. Kellogg Foundation. (2004, January 1). *Using logic models to bring together planning, evaluation, and action: Logic model development guide*. https://ag.purdue.edu/extension/pdehs/Documents/Pub3669.pdf

Woodward, C. (2010). *Logic model resource guide*. Quality Improvement & Innovation Partnership. http://www.hqontario.ca/portals/0/documents/qi/qi-rg-logic-model-1012-en.pdf

Wooley, C. M. (2009). Meeting the mixed methods challenge of integration in a sociological study of structure and agency. *Journal of Mixed Methods Research*, 3(1), 7–25.

World Bank. (2007). *Monitoring and evaluation: Tips for strengthening organizational capacity*. http://siteresources.worldbank.org/INTBELARUS/Resources/M&E.pdf

World Bank. (2009). *Community-driven development: Delivering the results people need*. http://siteresources.worldbank.org/IDA/Resources/IDA-CDD.pdf

World Health Organization. (n.d.). *A framework for strengthening evaluation and organizational learning*. https://www.who.int/docs/default-source/documents/evaluation/framework-for-strengthening-evaluation-and-organizational-learning.pdf?sfvrsn=720e4c8e_2

World Health Organization. (2006). *Constitution of the World Health Organization*. http://www.who.int/governance/eb/who_constitution_en.pdf

World Health Organization. (2022, March 28). *WHO coronavirus (COVID-19) dashboard*. https://covid19.who.int/

World Meterological Organization. (2022). *Four key climate change indicators break records in 2021*. https://public.wmo.int/en/media/press-release/four-key-climate-change-indicators-break-records-2021

Worthen, B. R., Sanders, J. R., & Fitzpatrick, J. L. (1997). *Educational evaluation: Alternative approaches and practical guidelines*. Longman.

Yarbrough, D., Shulha, L., Hopson, R., & Caruthers, F. (2011). *The program evaluation standards: A guide for evaluators and evaluation users* (3rd ed.). SAGE Publications.

Yin, R. K. (1989). *Case study research: Design and methods* (2nd ed.). SAGE Publications.

Yukon First Nations. (2014). *Yukon First Nations joint education action plan 2014–2024*. https://cyfn.ca/wp-content/uploads/2013/09/Approved-JEAP.pdf

Zamberg, I., Manzano, S., Posfay-Barbe, K., Windisch, O., Agoritsas, T., & Schiffer, E. (2020). A mobile health platform to disseminate validated institutional measurements during the COVID-19 outbreak: Utilization-focused evaluation study. *Journal of Medical Internet Research Public Health Surveillance*, 6(2), e18668. https://publichealth.jmir.org/2020/2/e18668/#ref11

Zimmerman, M. A. (2000). Empowerment theory: Psychological, organizational, and community levels of analysis. In J. Rappaport, & E. Seldman (Eds.), *Handbook of community psychology* (pp. 2–45). Kluwer Academic/Plenum.

Zimmerman, G. L., Olsen, C. G., & Bosworth, M. F. (2000). A 'stages of change' approach to helping patients change behavior. *American Family Physician*, 61(5), 1409–1416.

Zukoski, A., & Luluquiesen, M. (2002). Participatory evaluation. What is it? Why do it? What are the challenges? *Community Based Public Health Policy & Practice*, (5), 1–6.

Zulfiqar, A., & Bhaskar, S. B. (2016). Basic statistical tools in research and data analysis. *Indian Journal of Anaesthesiology*, 60(10), 662–669.

INDEX